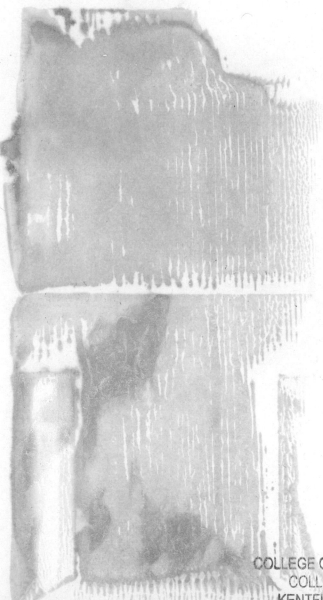

R. E. LEE

Books by
Douglas Southall Freeman

GEORGE WASHINGTON

LEE'S LIEUTENANTS

THE SOUTH TO POSTERITY

R. E. LEE

Charles Scribner's Sons

R. E. LEE

A BIOGRAPHY

By

Douglas Southall Freeman

Volume IV

CHARLES SCRIBNER'S SONS

NEW YORK   ·   LONDON

CONTENTS

CONTENTS

ILLUSTRATIONS

Between Pages 214 and 215

Lee's first note on the surrender

The McLean house, where the Army of Northern Virginia was surrendered

The pen with which the surrender of the Army of Northern Virginia was signed, and the sword General Lee wore at the time

General Lee's parole

Lee before the fire of the battle had faded from his eyes

Pampatike, the first home visited by General Lee, beyond the confines of Richmond, after his return from Appomattox

Derwent, the cottage lent to General Lee in June, 1865

Facsimile of the first page of a letter of August 24, 1865, in which General Lee conditionally accepted the presidency of Washington College

The "Old" President's house at Washington College

The "New" President's house at Washington College, occupied by General Lee during the last sixteen months of his life

Lee—the last phase

General Lee's office in the basement of the chapel at Washington College

View from the parlor into the dining-room where General Lee died

Death mask of General Lee

The chapel and campus of Washington College during the funeral of General Lee

The recumbent statue of Lee in the chapel of Washington and Lee University

The will of General Lee   *pages* 392-393

ILLUSTRATIONS

MAPS

R. E. LEE

CHAPTER I

LEE MAKES HIS LAST DESPERATE PLAN

No food, no horses, no reinforcement! As that dread spectre of ultimate defeat shaped itself, Lee did not content himself with reorganizing his army. Daily, as he sought to find provisions to keep his men from starvation, he wrestled with his strategic problem. Early was still in the Shenandoah Valley, guarding the Virginia Central with a few shivering *cadres* and under orders to create the impression, if he could, that his command was formidable.[1] Beauregard was seeking to muster a sufficient force to dispute Sherman's advance up the coast. Bragg had some 6500 effectives in eastern North Carolina.[2] These were the only troops of any consequence left in the South Atlantic states, except for the Army of Northern Virginia.

To dispose of Bragg and of Beauregard so that he could concentrate all his strength against the ragged divisions that defied him in front of Petersburg, Grant moved with swift assurance. He followed the strategy of partition. Having halved the Confederacy by seizing the line of the Mississippi and capturing Vicksburg, Grant had then divided the eastern half of the revolutionary states by sending Sherman through Georgia to the sea. Now, with only South Carolina, North Carolina, and Virginia to be subdued, he brought from Tennessee some of the troops that had wrecked Hood at Nashville. These he united with Terry's troops below Wilmington, placed the whole under Major General John M. Schofield[3] and directed him to advance westward against Lee's lines of communication along the seaboard from Weldon. If this operation were successful, Virginia would be severed from the Carolinas; and if Sherman moved northward, joined Schofield,

[1] *Early*, 459. General Early received these instructions on Jan. 2, 1865, when he visited Lee.
[2] O. R., 47, part 1, p. 1077.   [3] Jan. 31, 1865; O. R., 46, part 2, p. 314.

and marched with him to reinforce Grant, Lee would face three armies. By January 29 this danger had so far developed that Lee frankly warned the President. In case Grant were appreciably reinforced, he said, "I do not see how in our present position he can be prevented from enveloping Richmond." [4]

There was at the time only one ray of light—the possibility of a negotiated peace. Francis P. Blair, Sr., had been in Richmond on January 12 on his own initiative, in the hope that a settlement might be affected, and out of that visit had developed a proposal for the dispatch of a peace delegation to Washington. Three leading Southerners, Vice-President Stephens, Judge J. A. Campbell, and Senator R. M. T. Hunter, had gone to the Federal lines on the 29th and, after some parleys, had proceeded to Hampton Roads. There they conferred unofficially with President Lincoln. The whole South hung on the meeting, which, however, ended on the day it began, with no apparent possibility of an understanding.[5] The hopes of many were dashed, and the resolute saw in Mr. Lincoln's uncompromising stand a warning that the war would have to be fought to the finish; but there were some who hoped that out of the conference a tangible basis of peace might still develop. General Lee had watched the pourparlers, of course, with profound interest, but there is little evidence that he expected agreement. Knowing as he did the desperate plight of his army, the growing confidence of the North and the illimitable resources at the command of President Lincoln, it is hardly probable that he expected the Union to offer any other terms than surrender.

On the very day that the disappointed Southern commissioners came back to Richmond, General Lee had to confess to President Davis that he could not send reinforcements to Beauregard, and that Beauregard, with such resources as he could muster, would have to make an effort to defeat Sherman "wherever he can be struck to most advantage." [6] A little later, after he had seen the suffering of his hungry men during the operations of February

---

[4] *Lee's Dispatches*, 330. Lee believed at the time that the troops from Tennessee were moving to reinforce Grant directly, but in the same letter, considering the possibility that they might be intended for Sherman, he said, "Reinforcement to Sherman would be almost as bad in its consequences as to Grant."

[5] *O. R.*, 46, part 2, pp. 505 *ff.* contains the correspondence; the literature on the Hampton Roads Conference, as it was called, is large. It was on Feb. 5 that Mr. Davis notified the Confederate Congress of the outcome (*O. R.*, 46, part 2, p. 446).

[6] Lee to Davis, *MS.*, Feb. 4, 1865, *Duke Univ. MSS.*

5–7 around Hatcher's Run, he again put the Secretary of War on notice: "You must not be surprised if calamity befalls us." [7] Long conference with Mr. Davis and the secretary on February 13–16 disclosed no way of averting that calamity.[8]

Lee had always refrained from discussions with politicians on subjects that affected his military duties, but he now thought the situation so desperate that he determined to see Senator R. M. T. Hunter, a personal friend and one of the commissioners who had conferred with Mr. Lincoln in Hampton Roads. Visiting Hunter one evening, he talked with him nearly all night of the outlook for peace. If Hunter thought there was any prospect of peace, otherwise than by surrender, it was Hunter's duty, Lee said, to propose it. The senator had what seemed to him the best of reasons for not doing so, and he explained them. He had been to the President, he confided, and had told him that if peace could be had on any terms short of surrender, he should seek it. Davis had refused, and, as Hunter believed, had circulated a report that the senator had lost all hope of Southern victory and was in despair. Until this incident was cleared up, Hunter insisted, he would confer no more with the President. Lee repeated his suggestion and added that if he himself were to propose peace negotiations publicly, it would be equivalent to surrender. Hunter agreed, but argued that if Lee thought the "chance for success desperate," he should so advise the President. "To this," Hunter wrote, Lee "made no reply. In the whole of this conversation he never said to me he thought the chances were over; but the tone and tenor of his remarks made that impression on my mind. He spoke of a recent affair in which the Confederates had repelled very gallantly an attempt of the Federals to break his line. The next day, as he rode along . . . one of the soldiers would thrust forth his bare feet and say, 'General, I have no shoes.' Another would declare, as he passed, 'I am hungry; I haven't enough to

---

[7] O. R., 46, 2, 1210. In further correspondence with the War Department, during February and early in March, Lee usually included some "if" in referring to the probable evacuation of the line he had held since June, but he spoke once of reinforcements that could not be sent Bragg in North Carolina "until I abandon James River" (O. R., 46, 2, 1247). And once he told the secretary he did not consider "the abandonment of our present position as necessarily fatal to our success," provided sufficient supplies were forthcoming.

[8] For this visit, see 2 R. W. C. D., 422, Taylor MSS., Feb. 14, 1865. There is no record of the subjects of discussion.

eat.' These and other circumstances betraying the utmost destitution he repeated with a melancholy air and tone which I shall never forget." [9]

While the administration refused to face the dread reality, Schofield became a menace. Sherman was on the march. He entered Columbia, S. C., on February 17 and forced the evacuation of Charleston that night. Lee watched him with eyes that saw all too plainly what his advance boded. He wrote on February 19: "It is necessary to bring out all our strength, and, I fear, to unite our armies, as separately they do not seem able to make head against the enemy. . . . I fear it may be necessary to abandon our cities, and preparations should be made for that contingency." [10] The expedients of desperation were tried. Longstreet took advantage of a conference with the Federal General Ord to propose a conference between Lee and Grant in the hope that formal negotiations would eventuate. [11] Richmond was frantic with excitement; at headquarters hope fluctuated from day to day. [12] Lee repeated that the unhindered advance of Sherman would mean the severance of communications with the South and would force the evacuation of Richmond. [13]

General Bragg, in North Carolina, was so discredited by previous failure in the field that he could not rally the people of that state. General Beauregard, retreating from Charleston, was in ill-health. [14] He found that the militia of South Carolina would not cross the state line and that they consisted only of men between fifty and sixty and boys under seventeen, who were soon exhausted on the march. [15] There was the direst need of a coordination of these forces under some man who had the military confidence of the Carolinas. Lee knew that Johnston held the

[9] 4 S. H. S. P., 308–9.   [10] O. R., 47, part 1, p. 1044.

[11] Longstreet, 558–87, 647–49.

[12] Cf. Taylor MSS., Feb. 16, 1865: "My faith in this old army is unshaken"; ibid., Feb. 20, 1865: "They are trying to corner this old army. Like a brave old lion brought to bay at last, it is determined to resist to the death and if die it must, to die game. But we have not yet quite made up our minds to die, and if God will help us, we will yet prove equal to the emergency. . . . We are to have many hard knocks—we are to experience much that is dispiriting, but if our men are true—and I really think that most of them are—we will make our way safely, successfully, through the dark clouds that now surround us."

[13] O. R., 46, part 2, p. 1250.

[14] O. R., 46, part 2, p. 1245.   [15] O. R., 47, part 2, p. 1238.

good opinion of the people and was, perhaps, the only man who could bring out the last reserves, if even he could enlist them. Mr. Davis had not put Johnston at Lee's disposal and, indeed, had not acted on a joint resolution of Congress requesting him to restore Johnston to command of the Army of Tennessee.[16] Instead, Davis had written, though he had not sent Congress, a memorandum of some 4500 words in which he explained why he did not have confidence in Johnston as an independent field commander.[17] This would have kept Lee from acting in anything less than a final, overwhelming emergency, but now he decided to put the necessities of the South above the opinion of the President. Tactfully arguing that if Beauregard should be incapacitated he would have no one to take his place, Lee on February 21 asked the Secretary of War to order Johnston to report to him for assignment to duty.[18] This was promptly done, as Mr. Davis explained, "in the hope that General Johnston's soldierly qualities may be made serviceable to his country when acting under General Lee's orders, and that in his new position those defects which I found manifested by him when serving as an independent commander will be remedied by the control of the general-in-chief." [19]

On February 22 Lee placed Johnston in general charge of operations in the Carolinas, with instructions to collect the scattered troops in those states and to attack Sherman on the march, before he could form junction with Schofield.[20] If this proved an impossibility, then Johnston must join Lee or Lee must join Johnston, for it was accepted by all that Lee could not attempt to remain near Richmond once Sherman reached Roanoke River, the next strong defensive line south of the Appomattox.[21]

Johnston speedily found that his army was suffering heavily from desertion. Instead of having 29,000, as estimated, he could

[16] O. R., 47, part 2, p. 1304. [17] Ibid.
[18] O. R., 46, part 2, p. 1245. [19] O. R., 47, part 2, p. 1303.
[20] O. R., 47, part 2, pp. 1247, 1248, 1256–57. For some of the circumstances of Johnston's appointment, and for Johnston's fine pledge to serve under Lee, see Mrs. D. Giraud Wright: A Southern Girl in 1861, pp. 240–41.
[21] Lee to Breckinridge, Feb. 22: "The want of supplies alone would force us to withdraw when the enemy reaches the Roanoke" (O. R., 46, part 2, p. 1250). Lee to "a friend," July 27, 1868: "As regards the movements of General Sherman, it was easy to see that unless they were interrupted, I should be compelled to abandon the defence of Richmond; and with a view of arresting his progress I so weakened my force by sending reinforcements to South and North Carolina, that I had not sufficient men to man the lines. Had they not been broken, I should have abandoned them as soon as General Sherman reached the Roanoke" (21 Galaxy, 324).

5

count only about 15,000 effectives.[22] There was little likelihood
that he could break away and get to Virginia, and still less that he
could be subsisted on arrival.[23] By the harsh logic of elimination,
Lee must prepare to leave the Richmond front and to move
toward Danville to unite his army with Johnston's. Their one
hope would be to strike Sherman, to destroy him, and then together to face Grant. As early as February 21 Lee had been
planning to organize a base at Burkeville, the junction of the
Southside and the Richmond and Danville Railroads.[24] Before the
end of the month the plan of a movement to Johnston was uppermost in Lee's mind.

The coming of the blustery days of March found about 50,000
men under Lee's immediate command.[25] It was a pitiful army
with which to face such crushing odds—so pitiful that when
Longstreet reported that he believed Grant would confer with
Lee on a peace plan, the consent of the President was procured[26]
and a letter was dispatched to Grant on March 2, proposing an
interview.[27] Lee had no great expectations of a favorable answer.
He wrote the President: "I . . . hope that some good may result,
but I must confess that I am not sanguine. My belief is that he
will consent to no terms, unless coupled with the condition of our
return to the Union. Whether this will be acceptable to our people
yet awhile I cannot say." Was there a suggestion in that "yet

[22] O. R., 47, part 1, pp. 1053, 1055, 1058.   [23] O. R., 46, part 2, p. 1250.
[24] O. R., 46, part 2, pp. 1247, 1250; 2 Davis, 648–49, 676.
[25] This estimate, which is somewhat higher than most Southern writers have allowed,
is based on the returns of Feb. 27–March 1, including Ewell's command in the department of Richmond (O. R., 46, part 1, pp. 388–90 and ibid., 46, part 2, p. 1274). The
total was then 56,518 present for duty. Deduction of 6834 has been made as follows:
Desertions, 2000; March casualties, 500; losses and prisoners in the assault on Fort Stedman, 3500; captured on the picket lines, March 25, 834. That leaves 49,718. This
figure checks with Lee's statement that if, in effect, Grant and Sherman together had
160,000 men and Johnston brought 10,000 into Virginia, the Federals would outnumber
the combined forces by 100,000 (Lee's Dispatches, 345). Again, the total paroles at Appomattox were 28,231. Allowing for the 6800 deductions already made, and for 11,000
prisoners at Five Forks, Sayler's Creek, etc., this yields a total of 46,000, with casualties
not counted and the escape of a part of the cavalry left out of account. The forces supple-
menting approximately 36,000 muskets were: artillery around 5000, cavalry about 6500,
and miscellaneous units of sailors, marines, and heavy artillery, say, 2000. Taylor's estimate of infantry strength, 33,000 (Four Years, 187), was remarkably close considering
the paucity of the materials with which he worked in 1877. At no time after Jan. 1, 1865,
did Lee have present for duty more than 67,000, including those in the Valley (O. R., 46,
part 2, p. 1112; ibid., 46, part 3, p. 1331).
[26] Probably when Lee was in Richmond on Feb. 26–28, for which visit see Taylor
MSS., Feb. 28, 1865.
[27] O. R., 46, part 2, p. 824; ibid., 825; Longstreet, 558–87, 647–49.

awhile" that reunion was inevitable and, so far as he was concerned, not unacceptable as an alternative to the bloody finish of a hopeless war?[28]

Whatever hope he may have cherished of a favorable reception of his proposal was probably destroyed the day he wrote Grant. For on that same 2d of March, Sheridan attacked and overwhelmed the remnant of Early's little force at Waynesboro in the Shenandoah Valley. The Shenandoah Valley was irredeemably lost, and Sheridan was free to join Grant with his powerful mounted divisions.[29]

This news shook Lee to the depths. He wrestled with his conscience and his sense of duty. What should he do? His obligation to his government and to those half-frozen soldiers who must soon be overwhelmed in the trenches if the war went on—which came first? Long he debated it, on the night of March 3, pacing the floor of his quarters at Edge Hill. Longstreet and Hill were both distant. He could not discuss his problem with them, but he must unburden himself. With whom should he talk?

In desperation, though the hour was late and the night was blighting in its chill, he sent for John B. Gordon, who by this time was one of his most trusted lieutenants. It was 2 o'clock when Gordon arrived. "In [Lee's] room," Gordon wrote, many years later, "was a long table covered with recent reports from every part of the army. . . . He motioned me to a chair on one side of the table, and seated himself opposite me. . . . He opened the conference by directing me to read the reports from the different commands as he should hand them to me, and to carefully note every important fact contained in them. The revelation was startling. Every report was bad enough, and all the distressing facts combined were sufficient, it seemed to me, to destroy all cohesive power and lead to the inevitable disintegration of any other army that was ever marshalled. . . . Some of the officers had gone outside the formal official statement as to the numbers of the sick, to tell in plain, terse, and forceful words of depleted strength, emaciation, and decreased power of endurance among those who appeared on the rolls as fit for duty. Cases were given,

28 Lee to Davis, *MS.,* March 2, 1865, *Duke Univ. MSS.*
29 *Early,* 462 *ff.* For the ultimate fate of Early and the remnant of his force, see Appendix IV—ʟ

7

and not a few, where good men, faithful, tried and devoted, gave evidence of temporary insanity and indifference to orders or to the consequences of disobedience. . . . When I had finished the inspection of this array of serious fact, General Lee began his own analysis of the situation." [30] Of his 50,000 men, only 35,000 were fit for duty; Grant must have 150,000; Thomas was sending 30,000 east. "From the Valley," said Lee, "General Grant can and will bring upon us nearly 20,000, against whom I can oppose scarcely a vedette." Schofield and Sherman between them probably had 80,000; Johnston could only count on 13,000 to 15,000. Adding all the Union forces together, there would soon be in the seaboard states 280,000 Federal troops, to whom the Confederacy could oppose only 65,000.

"This estimate ended," Gordon wrote, "the commander rose, and with one hand resting upon the depressing reports, he stood contemplating them for a moment, and then gravely walked to and fro across the room. . . . He again took his seat facing me at the table and asked me to state frankly what I thought under these conditions it was best to do—or what duty to the army and our people required of us. Looking at me intently, he awaited my answer."

"General," said Gordon, "it seems to me there are but three courses, and I name them in the order in which I think they should be tried:

"First, make terms with the enemy, the best we can get.

"Second, if that is not practicable, the best thing to do is to retreat—abandon Richmond and Petersburg, unite by rapid marches with General Johnston in North Carolina, and strike Sherman before Grant can join him; or,

"Lastly, we must fight and without delay."

"Is that your opinion?" Lee asked.

Gordon reiterated his views and deferentially asked if he might inquire how Lee appraised the outlook.

"Certainly, General," Lee answered. "You have the right to ask my opinion. I agree with you fully."

A long discussion followed, in which Lee explained that he did not feel that he, as a soldier, had the right to urge political action

[30] *Gordon,* 385–88.

on the government. He did not tell Gordon that he had already written Grant, for that was a confidential matter between himself and the President, but at length, as Gordon argued that he should advocate peace negotiations, Lee said he would go to see the President the next day, which, as a matter of fact, he had already planned to do.[31]

Journeying to the capital the next morning, Lee doubtless reviewed with the President the possibilities of negotiating peace, but the discussion was probably cut short by the receipt of Grant's reply to Lee's letter of March 2. In this answer Grant declined a meeting. "I would state," said he, "that I have no authority to accede to your proposition for a conference on the subject proposed. Such authority is vested in the President of the United States alone." [32] Lee might have been willing to negotiate on the basis of a restoration of the Union, but if he canvassed this aspect of the subject with the President, he discovered quickly that Mr. Davis was determined to have the Confederacy go down in defeat rather than accept any terms that did not recognize Southern independence.

The conversation then turned to the dark necessity of evacuating Petersburg and Richmond. The chief executive faced this dread event with unshaken courage and, when Lee explained that he saw no alternative, Mr. Davis asked why Lee delayed: If the move had to be made, why should it not be undertaken forthwith? Lee replied that the condition of his animals was so reduced that they could not haul the wagon-train until the wet and muddy roads had dried somewhat.[33]

Then the two debated the best strategy of the inevitable retreat. Hood had proposed that the Army of Northern Virginia make for middle Tennessee, and Davis had forwarded Hood's letter to

---

31 *Gordon*, 387 *ff.;* Lee to Davis, *MS.*, March 2, 1865, *Duke Univ. MSS.* The chronology given in the text seems best to fit the confused facts. Gordon made no reference to the proposal parley with Grant and would almost certainly have remembered so important a matter if Lee had mentioned it. Gordon said (*op. cit.*, 385) that the interview occurred "during the first week in March." It must have been after March 2, for Lee told Gordon of the probable movement of 20,000 men from Sheridan, which he would hardly have reckoned upon if he had not already received intelligence of Early's defeat. Lee was in Richmond March 4–5 (2 *R. W. C. D.*, 439; W. A. Wash: *Camp, Field and Prison Life*, 316; *Taylor MSS.*, March 5, 1865). If Gordon was correct in saying that Lee went to Richmond the day after this interview, then the two were together on the evening of March 3. There is no record of any subsequent visit by Lee to Richmond early in March.
32 *O. R.*, 46, part 2, p. 825.　　　33 2 *Davis*, 648.

9

Lee for his criticism. Believing this course impracticable, Lee outlined the plan he was already formulating for a march to Johnston, a quick blow at Sherman and then an attack on Grant. To
accomplish this, he went on, it would be necessary to build up a
week's reserve of food in Richmond, to accumulate depots of supplies along the Southside and the Richmond and Danville Railroads, and to issue more corn to the horses even if this depleted
the scant stock the quartermaster general had on hand.[34]

This gloomiest of all the interviews between Lee and the Confederate President occurred on Saturday. The next day Lee wor-
shipped at Saint Paul's Church for the last time during the war,[35]
and then, bidding Mrs. Lee farewell, he returned to Petersburg.
Gordon, of course, was anxious to know the outcome of the conference, but he found his chief under no delusions. Lee explained
to the Georgian what had happened. "He said, nothing could be
done at Richmond," Gordon subsequently recorded. "The Congress did not seem to appreciate the situation. Of President Davis
he spoke in terms of strong eulogy: of the strength of his con-
victions, of his devotedness, of his remarkable faith in the possibility of still winning our independence, and of his unconquerable
will power. The nearest approach to complaint or criticism were
the words: 'You know that the President is very pertinacious in
opinion and purpose.'"[36]

"What, then, is to be done, General?" Gordon inquired.

Lee could only answer that they must fight.[37]

In preparing to fight, Lee had to balance one time-element
against another. He could not wait long, because Sheridan would
soon join Grant, and when that happened, the overpowering Federal cavalry could be employed to break Lee's communications
with the South and to prevent their restoration.[38] On the other
hand, the horses had to be conditioned, and the depots must be
prepared, as Lee had told the President, so that the movement to
join Johnston could be undertaken. The new commissary general
went vigorously to work building up the reserve that Lee needed.
St. John estimated that 500 tons of commissary supplies had to be
delivered daily in or near Richmond to subsist the army and to
collect the special reserve of seven days' rations, which General

[34] 2 *Davis*, 648–49. [35] Wash, *op. cit.*, 316.
[36] *Gordon*, 393. [37] *Ibid.* [38] *O. R.*, 46, part 3, p. 1319.

Lee wished to be held subject to the order of his commissary.
St. John affirmed that this delivery could be made if the military
lines then occupied by the army could be held, and he did his
utmost to make good his statement. "The condition of the railroads was only too well known," St. John said in his final report.
His assistant added: "The means of transportation were constantly
inadequate." Yet they contrived to improve the army ration, to
fill sizeable depots at Lynchburg, Danville and Greensboro, and
to lay down in Richmond most of the special store General Lee
desired. Perhaps, in doing this, St. John drew on the last food
stuffs that could be purchased with depreciated Confederate
money, but he made the immediate outlook for provisions better
than it had been for weeks.[39] While the commissaries were working to supply the army for a move, the general plan of a junction
with the forces in North Carolina was examined in every light
and the alternatives were debated.[40] By March 9 Lee concluded
that no "marked success" could be expected from Johnston's army.[41]
Two days later Johnston wrote frankly that if the Federal forces
in North Carolina were united, he could not prevent their march
into Virginia. With this bad news Johnston coupled a suggestion:
Instead of Lee's moving southward and giving battle with combined forces, would it be practicable for Lee "to hold one of the
inner lines of Richmond with one part of your army, and meet
Sherman with the other, returning to Richmond after fighting"?[42] Longstreet had made a somewhat similar proposal in

[39] St. John's own adverse opinion of the management of the commissary bureau was
greatly changed by personal observation. Some of the finest men in the service, he said,
were among its officers. "They were contending under extreme disadvantage with the
nearly crushing embarrassment of an insufficient supply of purchasing funds and very
difficult transportation. Otherwise the record would have been very different." See St.
John's and Williams's reports, Lee MSS—L; St. John in 2 Davis, 669–70.

[40] Secretary Seddon had resigned, in ill health and despair, effective Feb. 6, 1865,
and General John C. Breckinridge had succeeded him. The new head of the War Department had proposed, on Feb. 21, that the Appalachian area be stripped temporarily
of troops, who should be used to reinforce Johnston so that he could destroy Sherman.
"Something of this sort must be done," wrote Breckinridge, "or the situation is lost"
(O. R., 46, 2, 1245). Lee had to put this proposal aside as desirable, but impracticable,
because the troops that Breckinridge would have employed were scattered for lack of subsistence and could not be concentrated in time. Even if they could have been brought
together before Sherman reached the line of Lee's communications, their withdrawal
would expose to the enemy the districts they had occupied (O. R., 46, 2, 1250). This
letter is a very good example of Lee's condensed, clear argument on a military question.
This argument was rendered conclusive by the defeat of Early's command, which would
have been the chief reinforcement of Johnston.

[41] O. R., 46, part 2, p. 1295.   [42] O. R., 47, part 2, p. 1373.

February. It had then been left in abeyance.[43] Now, in the light of the information from Johnston, Lee began to canvass further the possibility of detaching part of his forces to assist his old comrade in crushing Sherman.

In particular, Lee had General Gordon make a study of the Federal centre around Petersburg, in order to ascertain whether the lines could be broken. When Gordon reported that this was feasible,[44] in the vicinity of the Federal Fort Stedman, Lee proceeded to work out a new plan. He was unwilling to risk a general offensive against the odds he faced in fortified positions, because he felt that he should conserve his strength for the open campaign, but he believed that if Gordon could penetrate the Federal lines after an assault by about half the army, one of two things would happen. Either General Grant would have to abandon the left of his line, or, what was more likely, he would have to shorten his front. This would make it possible for Lee to hold him with fewer men. Then, when Sherman was near enough to be reached quickly, Lee could detach picked troops to Johnston, effect a junction with that officer's little army and give battle to Sherman. If Sherman were beaten, Lee could then bring back his united forces to meet Grant. If Gordon did not succeed in breaking through the Federal lines, Lee would be in no worse plight for executing his previous general plan of joining Johnston with all his forces. For it was plainer than ever by this time that the Army of Northern Virginia would have to leave the Richmond defenses if it quietly awaited Sherman's approach to unite his army with Grant's.[45]

[43] Longstreet first suggested that Johnston be brought to Richmond (O. R., 46, part 2, p. 1233) and when told that more troops could not be subsisted there (O. R., 46, 2, 1250), he urged on Feb. 25 that local defense troops be used to hold the left of the Richmond line and that his corps be sent to strengthen the right. If Grant moved then, he could be met. If Grant did not move, part of the Confederate forces could be detached to support the army in North Carolina. Should that be followed by an attack on the Richmond front, Petersburg could be abandoned and Richmond and the line of the Appomattox be held. But, said Longstreet, he did not believe Grant would attack when he learned that Lee had sent troops to North Carolina. Rather was it likely that Grant would forthwith reinforce Sherman, lest he lose both Sherman and Richmond (O. R., 46, 2, 1253, 1258).

[44] Gordon, 397, and the same authority quoted in 2 Davis, 650. Gordon gave March 10 as the date of his interview, but his chronology was not very precise. The exact sequence of events in the development of the plan cannot be established absolutely.

[45] This is Lee's own explanation, which was not known until its publication in 1915 in Lee's Dispatches, 342 ff. It is plain from General Gordon's report in the Lee MSS., from his statement to President Davis (2 Davis, 650), and from his Reminiscences, p. 403, that he either was not told the full plan of his chief or else forgot some of the de-

Manifestly, the success of this revised plan was highly contingent. Everything depended on breaking the Federal front and on forcing Grant to shorten his line. But if this could be done the plan in obvious respects was an improvement on Longstreet's and on Johnston's. It involved less risk to Richmond, it did not demand the impossible in the way of supplies, and it took into account, as Johnston had not, the very definite limitations on the mobility of the army, both by road and by rail.

Lengthening March days brought no relief of any sort. Sheridan spread destruction over a wide area as he moved to rejoin Grant. Johnston's army proved to be weaker than the most pessimistic estimates.[46] Then, ominously, on March 23 Johnston reported that Schofield and Sherman had met at Goldsboro.[47] That town was equidistant 120 miles from Lee and from Greensboro, his main base of supplies in western North Carolina, and was only 110 miles from the nearest point on the Richmond and Danville Railroad. "Sherman's course," Johnston telegraphed, "cannot be hindered by the small force I have. I can do no more than annoy him. I respectfully suggest that it is no longer a question whether you leave your present position; you have only to decide where to meet Sherman. I will be near him." [48] The dreadful hour was drawing on. Sheridan, Lee believed, had already joined the Army of the Potomac. Grant was visibly preparing to attack on the Confederate right and to deprive Lee of the initiative. The Confederate commander could wait no longer, even for his horses to gain strength or for the heavy roads to dry. That night he gave his final approval to the plan for the attack on Fort Stedman.

tails. The student of Lee's campaigns will find it interesting to see how variously, in books written prior to the publication of Lee's confidential report to Mr. Davis, the biographers of Lee speculated on the reasons for the attack on Stedman.

[46] *O. R.*, 47, part 1, p. 1054.   [47] *O. R.*, 47, part 1, p. 1055.
[48] *O. R.*, 47, part 1, p. 1055.

CHAPTER II

Fort Stedman

(MARCH 25, 1865)

FORT STEDMAN was on the high ground known as Hare's Hill, at the crossing of the Federal lines and the Prince George Court-house road, three-quarters of a mile southeast of the Appomattox. The place could boast of no particular strength. It had no bastion and immediately adjoined Battery 10, which was open in the rear. The terrain behind the fort was almost as high as the parapet.[1] In the sketch that follows, the numerals represent the Federal batteries.

The distance to Fort Stedman from the Confederate lines, at the point known as Colquitt's Salient, was 150 yards, or probably less than at almost any other position on the whole of the defenses. Only 50 yards separated the pickets.[2] The nearness of the fort, which made a surprise attack possible, was one of the reasons General Gordon selected Stedman as the object of his assault. Another reason was that as he studied the enemy's works from the Confederate front he saw what he took to be three Federal forts in the rear of Stedman. Behind these was an open space. He believed that he could reach this cleared ground, form there, and take the three works in reverse. If he could do this and could spread his troops to the right and to the left for a sufficient distance, he argued that he would have a position of such strength and depth that he would divide the enemy's troops and could force the Federals to abandon that part of their fortifications to the south and southwest. In this way General Lee's immediate purpose would be served. The Federals would have to shorten their

---

[1] O. R., Atlas, Plate LXVII and LXXVII–2; Parke's report, O. R., 46, part 1, p. 316; Abbott's, ibid., 173. Gordon in his Reminiscences, 401 ff., probably magnified, and the Federal commanders, loc. cit., perhaps minimized the strength of the position.
[2] Parke, loc. cit.

front, and the Army of Northern Virginia would have a lessened stretch of lines to defend. Troops could then be detached from Lee to help Johnston.

Gordon developed an elaborate stratagem. Some of the obstructions in front of the Confederate works at Colquitt's were to

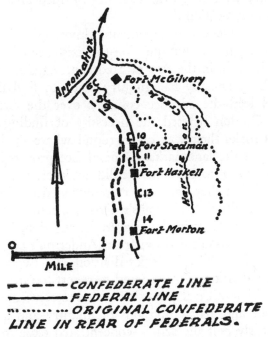

The opposing lines around Fort Stedman, March 25, 1865.

be secretly and noiselessly removed during the night preceding the attack, so as to afford sally ports. The Federal outposts were to be seized and silenced in the darkness before they could make outcry. Then fifty picked men were to chop down the abatis and *chevaux-de-frise* protecting Stedman. They were to rush the fort before daylight and were to be followed by three companies of 100 men each, wearing strips of white across their breasts to distinguish them in the darkness.[3] Having entered the work, these three companies were to pretend that they were Federals driven

[3] Major E. M. Williamson stated in *The Petersburg Progress-Index* of June 22, 1932, that General Gordon sent into Petersburg and purchased cloth with which to prepare these markings.

from the front positions and that they had been directed by the Federal commander to man the forts behind the lines. In this way Gordon hoped to reach and to occupy the Federal rear with little or no opposition. The main body of his infantry was then to move to the left and right, up and down the Federal line. This done, cavalry were to go through the fortified area and destroy Grant's communications.[4]

Lee left the tactical arrangements almost entirely to Gordon and apparently he did not question the existence of the forts that Gordon said were in the rear of Stedman. At Gordon's request, however, he personally had inquiry made to find three guides who could lead the advance columns over the terrain behind Stedman. Gordon stressed the necessity of finding individuals who could make their way over ground where shells and picks had destroyed the landmarks. General Lee procured three men and had them sent to Gordon. He did not know them personally, he explained, but they had been recommended to him.[5]

Grimes's, Walker's, and Evans's divisions, comprising Gordon's corps, were to be used in the assault. In addition, Ransom's and Wallace's of Johnson's division from Anderson's corps,[6] two brigades under Lane from Wilcox's division, and two under Cooke from Heth's division, were ordered to report to Gordon.[7] W. H. F. Lee's division of cavalry was instructed to come up from Stony Creek. Four and a half divisions of infantry and a division of cavalry—nearly half the army—concentrated close to the centre, around Colquitt's salient. This stripped the rest of the front almost bare of men and was in itself an evidence of Lee's desperation, especially as there were some indications of an impending Federal attack on Longstreet's front.[8]

On the afternoon of March 24, Gordon requisitioned Pickett's division also, which was then north of the James. Lee doubted whether Pickett could arrive in time to support Gordon, but, he wrote, "Still we will try," [9] and he promptly transmitted the order.[10] Other brigades could be brought up, he told Gordon, and disposed as needed. Showing none of the misgiving he must

[4] *Gordon*, 401 *ff*.
[5] *Gordon*, 405.
[7] Gordon's report, *Lee MSS.—K*.
[9] *Gordon*, 407.

[6] Anderson's report, *Lee MSS.—K*.
[8] *O. R.*, 46, part 3. p. 1337.
[10] *Lee MSS.—U*.

have felt over the employment of more than 50 per cent of his available infantry on a single mile of his long, long front, he concluded his letter to Gordon with characteristic words: "I pray that a merciful God may grant us success and deliver us from our enemies."[11] He directed Longstreet to be prepared to attack on the north side of the James the next morning and to take advantage of every circumstance that would prevent the transfer of troops to the south side of the river.[12]

Before dawn on the morning of March 25, the day set for the assault, General Lee rode over from the Turnbull house to the hill in the rear of Colquitt's salient, where Gordon was standing ready to give the signal to the men who crowded the trenches beneath him. The *chevaux-de-frise* had been quietly removed at the designated sally ports; the pickets had crept forward and were ready to fall on the Federal outposts before they could give the alarm; the 50 axemen were at hand; the selected 300 were all duly marshalled and distinguished by strips of white cloth. Almost on the second, at 4 o'clock, a single rifle, fired by a private at Gordon's word, sent the troops forward. Lee could only wait on the hill and listen and hope. Very soon a message came from Gordon, who himself had followed the charging troops: the men were in Fort Stedman and the 300 were on their way to the rear.[13] The sound of the firing must soon have apprised Lee that the attacking columns had spread 400 or 500 yards on either side of the salient they had stormed.[14]

The next news was of another sort: The officers of one party, Gordon reported, could not find the rear forts, on the seizure of which the success of the whole enterprise depended. The guide had been lost. Another courier brought a similar report from the other advance parties. Then followed confused fighting, not much of which Lee could see. Soon it was apparent the Federals had rallied, were hurrying up reserves, and were pouring into Fort Stedman and the adjoining part of the line a fire that was holding up the advance. Lee saw that an attempt to storm the Federal redoubts would be risky and, even if not repulsed, would

---

[11] *Gordon*, 407.
[12] Lee to Longstreet, March 24, 1865, *Lee MSS.—U.*
[13] *Gordon*, 410–11.
[14] The estimate of distance is that of Gordon in his report, *Lee MSS.—K.*

cost him heavily,[15] so, about 8 o'clock, he ordered Gordon to withdraw to his own lines. As the disappointed troops made their way back, they came under a cruel fire that dropped hundreds in their tracks.[16]

The survivors had a grim and humiliating story to tell "Marse Robert." The men had reached and had entered Stedman precisely as Gordon had planned. The main column had fought its way along the trenches on either side, but the selected 300 had failed to find the three forts in the rear for the all-sufficient reason that these forts did not exist. What Gordon had taken to be supporting forts were, in reality, old Confederate works that had been occupied and lost during the fighting of the 15th–17th of June, 1864. Futile search for these fortifications and the return to Fort Stedman had caused confusion and had given the Federals time to rally in their well-constructed works. Repeated attempts to storm Fort Haskell and Battery 9 had resulted in failure. From these works, from the reserve artillery on the hills in the rear, and from Batteries 4, 5, and 8, a smothering fire had been poured into those parts of the line that Gordon's men had occupied. Except at a very heavy loss of life it had not been possible to advance. To remain was useless in itself and involved continuing casualties, and extension of the line and ultimate capture. The officers of some commands found their men unwilling to cross the open ground between the lines and to return to their works. They preferred capture to running the gauntlet.[17]

[15] *Lee's Dispatches,* 344–45.

[16] *Gordon,* 411. Here Gordon spoke of the non-arrival of the supporting troops, presumably Pickett's, but he had been told in advance that it was doubtful whether Pickett could arrive in time. In this report, *Lee MSS.—K,* Gordon did not mention this, and, speaking of the two brigades from Heth and the two from Wilcox, merely said these "did not participate."

[17] Reports in *O. R.,* 46, part 1, pp. 155 ff., 172 ff., 316 ff., 355 ff.; 2 *Davis,* 650 ff.; *Thomas,* 38 ff. The Federal reports are authority for saying that some of the troops participating in the attack behaved badly and submitted to capture rather than return to their lines. Major Theodore Miller, a Union inspector of artillery, who was captured and held in a bomb-proof while the Confederates were in Fort Stedman, stated that "the number of stragglers and skulkers was astonishingly large." He saw "several instances where the authority of the officers who urged them on was set at defiance." After the order was given for Gordon's men to retire to their own lines, "officers ordered, threatened, and begged their men to fall back . . . in vain, for their only way lay across the field so effectually commanded by [the Federal] artillery." He claimed to have prevailed on his captors to remain and to help him escape, and he affirmed that he carried some 250 or 300 into the ranks of the advancing Federals (*O. R.,* 46, part 1, p. 359). Confirmatory evidence was offered by a Confederate captain of Gordon's corps who stated that after the attack had been delivered, the men hugged the works and would not go forward. This was warning, he thought, that the day of offensive movement was gone (Captain

And the failure of the attack was not all that had to be told. Immediately following the repulse of Gordon's assaults, and almost before the Confederates had returned to their works, the Federals advanced along the whole right of Lee's position nearly to Hatcher's Run and took the entrenched picket lines. In this counterstroke, they captured about 800 prisoners and held their ground against all attempts to drive them back to their main lines. The enemy was thus placed where he could advantageously launch a direct attack to break the Confederate front whenever he chose to do so. The total haul of prisoners at the picket posts and at Fort Stedman was 2783. The Union estimate of gross Confederate casualties of 4800 to 5000 was not greatly exaggerated.[18]

Lee waited till the worst was known, waited till it was plain he could hope for no advantage, and then, wearily, he turned Traveller's head toward the Turnbull house. He had not gone far when he met two horsemen approaching him. He identified them quickly, and smiled at them. They were Rooney and Robert, who had ridden ahead of their division, which had been ordered to follow the hoped-for advance of the infantry. The General thanked Rooney for coming so promptly on orders—his trooper-son had ridden nearly forty miles with half-starved men and bare-ribbed horses—and expressed his regret that the attack had not so developed that the cavalry could be used. "Since then," wrote Captain Robert Lee, nearly twoscore years afterwards, "I have often recalled the sadness of his face, its careworn expression."[19] The General did not tell his sons what the failure at Fort Stedman implied. Sadly he telegraphed Longstreet that Pickett would not be needed and that those of his men who had started from the north side should go into camp around Chester;[20] briefly he reported to the Secretary of War on the morning's events.[21] He did not probe the reasons for failure or blame either

---

J. C. G.: *Lee's Last Campaign,* 10). Gordon said nothing of this in his report, but stated, on the contrary, that "the troops behaved with commendable courage" (Gordon's report, *Lee MSS.—K*). General Lee telegraphed that "all the troops engaged . . . behaved most handsomely" (*O. R.,* 46, part 1, pp. 382–83), which can only mean that he, and Gordon as well, knew nothing of the failure that had been observed by some of those in closer touch with certain of the units.

18 *O. R.,* 46, 1, 155, 156, 196. The VI Corps made no report of these operations Union losses were 2080.

19 *R. E. Lee, Jr.,* 147.   20 *Lee MSS.—U.*

21 *O. R.,* 46, part 1, p. 382.

Gordon or his subordinates,[22] but in the events of the day he saw his plan destroyed utterly. "I fear now," he wrote the President on the 26th, "it will be impossible to prevent a junction between Grant and Sherman, nor do I deem it prudent that this army should maintain its position until the latter shall approach too near." Johnston, he went on, reported only some 13,500 infantry, a loss of 8000 men, largely by desertion. At that rate of attrition, Johnston would not cross the Roanoke with more than 10,000, "a force that would add so little strength to this army as not to make it more than a match for Sherman, with whom to risk a battle in the presence of Grant's army would hardly seem justifiable." Johnston estimated Sherman and Schofield at 60,000. Grant might have 100,000 and, Lee feared, did not have less than 80,000. "Their two armies united," he said, "would therefore exceed ours by nearly one hundred thousand." Besides, if Grant wished to bring Sherman's army to him without a battle, he could easily manœuvre in such a way that if Lee marched out to meet Sherman the Confederates would have to fight both armies.[23]

Thus Lee was thown back on the plan of evacuating the Richmond line and of moving with his whole force to join the command in North Carolina. Even this plan was now modified by the fact that when junction was formed, there would be no prospect of attacking and defeating Sherman alone, for Sherman would join Grant. As Lee had said when Longstreet proposed that Johnston be brought to Richmond,[24] concentration by the Confederates involved like concentration by the Federals. The plan of a march to unite with Johnston was now complicated, also, by the arrival of Sheridan's cavalry after it had refitted at White House on the conclusion of a long raid eastward from the Shen-

---

[22] There was, indeed, no basis for blame, other than that Gordon mistook the abandoned Confederate works in rear of Fort Stedman for Union fortifications. And here the Georgian was not wholly culpable, for he had come from the Valley long after the line had been stabilized and naturally knew little of the old, outer line of Petersburg which had been evacuated by Beauregard during the fighting of June 15–17. Lee was perhaps culpable for not having Gordon's findings checked by one of his own engineers, but he was not censurable for entrusting the operation to Gordon. It was to be undertaken on Gordon's front and, furthermore, there was no other corps commander to whom it could be assigned with better promise of victory. Longstreet was north of the James, it will be remembered, and Hill was sick. Anderson's handling of the assaults on fixed positions during the fighting around Fort Harrison had not been of a sort to indicate that he would make a success of the attack on Fort Stedman.

[23] *Lee's Dispatches*, 345–46.   [24] *O. R.*, 46, part 2, p. 1250.

andoah Valley.[25] The approach of the premier Federal cavalry
had been assumed on March 17.[26] On the very day of the attack
on Fort Stedman, Fitz Lee had notified Longstreet that Sheridan,
in his opinion, would be on Grant's left flank on the 28th or
29th.[27] There were many indications by the 27th that Sheridan
was moving to the south side of the James.[28]

The retreat from Petersburg must therefore begin. The sooner
it was undertaken, the greater the prospect of eluding Grant. But
there were obstacles, old and new, to a speedy withdrawal.
Gordon's men needed rest for the recovery of their morale. The
administration was not ready to evacuate Richmond. The roads
were still excessively bad. Although what Colonel Taylor had
guardedly styled "the dread contingency" had now become a
"foregone conclusion," even in his optimistic mind,[29] Lee had to
wait. He had sent pontoons forward,[30] he had surveyed the ordnance stores[31] and he had prepared maps for the retreat, but, for
the moment, all he could do was to strengthen the right flank,
against which, rather than against Richmond itself, he had long
believed the final attack would be delivered.[32] In spirit, he could
only repeat what he had written Mrs. Lee before the outlook had
become quite so dark: "I shall . . . endeavor to do my duty and
fight to the last."[33]

[25] See *supra*, p. 13.   [26] *O. R.*, 46, part 3, p. 1319.
[27] *Lee MSS.—U.*   [28] *Lee MSS.—U.*
[29] *Taylor's Four Years*, 145.   [30], [32] *S. H. S. P.*, 67.
[31] 38 *S. H. S. P.*, 5. In 122 *Harpers Magazine*, 333, Major A. R. H. Ranson stated
that he had been sent to Lynchburg in January, 1865, to provide a depot of ordnance
stores, but that these had been returned to Richmond in February.
[32] *O. R.*, 46, part 2, pp. 1189, 1203, 1247, 1251, 1265; *ibid.*, part 3, pp. 1337, 1338.
[33] Feb. 22, 1865; *R. E. Lee, Jr.*, 146.

CHAPTER III

FIVE FORKS: A STUDY IN ATTENUATION

(MARCH 29–APRIL 1, 1865)

THE week beginning March 27, 1865, was one on which the survivors of the Army of Northern Virginia were loath to dwell, because it was to them, in memory, the first stage of a gruesome nightmare; but to the student of war it is a most instructive period. It illustrated both the possibilities and the limitations of the employment of infantry to support cavalry in dealing with a turning movement. Further, it will long remain a classic example of the manner in which even the highest skill in reconcentration may not avail in holding a long line against a very powerful adversary. The events of the week, indeed, might well serve as the basis of a study in attenuation.

All Lee's intelligence reports on the 27th indicated that the anticipated Federal movement was about to start and that it was directed against the upper stretches of Hatcher's Run. This meandering stream covered Lee's right flank. Rising some fifteen miles west and southwest of Petersburg, it was not on the watershed of the Appomattox, but ran roughly parallel to that stream for about seven miles from west to east, and then turned to the southeast to become one of the affluents of the Nottoway. Between Hatcher's Run and the Appomattox ran the Southside Railroad, one of Lee's two essential lines of communication, via Burkeville, with the fragment of the Confederacy not yet occupied by the Federals.

The railroad, of course, was the prime objective of any attempt Grant might make on his left to drive Lee from Petersburg without a direct frontal assault. To reach the railroad, Grant's easiest course was to cross Hatcher's Run at a distance from Lee's lines, to march westward until he had reached a point beyond Lee's right flank, and then to strike northward. As the roads lay, this would carry Grant into a wooded country, cut by numerous small but troublesome watercourses, most of which were running high between muddy banks. The main features of the terrain as they affected Lee's military problem were as follows:

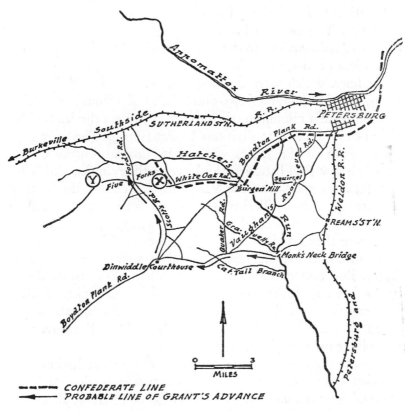

Terrain southwest of Petersburg to illustrate Grant's flanking operation against the Southside Railroad, March 27 ff., 1865.

Grant's easiest crossing was at Monk's Neck Bridge. Thence the way to the Southside Railroad led by Dinwiddie Courthouse and by Five Forks, where Lee already expected Grant's troops to appear. This route was only fifteen miles—say a march of a day and a half as the roads then were. To attempt to meet this advance by merely lengthening his front, Lee would be compelled to extend himself from the point marked with the encircled X to the encircled Y beyond Five Forks. This would be a prolongation of four miles, a distance Lee could not hope to cover adequately. Already he stretched this thin line almost as far as it would hold. On the twenty-seven and a half miles occupied by infantry, he could count an average of only 1140 men per mile. North of James River he had as defenders of his left flank Fitz Lee's division of cavalry. This numbered about 1800 mounted men[1] and was distant two days' march from the endangered right. Next the cavalry were Field's division of some 4600 men[2] and Kershaw's of 1800.[3] Their lines, which were fairly strong, extended slightly to the southwest of Fort Gilmer, two and a half miles from James River. It would take a minimum of twelve hours to get the leading brigade of either of these divisions to Petersburg. The only other forces north of the James were those around Chaffin's Bluff, namely a few field batteries, the heavy artillery units, which had very little transportation, the Virginia reserves, and the local defense troops. The artillerists were about 750 in number and the total of reserves and local defense troops was 3300, of whom about 1100 were then on the lines.[4] Altogether at this time Lee thus could muster above the James a total of approximately 9700 infantry, 1800 cavalry and 750 heavy artillery. Even to do this he had to call out all the reserves and local defense units. Without utilizing the local defense troops he could dispose about 7500 infantry. Exclusive of the cavalry, only Field or Kershaw could possibly be used to reinforce the right.

Between the James and the Appomattox, on and adjacent to the Howlett Line, were some heavy artillerists, a small detachment of naval gunners, and Mahone's division of infantry, about 3700 muskets. This infantry held nearly five miles of line and manifestly could not be reduced, for if the Federals broke through there they would cut the army in half and destroy communications between Richmond and Petersburg.

Gordon's corps, with artillery support, occupied a sector from

---

[1] Fitz Lee, March 23 (*Lee MSS—K*), gave the number as 2600 and said it was increasing daily, but he evidently included part of Rosser's division of 1200, who joined him but were sent on March 26 to W. H. F. Lee at Stony Creek (*F. M. Myers*, p. 367).

[2] *O. R.*, 46, part 1, p. 388, gave him 4799 present for duty as of March 1.

[3] According to *O. R.*, 46, part 1, p. 388, he had 1922 as of March 1.

[4] *O. R.*, 46, part 3, p. 1331; for organization of these commands see *O. R.*, 46, part 2, pp. 112, 1275.

the Appomattox River just east of Petersburg to the point where Lieutenant's Run passed through the lines, directly south of Petersburg and about one mile east of the Petersburg and Weldon Railroad. This was a front of slightly more than four miles, on which Gordon, after the losses in the affair at Fort Stedman, had only 5500 infantry,[5] a force that would have been hopelessly inadequate if the works had not been strong and all the ranges established. Beyond Gordon, in order from left to right, were Wilcox's and Heth's divisions of A. P. Hill's corps, extending from Lieutenant's Run to the works covering the Boydton plank road at Burgess Mill, on Hatcher's Run. This was a distance of more than eight miles, as the lines ran, and it was held by approximately 9200 officers and men.[6] To the right of Heth's division, protecting the White Oak and Claiborne roads in a bend of Hatcher's Run, lay Anderson's corps, which consisted of little more than B. R. Johnson's division of about 4800 infantry.[7] There was no cavalry on this flank. W. H. F. Lee's division, as already explained, was at Stony Creek, forty miles away by road. Its strength was approximately 2400. It was joined on the 28th by what was left of Rosser's division, some 1200 sabres, brought down from the Valley of Virginia.[8]

The only force that could be accounted a reserve was Pickett's division, which had been transferred to the north side of the James on March 14 to meet an anticipated attack by Sheridan.[9] The division, it will be recalled, had been ordered back to support the assault on Fort Stedman. One brigade, Steuart's, had reached Petersburg, but it was not needed in the operation and was held temporarily near the city. Two other brigades of the division were halted on Swift Creek, north of Petersburg. The remaining brigade, Hunton's, was still to the north of the James. The total strength of this scattered command was approximately 5000. It had suffered very heavily from desertion. The density of the

[5] Gordon's report, Lee MSS.—K.

[6] This allows 452 for desertions and casualties March 1–26 as a deduction from the 9652 reported present for duty March 1 (O. R., 46, part 1, p. 389).

[7] Anderson said (Lee MSS.—K) that he had about 6000 men when he was moved to the right, but that Wallace and Ransom's brigades lost about 1200 men while temporarily detached for the attack on Fort Stedman.

[8] F. M. Myers, p. 368. Myers gave the combined strength of the two divisions as 3000.

[9] O. R., 46, part 2, p. 1312.

infantry and the character of the various zones, as of March 27, were approximately as follows:

ZONE AND COMMAND	INFANTRY PER MILE OF DEFENDED LINE
North of the James—	
Cavalry on the left flank, 1800	
Longstreet, with Field's and Kershaw's division (chiefly in field works), 5 miles	1360[10]
Ewell, with Virginia reservists and siege artillery (in heavy earthworks), 2½ miles	740[11]
Howlett Line—	
Mahone's division (heavy works with naval and siege artillery support), nearly 5 miles	740
From the Appomattox to Lieutenant's Run—	
Gordon, with Walker's, Evans's, and Grimes's divisions (heavy works, enemy very close), 4 miles	1350
From Lieutenant's Run to Burgess's Mill—	
Wilcox's division of Hill's corps (some heavy works, chiefly field works), about 4½ miles	1100
Heth's division of Hill's corps (works of the same type as Wilcox's, though hardly as strong, except at Burgess's Mill), 3½ miles	1200[12]
Average density of this zone	1150
Beyond Burgess's Mill—	
Anderson, with Johnson's division (light field works on extreme right), 3 miles	1600
Average density (31,400 men on 27½ miles of line defended by infantry)	1140
Pickett's division, a quasi-reserve	5000
Cavalry at Stony Creek	2400
Ordered to Stony Creek, Rosser's division	1200

A pitiful situation, surely, for the only army of any consequence left to the Confederacy east of the Mississippi! What could Lee do with this scant force to meet the operation against his right? His first and obvious move, made on the 27th, was to transfer to that flank all the cavalry on the north side of the James, except Gary's brigade, which was left with Longstreet.[13] From Stony

[10] Even this coverage of the flank involved the virtual abandonment of two miles of the extreme left. If the extreme left were counted, Longstreet's density would have been only a little more than 900 per mile.

[11] This included the 750 heavy artillerists, who could be used as infantry.

[12] This assumption of 4½ miles for Wilcox and 3½ for Heth is believed to be correct, but it may have been that the density of the two divisions was about the same.

[13] F. Lee to Longstreet, March 27, 1865; *Lee MSS.—J;* F. Lee in *Proceedings . . . of the Court of Inquiry . . . in the Case of Governeur K. Warren* (cited hereafter as *War-*

Creek, of course, he could call up the rest of the cavalry, when needed, and thus could concentrate all his mounted troops on his extreme right. These three small divisions, however, could not possibly suffice to stop the movement, for on March 28 the report was that Federal infantry and artillery were continuing the march in great strength toward their left.[14] Lee must have suspected that these troops were from the north side of the James for he telegraphed for information from Longstreet,[15] whom he had cautioned five days before[16] to be on the alert and to be prepared to release all the troops he could possibly spare. As a second step in his effort to protect his right, Lee executed the plan he had adopted at Longstreet's suggestion[17]—to support his cavalry attack with an advanced and quasi-independent force of infantry. He knew he might have to increase this force, but he hoped if the enemy attacked he could do this without being compelled to draw troops from the line in such numbers as to make a break inevitable. The plan of operations was, in short, a compromise between a major detachment of force and a long extension of front. Pickett's division was selected for this service with the cavalry, and arrangements were made to shift other troops down the line to the right as operations required. Curiously enough, there is no record of any preliminary discussion as to who should command the force intended for the defense of the right.

It was on the 28th that Lee began to prepare for the movement of Pickett's division to the right.[18] He delayed dispatching the troops only in order to assure himself that Pickett could be moved there without too great risks to the north side.[19] He still had faith in his army and he told the administration that he believed it would have ten or twelve days in which to evacuate Richmond.[20] During the forenoon of the 29th Lee received word that hostile cavalry and infantry—there was no mention of artillery—had started a march southwestward from the Federal lines at Monk's

ren), 467. This movement, ordered on the 27th, began on the 28th. Rosser reached Stony Creek on the 28th.

[14] It is said that Lee owed his first information of this movement to a girl of eighteen, the daughter of poor parents living within the lines, who risked her life to communicate with his scouts (3 *Confederate Veteran,* 2-3).

[15] Lee to Longstreet, March 28, 1865, *Lee MSS.—U.*

[16] Lee to Longstreet, March 28, 1865, *Lee MSS.—U.*

[17] *O. R.,* 46, part 3, p. 1357.   [18] *Lee MSS.—I.*

[19] *O. R.,* 46, part 3, p. 1360.   [20] *O. R.,* 46, part 2, p. 1265.

Neck Bridge and had crossed Hatcher's Run.[21] From the early reports Lee was not certain of the immediate Federal objective.[22] He made his dispositions at once, however: Taking McGowan's brigade of Wilcox's division from its position on the line east of Hatcher's Run, he spread the other brigades over the ground McGowan had covered and moved him westward beyond Burgess's Mill. This arranged, Lee directed Pickett to move with the two brigades he had on Swift Creek, to pick up his third brigade in Petersburg and with these to go by train to Sutherland's station on the Southside Railroad, ten miles west of the city.[23] Rooney Lee's and Rosser's divisions of cavalry were ordered to join Fitz Lee's command on the extreme right.[24] A glance at the map will show that a cavalry raid on the Richmond and Danville Railroad around Burkeville was almost as easy as an attack on the Southside Railroad east of that point. Consequently, Lee directed Pickett's other brigade, Hunton's, which was still on the north side of the James, to cross to Manchester, away from the congestion of the Richmond yards and the allurements of Richmond streets, and to be ready to follow the rest of the division, or, if need be, to go directly on the Richmond and Danville Railroad to protect the Burkeville district.[25]

While these orders were being issued, Fitz Lee rode into Petersburg and reported the arrival of his division, which had been started the previous day from the extreme left. The commanding general told his nephew that Sheridan was in the vicinity of Dinwiddie Courthouse, was preparing to concentrate around Five Forks, and, in his opinion, intended to break up the Southside Railroad, which it was important to hold. Fitz Lee was to go there, where he would be joined by W. H. F. Lee and Rosser and by supporting infantry. He was to attack Sheridan—the one best way to break up the raid.[26] To insure co-ordination among the cavalry divisions, which had not been under unified command since Hampton had left Virginia,[27] Lee announced to his trooper-

---

[21] *O. R.*, 46, part 1, p. 1263. The best map is *O. R. Atlas, LXXVII.* Several detailed maps also appear in the *Atlas.* A section of the field, with contours, will be found in *Warren*, Part III.

[22] Lee to Longstreet, March 29, 1865, received 3:30 P.M., *Lee MSS.—U.*

[23] Pickett's report, *Lee MSS.—K.*

[24] Rooney Lee's report, *Lee MSS.—K;* for Rosser, see Fitz Lee in *Warren, 467.*

[25] Lee to Longstreet, *MS.,* March 29, 1865, *Lee MSS—U.*

[26] F. Lee's testimony, *Warren,* 467.   [27] *Ibid.*

kinsman that the latter was to take charge of the cavalry corps. No written orders were given Fitz Lee. He construed his verbal orders most strictly, as will presently appear, and he held General Lee's view of the situation long after the whole complexion of affairs had changed.

Later in the evening of the 29th, as a heavy rain began to fall,[28] word came from Anderson that the advancing Federals had extended their left to Dinwiddie Courthouse, which was six miles from their starting point. Anderson had sent out two brigades to meet the cavalry, who proved to be Gregg's, but he had been unable to drive them back[29] and had withdrawn to his works.[30]

This extension of the Federal left to Dinwiddie Courthouse, with no determined push northward toward the railroad, forced Lee to consider the possibility that instead of starting a raid, Grant was lengthening his line toward the southwest. The natural counter-move, of course, would be a corresponding extension of the Confederate front; but was that possible? Hunton could be and was called to Petersburg,[31] but beyond that, what could be done other than to bring over a part of Longstreet's corps? "Old Pete" was notified of the state of affairs and was told that he might be required to come to the southside with Field's division. Meantime, could Longstreet ascertain what troops were still in his front?[32] Longstreet's answer was that, as far as he could learn, the force on the northside was as usual, and that if Field were moved, the V. M. I. cadets and all the local defense troops should be called out to man the works.[33]

Soon the outposts reported that Federal artillery had also gone with the infantry and cavalry. Thereupon Lee took the further precaution of ordering to the extreme right the fine artillery battalion of Pegram with twenty guns.[34] Darkness fell in a continued downpour, with no further indication of what was ahead,

---

[28] O. R., 46, part 1, p. 53.

[29] O. R., 46, part 1, p. 1263; for the hour, ibid., 1287. This attack, which was opened at 3:20 P.M. by Wise's brigade of Johnson's division, was the real beginning of the Appomattox campaign.

[30] Anderson's report, Lee MSS.—K.

[31] O. R., 46, part 3, p. 1365.   [32] Lee to Longstreet, Lee MSS.—U.

[33] O. R., 46, part 3, p. 1363; O. R., 46, part 1, p. 1160. Longstreet did not know that Ord had crossed the James with three divisions of infantry and one of cavalry and was between the II and VI Corps on the south side of the river.

[34] McCabe in Warren, 511; Armistead C. Gordon: Memories and Memorials of W. Gordon McCabe (cited hereafter as Armistead Gordon), 1, 163.

except that on a large part of the Petersburg front heavy Federal demonstrations were begun. These were continued all night, as if Grant was feeling out the line in an effort to prevent the movement of troops to the right.[35]

The transfer that Lee had ordered during the day left the situation on the evening of the 29th as follows:

ZONE AND COMMAND	INFANTRY PER MILE OF DEFENDED LINE

North of the James—
Cavalry on the left flank, approximately 500[36]
Longstreet, with Field's and Kershaw's divisions (no change)... 1360
Ewell, with Virginia reservists and siege artillery (no change)... 740

Howlett Line—
Mahone's division (no change)............................ 740

From the Appomattox to Lieutenant's Run—
Gordon, with Walker's, Evans's, and Grimes's division (no change) 135ᴏ

From Lieutenant's Run to Burgess's Mill—
Wilcox's division of Hill's corps, diminished by McGowan's brigade, density reduced from 1100 per mile to.............. 888
Heth's division, strengthened by McGowan's brigade from Wilcox, density increased from 1200 to..................... 1550

Beyond Burgess's Mill—
Anderson, with Johnson's division (no change).............. 1600

Moving—
Pickett with 5000 infantry to join Anderson.[37]
Cavalry, 4200, to right flank.[38]

Although no alarming news greeted Lee on the rainy morning of March 30, he became convinced that he would have to strengthen his extreme right still more if he was to take the offensive against Sheridan. Any withdrawal from the line was, of course, exceedingly dangerous, but unless Lee was willing to have his right turned, what alternative was there? Grimly he ordered Gordon to take over two miles of trenches beyond the point where the flank of his troops rested;[39] and then, having discharged the gloomy business of the army at headquarters, he rode out to the

---

[35] Gordon's and Anderson's reports, *Lee MSS.—K.*
[36] Reduced to this figure by the transfer of all of Fitz Lee's division to the right flank.
[37] Hunton's brigade was moving up in rear of the other brigades. Pickett had only 3700 with him.
[38] This assumes a loss of 200 in the three divisions, on account of feeble horses, in the movement to the right.
[39] Gordon's report, *Lee MSS.—K.*

vicinity of Sutherland's. He found that Rooney Lee and Rosser had not arrived, but that Fitz Lee was advancing on Five Forks. Pickett had reached Anderson's headquarters and had reported to him on the night of the 29th. Lee promptly detached Pickett from Anderson and placed at Pickett's disposal Matt Ransom's and Wallace's brigades of Johnson's division, Anderson's corps, in addition to the three of Pickett's own division. Pickett was thereupon directed to march on Five Forks, to seize the initiative, and, with the cavalry, to march in the direction of Dinwiddie Courthouse for an attack on the flanking column of the enemy. Six of Pegram's twenty guns were to go with Pickett. The others were to remain at Burgess's Mill.[40] By these orders Lee definitely set up the mobile force to protect the right flank, roughly 6400 infantry and 4200 cavalry. Having done this—all that he could do—Lee rode back to Petersburg. "Don't think he was in good humor," an observant young officer wrote in his diary.[41]

Advancing to Five Forks, Fitz Lee saw nothing of the enemy. He then moved down the road toward Dinwiddie Courthouse, quickly established contact with the Federal infantry and horse and, after beating off two attacks, drove them back on their reserves.[42] This done, he returned to Five Forks, where he met Pickett. That officer had started from White Oak road for Five Forks, in accordance with General Lee's orders, but as his line of advance was closer to the Federals than that of Fitzhugh Lee, he was exposed to attack, in front and on the flank. The enemy made a rush on his wagon train, but was repulsed. Almost all the way to Five Forks he had to drive the enemy from his front. When at length he arrived it was nearly sundown.[43]

In conference, Fitz Lee and Pickett decided that as the remainder of the cavalry had not joined them, and as the men were very tired, having marched with little rest for eighteen hours, they would delay until the next morning, the 31st, the combined offensive General Lee had ordered. Two brigades were thrown out about three-quarters of a mile south of Five Forks to cover the front. To do this, the troops had, ominously enough, to drive back

<hr/>

[40] Pickett's report, *Lee MSS.—K;* McCabe in *Warren,* 511; Anderson's report, *Lee MSS.—K; Walter Harrison,* 135; C. *Wise,* 219.

[41] 1 *Armistead Gordon,* 163.   [42] *Warren,* 467; *Lee Dispatches,* 352.

[43] Captain W. Gordon McCabe, with the artillery, thought Pickett was needlessly cautious and lost time (1 *Armistead Gordon,* 163).

dismounted Federal cavalry who used repeating rifles and offered stiff resistance. Soon after this was accomplished, W. H. F. Lee and Rosser arrived at Five Forks with their cavalry.[44] Lee did not get a full report of all this, but by the close of the day he knew the mobile force on the right was facing tremendous odds. His information was that the units west of Hatcher's Run consisted of Sheridan's and Gregg's cavalry and of the V and parts of the II and VI Federal Corps.[45]

What could 10,600 hungry Confederates do against this host? Cool military judgment gave only one answer to that question, but so long as there was the least chance of success, Lee omitted no precaution. The removal of Johnson's two brigades to strengthen Pickett had left the infantry ten paces apart on the works within the bend of Hatcher's Run and west of Burgess's Mill. This position was important in itself and constituted the sector from which troops could be drawn most quickly in case further reinforcements had to be sent Pickett. Lee accordingly proceeded to place more troops there. McRae's brigade of Heth's division was passed from the eastern to the western side of Hatcher's Run and was held near Burgess's Mill. His sharpshooters were left behind.[46] Scales's brigade was moved from Wilcox's left to a position across the Boydton plank road, west of Hatcher's Run and just south of Burgess's Mill.[47] Hunton, who had come down from Manchester, was put in near the junction of the Claiborne and White Oak roads, within the works at the bend of the run.[48] The trenches abandoned by this shift to the right were taken over by Gordon in accordance with the orders Lee had given him that morning.[49] These changes left the density of the line and the disposition of the troops at midnight March 30–31 as follows:

---

[44] Pickett's report, *loc. cit.*

[45] *Lee's Dispatches,* 352. Lee's intelligence reports were in error. The II and the IV Corps were across Hatcher's Run, as reported, but the VI was still in the fortifications to the east of that stream. Lee had no notice, thus far, that one division of the XXIV also was across the run and that another division of the same corps and one of the XXV were directly east of the stream (Gibbon's report, *O. R.,* 46, part 1, p. 1173). The computation of the Union forces is easy except for the cavalry. Warren on March 31 had 17,073, Humphreys had 31,167, Turner's division of the XXIV was about 5500. If the cavalry, including MacKenzie, numbered 10,000, which there is every reason to believe it did, the total force beyond the run was 53,740. The odds were even greater than Lee assumed them to be.

[46] McRae's report, *Lee MSS.—I.*   [47] *Wilcox's MS. report,* 70.

[48] Hunton in *Warren,* 625.   [49] Gordon's report, *Lee MSS.—K.*

ZONE AND COMMAND	INFANTRY PER MILE OF DEFENDED LINE

North of the James—
Cavalry on the left flank, approximately 500
Longstreet, with Field's and Kershaw's divisions (no change)... 1360[50]
Ewell (with all local defense troops in position).............. 1320

Howlett Line—
Mahone (no change)..................................... 740

From the Appomattox to Lieutenant's Run—
Gordon, with Walker's and Evans's division, by extension of lines
    two miles to the right, density reduced on fronts of 4 miles
    from 1350 to.. 870

From Lieutenant's Run to Burgess's Mill—
Grimes's division of Gordon's corps, 2-mile front............. 870
Wilcox's division, further diminished by Scales's brigade but with
    line shortened to about 2¼ miles....................... 1100
Heth's division, strengthened by Scales's brigade, line approxi-
    mately 3¾ miles in length............................ 1785

Average density of this zone............................ 1370

Beyond Burgess's Mill—
Anderson, with Johnson's division, less Matt Ransom's and Wal-
    lace's brigades, but with Hunton's brigade of Pickett's division
    added, 3-mile front..................................... 1200
Mobile force set up beyond right of fortified position, at Five
    Forks, 6400 infantry and 4200 cavalry, 10,600 men.

On the morning of the 31st, when Pickett and Fitz Lee were to advance against the enemy seeking to turn the Confederate right, General Lee rode down the line as far as the fortifications within the angle of Hatcher's Run. When he arrived he found Union infantry in front of these works with their left "in the air" at a point about opposite the end of his own line. To take advantage of this carelessness, and to preclude the possibility of the Federals breaking through between Pickett's advancing column and Anderson's fortified position, Lee determined to attack and roll up the Union flank, though he had available for the task only four brigades, and those four, as it happened, from three divisions. Major General B. R. Johnson had two of these brigades, Wise's and Moody's, formerly Gracie's. Johnson accordingly was

[50] See notes to table page 26, *supra.*

33

put in command, under the general supervision of Anderson, who seems to have had little or no part in the action. McGowan's brigade, which was still close to Burgess's Mill, was moved over until it became the extreme right brigade. Moody was on Mc-Gowan's left. Then came Hunton. Wise was on the ground but not in line. The two right brigades were placed under McGowan, who was selected to deliver an assault, to turn the Federal left flank, and to drive the enemy across the front of the other brigades.

It had been raining since about 3 A.M.,[51] and was still raining when Lee made the arrangements for the attack. McGowan waited for the downfall to cease and then moved quietly out. He was getting himself into position, almost directly across the left flank of the infantry, under Lee's own eye, when firing broke out farther up the line. A lieutenant in Hunton's brigade, seeing the enemy, had sprung forward, had called on his men to follow him, and had opened the fight without waiting for orders. McGowan had perforce to launch his attack at once. The action had not progressed far when Lee saw that Hunton might lose contact with the troops on the line toward Petersburg, so he ordered Wise's brigade, which was available, to take position on Hunton's left. These tactics were successful. The troops on the Federal flank were quickly doubled up and thrown back across a branch of a nearby stream, Gravelly Run.[52] There the advance had to stop, however, as the Boydton plank road and strong Federal supports lay just beyond. Lee went with McGowan to the bank of the little watercourse, and after examining the terrain he determined to hold it if he could. Dispatching orders to that effect to General Hunton, he tried to get up some artillery and, if possible, some cavalry. Just then, unfortunately, the left of the attacking forces began to waver in the face of a strong Federal counterattack. Lee had to consent to a withdrawal which, at the end of the day, brought the troops virtually back where they had been in the morning. On parts of the line to the left of the point from

---

[51] 1 *Armistead Gordon*, 164.

[52] It probably was after this action that Lee met a Federal officer, Major J. A. Watrous, among the prisoners. "In a gentle voice, full of sympathy," Watrous wrote after the war, "he looked at me and asked, 'Are you badly wounded, Major?' I replied that I was, and Lee said, 'I am sorry, I am sorry, Major. Take good care of him, gentlemen'" (18 *Confederate Veteran*, 106).

which the advance had been made, brisk skirmishing occurred, but nothing more.[53]

Despite the outcome, this valiant fight under his very eyes had a stimulating effect on Lee. When General Hunton returned from the fray his scabbard had been bent almost double by a missile and he had three bullet holes through his clothes. Lee greeted him briskly: "I wish you would sew those places up," he said. "I don't like to see them."

"General Lee," said Hunton, "allow me to go back home and see my wife and I will have them sewed up."

The answer amused Lee. "The idea," he replied, "of talking about going to see wives; it is perfectly ridiculous, sir." [54]

Returning to the Turnbull house, Lee reported to the War Department the developments of the day. He had heard nothing from Pickett and Fitz Lee, and apparently he had caught no sound of their fire, but later in the evening he received news of what had befallen them while he had been directing the engagement in front of Anderson's corps. The troops around Five Forks had advanced southward toward Dinwiddie Courthouse, taking the initiative from the enemy. After a hard fight they had driven back the Federals, who were so numerous that Fitzhugh Lee was satisfied they constituted the whole of the cavalry corps. Pushing on, the Confederates had come within about half a mile of the courthouse. There darkness had halted them, and thence Pickett reported to Lee.[55] The showing of the men had been admirable. There was nothing to suggest either exhaustion or any wavering whatsoever.

The good showing made by his gallant old infantry on March 31 did not deceive General Lee. He realized on the morning of April 1 that the situation was increasingly critical, even though his troops had, as yet, been defeated nowhere on the right. In one

[53] O. R., 46, part 1, pp. 1287–88; Anderson's report, Lee MSS.—K; Hunton in Warren, 625; McGowan in ibid., 649.

[54] Autobiography of Eppa Hunton, 117. Another diverting incident occurred during this battle, when the gallant Walter Taylor stole off to indulge himself once more in the luxury of conflict. Riding out, he attempted to seize the flag of Orr's Rifles and to lead the charge, but Color-sergeant Dunlap flatly refused to give up the colors: if a fight was to be had, the sergeant did not propose to permit any one to deny him a part in its dangers (Norfolk Landmark, June 16, 1876, quoting The Abbeville [S. C.] Medium).

[55] O. R., 46, part 1, pp. 1263, 1299, Pickett's and W. H. F. Lee's reports, Lee MSS. —K.

of the last letters ever written in his autograph to the chief executive from the field, he explained the situation to Mr. Davis. By the extension of the Federal lines to Dinwiddie Courthouse he was cut off from the depot at Stony Creek, where, he reminded the President, forage for the cavalry had been delivered. It was more difficult to withdraw, for Sheridan's advance had deprived Lee of the use of the White Oak road, which was one of the most important highways on his right. The enemy was on his flank and potentially in his rear and was in position, with superior cavalry, to cut both the Southside and the Richmond and Danville Railroads. "This," he said, "in my opinion obliged us to prepare for the necessity of evacuating our position on the James River at once, and also to consider the best means of accomplishing it, and our future course." There was no longer any hope, he left Mr. Davis to infer, that time would remain for a slow removal of supplies from Richmond. He would like to have the President's views, he concluded, but felt that his presence at his head-quarters was necessary. If the President or the Secretary of War could come over for conference, he would be glad.[56]

Probably it was soon after he dispatched this letter—it certainly was not before—that Lee received a report from Pickett to the effect that he was being forced to withdraw from the vicinity of Dinwiddie Courthouse. This was bad news. As the Federals were certain to follow Pickett's withdrawal, every step of their advance would bring them toward Five Forks and thence, by what was known as Ford's road, dangerously close to the Southside Railroad. The whole distance by highway from Dinwiddie Courthouse to the railway was only seven and one-half miles—less than a day's march, even through such mud as at that season the armies had to encounter. If the railroad was to be saved, Pickett could not afford to give much ground. Lee accordingly wrote Pickett: "Hold Five Forks at all hazards. Protect road to Ford's Depot and prevent Union forces from striking the Southside Railroad." He added an expression of his regret that Pickett had been compelled to withdraw and could not hold his advantage.[57]

[56] Lee's Dispatches, 359–60.
[57] Text in Mrs. La Salle Corbell Pickett: Pickett and His Men, 386. This dispatch has not been found elsewhere.

The one prospect of saving a desperate situation continued to be the possibility that Grant might in some way expose himself to attack.[58] Lee proceeded to strengthen his position as far as practicable with artillery, on the sound principle that this was the first essential to a possible offensive in case Grant blundered. Pendleton was ordered to bring down to Petersburg a part of the reserve artillery and to dispose it behind the works held by Gordon,[59] whose troops were very close to exhaustion, inasmuch as more than one-half of them had to be continuously on duty.[60] Beyond Gordon's flank, A. P. Hill, who returned that morning from uncompleted sick leave,[61] resumed command of a corps that was little more than a shadow of itself. All Gordon's troops, plus that part of Hill's forces east of the north-and-south stretch of Hatcher's Run, now numbered only about 11,000 men. They occupied—it could not be said they held—fully eleven miles of works, from the Appomattox River to Hatcher's Run.[62]

Lee knew that this attenuation of his line was a desperate gamble with ruin, especially at a time when Pickett was retreating; and when he received word, early in the day, that troops from the XXIV Corps had been captured, he was quick to act. This corps belonged to Ord's army from the north side of the James, and if the XXIV had been transferred and no other had taken its place, then Longstreet could attack the enemy and force Grant to send troops back to the northside, or else Longstreet could despatch part of his command to strengthen the Petersburg front. A telegram presenting these alternatives to Longstreet was forwarded immediately.[63]

This done and the routine of the morning completed, Lee rode out again to the headquarters of Anderson's corps to watch at first-hand the developments there. He found that the troops which had been in Anderson's front the day before had moved to the right,[64] in the direction of General Pickett's front, but, so far

---

[58] Lee to Davis, April 2, 1865, *Lee MSS.—I.*

[59] *O. R.,* 46, part 1, p. 1280.   [60] Gordon's report, *Lee MSS.—K.*

[61] Heth's report, *Lee MSS.—K.* The late Mrs. Lucy Magill, daughter of General Hill, was authority for the statement that he had not completed his leave.

[62] They faced the VI and IX Corps, not counting any of the units still east of the run but intended for operations beyond it.

[63] Lee to Longstreet, April 1, 1865, *Lee MSS.—U.*

[64] Lee to Breckinridge, *O. R.,* 46, part 3, p. 1371.

as the records show, he heard nothing more from Pickett himself.

While at the headquarters of Anderson's corps, Lee received from Longstreet a reply to his telegram concerning the withdrawal of troops from the north side of the James. Longstreet had no sure information, but he was inclined to think the Federals had diminished their force. As he apprehended the Federal gunboats could prevent any successful offensive on his part, he thought it better if any troops could be spared to reinforce the southside.[65] Lee answered him with instructions to prepare for a troop movement to the Petersburg front if Longstreet found confirmation of the report that he faced reduced numbers.[66] A little later in the day Lee learned that some of his men had captured Federal troopers the contents of whose saddle pockets indicated that Kautz's cavalry was on the southside: would Longstreet ascertain what mounted units were on the northside?[67] Longstreet sent Gary's cavalry to make sure.[68] "Old Pete's" theory was that as Sheridan's cavalry was worn and Kautz's fresh, Sheridan probably had taken Kautz's and had left some of his tired troops in their place.[69]

At 4 o'clock that afternoon (April 1) heavy firing was heard from the right in the direction of Five Forks.[70] Theoretically, a cavalry brigade was in liaison between the Confederate right and the mobile force under Pickett and Fitzhugh Lee; practically, the mobile force had been cut off from the Southern lines since it had begun operations. There was, consequently, no knowledge at Anderson's headquarters as to what the sounds of action really meant. It must have been 5 o'clock and after when a young cavalry captain brought Lee the first intimation of what had happened across the damp, bleak flats among the pines. He was followed by a messenger from Fitz Lee, who reported that the

---

[65] O. R., 46, part 3, p. 1372.

[66] Lee to Longstreet, April 1, 1865, Lee MSS.—U.

[67] Lee to Longstreet, April 1, 1865, Lee MSS.—U.

[68] O. R., 46, part 3, p. 1377.

[69] O. R., 46, part 3, p. 1372. As a matter of fact, Lee was right and Longstreet was wrong. Kautz's division, commanded since March 20 by Brigadier General R. S. Mackenzie (O. R., 46, part 1, pp. 147–48), had arrived on Lee's right that very morning and had been in its first action there when the tell-tale saddle pockets had been taken. The division had been on the southside, in Grant's rear, since March 29 (O. R., 46, part 1, p. 1244).

[70] O. R., 46, part 3, p. 1288.

troops had been attacked in great force and that he had lost contact with Pickett.[71]

Lee accepted the news as indicating a reverse,[72] but he did not yet know that a dark and humiliating tragedy had been enacted around Five Forks in these grim stages: Pickett's withdrawal from in front f Dinwiddie Courthouse, ordered for 4 o'clock, had been begu at daybreak,[73] and had been carried out in good order, though followed up very closely by the Federals. The column had been halted, and line of battle had been formed in the position at Five Forks from which the advance had begun. Fitz Lee said in his report that this was done "on account of the importance of the location as a point of observation to watch and develop movements then evidently in contemplation for an attack on our left flank or upon the line of railroad communication . . . ,"[74] but the fact was that Fitz Lee thought the Confederate advance had broken up the Federal movement, at least temporarily. When he returned to Five Forks he was not looking for a Federal attack that afternoon.[75] Pickett must have been of the same mind, for he went off with Fitz Lee, about the middle of the day, to enjoy a shad-bake provided by General Rosser.[76] In their absence, shortly before 3 P.M., Federals were seen making their way toward the Confederate left. Soon they swept overwhelmingly down on the 6000 infantry,[77] who were badly placed and had very little artillery. Quickly the Union troops turned the left flank of the Confederates and routed or captured a large

---

[71] The substance of Fitz Lee's report can be reconstructed easily from Lee to Breckinridge, April 1, 1865, O. R., 46, part 1, pp. 1263–64.

[72] Anderson's report, Lee MSS.—K.

[73] Fitz Lee in Warren, 479.

[74] O. R., 46, part 1, p. 1300. Pickett wrote, after the surrender, that he would have preferred the position behind Hatcher's Run, where he had parked his wagons, and that he would have taken that position had not he received orders from General Lee to hold the road to Ford's. Pickett wrote, further, that he assumed Lee intended to send him reinforcements. He had reported early in the day, he said, that the enemy was trying to get in between him and the army. He stated that he asked in this telegram for a diversion, as otherwise he would be isolated (Pickett's report, Lee MSS.—K). No reference to the receipt of any such telegram is made by General Lee in his own dispatches that day, nor did he make any such dispositions prior to the news of the battle. as he would certainly have undertaken had he received such a warning of this character. Fitz Lee did not mention a dispatch of this sort, nor did he describe a condition that would have justified its transmission. The Federals did not record the capture of a dispatch of this purport.

[75] Warren, 481. [76] Irvine Walker, pp. 225 ff.

[77] Assuming 400 casualties and stragglers in the operation against Dinwiddie Courthouse.

part of them in a *coup de main*. The survivors retreated as best they could in the darkness to the Southside Railroad. There they were rallied.

Thus, in two calamitous hours, the mobile force that Lee had established to protect his right flank was swept away and virtually ceased to be. The Federals reported the capture of 3244 men and four guns.[78] The casualties were not large compared with those Lee had sustained in some of his great battles, but they were a very considerable fraction of his diminished army. His most strategic position had been lost. Fought in accordance with the plans made by two subordinates, and without Lee's participation or knowledge of what was happening, Five Forks was only one scene removed from the dread dénouement.[79]

[78] The loss in the V Federal Corps was 634 (*O. R.*, 46, part 1, p. 836). The casualties in Sheridan's cavalry were not separately reported but probably did not carry the total above 1000.

[79] Few battles in the Virginia campaigns provoked as much recrimination among the Confederate generals who participated. Pickett's report, which was not written until May, 1865, blamed General Lee for the position he (Pickett) selected and charged Fitz Lee with failure to use his cavalry in preventing the turning of the left flank (*Pickett and His Men*, p. 395). This report contained details of events that Captain W. Gordon McCabe, a historical critic who participated in the battle, insisted did not occur. Fitz Lee's report (*O. R.*, 46, part 1, p. 1298) did not blame Pickett but assailed Anderson for choosing the wrong line of advance—a charge that does not take into account the fact that as the position both of Pickett and of the Federals was unknown to Anderson, he could not have been expected to march in Warren's rear. What Fitz Lee claimed Anderson should have done is the counsel of perfection—after the event. Still later, in his life of General Lee, the cavalry commander modified his former view to the extent of saying that Pickett's "isolated position was unfortunately selected" (p. 376). Neither Fitz Lee nor Pickett ever made reference in print to their absence at the shad-bake, but Rosser, the host, admitted the facts, which General T. T. Munford repeatedly set forth in public and in private. They are reviewed fully in *Irvine Walker*, 226 ff. The fundamental cause of the defeat was, of course, the overwhelming strength of the attacking force, but if the ground had not been unfavorable the defeat would not have been a rout. The position would never have been taken up if there had been close liaison with Anderson, or if care had been taken in observing the advance of the enemy. As indicated, Fitz Lee gave the real secret of the fullness of the disaster when he said, in 1881, at the Warren Inquiry (*loc. cit.*): "When we moved towards Five Forks, hearing nothing more of the infantry's move which we had heard of the night before, I thought that the movements just there, for the time being, were suspended, and we were not expecting any attack that afternoon, so far as I know. Our throwing up works and taking position were simply general matters of military precaution." McCabe (*loc. cit.*, 603) stated that General Lee witnessed the rout at Five Forks, and in great indignation, affirmed that "when the troops were taken into action again, he would place himself at the head of them." McCabe also quoted an incident about Lee's orders for the arrest of the stragglers. This incident evidently refers to events after Sayler's Creek, not to Five Forks. And as General Lee did *not* see the rout, his reference to it, as given by McCabe, may be equally mistaken. The soldiers' viewpoint of the battle is given in *Walter Harrison*, 138–39, and in J. H. Hudson: *Sketches and Reminiscences*, 64 ff.

CHAPTER IV

THE BREAKING OF THE LINE

LEE heard the first incomplete report of Five Forks stoically on the afternoon of April 1, and, as was his habit when making his first adjustments to a new situation, in his deep voice he asked abstractedly of the cavalry officer who brought him the news, "Well, Captain, what shall we do?" [1]

The best he could do was little enough, and it entailed new risks: he must reinforce the cavalry with other infantry in place of Pickett's. At 5:45, Bushrod Johnson was ordered, through Anderson, to proceed at once to Church Crossing, near Ford's, and to support the cavalry.[2] Forty-five minutes later Johnson moved with three brigades—Wise's, Moody's, and Hunton's.[3] This meant the virtual abandonment of that part of the line within the bend of Hatcher's Run.

It meant even more, for as the few remaining units were spread out, they were so thinned as almost to be helpless. From Battery Gregg to Hatcher's Run the men were from ten to twenty feet apart, and at some points still farther. A single regiment of Scales's brigade and the sharpshooters of another, McRae's, were all that could be put in the position that Wise's and Hunton's brigades had occupied.[4] Lee's only chance of remanning the endangered, the all-but-abandoned works on the right was to bring Field's division of 4600 men from the north side of the James. He now ordered this, most urgently, and directed that Longstreet come with Field's men. In the last struggle he wanted near him that lieutenant, who, for all his stubborn self-opinion, was the best corps commander he had left. Lee must have put the extremity of his plight into that order, the text of which has been lost, for as it was transmitted through channels, it had an ominous ring.

[1] 28 *S. H. S. P.*, 110.
[3] *O. R.*, 46, part 1, p. 1288.
[2] Anderson's report, *Lee MSS.—K.*
[4] *Wilcox's MS. report*, 70.

"It is important beyond measure," Longstreet's adjutant general wrote Field, "that no time be lost." [5] As Field's departure would leave only one division of infantry, a single brigade of cavalry, and some heavy artillery north of the James, the tocsin was sounded in the capital and all the local defense troops, together with the state cadets, were ordered out to man the works below Richmond.[6] Ewell reassumed actively his general command on the northside.

Had Lee known early in the evening the full magnitude of the disaster that had befallen Pickett he might have ordered the evacuation of the Petersburg line before daylight. Even as it was, with the enemy on his right flank and the river behind him, he must have ridden back to the Turnbull house in full knowledge that what little hope remained to him hung on the arrival of Longstreet before Grant assaulted.

As compared with the state of affairs on March 27, here was the situation, in terms of the density of infantry, after Field started to move and the local defense troops took position:

ZONE AND COMMAND	INFANTRY PER MILE OF DEFENDED LINE	
	APRIL 1	MARCH 27
North of the James—		
Cavalry on the left flank, approximately 500; on March 27, 1800		
Kershaw's division, 1800, and 2200 of Ewell's local defense troops and reservists not previously on the line	600	1360
Ewell, with other reservists, on a front of 5 miles, local defense troops and heavy artillerists, on a front of 2½ miles	740	740
Howlett Line—		
Mahone's division	740	740
From the Appomattox to Lieutenant's Run—		
Gordon, with Walker's and Evans's divisions......	870	1350[7]
From Lieutenant's Run to Burgess's Mill—		
Grimes's division of Gordon's corps, 2 miles........	870	1350
Wilcox's division of Hill's corps, 2¼ miles..........	1100	1100

[5] O. R., 46, part 3, pp. 1374, 1375.

[6] O. R., 46, part 3, p. 1375. The hour of this dispatch, 7:30 P.M., makes it possible to fix the time of Lee's order for the dispatch of Field as subsequent to the receipt by Lee of the first news of the disaster to Pickett.

[7] On March 27 this corps front had extended only to Lieutenant's Run.

Heth's division of Hill's corps, diminished by casualties of March 31, approximately 250, and by McRae's sharpshooters and one regiment of Scales's	1565	1200
Average density of this zone	1262	1150

Beyond Burgess's Mill—

One regiment of Scales's brigade, McRae's sharpshooters, about 400 men on 3-mile front	133	1600

Moving April 1—

Anderson, with Wise, Hunton, and Moody, about 3500 men, to support the cavalry on the right.

Field's division, from the extreme left, about 4600 men, ordered to Petersburg.

Cavalry: north and west of Hatcher's Run, strength and condition unknown the evening of April 1 to Lee.

Pickett's command: A quasi-reserve on March 27; position and strength unknown to Lee on the evening of April 1.

South of the James River, on nearly 20 miles of line, Lee now had scarcely 16,000 infantry in position and none in reserve. From the Appomattox to Hatcher's Run, he had only 11,000. From Lieutenant's Run, where the works began to be less formidable, to the very end of his fortified position, where the Claiborne road crossed the western stretch of Hatcher's Run, he had no more than 12,500 infantry. These included the forces in the highly important position of Burgess's Mill. If Grant were held off one day longer, as he had been held off for nine months, there was still a chance of a safe withdrawal and a reconcentration. But if Grant turned the right, or discovered how thin was the line of infantry behind the works . . . then . . . but Lee could only tell General Grimes, who reported the weakness of his position, that he must do the best he could.

His orders given, Lee went to his quarters and partly disrobed, but he slept little, if at all.[8] He was exhausted, though not actually ill. He may have heard the shelling that began at 9 P.M. on Wilcox's front, the nearest point of which was only a little more than two miles from his headquarters. He probably knew nothing of a minor shift of part of McRae's force to the east of Hatcher's Run, next McComb, where danger seemed to be threatened.[9]

[8] This is inferred from Longstreet's description of conditions at headquarters on his arrival. (*Longstreet*, 604. See *Grimes*, 112.)

[9] *O. R.*, 46, part 1, p. 1285; *ibid., Atlas*, Plate LXXVII; report of Colonel E. Erson, *Lee MSS.—K.*

Perhaps he caught the sound of the picket firing that broke out at 1:45 on the morning of the fateful 2d of April. Soon A. P. Hill, who had been apprehensive because of the heaviness of the artillery fire, came out from his quarters, which were a mile and a half nearer Petersburg than Lee's.[10] About 4 o'clock Longstreet arrived in advance of Field's division, which was moving toward the city as rapidly as the creaking wheels of the decrepit railroad could turn. Lee was in bed, still feeling very unwell, but received Longstreet at once and reviewed for him the condition on the right. He directed Longstreet to take his troops, the instant they detrained, and to march for Hatcher's Run.[11]

Suddenly, while Lee was explaining the route of the division, Colonel Venable broke excitedly into the room. Wagons and teamsters, he said, were driving wildly down Cox's road toward Petersburg. An infantry officer had told him that Federal skirmishers had driven him from Harris's quarters, less than half a mile from Edge Hill.[12]

From Harris's quarters? Why, the huts of the Mississippians were a mile and a half in the rear of the main line! If the enemy were there, then the Federals had broken the line—broken it at a point that would put them in rear of the whole of the Confederate right!

Instantly the General sprang from his bed and hurried to the front door of the Turnbull house with Longstreet. It was an unusually dark morning.[13] Distant objects were vague. But long lines of men, like those of skirmishers, were visible, moving slowly toward Edge Hill from the southwest.[14] Were they retreating Confederates or advancing Union troops? Quick, Colonel Venable, mount and reconnoitre, and General Hill—but Hill was already running toward his horse. There must have been something desperate in the manner of Hill, for as the two hurried

---

[10] 11 *S. H. S. P.*, 566.

[11] *Longstreet*, 604; his report, *Lee MSS.—K.* Colonel Venable, 12 *S. H. S. P.*, 185, said that Longstreet arrived about 1 A.M., ahead of Hill, but he is contradicted both in *Longstreet, loc. cit.*, and in the contemporary report of the commander of the First Corps, which gave the time of his appearance at headquarters as "at daylight." Longstreet stated in 1896, *loc. cit.*, that he was ordered to Five Forks. In his report (April, 1865) he named Hatcher's Run. The earlier version, of course, is taken.

[12] Venable in 12 *S. H. S. P.*, 186.   [13] *O. R.*, 46, part i, p. 902.

[14] *Longstreet*, 605. Longstreet did not give the direction, but it can be inferred from the known line of the Federal approach.

off, Lee called to Venable to caution Hill not to expose himself.[15] Away they galloped. Other officers leaped into their saddles and sped after them. Couriers lashed their lean and frantic horses as they dashed away with orders.

Then, for a few moments, the line that stretched far across the gray fields halted as if in doubt. Anxiously Lee concentrated his gaze on it. Soon, in the growing light, the color of the men's uniforms was visible—blue. They were Federals. Could Longstreet use Field's division to stop them? No, "Old Pete" had to answer: Word had not yet come that any of Field's regiments had detrained, much less that they had arrived on the ground.[16] If that were so, the best that could be done for the moment was to rally the Confederate forces on Fort Gregg and Fort Baldwin, south of the Turnbull house and perpendicular to the main east-and-west line.[17] And as Fort Baldwin[18] was a mile and a quarter from the Appomattox, it was necessary for the troops south of Fort Baldwin and Fort Gregg to withdraw more to the east and to occupy the "inner line." In simplest terms, the general situation as then known to General Lee is sketched on page 46.

Going back to his private quarters, Lee dressed quickly and prepared to leave the Turnbull house, which was directly in the line of the Federal advance. When he reappeared, he was in full uniform and had on his sword.[19] Quickly he mounted his horse and rode down to the gate of Edge Hill and across the road, whence he had a good sweep of the country. He had not been there long, intent with orders for meeting the surprise, when a number of staff officers came up. Some of them were of Hill's entourage, and with them was Hill's dapple-gray horse. But the commander of the Third Corps was not astride the animal. Instead, Sergeant G. W. Tucker rode him—Tucker, who was

---

[15] *Taylor's Four Years*, 149; Venable in *S. H. S. P., loc. cit.*

[16] *Longstreet*, 605. Jos. R. Stonebraker: *A Rebel of '61*, pp. 94–95, noted that as Lee pointed out to Longstreet the position he wished Field to take, he reached into the rear pocket of his coat, took out a biscuit and ate it with his left hand. It probably was his only breakfast that day.

[17] Both these works had been constructed to cover the dam Lee had erected on Indian Town Creek and they were west of the "inner line" of redoubts that had been laid out in 1863 before the main defenses had been taken up.

[18] Also called Fort (or Battery) Whitworth.

[19] *Cooke*, 447. The same author, who saw Lee that morning, quoted but did not vouch for a tradition that Lee remarked he intended to have on his full harness if he had to surrender. No authority for this tradition has been found. It would appear to be a misplaced version of an incident at Appomattox mentioned on p. 118.

known throughout the army as Hill's daredevil courier, the man who had asked permission in the Wilderness campaign to go out to the skirmish line and kill a Federal cavalryman in order that he might get a horse to take the place of his own, which was dead. Tucker had no jest in him now: with heavy heart he told

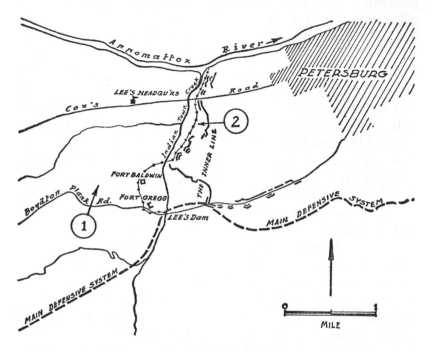

Situation on Lee's right-centre after the Confederate line had been penetrated on the morning of April 2, 1865.

1 The Federals were advancing on Lee's headquarters in the direction indicated by the arrow, but the point and the extent of the break were not known to Lee.
2 To halt the Federals, Lee planned to hold the front indicated by the dots and dashes, extending from the main defensive system, via Forts Gregg and Baldwin, to the Appomattox River and covering the old inner line west and southwest of Petersburg.

how Hill and himself had ridden on, after Colonel Venable had left them, and how they had encountered two Federals who had answered their call for "Surrender" with rifle shots. Hill had been hit and had toppled out of his saddle. Tucker had seen him on the ground, motionless, had caught his horse and had changed to it because the gray was fresher than his own mount. Lee listened intently. Grief showed itself in a sharp change of expression. Tears came to his eyes: "He is at rest now," he murmured, "and we who are left are the ones to suffer." Then he turned to Tucker and directed him to go with Colonel Palmer, Hill's adjutant general, so that Mrs. Hill might know the facts. "Colonel," he said to Palmer, "break the news to her as gently as possible." [20] To Major General Heth, Hill's senior division commander, Lee dispatched the grim announcement, with orders to report at once in person. As it happened, Heth was far down on the right, near Burgess's Mill, and found the enemy between him and headquarters when he attempted to get to the Turnbull house. As he failed to appear, Lee put the Third Corps under Longstreet. [21]

After the first irruption of the Federals there was a period of comparative calm west and southwest of Edge Hill. The tide of blue seemed, indeed, to be receding rather than advancing. It was probably at this time, though it is not certain, that Lee learned what had happened. Further fact, of course, sifted in with the hours. The Federals had started bombardment during the night, and at 4:45 had assaulted along nearly the whole of the line from the Appomattox River, on the Confederates' left, far around to the right on Hatcher's Run. The assaults had three aspects. On Gordon's lines, from the river to Fort Gregg, the enemy had gained the first line easily, but had there met with resistance of the most stubborn sort. At the very time that Lee was getting information of this, Gordon was counterattacking as vigorously as he had that day at Bloody Angle. [22] On his front, though the Federal advance could of course be pressed till the rear line was overrun, there was no immediate danger. Southwest of Fort

[20] Tucker's account, originally published in *The Philadelphia Weekly Times,* was reprinted in *The Culpeper Virginia Star,* Sept. 29, 1927, and subsequently in 11 *S. H. S. P.,* 564 *ff.* Venable's narrative is in 12 *ibid.,* 185; the version of "Courier Artillery, Second Corps," who met Hill and Tucker will be found in 12 *ibid.,* 184. The writer has also a fuller and later MS. account by this courier, the late G. Percy Hawes, of Richmond, Va. There are some minor conflicts of testimony as to Hill's departure from headquarters, but they are believed to be resolved correctly in the text. Colonel W. H. Palmer, Hill's chief of staff, stated in a letter of June 25, 1905, to Colonel Walter Taylor that Lee told him, "Go at once, Colonel, and get Mrs. Hill and her children across the Appomattox." When Colonel Palmer reached the Venable house, where Mrs. Hill was residing, he heard her singing. As soon as she saw him, she said: "The general is dead; you would not be here unless he was dead" (*Taylor MSS.*). Mrs. Hill was a sister of General John H. Morgan. For further details of the death and burial of Hill, see 19 *S. H. S. P.,* 183 and 27 *ibid.,* 34 *ff.*
[21] Heth's report, *Lee MSS.—K; Longstreet,* 608.
[22] Gordon's report, *Lee MSS.—K.* This report contains some unpublished detail.

Gregg, where the lines turned away toward Hatcher's Run, the assault had a second aspect. Thomas's and Lane's brigades of Wilcox's division, who occupied that part of the front, had simply been overwhelmed. Coming through at a little ravine below the Banks house, opposite the Federal Forts Fisher and Welch, at a point two miles southwest of the Confederate Fort Gregg,[23] the van of the Federals had pushed due north to the Boydton plank road and beyond. These were the troops that had first been seen from Lee's headquarters.[24] Two soldiers had actually gone half a mile farther to the Southside Railroad, where they had torn up a couple of rails. Most of Lane's and Thomas's men, and a few from Heth's division, falling back in front of the Federals and counterattacking more than once, had been ordered by General Wilcox toward Fort Gregg.[25] Some of them had gone the opposite way, toward the right. The Federals had turned in that direction much more heavily than to the Confederate left centre and were sweeping down the Boydton plank road and along the works towards Hatcher's Run. Near that stream the assault took on its third aspect. The fog had hung heavily along the run and had prevented a frontal assault at 4:45.[26] After 7 o'clock this fog had lifted and the Federals had gone forward. They first reached the line at a point about three miles southwest of the other break, and just to the east of Hatcher's Run at the first crossing of the Confederate lines over that stream.[27] The Federals met with little resistance here[28] and captured Davis's brigade and part of McComb's, both of Heth's division. The Confederates around Burgess's Mill, on the other side of Hatcher's Run, got away—Cooke's, Scales's, McGowan's, and a part of McRae's brigades. They marched northward to the Southside Railroad at Sutherland's Station, whither Anderson had gone and where Pickett had orders to join him.[29] The Federals who had turned toward the Confederate right, after the break-through on Lane's front at the Banks house, soon met those who had marched into the Confederate works on Hatcher's Run. There was a halt as the lines

[23] Lane's report, O. R., 46, part 1, p. 1285; Wright's report, ibid., 902–3.
[24] O. R., 46, part 1, p. 993.   [25] Wilcox's MS. report.
[26] O. R., 46, part 1, p. 1224.   [27] O. R., 46, part 1, p. 1221.
[28] Turner, O. R., 46, part 1, p. 1214.
[29] Wilcox's MS. report, 71; Heth's, Lee MSS.—K; Pickett's report, loc. cit., McRae's report, Lee MSS.—L.

were re-formed. Then a large part of the combined forces turned back toward Petersburg.

Lee did not have all this detail in the early morning, but he knew that the troops on Hatcher's Run were cut off from him,[30] and he could see that beyond the right of Fort Gregg he practically had no line. About the same time, presumably, Lee got his first full news of the magnitude of the disaster to Pickett the previous evening, though he had heard from the cavalry and knew something of it. Calamity was piled on disaster.[31]

Lee's situation now presented two obvious problems. One was to hold Petersburg until night and then to get out with the troops still on the lines. The other problem was to effect a new concentration with the forces cut off on the right, which forces he could not now help in their efforts to escape. He was not certain, shortly after 10 o'clock, that he would be able to maintain his position until night and he saw no prospect of doing more; but he determined, if he could hold out that long, to evacuate the whole front as soon as darkness fell, and to reconcentrate on the Richmond and Danville Railroad. In a few minutes of relative quiet[32] he dictated to his adjutant general a telegram for the Secretary of War, reviewing the facts, outlining his plan, and concluding significantly: "I advise that all preparation be made for leaving Richmond tonight. I will advise you later, according to circumstances." [33] Taylor in his turn, probably from his rough notes, dictated this fateful message to the telegraph operator, who sent it directly to the War Department in Richmond, where it was received at 10:40.[34] This was the dispatch that was carried to President Davis in Saint Paul's Church, Richmond, during the

[30] O. R., 46, part 3, p. 1378.

[31] The time of the receipt of any adequate report from Pickett is in doubt. Lee knew something of it, obviously, when he sent Breckinridge the telegram received April 2, at 10:40 A.M. Gordon said Lee notified him (see infra, p. 50) not to sacrifice more lives in another general counterattack. According to Parke (O. R., 46, part 1, p. 1018), Gordon delivered his heaviest counterattack at 11 o'clock. Having received Lee's orders soon thereafter, Gordon returned to the defensive. Assuming the wires down, it took an hour to get word from headquarters to Gordon. That would indicate that full news from Pickett had been received not long before or after 10 o'clock.

[32] Longstreet, 607.

[33] O. R., 46, part 3, p. 1378. Reagan, op. cit., 196–97, stated that he had informed the President, on his way to church, of the situation at Petersburg. The receipt of the dispatch, therefore, simply confirmed what Reagan had told Mr. Davis.

[34] The writer once asked Colonel Taylor if he knew what had become of the original of this dispatch. He answered that there probably had been no original, as he had dictated virtually all the orders for the evacuation to the operator without writing them out.

morning service. He read it, got up quietly, and left the building.

About the time Lee sent this warning to the President, General Gordon forwarded a report of conditions on his front. He had met the enemy's assaults with local counterattacks, he said, and was preparing a larger operation. As this would be costly of life, he asked whether General Lee's future movements depended on the recapture of his original line. Lee sent back answer that the enemy's gains on the right would necessitate a withdrawal and that Gordon should sacrifice no more men needlessly,[35] but should close the breach the Federals had made in his line and should be prepared to quit at nightfall.

Thus far Lee had maintained his equanimity. When a staff officer came up, asked some question of one of his subordinates, and formally saluted the General, Lee raised his hat in acknowledgment and gave the answer "in a voice entirely measured and composed." [36] He was "self-contained and serene," wrote Colonel Taylor, and "he acted as one who was conscious of having accomplished all that was possible in the line of duty, and who was undisturbed by the adverse conditions in which he found himself." [37]

New tests of his self-control lay ahead, for the Federals, who had been inactive and had almost disappeared after their first rush toward the Turnbull house, began to move forward again. Their evident purpose was to storm or mask Fort Gregg and Fort Baldwin and to close in north of these works, past Lee's headquarters, to the Appomattox River. Shell began to come over. One of them went through the house itself. Federal infantry were massing. Assaults were brewing. Guns that Lee had ordered down from the Howlett Line the previous day[38] had gone into action nearby, some of them in the garden of the Turnbull house. They were served under Lee's eye in a manner to win the enemy's praise, and they seemed to hold up the Federal flanking movement.

Soon Taylor and the telegraph operator were leaving the house. Musketry fire was mingling with the shell. Even the artillery was about to withdraw. Lee himself must turn his back on the

---

[35] Gordon's report, *Lee MSS.—K; Gordon,* 420.
[36] *Cooke,* 447. Cooke himself was the questioner.
[37] *Taylor's General Lee,* 275.   [38] *O. R.,* 46, part 1, p. 1280.

enemy and go within the inner lines. Carefully sending away a chair he had borrowed,[39] and manifestly unwilling to start, he remained until the enemy was so close that Traveller had to be put to a gallop. "This is a bad business, Colonel," he said to one of his staff, in a tone still untroubled. Ere long the Turnbull house was aflame—by design, he thought, and much to his regret.[40] A little way, and he reined in his gray, but evidently his cavalcade had been seen and recognized, for the Federals pursued it with a hot fire.[41] Soon a shell exploded only a few feet behind, killed a horse and scattered fragments. Lee's face became flushed as it did when he was angry, he turned his head over his right shoulder, and his eyes were gleaming. He wanted to charge his pursuers, but he quickly recovered himself, and rode through the inner line, where a thin, "scratch" force received him with cheers as warm as those of that great high noon of his glory at Chancellorsville. "Well, Colonel," he is said—perhaps apocryphally—to have told one of his officers, "it has happened as I told them it would at Richmond. The line has been stretched until it has broken." [42]

Now came one of the most dramatic incidents of an overwhelming day. Some 400 to 600 troops of Wilcox's division and of Harris's brigade[43]—men who had previously been rallied and employed in counterattacks that had delayed the enemy's advance —were put into Fort Gregg and were told to hold it to the last extremity. They made a Homeric defense. Using their few field

[39] The chair was of special design, with a wide right arm and had a pivoted table attached to the left in such a way that it could be used in front of the chair (*Mrs. Campbell Pryor's MS. Memoirs*, 8–9).

[40] *Taylor's Four Years*, 150. The site was occupied by the 2d Brigade, 2d Division, VI Corps (*O. R.*, 46, part 1, p. 971).

[41] In *Following the Greek Cross*, 258, T. W. Hyde stated that Lee was plainly seen by the Federals.

[42] *Cooke*, 447–48. This is the best and the only account of reasonable adequacy by an eye-witness. Both *Long*, p. 410, and *White*, p. 418, quoted Cooke but did not credit him. Longstreet's chronology of the day was somewhat confused. In his *Four Years*, p. 150, Taylor inferentially gave a later hour for the evacuation of the Turnbull house than in his *General Lee*, p. 272, where the sequence of events is somewhat jumbled. The writer has not attempted to fix the exact time of the ride to the inner lines, but he is satisfied it was later than has been supposed. The only satisfactory check on the time is that given by the various Federal commanders. It may have been 11 A.M. or 12 M. before the Federal line was well-formed on the Confederate right between Fort Gregg and the river. It was 1 o'clock when the attack on Gregg was ordered, and 3:30 when the Federals reached the Appomattox (*O. R.*, 46, part 1, pp. 911, 927, 1179) Lee did not leave the house until about the time the artillery limbered up. That was not long before the attack on Gregg.

[43] *Wilcox's MS. report*, 738. Harris's brigade belonged to Mahone's division.

51

guns as long as they could, they then employed their muskets, and in the final assault at 1 o'clock, their bayonets. Against them was directed a full division. At one time, in the hand-to-hand fighting on the parapet, six Federal flags were to be counted. "And still the fighting continued. At length the little battery was entirely surrounded, and from the loopholes in the palisades enclosing the gorge a spirited and telling fire was delivered upon the enemy at short range; after the complete surrounding of the battery, the struggle continued fifteen or twenty minutes."[44] When the Federals at last entered Fort Gregg, they found fifty-five dead and took about 300 prisoners, including the wounded.[45]

Just before the attack on Fort Gregg began, Benning's brigade, which was the van of Field's division, reported to Longstreet and was put in to fill a gap on the Confederate right, between Fort Baldwin and the Appomattox River. Along with the men already on the line they fought desperately but against such heavy odds that their officers kept calling for reinforcements. Lee had each time to send the same answer—that he had none. Finally, when Colonel Palmer came up from Longstreet, and asked for troops to be employed around Battery 45, Lee's patience failed him. He was standing at the time on the bluff above Town Creek, in the thickest of the fire, near the Whitworth house, but, as always, he seemed oblivious to the danger. "I have received that message several times," he said to Palmer, "and I have no troops to send." Palmer saluted formally. "I cannot help it, General, how often you have heard it; I am compelled to deliver you General Longstreet's message." Lee's manner softened, but his necessity continued. The men must fight it out where they were.[46] And they did. Shortly thereafter a broken line was taken up in rear of the forts from Battery 45 to the Appomattox. This line was stabilized during the early afternoon.[47]

[44] *Wilcox's MS. report,* 75.
[45] *O. R.,* 46, part 1, p. 1174. For details of the defense and statements of the part played by different commands, see *S. H. S. P.,* 105, 403; 3 *ibid.,* 19 *ff.,* 82 *ff.;* 4 *ibid.,* 18; 8 *ibid.,* 475; 9 *ibid.,* 102. In the *Guide to the Fortifications and Battlefields Around Petersburg,* 22, it is stated that Lee called his staff around him, pointed to Fort Gregg, and asked them to witness a most gallant defense.
[46] W. H. Palmer to W. H. Taylor, *MS.,* June 25, 1905, *Taylor MSS.*
[47] This is a later hour than is usually assumed but it is fairly well established by *Wilcox's MS. report, loc. cit.,* and Longstreet's, *Lee MSS.—K,* as well as by Penrose's report, *O. R.,* 46, part 1, p. 927, of the hour at which his command, which was on the extreme Federal left, rested its flank on the river. Pendleton must have been in error in his statement of the time (*O. R.,* 46, part 1, p. 1280).

As soon as he was reasonably sure that he could hold Petersburg until nightfall, Lee went to the McIlwaine or Dupuy house, one mile from the city,[48] and proceeded to arrange the details of the evacuation. This was a more difficult task than the withdrawal from Maryland in 1862, or the retreat after Gettysburg, owing to the condition of the men, of the animals, and of the roads, and to the necessity of destroying many supplies and guns that could not be moved. The march was to be directed to Burkeville, and the point of reconcentration was to be Amelia Courthouse, a village distant forty miles from Petersburg, on the railroad from Richmond to Danville.

A retreat to Amelia meant that all the units except Anderson's corps and Mahone's division would have to make two crossings of a river, with all the encumbrance of their heavy wagon trains. The reservists and those of Longstreet's troops left on the north side of the James must pass over that river and then over the north-and-south stretch of the Appomattox, just east of Amelia Courthouse. The divisions from Petersburg had to get north of the Appomattox, and, turning westward, had to negotiate that stream again. Anderson's corps could strike out up the south bank of the Appomattox and could reach Amelia Courthouse without crossing the river.

The roads from the different parts of the line to Amelia Courthouse had been studied by Lee's engineers, and the condition of the bridges, as already noted, had been reported as of March 30.[49] The task of the staff was primarily that of routing the commands so as to minimize congestion on any particular road. Of the three spans on the upper Appomattox, Goode's and Bevill's were passable. The state of the third, that at Genito, being in doubt, Lee ordered pontoons sent to Mattoax by railroad. Thence engineers were to transport them to Genito bridge and were to put them down so that the wagon train from Richmond could pass.[50] Orders were to destroy all bridges after the last Confederate forces had crossed. In the case of Ewell, who would be in charge of all

---

[48] 22 *S. H. S. P.*, 70, 71. The old Dupuy property was the country home of Captain Robert D. McIlwaine and was known as the "Cottage Farm." For tracing its interesting history, the writer is indebted to his distinguished friend, Arthur Kyle Davis, LL.D., of Petersburg, Va.

[49] *O. R. Atlas,* Plate LXXVIII.   [50] 32 *S. H. S. P.,* 68.

53

the troops leaving Richmond, supplementary instructions were given to avoid any alarm of preparation in the capital.[51] The evacuation of Petersburg was to begin immediately after dark. All guns were to be out of the works in front of that city by

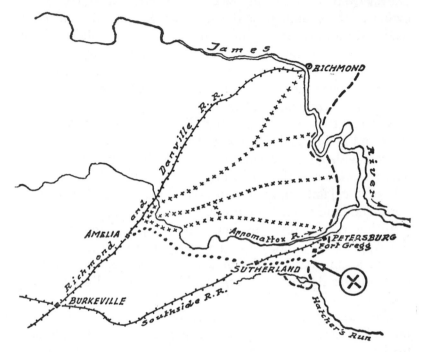

Proposed lines of retreat of the Army of Northern Virginia, April 2, 1865, for a reconcentration on the Richmond and Danville Railroad. The encircled X and the arrow indicate where the line was broken. The dotted line shows how Anderson could move on Amelia Courthouse and avoid a crossing of the Appomattox. A more detailed sketch of the routes of the other units appears on page 62.

8 o'clock and were to be across the Appomattox by 3 A.M.[52] The special orders were issued as rapidly as possible. The general order was drafted more slowly and was revised with some care, though not materially changed.[53]

[51] O. R., 46, part 3, p. 1380. [52] O. R., 46, part 1, p. 1280.

[53] Several drafts are in the Lee MSS.—N. What appears to be the original is in pencil on scraps of paper in the autograph of Colonel Walter H. Taylor. Among the Taylor MSS. is an undated clipping of an article by Colonel John A. Sloan in which it is stated that the final order was dictated to Colonel Taylor about 3 P.M. on the portico of Captain McQuain's house, to the left of but near Cox's road, one-half to three-quarters of a mile from Petersburg. "McQuain," of course is an error for "McIlwaine." Longstreet, Wilcox, and Heth were said to have been present with Lee. It probably was here that

Its composition was interrupted by many calls for counsel and direction. Mr. Davis, going from the church to the War Department, telegraphed that a move from Richmond that night would "involve the loss of many valuables, both for the want of time to pack and of transportation." [54] It was a plain request for more time, despite warnings repeatedly given since February 21. Lee's nerves were beginning to feel the strain of a day in purgatory, and when he read the President's message he tore it into bits. "I am sure I gave him sufficient notice," he said,[55] but he replied calmly that it was "absolutely necessary" to abandon the position that night. Lee thought at the time that the President would go with the army and he made arrangement to acquaint him with the route and to supply him with a guide.[56]

Rumors of the proposed move were getting afoot. The naval commander at Drewry's Bluff had heard of the stir among the infantry, and as he had no orders from his department, he asked for suggestions, through Mahone, who held the adjacent lines.[57] From the bureau of subsistence in Richmond came an inquiry to Colonel Cole as to the proper route for the reserve rations that had been accumulated.[58] Lee probably never saw this message. Soon there came the mayor and two members of the Petersburg city council to inquire what was to be done and what action they should take. Lee found them at the house when he returned from a brief absence, and he took pains to say nothing that would create needless panic in the town. With polite reticence he said he would communicate with them officially at 10 P.M.[59] Reminders there were, in the midst of it all, that Petersburg was not the only city in anguish. From Lieutenant General Taylor in Alabama, Lee received telegrams predicting the fall of Mobile.[60]

W. W. Chamberlain, *op. cit.*, 120, saw Lee with Longstreet. While the orders were being prepared, Colonel W. H. Palmer was asked by Colonel Taylor to assist in writing them out. While doing so, Palmer found a word he could not read and he went to Taylor to decipher it. Lee saw him. "Colonel Palmer," he said, "I wish you would leave Colonel Taylor alone, he is engaged on an important order and I don't want him disturbed." Palmer replied, "Colonel Taylor has asked me to assist him, and there is an indistinct word." Lee promptly apologized: "I did not understand," he said (W. H. Palmer to W. H. Taylor, *MS.*, June 25, 1905, *Taylor MSS.*).

54 *O. R.*, 46, part 3, p. 1378.
55 Charles S. Venable to Walter H. Taylor, *MS.*, March 29, 1878, *Taylor MSS.*
56 *O. R.*, 46, part 3, p. 1378.
57 *Lee MSS.—I.*   58 St. John's report, *Lee MSS.—L.*
59 22 *S. H. S. P.*, 70–71.   60 *Lee MSS.—U.*

Another message now from the President: Would the Danville Railroad be safe that night? Lee thought so and notified him it could be used until the next day.[61] The admission was gloomy, but so was the situation, yet Lee did not abate his efforts. Receiving a letter of the previous day from Mr. Davis, he found time at 3 o'clock to dictate an immediate reply, in which he discussed plans for raising Negro troops, as if the war would go on indefinitely. In a later paragraph he told what had happened and explained: "I do not see how I can possibly help withdrawing from the city to the north side of the Appomattox tonight." He concluded characteristically: "I regret to be obliged to write such a hurried letter to your Excellency, but I am in the presence of the enemy, endeavoring to resist his advance," as though the exactions of the greatest crisis in the army on which his government depended for its existence would not have excused sentences far more disjointed than his calm lines. He was full of courtesy still —and still full of fight.[62]

The afternoon was passing. Duties for the desperate night had to be apportioned. Lee called his entire staff together, explained the plans for the evacuation and assigned to each his work.[63] There was one staff officer, however, who had plans of his own for the evening. That was Colonel Walter Taylor. He worked furiously until the last orders were out and awaiting execution. Then he came to Lee and preferred as strange a request as ever adjutant general put forward on the day of a general troop movement: Would the General excuse him that evening and permit him to go over to Richmond? He would overtake the army early in the morning, but tonight—tonight he wanted to get married! He explained that the home of his affianced was within the enemy's lines and that she was alone in Richmond, working in one of the government offices, and wished to follow the fortunes of the Confederacy if the front should be restored farther south. Thereupon General Lee, said Taylor, "promptly gave his assent." [64] Thus it came about that on the night when the whole army was

[61] O. R., 46, part 3, p. 1378.
[62] 2 Davis, 660–61; Jones, 309. A very beautiful and careful copy of this letter, on good paper, in Taylor's autograph, is among the Lee MSS.—I. It is an interesting proof of the order that ruled at headquarters.
[63] Major G. B. Cooke, in Richmond News Leader, Jan. 19, 1923.
[64] Taylor's General Lee, 277.

to move, and over strange roads, Lee acted as his own adjutant general.

When the dreadful day ended the lines were still holding. The enemy's attacks had died away, as if Grant knew that the morning would yield him the city, without the shedding of more blood. Lee sent the last word to the War Department: "It is absolutely necessary that we abandon our position tonight, or run the risk of being cut off in the morning. I have given all the orders to officers on both sides of the river, and have taken every precaution that I can to make the movement successful. It will be a difficult operation, but I hope not impracticable."

In the spirit of that final statement, soon after night fell, the troops began quietly to move out of the city. Lee mounted Traveller and passed over the bridge to the north side of the Appomatox[65]—for the last time as a soldier. He was next to see Petersburg as a silent guest at a wedding party, in the midst of gaiety depressed by the memories of a suffering city, of a starving army, and of a dying cause.

His heart was heavy but his manner was calm as he rode to the mouth of the Hickory road, where Gordon was to take the right fork and Longstreet the left if they slipped successfully away from their positions. Lee drew rein between the forks and in person superintended the movement. In darkness, the columns pressed on, with no drum for their step, no word from the sergeants. Their march was to the growl of the Federal guns on the lines and to the groan of heavily laden wagons. The different commands could not be distinguished in the blackness. Pickett was not there, nor Johnson's division, nor Kershaw's, nor more than a fragment of Heth's or of Wilcox's. Mahone was moving by a different road. But the ghosts of others walked the night— Perry's Alabamians, Benning's Georgians, and that glorious old Texas brigade that Hood and then Gregg had commanded. There was the remnant of Rodes's division and there the wreck of Early's, with what was left of the renowned "Stonewall Brigade." Lee waited till the rear was well closed up before he rode on.[66]

[65] He probably went over the Battersea Bridge, as that was nearer the Dupuy house, but this is not certain.
[66] *Cooke*, 449; *History of the Sixtieth Alabama Regt.*, 100.

CHAPTER V

THE THREAT OF STARVATION

WHEN he evacuated Petersburg on the night of April 2, 1865, Lee had with him probably not more than 12,500 infantry—fewer men than in any of the five Federal corps on the south side of the James—and on the whole of the front he had only from 28,000 to 30,000 infantry moving or preparing to move. After the heavy losses on the right on April 1, and the casualties sustained in the Federal assault of April 2, he could not have mustered even that number had not the local defense troops and many of the detailed men and convalescents quit Richmond and joined in the retreat. Not all of these, of course, were efficient troops. Nor, for that matter, could all the units of the veteran army itself be accounted fit. Wilcox's and Heth's divisions, two of the largest in the army, had been shattered and divided. Pickett's had almost ceased to exist. Johnson's was worn by long service in the trenches. For stiff fighting the next day, in case he was immediately pursued, Lee could have relied only on Field's division of Longstreet's corps and on Gordon's small and weary corps. Of the troops ordered to join Lee at Amelia Courthouse from quiet sectors, two divisions and no more than two—Mahone's and Kershaw's—were in good condition, and Kershaw's was very thin. Nearly all the cavalry were close to exhaustion and were still detached. The only exception was Gary's small brigade which was to accompany the infantry from the north side of James River. The artillery counted about 200 guns,[1] some of them on weak carriages, pulled by feeble horses in rotten harness.[2] The wagons exceeded 1000, most of them with four animals.[3] When the trains were fully

[1] O. R., 46, part 1, p. 1283.
[2] All the guns that could not be removed were rendered useless, O. R., 46, part 1, p. 1281. The ammunition depots, etc., in and around Richmond and Petersburg were destroyed—Baldwin's report, Lee MSS.—L. A good account of the explosion of the magazines will be found in Captain J. C. G., Lee's Last Campaign, 27.
[3] Corley's report, Lee MSS.—L.

spread out they occupied thirty miles of road,[4] heavy impedimenta for an army whose escape required speed.

Despite all this, the start was auspicious.[5] After day broke on April 3 and the men had been rested by the roadside, a curious spirit, half of elation, spread down the ranks. Lee himself is credited, though not on specific authority, with saying, "I have got my army safe out of its breastworks, and in order to follow me, the enemy must abandon his lines, and can derive no further benefit from his railroads or James River."[6] He appeared to be relieved that he was on open ground again and he seemed confident he would be able to reach Johnston.[7] Everything, however, depended on a speedy and uninterrupted retreat. The infantry, having subsisted on the meagrest of rations, while remaining for the most part in fixed positions, could not endure fighting by day and marching by night. The teams would soon break down on the muddy roads.

There was nothing on the first day to indicate a rapid or vigorous pursuit,[8] but if that lead of one day were lost all might be lost. For it was now more manifest than ever that when Grant found the direction of the army's retreat and set out after Lee, all the advantage would be with the Federals. Lee's route above the Appomattox was westerly, but it was twenty degrees farther north than was that of Grant, moving below the river. Lee's immediate objective, Amelia Courthouse, could be reached before Grant could overtake him, but beyond Amelia, Lee's road turned to the southwest, down the Richmond and Danville Railroad, and crossed the low trajectory of Grant's march. From Petersburg to Burkeville, the junction of the Southside and of the Richmond and Danville Railroads, the distance Lee had to cover was fifty-five miles, by way of Goode's bridge. Grant's route from Sutherland Station to Burkeville, via the Namozine road, was thirty-six miles, nineteen miles shorter than Lee's. That is to say, Lee operated on the arc and Grant on the chord;[9] Lee had to follow the dotted and Grant the black line, as shown on page 60.

---

[4] *McCabe*, 630.
[5] The routes are given in *O. R.*, 46, part 3, p. 1379; and *ibid.*, *Atlas*, Plate LXXVIII.
[6] *Cooke*, 451.   [7] *McCabe*, 616.
[8] *Taylor's General Lee*, 280.
[9] General W. H. Stevens pointed this out in his report, *Lee MSS.—L.*

Lee's total distance to the Roanoke River,[10] the nearest point where he could hope to meet Johnston, was 107 miles. Grant's was 88.

In the knowledge that the time-factor would settle the campaign—and with the campaign the war—Lee urged the troops to their best effort. He was in the vicinity of Summit when a message arrived from Judge James H. Cox of Clover Hill inviting Lee and Longstreet and their staff officers to dine with him. Men who had subsisted for weeks on the stern fare of the trenches were

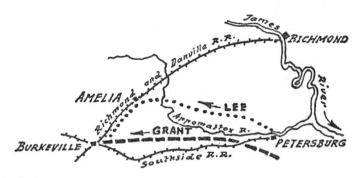

Sketch showing lines of advance of the opposing armies to Burkeville, April, 1865.

delighted at this prospect of enjoying the hospitality of a Virginia home of distinction, and they gladly rode over to Clover Hill through a mile of woods. The house was crowded with guests and, despite the excitement of the retreat, the place took on a festive air for an hour. When the mint juleps were served, the General barely touched his and enjoyed, instead, a glass of ice water. "Do you know," he said to Miss Kate Cox, the daughter of the house, "that this glass of cold water is, I believe, far more refreshing than the drinks they are enjoying so much?"

Soon, of course, the conversation centred on the movement of the army. "General Lee," said Miss Cox, "we shall still gain our cause; you will join General Johnston and together you will be victorious."

"Whatever happens," Lee answered quietly, "know this—that

[10] This stream is called the Roanoke below Clarksville, Va., near which the Dan and Staunton Rivers unite. Lee could hope to reach the Staunton northeast of South Boston. The best small-scale map for the whole ground of the retreat is that in *O. R. Atlas*, Plates CXXXVII and CXXXVIII.

no men ever fought better than those who have stood by me."

Miss Kate had been assigned to sit by Longstreet and to help him cut his food, for he was still unable to use his right arm; but when dinner was announced Lee insisted that she stay by his side. As coffee was passed at the close of the meal, Lee put cream in his.

"General Lee," said the vivacious Miss Kate, "do you take cream in your after-dinner coffee?"

The weary soldier smiled. "I have not taken coffee for so long that I would not dare to take it in its original strength." Kate understood this better when one of the staff confided to her that Lee sent all his coffee to the hospitals.

Soon, of course, the officers of the little cavalcade had to turn their backs on the pleasant Cox home and rejoin the long line of ragged men streaming westward through the spring mud.[11] Already, Lee found, some of the half-starved teams were collapsing as they tried to pull the heavy ordnance wagons. Men too weak to keep up with the column were beginning to straggle.[12] Then the discovery was made that the high water had covered the approaches to Bevill's bridge over the Appomattox, twenty-five miles northwest of Petersburg. This was not a light matter. For Bevill's was the nearest of the three bridges across the north-and-south stretch of the Appomattox on the roads to Amelia. Longstreet's and Gordon's troops had been ordered to use this bridge, while Mahone, his train, and Gordon's wagons crossed at Goode's, the next span up the river. Ewell and the men from Richmond, according to the plan, were to have their pontoons at Genito crossing, two miles and a half above the railroad trestle at Mattoax.[13] With Bevill's bridge impassable, Longstreet and Gordon had to be rerouted via Goode's.[14] This taxed that bridge and caused congestion and delay which were increased as the fall of the flood-waters lowered the pontoons and made it necessary for the engineers to readjust the approaches.[15] To make a bad condition worse, Lee learned, late in the afternoon, from a

[11] Kate V. C. Logan: *My Confederate Girlhood*, 69 ff.
[12] Baldwin's report, *Lee MSS.—L;* Dispatch of Captain A. R. H. Ranson, *Lee MSS.—N.*
[13] O. R., 46, part 3, p. 1379.   [14] Longstreet's report, *Lee MSS.—K.*
[15] 32 *S. H. S. P.*, 68. This is an important article by Colonel T. M. R. Talcott, who commanded the engineer troops.

61

Mr. Haxall, who lived near Goode's bridge, that pontoons had **not** been laid at Genito. It developed that the engineer bureau had not dispatched the boats to Mattoax as directed. Ewell's **men** were moving toward a stream they could not cross. Lee had **to**

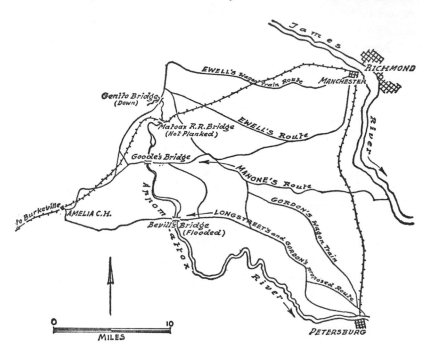

Sketch showing the routes to the bridges across the Appomattox above Petersburg and **the** condition of those bridges, April 3, 1865.

dispatch a courier to Ewell to acquaint him with the facts and to instruct him, if he could do no better, to move down to Goode's bridge and use that.[16] The situation is set out graphically in the sketch on this page.

By nightfall on the 3d the troops from Petersburg had covered an average of not less than twenty-one miles. Longstreet had crossed Field's and Wilcox's men over the Appomattox at Goode'ᶳ and had taken up a line to the west of the bridge in order to cover the passage of the wagons and of the artillery.[17] Gordon, who waᶳ

[16] The dispatch, as it happened, did not reach Ewell that night (*O. R.,* 46, part 3, p. 1382).
[17] Longstreet's report, *Lee MSS.—K.*

behind Longstreet, acted as rearguard of the principal column the next day and the next.[18] Mahone had left the Howlett Line a little before daylight on the 3d and was well on the road to Goode's bridge. Lee had heard nothing from Ewell, who was supposed to be marching to Genito bridge with Custis Lee's command and Kershaw's division. It is doubtful whether Lee had seen against the sky any reflection of the great fire that had been starting in Richmond as Kershaw had moved out. He certainly did not know, though of course he assumed, that the Federals that morning had reached the objective of nearly four years' fighting and had entered the capital city.

Anderson by this time, the night of the 3d, had approached Bevill's bridge. Then Lee learned through an exhausted staff officer the confused story of what had happened on the extreme right after the line had been broken early on the morning of the 2d. In obedience to orders, after Pickett had been defeated at Five Forks, Anderson had started about dark on April 1 to go to Church Crossing, near Ford's Station on the Southside Railroad, to support the cavalry.[19] Meantime, after the battle, what was left of Pickett's command—nearly all of it had been captured—had found its way to the Southside Railroad, whence it proceeded to Exeter Mills in the hope of crossing the Appomattox and rejoining the army.[20] At the mills, Pickett had found no bridge and had discovered that the river was too high to be forded. Anderson had reached Church Crossing at 2 A.M. on the morning of April 2 and had formed a junction with Fitz Lee's cavalry, but had received no word of Pickett. Couriers were dispatched to find Pickett and to give him orders to report to Anderson.[21] Pickett was duly located, very early in the morning of April 2, and he set out to march to Anderson, but he had not gone far before he met stragglers from Heth's and Wilcox's divisions. These men, who had been forced from the line in the Federal assault on the morning of April 2, had been turned to the Confederate right while the rest of their commands had been driven toward the left, that is, toward Fort Gregg. Pickett subsequently stated that he ascertained from these men what had happened and

18 Gordon's report, *Lee MSS.—K.*   19 Anderson's report, *Lee MSS.—K.*
20 Pickett's report, *Lee MSS.—K.*
21 Pickett in his report, *Lee MSS.—K*, said his orders were to report at Sutherland's.

63

that he decided to continue up the river and join Anderson, who, as he learned, was moving toward Amelia Courthouse. So Pickett changed his route and carried the débris of his command farther up the south bank of the Appomattox. That night, April 2, Hunton's brigade, which had been having hard fighting, rejoined Pickett.[22] Anderson, for his part, on the morning of that same fateful 2d of April, found only a strong cavalry force in front of his infantry and of Fitzhugh Lee's command. But the horses of the Confederate troopers were so weary, and the men were so tired, that he did not consider it wise to take the offensive until soldiers and mounts had rested. While he was waiting, information of the disaster at Petersburg reached him. Later he got orders to retire behind the Appomattox at Bevill's, which was the nearest bridge across that stream.[23] On the 3d, accompanied by the cavalry, Anderson began to carry out these orders, and, after a day of many disturbances,[24] reached the vicinity of Bevill's bridge. There he caught up with Pickett.

During the time Pickett was marching up the Appomattox on the 2d, while Anderson was resting at Church Crossing, preparatory to a similar move, the broken parts of Wilcox's and Heth's divisions—McGowan's, Scales's, MacRae's, and perhaps some of McComb's stragglers—got together under General Heth at Sutherland's Tavern. They numbered about 1200 muskets[25] and they proceeded to construct a hasty line by piling up fence rails. Two attacks they succeeded in beating off, but when the enemy turned their left flank and got in their rear they had to retreat hurriedly. Many were captured; a remnant got across the river. They kept moving, at intervals, until the night of the 3d, when they rejoined their divisions at Goode's bridge.[26] Although there thus were three points of concentration—Church Crossing, Sutherland's Tavern, and Exeter Mills—Anderson, who had nearly all the cavalry of the army with him, could not get the troops together. Each command fought or marched alone, in an effort to escape. But now, at last, on the night of the 3d, Lee was in touch with all the units that had made their way from the Petersburg line, and he had no reason to suppose the forces from the Richmond and Howlett

[22] Pickett's report, *loc. cit.* [23] Anderson's report, *Lee MSS.—K.*
[24] *O. R.,* 46, part 1, p. 1289; *O. R.,* 46, part 3, p. 1381.
[25] Cooke's report, *Lee MSS.—K.* [26] *Wilcox's MS. report,* 72.

lines would not speedily overtake him. It looked as if the reconcentration would be effected at Amelia Courthouse with no further losses.[27]

About 7 o'clock the next morning, April 4, Lee learned that the courier who had been sent to Ewell with orders the previous evening had come back and had reported that he had not been able to hear anything of the troops moving from Richmond. Lee did not know what this implied, so he sent the dispatch off again with a postscript in which he gave Ewell discretionary orders to cross the river where he could, and to move as soon as practicable to Amelia Courthouse.[28] To cover the possibility that Ewell might be compelled to use Goode's bridge, Lee directed that Mahone's division should remain there and should preserve the crossing until it was known that Ewell was over the Appomattox.

After Longstreet passed the rest of his command over Goode's bridge,[29] early in the morning of the 4th, he soon met enemy cavalry. Contact meant, of course, that Grant would speedily be apprized of the army's position. Indeed, he might already have learned it. Skirmishing began and continued intermittently on the left flank as the column moved toward Amelia Courthouse, eight and a half miles away. Lee himself crossed the stream shortly after 7:30.[30] Near the bridge a young staff officer came up on his horse to report his command in good condition and awaiting orders. Lee heard him through and then, looking straight at him, asked: "Did those people surprise your command this morning?" The staff officer, much astonished, answered in the negative and inquired if General Lee had received any such report. The General answered that he had not, but that, judging from appearances, something urgent had kept the young men around headquarters from making their toilet, so he thought perhaps they had been surprised. Then he pointed to the officer's boots. On one leg the trousers were stuffed hastily into the boot. On the other they were outside. The youngster had been unconscious of this and, when he looked, he blushed shamefacedly, took his rebuke in silence, saluted, and started to ride off. Seeing the officer's

---

[27] Lee probably bivouacked at Hebron Church, six miles from Goode's bridge (*O. R.,* 46, part 3, p. 1382).

[28] *O. R.,* 46, part 3, p. 1382.

[29] Longstreet's report, *Lee MSS.*—K.

[30] *O. R.,* 46, part 3, p. 1382.

mortification, Lee called him back and told him that he only intended to remind him that on a retreat those who were near the commanders must take particular care to avoid anything that looked like demoralization.[31]

General Lee then rode on with the advance of Longstreet's corps. Gordon's veterans followed. The troops had now been out of the trenches thirty-six hours, with their wagon train strung out on the muddy roads behind them. The little bread and meat they chanced to have with them at the time of the Federal onslaught of the 2d had been consumed. The men were hungry, and for such long marches as they were expected to make they needed ample food. That had been anticipated in advance of the retreat. The commissary general had carried out his instructions to collect a special reserve of rations in Richmond and had accumulated some 350,000 there. Lee's expectation was to supply the troops from this reserve as the men arrived at Amelia Courthouse. Then he expected to move directly down the railroad toward Danville. At other points on the railway, as he advanced, additional supplies were to be sent him. Having changed his base to Danville, he reasoned that, as he marched, his line of communications would be shortened hourly.

On reaching Amelia Courthouse, during the morning of April 4, still with the van of Longstreet's corps, Lee's first thought was for the commissary stores. He found ordnance supplies in abundance—96 full caissons, 200 boxes of artillery ammunition, and 164 boxes of artillery harness[32]—but no food. More than 30,000 hungry men were moving on a village where there was not an army ration!

This meant, at the least, a full day's delay, for the army must be fed, and the only way to do this was to halt the march, send out the wagons into the impoverished country round about, and impress what could be found. And a day's delay entailed the loss of the army's advantage in time. Even that might not be all. For if the enemy should come up during the night and cut the railroad ahead of the army, where could rations be found for the next day, or the next? The possibilities alarmed Lee as had nothing that had occurred up to that time on the retreat. His anxiety

---

[31] 21 *S. H. S. P.*, 97.   [32] Baldwin's report, *Lee MSS.—L.*

showed itself in his face. He began to look haggard, though his general bearing was as calm and, to some eyes, as confident as ever.[33]

It was, of course, no easy task to disentangle wagons from the train and to send them out foraging over roads about which the teamsters knew nothing, but this was done at once. Lee in person addressed to the planters of the surrounding country an appeal for help in these terms:

Amelia C. H., April 4, 1865.

To the Citizens of Amelia County, Va.

The Army of Northern Virginia arrived here today, expecting to find plenty of provisions, which had been ordered to be placed here by the railroad several days since, but to my surprise and regret I find not a pound of subsistence for man or horse. I must therefore appeal to your generosity and charity to supply as far as each one is able the wants of the brave soldiers who have battled for your liberty for four years. We require meat, beef, cattle, sheep, hogs, flour, meal, corn, and provender in any quantity that can be spared. The quartermaster of the army will visit you and make arrangements to pay for what he receives or give the proper vouchers or certificates. I feel assured that all will give to the extent of their means.

R. E. LEE, General.[34]

The only other thing Lee could do immediately to procure food was to order supplies sent up the Richmond and Danville Railroad from Danville. A dispatch directing the immediate shipment of 200,000 rations to Amelia was sent by Colonel Cole for transmission from Jetersville, seven miles below Amelia.[35]

---

[33] Cooke, 452; W. M. Owen, 375; Eggleston, 147; W. A. McClendon: Recollections of War Times, 229.

[34] 7 Confederate Veteran, 223.

[35] O. R., 46, part 3, pp. 560, 561. This message probably was sent to Jetersville because the telegraph line had been cut between Jetersville and Amelia before the dispatch could be put on the wire at Amelia. But of the exact point where the line was broken there is no definite information. A detachment of the 1st Maine Cavalry was sent out early on April 4 to "tap the railroad," but no report of when and where it struck the line is printed (O. R., 46, part 1, p. 1157). The message was not telegraphed from Jetersville, either because the wire was down below that point or else because the operator knew the Federals were "listening in." On his arrival at Jetersville, Sheridan found the dispatch, sent it to Burkeville and had it transmitted to Danville, in the hope that the supplies would be forwarded and captured. The commissary in Danville, however, soon discovered the condition of the railroad and made no shipment (2 Grant, 465. See also

Some of the troops were silent and depressed when they received no rations, but in the Second Corps they still had heart enough to cheer Lee when he passed.[36] The veterans, in the main, were as cheerful as of yore. They still, as one observer testified of those he saw, were "in excellent morale, and had never been readier for desperate fighting than at that moment. Men and officers were tired and hungry, but laughing; and nowhere could be seen a particle of gloom, of shrinking, or ill-humor, sure symptoms in the human animal of a want of 'heart of hope.' "[37]

Proud as Lee must have been of the spirit his men displayed, he knew that it could not long be sustained in the face of continued hunger and attack. He must recover as many hours as he might of the day's lead he was losing. This could be done only by rapid marching. And rapid marching could be made possible, if possible at all, only by a reduction of the wagon train and artillery which had encumbered the road and had slowed down the retreat, while calling for the detachment of heavy guards. So, during the morning of the 4th,[38] General Pendleton was set to work bringing down the artillery to the needs of the army, and Colonel Corley was directed to do the same thing with the wagons. The excess animals were to be used to help those that remained with the trains. The surplus guns were to be moved by rail to Danville, if practicable. The wagons that were not required with the troops were to be sent around the army in such a way that, though they would have a longer route, the army would be between them and the Federals. Lee's own road was to be southwest, along the railroad. The wagons were to cross the railroad, strike west, and then, at a safe distance, turn south. The soldiers, in other words, were to follow the hypotenuse to the acute angle at Danville, while the wagons were to go around the right angle.

In case the artillery could not be sent by rail, it was to follow the

J. S. Wise: *End of an Era*, pp. 416–18). Grant's statement that he learned of this dispatch to Danville and notified Sheridan (2 *Grant*, 464), obviously was at variance with the facts. The Federal commander evidently confused this incident with one when he sent information to Sheridan from Wilson's (*O. R.*, 46, part 3, p. 557). Sheridan in his report (*O. R.*, 46, part 1, p. 1107) said the supplies were ordered by Cole to Burkeville from Lynchburg and from Danville, but he wrote this May 16. The account he gave on the day of the finding of the dispatch is of course to be preferred, especially as it conforms to Lee's general statement (*O. R.*, 46, part 1, p. 1265). For the reason why Lee found no supplies at Amelia, see Appendix IV—2.

[36] Jos. R. Stonebraker: *A Rebel of '61*, p. 95.
[37] Cooke: *Wearing of the Gray*, 594.   [38] *O. R.*, 46, part 1, p. 1281.

route of the wagon trains. This seemed the safest course to follow and the only one that gave any promise of speeding up the movement of the army.[39]

While this work was being done, during the forenoon of the 4th, Hill's corps was arriving at Amelia. Wilcox's division reported at 1 o'clock.[40] Some units of Heth's division were up by 4 P.M.—among them MacRae's brigade, now reduced to about 150 men.[41] Gordon was halted at Scott's shop, about five miles from Amelia.[42] Mahone was still at Goode's bridge waiting for Ewell.[43] Anderson and most of the cavalry, harried by skirmishing,[44] were marching up from the southeast and at nightfall would be about five miles distant.[45] Some of the mounted units were beginning to put in an appearance at Amelia.[46] Only the position of the troops from Richmond remained in doubt. They had now been on the road nearly two days and had not reported.

But the enemy was advancing, too. That was as ominous as the lack of provisions. South of the railroad and beyond Amelia, on the way to Burkeville, the Federal cavalry were to be seen. Longstreet moved out Field, Wilcox, and Heth and attempted to bring on a fight, but he found the Unionists wary.[47] Lee, himself, anxious to know the strength of the bluecoats, set out to reconnoitre behind the Fourteenth Virginia Cavalry, of Rooney's Lee's division. He went some distance down the Avery Church road and soon found himself where the regiment was skirmishing with a Federal mounted outpost. Just as he rode up, the Federals dashed up and were met with a countercharge. Probably before he realized it, the General was spurring fast toward the approaching squadrons. Most of the Federals veered off, after an exchange of shots, but one of them rode straight on. In an instant three or four pistols were turned on him. Lee divined what had happened. "Don't shoot," he cried out. The men heard him and lowered their weapons. One of them caught the Federal's bridle

[39] The original order, which is in Colonel Venable's handwriting, is among the *Lee MSS.—L.* It is printed *O. R.*, 46, part 3, p. 1384. *Cf. ibid.*, 46, part 1, p. 1281.

[40] *Wilcox's MS. report*, pp. 78–79.   [41] McRae's report, *Lee MSS.—L.*

[42] *O. R.*, 46, part 3, p. 1385.   [43] *O. R.*, 46, part 3, p. 1385.

[44] *O. R.*, 46, part 1, pp. 1300–1301.

[45] Anderson in *Lee MSS.—K*; Johnson in *O. R.*, 46, part 1, p. 1289. The halt for the night was near Washington Academy, at the junction of the Bevill's Bridge and Tabernacle Church roads.

[46] *F. M. Myers*, 371.   [47] Longstreet's report, *Lee MSS.—K.*

and brought the horse to a halt. Then they saw what had prompted Lee to give the order: the Federal was wounded and unable to control his runaway mount.[48]

At nightfall the Federals withdrew from in front of Amelia, and Longstreet's troops were able to leave their line of battle.[49] But there was rest neither of mind nor of body for Lee. His tents were pitched in the large yard of a house occupied temporarily by Mrs. Francis L. Smith, a refugee from Alexandria, whose husband was one of General Lee's countless kinsmen.[50] It was a quiet place of trees and grass and at another time it would have been a pleasant camp site. As it was, Lee was busy with troop dispositions and was wretched over the hunger of his men. Always sensitive to their suffering, he must have been tortured to know that after struggling for two days through the mud on a march of from thirty-five to forty miles, they should have to sleep on empty stomachs and with no assurance of food on the morrow.

Now, at last, came word from Ewell. He had reached the Appomattox and had found no bridge on his designated route, but he had gone to Mattoax and reported from that point, telling General Lee that the engineers were planking the railroad bridge so that he could cross there.[51] Lee answered with instructions and encouragement.[52] He surmised that Ewell would have passed the stream by the time he wrote, 9 P.M., and in this he was not greatly mistaken. Kershaw of Longstreet's corps and the scratch division of Custis Lee, 6000 men altogether,[53] were behind the Appomattox by night.[54] Mahone, who had been holding the bridge at Goode's, passed over also and set out for Amelia.[55] In anticipa-

[48] 33 S. H. S. P., 375–76. This story sounds apocryphal, but its circumstances check with facts that can be established. The time of day is based on the hour of the Federals' advance, according to their own reports.

[49] Longstreet's report, Lee MSS.—K.

[50] An odd fact about this camp site is told by Captain F. M. Colston (38 S. H. S. P., 5). Dispatched to Amelia at the end of February to survey the ordnance supplies there, he had spent the night at Mrs. Smith's. She had remarked her acquaintance with the Lees but had said that she had not seen the General since the commencement of the war. Glancing out at the lawn, Captain Colston remarked that before the war was over General Lee might be camped under her trees. After the close of hostilities, Mrs. Smith insisted that Colston had knowledge at the time of his visit of Lee's intention to evacuate Petersburg. He denied it. "We never talked retreat," he wrote in recounting the coincidence.

[51] Reconstructed from Ewell's and Custis Lee's reports and from General Lee's answer, O. R., 46, part 3, pp. 1384–85. See the sketch-map on page 62.

[52] O. R., 46, part 3, pp. 1384–85.　　　[53] O. R., 46, part 1, p. 1295.

[54] Kershaw's report, O. R., 46, part 1, p. 1283; Stevens report, Lee MSS.—L.

[55] Stevens, loc. cit.

tion of the approach of Ewell's wagon train, which was moving by a roundabout road, Lee at 11 o'clock issued orders for it to follow some of the roads designated for the first stages of the movement of the surplus wagons and artillery, on the right of the Richmond and Danville Railroad. This general route was prescribed for the wagon train of Mahone and of the rest of the Third Corps.[56]

The situation, then, at the end of a torturing day was this: The reconcentration was nearly complete, but it was bringing more men together where no food was available. If the troops were to be fed at all, it was from what the wagons could collect in the adjacent country, and from what might be sent from Danville in answer to Cole's telegram. Should food be forthcoming on the morrow, then the army could move down the railroad and, being no longer slowed down by so large a wagon train, might regain some of the time it had lost in seeking provisions around Amelia. Still again, if they had good fortune, the excess wagons and artillery on the right of the railroad might reach their destination unharmed. There were many "ifs," however, and nearly all of them were contingent on the enemy's movements. Those movements, as yet, had disclosed nothing more formidable than cavalry that had disappeared when darkness came. Although the odds were all against Lee, there was still a chance of escape: twenty-four hours would dim it or bring it nearer reality. The Staunton River, a strong line, was distant only four days' forced marching, and beyond it lay Danville, where a million and a half rations were stored.[57]

On the morning of April 5, a showery, unhappy day,[58] the wagons began to come in from foraging. One glance at them told the tale: they were almost empty. The farmers had scarcely anything to give or to sell. The country had already been stripped of food and of provender. It was worse than a disappointment; it was a catastrophe. Often the loyal old army had been hungry, but now starvation seemed a stark reality. Wet and gloomy, the men were slow to take their places in the ranks and to test what was, perhaps, their last hope—that of marching down the road

[56] *O. R.,* 46, part 3, p. 1384.
[57] St. John's report *Lee MSS.—L.* Danville was distant 104.5 miles by railroad.
[58] Waldrop in 3 *Richmond Howitzers,* 57.

far enough to find the provisions that had been ordered from Danville.

At length the surplus artillery and the wagons were started on their roundabout way to Danville, west of the railroad and beyond the right flank of the army. The caissons and boxes of shells that had been found at Amelia were destroyed, except such as could be used to renew the supply of the guns with the troops.[59] The trains of most of the infantry were also sent to the right and, as planned, were to move on a narrower arc than the other vehicles.[60] W. H. F. Lee's cavalry division, which had come up, was dispatched down the railroad. Gary's brigade was ordered to protect the wagon train.[61] Gordon's infantry were to continue to cover the rear.[62]

Then Longstreet began to move southwestward, behind a cavalry screen, toward Jetersville and Burkeville, the road of escape to Danville. He was followed by Mahone and presumably by Pickett.[63] After them marched the rest of Anderson's troops, who had now arrived.[64] While the column was extended, Ewell reported with Kershaw and Custis Lee from Richmond.[65] He was put in rear of Anderson but did not move until later in the day. These troops of Ewell's had outmarched their wagon train, which had contained 20,000 good rations for Custis Lee's division. The men did not know it until the next day, if then, but that precious wagon train, when within four miles of Amelia, was struck by Federal cavalry and destroyed.[66]

Before these dispositions for the march down the railroad were made, rumors came that the vehicles to the westward had been attacked—bad news, if true, for it meant that the Federal cavalry had crossed the railroad ahead of the Confederate infantry and had worked their way well around to the right flank. Fitz Lee reported after these rumors reached headquarters at Amelia. He

[59] O. R., 46, part 1, p. 1281; Baldwin's report, Lee MSS.—L.

[60] Those of the Third Corps and of Anderson were routed on a wide arc from the start of the day's march. It is not clear when the others were put on the same roads, but they probably were kept close to the army until it was halted.

[61] O. R., 46, part 1, p. 1301.   [62] O. R., 46, part 1, p. 1296.

[63] Stevens's report, Lee MSS.—L; O. R., 46, part 3, p. 1385.

[64] Anderson's report, Lee MSS.—K; O. R., 46, part 1, p. 1288.

[65] O. R., 46, part 1, p. 1283. To Custis Lee, who had the heavy artillerists of the Richmond defenses as one of his brigades, the naval battalion and Smith's artillery from the Howlett line were immediately attached (O. R., 46, part 1, p. 1296).

[66] O. R., 46, part 1, p. 1296.

had not seen his uncle since the morning of March 29, at Petersburg, and he had lost many troopers meanwhile. But this was no
time for reminiscence or explanation. He was ordered to take
his own division and Rosser's and to proceed at once in the direction of Paineville, near which the wagon train was supposed to
be moving.[67]

General Lee kept his headquarters at Amelia until the infantry
were well on the road toward Jetersville, the next station beyond
Amelia on the Richmond and Danville Railroad. From the village he may have heard the sound of the skirmishing that marked
the advance.[68] About 1 P.M. he rode forward with Longstreet,
and at a distance of about seven miles from Amelia came upon
the enemy, entrenching on a well-chosen position.[69] The Federals
had overtaken Lee. The road of the army's escape was blocked.[70]

[67] O. R., 46, part 1, pp. 1300–1301.
[68] Longstreet's report, Lee MSS.—K.   [69] Alexander, 595.
[70] In her memoir of her husband (2, 595), Mrs. Davis quoted a story that when the
Federals entered Richmond they found in the Executive Mansion a confidential report,
prepared by General Lee, in which he set forth for the information of Congress the route
he proposed to follow on his march to join Johnston. This information is said to have
been used by the Federals and is alleged to have facilitated the pursuit. General Custis
Lee is given as authority for this statement, which he is said to have received from General Benham of the Federal army. This tale was repeated by various Southern writers and
attracted the attention of James Ford Rhodes (see Livermore, quoted infra). Among the
later writers to give currency to the report were Doctor R. H. McKim (A Soldier's Recollections, 265 ff.) and Thomas Nelson Page (op. cit., 548). The facts were examined by
Colonel Thomas L. Livermore (Proceedings of the Massachusetts Historical Society, 1906,
pp. 87 ff.) and the story was conclusively shown to be without foundation. In addition to
the reasons given by Colonel Livermore for dismissing the alleged discovery as a fable, it
might be said that never, in his whole military career, did General Lee outline his strategic plans "for the information of Congress." Only to the President or to the Secretary of
War, and then in cautious terms, did he ever speak of what he intended to do. In this instance, it is manifest that the alleged letter was confused with a general report Lee had
made to Secretary Breckinridge on the military outlook. This paper was of interest to
the Federals but of no value in shaping the pursuit. It might be added that those who
circulated the story did Grant little honor in assuming that if he knew Lee's route he did
not march after him with greater assurance. Grant did well, but he would have done
much better if he had possessed such information of Lee's plans as McClellan found at
Frederick (see supra, vol. II, p. 410).

CHAPTER VI

"HAS THE ARMY BEEN DISSOLVED?"

OFTEN enough, before that 5th of April, 1865, the advance of the Army of Northern Virginia had been halted and word had been sent back that the enemy was at bay. This time Lee was the pursued and not the pursuer. Unless the Federal position could be quickly forced or turned, the hope of getting supplies from Danville was at an end, and that, in the desperate situation of the retreating forces, might mean an overwhelming disaster with results too horrible to contemplate.

Hastening to the front as soon as he received report of the enemy's presence, Lee found his son Rooney on the ground, with some information as to Federal forces. They were Sheridan's men, the cavalryman reported—how Lee's weary heart must have sunk at the words—and infantry were close by, moving in the general direction of Burkeville.[1] Grim-faced and silent, Lee made a reconnaissance of the Federal position, made it carefully and slowly as was required where so much depended upon the decision. He called in the farmers from the neighborhood and talked to them of the country ahead, but he found they knew little of it. Should he try once more the "antique valor" of his infantry, as he had at Second Manassas and at Chancellorsville? Should he stake everything on one last assault, throw all his men forward, like the "Old Guard" at Waterloo, and either win a crushing victory or die where the flags went down? Doubtless the blood of his old cavalier ancestors battled momentarily with his judgment as a commander, but judgment triumphed over impulse and, at length, he put down his glasses: he could not afford to attack with his weakened troops.[2]

[1] *O. R.*, 46, part 1, p. 1265. Besides Sheridan's cavalry, the V Corps was already in position (*O. R.*, 46, part 1, p. 839), while the II Corps was just coming on the field (*O. R.*, 46, part 1, p. 681). The VI Corps was nearly within striking distance (*O. R.*, 46, part 1, p. 905).

[2] *Longstreet*, 610; *Alexander*, 595. The ground appears on *O. R. Atlas*, Plate LXXVII, 4. Lee's decision doubtless will be sustained by all who examine the terrain and justly

74

If he could not attack the Federal position, what should he do? What alternative was there? Deprived of the use of the Richmond and Danville Railroad, his main reliance for supplies, he must speedily get provisions if he was to continue fighting. How could he victual the men and at the same time proceed with his retreat? It was the last major strategical question that he put to himself, and it was answered in a manner that accorded with his fame. The railroad supply-lines left to him before he had quit Petersburg had formed a rough Saint Andrew's cross, thus:

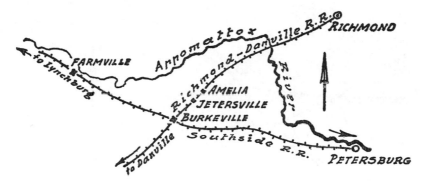

Sketch of the railroads crossing at Burkeville.

The lines met at Burkeville, the junction that had been in his mind since February. He had lost his base at the upper end of the Richmond-Burkeville stretch of the Richmond and Danville, and he was cut off from the Burkeville-Danville division. Behind him, the Federals in their first irruption had reached and had rendered useless the Burkeville-Petersburg part of the Southside Railroad. All that was left to him of the four arms of the cross was that to the northwestward, from Burkeville toward Lynchburg. He determined to strike across to that "arm" of the cross, to order supplies down it from Lynchburg, and then, having fed his army, to turn southwestward in the direction of Danville again. He would move on the dotted line shown on page 76.

appraise the condition of the army. Had he hurled his little army against the Federal position, he might have carried it—for his men had stormed worse places against as heavy odds—but he would merely have been driving himself into a sack, the neck of which could easily have been closed behind him. The least that could have happened to him would have been the complete loss of his wagon train and the almost certain envelopment of his left flank.

75

But how was he to get away from the enemy that stood across his path and was getting stronger every hour? He had lost his day's lead at Amelia: manifestly he could only regain it by a night march. In this desperate throw against fate, everything depended on speed—and speed was the last thing that could be expected of an army in which the horses were ceasing to struggle any more and the men were beginning to drop from hunger.[3]

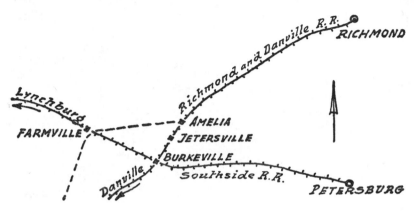

Sketch to illustrate how Lee planned to avoid Burkeville and to strike for Danville, via Farmville.

There was, however, nothing left to do but to try it. Orders were given accordingly, though they may not have reached all the commands.[4]

Longstreet retraced his steps a short distance up the railroad and turned to the left. The other corps took the same general route—only to find the roads jammed and progress almost impossible. It developed that the rumored attack on the wagon train had been a disastrous reality. Federal cavalry[5] had swept down upon the trains before they had reached Paineville, on the road to Farmville, and had driven off the guards. About 200 wagons had been burned, and 320 soldiers, in addition to 310 Negro teamsters, had been made prisoner. This attack on a narrow road in swampy ground blocked the way and stopped all

[3] Lawley, *Fortnightly Review*, September, 1865; *McCabe*, 619.

[4] Longstreet said, *op. cit.*, 610, that he got no orders. It is hard to see how he led the movement without them.

[5] It was the 1st Brigade of the 2d Division (*O. R.*, 46, part 1, pp. 114, 1145).

movement of the trains. Six hours passed before the wheels of the wagons began to turn again. It was after night when the trains got to Paineville, distant only about ten miles by road from Amelia.[6] This long tie-up made it necessary to reroute some of

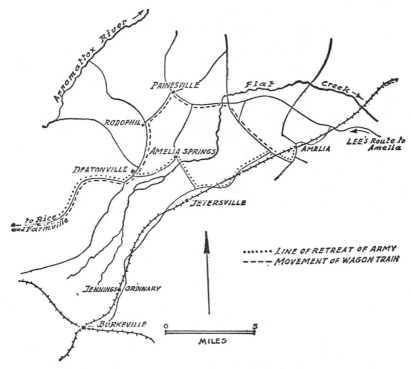

Routes from Jetersville and Amelia Courthouse, as selected by Lee, April 5, 1865, for his retreat toward Farmville.

the wagons on the road the infantry were following toward Amelia Springs.[7] The above sketch shows the terrain.

The forced night march of April 5–6, now Lee's chief hope of escape, almost immediately became a slow stumble over crowded roads where confusion ruled and panic easily was spread. A black stallion, running away with a fence rail swinging from his bridle,

[6] Stevens's report, *Lee MSS.—L;* Baldwin's report, *Lee MSS.—L;* Stevens said that "over 100" wagons were destroyed, including all reserve ordnance and medical supplies. The route of the wagons, best followed on *O. R. Atlas,* Plate XCIII, is given by Stevens as Paineville-Rodophil-Deatonsville and Rice.

[7] This is plain from Lee's reference to Gordon's route in *O. R.,* 46, part 3, p. 1387.

set men to shooting at one another in the darkness.[8] Worse still, as the engineers had not considered the possibility of an advance on the road from the railway to Amelia Springs, they had not strengthened the bridge over a troublesome little stream known as Flat Creek, which crossed the road just before the springs were reached. The bridge broke down and halted the artillery and the wagons, though the infantry could ford the watercourse and keep on. Lee ate his supper at Selma, the home of Richard Anderson, about two miles from Amelia Springs. Anticipating a clash, he urged the hospitable family to seek safety in the cellar.[9] Then he hurried to the creek and sent for the engineer troops, who were still at Amelia Courthouse, where they had arrived that day.

Probably while he was waiting for the engineers to come up, a courier brought Lee a message from Gordon: two spies had been captured, and from one of them had been taken dispatches that Gordon considered sufficiently important to forward for Lee's inspection. The small envelope was marked for quick delivery and was addressed to the Federal General Ord. Inside were two yellow tissue sheets, copies of messages of no great consequence, and a single white sheet on which in a sprawling hand was a note to Ord dated "Jetersville, April 5, 1865—10:10 P.M." It directed that officer to move at 8 A.M. the next morning and to take a position from which he could watch the roads between Burkeville and Farmville. "I am strongly of the opinion that Lee will leave Amelia tonight to go south. He will be pursued at 6 A.M. from here if he leaves. Otherwise an advance will be made upon him where he is." This was signed "U. S. Grant, lieut-genl."

There was no mistaking the meaning of this: Grant himself was at Jetersville, Ord at Burkeville. The Army of the James as well as the Army of the Potomac was nearby in sufficient strength to pursue or to attack. It was the first certain information Lee had that Ord's troops from the north side of the James, the most distant Federal units, were on his heels. The news showed the

---

[8] *Alexander,* 595.

[9] Information from Gilliam Anderson, Esq., through the writer's generous friend, M. R. Turner of Blackstone, Va. The late Mrs. G. T. Crallé, née Eliza Gilliam Willson, was a young guest at Selma and was stationed on the porch to keep out intruders while Lee ate his supper in the basement dining-room. While he was at the meal, Colonel Marshall came up on an important mission. Miss Willson refused to let him enter the house. He hesitated a moment, then took up a Confederate flag and wrapped it around her. She then decided that he was a safe visitor and permitted him to pass.

vigor of the pursuit and reinforced the urgency of speed and still more speed. Lee remained at the crossing until the engineers had arrived and had given assurance that the material for repairing the bridge was close at hand.[10] Thence he rode on to Amelia Springs,[11] just beyond Flat Creek, and there he at once adjusted his dispositions, so far as practicable, to the new development.

The first obvious danger was, of course, that the wagon train would slow down the retreat of the army so much that the rear troops might be cut off. There was no way to be rid of the wagons because the roads were few. The one route that was not to be used by the army led to the Appomattox at a point where, so far as Lee could ascertain, there was no bridge. The wagons, therefore, had to be taken along, and the rear closed up as well as was possible. Part of the cavalry could be utilized to cover the retreat and, as it happened, could use crossroads that were well-suited for defense. Special pains must be taken to destroy the bridges. All this General Lee explained in a letter he wrote General Gordon at 4 A.M. in his own hand. "I will try to get the head of the column on," he concluded, "and to get provisions at Rice's Station or Farmville." [12]

When he handed Gordon's staff officer this letter, Lee thought a moment before giving an answer to a verbal question Gordon had forwarded concerning the disposition of the spies. Having been caught in Confederate uniform, and having acknowledged themselves Federal spies, these men were liable to immediate military execution. Gordon had asked whether this should be carried out. Lee pondered. "Tell the General," he said at last, "the lives of so many of our men are at stake that all my thoughts now must be given to disposing of them. Let him keep the prisoners until he hears further from me." Subsequently, the officers who carried and received this message concluded that Lee deferred a de-

10 *O. R.*, 46, part 1, p. 583; 32 *S. H. S. P.*, 69; *Gordon*, 425 ff. The originals of the captured dispatches are in the Lee MSS. Both Gordon, *loc. cit.*, and Hunter, cited in a note to 32 *S. H. S. P.*, 69, were in error as to the date of the capture of this dispatch. The date of Grant's dispatch and that of Lee's answer to Gordon (*O. R.*, 46, part 3, p. 1387) make this plain. There would, of course, have been no particular value on the night of April 6–7 to a dispatch written from Jetersville on the night of the 5th–6th, for by the later date the attack at Sayler's Creek had demonstrated the presence of the Federal infantry.
11 Some of the Federal accounts styled the place "Sulphur Springs."
12 *O. R.*, 43, part 3, p. 1387. The terms "Rice," "Rice's," and "Rices' Station" are used indiscriminately in the reports and correspondence. The correct name is Rice.

cision in the belief that if the fate of his own army was to be settled speedily, he should not take the lives of his enemies needlessly.[13]

The second danger Lee had to consider on the night of April 5–6 was one he discussed with Fitz Lee, who had driven off the Federal attack on the wagon train near Paineville and had now ridden ahead of his command to Amelia Springs. This danger was that Sheridan would attack and destroy the wagon train as it groaningly crept to the southwest the next day. Already it was apparent that the United States cavalry had ceased operating against the Confederate rear and were preparing to move on a route parallel to Lee's left marching flank—a direful prospect. The only defense was caution in seeing that each command kept contact with the unit ahead and, exercising the greatest vigilance, stood ready to beat off attacks.[14] Fitz Lee was to send all except one division of his cavalry toward Rice after Longstreet, but he was to remain in person to explain the situation to the first infantry commander to arrive. The division left behind was to guard the rear.[15]

In a word, the condition presented by the captured dispatch could not be removed strategically and had to be met tactically. With speed his one remaining weapon, Lee was confirmed in his decision that the movement of the whole army must continue through the night and on into the day with only such brief rest as was imperative. Longstreet was to remain in the van, and Lee determined to march with him in the hope of expediting the retreat. Behind Longstreet were to come Anderson, Ewell, and, in the rear, the alert, hard-hitting Gordon. Beyond Deatonsville, five miles west of Amelia Springs, all these troops and all the wheeled vehicles would have to use one road. And to this road, unfortunately, another ran almost parallel, just where the Federals could use it for dashes against the wagon trains. It was the gloomiest outlook Lee had yet faced on the retreat. Desperate since he had reached Amelia Courthouse and had found no provisions there, his situation might easily be rendered hopeless within twenty-four hours.

Commissary General St. John reported at headquarters while

---

[13] 21 S. H. S. P., 98; 32 ibid., 69.
[14] O. R., 46, part 1, pp. 1301–2. [15] O. R., 46, part 1, p. 1302.

Lee was at Amelia Springs. St. John had left Richmond not long before the Federals had entered the city on the morning of April 3, and he had been trying to hasten forward the wagons he had loaded in Richmond with the provisions he had not been able to send up the Danville Railroad on April 2 in answer to Colonel Cole's belated message.[16] From St. John, probably, Lee learned for the first time why the rations had not been await- ing him at Amelia. He learned, also, that part of those that had been brought from the evacuated capital had been captured by the Federals near Clementown bridge.[17] The only encourage- ment St. John could give was that he had 80,000 rations at Farmville, which was nineteen miles away. This food had been en route to the army when the Southside Railroad had been cut. After the cars had been halted at Burkeville, they had been switched back up that line toward Farmville. Their contents would be available as soon as the army reached the railway. Should they be left at Farmville, asked General St. John, or should they be moved farther down the railroad, closer to the army? Lee said frankly that the military situation made it im- possible to answer. What he apprehended, of course, was that the Federal cavalry might reach the railroad before he did, and might destroy the train. St. John accordingly went on to Farm- ville to prepare for the coming of the army and for the issuance of rations there.[18]

It was now the early morning of April 6, a dreadful day in the history of the Army of Northern Virginia. While Lee had been giving his orders and conferring at Amelia Springs, the column had been moving painfully forward—soldiers, wagons, and guns mingled together, men and horses tottering in their weakness and their misery. Straggling was perceptibly worse. The number of broken-down teams was larger. Many of the department clerks and reservists in Ewell's corps, who were unaccustomed to marching, had to quit the road. Starting on the 3d with about 6000, Ewell now had less than half that strength.[19] As Lee rode forward to

[16] See *supra*, p. 55 and Appendix IV—2. [17] St. John's report, *Lee MSS.*—L.
[18] St. John's report, *loc. cit.*, R. and F., 2, 671–72. It is possible that the Secretary of War was with the commissary general at this interview. Breckinridge certainly saw Lee the next day (*cf. O. R.*, 46, part 3, p. 1389).
[19] *O. R.*, 46, part 1, p. 1295.

join Longstreet there was something akin to despair in the eyes
that were turned on him, and there was delirium in the loyal
cheers that greeted him.

Continuing to the vicinity of Rice, which is about twelve miles
southwest of Amelia Springs and on the Southside Railroad, Lee
awaited there the coming of the First Corps. Longstreet arrived
during the forenoon with his men, after what must have been a
very good march. "Old Pete" had information that some 600 or
700 mounted Federals had passed up the road toward Farmville,
which is eight and a half miles by rail from Rice, and about
seven by the old highway. The object of these troops presumably
was to burn the bridges over which part of Lee's army would pass
in reaching that town. Longstreet immediately sent off cavalry
in pursuit of these bluecoats.[20] Hearing, also, that the enemy was
in force about four miles to the southeastward, he took up line
of battle covering the roads to Rice and at right angles to the railway.[21]

This intelligence of the nearness of the Federals was bad news
for Lee. Still more ominous was a development about 10 A.M.
After Longstreet had come up, Wilcox's and Heth's divisions had
reported, and then Mahone. But Pickett, whose men were at the
head of Anderson's little corps, had not closed on Mahone, as the
marching orders required. Instead, there was a gap, and, after a
little, word that the wagon train had been assailed some two
miles back on the road. Lee heard of this while he was with
General Pendleton. He at once directed that officer to collect what
men he could and to see if he could stop the attack on the trains.[22]
Soon it was apparent that the Federals had fired the wagons they
had reached. How strong they were and what support they had,
Lee did not know. But the outlook was grim. With the column
broken, the presence of Union cavalry on the flank of a far-spread
wagon train meant danger and inevitable delay—at a time when
speed was everything. Besides, Lee was militarily in the dark,
ahead of half his army.

While waiting anxiously for the arrival of the head of Anderson's column Lee examined the roads and the terrain around

[20] *O. R.*, 46, part 1, p. 1302.
[21] Longstreet's report, *Lee MSS.—K.*   [22] *O. R.*, 46, part 1, p. 1281.

82

him. It was bad ground for a retreat. The meandering Appomattox found its way among hills that now were close to its channel, and now set forbiddingly back from it, high and difficult of approach. The country on either side of the river was rolling and cut by many smaller streams. Some of these bogged between the hills. Others, mere branches in themselves, ran between declivities so steep that heavy bridges were necessary. The roads converged in the general direction of Farmville, and were straightest and best from the very direction of the Federal approach. There could hardly have been a stretch of Virginia countryside better suited for an attack by cavalry on an encumbered column of infantry.[23] Particularly dangerous was the ground northwest of Rice, still to be traversed by the centre and the rearguard. There were located the two forks and the watershed of a little stream called Sayler's Creek that flows northward into the Appomattox at a point where the river makes a loop to the southward as shown on the map, page 87.

The crossings of this watercourse were much exposed. The bridges were weak and narrow. To the west of the creek were hills that presented a hard pull for teams and were not as strong a defensive position as they seemed, because they were easily taken in rear. Over nearly the whole of the landscape grew dark pine woods, broken by scattered plantations and a few small farms—just the setting for a military tragedy.

In examining this ground General Lee rode during the early afternoon, virtually without escort, toward the Appomattox River and the mouth of Sayler's Creek. There he found himself with Roberts's cavalry brigade.[24] This little command of North Carolinians was not engaged, but it was watching something as ominous as it was unexpected—a fight in progress on the other side of the creek, between Gordon's corps and unidentified units of the enemy. Gordon was the rearguard: if he was being assailed, where were the central divisions? What had happened to them? Lee dismounted near a cabin, held Traveller by the bridle and with the other hand took out his glasses to survey some white objects he saw in the distance.

---

[23] Map in *O. R. Atlas,* Plate LXXVIII, 4.
[24] William P. Roberts in February, 1865, had been commissioned brigadier general and had been assigned a small brigade in Rooney Lee's division.

A young captain came up at the moment. "Are those sheep or not?" Lee asked doubtfully.

"No, General," said the possessor of younger eyes, "they are Yankee wagons."

Lee looked again through his glasses and then said slowly: "You are right; but what are they doing there?" What did it mean that the Federal wagon trains, which normally followed the troops, were already up—and no word from Anderson or Ewell, who were marching ahead of Gordon? [25]

Riding back in a few minutes, toward the line on which these corps should be moving, Lee soon met General Mahone, who had been engaged the previous evening in a verbal encounter with Colonel Charles Marshall. Lee had thought Mahone in the wrong and he proceeded now to remonstrate with him on the tone he had employed. While they were talking, Colonel Venable rode up and asked if Lee had received his message.

"No," said the General.

Then Venable told him that the enemy had captured those of the wagons that were between the branches of Sayler's Creek.

"Where is Anderson?" exclaimed General Lee. "Where is Ewell? It is strange I can't hear from them." Then he turned. "General Mahone," he said, "I have no other troops. Will you take your division to Sayler's Creek?"

Mahone gave the order, the men started, Lee and Mahone went ahead of them, Colonel Venable behind the two. They rode on a high ridge leading northward to the Appomattox, and then they turned to the right and came to the elevation overlooking the creek. The landscape opened up on the instant for a long distance across the valley. Lee stopped and straightened himself in his saddle and stared at what he saw. It was such a sight as his eyes had never beheld in the years of his command of the Army of Northern Virginia: streaming out of the bottom and up the ridge to them were teamsters without their wagons, soldiers without their guns, and shattered regiments without their officers, a routed wreck!

"My God!" cried Lee, as if to himself; "has the army been dissolved?"

[25] 28 *S. H. S. P.,* 110–111.

Mahone, whose heart was in his mouth, swallowed and struggled and at last answered stoutly: "No, General, here are troops ready to do their duty."

Lee regained his poise on the instant. "Yes, General," he said, "there are some true men left. Will you please keep those people back?"

As Mahone hurried away to draw a line of battle, Lee spurred forward to rally the men who were running toward him. Either from the ground where the bearer had dropped it in his flight, or else from the hand of some color-bearer, Lee took a battle flag and held it aloft. There on Traveller he sat, the red folds of the bunting flapping about him, the soldiers in a mob in front of him, some wild with fear, some exhausted, some wounded. A few rushed on; others looked up and, recognizing him, began to flock around him as if to find shelter in his calm presence. Did it flash over him then that this was the last rally of the great Army of Northern Virginia?[26]

[26] The best account is Mahone's in *Longstreet*, 614–15. See also 32 *S. H. S. P.*, 71; *cf. O. R.*, 46, part 1, p. 1290.

CHAPTER VII

A Letter Comes to Headquarters

THERE on the hill above Sayler's Creek the fugitives gathered fast. For all of them, as for Pickett's survivors after the fatal charge at Gettysburg, Lee had encouragement. Mahone's men would protect them, he said; the enemy would not overtake them. They must go to the rear and form again. "It's General Lee," the encouraged soldiers began to cry. "Where's the man who won't follow Uncle Robert?" [1]

Mahone soon returned and took the battle flag from the General's hand.[2] Lee reached for his binoculars and began to study the valley and the hills beyond it, in the hope of discovering how he should dispose his thin line to halt the enemy's advance. Presently, in the backwash of the retreating troops, there arrived a "general of exalted grade," whose name merciful history does not record. Lee was sweeping the field with his glasses at the moment, the reins loose on Traveller's neck, "his attitude full of alertness and pugnacity." Not a glance did he give to the newcomer.

"General Lee," said one of his staff officers, "here is General ——."

Lee did not lower his glasses or honor the beaten commander with a nod. All he did was to move his right hand to the rear in a gesture of biting reproach. "General," he said slowly, "take those stragglers to the rear, out of the way of Mahone's troops. I wish to fight here." [3]

The character of the *débâcle* was not yet known, but its magnitude was obvious. Gordon presumably was still fighting at the lower crossing of the creek, but Ewell and Anderson somehow had met disaster. The capture of their commands was the most natural thing to surmise, for those refugees who came up to Lee

---

[1] *Wearing of the Gray*, 596.   [2] *Longstreet*, 615.
[3] Colonel W. E. Cameron, an eye-witness, in *Norfolk Landmark*, Nov. 25, 1894.

brought with them tales of whole divisions surrounded and Federals springing up everywhere with cries of "Surrender."

What should be done? Lee put the question to Mahone as he always did to whosoever was nearest him when he was "think-

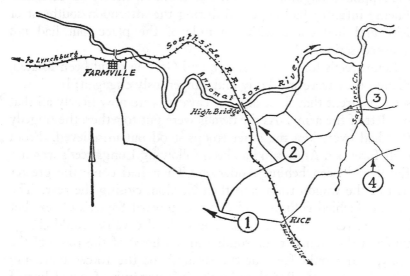

Sketch of Lee's proposed movements after the disaster of Sayler's Creek, April 6, 1865.
(1) Longstreet was to march on Farmville. (2) Mahone with his division and the stragglers was to cross at High Bridge. (3) Gordon, if he escaped, was to follow Mahone. (4) The scene of the disaster to Ewell.

ing aloud" on some military problem. Mahone had a suggestion. Together they worked out a plan for Longstreet to march on to Farmville, while Mahone held his position. Later in the night Mahone was to withdraw through the woods and cross the Appomattox on the Southside Railroad bridge. He was to hold the crossing until all the troops, guns, and wagons had passed, and then the engineers were to burn both that high span and the lower wagon bridge under the hill. Colonel Talcott, who was nearby, was immediately called up and assigned to this duty.[4] No provision could be made as yet for Gordon, for the outcome of his battle was not yet plain. The bridges, of course, were to be held for him if he got away. In sketch, the plan is shown above.

It was now nearly dusk. Worn and already so tired that he had

[4] *Longstreet,* 615. 32 *S. H. S. P.,* 71.

stretched himself on the ground to rest during the evening,[5] Lee rode back to Longstreet's lines at Rice.[6] He found all quiet there. The cavalry that had been sent off during the morning had over-taken the Federals who were aiming to burn the high bridge over the Appomattox, and had killed or captured nearly all of them.[7] Enemy infantry had appeared during the afternoon southeast of Rice and had come within a mile of the place, but had not attacked seriously.[8]

Longstreet's forces were intact, and Gordon's had been located, though they were still hotly and dangerously engaged; but it was soon apparent that these and the cavalry were now nearly all that was left of the army. As the details were put together, the tragedy that had overtaken the other troops stood out unrelieved. From early forenoon Anderson had been following Longstreet's wagons. Ewell had been behind Anderson. Then had come the greater part of the wagon train, and then Gordon, closing the rear. The long, enfeebled column had crept on toward Sayler's Creek, but had been repeatedly engaged. The Federal cavalry would charge up from the Genito road, south and southeast of the route of the army, and would feel out the strength of the forces marching with the wagons. Repulsed by the infantry, who formed line of battle to protect the trains, the Federals would ride on ahead and strike again and still again, always in search of some weak spot.

About 11 A.M., the Union troops were attacking Gordon so vigorously in the rear and were demonstrating so heavily that Anderson and Ewell halted where they were in order to permit the wagons to pass and thereby to keep Gordon from being cut off while covering the trains. Anderson had orders that he should close on Mahone's division, which was the rear command under Longstreet, but Anderson did not notify Mahone that he was halting. As a consequence, Mahone marched on and left behind him an hourly-widening gap between him and the van of Pickett's division, the leading unit of Anderson's command. Unprotected wagon trains were moving through this gap, near the large Harper plantation,[9] on the upper stretches of Sayler's Creek and

---

[5] 38 S. H. S. P., 11.   [6] Alexander, 597.   [7] O. R., 46, part 1, p. 1302.

[8] Longstreet's report, Lee MSS.—K; O. R., 46, part 1, pp. 1175, 1181, 1187. While apparently not identified as such, these troops were of the XXIV Federal Corps.

[9] O. R., 46, part 1, p. 1132.

The terrain of the Sayler's Creek area, the routes of the Army of Northern Virginia through it, and the approximate line of Ewell's corps when attacked, April 6, 1865.

between the branches, when Federal cavalry bore down on them. The bluecoats reached the wagon train and burned a small part of it. This was the attack General Lee had asked General Pendleton to try and repulse when he had heard of it during the forenoon. The irruption of the Federals, of course, partially blocked the

89

road, caused Anderson's troops to halt, and made progress slower, but at length, about 2 P.M., the remaining wagons ahead of Anderson began to move once more. Gordon was then close on Ewell's rear, and all the wagon trains between Ewell and Gordon seemed to be safe.

When the leading troops of Anderson's command reached the point where the wagons had been fired, they found Union cavalry across the road in great strength. General Wise at once extemporized an assault with his brigade and drove the Federals to the south, but he was greatly outnumbered, and as he had not communicated to his immediate superior his intention of attacking, he was not supported by the rest of Johnson's division and had to withdraw. Meantime, and apparently with no knowledge of what Wise was doing, Anderson rode back to the head of Ewell's column to find its commander, and to tell him that the enemy held the road ahead. Ewell had already heard this from Fitz Lee, who chanced to be passing, and he had directed the wagon trains to leave the main route of the army east of Sayler's Creek and to take a more northerly road, over a lower crossing, so that they would escape the obstacle of the burned vehicles. No word of this change of the route of the wagon trains, however, was sent to Gordon, who was following Ewell but was not in direct touch with him.

When Anderson and Ewell met, it was clear that they must either attack and drive off the enemy or else leave the road, skirt around the Federals and seek a way that would lead to Farmville. Ewell was for the latter course, but as he had not been over the ground and as Anderson had, he left the decision to the South Carolinian. Anderson chose to deliver a joint attack to clear the line of march. Before the dispositions for this could be made, however, Federal troops began to appear in large numbers in Ewell's rear. This was because Gordon, who had been following Ewell and had been heavily engaged, had assumed, in the absence of any word to the contrary, that the route of the wagons was that of the infantry, as it had been all day. He had filed off after the trains; the Federals had found the gap and had plunged in. The result was that while Anderson was about to be attacked in front, Ewell's corps was to be assaulted from the rear. Per-

90

ceiving this, Anderson told Ewell that he, Ewell, would have all he could do on his line and that the attack to clear the road ahead would have to be made with Anderson's own command. Anderson rode away for this purpose and Ewell prepared his line of battle to resist the Federal assault. Back to back, the corps made ready—Anderson facing west, Ewell east. In Ewell's command was the naval battalion under Commodore Tucker, which answered orders with the sailor's "aye, aye, sir." Here, also, were heavy artillerists from the James River defenses, some of whom had probably never been under musketry fire in their whole career as soldiers. Custis Lee commanded them and the local defense troops. The other division was Kershaw's, consisting of a remnant—some 1600—of the veterans of the First Corps.

Anderson's attack was not well organized and failed almost before it was launched. Ewell's defense was stubborn and included one spirited counterattack, but it was in vain. Anderson's troops were captured, except for Wise's brigade and a few scattered individuals who escaped through the woods—the men whom Lee had seen from the other side of Sayler's Creek. Ewell's corps was taken in front, in flank, and in rear, and after hand-to-hand fighting, where the bayonet was used, was forced to surrender. Ewell lost 2800 in this way, Anderson perhaps 1500. The two corps as fighting units virtually ceased to exist.[10] Lee told only the sombre truth when he said to Pendleton, "General, that half of our army is destroyed." [11]

---

[10] Ewell's, Kershaw's, B. R. Johnson's, Custis Lee's and Fitz Lee's reports are in *O. R.*, 46, part 1, pp. 1283 ff. Anderson's is in *Lee MSS.—K;* Wise's account is in 25 *S. H. S. P.*, 17 ff. The same volume (p. 39) contains another useful narrative. Facts of interest as to numbers, positions, and time of the various attacks will be found in Wright's report, *O. R.*, 46, part 1, p. 906, Olcott's *ibid.*, p. 937, Devin's, *ibid.*, p. 1125, Custer's, *ibid.*, 1132. The story of the sailors and heavy artillerists has been admirably told in *Stiles*, 328 ff. Cf. also G. *Wise*, 234–35.

[11] *Pendleton*, 401. Could Lee have prevented the disaster at Sayler's Creek? Was he to blame for it? Probably not. He undoubtedly regarded speed as the essential of the retreat. With speed there was at least a chance of escaping with the van. Without rapidity of retreat, there was the certainty of early ruin. Lee, said Grant, "never permitted the head of his columns to stop because of any fighting that might be going on in his rear. In this way he came very near succeeding in getting to his provision trains and eluding us with at least part of his army" (2 *Grant*, 472). If that was good strategy, as his adversary believed, then Lee cannot be held culpable for riding ahead. His orders seem to have been about the best he could have drawn with the situation as it was. Neglect of his orders rather than a defect in them opened the two gaps through which the Federals struck in front and in rear. Gordon's mistake in following the wagons rather than the troops was a natural one, inasmuch as Ewell had not advised him of a change of route. Anderson's and Pickett's failure to see that Mahone was informed when Pickett

The weary commander probably was still gathering the details of the disaster to Ewell and to Anderson on Sayler's Creek when this note came from Gordon, marked 5 P.M.:

"I have been fighting heavily all day. My loss is considerable and I am still closely pressed. I fear that a portion of the train will be lost as my force is quite reduced & insufficient for its protection. So far I have been able to protect them, but without assistance can scarcely hope to do so much longer. The enemy's loss has been very heavy." [12]

As he had covered the rear, Gordon had been so closely pursued that he had been forced before noon to halt a division, to throw up works across the road, to pass the other divisions through, and then to repeat the process with the second division and the third. Once he was compelled to form line of battle along the hills at Deatonsville, and with Jones's artillery and W. H. F. Lee's division of cavalry, to retard the enemy until the road in front of him was clear of wagons for a mile. Then he set out again and having turned to the right as already noted, caught up with the wagon trains at an exceedingly bad crossing near the mouth of Sayler's Creek. The cavalry had been withdrawn by this time, so his three small and tired divisions had to hold off the Federals on the east side of the creek until the wagons got over. The direct assault of the enemy[13] was successfully repulsed. Soon afterward, however, the Federals who had overrun Ewell's front massed for a new charge on Gordon. It was at this juncture that he wrote Lee.

halted was, of course, a serious lapse. Mahone, also, must take his share of the blame. Throughout the campaign, as one reads the reports, one has the feeling that from weariness or despair or other cause, Anderson was scarcely responsible. In his report he mentioned more than once the hopelessness of the troops who, he said, "entered upon the campaign of 1865 with but little of the spirit of former days" (Anderson's report, Lee MSS.—K). It is probable that Anderson himself was oppressed by the feelings he thought were crippling his men. Had he been normal, in vigor of attack, Anderson might have saved the day by clearing the road before the Federals appeared in Ewell's rear. The old efficiency of organization was vanishing, and so was the offensive power of the army. Officers were failing as the men were. The limit of human endurance was passed with all except the strongest. It may seem ungenerous and worse to assess culpability on soldiers who had been marching for four days and for parts of three nights, and starving in the hour of their nation's death. Yet the happenings of April 4–9 show how ceaseless strain on the nerves of soldiers deadens initiative and destroys judgment even when men still can march and ride and seem to be themselves.

[12] Lee MSS.—L.

[13] The attacking force consisted of part of the II Corps.

Probably before the dispatch was received—Lee could not have given assistance even had word come earlier—Gordon was again attacked. Once more he drove back his assailants, but about 6 o'clock he was assaulted heavily in front and on both flanks. His exhausted divisions broke, got across the creek as best they could, and formed again, after a fashion, on the west bank, in the darkness.[14]

Gordon lost by capture some 1700.[15] These, added to the men taken from Ewell and Anderson and those who straggled and fell into the hands of the enemy during the day, brought the Federals' haul of prisoners to at least 6000. With the killed and wounded counted in, the day had cost Lee not less than 7000 and perhaps 8000 men.[16] The Southern commander now had only six divisions that could be counted as fighting organizations and but two of these, Field's and Mahone's, were of any size. The cavalry mounts were nearly dead, though the troopers who had been able to keep their horses going were still capable of putting up a fight. The artillery was reduced by about 50 per cent in personnel and still further in guns. To oppose on the morrow four corps of infantry and four divisions of cavalry—a total of 80,000 men, all within striking distance and with sufficient food and ammunition—Lee could not muster more than 12,000 reliable muskets and 3000 sabres. Every hour was to see that number perceptibly diminished, for men who had held their nerves under control and had silenced their protesting stomachs were dropping fast. Each halt meant that some soldiers would not be able to obey the "Fall in" when the column moved forward again.

Lee permitted himself no inferences that night. Nor, where everything was contingent on hour-by-hour developments, could he plan far ahead. Obviously there was still a chance of escaping with what remained of the army, if he could rest and reorganize his men. For then he could widen in the direction of Lynchburg the arc of his retreat to the southwest and might still outmarch the enemy. At the least, he could execute the first part of this movement. He could cross to the north bank of the Appomattox, burn

---

[14] The best account is Gordon's own, *Lee MSS.—K.* Cf. *O. R.*, 46, part 1, pp. 682, 779. The evidence as to the time of Lee's receipt of his dispatch of 5 P.M. is inferential.
[15] *O. R.*, 46, part 1, pp. 682, 784.
[16] Grant (*O. R.*, 46, part 1, p. 55) merely approximated the prisoners.

the bridges near Farmville, and give his men the repose that was now as much a necessity as food. He might even in this way deceive the enemy and get a new lead.

So long as this chance was open to him, his sense of duty did not permit him to consider any alternative. Soon after he returned to Rice, about sundown, he gave orders for Longstreet to resume the retreat via Farmville, in the direction of Lynchburg.[17] The guns were withdrawn,[18] and the troops started moving shortly after dark. Field's, Heth's, and Wilcox's divisions, together with the wagon trains of the whole army, were now put on the road— a very bad one at that.[19] The cavalry moved in Longstreet's rear.[20] The orders to the officers collecting the scattered units were that they should get the men across the Appomattox and re-form them there.[21] Mahone and Gordon were to go over the river via the High Bridge.[22] From Lynchburg, the post-commandant had wired that the Federals were advancing down the Virginia-Tennessee Railroad and that he wished to know if reinforcements could be sent. Lee answered that this could not be done, that Lynchburg must be held, if practicable, and that, if it could not be, supplies should be sent to Farmville or as far down the road toward that town as possible.[23]

Long after the leading troops had resumed the march toward Farmville, Lee remained at his temporary headquarters in a field north of Rice. He had a camp-fire of fence-rails close to his ambulance. For a time he stood by the wheel of the vehicle, looking into the fire and dictating to his military secretary, Colonel Marshall, who was sitting by a lantern in the ambulance, writing out Lee's orders on a lap-desk.[24]

[17] *Alexander,* 597.
[18] *O. R.,* 46, part 1, p. 1281. [19] Longstreet's report, *Lee MSS.—K.*
[20] *O. R.,* 46, part 1, p. 1303. [21] *O. R.,* 46, part 1, p. 1292.
[22] Gordon's report, *Lee MSS.—K; Longstreet,* 615.
[23] *Lee MSS.—L.*
[24] John S. Wise: *End of an Era,* 429. Mr. Wise gave an account of an interview with Lee in which he stated that he told the General he came on indirect orders from President Davis and wished a report for the President of General Lee's progress and plans. In the course of this interview Wise quoted Lee as saying: "A few more Sayler's Creeks and it will all be over—ended just as I expected it would end from the first." Wise was eighteen at the time. He went to Danville, where he visited Mr. Davis. Recalling the visit, the Confederate President wrote (2 *Davis,* 678): ". . . little if any reliable information in regard to the Army of Northern Virginia was received until a gallant youth, the son of General Henry A. Wise, came to Danville and told me that, learning Lee's army was to be surrendered, he had during the night mounted his fleet horse, and, escaping through and from the enemy's cavalry, some of whom pursued him, had come quite alone to

Soon afterward, Lee rode on to Farmville and went to the home of Patrick Jackson on Beech Street, where he sought a few hours' rest. Very early on the morning of April 7, as he prepared to leave, his hostess met him with an invitation to breakfast. He declined with his wonted courtesy, on the ground that he did not feel like eating. Mrs. Jackson pressed him: "Isn't there something we can fix for you, General?" Her manner was so earnestly solicitous that he confessed he had for days been wanting a cup of tea. Fortunately—and most oddly in the general distress of the times—the family had a little tea that had been put away against the day of need. It was quickly brought forth and brewed. Lee drank it gratefully.[25]

It must have been from Mrs. Jackson's that Lee directed Traveller to the home of Mrs. John T. Thornton, which was nearly opposite. Dismounting, he entered and greeted the widow of one of the most gallant of his regimental cavalry commanders, killed two years and a half previously during the Maryland expedition. "I have not time to tarry," he said with deep emotion, "but I could not pass by without stopping for a moment to pay my respects to the widow of my honored soldier, Colonel Thornton, and to tender her my deep sympathy in the sore bereavement which she sustained when the country was deprived of his invaluable services." [26] Then he went on to survey the situation.

One relief, if only one, was in sight. General St. John had reached Farmville from Amelia Springs the previous day. He had found the provisions sent from Burkeville on the approach of the enemy, 80,000 rations of meal and about 40,000 of bread, and he had set about collecting voluntary contributions of grain, which he had the mills grind at once. He had dispatched three couriers to Lee on the afternoon of the 6th with a report and a request for protection of the trains, though apparently none of

warn me of the approaching event." When first published, Wise's statement was challenged (3 *Publications of the Southern History Association*, 230). In the *Taylor MSS.* is a lengthy memorandum on this incident. Written by Colonel Walter Taylor, it disputes the accuracy of Wise's memory. It says, in part: "I was close to General Lee during those four years and can and do say that he never gave the slightest indication of such a belief [in the inevitability of Southern failure] as he is here represented to have entertained, although he fully appreciated the serious character of the work in hand and never underestimated the power of the other side in the contest; and it is entirely at variance with the general trend of thought that characterized his confidential interchange of ideas with those nearest to him" (*Taylor MSS.*, undated).

[25] Statement of Miss Mary Jackson, of Farmville, Va.   [26] *Jones*, 326.

these reached Lee. Now General St. John turned over all he had to Lee's commissary for issue to the troops, many of whom had received no regular rations since April 2,[27] five days previously. The starving time, it seemed, at last was over! The wagon train was arriving,[28] the artillery was coming up,[29] the head of Longstreet's column was close at hand. There was, however, a touch of new personal suspense for Lee in a meeting with Custis's courier, Dick Manson. When Lee asked eagerly how his son had fared in the battle of Sayler's Creek, Manson could only answer that he had been sent off the previous morning and did not know what fate had befallen his commander.[30]

Lee now rode to the north side of the Appomattox to locate the troops that had escaped the disaster at Sayler's Creek and had been ordered to cross the Appomattox at High Bridge. He soon found Major General Bushrod R. Johnson, who reported that his division had been destroyed; but very shortly Lee saw marching toward him in good order the largest of the brigades of Johnson's division, headed by General Wise. That veteran was afoot, wrapped in a gray blanket in lieu of a cloak, wearing a strange hat cocked on one side, and showing plainly on his face the red of the mud-puddle in which he had washed.

Weary as he was, Lee scarcely could repress his smile at the appearance of Wise. Calmly he asked what was the condition of Wise's command.

"Ready for dress-parade," answered Wise proudly, and proceeded to demand provisions for his troops.

Lee promised food and directed him to deploy his men across the hill. Wise, he went on, was to organize and take command of the stragglers who, despairingly and in large numbers, were streaming toward them. There followed a colloquy in which Wise sought to make it plain that General Bushrod Johnson, who was still sitting nearby, was to be accounted a straggler and had left his troops.

"Do you mean to say, General Lee," inquired Wise, "that I must take command *of all men of all ranks?*"

[27] St. John's report, *Lee MSS.*—L.
[28] Stevens's report, *Lee MSS.*—L.   [29] *O. R.,* 46, part 1, p. 1281.
[30] R. W. Manson to H. N. Phillips, *MS.,* July 5, 1926, copy of which Mr. Phillips graciously gave the writer.

Wise was satisfied that Lee, as he understood the significance of his question, turned his head to conceal another smile.

"Do your duty, sir," was all Lee said.[31] He added, privately no doubt, that General Wise would do well to wash his face again.[32] Behind Wise's brigade and the stragglers, but probably not reported at this hour, the survivors of Gordon's corps were moving up. They had crossed at High Bridge, as directed, were marching along the railroad track,[33] and would be ready to rejoin the rest of the army when Longstreet moved to the north side of the Appomattox.[34]

Ere long, General Breckinridge, the Secretary of War, arrived at temporary headquarters.[35] Lee at once went into conference with him, but neither he nor Breckinridge left any account of the interview. Breckinridge got the impression that Lee's move across the Appomattox was for temporary relief, and he reported to Mr. Davis the next day that Lee on the 7th would "still try to move around toward North Carolina." The secretary, himself a soldier of ability, was quick to see the desperate plight of the army. "The straggling has been great," he telegraphed, "and the situation is not favorable." [36]

Longstreet's troops were now coming into Farmville, and the advanced units were marching across the bridge and to the northside, where they were to halt and cook their long-awaited rations. The cavalry was following them, with the understanding that when they had passed, the two bridges—that of the railroad and that on the plank road—were to be burned. If this were done and if the two crossings at High Bridge had been destroyed, as previously ordered, then Lee would have at least some chance to rest his army and to resume his march ahead of the enemy, because the river could not be forded by infantry, though it was passable by cavalry. The sketch on page 98 shows the position of the bridges.

---

31 *MS. Memoirs* of W. B. Freeman, who witnessed part of the encounter; Wise's statement in 25 *S. H. S. P.*, 19. There is another version of this colloquy, or an account of a second in J. S. Wise: *End of an Era*, 433–35. The writer has followed the earlier narrative of the senior Wise.

32 *End of an Era*, 434.   33 Captain J. C. G., *Lee's Last Campaign*, 34.

34 Gordon's report, *Lee MSS.—K.*

35 J. S. Wise, *op. cit.*, 431, identified the headquarters as north of the Appomattox "in the forks of the road." The identification cannot be precise, but the house probably was that long occupied by R. D. Thaxton.

36 *O. R.*, 46, part 3, p. 1389.

Just at this hopeful moment came dire news. All Lee's plans were suddenly set at nought. Federal infantry were already on the north bank of the river, and were moving rapidly upstream toward the flank of the tired forces that were frying their bacon

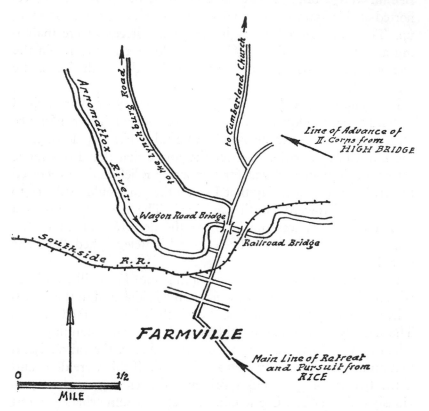

The river and roads north of Farmville showing, in particular, the location of the two bridges across the Appomattox.

in the belief that at last they were safe from alarms. It developed that a grievous blunder had been made. Down the river, at High Bridge, where General Mahone had been stationed as rearguard, the railroad span had been set afire in time to be burning freely before the enemy reached it, but the wagon bridge in the valley, a much smaller affair, had been lighted too late. Barlow's division of the II Corps had gone down to it, had put the

98

flames out and had marched rapidly across it. By 9 o'clock the 1st Division of the same corps was moving easily over it. The delay in setting the wagon bridge afire seems to have been due to misunderstanding of the usual sort. The engineers had been directed to burn the bridges on word from General Mahone. He either forgot to give the orders in time or else thought the engineers were to act without him.[37] Mahone made an attempt to retake the bridgehead, but failed.[38] Thereupon he was forced to withdraw, though he put up stiff resistance to the Federal advance, some three miles from Farmville.[39] Gordon's corps, which was ahead of Mahone, had light skirmishing.

General Lee exploded when he got word of the blunder. With vehemence unrestrained he voiced his opinion of the act and its authors:[40] The last hope of the shattered army was being allowed to slip away! Lee's rage was soon subdued, however, and his mind was put to work to redeem once more—it was to be nearly the last time—the military mistakes of others. He sent for Alexander, told him what had happened, showed him on the map where the Federals could strike the road of the Confederate retreat three miles ahead, and directed him to move artillery to protect the position. When Alexander pointed out that the Federals on the south side of the river would have a shorter march, Lee neither resented the observation nor stopped to explain that he had no choice of route because he had to keep close to the railroad in order to meet his supply trains and to feed his men.[41] He merely folded up his map and said there would be time enough to look after that.

In telling Alexander to send forward the guns to the place he designated, Lee also entrusted to him the destruction of the two

---

[37] Mahone's defense is hinted in *Longstreet*, 615. Talcott gave his version in 32 *S. H. S. P.*, 71. Talcott was in error, however, in saying that General Lee's reported indignation was over the failure to burn a bridge higher up the river. The only other bridges that mattered were those at Farmville, concerning the condition of which at the time of the Federals' approach there is an adequate account in *O. R.*, 46, part 1, p. 652. For Humphreys's report as to the High Bridge affair, see *O. R.*, 46, part 1, p. 683. A full narrative of the steps taken to save the High Bridge from complete destruction will be found in Livermore's *Days and Events*, 449 ff. For the hour of the crossing of the troops, see *O. R.*, 46, part 1, p. 713.

[38] *O. R.*, 46, part 1, p. 758.

[39] *O. R.*, 46, part 1, p. 787. Mahone in his report, *Lee MSS.—L*, merely referred to two fights early in the day.

[40] *Long*, 413.　　　　　　　　　[41] *Alexander*, 597–98.

bridges at Farmville, that of the railway and that on the plank road. Alexander was enjoined to see that the crossings were not burned before the Confederate cavalry had passed, and that they were not to be left so long that the Federals could extinguish the fire and utilize them.[42]

The order was given none too soon. Federal cavalry—they proved to be Crook's[43]—were pressing so closely behind the Confederates' horses that Fitz Lee had to make a stand on the outskirts of Farmville and in the very streets of the town to permit Longstreet's rearguard and the stragglers to clear the bridges.[44] By 11 A.M. the advance of that troublesome, fast-moving VI Corps was on the hills overlooking Farmville from the south.[45] The bridges were then fired and caught aflame rapidly, before the Confederate cavalry could break off the skirmish and cross.[46] The arrival of the Federals caused a near-stampede among the teamsters and scattered units on the north side of the river and prompted General Lee to order an immediate resumption of the retreat. He was concerned for the moment, also, lest part of the cavalry had been cut off and lost, and he insisted that the head of Longstreet's column start at the double quick. The issue of rations had to be suspended, even though a large part of the army had received nothing.[47] In retrospect, at least, Longstreet attributed Lee's precipitancy to something akin to panic and he stated that he tried to reassure his chief by telling him that the cavalry would certainly find and use a nearby ford. Longstreet apparently did not realize how close the danger was. Envelopment was threatened; no time was to be lost.[48] The cars containing provisions were sent farther up the railroad[49] in the hope that they might be overtaken on the march, which was to be north of and then approximately parallel to the line.[50]

Lee went up the road with Longstreet's column some two miles

---

[42] *Alexander*, 599. [43] Formerly Kautz's.

[44] Longstreet's report, *Lee MSS.—K; E. M. Boykin: The Falling Flag* (cited hereafter as *Falling Flag*), 32–33.

[45] *O. R.*, 46, part 1, p. 652.

[46] *Longstreet, loc. cit.;* Fitz Lee's report, *O. R.*, 46, part 1, p. 1303. McRae, who apparently was near the rear, said in his report, *Lee MSS.—L*, that he arrived "about noon."

[47] Charles Marshall: *Appomattox. An Address . . . Jany. 19, 1894* (cited hereafter as *Marshall's Appomattox*), 7.

[48] *Longstreet*, 616. [49] St. John's report, *Lee MSS.—L.*

[50] Inquiries were made to Lynchburg and to Danville as to the reserve ordnance stores there, but elicited no reply, according to Baldwin's report, *Lee MSS.—L.*

and a half to the coal pits north of Farmville. There, to his relief, he found the cavalry and learned that the Confederates had located a ford some miles above the plank-road bridge and had crossed safely.[51] The cavalry at the moment were covering the wagon train which was moving toward the main highway over "Lackland's Mill road," described by Stevens as "terribly bad." [52] Lee sat down under an oak tree and was resting his back against it when Federal cavalry, who had used the ford by which Fitz Lee had crossed, advanced for another attack on the wagons. The troubled commander slowly got up, mounted his horse and rode past the Confederate troopers, who gave him a cheer. He lifted his hat in acknowledgment and soon paused to watch the fight.[53] Under his eyes, one division met the oncoming Federals in front and another took them in flank. The enemy's attack was broken up brilliantly. Many of the Federals were captured, including their commander, Brigadier General J. Irvin Gregg.[54] The survivors were routed. Lee's spirits, which always rose when action was joined, were much improved by this success. "Keep your command together and in good spirits, General—don't let them think of surrender—I will get you out of this," he told his son Rooney Lee after General Gregg had been taken.[55] It was a courageous remark, but it was ominous in that it showed General Lee knew the men were talking of surrender. It was the first time, too, so far as is known, that Lee in his own conversation had recognized such a contingency on the retreat.

Lee held the cavalry where it could meet another attack,[56] and he sent Mahone's division to the position taken by the artillery which Alexander had duly sent forward to the point where the road of the Federal advance met the road of Lee's march. This position was near Cumberland Church and Price's farm,[57] a little more than three miles north of Farmville. Mahone drew up line of battle there, entrenched, and prepared to cover the passage of the wagons and of the army.[58] Gordon's corps, which had now

[51] This, presumably, was at Sandy Ford, four miles above the plank-road bridge.
[52] Stevens's report, *Lee MSS.*—L.
[53] 32 *S. H. S. P.*, 310; *Napier*, 223.   [54] *O. R.*, 46, part 1, p. 1303.
[55] *Cooke*, 455. *Long*, 415, evidently followed Cooke.
[56] *O. R.*, 46, part 1, p. 1303.
[57] *O. R.*, 46, part 1, p. 793.   [58] *Alexander*, 599.

come up, moved by the left flank through the woods to protect the wagons.

Owing to the condition of the animals and to the badness of the road by which the wagons were moving, the march was exceedingly slow in getting under way. The army had virtually no start when Federal infantry began to appear in much strength on Mahone's front. In the afternoon they attacked and tried to turn the division's left, which was almost "in the air." The cavalry who were covering the flank were driven in, and a battery was taken temporarily. The whole of the infantry had to stop, and both Gordon and Longstreet had to send Mahone help. He then beat off the attack and delivered a countercharge in which he took some prisoners.[59] Lee congratulated the men,[60] but he could not presume on this momentary advantage. He did not dare attempt his usual solution of such a problem, namely, an offensive against the troops that threatened his road. The wagons were still close at hand, most of the infantry had been moving with little or no rest for a minimum of eighteen hours, and some of them had been almost constantly on the move since nightfall of the 5th— more than forty hours. The strength of the Federals on the right and rear of the army was not known. Lee did not feel that he could afford to withdraw Mahone from his strong position until darkness. The failure to burn the wagon bridge below High Bridge was costing him dearly! For the Federals south of the river had been somewhat mystified by his movements and, if Humphreys's II Corps had been kept back at High Bridge, Lee might have had something of the advantage that McClellan gained by crossing to the south side of the Chickahominy on the night of June 27, 1862. As it was, the start that had been so vigorously begun at the double-quick near Farmville came to this maddening halt within four miles and in plain sight of the enemy!

Lee did not complain because of his inability to move from Cumberland Church, but at least once in the afternoon he displayed the petulance that always was the surest sign of a battle for self-mastery. He had ridden out toward Mahone's line and

---

[59] Mahone's report, *Lee MSS.—L*; Gordon's report, *Lee MSS.—K*; 1 *N. C. Regts.*, 685.
[60] *Grimes*, 116; 1 *N. C. Regts.*, 265.

was watching the fire of one of Chamberlayne's batteries, when a staff officer from Gordon came up the side of the hill next the enemy. Lee waited until the officer had given his message and then he pointed out his mistake in exposing himself unnecessarily. The officer answered that he was ashamed to shelter himself when he saw the commanding general sitting in plain view of the Federals. Lee flared up and answered rather sharply: "It is my duty to be here. I must see. Go back the way I told you, sir!" A small incident surely, but it was remembered and repeated: evil was the day when "Marse Robert" employed even that mild tone of rebuke! [61]

As darkness fell, Lee went to a cottage near Mahone's lines and close to Cumberland Church to spend the night.[62] Longstreet soon joined him there.[63] About half-past nine or perhaps a little later, a courier came up from Mahone's front with a dispatch for the commanding general. Lee opened it himself and read:

Headquarters Armies of the United States.

April 7, 1865—5 P.M.

General R. E. Lee,
    Commanding C. S. Army:

  General: The results of the last week must convince you of the hopelessness of further resistance on the part of the Army of Northern Virginia in this struggle. I feel that it is so, and regard it as my duty to shift from myself the responsibility of any further effusion of blood, by asking of you the surrender of that portion of the C. S. Army known as the Army of Northern Virginia.

  Very respectfully, your obedient servant,

U. S. GRANT,
Lieutenant-General,
Commanding Armies of the United States.[64]

[61] *Long*, 415–16. The date and approximate time of day can be fixed by the reference to the name of the battery.

[62] *Alexander*, 600. As far as can now be determined this was the Blanton house, near Blanton's shop in Cumberland County, about three miles from Farmville (*Farmville Herald*, Feb. 5, 1926).

[63] *Longstreet*, 617.

[64] *O. R.*, 46, part 3, p. 619; *Longstreet*, 619. The time of the arrival of the message, which had been offered by flag of truce shortly after 5 o'clock but could not be received until later because of the firing, is fixed fairly well by the narrative of the men who met the Federal bearer. See 20 *S. H. S. P.*, 60. *Cf.* 19 *S. H. S. P.*, 270; *Sorrel*, 300. None of the originals of Grant's letters is in the Lee papers.

General Lee studied it without a word or sign and then silently passed it to Longstreet, who was sitting near him. Longstreet read it, also, and handed it back.

"Not yet," he said.[65]

[65] *Longstreet,* 619.

CHAPTER VIII

The Last Council of War

"Not yet"—Longstreet's answer bespoke his chief's mind. As long as there was a prospect of escape Lee felt it was his duty to fight on. He would not yield one hour before he must. But might it be possible, on the basis of Grant's letter, to negotiate an honorable peace? Might Grant be willing to do now what he had refused to do a month before—confer and see if a way could be found to end the slaughter? Perhaps the chance was remote, but if there was a chance, Lee must avail himself of it. He could not assume, in Grant's words, "the responsibility of any further effusion of blood." With no reply to Longstreet, he took a single sheet of cheap, ruled note paper that bore a raised watermark in the upper left-hand corner, and wrote this answer:

Genl   7th Apl '65

I have recd your note of this date. Though not entertaining the opinion you express of the hopelessness of further resistance on the part of the Army of N. Va.—I reciprocate your desire to avoid useless effusion of blood, & therefore before considering your proposition, ask the terms you will offer on condition of its surrender

Very respy your obt. Servt

R. E. Lee
Genl

Lt. Genl. U. S. Grant
    Commd Armies of the U. States[1]

Lee sent this reply promptly and did not show it to Longstreet, or, so far as is recorded, to any one else, though the nature of the

---

[1] *MS.*, office of the U. S. Adjutant General. It is worth noting that the original contains the full conclusion used in letters of the time, "Very respectfully your obedient servant" and also the formal address to General Grant by his military title. These are not published in the version given in *O. R.*, 46, part 1, p. 619, though Grant's polite conclusion to the preceding letter is printed.

message from Grant was guessed if its purport was not actually known.[2] Within an hour after the flag of truce had been met, the answer had been presented on the lines to the waiting staff officer, who was none other than Lee's old friend and former adjutant at West Point, Seth Williams, Grant's inspector general.

The wagons had passed on now and had halted in the neighborhood of New Store, close to the southwestern edge of Buckingham County, nearly twenty miles from Farmville, but they were much scattered because of "the wretched road and jaded condition of the animals."[3] Broken-down caissons and wagons were abandoned and sometimes were not even pulled out of the road before they were fired.[4] The troops who still carried their muskets had hardly the appearance of soldiers as they wearily tramped along, their clothes all tattered and covered with mud, their eyes sunken and lustreless, and their faces pale and pinched from their ceaseless march. "Many of the men who had thrown away their arms and knapsacks were lying prone on the ground along the roadside, too much exhausted to march further, and only waiting for the enemy to come and pick them up as prisoners, while at short intervals there were wagons mired down, their teams of horses and mules lying in the mud, from which they had struggled to extricate themselves until complete exhaustion had forced them to be still and wait for death to glaze their wildly starting eyes, and still their quick gasping and panting for the breath which could scarcely reach some of them through the mud that almost closed their nostrils; but through all this a part of the army still trudged on, with their faith still strong, and only waiting for General Lee to say whether they were to face about and fight. . . ."[5]

With straggling as it was, and with the enemy known to be close on his heels, Lee deemed it desirable to send ahead Gordon's tired men and the various scattered units and to bring from van to rear the corps of Longstreet which had suffered less and was in fair fighting condition. Nothing was left of the infantry now but the starved remnant of these two corps and a few small brigades

---

[2] Colonel Marshall, in his *Appomattox*, 7, said there was some difference of opinion among officers as to what the answer should be. That reference, obviously not conclusive, is the only one the writer has found indicating that the dispatch may have been seen by others besides Longstreet or may have been discussed.

[3] Stevens's report, *Lee MSS.*—L.

[4] *Longstreet*, 620.   [5] *F. M. Myers.* 388–89.

kept together by the spirit of their officers and the persistence of
their morale. By 11 P.M. Gordon's men had passed up the road
toward Lynchburg, and Longstreet resumed the march.[6] The
cavalry closed the rear[7]—kept there because the immediate danger
from the troops following them was greater at that time than that
from any force that might be moving parallel to the route of the
retreat. At 1 A.M., from New Store, the wagons started once again.[8]

It was now Saturday, April 8, the beginning of the sixth day
after the evacuation of Petersburg. Lee's objective remained the
same—Danville and union with Johnston—but his hope of attaining that objective had dwindled until now it hung on a double
contingency. The meandering Appomattox River along the line
of Lee's retreat was narrowing fast. A few miles more of the
march and the river would cease to be a protecting barrier against
that part of Grant's army moving south of the stream and parallel
to Lee. Beyond the headwaters of the Appomattox, across a watershed to the west, lay the James River, with Lynchburg at the
nearest point of Lee's approach. This watershed was about twelve
miles wide. Directly over it ran the Southside Railroad, on which
were the provision trains that had been sent from Lynchburg, as
well as the cars that had been hurried from Farmville on the
Federals' approach. If, therefore, Lee was to escape, he had to
cross the watershed between the Appomattox and the James before the enemy got there and closed the way. And if he was to
keep his army from literal starvation, he had to meet at some point
on the railroad over that watershed the trains of provisions that
were being moved to meet him. The most convenient place to
reach the trains was where the road of his march crossed the
railway at a station called after the county and the river, Appomattox. The terrain was as shown in the sketch on page 108.

Would Lee reach Appomattox Station before the Federals and
would he procure food there or nearby? If he did, he might feed
the men, turn south and even yet reach Danville and join General
Johnston. But if he found the Federals across the watershed in
sufficient strength to block his advance and to seize his provisions,

[6] Longstreet's report, *Lee MSS.*—K. *Cf. Longstreet*, 619.
[7] *O. R.,* 46, part 1, p. 1303.
[8] Stevens's report, *Lee MSS.*—L.

that was the end. James River would then cut off his retreat. There could be nothing beyond that point, no alternative to which, as in the past, he could turn quickly if his chosen plan had to be laid aside.

Lee had no way of judging that morning precisely what were the chances of reaching Appomattox Station and of getting his provisions. General St. John had started out for Danville on the

The watershed between the James and Appomattox Rivers east of Lynchburg, with special reference to the line of the Southside Railroad.

7th and had made a wide circuit ahead of the army, in order to avoid the Federals. At Pamplin's Station, eighteen miles west of Farmville, he had found the cars sent up from Farmville. He thought they should go farther west and he communicated with General Lee. But the situation was so uncertain that Lee had not been willing to send them on toward Lynchburg.[9] Perhaps he decided not to have these rations sent westward because he intended to halt at Appomattox Courthouse the supplies sent down from Lynchburg. With supplies both at Appomattox and at Pamplin's he stood a better chance of feeding the men.

As for the possibility of marching to Appomattox before the Federals could close the way, that depended on how many of the enemy were pursuing on the north side of the river and how many were moving and at what speed on the south side, by a somewhat shorter route. The Confederate intelligence service had broken

[9] St. John's report, *Lee MSS.—L.*

108

down with the rest of the staff. None of the cavalry was ahead. Lee had no means of ascertaining the grim truth that two Union corps[10] were now on the north bank, following him closely, while the cavalry corps, the V, the XXIX, and part of the XXV were hurrying forward, unencumbered by wagons and weak horses, in an effort to beat him to Appomattox Station.

Toward that point the march continued slowly through bright sunshine during the morning hours of the 8th.[11] The Federals in the rear did not push the cavalry. The infantry were only a little disturbed on the left flank,[12] and there only by horsemen. Lee's manner was as composed as ever, and when he received the salute of a cavalry command he passed, it was, as one officer wrote, "with a calm smile that assured us our confidence was not misplaced." [13]

The situation was so quiet that General Lee halted during the forenoon and stretched himself out on the ground to rest. While he was there, General Pendleton approached and told him that a number of his officers had met the previous evening and had considered the situation. They had concluded that the army could not cut its way through the Federals or disband and reassemble, and that, consequently, further bloodshed would be futile.[14] They had deputized Pendleton to acquaint Lee with their deliberations and to tell him that, in their opinion, he ought to stop the fighting and open negotiations for the surrender of the army. Pendleton did not say so, but the officers had acted in a desire to save Lee the humiliation of making the first move toward surrender. They were willing to assume the responsibility of advising that course if thereby they might relieve him. Lee did not like the suggestion. What he answered is a matter of dispute. Early writers quoted him as saying, "Surrender? I have too many good fighting men for that!" Pendleton stated that Lee replied substantially: "I trust it has not come to that! We certainly have too many brave men to think of laying down our arms. They still fight with great spirit, whereas the enemy does not. And, besides, if I were to intimate to General Grant that I would listen to terms, he would at once regard it as such an evidence of weakness that he

10 II and VI.
11 *Falling Flag,* 45.
13 *Falling Flag,* 46.

12 *Longstreet,* 620.
14 *Gordon,* 443.

would demand unconditional surrender—and sooner than that I am resolved to die. Indeed, we must all determine to die at our posts." [15] The manner must have been sterner than the words, for when General Pendleton talked of the interview shortly after it ended, he had the air of a man who had been decidedly snubbed and was embarrassed to have to tell of it.[16] Longstreet and Gordon had not attended the conference nor did they share the opinion of those for whom Pendleton spoke. Longstreet stated that when he was asked to broach to General Lee the subject of surrender, he refused with a sharp reminder that in proposing such action the officers were violating the articles of war and were liable to court-martial.[17]

The day wore on, with less of incident than any since the retreat had begun. During the early afternoon word came from Fitz Lee that his rearguard was about two miles behind the infantry and that the enemy was two miles behind him. Only infantry was pursuing him, he said, and they were of the II Corps. The Federal cavalry had probably gone to the Confederate left: had not he better leave a cavalry picket on the road and come

[15] *Pendleton*, 402. The difference between Pendleton's version and the briefer "Surrender," etc., is not important; but in *Jones*, 297, there is an elaborate version in which, after quoting substantially what Pendleton wrote, Jones went on to attribute to Lee this language: "General, this is no new question with me. I have never believed we could, against the gigantic combination for our subjugation, make good in the long run our independence unless foreign powers should, directly or indirectly, assist us. This I was sure it was their interest to do, and I hoped they would so regard it. But such considerations really made with me no difference. We had, I was satisfied, sacred principles to maintain and rights to defend, for which we were in duty bound to do our best, even if we perished in the endeavor." Pendleton's own language is, of course, to be preferred to Jones's account of what he remembered Pendleton had told him. Moreover, Jones clearly misunderstood at least that part of Pendleton's remarks that relate to Lee's alleged belief that foreign intervention was the only means of winning Southern independence and might reasonably be expected. Lee held no such views. What he said in South Carolina in the winter of 1861–62 has already been quoted (see vol. I, p. 621). In addition, he wrote Mr. Davis on July 6, 1864, "As far as I have been able to judge this war presents to the European world but two aspects, a contest in which one party is contending for abstract slavery and the other against it. The existence of vital rights involved does not seem to be understood or appreciated. As long as this lasts, we can expect neither sympathy nor aid. Nor can we expect the policy of any government towards us to be governed by any other consideration than that of self-interest. Our safety depends upon ourselves alone. If we can defeat or drive the armies of the enemy from the field, we shall have peace. All our efforts and energies should be devoted to that object" (*Duke Univ. MSS.*). This speaks for itself.

[16] *Alexander*, 600–601.

[17] *Longstreet*, 620; *Gordon*, 433. General Schaff (*Sunset of the Confederacy*, cited hereafter as *Schaff*, 141) had a very interesting critique of the several accounts of this interview and of the conference that led to it. He inclined to the belief that both Gordon and Longstreet were to some extent party to the proposal, and he called attention to the fact that neither of them entered a denial until long after Pendleton's death.

forward with his troops?[18] Some two hours later a further dispatch from Fitz Lee brought news that the enemy's cavalry had
reached Prospect Station, twenty miles east of Appomattox. They
would arrive at Appomattox by 10 A.M. of the 9th at the earliest.
Rooney Lee and Gary should push on to Appomattox, Fitz Lee
wrote. He would come forward himself as quickly as he could
get past the column.[19] If this was a correct forecast, the race to
Appomattox would be close! The enemy's cavalry and the Confederate advance would get there within a few hours of each other.

During the same afternoon of the dragging march toward Appomattox there disappeared from Confederate command an officer
who had played no small part on the bloody stage of northern
Virginia. Throughout the operations from March 29 onward,
despair had seemed to dominate the heart of Richard H. Anderson, "Fighting Dick." As already indicated,[20] he nowhere had
fought with his old vigor. After the action at Sayler's Creek he
had spent the 7th trying, as he said, to get together the fragments
of his command.[21] While he had been looking for Pickett, that
officer had been searching for him, and, at length, had rejoined
Longstreet with a handful of men, only about sixty of whom, as
he subsequently reported, had muskets when the end came. These
survivors were assigned to Mahone.[22] After Wise had collected
what was left of Johnson's division, the largest of Anderson's
units, it was attached to Grimes's division of Gordon's corps.[23]
Thus was Anderson left without a command, and on the afternoon of the 8th he was formally relieved and notified that he
could return to his home, or any other place he might select, and
report thence to the Secretary of War.[24] The specific reasons for
Lee's action were not given—whether he thought Anderson disqualified for further command because of his despair, or whether
he considered him culpable for what had happened at Sayler's
Creek.[25] Whatever the cause, Anderson did not dispute the ac-

---

18 *Lee MSS.—N*, dated 1 P.M.
19 *Lee MSS.—N*, dated 3 P.M.   20 See *supra*, p. 92.
21 Anderson's report, *Lee MSS.—K;* Pickett's report, *ibid.*
22 Pickett's report, *Lee MSS.—K;* Pickett to Latrobe, April 11, 1865, *Lee MSS.;* William Mahone to W. H. Taylor, Nov. 29, 1891, quoting *MS.* order of April 8, 1865,
Taylor MSS.
23 *O. R.,* 46, part 1, p. 1291; *Grimes,* 117.   24 Anderson's report, *Lee MSS.—K.*
25 There is no reason to believe that intemperance had anything to do with it. One
of the members of his staff told C. Irvine Walker, Anderson's biographer, that during his
period of command in Virginia, Anderson did not drink.

tion. After the war, in a personal struggle of the bitterest sort against poverty, he remained on friendly terms with his old chief.[26] At the same time that Lee relieved Anderson of command, he took the same action regarding Pickett and Bushrod Johnson, but the order concerning Pickett apparently never reached him. As late as April 11 he signed himself, "Maj. Genl. Comdg." Lee thought the order had been given Pickett, and when he saw him later he is said to have remarked, "I thought that man was no longer with the army." [27]

About dark[28] Lee received another note from Grant. It had been passed through the lines before noon[29] but had been delayed in reaching General Lee. It came sealed, its contents not known to those who handled it,[30] and was in answer to Lee's request of the previous evening for a statement of Grant's terms. With the aid of a wax-taper that Colonel Venable lighted, Lee quietly read the paper. Grant stated, in simple terms, that as peace was his great desire, the only condition on which he would insist would be that the officers and men who were surrendered should be disqualified to bear arms until properly exchanged. Grant added that he would meet Lee, or, he offered thoughtfully, would designate officers to meet others named by Lee to arrange the terms for the surrender of the Army of Northern Virginia.[31]

Lee said nothing for a few moments. Then he asked Colonel Venable, "How would you answer that?"

"I would answer no such letter," Venable replied.

"Ah, but it must be answered," Lee said.[32]

Lee was not yet willing to consider surrender, but the hope of a general settlement that had shaped his action on receipt of Grant's first letter did not seem wholly destroyed by Grant's language. It might not be impossible to make honorable terms for all the Confederate forces. So, from the roadside where the mes-

---

[26] Cf. his letter of June, 1866 to Lee, covering his final report, Lee MSS.—K.

[27] Lee MSS.; personal statements to the writer by Colonel W. H. Taylor and Major Giles B. Cooke; W. H. Taylor to W. H. Palmer, MS., June 17, 1911. W. H. Palmer to W. H. Taylor, MS., June 24, 1911, Taylor MSS. These two writers recalled the issuance of the order.

[28] Alexander, op. cit., 601, said the letter came late in the afternoon, but Colonel Venable in a letter to Colonel Taylor, March 9, 1894, stated it arrived after dark (Taylor MSS.).

[29] O. R., 46, part 3, p. 643.

[30] O. R., 46, part 3, p. 643.

[31] O. R., 46, part 3, p. 641.

[32] Venable to Taylor, loc. cit.

sage reached him, on a sheet similar to the one he had used the night before, Lee wrote in his own hand this letter, of which Colonel Marshall took a copy on a bit of scrap paper:

8^h Ap^l '65

Genl

I recd at a late hour your note of today. In mine of yesterday I did not intend to propose the surrender of the Army of N. Va —but to ask the terms of your proposition. To be frank, I do not think the emergency has arisen to call for the surrender of this Army, but as the restoration of peace should be the sole object of all, I desired to know whether your proposals would lead to that and I cannot therefore meet you with a view to surrender the Army of N. Va.—but as far as your proposal may affect the C. S. forces under my command & tend to the restoration of peace, I shall be pleased to meet you at 10 A. M. tomorrow on the old stage road to Richmond between the picket lines of the two armies.

Very respy your Obt Sevt

R. E. LEE

Genl.

Lt. Genl U. S. Grant
Commg Armies of the U. S.[33]

This letter was delivered to General Humphreys' lines, beyond the Confederate rearguard.[34] Before it was dispatched, the leading brigades of Gordon's command, very weary, had halted at 3 P.M. about one mile from Appomattox Courthouse.[35] Ahead of Gordon were surplus wagons and, beyond the courthouse, the artillery under General R. L. Walker that had been started from Amelia Courthouse on the 4th and had now been overtaken.[36] Longstreet's corps stopped behind Gordon, about nightfall, his rearguard six miles from the courthouse.[37] Lee and his staff turned out from the road into thick woods, with Longstreet and his officers, and made his camp on the left of the highway, about

---

[33] *MS.,* office of the U. S. Adjutant General; Marshall's copy in *Lee MSS.—M.* In some of the printed versions of this letter—Fitz Lee's and Alexander's, for example— "desired" is put in the present tense, with an obvious change of meaning.

[34] *Alexander,* 601. [35] *O. R.,* 46, part i, p. 1291.

[36] *O. R.,* 46, part i, p. 1282; Stevens's report, *Lee MSS.—L.*

[37] Longstreet's report, *Lee MSS.—K.*

two miles from the courthouse.[38] Lee's ambulance and the head-quarters wagons were entangled somewhere among the trains. There were no tents, no tables, no camp stools, no cooking utensils, and practically no food. The moon was now up[39] and the air was chill, though the day had been warm for the season. A fire was lighted. Lee and the others sat around it on the ground.[40]

About 9 o'clock there came a sudden roar of artillery from the front where, until that time, all had been quiet. The sound probably was heard at Lee's headquarters and told its own story.[41] If it was not heard, what had happened was soon written on the skies. For against the clouds, in front as well as in rear and on the left flank, the light of camp-fires was reflected.[42] And soon there came confirmation in messages from the front. The enemy was across the line of the army's advance over the watershed! Federal troops had come up from the south, and had attacked and had captured some of the surplus artillery as well as the wagon train of Rooney Lee's division.[43]

Although this news might mean the extinction of the last spark of hope, Lee received it so quietly that none of those who were with him that evening recorded what he said in comment. He sent orders to Fitz Lee to pass the cavalry to the front and directed him to report in person at headquarters.[44] The rearguard, left without cavalry, proceeded to dig and to man field works across the road of the Federal pursuit.

Ere long Fitz Lee arrived, as did Gordon, on a like summons. With these and with Longstreet, began Lee's last council of war. The commander stood by the fire. Longstreet sat on a log, smoking his pipe. Gordon and Fitz Lee stretched themselves out on a blanket.[45] Staff officers and perhaps some of the brigade and division commanders sat nearby but not within earshot.[46]

---

[38] 2 *S. H. S. P.,* 357. For a detailed description of the site, see *Schaff,* 163.
[39] *Falling Flag,* 49.   [40] *Schaff, loc. cit.*
[41] It was plainly audible at the headquarters of General Bryan Grimes (27 *S. H. S. P.,* 94). He was east of Appomattox Courthouse and probably not more than a mile from Lee.
[42] MS. *Memoirs of W. B. Freeman.*
[43] *O. R.,* 46, part 1, p. 1282; Stevens's report, *Lee MSS.—L.*
[44] *O. R.,* 46, part 1, p. 1303.
[45] *Cooke,* 459; *Long,* 420; Gordon: *Modern Eloquence,* 5, 491.
[46] Probably it was the proximity of these men that led Gordon into the error (*Reminiscences,* 435) of asserting that General Pendleton and a number of staff officers attended the council.

Lee explained the condition of affairs as far as he knew it and read to his chiefs of corps the correspondence with Grant.

What, he then asked, did they advise him to do?[47]

There could, of course, be only one answer from men who were determined to fight as long as any hope remained. That answer was to attack as soon as possible, to attempt to cut a way through, and, if successful, to resume the march. Should it be found that the troops ahead were only cavalry, Fitz Lee's men could charge them, with Gordon in support, and could clear the road for the rest of the soldiers. But if the Federal infantry had outmarched the weary survivors of the Army of Northern Virginia, and stood in force across the road, too strong to be driven, the troops would then be virtually surrounded and only one thing remained to be done—surrender. The word could not be avoided now.

From this decision, reached without heroics, there was no dissent. Details were worked out quickly. The advance was to begin at 1 A.M. Fitz Lee was to drive the enemy from his front, wheel to the left, and cover the passage of the trains, which were to be reduced to two battalions of artillery and the ammunition wagons. Gordon was then to move ahead, and Longstreet was to close up and be ready to repel any attack by the forces moving on the Confederate rear.[48] The route was to be via Campbell Courthouse and Pittsylvania, and not by Lynchburg, on which a separate Federal column was moving along the Virginia and Tennessee Railroad, and from which all provisions had been sent to meet General Lee's advance. The surplus wagons, however, were to go toward Lynchburg on the bare chance that they might escape while the enemy was pursuing the army.[49]

The orders were given. The conference was ended. Hope had seemed lost half a dozen times, only to find through Lee's resourcefulness something new on which to fix itself; hope had sustained the army on all that dreadful march; hope was now reduced to the possibility that only Union cavalry and none of the blue-coated infantry stood in the way. Yet, though the army was merely the ghost of other days, somehow that hope would not down altogether.

[47] Gordon, loc. cit.; O. R., 46, part 1, p. 1303.
[48] O. R., 46, part 1, pp. 1266, 1303.
[49] Marshall's Appomattox, p. 11; Colston to Lee, April 8, 1865, 4 P.M.; Lee MSS.—M.

Gordon and Fitz Lee rode off. Longstreet prepared to make his bed on the ground, with his saddle for his pillow and the saddle blanket for his covering. Something as nearly approaching peace as ever there comes in war was about to settle over the bivouac among the trees when one of Gordon's staff officers returned to explain that his chief had neglected to ask where he was to halt and camp the next night—as though it were certain he would break through and resume the march. Did General Lee have any directions for him on this point?

"Yes," said Lee grimly. "Tell General Gordon I should be glad for him to halt just beyond the Tennessee line," some 175 miles away.[50]

It was then about midnight, the beginning of one of the three or four most memorable dates in American history, April 9, 1865, Sunday, Palm Sunday. And the oaks in the forest were tasseling in rebirth.[51]

[50] *Gordon,* 436.   [51] *Falling Flag,* 55.

CHAPTER IX

THE NINTH OF APRIL

DURING the night, after the vanguard was moved forward to meet anticipated attack,[1] the reflection of the camp fires on the clouds and the mutter of moving men indicated the massing of a large force on the Confederate front and left.[2] Lee, with his usual care, reasoned that this might call for a change in the plan that had been worked out at the council a few hours before, so he ordered the chief of the cavalry corps to feel out the strength of the enemy and, if need be, to suspend his advance until daylight, when he could better ascertain the situation.[3] Then Lee sought a little sleep.

Shortly after 1 o'clock, from the road nearby, there came the weary staccato of the march. It was not noisy, for the men were too tired and too depressed to indulge in banter. So nearly silent were the passing troops that it was impossible to tell to what command they belonged. But presently through the darkness came a voice and a scrap of doggerel:

> "The race is not to them that's got
> The longest legs to run
> Nor the battle to that people
> That shoots the biggest gun."

The intonation was unmistakable, and the words were familiar in the army as part of the so-called "Texas Bible." The elocutionist who was reciting the lines for his solace must be a member of the famous old "Hood's brigade" of the First Corps. Longstreet's men evidently were going forward unseen, to close the rear in the final attempt to break through.[4] If General Lee heard the

---

1 *O. R.*, 46, part 1, p. 1292.
2 *O. R.*, 46, part 1, p. 1266. Lee here reported the concentration but not his reasons for knowing it was being effected. These reasons are gathered from the statements of survivors.
3 *O. R.*, 46, part 1, p. 1266.   4 *Marshall's Appomattox*, 12.

soldier, as at least one other at his bivouac did, he may have remembered how he had written Mrs. Lee in kindred, if nobler words, when the last Federal offensive was in the making, "trusting to a merciful God, who does not always give the battle to the strong, I pray we may not be overwhelmed. I shall . . . endeavor to do my duty and fight to the last." [5]

Soon the groups among the trees were all awake. The younger men stirred up the fire and, from a single tin cup, performed their toilet and ate, in turn, a gruel of meal and water that each mixed and warmed over the burning sticks. General Lee dressed himself faultlessly, and put on his handsomest sword and his sash of deep, red silk, but he was not seen eating any breakfast. Perhaps he had none. "I have probably to be General Grant's prisoner and thought I must make my best appearance," he later told General Pendleton, when that officer came up and expressed his surprise at Lee's attire. Lee thoughtfully urged the artillerist to get some rest and in the morning to be guided by circumstances. [6]

Then, about 3 o'clock, Lee started to the front, where already the guns were announcing Gordon's preparations for an advance. Lee had not far to go, for what was left of the Army of Northern Virginia was now on and alongside a single road, the van not more than four miles, at that hour, from the rearguard. [7] He had less than 8000 armed infantry left in the ranks, [8] though other thousands, too exhausted to bear them, had stuck their guns into the ground with the bayonets and were dragging slowly about, looking for food, [9] or were hanging to the wagons, now reduced by capture and loss to 744. [10] Gordon's corps, 7500 on March 25, was now about 2000. [11] Field's division, the largest in the army and the one that had sustained the least fighting on the retreat, had present for duty only 3865 of an "aggregate present and absent" of 11,017. The number of Field's men reported "absent in C. S. lines" that day, 4497, was larger than the number present for duty. [12] Pickett had only 60 armed men, though he subse-

---

[5] See *supra*, p. 20; *R. E. Lee, Jr.*, 146.   [6] *Pendleton*, 404.

[7] The map in *Schaff*, 222, seems to be accurate though it does not show Gordon's exact position.

[8] Baldwin's report, *Lee MSS.—L; O. R.*, 46, part 1, p. 1266. Lee thought the number around 15,000. See *infra*, p. 122.

[9] J. H. Claiborne: *Seventy-five Years in Old Virginia*, 281.

[10] Corley's report, *Lee MSS.—L.*

[11] Gordon's report, *Lee MSS.—K.*   [12] Field's report, *Lee MSS.—L.*

quently reported about 740 others present at Appomattox without their muskets.[13] The artillerists were 2073 officers and men, with 61 guns and 13 caissons.[14] These had an average of 93 rounds of ammunition,[15] which the chief ordnance officer reported "were the sole dependence in the State of Virginia." [16] The cavalry were between 2100 and 2400.[17]

As Fitz Lee had availed himself of the discretion the commanding general had given him, and had delayed his advance until nearly daylight, it was 5 o'clock when the attack opened,[18] about half a mile west of the courthouse.[19] When Lee arrived in rear of Gordon's command the battle was on, the artillery was in action, and the countryside was echoing with volleys that must have sounded much more like those of infantry than like those of cavalry. There was a fog, however, that concealed the landscape, though Lee was on high ground. The course of the action could not be seen. Lee waited until perhaps 8 o'clock, and then, as the sound of battle was not receding and no word had come from Gordon, he sent Colonel Venable to study the situation and to ask what might be expected.

Venable found that this had happened: Gordon had gone forward, had passed through the village of Appomattox Courthouse, and had soon found a breastwork across the road with Federals behind it. He had not known whether they were foot or dismounted horse,[20] but after a short pause, he had attacked, with the cavalry on his right and with the skeleton divisions of Johnson, Grimes, Evans, and Walker in order to the centre and left. They had echeloned by the right flank, had advanced quickly, had driven the enemy, had captured two guns, had cleared the road, and then had wheeled by the left flank into line of battle to cover the passage of the wagons, as Lee had directed. Scarcely had this been done than the cavalry had discovered a heavy force of infantry, concealed in a woodland in rear of Gordon's right flank. The in-

---

[13] Pickett's report, Lee MSS.—K. See supra, p. 111.

[14] Pendleton's report, Lee MSS.—L; Colonel Baldwin in his report, Lee MSS.—L, stated that the guns numbered sixty-three.

[15] O. R., 46, part 1, p. 1267.

[16] Baldwin's report, Lee MSS.—L.   [17] O. R., 46, part 1, p. 1303.

[18] Longstreet, op. cit., 623, attributed the delay to mere tardiness, overlooking Lee's statement in O. R., 46, part 1, p. 1266, that he had sanctioned it.

[19] O. R., 46, part 1, p. 1303.   [20] Grimes in 27 S. H. S. P., 94.

fantry had soon moved, with Union troopers in support, against the Confederate cavalry connecting with Gordon's right and had driven the mounted Confederates back. The enemy in the wood, speedily identified as infantry, had advanced by the left flank in the direction of the courthouse. The Federals' purpose seemed to be to close on Gordon's rear and to cut him off from Longstreet, who had now come up as far as the crowded condition of the road permitted, and was on the other side of the Appomattox, a small stream at that point.[21] Simultaneously with this move on the Confederate right, the enemy's cavalry had moved toward Gordon's left and had begun to envelop that flank. General Long and Colonel Thomas Carter with their guns had been able to hold up this advance until General Evans could about-face part of his command and go to meet the approaching blue-coats—go, ominously enough, in the direction exactly opposite that of the original advance.[22]

This was the situation explained to Venable.[23] He surveyed it hastily and soon was back with Gordon's report of it: "Tell General Lee," Gordon said, "I have fought my corps to a frazzle, and I fear I can do nothing unless I am heavily supported by Longstreet's corps." [24]

Lee heard in silence this report, which was the more conclusive because Gordon was one of the most daring leaders in the Army of Northern Virginia. If Gordon could "do nothing," unless "heavily supported by Longstreet's corps," which was already holding off two corps on Lee's rear, then . . . "Then," said Lee, oblivious to the presence of his staff officers about him, "there is nothing left me to do but to go and see General Grant, and I would rather die a thousand deaths." [25]

[21] Longstreet's report, *Lee MSS.—K.*

[22] There had been no opportunity of ascertaining the different Federal units, but had Gordon known it, those on his right were of Ord's command, which had just come up (*O. R.,* 46, part 1, p. 1162). Those supporting the cavalry on his left and joining Ord's right were the V Corps (*O. R.,* 46, part 1, p. 841), with Chamberlain's brigade on the extreme right, beyond the cavalry.

[23] This description paraphrases Gordon's report, *Lee MSS.—K. Cf. Gordon,* 436- 37 and Grimes's account in 27 *S. H. S. P.,* 94.

[24] Venable, in *Long,* 421. As given in *Gordon,* 437–38, written long after the war, the message was "Tell General Lee that my command has been fought to a frazzle, and unless Longstreet can unite in my movement, or prevent those forces from coming upon my rear, I cannot long go forward."

[25] Venable in *Long,* 421.

His words meant the end! When Lee, the resourceful, the ever-striking, saw nothing ahead but surrender, who else could cherish hope longer? Restraint was broken under the weight of the tragedy. Men spoke in the grief of their hearts. "Oh, General," said some one who doubtless had proudly fed his soul on the thought that the Confederates, like Washington and his comrades-in-arms, had been writing the story of a new nation, "Oh, General, what will history say of the surrender of the army in the field?"

"Yes," answered Lee, simply, "I know they will say hard things of us: They will not understand how we were overwhelmed by numbers. But that is not the question, Colonel: The question is, is it right to surrender this army. If it is right, then I will take all the responsibility." [26]

But he did not take it as calmly as his brave answer indicated. He looked over the field, about the time the fog was lifting, and he exclaimed as though he were tempted to a desperate act: "How easily I could be rid of this, and be at rest! I have only to ride along the line and all will be over!" His voice was almost hopeless, and he was scarcely able to control his feelings, but he stopped and gripped himself and, after an inward struggle, said with a deep sigh: "But it is our duty to live. What will become of the women and children of the South if we are not here to protect them?" [27]

After a little, he sent a messenger for Longstreet, and, by a dying fire of fence rails, he waited for "Old Pete" to arrive. When Longstreet rode up, Lee saluted him, but he had a look of deep depression that Longstreet observed. Lee told the chief of the First Corps how matters stood, with Gordon blocked, no food at hand and the rearguard facing a large part of Meade's army, and he ended with the statement that he did not think it was possible to get on. What was Longstreet's view? It was quickly given in a counter-question: Would the sacrifice of the Army of Northern Virginia help the cause elsewhere? Lee did not think so. Then, answered Longstreet, your situation speaks for itself.[28]

Mahone was nearby, shivering. Lee asked for his opinion. Mahone stirred up the fire and took pains to explain that he was

---

[26] Venable in *Long*, 422. [27] *Chesnay*, 127; *Cooke*, 461.
[28] Longstreet, *op. cit.*, 625, did not attempt direct quotations in this passage.

a-tremble because he was cold, rather than scared. After a number of questions, he stated the same conclusion as Longstreet.[29]

Soon Alexander appeared. Lee called to him, walked over to a felled oak, peeled off the bark, sat down, took out his map from his breast pocket and said to the young chief of artillery of the First Corps, who had not yet learned of Gordon's plight or of Lee's decision, "Well, we have come to the junction,[30] and they seem to be here ahead of us. What have we got to do today?"

Alexander answered that the men of the First Corps were still in condition to fight and were ready to do their part if Lee saw fit to try and cut his way through the Federals.

"I have left only two divisions, Field's and Mahone's, sufficiently organized to be relied upon," Lee answered. "All the rest have been broken and routed and can do little good. Those divisions are now scarcely 4000 apiece, and that is far too little to meet the force now in our front."

Thereupon Alexander proposed, as an alternative to surrender, that the men take to the woods with their arms, under orders to report to governors of their respective states.

"What would you hope to accomplish by that?" Lee queried.

It might prevent the surrender of the other armies, Alexander argued, because if the Army of Northern Virginia laid down its arms, all the others would follow suit, whereas, if the men reported to the governors, each state would have a chance of making an honorable peace. Besides, Alexander went on, the men had a right to ask that they be spared the humiliation of asking terms of Grant, only to be told that U. S. "Unconditional Surrender" Grant would live up to the name he had earned at Fort Donelson and at Vicksburg.

Lee saw such manifest danger in this proposal to become guerillas that he began to question Alexander: "If I should take your advice, how many men do you suppose would get away?"

"Two-thirds of us. We would be like rabbits and partridges in the bushes and they could not scatter to follow us."

"I have not over 15,000 muskets left," Lee explained. "Two-thirds of them divided among the states, even if all could be collected, would be too small a force to accomplish anything. All

[29] *Longstreet*, 625.
[30] That is, the junction of the roads being followed by the two armies.

could not be collected. Their homes have been overrun, and many would go to look after their families.

"Then, General," he reasoned further, "you and I as Christian men have no right to consider only how this would affect us. We must consider its effect on the country as a whole. Already it is demoralized by the four years of war. If I took your advice, the men would be without rations and under no control of officers. They would be compelled to rob and steal in order to live. They would become mere bands of marauders, and the enemy's cavalry would pursue them and overrun many sections they may never have occasion to visit. We would bring on a state of affairs it would take the country years to recover from. And, as for myself, you young fellows might go to bushwhacking, but the only dignified course for me would be to go to General Grant and surrender myself and take the consequences of my acts."

Lee paused, and then he added, outwardly hopeful, on the strength of Grant's letter of the previous night, whatever his inward misgivings, "But I can tell you one thing for your comfort. Grant will not demand an unconditional surrender. He will give us as good terms as this army has the right to demand, and I am going to meet him in the rear at 10 A.M. and surrender the army on the condition of not fighting again until exchanged." [31]

Alexander went away a humbler man. "I had not a single word to say in reply," he wrote years afterwards. "He had answered my suggestion from a plane so far above it, that I was ashamed of having made it." [32]

It was soon after General Lee had been talking to Longstreet and to Mahone[33] that his adjutant reported. Taylor had returned to the army on the 3d, after his marriage in Richmond the preceding night, and he had been busy with a thousand duties on the retreat. The evening before he had been sent off to park the trains and he had just now rejoined the headquarters staff.

"Well, Colonel," said Lee, in his usual formula, "what are we to do?"

[31] *Alexander*, 604–5. Alexander's quotation marks are not, of course, to be taken literally, but there is no reason to believe they in any way misrepresent the substance of Lee's remarks.
[32] *Alexander*, 605.
[33] This is established by his reference to "these gentlemen around me" in the dialogue that followed. It is not certain whether the conversation with Alexander preceded or followed that with Taylor. The writer thinks the order given in the text is correct.

Taylor expressed the belief that if they rid themselves of the trains, they might still escape.

"Yes," said Lee, "perhaps we could; but I have had a conference with these gentlemen around me, and they agree that the time has come for capitulation."

"Well, sir, I can only speak for myself; to me any other fate is preferable——"

"Such is my individual way of thinking," Lee broke in.

"But," Taylor added, "of course, General, it is different with you, you have to think of these brave men and decide not only for yourself but for them."

"Yes," replied Lee, "it would be useless and therefore cruel to provoke the further effusion of blood, and I have arranged to meet General Grant with a view to surrender and wish you to accompany me." [34]

Lee seems to have unburdened himself somewhat by talking in this frank manner with his associates-in-arms, but he was still abstracted and manifestly sick at heart when he mounted Traveller at 8:30 or about that time.[35] He was going to meet Grant, and if the Federal chief was not willing to discuss a general peace, then Lee would have to ask terms for the Army of Northern Virginia alone. Those terms were not to be negotiated: if his adversary so willed, they could be imposed.

The rendezvous that Lee had set with Grant, in his note of the previous evening, was on the old state road, between the picket lines. It was in that direction he now went, accompanied by Taylor, Marshall, and Sergeant Tucker, chief courier of the Third Corps.[36] They passed along the road where Longstreet's corps had halted, for the last time in its famous career, because it had found the way ahead blocked by the wagon train that had stopped when Gordon's advance had encountered the enemy in superior force. Soon the four riders came to a stout breastwork of logs that the Confederate rearguard had erected across and on either side of the road to hold off the Federals, whose appearance was expected at any time. The men recognized Lee and cheered him as he passed through their line.

The courier then went ahead with his white flag. Marshall and

[34] *Taylor's Four Years*, 151–52.   [35] *Alexander*, 606.
[36] W. H. Palmer to W. H. Taylor, *MS.*, June 24, 1911—*Taylor MSS.*

Taylor followed, and, a little behind them, Lee. It was, as far as the records show, the first time during the war between the states that Lee personally had ever appeared for any purpose under a flag of truce. The little group of horsemen had gone a little more than half a mile[37] and had just turned a bend in the road, when they saw a line of Federal skirmishers approaching them. Marshall immediately went out in the expectation of meeting General Grant and his staff. Instead, after a little, the skirmishers halted and a single Union officer and his flag-bearer came forward. The officer proved to be Lieutenant-Colonel Charles A. Whittier, Assistant Adjutant General on the staff of Major General A. A. Humphreys, commander of the II Corps. Colonel Whittier had no verbal message from General Grant and no instructions to conduct the party to a meeting place. Instead, he merely brought a letter, which he delivered. He would wait, he said, in case Lee wished to send an answer. Marshall jogged back and gave the dispatch to Lee, who opened it and read as follows:

Headquarters Armies of the United States
April 9, 1865.

General R. E. Lee,
   Commanding C. S. Armies:

General: Your note of yesterday is received. As I have no authority to treat on the subject of peace the meeting proposed for 10 A.M. today could lead to no good. I will state, however, General, that I am equally anxious for peace with yourself, and the whole North entertain the same feeling. The terms upon which peace can be had are well understood. By the South laying down their arms they will hasten that most desirable event, save thousands of human lives, and hundreds of millions of property not yet destroyed. Sincerely hoping that all our difficulties may be settled without the loss of another life, I subscribe myself,
Very respectfully, your obedient servant,
U. S. GRANT,
Lieutenant-General U. S. Army.[38]

[37] *Humphreys*, 395.
[38] *O. R.*, 46, part 3, p. 664. At Grant's headquarters there had been a warm discussion of Lee's previous letter. Grant had not been disposed to raise a question, as he believed Lee was simply seeking to find an easy and honorable way of surrendering the army, but General John A. Rawlins had insisted on this form of reply (J. H. Wilson: *John A. Rawlins*, 317 *ff*.).

There was not to be even the poor comfort of an approach to the surrender of the army of Northern Virginia through a discussion of peace on all the fronts! The humiliation must be complete. Lee had to make a formal and unqualified offer to yield up the arms of his men. But he did not hesitate a moment. Having concluded that it was his duty to prevent further bloodshed in his army, he faced that duty precisely as he met any other, in a determination to do his best for the soldiers, without any evasion or attempt to shield himself. He bade Colonel Marshall get out pencil and paper so that he could dictate a note in which he would try to insure for the soldiers the generous terms of parole that the Federal commander had offered in his note of the 8th, though Grant had not repeated them in this new letter.

This omission gave Lee much concern. Disappointed that Grant had not come to meet him, he began to be apprehensive that his adversary had refused to appear because he now felt that he had the army virtually surrounded and could impose harsher conditions. Lee's misgivings may have been increased, when at that very moment, there came a roar of artillery from the front, as if the enemy were attacking. He started a reply, which Marshall took down in pencil on a broad sheet of paper, but while he was dictating there came a rush of horse's hoofs and a one-armed man in gray dashed from around the bend and went a hundred yards beyond them before he could pull in his mount. Lee knew the horses of most of his officers and he probably had no difficulty in identifying the superb animal that now came heavily back, half dead from the wild speed to which the officer on her back had forced her.

"What is it, what is it?" Lee cried to the soldier, whom he recognized. "Oh, why did you do it? You have killed your beautiful horse!" [39]

The officer, Colonel John Haskell, explained that Longstreet had dispatched him—telling him to kill his mare if need be—to say that Fitz Lee had just sent word he had found a road by which the army could escape. Lee either did not credit the report or else did not believe the infantry could safely follow where the cavalry might go. He went on with his letter, which was hur-

[39] *Alexander,* 606; *Humphreys,* 393.

126

riedly finished, as the sound of firing from the front grew ominously:

April 9th, 1865

General,

I received your note of this morning on the picket line whither I had come to meet you and ascertain definitely what terms were embraced in your proposal of yesterday with reference to the surrender of this army. I now request an interview in accordance with the offer contained in your letter of yesterday for that purpose.

Very respectfully

Your obt. servt

R. E. LEE

Lt. Gen U. S. Grant
Comdg U. S. Armies

Lee received the text from Marshall and signed it in a large, bold hand, probably because he did not have his glasses on.[40] He did not wait for Marshall to make a copy of this letter,[41] but he took time to direct his secretary to express to General Grant, through Colonel Whittier, his regret at not seeing him.

As Marshall carried the letter to Whittier, who was waiting a short distance away, he saw the Federal skirmishers again advancing. He knew that if they went forward they would soon strike the Confederate rearguard, and that a needless battle would occur, so he explained to Whittier the purport of the letter and told him he hoped hostilities might be suspended until the communication reached Grant. Whittier took the letter and went off, with a promise to bring an answer from his commanding general.[42] Lee waited in the road. Probably at that time, while Whittier was within the Union lines, there came another message from the front: Fitz Lee reported his previous information erroneous. There was no road by which the infantry could get away.[43] Lee then remembered he had omitted to notify Gordon that he intended to ask for a suspension of hostilities and that he had failed to authorize him or Longstreet to send out a flag of truce, pending the surrender. It must have been by the courier who brought the second message from Fitz Lee that the com-

[40] MS., office of the U. S. Adjutant General.
[41] The copy in the Lee MSS. is from memory.
[42] Marshall's Appomattox, 17.   [43] Alexander, 607.

manding general sent back word to his corps commanders to seek an armistice.[44]

Colonel Whittier soon returned and said he was directed to state that the attack had been ordered and his commanding officer had no discretion but must deliver it. A letter could not reach General Grant, he explained, in time for orders to be received from him before the hour set for the attack.[45] Marshall expressed his regret at this and asked Whittier to request his superior to read Lee's letter to General Grant, as he felt that, in the circumstances, the commanding officer might feel justified in suspending the order and in avoiding a useless sacrifice of life.[46] Whittier disappeared again with this appeal.

Lee waited with his companions. Time passed. The Federal skirmishers drew closer. A flag of truce came out from the Federal lines with a request that the Confederates withdraw, as the advance was under way and the attack was about to be delivered. It was probably through this messenger that Lee sent another note to General Grant. This, like the other, he dictated to Colonel Marshall and signed in pencil. It read:

General,   9th April 1865

I ask a suspension of hostilities pending the adjustment of the terms of the surrender of this army, in the interview requested in my former communication today.   Very respectfully,
Your obt. servt.,

Lt. Gen. U. S. Grant   R. E. LEE
Comdg. U. S. Army.   Genl.

[44] *Longstreet*, 626–27. The conclusion as to who carried the message is reached by elimination. Taylor said (*General Lee*, 289) that both he and Marshall rode back with General Lee. Colonel Haskell's horse was in such condition that he could not have transmitted so important a dispatch speedily. Sergeant Tucker of course remained with the flag of truce. The second messenger from Fitz Lee was, therefore, the only one who could have borne the order, which was certainly received before Lee returned to the front. It is proper to remark at this point that Marshall and Taylor each made an error in their report of this ride to the rear. Taylor stated (*Four Years*, 152) that Colonel Whittier told him Grant was prevented from meeting Lee on that road but requested that General Lee meet him on the other road. This error is in keeping with Miss Mason's statement (*op. cit.*, 307) that Lee never received Grant's dispatch beginning "your note of yesterday." Lee's own language, as already quoted, is proof that he did receive the letter, and not merely a message. Colonel Marshall's error was in confusing (*Appomattox*, 17) the message from Gordon, early in the morning, with that from Longstreet and Fitz Lee through Colonel Haskell.
[45] *Marshall's Appomattox*, 17.
[46] *Marshall's Appomattox*, 17; C. A. Whittier to Nelson A. Miles, Feb. 15, 1896, quoted in N. A. Miles: *Personal Recollections*, 44.

Although the Federals still came steadily forward, Lee waited under the flag of truce for an answer. Determined that not another life should be lost if he could prevent it, he remained where he was until the head of the Federal column was plainly visible not more than one hundred yards away. Then came a peremptory warning that he must withdraw immediately as the advance could not be halted. Very reluctantly, and apprehensive that this meant a waste of life in another battle and harsher terms of surrender, Lee turned his horse's head and rode back up the road and through the Confederate rearguard, where he found Longstreet awaiting the Federals' attack. The wagon trains had been parked, and part of the troops from the rear of the First Corps had been moved forward and had formed a line of battle behind Gordon's command and to the east of the north fork of the Appomattox, so that Longstreet's troops were now equally prepared for attack from in front or from behind.[47]

Lee remained near the rear of Longstreet's position until after 11 o'clock, when it seemed that the opening of the attack was only a matter of moments, though the Confederate guns were silent and the infantry were under orders not to fire. Just when it appeared certain that the action would open, Colonel Whittier appeared again under a white flag opposite Field's division. He brought a note from Meade, the text of which, unfortunately, has been lost. As far as it can be reconstructed inferentially, the note expressed agreement to an informal truce on Meade's lines for an hour and suggested that Lee might be able to communicate more quickly with Grant if he sent a duplicate of his letter through some other part of the line.

With this assurance and suggestion, Lee rode back toward the front. He stopped in a small apple orchard at the foot of the hill and a short distance in advance of the line of battle that had been drawn up facing westward. From this point Lee now sent Grant his third note of the day, written, as were the others, by Colonel Marshall in pencil and signed by the General. Here it is:

> Hd Qrs A N Va
> 9th April 1865

General, I sent a communication to you today from the picket

---

[47] Longstreet's report, Lee MSS.—K; Longstreet, 625–26; Alexander, 608.

line whither I had gone in hopes of meeting you in pursuance of the request contained in my letter of yesterday. Maj. Gen. Meade informs me that it would probably expedite matters to send a duplicate through some other part of your lines. I therefore request an interview at such time and place as you may designate, to discuss the terms of the surrender of this army in accord with your offer to have such an interview contained in your letter of yesterday.

Very respectfully
Your obt servt
R. E. Lee
Genl.[48]

Lt. Gen. U. S. Grant,
　　Comdr. U. S. Armies.

If this letter went even further than did Lee's earlier communication requesting an interview, it was because his experience of the morning had made him fearful of sterner terms and because, in the second place, the desperate situation had become so much worse that his army could easily be destroyed, no matter how dearly the men sold their lives. Unknown to the commanding general, Fitz Lee had gone off with nearly all the cavalry, determined that he would not share in the surrender.[49] Gordon's troops had withdrawn from their advanced position[50] and had fallen back across the north fork of the Appomattox[51] to rally on Longstreet. As the Federals had pressed closely in on the south and had worked around to the northwest, what was left of the Army of Northern Virginia was almost enveloped. That the enemy did not proceed to attack was due to the fact that an informal truce in front, similar to the one in the rear, had been allowed by Sheridan and Ord.[52]

Lee was very tired after the strain of the morning, and he now stretched himself out under the apple-tree on a pile of fence rails that Alexander[53] had arranged for him and had covered with blankets.

From this position Lee saw some Confederate troops crossing

[48] O. R., 46, part 3, p. 665. For a discussion of the conflicting evidence regarding this exchange of notes, see Appendix IV—3.

[49] O. R., 46, part 1, p. 1303.　　[50] Gordon's report, Lee MSS.—K.

[51] Lee's report, O. R., 46, part 1, p. 1266.

[52] Gordon, 439; Longstreet, 627.　　[53] Alexander. 609.

a nearby creek, and he inquired who they were. He was told they were his engineer regiment, commanded by his young friend and former staff officer, Colonel T. M. R. Talcott. Lee sent for Talcott and told him that he considered it his duty to go to see General Grant and to stop further sacrifice of life.[54] At Taylor's instance, as a crowd was beginning to gather, Talcott threw out a cordon around the tree.

Very soon there arrived under a flag of truce Brigadier General James W. Forsyth, Sheridan's chief of staff, who came to say that the Union cavalry commander was doubtful of his authority to recognize the informal truce and wished to communicate with General Meade. As the route through the Confederate army was the shortest, he requested permission to go that way. Lee acquiesced and sent Colonel Taylor to accompany him—the Federal Assistant Adjutant General with his own A. A. G., the strictest military etiquette.[55]

To Longstreet, who came up about this time, Lee confided his fear that Grant might be disposed to demand stiffer terms, inasmuch as he had declined those offered the previous day. Longstreet did not think so. He had known Grant intimately before the war and he told his chief that the Federal general would impose only such terms as Lee himself would in reversed circumstances. Lee did not seem altogether satisfied, and continued to converse with Longstreet in broken sentences for some time. They were still together when Forsyth and Taylor returned from their ride to Meade's lines in the rear. Forsyth doubtless brought verbal assurance and may have transmitted General Meade's definite written acceptance of a truce until 2 o'clock.[56]

And now, about 12:15 P.M., with another flag of truce, came a single staff officer, accompanied by a Confederate escort, probably Colonel John Fairfax.[57] He rode from the front, the direction whence Grant's messenger was expected to arrive. His mission was correctly guessed from the moment of his appearance.

[54] 32 S. H. S. P., 72.

[55] *Taylor's Four Years*, 152. Colonel Taylor was of opinion, on his ride to the rear, that the Federals had not advanced as far toward Longstreet's rear as some writers have claimed (W. H. Taylor to E. P. Alexander, *MS.*, Aug. 24, 1906, *Taylor MSS.*).

[56] Meade's letter, O. R., 46, part 3, p. 666, shows that Forsyth was with him when it was written. As Forsyth was returning directly and was concerned in the very subject of the correspondence he naturally would bring the letter.

[57] This is Major Giles B. Cooke's recollection.

"General," said Longstreet to Lee, as the rider approached, "unless he offers us honorable terms, come back and let us fight it out."

Lee said nothing, but in his bearing there was something—the prospect of another fight perhaps—that made Longstreet think he had heartened his chief.[58]

Lee sat up as the Federal officer dismounted. In the eyes of his companions he had never looked grander than at that moment.[59]

"General Lee," said the officer's escort, "allow me to introduce you to Colonel Babcock."

Lee raised himself to his full height and bowed. Lieutenant-Colonel Orville E. Babcock, A. D. C. to General Grant, saluted[60] and delivered a letter,[61] which General Lee read, as follows:

> Headquarters Armies of the U. S.
> April 9, 1865
>
> General R. E. Lee,
>   Commanding C. S. Army:
> Your note of this date is but this moment (11:50 A.M.) received. In consequence of my having passed from the Richmond and Lynchburg road to the Farmville and Lynchburg road I am at this writing about four miles west of Walker's church, and will push forward to the front for the purpose of meeting you. Notice sent on this road where you wish the interview to take place will meet me.
>   Very respectfully, your obedient servant
>   U. S. GRANT,
>   Lieutenant-General[62]

There was at least no suggestion in this letter of other terms than those that had been offered the day before! Babcock supplemented its considerate language with a very courteous message: he had been sent by General Grant, he said, to make any arrangement General Lee might desire for a conference, whether within the Union or within the Confederate lines.

[58] *Alexander*, 609; *Longstreet*, 628.
[59] Major Giles B. Cooke in 1 *Macrae*, 192; Frank Potts to Reverend Doctor John Potts, April, 1865, *Palmetto Leaf*, Jan. 8, 1927; reprinted as the *Death of the Confederacy*, cited hereafter as *Frank Potts; cf. Owen*, 385.
[60] *Taylor's General Lee*, 290; 1 *Macrae*, 192.
[61] So Marshall and Taylor; Horace Porter, who was not a witness, said (4 *B. and L.*, 735) Colonel Babcock handed the communication to one of Lee's staff.
[62] *O. R.*, 46, part 3, p. 665.

Grant already had offered, it will be remembered, to have the surrender arranged through officers designated for that purpose, in order that the Confederate leader might be spared humiliation, but Lee probably never thought of passing on to others this unpleasant task. He meant literally what he had said to Alexander —that he would go to General Grant and surrender himself and take the consequences of his acts.[63] Marshall thought that Lee subconsciously was impelled to this personal surrender by reason of his father's unfavorable reference in his *Memoirs* to Cornwallis's failure to appear on the day of the surrender at Yorktown.[64]

Making ready to proceed, Lee took from his breast pocket the folded map with which he had fought the campaign and gave it to Colonel Venable, who, a little later, burnt it. Lee questioned, also, whether the truce that had been granted would last long enough to cover the necessary interview. Babcock met this by writing in Grant's name a dispatch to Meade to continue the truce until further orders.[65]

On such a mission as he was now about to begin, Lee naturally would be accompanied by his adjutant general and by his military secretary, but Colonel Taylor had no heart for being present at a surrender. He begged off on the ground that he already had ridden twice through the lines that morning.[66] Lee excused him with his usual consideration for the feelings of others. In the company of Marshall, Babcock, and Tucker, the daring orderly, Lee started up the road, and beyond the thin and silent line of battle on the hillside.[67] At the stream, Traveller wanted to drink. Lee waited until his faithful mount had his fill.[68] Then he went on.

How often he had ridden that strong steed and in scenes how various! Up Malvern Hill, when the very earth seemed alive with the crawling wounded; over Thoroughfare Gap while "Stonewall's" guns were growling, and after the spinning wheels

---

63 See *supra*, p. 123.   64 *Marshall's Appomattox*, p. 8.

65 *Alexander*, 603 n. and 610. Alexander stated that this message was sent by Colonel Forsyth. As Forsyth proceeded, according to Taylor (*General Lee*, 290), back into his own lines, where he naturally would go at once to report to Sheridan, Alexander must have confused Forsyth's ride before Babcock's arrival with that of another officer subsequently.

66 *Taylor's Four Years*, 152.   67 *Marshall's Appomattox*, 18.

68 W. H. Palmer to W. H. Taylor, *MS.*, June 24, 1911—*Taylor MSS.*

of the pursuing guns at Second Manassas; across South Mountain; among the bloody ridges of the Antietam; with the mists enveloping him at Fredericksburg; confident and calm when the cheering thousands acclaimed him in the woods of Chancellorsville; out on the hill at Gettysburg; along the mournful byways of the Wilderness; down the Telegraph road toward Cold Harbor; over the James and over that same Appomattox, sullen and tawny, at Petersburg. Jackson had ridden with him, the battle light in his eyes, the laughing Stuart, the nervous Hill, the diligent Pender, the gallant Rodes—all of them dead now, and he alone, save for those silent companions, was on his last ride as commander of the Army of Northern Virginia. Thirty-nine years of devotion to military duty had come to this . . . and this, too, was duty.

As the little cavalcade passed toward the village of Appomattox, Lee had to arouse himself and arrange the details: Grant had left it to him to select the place of meeting. Would Marshall go ahead and find a suitable house? Obediently, the colonel trotted off. Lee remained with Babcock. They did not talk— how could they? [69]

After a while the orderly returned to say that Colonel Marshall had found a room for the conference. Lee went on and, under the soldier's guidance, drew rein beyond the courthouse in the yard of a house on the left-hand side of the road to Lynchburg. The residence belonged to Major Wilmer McLean, who, by the oddest chance, had owned the farm on Bull Run where, in the first battle of that name, the initial clash had occurred. Major McLean had removed from that exposed position and had purchased a property at Appomattox—only to find that the march of the armies he had sought to avoid was now about to end, as it had begun, at his door.[70]

Lee dismounted in the yard and after the orderly took Traveller, he walked toward the wide steps that led to the covered porch which ran the whole width of the house. Entering the central hall, at the top of the steps, he turned into the front room on his

[69] Marshall is the only authority for this part of the ride.
[70] *Marshall's Appomattox*, 18; *Alexander*, 610. Major McLean happened to be the first white civilian Colonel Marshall met in the village. When Marshall told him what was wanted, McLean first conducted him to a different house. Marshall found this vacant and in very bad repair and told McLean it would not serve the purpose. Thereupon McLean offered his own, well-furnished residence.

left, a typical parlor of a middle-class Virginia home.[71] Colonel
Marshall went with him. Colonel Babcock accompanied Lee,
also, with the explanation that as General Grant would soon arrive, the orderly could easily direct him to the place. Lee walked
diagonally across the room and sat down close to a small table in
the corner beyond the front window and farthest from the hall.[72]
He put his hat and gauntlets on the table, and there he waited.
Babcock and Marshall remained in the room and, no doubt,
seated themselves at his invitation.

Half an hour passed, perhaps the longest half hour in Lee's
whole life. If there was any conversation, it was in snatches and
was slow, labored, and vague.[73] About 1:30 o'clock there was a
clatter in the road, the sound of the approach of a large body of
mounted men. They drew nearer, they halted, they dismounted.
Some of them climbed the steps. Babcock went to the door and
opened it. A man of middle height, slightly stooped and heavily
bearded, came in alone. He was dressed for the field, with boots
and breeches mud-bespattered.[74] He took off his yellow thread
gloves as he stepped forward. Lee had never seen him to remember him but he knew who he was and, rising with Marshall, he
started across the room to meet General Grant. They shook hands
quietly with brief greetings. Then Grant sat down at the table
in the middle of the room, and Lee returned to his place. Marshall stood to the left and somewhat behind him. Babcock had a
few whispered words with Grant, then went from the room and
out on the porch. He soon was back, followed by a full dozen
Federal officers, Sheridan and Ord among them. These newcomers arranged themselves behind Grant and in sight of Lee
as quietly as boots and spurs and clanking swords permitted.
Grant made no reference to their coming. Lee showed no sign
of resentment at their presence.

The conversation began: "I met you once before, General Lee,"
Grant said in his normal tones,[75] "while we were serving in Mex-

71 The photograph of the house, used in the text, is perhaps the best, but one of much
excellence appears, along with other good pictures of the retreat, in the *Photographic
History of the Civil War*, 3, 315. The reader should be warned, however, that the legends
under these particular cuts are singularly inaccurate.

72 4 *B. and L.*, 735.   73 Babcock never wrote of Appomattox.

74 *Cf.* A. J. McKelway in 52 *Harpers Weekly*, 411.

75 Grant subsequently admitted that he was "much embarrassed" during the interview (J. T. Austin: *Moses Coit Tyler*, 60–61).

ico, when you came over from General Scott's headquarters to visit Garland's brigade, to which I then belonged. I have always remembered your appearance, and I think I should have recognized you anywhere."

"Yes," answered Lee quietly, "I know I met you on that occasion, and I have often thought of it and tried to recollect how you looked, but I have never been able to recall a single feature."

Mention of Mexico aroused many memories. Grant pursued them with so much interest and talked of them so readily that the conversation went easily on until the Federal was almost forgetting what he was about.[76] Lee felt the weight of every moment and brought Grant back with words that seemed to come naturally, yet must have cost him anguish that cannot be measured.

"I suppose, General Grant," he said, "that the object of our present meeting is fully understood. I asked to see you to ascertain upon what terms you would receive the surrender of my army."

Grant did not change countenance or exhibit the slightest note of exultation in his reply. "The terms I propose are those stated substantially in my letter of yesterday—that is, the officers and men surrendered to be paroled and disqualified from taking up arms again until properly exchanged, and all arms, ammunition and supplies to be delivered up as captured property."

Lee nodded an assent that meant more than his adversary realized. The phantom of a proud army being marched away to prison disappeared as Grant spoke, and the hope Lee had first expressed to Taylor that morning was confirmed. "Those," said he, "are about the conditions I expected would be proposed."

"Yes," Grant answered, "I think our correspondence indicated pretty clearly the action that would be taken at our meeting; and I hope it may lead to a general suspension of hostilities and be the means of preventing any further loss of life."

That, of course, was a theme that Lee's conception of his duty as a soldier would not permit him to discuss. It was his to obey orders and to direct the forces in the field. The civil authorities had the sole power, he held, to make peace of the sort General Grant had in mind. So he merely inclined his head again.

Grant talked on of peace and its prospects. Lee waited and

---

[76] 2 *Grant,* 490. General Ely S. Parker, on the other hand, in his *Narrative* (see Bibliography) asserted in 1893 that the conversation lagged.

then, courteously, but in a manifest desire to finish the business in hand, he said: "I presume, General Grant, we have both carefully considered the proper steps to be taken, and I would suggest that you commit to writing the terms you have proposed, so that they may be formally acted upon."

"Very well, I will write them out."

Lee sat in silence and looked straight ahead as Grant called for his manifold order-book, opened it, lit his pipe, puffed furiously, wrote steadily for awhile with his pencil, paused, reflected, wrote two sentences and then quickly completed the text.[77] Grant went over it in an undertone with one of his military secretaries, who interlined a few words. Lee did not follow any of this. He sat as he was until Grant rose, crossed to him, and put the manifold book in his hands, with the request that he read over the letter.

Lee probably was at his tensest then, for he busied himself with little mechanical acts as though to master his nerves. He placed the book on the table. He took his spectacles from his pocket. He pulled out his handkerchief. He wiped off the glasses, he crossed his legs, he set his glasses very carefully on his nose, and then he took up the order book for a slow, careful reading:

"Appomattox C. H., Va.

Apr. 9th, 1865.

"Gen. R. E. Lee,
 "Comd. C. S. A.
"Gen.

"In accordance with the substance of my letter to you of the 8th instant I propose to receive the surrender of the Army of N. Va. on the following terms, to-wit:

"Rolls of all the officers and men to be made in duplicate, one copy to be given to an officer designated by me, the other to be retained by such officer or officers as you may designate. The officers to give their individual paroles not to take up arms against the"

—At this point, Lee turned the page and read on—

[77] For the reason for Grant's pause in his writing, see *infra*, p. 142, note 89.

"Government of the United States until properly and each company or regimental commander sign a like parole for the men of their command."

Lee stopped in his reading, looked up, and said to Grant: "After the words 'until properly,' the word 'exchanged' seems to be omitted. You doubtless intended to use that word."

"Why, yes," answered Grant, "I thought I had put in the word 'exchanged.'"

"I presumed it had been omitted inadvertently, and with your permission I will mark where it should be inserted."

"Certainly."

Lee felt for a pencil, but could not find one. Colonel Horace Porter stepped forward and offered his. Lee took it, thanked him, placed the book on the table, inserted the caret, and resumed his reading:

"The arms, artillery and public property to be parked and stacked and turned over to the officer appointed by me to receive them.

"This will not embrace the side arms of the officers, nor their private horses or baggage. This done each officer and man will be allowed to return to their homes not to be disturbed by United States authority so long as they observe their paroles and the laws in force where they may reside.

Very respectfully,
U. S. GRANT, Lt Gl." [78]

There was a slight change in Lee's expression as he read the closing sentences, and his tone was not without warmth as now he looked up at Grant and said: "This will have a very happy effect on my army."

"Unless you have some suggestions to make in regard to the form in which I have stated the terms," Grant resumed, "I will have a copy of the letter made in ink and sign it."

Lee hesitated: "There is one thing I would like to mention. The cavalrymen and artillerists own their own horses in our army. Its organization in this respect differs from that of the United

---

[78] A reproduction of the original. with Lee's caret duly appearing, is in 2 *Grant*, 497.

States. I would like to understand whether these men will be permitted to retain their horses."

"You will find," answered Grant, "that the terms as written do not allow this. Only the officers are allowed to take their private property."

Lee read over the second page of the letter again. For months he had agonized over his field transportation and cavalry mounts. He knew what the army's horses would mean to the South, stripped as it had been of all draft animals, and he wanted those of his men who owned mounts to have them for the spring plough-ing. His face showed his wish. His tongue would not go beyond a regretful "No, I see the terms do not allow it; that is clear."

Grant read his opponent's wish, and, with the fine considera-tion that prevailed throughout the conversation—one of the noblest of his qualities, and one of the surest evidences of his greatness—he did not humiliate Lee by forcing him to make a direct plea for a modification of terms that were generous. "Well, the subject is quite new to me. Of course, I did not know that any private soldiers owned their animals, but I think this will be the last battle of the war—I sincerely hope so—and that the sur-render of this army will be followed soon by that of all the others, and I take it that most of the men in the ranks are small farmers, and as the country has been so raided by the two armies, it is doubtful whether they will be able to put in a crop to carry them-selves and their families through the next winter without the aid of the horses they are now riding, and I will arrange it this way: I will not change the terms as now written, but I will instruct the officers I shall appoint to receive the paroles to let all the men who claim to own a horse or mule take the animals home with them to work their little farms."

It could not have been put more understandingly or more gen-erously. Lee showed manifest relief and appreciation. "This will have the best possible effect upon the men," he said, "it will be very gratifying and will do much toward conciliating our people."

While Grant set about having his letter copied, Lee directed Marshall to draft a reply. In the wait that followed, Grant brought up and introduced the officers who had remained silent in the background. Lee shook hands with those who extended theirs and bowed to the others, but he spoke only to General Seth Williams, a warm friend during his superintendency at West Point. He talked to Williams without apparent effort, but when that officer introduced a pleasantry of the old days, Lee had no heart for it. He could not jest as his army was surrendering and his country dying. He only inclined his head ever so little at Williams's joke, and he did not smile. When Colonel Parker was presented, it seemed to Horace Porter that General Lee looked at him longer than at the others. It was Porter's belief that General Lee thought the Indian a Negro and was surprised to find an African on Grant's staff.[79]

When the introductions were over, Lee turned again to Grant. "I have a thousand or more of your men as prisoners, General Grant, a number of them officers whom we have required to march along with us for several days. I shall be glad to send them into your lines as soon as it can be arranged, for I have no provisions for them. I have, indeed, nothing for my own men. They have been living for the last few days principally upon parched corn, and are badly in need of both rations and forage. I telegraphed to Lynchburg, directing several train loads of rations to be sent on by rail from there, and when they arrive I should be glad to have the present wants of my men supplied from them."

There was a stir among the listeners at this remark, and they looked at Sheridan, for, unknown to Lee, he had the previous night captured at Appomattox Station the rations that had come down from Lynchburg. Those that had been sent up from Farmville had been found by the Federals farther down the road.[80] Grant did not add to Lee's distress by a recountal of these seizures. He merely said, "I should like to have our men within our lines as soon as possible. I will take steps at once to have your army supplied with rations, but I am sorry we have no forage for the animals. We have had to depend upon the country for our supply of forage. Of about how many men does your present force consist?"

Lee reflected for a moment: "Indeed, I am not able to say. My

[79] Parker, *op. cit.,* stated that the introductions were made when Grant's officers entered the room.
[80] St. John's report, *Lee MSS.—L; Gibbon,* 311; *O. R.,* 46, part 1, p. 1109.

losses in killed and wounded have been exceedingly heavy, and besides, there have been many stragglers and some deserters. All my reports and public papers, and, indeed, my own private letters, had to be destroyed on the march to prevent them from falling into the hands of your people.[81] Many companies are entirely without officers, and I have not seen any returns for several days; so that I have no means of ascertaining our present strength." [82]

Grant had estimated Lee's numbers at 25,000 and he asked, "Suppose I send over 25,000 rations, do you think that will be a sufficient supply?"

"I think it will be ample," Lee is said by Horace Porter to have replied. "And it will be a great relief, I assure you," he added instantly. Colonel Marshall's memory of Lee's answer was that he said 25,000 rations would be "more than enough." [83]

General Sheridan then came forward and requested that he might copy two dispatches he had sent Lee that day, in such a hurry that he had not written them out for his records. These dispatches were protests against alleged violations of the truce.[84] Lee took out the dispatches from his pocket and said he was sure that if the truce had been violated it was through a misunderstanding.

By this time, Marshall had finished his draft of Lee's acceptance of Grant's terms of surrender. It began with a sentence which would indicate that the agreement had been reached by correspondence. Lee modified this because he thought it would create a false impression. He made, perhaps, a few other changes, and then he had Marshall copy the document. The Federals had bor-

---

[81] Lee left Petersburg, according to Doctor J. H. Claiborne (*Seventy-Five Years in Old Virginia,* 279), with his headquarters wagon, his ambulance and a carriage, the last-named probably the vehicle he had used in his illness during the last week of May, 1864. In a panic, on April 7, the teamsters or clerks had destroyed all the records of army headquarters (*Jones,* 180, quoting Lee), except probably those that were in the General's military chest. The letter-books and a few other papers were preserved. With the documents sent Lee after the war, when he was planning to write a history of his campaigns, these form the corpus of the *Lee MSS.* quoted so many times in these pages. Among the papers destroyed must have been most of the reports and much of the correspondence covering the period from May 4, 1864. Apparently all headquarters correspondence prior to that date had been sent to the archives in Richmond, whence it was shipped farther south for safety. It is now in the records of the War Department, Washington.

[82] This is taken, with the rest, from Horace Porter's well-known account (4 *B. and L.,* 735 *ff.*). It does not seem reasonable to accept all else that Porter said as direct quotation and to omit this. The collateral evidence, however, is against its literal accuracy. Lee would hardly have failed to take into account his losses of prisoners and, besides, he had watched as closely as he could the decline in his numbers.

[83] 4 *B. and L.,* 742; *Marshall's Appomattox,* 18.

[84] There is no mention of these dispatches in the *Official Records* and no reference to them in the narratives of any of those who were near Lee that day.

rowed Marshall's ink in order to write their answer, and now, Marshall, having no paper with him, had to procure some from their stock.

The finished letter was now brought Lee and was read over by him:

"Lieut-Gen. U. S. Grant,
    "Commanding Armies of the United States.

"General: I have received your letter of this date containing the terms of surrender of the Army of Northern Virginia as proposed by you. As they are substantially the same as those expressed in your letter of the 8th instant, they are accepted. I will proceed to designate the proper officers to carry the stipulations into effect.

"Very respectfully, your obedient servant," [85]

Lee put his signature to this without a quiver. Marshall sealed it and went over to Parker, who already had Grant's letter waiting for him, duly signed and in an addressed envelope. They made the exchange and the surrender was complete.[86] It was then about 3:45 P.M.

The rest was casual and brief. Grant explained why he was without his sword.[87] Lee is said to have remarked that he usually wore his when with the army in the field.[88] Then Lee requested that Grant notify Meade of the surrender, so that firing might not break out and men be slain to no purpose. He requested also, that pending the actual surrender, the two armies be kept separate, so that personal encounters would be avoided. Grant acquiesced immediately and suggested that time might be saved if two of his officers rode to Meade through the Confederate lines.[89]

---

[85] O. R,. 46, part 3, p. 666.   [86] Parker, op. cit.   [87] Cf. Parker, op. cit.
[88] There was, however, some misunderstanding here as Lee rarely wore a sword.
[89] This account, in the main, follows Horace Porter, loc. cit. Parker's Narrative, written in 1893, is substantially the same but presents what would seem to be a less logical sequence of events. The myth of a tender of Lee's sword and its return by Grant was, of course, so exploded by Grant (op. cit., 2, 494) and by Marshall (29 S. H. S. P., 269–73; cf. 9 ibid., 139–40) that reference to it in the text has not been considered necessary. The sword, by the way, did not have a hilt "studded with jewels," as Porter thought. It was Lee's "Maryland sword," fully described by Fitz Lee (op. cit., 394). It is now in the Confederate Museum, Richmond. Talking after the war with John Randolph Tucker, Lee answered in this way a question as to whether Grant had returned his sword. "No, sir," he said, "he had no opportunity of doing so. By the terms the side arms of officers

Lee thereupon rose, shook hands with General Grant, bowed to the spectators and passed from the room. He went through the hall to the porch, where several Federal officers at once sprang to their feet and saluted. Putting on his hat, Lee mechanically but with manifest courtesy returned their salute and with measured tread crossed the porch. At the head of the steps, he drew on his gauntlets, and absently smote his hands together several times as he looked into space—across the valley to the hillside where his faithful little army lay. In a moment he aroused himself and, not seeing his mount, called in a voice that was hoarse and half-choked, "Orderly! Orderly!" Quickly Tucker answered from the corner of the house, where he was holding Traveller's rein as the steed grazed. Lee walked down the steps and stood in front of the animal while the man replaced the bridle. Lee himself drew the forelock from under the brow band and parted and smoothed it. Then, as Tucker stepped aside, Lee mounted slowly and with an audible sigh.[90] At that moment General Grant stepped down from the porch on his way to the gate, where his horse was waiting. Stopping suddenly, Grant took off his hat, but did not speak. The other Federals followed the courteous example of their chief. Lee raised his hat, without a word, turned his horse and rode away to an ordeal worse than a meeting with Grant—the ordeal of breaking the news to his soldiers and of telling them farewell.

By no means all the men were prepared for the surrender. The rapidity of the retreat, the failure of rations, and the dwindling of brigades to companies had spelled disaster in the minds of the intelligent. The circle of fire reflected on the clouds the night of the 8th had convinced the discerning that the army was virtually surrounded. The halt of the morning and the frequent passage of flags of truce had confirmed their fears of capitulation. Yet such

were exempt from surrender, and I did not violate those terms by tendering him my sword. All that was said about swords was that General Grant apologized to me for not wearing his sword, saying it had gone off in his baggage, and he had not been able to get it in time" (J. William Jones in *Richmond Times-Dispatch,* Jan. 20, 1907). Badeau (*Grant in Peace,* 18–23) stated on Grant's authority that the Federal commander glanced at Lee's sword during the composition of the terms of surrender, reasoned that it would be a humiliation to Lee to surrender his weapon, and thereupon wrote the sentence exempting officers' side arms.

90 George A. Forsyth: "The Closing Scene at Appomattox Court House," *Harpers Magazine,* April, 1898, pp. 708–10.

was the faith of the army in itself and in its commander that many were unwilling to believe the end had come.

Lee came toward them, down from the ridge, across the little valley, up the hillside through the pickets, and into the line. He was as erect as ever, but he was staring straight ahead of him, with none of the cheerfulness and composure that usually marked his countenance even in the most dreadful moments of his hardest battles.[91] The men started to cheer him, as they often did when he rode among them, but somehow their cheers froze in their throats at the sight of him.[92] They hesitated a moment as he rode fixedly on, and then without a word they broke ranks and rushed toward him.

"General," they began to cry, "are we surrendered?"

The question was like a blow in the face. He tried to go on, but they crowded about him, bareheaded. He removed his hat in acknowledgment and attempted once more to proceed. The road was too full of frenzied, famished faces. He had to halt and answer his loyal old soldiers. "Men," he said, "we have fought the war together, and I have done the best I could for you. You will all be paroled and go to your homes until exchanged."[93] Tears came into his eyes as he spoke. He attempted to say more but even his amazing self-mastery failed him. Moving his lips in a choking "good-bye," he again essayed to ride on to the orchard from which he had come.

"General, we'll fight 'em yet," they answered.

"General, say the word and we'll go in and fight 'em yet."[94]

Everywhere as the news spread, each soldier reacted to it in his own fashion. Some wept, openly and without abashment. Others were dazed, as though they did not understand how the Army of Northern Virginia, Lee's army, could surrender. To Field's divi-

---

[91] Major A. R. H. Ranson in 122 *Harper's Monthly*, 335.   [92] E. A. Moore, 290.

[93] 38 *S. H. S. P.*, 12. Of the many versions of his words, the writer has taken that of Captain Frederick M. Colston. That officer said he climbed to a wagon hub and heard Lee distinctly, though he stated that Lee added some other words he forgot. Lawley's contemporary version (*Fortnightly Review*, September, 1865, p. 9) is almost identical. A fuller version, Peacock's, which appears in 19 *S. H. S. P.*, 269, may include some of Lee's remarks later in the day: "Yes, my men, you are surrendered. The odds against us were too great. I would not lead you to fruitless slaughter. Private property will be respected; officers will retain their side arms and horses. All will be paroled and transported to your homes and may you find your families and loved ones well. Good-bye, my men, good-bye."

[94] Major Giles B. Cooke, quoted in 1 *Macrae*, 193

sion, which had suffered little on the retreat, it seemed incomprehensible.[95] To others, it was as the very end of the world. "Blow, Gabriel, blow!" cried one man, and threw down his musket as General Grimes told him what had happened. "My God, let him blow, I am ready to die!" [96]

Some blasphemed and some babbled, but all who could do so crowded to say farewell to Lee. Catching hold of his hands, they looked up at him and cried the more. They touched his uniform or his bridle rein, if they could not grasp his hand, and if they could not reach him, they smoothed Traveller's flank or patted his neck. And in a confused roar, half-sob, half-acclamation, they voiced their love for him, their faith in him, their good-bye to him as their commander.[97]

Passing on slowly, agonizingly, he stopped at the apple orchard, where Talcott's engineers were still doing duty, and passed the cordon they had formed around the place. Lee saw Talcott among his men and had sufficient composure to tell the colonel what the terms were. Grant would soon send rations, he said. Talcott must keep his men together and must make them as comfortable as possible until they were paroled.[98]

Then Lee retired a short distance into the orchard away from the road, and there he began to feel the reaction. He could not sit down or rest but kept pacing up and down under a tree. To one at least of those who watched him, Blackford of the engineers, he seemed in "one of his savage moods." Blackford added, "when these moods were on him it was safer to keep out of his way." The staff officers did not disturb him. He walked and turned and walked again and turned, battling with his own emotions. Presently, through the abandoned lines, there began to arrive Federal officers, generally in groups of four or five. Some knew him and wished to greet him. Others were drawn by curiosity to gaze at the old lion, captured at last. They went to Taylor or to Venable, who had field headquarters under another tree, and asked to be presented to the General. Taylor brought them

[95] *Longstreet*, 629.   [96] 27 *S. H. S. P.*, 96; *Grimes*, 122.
[97] Gordon must have come up about this time. On the authority of Gordon, after the war, Jones quoted Lee as saying at this time, "I could wish that I were numbered among the fallen in the last battle!" But this was too rhetorical for Lee (*Jones*, 346; *Cf. Gordon*, 282).
[98] 32 *S. H. S. P.*, 72.

over. At their approach, Lee halted, drew himself up and stood at attention. He "glared" at them, according to Blackford, "with a look few men but he could assume." [99] They approached and took off their hats. He merely touched the rim of his hat in return and sometimes did not seem to Major Blackford to do even that. The interviews all were brief and manifestly not to his liking. In the hour of the supreme tragedy of his career as a soldier, Lee did not wish to see strangers or to be stared at, it mattered not with what deference.

He probably had halted at the apple orchard to be accessible for the necessary business of the surrender, and he waited until the Federal wagons had begun to arrive with the rations.[100] It may have been while he was there that he received from Grant's headquarters a copy of the order appointing the three Federal commissioners to arrange the details of the surrender.[101] His own representatives, Longstreet, Gordon, and Pendleton, were named the same day, it is not known where or at what hour.[102]

The sun was now near its setting. The immediate duties were done. Lee mounted Traveller and started toward his headquarters, which were under a large white oak, about a mile to the rear. As he went, the scenes of his return from the interview with General Grant were repeated in heightened pathos. For now the whole army knew that the surrender had occurred, and most of the intelligent men had been given time to reflect what that act meant to him who was, in their eyes, both cause and country. "There was," Blackford wrote, "a general rush from each side of the road to greet him as he passed, and two solid walls of men were formed along the whole distance. Their officers followed, and behind the lines of men were groups of them, mounted and dismounted, awaiting his coming. . . . As soon as he entered this avenue of these old soldiers, the flower of the army, the men who had stood to their duty through thick and thin in so many battles, wild, heartfelt cheers arose which so touched General Lee that

[99] *Memoirs of Life in and out of the Army in Virginia.* . . . Compiled by Susan Leigh Blackford (cited hereafter as *Blackford*), vol. 2, Appendix, p. iv.

[100] *Blackford, loc. cit.*

[101] The copy in *Lee MSS.—N* is in Colonel Parker's handwriting, *O. R.,* 46, part 3, p. 666.

[102] *O. R.,* 46, part 3, pp. 666–67. It is not plain whether he sent for Longstreet from the apple orchard or later in the evening from his headquarters to get his advice as to distribution of the money in the custody of the chief of ordnance (*Longstreet,* 628).

tears filled his eyes and trickled down his cheeks as he rode his splendid charger, hat in hand, bowing his acknowledgments. This exhibition of feeling on his part found quick response from the men whose cheers changed to choking sobs as, with streaming eyes and many evidences of affection, they waved their hats as he passed. Each group began in the same way, with cheers, and ended in the same way, with sobs, all along the route to his quarters. Grim, bearded men threw themselves on the ground, covered their faces with their hands and wept like children. Officers of all ranks made no attempt to conceal their feelings, but sat on their horses and cried aloud. . . . Traveller . . . took as much pleasure in applause as a human being, and always acknowledged the cheers of the troops by tosses of his head and the men frequently cheered him for it, to which he would answer back as often as they did. On this, Traveller's last appearance before them, his head was tossing a return to the salutes all along the line. . . . One man . . . extended his arms, and with an emphatic gesture said, 'I love you just as well as ever, General Lee!' " [103]

They thronged about him when he reached his headquarters, and when he dismounted all who were in sight of his camp hastened up.

"Let me get in," they began to cry. "Let me bid him farewell."

Lee stood with Long and Stevens and a few other old personal friends, and he sought to keep his composure, but as man after man crowded around him, each with warm words, his eyes filled anew with tears. In broken phrases he told his veterans to go home, to plant a crop and to obey the law, and again and again he tried to say farewell. But they would not have it so. One handsome private, a gentleman in bearing, for all his dirt and rags, shook hands and said, "General, I have had the honor of serving in this army since you took command. If I thought I were to blame for what has occurred today, I could not look you in the face, but I always try to do my duty. I hope to have the honor of serving under you again. Good-bye, General; God bless you."

On the instant another gripped his fingers. "Farewell, General

---

[103] *Blackford*, II, Appendix, p. vi. Most of those who have written of this historic scene apparently have overlooked the fact that there were two rides through the army. Consequently the remarks Lee made when stopped on his ride through Gordon's command, on his way back to the apple orchard, are usually quoted as though spoken just before he went to his tent.

Lee," he said, "I wish for your sake and mine that every damned Yankee on earth was sunk ten miles in hell!"

This forthright profession relieved the strain. In the stir that followed, Lee lifted his hat once more in salute and went into his tent . . . to be alone.[104]

[104] *Blackford*, II, Appendix, p. vi; *Frank Potts*, 14–15.

CHAPTER X

THE FINAL BIVOUACS

ON the morning of April 10, 1865, rain was falling steadily—a rain that prepared Virginia fields for new planting, even though in the dark woods around Appomattox, along the red clay roads, it seemed to deepen the gloom that enshrouded the dead army.

Lee went about the duties of April 10 calmly but with an occasional evidence of abstraction. He felt that he should prepare a report of the campaign, and he sent a circular to the corps chiefs directing them to prepare brief accounts of their operations from March 29 "to the present time." Longstreet and Gordon were to procure and to forward reports from the division commanders, including those who had been assigned to their corps after the retreat had begun. The only reference in this circular to the surrender was the statement of Taylor, who wrote it, that Lee wished the documents "before the army is dispersed, that he may have some data on which to base his own report."[1] Lee must have sent a somewhat similar circular to the principal officers of the general staff whom he directed to report the extent and condition of the supplies and equipment in their charge on April 8.[2]

About 10 o'clock Lee called for the draft of a farewell address to the army which he had instructed Marshall to write after the crowd had scattered and night had fallen on the 9th, when he had sat for a short time with some of his staff officers around a camp fire outside his tent. The draft was not forthcoming. Marshall had been so occupied amid all the coming and going around the camp that he had found no time for the task. Lee told him to go into his ambulance, which had been drawn up near his

[1] Copy of the circular in *Pickett and His Men*, 393.
[2] This is safely inferred from the reference of nearly all the officers of the general staff to the status of affairs at that time.

149

headquarters tent, and to stay there until he finished the document. To make it certain that Marshall would not be interrupted, and to keep intruders away, Lee posted an orderly by the door of the ambulance.[3]

Soon there came word that General Grant had ridden over from the courthouse to call on him and that he had been stopped and told he must wait until General Lee's instructions could be given the pickets who had been put out the previous day to prevent personal collisions among the men of the two armies. Chagrined at this display of a lack of proper consideration for a distinguished visitor, Lee immediately mounted Traveller. Wearing the uniform he had used the previous day, and wrapped in a blue military overcoat, he proceeded at a gallop to meet Grant. He found him on a little knoll to the right of the road to Lynchburg, just south of the north fork of the Appomattox and between the lines of the two armies. As he approached, Lee lifted his hat, as did Grant. The officers who had attended the Federal commander were equally polite, and, after a moment, withdrew in a semicircle behind Grant, out of earshot. Grant began by telling Lee that his interest was in peace and in the surrender of the other Confederate armies. Lee replied that the South was a large country and that the Federals might be compelled to march over it three or four times before the war was entirely ended, but the Federals could do this, he said, because the South no longer could resist. For his own part, he hoped there would be no further sacrifice of life, but he could not foresee the result. Thereupon Grant said there was no man in the South whose influence with the soldiers and with the people was as great as Lee's, and that if Lee would advise the surrender of all the armies he believed they would lay down their arms. Lee knew far better than Grant possibly could the weakness of the Confederate forces still in the field. Weeks before, he had told the Secretary of War that he did not believe the troops east of the Mississippi, outside the Army of Northern Virginia, could offer effective resistance.[4] But Grant's proposal had to do with a question the President would have to decide, a question that Lee felt he could not urge on his own initiative. He promptly said that he could not advise the remaining Confederate

---

[3] Marshall in 4 B. and L., 747.   [4] Cf. O. R., 46, part 2, p. 1295.

armies without first consulting the President. Grant understood Lee's viewpoint and did not attempt to persuade him.[5]

Shifting the subject, Lee talked of the paroling of the army and asked that the instructions of the officers who were arranging the details of the surrender should be made so explicit that no misunderstanding could arise. Grant called up Gibbon, one of the commissioners, and gave assurance that this would be done.[6] Then, as Lee was preparing to say farewell and to return to his lines, General Sheridan, General Rufus Ingalls, and General Seth Williams, who were anxious to have a closer look at the Army of Northern Virginia, asked General Lee if they might go over and call on some of their old army friends. General Lee immediately consented, and, after a little, lifted his hat once more to General Grant and rode off. The conversation had lasted more than half an hour and, according to Grant, was "very pleasant." [7]

Lee did not see his adversary again until May 1, 1869, when he made a visit to Baltimore and stopped in Washington on his way home to call on Grant at the White House, where he had been advised the President would be glad to receive him.[8] It is a curious fact that the two whose names are more closely linked than those of any two opponents in American history, Marshall and Jefferson

---

[5] 2 *Grant,* 497. Horace Porter's account (4 *B. and L.,* 745) was based on his recollection of what Grant told his staff that evening after the interview. There is nothing in Porter's narrative that could not have been said, but internally it seems a bit embroidered with time, and it has the emphasis in the wrong place. As Porter's is second-hand, Grant's version must, of course, be preferred to it. Porter's statement is as follows: "Grant began by expressing a hope that the war would soon be over, and Lee replied by stating that he had for some time been anxious to stop the effusion of blood, and he trusted that everything would be done to restore harmony and conciliate the people of the South. He said the emancipation of the Negroes would be no hindrance to the restoring of relations between the two sections of the country, as it probably would not be the desire of the majority of the Southern people to restore slavery then, even if the question were left open to them. He could not tell what the other armies would do or what course Mr. Davis would take, but he believed it would be best for their other armies to follow his example, as nothing could be gained by further resistance in the field. Finding that he entertained these sentiments, General Grant told him that no one's influence in the South was so great as his, and suggested to him that he should advise the surrender of the remaining armies and thus exert his influence in favor of immediate peace. Lee said he could not take such a course without consulting President Davis first. Grant then proposed to Lee that he should do so, and urge the hastening of a result which was admitted to be inevitable. Lee, however, was averse to stepping beyond his duties as a soldier, and said the authorities would doubtless soon arrive at the same conclusion without his interference." Other second- or third-hand accounts are Gibbon's, *op. cit.,* 326–27, and Dana's in *O. R.,* 46, part 3, pp. 716–17. The last-named seems to be based chiefly on staff gossip.

[6] Gibbon, 326–27, 341–42, confusing much that was said on the 9th with the conversation on the 10th.

[7] 2 *Grant,* 497.   [8] *R. E. Lee, Jr.,* 349.

not excepted, should have seen each other only four times, or perhaps five times, during their lives.

General Lee was returning to his camp and was close to it when
he met a cavalcade in blue and was greeted with a cheery "good
morning, General" from a bearded man, who removed his cap as
he spoke. For the moment Lee did not recognize the speaker,
but the latter recalled himself as none other than George Gordon Meade, commanding the Army of the Potomac, and an old
friend of kindly days.

"But what are you doing with all that gray in your beard?"
Lee asked.

"You have to answer for most of it!" Meade magnanimously
replied.[9]

It was explained quickly that Meade had ridden over on a visit
of courtesy and, not finding Lee at headquarters, was just starting back when he met him. Meade introduced his two aides,
Colonel Theodore Lyman and Captain George Meade, his son.
Lee shook their hands "with all the air of the oldest blood in the
world," according to Lyman. "In manner," Lyman observed, Lee
was "exceedingly grave and dignified—this, I believe, he always
was; but there was evidently added an extreme depression, which
gave him an air of a man who kept up his pride to the last, but
who was entirely overwhelmed. From his speech I judge he was
inclined to wander in his thoughts."[10]

As Lee and Meade rode toward the Confederate headquarters,
the graycoats began to cheer and to yell, as they had done whenever Lee had appeared that day.[11] Unwilling to appear in a false
light, Meade said to his color bearer, who had the flag rolled up,
"Unfurl that flag." Quickly the answer came from a cadaverous
soldier by the roadside: "Damn your old rag! We are cheering
General Lee."[12]

[9] There are numerous versions of this episode. Long, 426, quoted that of Colonel de
Chenal. In 2 Meade, 270, there is a brief reference to the meeting. The account the
writer has preferred is that of Colonel Theodore Lyman, written April 23, 1865, when
the events were still fresh in his mind. His version appears in his letters, which are of
extraordinary interest, published under the title Meade's Headquarters, 1863–1865, edited
by George R. Agassiz. The assumption that Lee was returning from the interview with
Grant when he met Meade is fully borne out by Grant's and Lyman's statements of the
roads they followed. A very good account of Meade's ride through the lines is given by
General Field in 14 S. H. S. P., 562. Field escorted Meade to Lee's tent.
[10] Lyman, op. cit., 360–61.
[11] W. A. McClendon: Recollections of War Times, 234.   [12] Mixson, 120.

Lee invited Meade into his tent and chatted with him for some time. The talk was of the recent fighting and of the siege of Petersburg. As one professional soldier to another, Meade asked how many men Lee had in front of him on the morning of April 2. Lee replied that by the last returns he had 33,000 muskets.

"You mean that you had 33,000 men in the lines immediately around Petersburg?" Meade said.

Lee answered that the 33,000 were all he had on the whole line from the Chickahominy to Dinwiddie Courthouse.

Meade expressed his surprise and said candidly that he had on the south side of the James over 50,000 men.

Lee found consolation in knowing that he actually had fought against as heavy odds as he had supposed. After his visitor had left, Lee told Taylor and Long what Meade had said, and he inquired particularly of Taylor if his memory was correct and that he had only 33,000 infantry at the date of the last return. Taylor confirmed the figures.[13]

Later in the day Lee had another visitor in the person of the ablest of the Federal artillerists, General Henry J. Hunt. He found Lee "weary and care-worn, but in this supreme hour the same self-possessed, dignified gentleman that I had always known him." Lee conversed pleasantly with Hunt for half an hour, until General Wise and, after him, General Wilcox, came in. The last-named offered to accompany Hunt to the station of Long, who had been a lieutenant in Hunt's battery before the war. Lee had already informed Hunt where he might find his former subordinate. "Long will be very glad to see you," he said, and he went on to tell what had befallen that officer.[14]

After dining frugally with his staff,[15] Lee had still other visitors and not a few routine duties. He received the formal terms of surrender as accepted by his commissioners and forwarded by Colonel Latrobe,[16] and from Grant's headquarters he got a copy of the Federal order under the terms of which paroled Confederates were to be allowed to pass through the Federal lines and

---

[13] *Taylor's Four Years,* 154; *cf.* a different and later account in *Long,* 426. For the version of F. M. Colston, to whom Taylor repeated what Lee told him, see 38 *S. H. S. P.,* 13.

[14] Hunt, quoted in *Long,* 426-27.

[15] Major Giles B. Cooke in *Richmond News Leader,* Jan. 19, 1923, p. 14.

[16] *Lee MSS.—N;* text in *O. R.,* 46, part 3, pp. 685–86.

to travel free on government transports and military railroads in order to reach their homes.[17]

When Marshall had finished his pencilled draft of the farewell order, Lee went over it, struck out a paragraph that seemed to him calculated to keep alive ill-feeling, and changed one or two words. Marshall then wrote a revised draft, which he had one of the clerks at headquarters copy in ink. General Lee signed this and additional copies made by various hands for the corps commanders and for the chiefs of the bureaus of the general staff. Other individuals made copies of their own which they brought to General Lee to sign as souvenirs.[18] This accounts for the multiplicity of "originals," most of which are owned by persons who believe them the authentic first draft. As a matter of fact, there is no "original." Marshall probably destroyed or misplaced the pencilled text which General Lee revised. The language of the eliminated paragraph is not even known. An amended draft, in Marshall's autograph, is in the hands of his descendants, but cannot be affirmed positively to be the paper given by Marshall to the copyist.[19] In hasty transcription and frequent reprinting the language of the order has assumed several versions. That which follows is from General Lee's letter book, into which it was copied, after Appomattox, by Custis Lee.

Hd. qrs. Army of N. Va.
April 10, 1865

General Orders }
No. 9

After four years of arduous service marked by unsurpassed courage and fortitude, the Army of Northern Virginia has been compelled to yield to overwhelming numbers and resources.

I need not tell the brave survivors of so many hard fought battles, who have remained steadfast to the last, that I have consented to this result from no distrust of them; but feeling that valor and devotion could accomplish nothing that could compensate for the loss that must have attended the continuance of

[17] *Lee MSS.—N.* Lee discussed with Gibbon and with Longstreet the possible embarrassment of his soldiers because their paroles were not signed by Federal officers (*Gibbon,* 336).

[18] General Perry, for instance, 20 *S. H. S. P.,* 61; *cf.* Ranson in 122 *Harper's Monthly Magazine,* 336.

[19] Reproduced in *Marshall,* 276–77.

the contest, I determined to avoid the useless sacrifice of those whose past services have endeared them to their countrymen.

By the terms of the agreement, officers and men can return to their homes and remain until exchanged. You will take with you the satisfaction that proceeds from the consciousness of duty faithfully performed; and I earnestly pray that a Merciful God will extend to you His blessing and protection.

With an unceasing admiration of your constancy and devotion to your Country, and a grateful remembrance of your kind and generous consideration for myself, I bid you all an affectionate farewell.

(Sgd) R. E. LEE
Genl.[20]

The next day, April 11, Lee began to receive the reports of his subordinates. Some of them were hurried and perfunctory, but others were well-considered. Those of the field officers concerned operations only. The general staff wrote in some instances of the problems of the retreat, and confirmed Lee's judgment as to the necessity of surrendering when he did. General W. H. Stevens, the chief engineer, was most explicit. "From a careful study of our position and resources," he wrote, "the route pursued was the only one open to a chance of success, and I give it as my opinion that to have prolonged the effort to escape would have resulted in consequences frightful to contemplate and perhaps criminal to have ordered." The trains and army were surrounded: "To have attempted to cut a passage would have resulted in a frightful loss of life, giving no results at all commensurate with such a loss." [21] The report of the chief of ordnance, Lieutenant Colonel B. G. Baldwin, showed to what a pitiful number of armed men the divisions had been reduced, and how scanty was the ammunition available in Virginia for them and for the artillery.[22] Mahone affirmed that his men, to the very end, were well in hand and ready to give battle, but he revealed that from

---

[20] Marshall's own account, written in 1887, appears in 4 *B. and L.,* 747. The view here expressed as to the "originals" is based on lengthy investigations by the late W. W. Scott and by Virginius Dabney of Richmond. Mr. Dabney's conclusions were summarized in *The Richmond News Leader* of Sept. 27, 1924, p. 26, and Nov. 12, 1924, p. 20. Mr. Dabney kindly placed at the writer's disposal the large correspondence he collected in preparing his articles.

[21] *Lee MSS.—L.*   [22] See *supra,* p. 119.

his command, one of the two divisions on which Lee had felt he could count as late as the morning of the 9th, 39 officers and 1231 enlisted men were missing.[23] Speaking of the army as a whole, straggling, said Stevens, "from the start was frightful" [24]—a hackneyed but accurately descriptive adjective repeated several times in his report.

With this material and doubtless with Marshall's assistance in the usual way, Lee set about preparing his own report. When completed, it was a document of some 1200 words and was designed to be preliminary to a longer report that Lee then purposed to write. The only personal reference was in the opening sentence: "It is with pain that I announce to your Excellency the surrender of the Army of Northern Virginia." With no further preliminaries, he sketched operations from the arrival at Amelia Courthouse to the surrender. The outcome was attributed primarily to failure to find at Amelia the provisions he expected would be there. The army, he explained, had been forced to halt a day in order to seek food in the surrounding country. "This delay," he said, "was fatal, and could not be retrieved." The nearest approach to blame for any individual was the statement, in reference to Sayler's Creek, that "General Anderson, commanding Pickett's and B. R. Johnson's divisions, became disconnected with Mahone's division, forming the rear of Longstreet."

Proceeding then to the events that ended in the capitulation, he said of his action in accepting Grant's terms: "I deemed this course the best under all the circumstances by which we were surrounded. On the morning of the 9th, according to the reports of the ordnance officers, there were 7892 organized infantry with arms, with an average of 75 rounds of ammunition per man. The artillery, though reduced to sixty-three pieces, with ninety-three rounds of ammunition, was sufficient. These comprised all the supplies of ordnance that could be relied on in the State of Virginia. I have no accurate report of the cavalry, but believe it did not exceed 2100 effective men. The enemy was more than five times our numbers. If we could have forced our way one day longer, it would have been at a great sacrifice of life, and at its end I did not see how a surrender could have been avoided. We

<hr />

[23] *Lee MSS.—L.* [24] *Lee MSS.—L.*

had no subsistence for man or horse, and it could not be gathered in the country. The supplies ordered to Pamplin's Station from Lynchburg could not reach us, and the men, deprived of food and sleep for many days, were worn out and exhausted." That was the closing sentence.[25]

This report is dated April 12, "near Appomattox Courthouse," and it doubtless was finished and signed that morning. By the time it was completed Lee had said farewell to many of his officers, had given his autograph to some of them,[26] had written his pledge not to take up arms against the United States "until properly exchanged," [27] and had signed Taylor's individual parole, the only one that required his personal attention. Taylor as A. A. G. had attested those of the other staff officers.[28]

As the paroling had begun on April 10, Lee might have started home that day. He never explained why he remained until the 12th, but doubtless he stayed because he did not wish to leave his men to bear without him the humiliation of stacking their arms and giving over their cherished old battleflags. He did not witness that sad ceremony on the morning of April 12, for it occurred out of sight of his camp and nearer Appomattox,[29] but he did not break camp till the surrender was over and his tearful soldiers had turned away from the field of their last parade.

[25] *O. R.,* 46, part 1, p. 1265.   [26] For instance, 38 *S. H. S. P.,* 14.
[27] Original in Confederate Museum, Richmond; text in *O. R.,* 46, part 1, p. 667. None of those around Lee mention the time of the signing of this parole or the circumstances attending it. As there are among the Lee papers several blank Federal paroles of the same form as that signed by himself and his personal staff, it seems likely that the printed sheets were sent him and received the signatures at his headquarters.
[28] 38 *S. H. S. P.,* 13; *Taylor's General Lee,* 296.
[29] The Confederates left their wagons parked and their artillery in the road, and marched to an open field near the courthouse, under the command of General Gordon. As they approached the ground where they were to stack arms and pile up their ragged battleflags, General Joshua L. Chamberlain, who commanded the Maine brigade that faced the field, gave orders for his men to present arms. Gordon immediately saluted and passed a like order down the ranks of the heartbroken survivors of the Army of Northern Virginia. The veterans wept as they placed on the ground the flags they had so often borne victoriously forward. Some of the soldiers, rather than surrender their banners, tore them into bits and divided them among themselves. In a few instances, color bearers concealed the flags under their shirts and bore them home as relics. In one North Carolina regiment, as General Bryan Grimes shook hands with each man in turn, one soldier said to him, "Good-bye, General; God bless you; we will go home, make three more crops and then try them again" (Grimes, quoted in 5 *N. C. Regts.,* 256). Most of the men realized, however, that the defeat of the army meant the end of all hope of a separate Southern government and left Appomattox, grateful for the consideration shown them and determined to labor peaceably for a restored Union. Both General Chamberlain (*Passing of the Armies,* 260 *ff.*) and General Gordon (*op. cit.,* 448 *ff.*) left moving accounts of the surrender (*cf. Jones,* 308).

There was no theatrical review, no speech-making, no pledge to keep the cause alive in loyal hearts. All that was behind Lee. Quietly and unceremoniously he left his last headquarters on the 12th and started home.[30] With him rode Taylor, Marshall, and Cooke, the last-named sick and in an ambulance lent by the Federals. They took with them their headquarters wagon and General Lee's old ambulance, which Britt drove.[31] Colonel Venable started with them but parted company very soon, as his route to reach his family in Prince Edward County was different from theirs. Some Federal officer, probably Gibbon, who was the senior Union general remaining at Appomattox, sent over a handsomely mounted escort of twenty-five cavalrymen to attend Lee to Richmond if he desired it. When Lee declined, the troopers still insisted on doing him the honor of accompanying him some distance from the camp.

The worst of the strain was over now. Rest had begun to restore the nerves of the men, who had scarcely relaxed from the time they left Petersburg until they surrendered.[32] They already had exhausted the fighting and its outcome as a theme of conversation, and as they went homeward through the budding trees, away from the sounds of rumbling wagon trains and marching columns, they talked freely and of many things,[33] but little of the

[30] *Taylor's General Lee*, 296–97; *Statement of Major Giles B. Cooke to the writer.* The movements of General Lee immediately after the surrender are variously given by the biographers. Taylor in his *Four Years*, 154, stated that his chief arrived in Richmond April 12. McCabe (*op. cit.*, 636) and Miss Mason (*op. cit.*, 316) gave the same date, as, inferentially, did Cooke (*op. cit.*, 466). All of them apparently were misled by contemporary newspaper accounts, which confused the return of General Lee with that of Custis. Obviously, the General could not have returned so soon to Richmond, as the journey by road was nearly 100 miles and he was certainly at Appomattox on the 10th. Colonel Taylor evidently saw his error, for in his later *General Lee*, 296, he wrote that Lee left Appomattox on the 12th. Lawley (*Fortnightly Review*, September, 1865, p. 10) also gave the 12th as the date of departure. Both Captain R. E. Lee (*op. cit.*, 155) and the Richmond correspondent of *The New York Herald* (cited *infra*, p. 163, n. 47) put the time of the General's arrival in Richmond as the 15th. Inasmuch as he is known to have spent three nights on the road, this would make the 12th the date of breaking camp at Appomattox. The only contemporary witness who gives a positively contrary date is Major Giles B. Cooke. In his *Just Before and After Lee Surrendered*, 7, he quoted his diary, which fixed the time for the start as the 11th. It is manifest, however, from the internal evidence of this entry that it was made at some time subsequent to the 13th, perhaps several days thereafter. The major must have been wrong in his chronology by one day. Furthermore, the date of Lee's report to President Davis is almost conclusive evidence. This is headed "Near Appomattox Court-House, Va., April 12, 1865."

[31] Giles B. Cooke: *Just Before and After Lee Surrendered to Grant*, 7.

[32] Lyman, *op. cit.*, p. 361, quoted Marshall as saying he got no sleep whatever for seventy-two hours.

[33] *Taylor's General Lee*, 297; W. H. Taylor to Charles M. Graves, MS., Nov., n.d., 1904—*Taylor MSS.*

war. When Lee did speak of the struggle and its outcome, his thought, as always, was of those around him rather than of himself. He urged the young officers to go home, to take whatever work they could find, and to accept the conditions necessary for their participation in the government.[34]

The road they were following led northeastward from Appomattox to Buckingham Courthouse and thence eastward to Cumberland Courthouse, where it struck the old stage road from Lynchburg to Richmond by way of Farmville. As evening drew on, General Lee passed through Buckingham Courthouse, where he was identified and greeted. Two miles beyond the village he came, according to Lawley, to the bivouac of Longstreet,[35] and there he decided to make his camp, in woods owned by Mrs. Martha Shepherd. Although his tent was speedily and quietly pitched, the coming of even so small a cavalcade attracted attention. Mrs. Shepherd learned who her visitor was and sent him an invitation to spend the evening at her home. For fear of inconveniencing her, he declined, precisely as he had scores of times during the war. If Lawley was correct in saying that Longstreet was camped in the same woods, the two spent their last evening together and parted the next day to meet no more, though they continued to correspond irregularly. Longstreet was bitter. Acknowledging that for months he had felt the Southern cause hopeless, he affirmed that the next time he fought he would be sure it was necessary.[36] If this remark came to Lee's ears he overlooked it. "My interest and affection for you will never cease," Lee wrote Longstreet the next January, "and my prayers are always offered for your prosperity." [37]

In some way the news of Lee's coming spread ahead of him. Women hastened to cook provisions and brought them out to the road, where they waited for him. "These good people are kind, too kind," he is reported to have said. "Their hearts are as full as when we began our first campaigns in 1861 They do too much

[34] *Taylor's General Lee,* 297.

[35] Lawley, *loc. cit.,* 10. Major Cooke, who accompanied General Lee on this part of the journey, has no recollection of overtaking Longstreet. He is satisfied that if Longstreet was camped in the same woods he was not close to Lee.

[36] *Philadelphia Weekly Times,* July 27, 1879, p. 8. Longstreet denied having said, as some other officer alleged, that if there were another war he would not fight under Lee.

[37] *Longstreet,* 654-5.

—more than they are able to do—for us." His only concern over food was about some oats he had procured for Traveller,[38] and was afraid some one else might take. As the day wore on, Traveller cast a shoe and became lame. Lee soon stopped at Flanagan's Mill, Cumberland County, where he spent the night under the friendly roof of Madison Flanagan. The mount was shod that night and was ready for the road the next morning.[39]

On the 14th Major Cooke, who was still sick, bade his chief farewell and turned off the road.[40] Accompanied now only by Taylor and Marshall and the drivers, Lee continued on his way. Ere long he overtook one of his youthful veterans, limping barefooted along the same road. The boy had procured a mule at Appomattox, along with his parole, but had lost the animal when it had bolted from him. "My boy," said Lee, "you are too badly off for the long journey ahead of you; you have no shoes. I am going to spend the night at the home of my brother, Charles Carter Lee, who lives a few miles ahead at Fine Creek Mills. I will find you a pair of shoes and you must stop there to get them." [41]

At evening Lee reached his brother's farm in Powhatan County. He was made welcome, of course, but as the house was crowded he insisted on using his own tent. He was then invited to "spend the night" in familiar Virginia phrase, at the residence of John Gilliam, whose farm adjoined that of C. C. Lee. He asked, instead, that the available room be given a sick officer and his wife, who had driven up. Learning from his brother's family that the Gilliams were disappointed at his refusal and were very anxious that he at least eat a meal at their table, he sent word that if it were agreeable he would take breakfast with them. Then, having procured a pair of shoes for the soldier to whom he had promised them, he went into camp, immediately in front of the Gilliam home. It was his final bivouac, the last night he ever slept under canvas.

The next morning he ate with the Gilliam family. It probably was at this time, and in answer to a question from Mr. Gilliam,

[38] *Cooke,* 465, 466.
[39] Statement of Doctor T. Latané Driscoll, grandson of Lee's host. Doctor Driscoll courteously verified all the facts of this forgotten halt on the road to Richmond.
[40] Statement to the writer.
[41] Judge D. C. Richardson, giving his own experience, in 38 *Virginia Magazine,* 69.

that he said many people would wonder why he did not make his escape before the surrender, when that course was practicable. The reason, he explained, was that he was unwilling to separate his fate from that of the men who had fought under him so long.[42] He was unrestrained in his conversation and made much of a little girl of about ten, the daughter of the Gilliams, who was presented to him. He took her on his knee and caressed her. "Polly," he said, "come with me to Richmond and I will give you a beau."[43]

The company was swelled that morning by the arrival of Rooney Lee and the General's nephew, John Lee.[44] Riders and vehicles soon got under way—there were twenty horses altogether —and went down the River road, through Powhatan and Chesterfield Counties. As they neared the capital of the dying Confederacy, in the midst of a gloomy spring downpour, General Lee and two of his officers went ahead of the wagons and of the ambulance. Ere long they reached Manchester, which was then a separate municipality on the south side of James River, opposite Richmond. While the rain was at the heaviest he passed in the town the home of a Baptist minister who chanced to see the General, and later wrote of the scene in these moving words: "His steed was bespattered with mud, and his head hung down as if worn by long travelling. The horseman himself sat his horse like a master; his face was ridged with self-respecting grief; his garments were worn in the service and stained with travel; his hat was slouched and spattered with mud and only another unknown horseman rode with him, as if for company and for love. Even in the fleeting moment of his passing by my gate, I was awed by his incomparable dignity. His majestic composure, his rectitude and his sorrow, were so wrought and blended into his visage and so beautiful and impressive to my eyes that I fell into violent weeping. To me there was only one where this one was. . . ."[45]

The streets through which General Lee rode in Manchester

---

[42] 17 S. H. S. P., 361–62.

[43] Cf. "Lee and the Ladies," 78 Scribner's Magazine, 468; personal statements of the Gilliam family received through the kindness of Miss Nannie Jones of Richmond; note in 15 S. H. S. P., xxvii; MS. Recollections of Miss Polly Gilliam.

[44] R. R. Lee to the writer, MS. Dec. 16, 1925. Mr. Lee was then at the home of his father, Charles Carter Lee.

[45] William E. Hatcher: Along the Trail of the Friendly Years, 118–19. Doctor Hatcher must have been mistaken in saying Lee had only one companion.

cut off his view of Richmond until he was close to the James River, which he had made renowned in military history. Then he could see how deep and how hideous were the scars on the face of the city. Both bridges were gone: a line of Federal pontoons afforded the only crossing. Nearly the whole waterfront had been consumed in the fire of April 2–3 that had followed the evacuation. Arsenal, factories, flouring mills, tobacco warehouses, stores, dwellings—all were destroyed. On his left, in the middle of the stream, Belle Isle prison camp lay deserted. Beyond it, as his eyes swept along the river, the Tredegar Iron Works was intact, but east of it were gaunt, blackened walls, the only sentinels over the once-busy plants that had supplied him with shell and with small arms. Thence eastward for nearly a mile the fire had levelled the city from the north bank of the James to the hill beyond the business district. Scarcely a wall now stood shoulder-high in the whole area, for safety had required the wrecking of those the flames and the fall of floors had left standing. The streets that had shown the proudest bustle in the days of the Confederacy now were mere tracks amid débris that had been hastily pushed back to the sidewalk to afford a passageway. They seemed to divide plots of tangled roofing and charred timbers in a garden of desolation. Above them, as boldly set as if the terraces of gray and black and red had been made for no other purpose than to display it, was the sharply cut façade of the capitol that Jefferson had designed, the capitol in which Houdon's statue of Washington stood, the capitol where Lee himself had received command of the Virginia troops, the capitol where Jackson's body had lain in state after Chancellorsville, the capitol through whose corridors had run the defiant voices of the Confederate Congress, swearing that the new nation should never know subjection and would never seek reunion. And now over its roof, in the easy pride of assured possession, the Union flag was flying. Against the gray sky of the dark April afternoon, above the waste and wretchedness of the city, that colorful flag must have seemed to dominate Richmond as the symbol of conquest.[46]

[46] The fullest accounts of the evacuation of Richmond, the fire, and the arrival of the Federals are: Alex. W. Weddell: *Richmond, Virginia, in Old Prints,* 171 *ff.;* Mrs. Mary A. Fontaine to Mrs. Marie Burrows Sayre, April 30, 1865, *Calendar of Confederate Papers,* 274 *ff.;* W. A. Christian: *Richmond: Her Past and Present,* 259 *ff.;* Mrs. Emmie Crump

General Lee probably was forced to wait a while at the pontoon bridge, for his wagons and companions overtook him and followed him across the river and up the streets of Richmond. If there was a halt, General Lee did not prolong it an unnecessary minute, for he was anxious to avoid a demonstration of any sort. Rumor had spread on the 12th that he had arrived, but it had been ascertained then that the General Lee who had come to town was Custis, who had been carried as a prisoner of war from Sayler's Creek to City Point and had been allowed to visit his mother.[47] Still, it had been the supposition of all loyal Confederates that Lee would return directly from Appomattox to his family in Richmond. A certain informal lookout for him had been kept. Now word spread quickly that he was riding uptown. As many as could reach Main Street before he passed, hurriedly turned out to see him.

What met their gaze was not a pageant to stir martial ardor. He had put aside his best uniform and had on one that had seen long service, but he still wore a sword, though apparently not the handsome weapon he had carried at Appomattox. His mount was Traveller. With him now rode five others, Taylor, Marshall, and Rooney Lee among them. These officers also carried their side arms, but all their horses were gaunt and jaded. Behind them rattled the General's old ambulance and the wagons the Federals had permitted the officers to bring away from Appomattox for the transportation of their personal effects. In these vehicles, along with the possessions of the others, were General Lee's camp equipment and those of the headquarters records that had escaped destruction on the road to Appomattox. No attempt was made to dress up the vehicles for a formal showing. One of them, lacking a canvas, was covered with an old quilt. But those who looked at the sad little procession understood and choked and wept. Along a ride of less than a mile, from the pontoons to the residence at 707 East Franklin Street, the crowd grew thicker with each block. Cheers broke out, in which the Federals joined heartily. Hats went off, and uniform caps of blue along with them. General Lee acknowledged the greetings by uncovering repeat-

Lightfoot: *Evacuation of Richmond, MS.* Numerous papers on the subject will be found in 13, 23, 24, 25, and 32 *S. H. S. P. Cf. E. A. Moore,* 277.
[47] *New York Herald,* April 16, 1865, p. 2, col. 4.

edly, but he was manifestly anxious to finish his journey as quickly as he could.

Arriving in front of the house, he turned his horse over to one of the men attending the wagons.[48] The heart-broken civilians of Richmond, widows, old men, maidens, thronged him as the soldiers had at Appomattox. They wanted to speak to him and to shake his hand, and if that was impossible, at the least to touch his uniform. He grasped as many outstretched palms as he could. In a moment, with his emotions strained almost to tears, he made his way to the iron gate, and up the granite steps. Bowing again to the crowd, he entered the house and closed the door. The cheers of the crowd died out, and it began to scatter. His marching over and his battles done, Robert E. Lee unbelted his sword forever.[49]

[48] Request was speedily made to the post quartermaster, Lieutenant H. S. Merrell, for forage and stabling for all twenty of the animals—the first official notice the Union authorities had that he had reached Richmond. He "looked exceedingly robust," to a Federal newspaper correspondent who saw him for the first time as he prepared to enter the house. He was "certainly a most splendid specimen of a soldier and gentleman."

[49] *New York Herald,* April 18, 1865, p. 5, col. 2; eye-witness, Mrs. Julia Page Pleasants, in Mary Newton Stanard's *Richmond,* p. 213; *cf.* 34 *Virginia Magazine,* 9.

CHAPTER XI

THE SWORD OF ROBERT E. LEE

AMID the deep shadows of some of the old tombs in European cathedrals the observant traveller occasionally sees a sword that bears the marks of actual combat. Hacks and gaps there still remain, not made, like Falstaff's, to adorn a tale of pretended valor, but won in war when furious blade met challenging steel. No scratch was on the sword that General Lee laid away that April day in Richmond on his return from Appomattox. His weapon had never been raised except in salute. Rarely had it been even drawn from its scabbard. Yet it was the symbol of a four-year war, the symbol of an army and of a cause. Where it had been, the red banners of the South had flown. About it all the battles of the Army of Northern Virginia had surged. As he puts it down, to wear it no more, the time has come, not to fix his final place as a soldier, but to give an accounting of his service to the state in whose behalf alone, as he had written on another April day, back in 1861, he would ever have drawn his blade in fratricidal strife.

Had his sense of duty held him to the Union, as it held Winfield Scott and George H. Thomas, how much easier his course would have been! Never, then, after the first mobilization, would he have lacked for troops or been compelled to count the cost of any move. He would not have agonized over men who shivered in their nakedness or dyed the road with shoeless, bleeding feet. Well clad they would have been, and well fed, too. They would not have been brought down to the uncertain ration of a pint of meal and a quarter of a pound of Nassau bacon. The superior artillery would have been his, not his adversary's. On his order new locomotives and stout cars would have rolled to the front, swiftly to carry his army where the feeble engines and the groaning trains of the Confederacy could not deliver men. He would have enjoyed the command of the sea; so that he could have advanced his base a hundred miles, or two hundred, without the anguish of a single, choking march. If one jaded horse succumbed on a raid, the teeming prairies would have supplied two. His simplicity, his tact, his ability, and his self-abnegation would have won the confidence of Lincoln that McClellan lost and neither Pope, Burnside, nor Hooker ever possessed. He would, in all human probability, have won the war, and now he would be preparing to ride up Pennsylvania Avenue, as was Grant, at the head of a victorious army, on his way to the White House.

But, after the manner of the Lees, he had held unhesitatingly to the older allegiance, and had found it the way of difficulty. Always the odds had been against him, three to two in this campaign, two to one in that. Not once, in a major engagement, had he met the Federals on even terms; not once, after a victory, had his army been strong enough to follow it up. To extemporize when time was against him, to improvise when supplies failed him, to reorganize when death claimed his best lieutenants—that had been his constant lot. From the moment he undertook to mobilize Virginia until the last volley rolled across the red hills of Appomattox, there had been no single day when he had enjoyed an advantage he had not won with the blood of men he could not replace. His guns had been as much outranged as his men had been outnumbered. He had marched as often to find food as to confound his foe. His transportation had progressively declined as his dependence upon it had increased. The revolutionary government that he espoused in 1861 had been created as a protest against an alleged violation of the rights of the states, and it made those rights its fetish. When it required an executive dictatorship to live, it chose to die by constitutionalism. Fighting in the apex of a triangle, one side of which was constantly exposed to naval attack by an enemy that had controlled the waterways, he had been forced from the first to accept a dispersion of forces that weakened his front without protecting his communications. Always, within this exposed territory, his prime mission had been that of defending a capital close to the frontier. With poverty he had faced abundance; with individualism his people had opposed nationalism.

Desperate as his country's disadvantage had been, it had been darkened by mistakes, financial, political, and military. Of some of these he had not been cognizant, and of others he had not spoken because they lay beyond a line his sense of a soldier's duty forbade his passing. Against other errors he had protested to no purpose. From the first shot at Sumter he had realized that the South could only hope to win its independence by exerting itself to the utmost; yet he had not been able to arouse the people from the overconfidence born at Bull Run. Vainly he had pleaded for the strict enforcement of the conscription laws, exempting no able-bodied man. Times unnumbered he had pointed out that concentration could only be met by like concentration, and that the less important points must be exposed that the more important might be saved. On the strategy of particular campaigns he had been heard and heeded often; on the larger strategy of full preparation, his influence had not been great, except as respected the first conscription act. Regarding the commissary he might as well not have spoken at all, because Mr. Davis held to Northrop until it was too late to save the army from the despair that hunger always breeds.

Lee had himself made mistakes. Perhaps no one could have saved Western Virginia in 1861, but he had failed to recover it. With it the Confederacy had lost the shortest road to the Union railway communications between East and West. In his operations on that front and during the Seven Days, he had demanded professional efficiency of an amateur staff and had essayed a strategy his subordinates had been incapable of executing tactically. After Second Manassas he had overestimated the endurance of his men, and in Maryland he had miscalculated the time required for the reduction of Harpers Ferry. Longstreet had been permitted to idle away in front of Suffolk the days that might have been spent in bringing his two divisions back to Chancellorsville to crush the baffled Hooker. In reorganizing the army after the death of Jackson, Lee had erred in giving corps command to Ewell. Apart from the blunders of that officer and the sulking of Longstreet at Gettysburg, he had lost the Pennsylvania campaign because his confidence in his troops had led him to assume the offensive in the enemy's country before his remodelled machine had been adjusted to his direction. At Rappahannock Bridge he had misread the movements of the Federals, and in the Wilderness, on the night of May 5–6, 1864, he had left Wilcox and Heth in a position too exposed for their weary divisions to hold. Wrongly he had acquiesced in the occupation of the Bloody Angle at Spotsylvania. Incautiously, that blusterous 11th of May he had withdrawn his artillery from Johnson's position. The detachment of Hampton and of Early, however necessary, had crippled him in coping with Grant when the Army of the Potomac crossed the James. He had strangely underestimated Sheridan's strength in the Shenandoah Valley, and he had failed to escape from Petersburg. Until the final retreat, none of these errors or failures, unless it was that of invading Pennsylvania so soon after the reorganization of the army, affected the outcome of the war, but together they exacted of the South some of its bravest blood.

Deeper still had been the defect of Lee's excessive amiability. When every hour of an uneven struggle had called for stern decision, he had kept all his contention for the field of battle. The action opened, he was calm but terse and pugnacious; the fighting ended, he conceded too much in kind words or kinder silence to the excuses of commanders and to the arguments of politicians. Humble in spirit, he had sometimes submitted to mental bullying. Capable always of devising the best plan, he had, on occasion, been compelled by the blundering of others to accept the second best. He had not always been able to control men of contrary mind. His consideration for others, the virtue of the gentleman, had been his vice as a soldier.

Perhaps to this defect may be added a mistaken theory of the function of the high command. As he explained to Scheibert, he believed that the general-in-chief should strive to bring his troops together at the right time and place and that he should leave combat to the generals of brigade and division. To this theory, which he had learned from Scott, Lee steadfastly held from his opening campaign through the battle of the Wilderness. It was for this reason, almost as much as because of his consideration for the feelings of another, that he deferred to Longstreet at Second Manassas and did not himself direct the attacks of the Confederate right on July 2 and 3 at Gettysburg. Who may say whether, when his campaigns are viewed as a whole, adherence to this theory of his function cost the army more than it won for the South? If this policy failed with Longstreet, it was gloriously successful with Jackson. If the failure at Gettysburg was partly chargeable to it, the victory at Chancellorsville was in large measure the result of its application. Not properly applicable to a small army or in an open country, this theory of command may have justified itself when Lee's troops were too numerous to be directed by one man in the tangled terrain where Lee usually fought. Once adopted where woods obscured operations, Lee's method could not easily be recast for employment in the fields of Pennsylvania.

When Lee's inordinate consideration for his subordinates is given its gloomiest appraisal, when his theory of command is disputed, when his mistakes are written red, when the remorseless audit of history discounts the odds he faced in men and resources, and when the court of time writes up the advantage he enjoyed in fighting on inner lines in his own country, the balance to the credit of his generalship is clear and absolute.

In three fast-moving months he mobilized Virginia and so secured her defense that the war had been in progress a year before the Unionists were within fifty miles of Richmond. Finding the Federals, when he took command of the Army of Northern Virginia on June 1, 1862, almost under the shadow of the city's steeples, he saved the capital from almost certain capture and the Confederate cause from probable collapse. He repulsed four major offensives against Richmond and by his invasion of Pennsylvania he delayed the fifth for ten months. Ere the Federals were back on the Richmond line again—two years to the day from the time he had succeeded Johnston—Lee had fought ten major battles: Gaines's Mill, Frayser's Farm, Malvern Hill, Second Manassas, Sharpsburg, Fredericksburg, Chancellorsville, Gettysburg, the Wilderness, and Spotsylvania. Six of these he had indisputably won. At Frayser's Farm he had gained the field but had not enveloped the enemy as he had planned. Success had not been his at Malvern Hill and at Sharpsburg, but only at Gettysburg had he met with definite defeat, and even there he clouded the title of his adversary to a clear-cut victory.[1] During the twenty-four months when he had been free to employ open manœuvre, a period that had ended with Cold Harbor, he had sustained approximately 103,000 casualties and had inflicted 145,000. Holding, as he usually had, to the offensive, his combat losses had been greater in proportion to his numbers than those of the Federals, but he had demonstrated how strategy may increase an opponent's casualties, for his losses included only 16,000 prisoners, whereas he had taken 38,000.[2] Chained at length to the Richmond defenses, he had saved the capital from capture for ten months. All this he had done in the face of repeated defeats for the Southern troops in nearly every other part of the Confederacy. In explanation of the inability of the South to capitalize its successes, one British visitor quoted Lee as saying: "The more [the Confederates] followed up the victory against one portion of the enemy's line the more did they lay themselves open to be surrounded by the remainder of the enemy." Lee "likened the operation to a man breasting a wave of sea, who, as rapidly as he clears a way before him, is enveloped by the very water he has displaced." These difficulties of the South would have been even worse had not the Army of Northern Virginia occupied so much of the thought and armed strength of the North. Lee is to be judged, in fact, not merely by what he accomplished with his own troops but by what he prevented the hosts of the Union from doing sooner elsewhere.[3]

The accurate reasoning of a trained and precise mind is the prime explanation of all these achievements. Lee was preeminently a strategist, and a strategist because he was a sound military logician. It is well enough to speak of his splendid presence on the field of battle, his poise, his cheer, and his manner with his men, but essentially he was an intellect, with a developed aptitude for the difficult synthesis of war. The incidental never obscured the fundamental. The trivial never distracted. He had the ability—who can say how or why?—to visualize his fundamental

[1] See *supra*, vol. III, p. 154, note 101.
[2] Prisoners are reckoned in the total estimates, which, compiled from a variety of sources, cover roughly the period June 1, 1862–May 31, 1864.
[3] Herbert C. Saunders, 1866, quoted in *R. E. Lee, Jr.*, 232–33.

problem as though it had been worked out in a model and set before his eyes. In Richmond, during May, 1862, to cite but one instance, he saw clearly where others saw but dimly, if at all, that Jackson's little army in the Valley was the pawn with which to save the castle of Richmond.

Once his problem was thus made graphic, he projected himself mentally across the lines to the position of his adversary. What was the logical thing—not the desirable thing from the Confederate point of view—for his opponent to do? Assuming that the Federals had intelligent leadership, he said, "It is proper for us to expect [the enemy] to do what he ought to do."[4] After he had studied the probabilities, he would turn to his intelligence reports. Prisoners' statements, captured correspondence, newspapers, information from his spies, dispatches from the cavalry outposts—all these he studied carefully, and often at first hand. Every stir of his enemy along the line he canvassed both for its direct meaning and for its relation to other movements.

In assembling this information he was not more adept than many another capable general, and in studying it he was not more diligent, but in interpreting it he excelled. Always critical of the news that came from spies, few of whom he trusted, he was cautious in accepting newspaper reports until he learned which correspondents were close-mouthed or ill-informed and which were reckless or well-furnished with fact. When he discovered that the representative of *The Philadelphia Inquirer,* for example, knew what he reported and reported what he knew, he attached high importance to his statements. A credulous outpost commander received scant attention when he forwarded countryside rumor; but Stuart's "sixth sense" Lee soon learned to appreciate, and when that tireless officer affirmed that the enemy was marching toward an objective he named, Lee rarely questioned it. The infantry were apt to move quickly in the hoof-prints made by Stuart's returning courier. If Lee's strategy was built, in large part, on his interpretation of his intelligence reports, that interpretation was facilitated more by Stuart and Stuart's scouts than by anything else.

Lee did not rely so much as has been supposed upon his knowl-

[4] *O. R.,* 25, part 2, p. 624.

edge of his adversaries. He knew that McClellan would be meticulous in preparation, and that Meade, making few mistakes himself, would be quick to take advantage of those of which he might be guilty. But these were the only Federal generals-in-chief with whom he had been closely associated before the war. The others, save Grant, were in command for periods so brief that he scarcely knew them before they were gone. Grant's bludgeoning tactics and flank shifts he quickly fathomed, but he was progressively less able to combat them as his own strength declined.

Whether it was the cooking of rations in the Federal camps, coupled with verified troop movements on the Baltimore and Ohio; whether it was the ascent of transports on the James and a knowledge that McClellan would not renew his attack on Richmond until he felt himself strong enough to sustain the offensive; whether it was the gabble of deserters and a careful report of what Stuart himself had seen of dust clouds and covered wagons —whatever the information on which Lee acted, it was almost always cumulative. In nothing was he more successful, as an analyst of intelligence reports, than in weighing probabilities, discarding the irrelevant, and adding bit by bit to the first essential fact until his conclusion was sure. The movement from the Wilderness to Spotsylvania was perhaps the most dramatic example of this method, but it was only one of many where Lee built up his strategy from information steadily accumulated and critically examined.

Having decided what the enemy most reasonably would attempt, Lee's strategy was postulated, in most instances, on a speedy offensive. "We can only act upon probabilities," he said, "and endeavor to avoid greater evils,"[5] but he voiced his theory of war even more fully when he wrote, ". . . we must decide between the positive loss of inactivity and the risk of action."[6] His larger strategy, from the very nature of the war, was offensive-defensive, but his policy was to seize the initiative wherever practicable and to force his adversary to adapt his plans thereto. If a "fog of war" was to exist, he chose to create it and to leave his opponent to fathom it or to dissipate it.

Once he determined upon an offensive, Lee took unbounded

[5] O. R., 19, part 2, p. 715.　　　　[6] O. R., 27, part 3, p. 868.

pains to execute it from the most favorable position he could occupy. As far as the records show, he never read Bourcet, but no soldier more fully exemplified what that master taught of the importance of position. The student can well picture Lee in his tent, his map spread on his table before him, tracing every road, studying the location of every town and hamlet in relation to every other and choosing at last the line of march that would facilitate the initial offensive and prepare the way for another. A monograph of high military value might be based entirely on his use of the roads of Piedmont Virginia and the gaps of the Blue Ridge, now to further his own strategic plan, now to block that of the enemy. All this might be termed the "grand strategy of position." Of his great aptitude for reconnaissance and of the wise strategic employment, in combat, of ground that had been previously selected, or occupied from necessity, enough has already been said in comment on particular campaigns. Lee's career does not prove that a soldier must be a great military engineer to be a great strategist, but it does demonstrate that if a strategist is an engineer as well he is doubly advantaged.

If Lee on occasion seemed "slow" to his restless and nervous subordinates, it was because some unvoiced doubt as to the enemy's plan or his own best position still vexed his mind. For when his military judgment was convinced, he begrudged every lost hour. Herein was displayed the fourth quality that distinguished his strategy, namely, the precision of his troop movements, the precision, let it be emphasized, and not the speed nor always the promptness of the march. The army as a whole, under Lee's direction, could never cover as much ground in a given time as the Second Corps under Jackson or under Ewell. It was very rarely that the whole force completed, under pressure, what "Old Jack" would have regarded as an average day's march. Usually Lee had to ride with Longstreet to accomplish even as much as was credited to the slow-moving commander of the First Corps. Lee, however, could calculate with surprising accuracy the hours that would be required to bring his troops to a given position. This was true, also, of the various units in a converging movement unless the units were Longstreet's and were not operating under Lee's own eye. After the Seven Days' campaign had acquainted him with his men and their leaders, Lee made only three serious mistakes in logistics. One of these was in the time required to occupy Harpers Ferry and to reconcentrate the army at Sharpsburg. The next was in calculating when the First Corps would arrive at Gettysburg, and the third was in estimating the hour at which that same corps would overtake A. P. Hill in the Wilderness. In two of these three instances, Lee based his advance on Longstreet's assurances, which were not fulfilled. Against these three cases of the failure of Lee's logistics are to be set his transfer of the Army of Northern Virginia to meet Pope; the movement down the Rappahannock to confront Burnside at Fredericksburg; the quick and sure detachment of Anderson and then of Jackson at Chancellorsville; the convergence of Hill's and of Ewell's corps at Gettysburg; the march from the Wilderness to Spotsylvania; the shift to the North Anna, and thence to the Totopotomoy and to Cold Harbor, and the careful balancing of force north and south of the James during the operations against Petersburg—the list is almost that of his battles. Had his mastery of this difficult branch of the art of war been his only claim to distinction as a soldier, it would of itself justify the closest scrutiny of his campaigns by those who would excel in strategy.

His patient synthesis of military intelligence, his understanding employment of the offensive, his sense of position and his logistics were supplemented in the making of his strategy by his audacity. Superficial critics, puzzled by his success and unwilling to examine the reasons for it, have sometimes assumed that he frequently defied the rules of war, yet rarely sustained disaster in doing so because he was confronted by mediocrity. Without raising the disputable question of the capacity of certain of his opponents, it may be said that respect for the strength of his adversaries, rather than contempt for their abilities, made him daring. Necessity, not choice, explains this quality. More than once, in these pages, certain of his movements have been explained with the statement that a desperate cause demanded desperate risks. That might well be written on the title-page of his military biography, for nothing more surely explains Lee, the commander. Yet if "daring" is an adjective that has to be applied to him again and again, "reckless" is not. Always in his strategy, daring was meas-

ured in terms of probable success, measured coldly, measured carefully. If the reward did not seem worth the risk, nothing could
move him—except the knowledge that he had no alternative.
In detaching Jackson for the march against Pope's communications, and in dividing his forces at Chancellorsville, examination
of the circumstances will show that daring was prudence. In
ordering Pickett's charge at Gettysburg, he felt that he had a fair
chance of success if he attacked, and ran worse risks if he did not.
The same thing may be said of the assault on Fort Stedman. From
the Seven Days to Gettysburg, his daring increased, to be sure, as
well it might, with his army performing every task he set before
it; but the period after Gettysburg affords proof, almost incontro-
vertible, that he never permitted his daring to become recklessness. Throughout the spring and early summer of 1864, he felt,
as he said on the North Anna, that he must "strike a blow"; but
each time, save on May 5–6, his judgment vetoed what his impulse
prompted.

These five qualities, then, gave eminence to his strategy—his
interpretation of military intelligence, his wise devotion to the
offensive, his careful choice of position, the exactness of his logistics, and his well-considered daring. Midway between strategy
and tactics stood four other qualities of generalship that no student of war can disdain. The first was his sharpened sense of the
power of resistance and of attack of a given body of men; the second was his ability to effect adequate concentration at the point of
attack, even when his force was inferior; the third was his careful
choice of commanders and of troops for specific duties; the fourth
was his employment of field fortification.

Once he learned the fighting power of his army, he always disposed it economically for defense, choosing his position and for-
tifying it with the utmost care, so as to maintain adequate reserves—witness Fredericksburg. Only when his line was extended by the superior force of the enemy, as at Sharpsburg and
after the Wilderness, did he employ his whole army as a front-
line defense. In receiving attack, he seemed to be testing, almost
with some instrument of precision, the resistance of every part of
his line, and if he found it weakening, he was instant with his
reserves. Over and again, in the account of some critical turn of

action, it is stated that the reserves came up—rather accidentally than opportunely—and restored the front. Behind this, almost always, was the most careful planning by Lee. On the offensive it was different. "It is only by the concentration of our troops," he said in November, 1863, "that we can hope to win any decisive advantage." [7] He was writing then of the general strategy of the South, but he applied the same principle to every offensive. At Gaines's Mill and at Malvern Hill he early learned the wastefulness of isolated attacks, and thereafter, confident of the *élan* of his troops, it was his custom to hurl forward in his assaults every man he could muster, on the principle that if enough weight were thrown against the enemy, there would be no need of reserves. The final attack at Second Manassas and the operations of May 3 at Chancellorsville illustrate this. Only when he was doubtful of the success of an assault, as on the third day at Gettysburg, did he deliberately maintain a reserve. In partial attacks he somehow learned precisely what number of men would be required, with such artillery preparation as he could make, and he rarely failed until the odds against him became overwhelming.

For swift marches and for desperate flank movements, Lee relied on the Second Corps as long as Jackson lived; to receive the attack of the enemy he felt he could count equally on the First. Within the corps he came to know the distinctive qualities of the different divisions, and even among the divisions he graded the brigades. He was guided less in this, perhaps, by the prowess of the men than by the skill and resourcefulness of the different general officers. If danger developed unexpectedly in some quarter, his first question usually was, "Who is in command there?" [8] and he shaped his course according to his knowledge of the type of leadership he could anticipate.

Whether that leadership was good or bad, Lee gradually developed fortifications to support it. The earthworks he threw up in South Carolina were to protect the railroad he had to employ in bringing up his army. Those built around Richmond, in June, 1862, were designed in part to protect the approaches from siege tactics and in part to permit of a heavy concentration north of the Chickahominy. The works were too light to withstand the con-

[7] *O. R.*, 29, part 2, p. 819.   [8] *Cf. Cooke*, 368.

tinued hammering of siege guns, but, quickly constructed, they served admirably to cover his men and to discourage assault. They thus were midway between permanent fortifications of the old type and the field fortifications he subsequently employed. The same might be said of the works he constructed at Fredericksburg. His digging of trenches in the open field, while actively manœuvring, began with the first stage of the Chancellorsville campaign and was expanded at Mine Run. After May, 1864, when increasing odds forced him unwillingly to the defensive, he made the construction of field fortifications a routine of operations. The trenches, well laid, well sighted, and supplied where possible with abatis, served both a strategical and tactical object. They were strategical in that they made it possible for him to detach troops for manœuvre; they were tactical in that they enabled him successfully to resist a superior force with a steadily diminishing army. General Sir Frederick Maurice has held this to be Lee's major contribution to the art of war.

As a tactician, Lee exhibited at the beginning of hostilities the weaknesses that might be expected of one who had been a staff officer for the greater part of his military career. Until he lost many of his most capable officers he held strictly to his theory of the function of the high command—that of bringing the troops together in necessary numbers at the proper time and place. Yet he continued to learn the military art as the war progressed, and of nothing did he learn more than of tactics. He overcame his lack of skill in the employment of his cavalry. In the end he was deterred from elaborate tactical methods only because, as he confided to Hill in their conversation at Snell's Bridge,[9] he did not believe the brigade commanders could execute them. He was often desirous of delivering an attack perpendicular to the line of the enemy and of sweeping down the front. This was his plan for the Confederate right on the second day at Gettysburg, and it was often suggested to his mind thereafter, but it was never successfully executed on a large scale. His subordinates could not get their troops in position for such a manœuvre. Almost invariably the attack became frontal.

Predominant as was strategy in the generalship of Lee from the

9 See *supra*, vol. III, p. 331.

outset, and noteworthy as was his later tactical handling of his troops on the field of battle, it was not to these qualities alone that he owed the record he closed that day when he unbelted his sword after Appomattox. It had been as difficult to administer the army as to use it successfully in combat. Never equipped adequately, or consistently well-fed after the early autumn of 1862, the Army of Northern Virginia had few easy marches or ready victories. Lee had to demand of his inferior forces—as he always affirmed the administration had to exact of the entire population —the absolute best they could give him. The army's hard-won battles left its ranks depleted, its command shattered by death or wounds, its personnel exhausted, its horses scarcely able to walk, its transportation broken down, its ammunition and its commissary low. That was why its victories could not be pressed. Earnestly, almost stubbornly, he had to assert, "The lives of our soldiers are too precious to be sacrificed in the attainment of successes that inflict no loss upon the enemy beyond the actual loss in battle." [10]

On him fell the burden of an endless reorganization that is as much a part of his biography as it is of his title to fame. Out of the wreckage of battle, time after time, he contrived to build a better machine. He did not work by any set formula in administering the army, but by the most painstaking attention to the most minute details. Hungry men had to be restored by better rations: if the commissary could not provide them, he would seek them by raids or by purchases in the surrounding country, even if he had to send out details to thresh wheat and to grind it at the country mills. Rest was imperative: he would choose a strategically sound position, where the troops could have repose without uncovering the approaches to Richmond. To select men to succeed the general officers who fell in action, he would confer with those who knew the colonels of the regiments and he would examine each officer's record for diligence, for capacity, and for sobriety. Had the men worn out more shoes than they had been able to capture from the enemy? Then he would present their plight to the administration and would continue writing till the footgear was forthcoming, or else he would organize his own cobblers, save and tan the skins of the animals the commissaries had

[10] O. R., 21, 1086.

slaughtered, and out of them would seek to make shoes that would keep his men, at least, from having to march barefooted over snowy roads. If state pride demanded that troops from the same area be brigaded together and commanded by a "native son," he might disapprove the policy, but he would shift regiments and weigh capabilities and balance fighting strength until the most grumbling congressman and the most jealous governor were satisfied. The very soap his dirty men required in the muck of the Petersburg trenches was the subject of a patient letter to the President. His mobilization of Virginia, though it was among his most remarkable achievements and afforded sure evidence of his rating as an administrator, was equalled by the speed and success of his reorganization of the army after the Seven Days, after Sharpsburg, and after Gettysburg.

One aspect of his skill in administration deserves separate treatment as a major reason for his long-continued resistance. That was his almost uniform success in dealing with the civil government, a sometimes difficult business that every military commander must learn. Although the front of his army may be where the general-in-chief can direct every move, its rear stretches back far beyond the most remote bureau of the War Department. Few generals are ever much stronger than their communications with the authorities that sustain them, and few are greater, in the long view, than the confidence they beget. Often and tragically, both North and South illustrated this maxim during the War between the States. It was by the good fortune of former association that Lee had the esteem of President Davis; it was by merit that he preserved that good opinion, by merit plus tact and candor and care. During the war, General Lee received a few sharp messages from Mr. Davis, and he must have known him to be nervous, sensitive, and jealous of his prerogatives; yet it cannot be said that Lee found Davis a difficult man with whom to deal. This was because Lee dominated the mind of his superior, yet applied literally and loyally his conviction that the President was the commander-in-chief and that the military arm was subordinate to the civil. He reported as regularly to the President as Stuart or Jackson, those model lieutenants, reported to him. Reticent toward his own staff about military matters, he rarely made a move without explaining his full purpose to the President in advance. In judgment he always deferred to Mr. Davis. The detachment of troops frequently diminished the army's power of resistance, and sometimes threatened its very life, but Lee usually closed his reasoned protest with the statement that if the executive thought it necessary to reduce the forces under his command, he would of course acquiesce. Although he was entrusted with the defense of the capital of the Confederacy, and had constantly to seek replacements, Lee never put the needs of his army above those of the Confederacy. Steadfastly he worked on the principle he thus stated: "If it is left to the decision of each general whether he will spare any troops when they are needed elsewhere, our armies will be scattered instead of concentrated, and we will be at the mercy of the enemy at all points." [11] He never vexed a troubled superior by magnifying his difficulties. If, to the unsympathetic eye, there frequently is a suggestion of the courtier in the tone of Lee's letters to the President, it was because of Lee's respect for constituted authority.

Dealing with four Secretaries of War in order—Walker, Benjamin, Seddon, and Breckinridge—Lee encountered little or no friction. Benjamin was reputed to be the most exacting of them all in that he was charged with desiring to dictate the strategy as well as to administer the department. Johnston's friends have said if that officer had not forced the issue with Benjamin, no other general in the field would have been free to command his army. Lee had no occasion to fear this would be so. His relations with Benjamin, though never close, were consistently pleasant. To each of the secretaries Lee reported and before each of them he laid his difficulties. Usually he was candid with them as to his plans, so much so, indeed, that often if a letter were not addressed to the "Hon. Secretary of War," one would think it were intended for the confidence of the President. Only when important moves were afoot and secrecy was imperative was Lee ever restrained in addressing the war office.

Increasingly as the emergencies demanded, Lee addressed directly the administrative heads of the bureaus of the War Department, without reference to the secretary, but in so doing he

[11] *O. R.,* 29, part 2, p. 820.

escaped clashes with their superior. Colonel Northrop, of course, was a thorn in his flesh. In correspondence with him Lee was always courteous and always restrained. In a long controversy over the impressment of food from farmers,[12] Lee simply held his ground in the face of all the arguments of Colonel Northrop. Sometimes, when the commissary general insisted that rations be reduced, Lee ignored the suggestion and, from available supplies, fed his men what he considered necessary to restore their vitality or to maintain their health. This provoked complaining endorsements by Northrop on papers meant for the President's eye, but it brought Lee no rebuke from Mr. Davis. Northrop was Lee's one outspoken critic in the administration. Most of the others were his open admirers.

With Congress, Lee had little directly to do. Perhaps it was fortunately so. He often captivated politicians, and at one time, it will be remembered, he virtually acted for the administration in dealing with that difficult and positive individual, Governor Zebulon Vance of North Carolina; but Lee had seen too much of Congress in Washington to cherish any illusions regarding it in Richmond. He had, in fact, an ineradicable distrust of politicians. Although he rarely broke the bounds of his self-imposed restraint, he was convinced that Congress was more interested in the exemptions than in the inclusions of the conscript laws. In the winter of 1864–65, he thought the lawmakers were playing politics when the existence of the Confederacy depended upon the enlistment of every able-bodied man. His outburst in his conversation with Custis Lee, after his conference with the Virginia delegation in Congress, revealed many things that he had long felt but had not said.

Next in order, among the reasons for Lee's success as a soldier, is probably to be ranked his ability to make the best both of the excellencies and of the limitations of his subordinate officers. Thanks to the President's understanding of the need of professional training for command, and thanks, also, to the wisdom of his own early selections, Lee had some of the best graduates of West Point among his officers. He saw to it that such men held the posts of largest responsibility. At one period of his warring,

[12] See *supra*, vol. III, p. 251.

a council of his corps and divisional commanders would almost have been a reunion of alumni of the Military Academy. Yet these officers were not all of them outstanding in ability, nor were they sufficient in number to command the divisions, much less the brigades. Even when he availed himself of the well-schooled former students of the Virginia Military Institute, and of like schools in other states, he had to entrust the lives of many thousands of his men to those who had received no advanced training in arms prior to 1861. Along with the individual jealousies, ambitions, and eccentricities that have to be encountered in every army, he had to cope with political generals and with those who had a measure of class antagonism to the professional soldier. Perhaps Lee's most difficult labor was that of taking a miscellaneous group of Southern individualists, ranging in capacity from dullness to genius, and of welding them into an efficient instrument of command.

No commander ever put a higher valuation on the innate qualities of leadership. "It is," he wrote, "to men . . . of high integrity and commanding intellect that the country must look to give character to her councils." [13] He was not quick to praise but he was sparing in criticism. When he offended the *amour propre* of any officer, he made amends. Unless a man was grossly incapable, he was slow to relieve him of command. He preferred to suffer the mediocrity he knew than to fly to that of which he was not cognizant. If a general was disqualified by slowness, by bad habits, or by obtuseness, Lee sought quietly to transfer him to a post where his shortcomings would be less costly. In some instances, perhaps, officers did not know that they owed their change of command to the fact that Lee had weighed them and had found them wanting. Indecision, notorious ill-temper, intemperance, and a pessimistic, demoralizing outlook were the qualities he most abhorred in a soldier. "I cannot trust a man to control others who cannot control himself," he said, and, in the saying, explained why some men of capacity, even of brilliance, never rose high in his army or remained long with it. For personal cowardice he had a soldierly scorn, but he rarely encountered it. There was only one brigadier general in his army, and

13 *O. R.*, 21, 1067.

none above that grade, concerning whose personal courage in the presence of the enemy there ever was serious question.

Lee would listen patiently to suggestions from any quarter, even when they were given by those who seemed disposed to usurp his function as commanding general; and he was always patient in dealing with personal idiosyncrasies, unless they touched his sense of honor and of fair play. Whatever the station of an officer, Lee endeavored to see that full justice was done him, though he avoided personal dealings, if he could, with those who had no merit with which to sustain their grievances.

Except perhaps in the case of Longstreet, the more a soldier was capable of doing, the more Lee demanded of him. Never brusque unless with extreme provocation, Lee was least suave and most exacting in dealing with those whose conception of duty he knew to be as high as his own. Once he got the true measure of Jackson, he would have considered it a reflection upon that officer's patriotism to bestow soft words or to make ingratiating gestures. He had a personal affection for the praise-loving Stuart, but he rarely put flattery or flourishes into his letters to that remarkable man. Yet when a dull brigadier or a stupid colonel came to his quarters, Lee did his utmost to hearten him. For young officers he always had kind words and friendly, considerate attention, except when it was manifest that they needed a rebuke. If he had nothing else to give an exhausted lieutenant who brought dispatches through the burning dust of a July day, he would proffer him a glass of water in the same tones he would have employed in addressing the President. Although he realized that a trained and disciplined officers' corps was the greatest need of the army, he was almost alone among the higher commanders of the Confederacy in realizing that the volunteer leaders of a revolutionary force could not be given the stern, impersonal treatment that can be meted out to the professional soldiers of an established government. How different might have been the fate of Bragg and perhaps of the Confederacy if that officer had learned this lesson from Lee!

Lee's social impulses aided him in dealing with his officers. He kept a frugal table, as an example to the army, and he entertained little, but he was an ingratiating host and a flawless guest.

Mindful of the amenities, he never failed to show captivating courtesies to the wife of any officer of his acquaintance when she visited the army. His calls were always prompt and cordial, and in talking to the wife he usually had more kind things to say of the husband than he ever voiced to the soldier in person. If grief came in the loss of a child, he was among the mourners. When a general was wounded, his were the most encouraging words to the alarmed wife. At every review held in the season when the "ladies of the army" might visit it, he personally arranged that they should witness the ceremonies from a point of vantage, and usually he rode over to speak to them. His subordinates respected him for his ability and his rectitude; their wives made them love him.

All that can be said of Lee's dealings with his officers as one of the reasons for his success can be said in even warmer tones of his relations with the men in the ranks. They were his chief pride, his first obligation. Their distress was his deepest concern, their well-being his constant aim. His manner with them was said by his lieutenants to be perfect. Never ostentatious or consciously dramatic, his bearing, his record of victories, his manifest interest in the individual, and his conversation with the humblest private he met in the road combined to create in the minds of his troops a reverence, a confidence, and an affection that built up the morale of the army. And that morale was one of the elements that contributed most to his achievements. The men came to believe that whatever he did was right—that whatever he assigned them they could accomplish. Once that belief became fixed, the Army of Northern Virginia was well-nigh invincible. There is, perhaps, no more impressive example in modern war of the power of personality in creating morale. More than one writer has intimated that Lee's forbearance in dealing with Longstreet showed him too much of a gentleman to be a commander of the very first rank. It would be well for these critics to remember that the qualities of a gentleman, displayed to those in the ranks, contributed to far more victories than Longstreet ever cost Lee.

The final major reason for Lee's successes in the face of bewildering odds is akin to the two just considered. It was his ability to maintain the hope and the fighting spirit of the South. The confidence aroused by the first victory at Manassas sustained the South until the disasters at Fort Henry and Fort Donelson. Thereafter, for a season, the belief was strong that Europe's need of cotton would bring recognition and intervention. As months passed with no hopeful news from France or from England, while the Union forces tightened their noose on the Confederacy, the Southern people looked to their own armies, and to them alone, to win independence. Vicksburg fell; the Confederacy was cut in twain. The expectations raised by the victory at Chickamauga were not realized. The Army of Tennessee failed to halt the slow partition of the seceded states. Gradually the South came to fix its faith on the Army of Northern Virginia and on its commander. Elsewhere there was bickering and division; in Virginia there was harmony and united resistance. The unconquered territory was daily reduced in area, but on the Rapidan and the Rappahannock there was still defiance in the flapping of each battle flag. The Southern people remembered that Washington had lost New York and New England, Georgia and South Carolina, and still had triumphed. Lee, they believed, would do no less than the great American he most resembled. As long as he could keep the field, the South could keep its heart. So, when the despairing were ready to make peace and the cowardly hid in the swamps or the mountains to escape the conscript officer, the loyal Confederate took his last horse from the stable for his trooperson, and emptied his barn of corn in order that "Lee's army" might not starve. Morale behind the line, not less than on the front of action, was sustained by Lee. Conversely, he could count upon a measure of popular support that neither the President, the Congress, nor any other field commander could elicit.

The qualities that created this confidence were essentially those that assured Lee the unflagging aid of the President, the loyalty of his lieutenants, and the enthusiastic devotion of his men. But the order in which these qualities were esteemed by the civil population was somewhat different. Mr. Davis and the corps commanders knew that Lee was better able than any other Southern soldier to anticipate and to overthrow the plans of the enemy; the men in the ranks were satisfied he would shape his strategy to defeat the enemy with the least loss to them. The people in the Southern towns and on the farms of the Confederate states saw, in contrast, a series of military successes they were not capable of interpreting in terms of strategy or of tactics. They understood little of all the subtle factors that entered into army administration and into the relations of commander with President and with soldiers. But for them the war had taken on a deeper spiritual significance than it had for some of those who faced the bloody realities of slaughter. In the eyes of the evangelicals of the South, theirs was a contest of righteousness against greed, a struggle to be won by prayers not less than by combat. They saw in Lee the embodiment of the faith and piety they believed a just Heaven would favor. A war that would make a partisan of God works other changes no less amazing to the religious concepts of a nation, and among the Southern people, during the last year of the struggle, it lacked little of lifting Lee to be the mediator for his nation. The army, seeing him in battle, put his ability first and his character second. The civilian population, observing him from afar, rated his character even above his ability.

These, then, would seem to be the signal reasons why Lee so long was able to maintain the unequal struggle of a Confederacy that may have been foredoomed to defeat and extinction. To recapitulate, the foundation stone of his military career was intellect of a very high order, with a developed aptitude for war. On that foundation his strategy was built in comprehensive courses. Visualizing a military problem with clarity, he studied every report that would aid in its solution. If it were possible, he put his solution in terms of the offensive. With care he would select his position; with skill he would reconnoitre it; with precision of logistics he would bring his troops to it, and with daring he would engage them. For every action he sought to concentrate adequately, and for every task he endeavored to utilize the lieutenant best suited. In combat, however excellent his constantly improving tactics, he begrudged the life of each soldier he had to expose, yet he hurled his whole army into the charge, sparing not a man, when his daring gave him an opening for a major blow. As his numbers diminished and he was forced to the defensive, he perfected a system of field fortification that had a strategic no less than a protective value. A diligent army administrator, self-controlled and disciplined in his dealings with his superiors, he chose his subordinates wisely and treated them with a justice that Washington himself could not have excelled. He had, besides, a personality and a probity that combined with his repeated victories to gain for him the unshakable confidence of his troops and of the civil population. The tactics he employed in the 1860's belong to the yesterday of war, but the reasons for his success remain valid for any soldier who must bear a like burden of responsibility, whether in a cause as desperate or where the limitless resources of a puissant government are his to command.

When the story of a soldier is completed, and the biographer is about to leave the last camp-fire of a man he has learned to respect and to love, he is tempted to a last word of admiring estimate. May he not, by some fine phrase, fan into enduring flame the spark of greatness he thinks he has discovered in the leader whose councils he has in spirit shared? May he not claim for him a place in the company of the mighty captains of the past? Yet who that reverences historical verities can presume to say of any soldier who rises above the low shoulders of mediocrity, "In this he outshone or in that he rivalled another who fought under dissimilar conditions for a different cause in another age?" Circumstance is incommensurable: let none essay to measure men who are its creatures. Lee's record is written in positive terms; why invoke comparatives? The reader who can appraise the conditions under which he fought can appraise the man. Others need not linger at the door or watch him take off his sword, or strain to hear the words he spoke to Mrs. Lee in the first moment of their meeting.

CHAPTER XII

Two Decisions

GENERAL LEE did not break down when, on his return from Appomattox, he sat down behind the closed door of the house in Franklin Street, a paroled prisoner of war. He was exhausted in body, heavy of heart, and troubled for the future of the defeated Southern people. But there was for him no pacing of the floor, no moody musing, no reproaches, no despair. Inwardly, he must have suffered more than was realized even by those who knew him best. Outwardly he seemed, for the time, merely a very tired man who had passed through a bitter experience about which he did not wish to talk, though he would converse freely on other subjects. He spent long hours in bed and for some days did not leave the house. The remainder of the time he who had passed so many days in the saddle or in bivouac sat quietly in a chair in the back parlor, with some of his family around him. A week before, carnage, clamor, and the anguish of his country's death spasm. Now, four walls, silence, and a slow fire on the hearth.

Meantime the agonized city was close to chaos. The old government and the familiar landmarks were gone. Blue coats ruled where only gray had been honored. The Negroes, who had nearly all left their former masters' homes, were still half-intoxicated with their new freedom. Nobody had any money and few had any provisions.[1] In the fire of April 2–3 the public supplies of the Confederacy and the stock of the principal stores had been destroyed or looted. Many of the people were dependent for food on the relief agencies set up after the Federals had entered Richmond.[2] Lack of information was worse even than lack of

[1] *Mrs. McGuire,* 358.
[2] From April 8 to April 15, inclusive, according to the relief committee, tickets for 85,555 rations were issued (*Miss Brock,* 373).

food. No trains were running, for the railroads had all been cut
or their rolling stock burned. The mail system had been wiped
out; the telegraph was in the hands of the Federals. Only one
newspaper was being printed, and that one, *The Whig,* had
turned coat.[3] All military operations were screened. The people
did not know how Johnston's army was faring, nor what had become of the Confederate troops in Virginia who were not at
Appomattox, nor when and how the thousands of prisoners who
were eating out their hearts in Northern camps would get home
again. The men who had remained in the city after its evacuation
—cripples, clerks, and gray-beards—seemed to be dazed, and unable, as yet, to realize that the heart of the Confederacy was beating no more. Women stayed at home and worked and wept.
The days were torture and the nights were dread. Darkness was
on the streets as in the houses, for the conflagration had destroyed
many of the gas mains.[4] Everywhere was suspense or despair,
a tension heightened on the one side by suspicion that the South
inspired the assassination of Lincoln, April 14, 1865, and on the
other by resentment that so foul a charge could be credited.

Then, slowly, like a man brought back from the maw of death,
the city began again to live. Convalescents hobbled about the
streets, released at last from the hospitals. The survivors of the retreat to Appomattox limped back and continued to arrive until
Halleck estimated there were in the city between 10,000 and
15,000 former Confederates.[5] Negroes flocked in from the plantations and swelled to 40,000 or 50,000 the colored population.
Federal units on the march were often given a day in Richmond,
and with their equipment and numbers amazed a city that had
become accustomed to thin brigades and starving horses. The
railroads were repaired and tourists descended in swarms. Adventurers and speculators, writers and artists, sharpers and
schemers appeared every day in larger numbers.

There was, so far, no work for any one. Returned soldiers
walked the streets but might not stop and talk one to another, for after the murder of President Lincoln orders had been
given that no more than two men should be allowed to fore-

[3] *New York Times,* April 11, 1865, p. 4.
[4] *New York Times,* April 14, 1865, p. 2.   [5] *O. R.,* 46, 3, 1295-96.

gather in a public place.[6] They needed leadership, did those **Confederates** whose name, a few brief weeks before, had been **terror** to the North. No country was theirs and no cause, and they looked often and wistfully at the tall brick residence on Franklin Street, because, in defeat as in victory, they regarded Lee as still and always their leader. In front of the house a Federal sentinel usually stood, while a changing knot of curious strangers peered at the windows. These newcomers, especially the excursionists, trooped to Libby prison, and gaped at the fire-swept area, and gazed at the Capitol, and then, if they could, sought to get a glimpse of him who embodied in their eyes the diabolical "rebellion" against which their press and their preachers had declaimed. The staid building, with the door he had shut behind him, was as much the centre of that stricken city as ever his tent had been the headquarters for that city's defense. The whole bewildered life of Richmond, of Virginia, and of the South, revolved in those days about that street, about that house, and about one man in it.

The people did not let him sit long in the back parlor to rest from the strain those last months had put upon his arteries and heart. Before the first physical reaction was over, his doorbell was ringing. Rooney, Robert, and Dan Lee, his fine nephew of the navy, formed themselves into a staff of ushers[7] and tried to save him from those who had no claim upon his time; but between the insistence of visitors and the General's sense of social obligation, they could do little to relieve him. His own people came to him, to comfort and to be comforted. Women whose sons or husbands were still among the missing besought his help, and, of course, could not be turned away. A Confederate imprisoned in Richmond asked General Lee to use his efforts to get him and his comrades released. "But if you can't," he wrote, "just ride by the Libby, and let us see you and give you a good cheer. We will all feel better after it." The General could not grant their wish, but he was moved by their distress and that of

---

[6] *De Leon,* 368. General Lee made no public comment on the assassination of President Lincoln because of his desire to avoid everything that might make him conspicuous, but he was shocked by the act, and subsequently he wrote: "It is a crime previously unknown to this Country, and one that must be deprecated by every American" (R. E. Lee to Count Joannes, Sept. 4, 1865, *Jones,* 204).

[7] They doubtless had abundant helpers, for when kinsmen or friends came to Richmond without shelter or money, they were cared for on pallets at the Lee house till they were able to go home.

the prisoners taken on the retreat to Appomattox. In their behalf he wrote General Grant asking that all who had been captured after April 2 should have the terms allowed at the McLean House.[8]

Often at night, for exercise and for the solace of starry skies, the General would walk through the mournful residential districts of the city, accompanied only by Mildred, and sometimes he would stop at the home of some understanding friend.[9] One evening, when he called at General Chilton's home, from which not a glint of light was to be seen, he found a welcome as bright as the house was dark. A candle was lighted, and there before him stood Channing Smith, one of the most daring of the cavalry spies, who belonged then to Mosby's unsurrendered Rangers. Lee was surprised to see the boy, and the young trooper was shocked at the sight of the old commander to whose tent he had brought so many reports. "O! What a change in his appearance!" Smith wrote. "The last time I had seen him he was in the fullest glory of his splendid manhood, and now pale and wan with the sorrow of blighted hopes. I could not help nor was I ashamed of the tears which filled my eyes." Smith had a message from Mosby, a message and a question: What should the Rangers do? Should they surrender or fight on?

Lee answered: "Give my regards to Colonel Mosby, and tell him that I am under parole, and cannot, for that reason, give him any advice."

"But, General," said the young scout, "what must *I* do?"

"Channing," replied the General, "go home, all you boys who fought with me, and help to build up the shattered fortunes of

[8] R. E. Lee to U. S. Grant, April 25, 1865; *O. R.*, 46, 3, 1013.

[9] Mrs. Mary Pegram Anderson in *Richmond Times-Dispatch*, Jan. 20, 1907. Mrs. Robert Dabney Minor, wife of a gallant officer of the *Virginia*, invited Lee to call, with the promise that if he did so she would give him a "nice cup of tea," still a rarity among impoverished Richmonders. Lee duly called with Agnes—more for the company than for tea—and fortunately found Captain Minor at home. While the two were engaged in conversation, Mrs. Minor brewed the tea, but when she returned she brought only three cups, one for the General, one for her husband, and one for Agnes. "I'll not drink any until you get yourself a cup," the General announced. Mrs. Minor duly rose, left the room and came back with a full cup. Seating herself on an ottoman at the General's feet, she sipped and chatted with the rest. General Lee never knew that the young woman had discovered that she had only enough tea for three cups and that, when the General insisted that she drink, she had resourcefully filled her cup with muddy James River water, which she drank from her spoon as if it had been the finest Orange Pekoe.— *Statement of Miss Annie Minor of Richmond.*

our old state." [10] That was as far as Lee had found his way at this time: in the crisis of defeat, as in the day of the threat of war, his first thought was of Virginia.

Many put the same question that puzzled Channing Smith. Old officers called to bid their chieftain farewell, some of them bound for distant states, and convinced they would never see him again. Ministers and public men asked his counsel. Friends of his daughters came to beg souvenirs.[11] Every group of his departing soldiers sent a delegation or moved *en masse* on his quarters to pledge him their love and their loyalty. Two came one day, ragged and diffident, telling him they represented sixty who were around the corner, too tattered to enter a private dwelling. Their homes were in the mountains, they explained, and they owned land. They wanted him to come and live among them, that they might work for him and guard him from his foes.

"You would not have your general run away and hide," he answered, deeply stirred. "He must stay and meet his fate." His parole protected him, he went on, and he relied on General Grant's word. At last, unwillingly, they went on their way, enriched with clothing he gave them from his own scant store.

"One day," it has been recorded by Colonel Clement Sullivane, aide to Custis Lee, "all visitors were turned away, generals and statesmen, high and low alike, with the statement that General Lee had such an arrearage of correspondence that he must dispatch it, and he had given instructions during the day to excuse him to all visitors. I was seated at a window in the parlor only a few feet from the door; and as the windows and doors were all open, I could see and hear all that passed. By and by a tall, ragged Confederate soldier, with his left arm in a sling, came up the steps and was met at the door by Custis Lee. He asked to see General Lee. 'I am sorry,' replied Custis, giving him the familiar explanation. The soldier hesitated a moment and then said that he belonged to Hood's Texas brigade, that he had followed General Lee for four years, that he was about to set off and walk to Texas, and he had hoped before he left to shake his old commander by the hand and bid him good-bye; but if he couldn't, he

[10] Smith in 35 *Confederate Veteran*, 327.
[11] *Cf.* De Leon, *Belles, and Beaux and Brains of the 60's*, 418–19.

couldn't, and it could not be helped, and with this he turned away and went down the steps. Custis Lee hesitated a few moments and then called to the soldier to come back, that possibly General Lee would make an exception in his case, and he would see. So he ushered him into the parlor and went off upstairs. I offered the old soldier a seat and entered into a friendly conversation with him about his wounds, etc. Presently I heard the stately step of General Robert E. Lee descending the stairway. As we both arose on his entrance into the room, he bowed gravely to me and then advanced to the Texan, with his hand extended. The poor fellow grasped it, looked General Lee straight in the eye, struggled to say something, but choked and could not, and, wringing Lee's hand, he dropped it as he burst into tears; then, covering his face with his arm, he turned away and walked out of the room and the house. General Lee gazed after him for a few moments motionless, his fine, deep, dark eyes suffused and darkened with emotion, and then, again gravely bowing to me, he left the room and returned upstairs. Not a single word was spoken during the meeting by any of the three participants. . . ."[12]

Others wished to see the face on which the Texan had gazed, and if they might not behold him in the flesh, they wanted pictures of Lee. Photographers importuned him—among them Brady, for whom he sat in the rear of his home, with his son Rooney and Walter Taylor standing by. It was a stern picture. The jaw was strongly set and a shadow both of anguish and of defiance lingered on his face.

Journalists dogged him. Federal officers climbed his steps, some from ill-concealed curiosity and some to pay an honest tribute to him as soldier and as man. He disliked these interviews, but he did not feel he could decline them, and once, when he thought the young men of the household had denied him to three Union officers whom he should have received, he had his nephew ride across the river in what proved to be a futile attempt to find them and to apologize to them.[13]

One Irish bluecoat who called at the house proved to be an old

[12] 28 *Confederate Veteran*, 459–60.
[13] Major T. T. Graves, of Weitzel's staff, one of the first two officers to enter Richmond, was sent by Weitzel to offer help to Fitz Lee, with whom he had been at West Point. Graves, from the front parlor, saw General Lee in the back parlor "with a tired, worn expression on his face . . . leaning over" (4 *B. and L.*, 728).

regular of the Second United States Cavalry, Lee's own former regiment. He had a Negro with him, carrying a heavily laden basket of provisions. He told Captain Robert Lee, who met him, that he had heard down the street the Lees were in need of food, and that as long as he had a cent, his colonel should not want. The General heard the conversation and came into the hall. He was met with a salute from his old-time soldier, and had much difficulty in persuading the Irishman that he was not hungry. In the end he had to accept the basket, with the understanding that he would send it to the sanitary commission, which was caring for the sick. The veteran tried to embrace Lee on leaving and cried, "Good-bye, Colonel! God bless ye! If I could have got over in time, I would have been with ye!" [14]

Not one of all these visitors observed in General Lee any evidence of collapse, or even the slightest wavering in his self-control. Men saw new lines in his face and sadness in his eyes, but if they were discerning, they were quick to observe that this did not come from any rage at his defeat or from any personal humiliation over the surrender. He grieved then and to the end of his days, sometimes so deeply that he had to get up from his bed and pace the floor until he was weary, but it was never in self-pity. It was always for the victims of the war—old people left childless and poor, young mothers doomed to struggling widowhood, orphans whose fathers' bones lay on distant fields. The sorrows of the South were the burden of his life, manifest from the hour he came home, never eased until the autumn of 1867, and never removed until his death. Not a day in the last five years of his life can be understood unless it be remembered that the weight on his heart was that of others' woes. For himself, he summed it up when he told one of the chaplains at Washington College, "Yes, all that is very sad, and might be a cause of self-reproach, but that we are conscious that we have humbly tried to do our duty. We may, therefore, with calm satisfaction, trust in God, and leave results with Him." [15] To that view he held, regardless of what the effort cost him.

He had no intention of further, futile resistance. All too plainly he saw it would be vain. Throughout his life he had submitted

[14] *R. E. Lee, Jr.*, 157 ff.; *Miss Mason*, 318 ff.   [15] *Jones*, 144.

himself to existing authority, and he would do so now. But what of the future of the South, and what of those thousands of hot-blooded young men who had fought so passionately against the Union they were now commanded to respect as the only government in existence? What of those whose lives might be at the mercy of the liberated Negroes? He must shape his course to serve them.

On April 26 Johnston surrendered. A week thereafter, as if to evidence the belief that its service would no longer be needed, the Army of the Potomac approached Richmond in all its might. It was on the march to Washington, where it was to be reviewed and disbanded. Ahead of the endless divisions rode General Meade, willing then as always to practise the lofty doctrine of reconciliation. In Meade's entourage was Markoe Bache, who happened to know Custis Lee and called on him. In some way, the suggestion of a visit by Meade to Lee was made, whereupon Custis, of course, said that his father would be glad to see the General. On May 5, the forthright commander called and had a long conversation with Lee. In the frankness of old friendship, he urged Lee to take the oath of allegiance, not only to establish his own status but for the influence his action would have on the South. Lee replied, in the same spirit, by telling Meade what he had been thinking—that he had no personal objections to renewing allegiance to the United States, and that he intended to submit to their authority, but that he did not propose to change his footing as a paroled prisoner of war until he knew what policy the Federal Government intended to pursue toward the South. Meade argued that the government could make no decision of policy until it was satisfied the Southern people had returned to their allegiance. The best evidence of an intention to obey the Federal law, he contended, would be the oath. Lee did not combat this logic, nor did he deny that the military power of the Confederacy was destroyed. With the realism that always marked his acts, he agreed that the government of the United States was the only one that possessed any authority. Those who proposed to live under it should acknowledge it by the oath. But he would wait and see how the Federal Government itself acted. Then the question turned to the condition of the Negroes, concerning which the two talked at length. When Meade left he was, as he wrote, "really sad to think of [Lee's] position, his necessities, and the difficulties which surround him." [16]

Both men doubtless thought often of this conversation. What Lee had said, he had determined from the very day of the surrender to make the first rule of his conduct. No matter what happened, he would not abandon Virginia, as many heavy-hearted Confederates were planning to do.[17] He would remain with his state and share her fate. "Now, more than at any other time," he told a friend, "Virginia and every other state in the South needs us. We must try and, with as little delay as possible, go to work to build up their prosperity." He similarly counselled others.[18]

That was not all he decided, even when the memory of Appomattox still burned: he would, as a corollary, do nothing that would inflame the victors against the South. As he was hated by the North and was accounted responsible for the death of many of its sons, he would efface himself from public affairs, lest Virginia be hurt when his enemies struck at him. No word, no act of his, he resolved, should bring injury to her, or add to the woes

[16] 2 Meade, 278–79.   [17] Cf. De Leon, 369.

[18] Jones, 145; R. E. Lee, Jr., 163; Avary: Dixie After the War, 68; personal statement of G. Percy Hawes, Oct. 5, 1925; Margaret J. Preston in 38 Century Magazine (cited hereafter as Mrs. Preston), 271–72. Among those whom he thus advised at a later date was General Early, who had left the country and was then in Mexico. Another was Captain Matthew Fontaine Maury, the inventor and oceanographer, who had been on a mission in Europe at the end of the war and had accepted an appointment from Maximilian of Mexico as imperial commissioner of agriculture (Lewis: Matthew Fontaine Maury, 190). General Lee was careful not to dispute the wisdom of the acts of individuals in emigrating and he did not think that Maury should attempt to return at once to the United States (Lewis, op. cit., 188). Neither did he want to throw cold water on a great scheme of land settlement that Maury was maturing. But his own decision and his counsel to others were alike explicit. "As long as virtue was dominant in the republic," he wrote Maury, "so long was the happiness of the people secure. I cannot, however, despair of it yet. I look forward to better days, and trust that time and experience, the great teachers of men, under the guidance of an ever-merciful God, may save us from destruction, and restore to us the bright hopes and prospects of the past. The thought of abandoning the country and all that must be lost in it is abhorrent to my feelings, and I prefer to struggle for its restoration and share its fate, rather than give up all as lost. I have a great admiration for Mexico; the salubrity of its climate, the fertility of its soil, and the magnificence of its scenery, possess for me great charm; but I still look with delight upon the mountains of my native state . . . [Virginia] has need for all of her sons, and can ill afford to spare you" (R. E. Lee to M. F. Maury, Sept. 8, 1865; Jones, 206. Cf. ibid., 202, 208, 215, for somewhat similar letters to Colonel Richard L. Maury, General C. M. Wilcox, and General Early. Cf. also, R. E. Lee, Jr., 163). To Beauregard he wrote, still later in the year, after he had gone to Lexington: "I am glad to see no indication in your letter of an intention to leave the country. I think the South requires the aid of her sons now more than at any period of her history. As you ask my purpose, I will state that I have no thought of abandoning her unless compelled to do so" (Jones, 207).

of a defeated people. He would seek, also, to moderate the opinion of the South while not exciting that of the North. The old, bitter issues he would not discuss; the finished battles he would not revive. Nothing that he said or did should make it more difficult than it was to live under the government of the victorious Union. If men asked his counsel, he would advise silence, hard work, quiet behavior and avoidance of everything that might arouse the spirit of resistance or react against the defenseless. When visitors denounced the Federals, his was the first voice of moderation and his the first acknowledgment of generosity. "General Grant has acted with magnanimity," he said.[19]

This rule of conduct, which after Appomattox he never relaxed for a moment, he applied in small things as in large. When neighborhood youths set upon a juvenile "Yankee" whom they caught alone in the street in front of Lee's home, the General came out and reproved them for attacking an "innocent little boy that had never done harm to any one." He told the attackers that as Virginia gentlemen they should treat the stranger civilly, even if he was a Northerner. He took the frightened lad into his house and kept him there until the assailants had gone away.[20] His conciliatory attitude soon became known. Halleck heard while in Richmond that Lee intended to take the oath of allegiance, and both he and Grant predicted that if Lee did so, most Southerners would follow his example.[21]

Where and how could he best lead the life he had shaped for himself? He was not penniless, for in the general wreck of Southern fortunes, he had saved some of his modest investments;[22] but their yield was uncertain and was not enough to maintain the family in Richmond, even had he desired to stay there. His inclination and his financial circumstances alike disposed him to leave the old capital, with its curious crowds and its Federal garrison. "I am looking for some little quiet house in the woods," he wrote General Long, "where I can procure shelter and my daily

[19] T. N. Page: *Robert E. Lee, Man and Soldier*, 640.

[20] Judge Daniel Grinnan, quoting W. A. Stanard, who got the story from the "little Yankee" sixty years after; *American Issue*, Virginia Edition, Feb. 21, 1925.

[21] Halleck to Grant, May 5, 1865; II *O. R.*, 8, 534-36.

[22] He was one of the earliest depositors in the new First National Bank of Richmond. His signature slip is still preserved in its records.

bread if permitted by the victor. I wish to get Mrs. Lee out of the city as soon as practicable." [23] This last was no small consideration. Mrs. Lee had never doubted the success of the Southern cause. [24] The final defeat had been a bewildering blow, especially as the evacuation of Richmond had forced her temporarily to leave her home, which was threatened by fire. [25] She rallied courageously, however. "I feel," she wrote about a week after the General's return, "that I could have blessed God if those who were prepared had filled a soldier's grave. [Now] I bless Him that they are spared, I trust for future usefulness to their unhappy country. . . . For my part, it will always be a source of pride and consolation to me to know that all mine have perilled their lives, fortune, and even fame in so holy a cause." [26] Brave as she was, General Lee felt it was not prudent to keep her amid the excitements and irritations of the occupied city, and he sent Rooney to the Pamunkey to see if place could be found for her there. [27] As his son's report was not encouraging, the General decided to make some inquiries of his own.

Late in May, [28] without sending any word in advance, he mounted Traveller, and, all alone, rode out of Richmond, across the Chickahominy and on toward the Pamunkey. The first part of his journey lay past Mechanicsville, scene of his initial major engagement as commander in eastern Virginia. A little farther, and Lee passed through the gray earthworks that Early's men had thrown up almost precisely a year before, while Grant was moving toward Cold Harbor, where the field was covered with fallen Federals. Bloody scenes they were, and grim memories they may have awakened, but if so, they were hidden in his own heart. The country changed somewhat, and the battle-grounds were left behind, as the morning wore away. At 3 o'clock he drew rein in the yard of Pampatike, [29] home of his cousin, the gallant artil-

[23] *Long,* 439.
[24] Mrs. R. E. Lee to Mrs. R. H. Chilton, *MS.,* May 6, 1867; *Chilton Papers.*
[25] Mrs. Mark Valentine in 10 *Confederate Veteran,* 279–81.
[26] Mrs. R. E. Lee to Miss Mary Meade, *MS.* [April] 23, [1865], for a copy of which the writer acknowledges the kindness of Matthew Page Andrews of Baltimore, Md.
[27] *Ibid.*
[28] Or perhaps early in June, as R. E. Lee, Jr., stated (*op. cit.,* 166). The reason for thinking he left late in May is that he had not seen President Johnson's amnesty proclamation of May 29 at the time of his departure.
[29] The name is pronounced with the accent on the "ti," and with the "i" of the "tike" given the same value as in the name "Ike."

lerist, Colonel Thomas H. Carter, whose name has often appeared in these pages.

The General was recognized and welcomed on the instant and soon was in the circle of admiring relations. He was pleased when they told him Mrs. Carter had wept when her husband came back safe from Appomattox, because she grieved to think he could no longer fight for his country. Lee applauded her, but he did not talk much about the war. Instead, he chatted about Mexico and much about the farm he wished to purchase, and often of the kin of the Carters and of the Lees. Colonel Carter, in the matter of a farm, recommended Clarke County if the General desired a grass country, and Gloucester if he preferred salt-water. Lee declared for the grass. In his turn, he advised his cousin not to depend for labor on the Negroes, ninety and more in number, who still lived at Pampatike. The government would provide for them, said Lee. In their place, Carter should employ white help. Carter argued politely that this was the counsel of perfection: he had to use what he could get. The General held on. "I have always observed," said he, "that wherever you find the Negro, everything is going down around him, and wherever you find the white man, you see everything around him improving." [30]

He played for hours with two small daughters of the house, aged three and five, who, at his special request, were sent up to his room in the early morning to visit him before he arose. He delighted, too, in watching Traveller, after the horse had been turned out on the lush lawn to graze and to wallow. "I am sure the days passed here," said the son who must have shared some of them with him, "were the happiest he had spent for many years." [31]

As news spread that the General was at Pampatike, invitations began to pour in. One was to dinner with Mrs. Corbin Braxton of Chericoke, widow of a grandson of Carter Braxton, a signer of the Declaration.[32] Along with the General and the Carters, she

[30] *R. E. Lee, Jr.,* p. 168.   [31] *R. E. Lee, Jr.,* p. 166.
[32] Honorable Henry T. Wickham has given the descent and the relationship as follows: Carter Braxton the signer married as his second wife, Elizabeth Corbin. Their son George married Mary Carter, daughter of Charles Carter of Shirley by his first marriage to Mary W. Carter of Cleve. The son of George and Mary Carter Braxton was Corbin Braxton. His wife, General Lee's hostess, was Mary Tomlin. Corbin Braxton was thus Lee's half-first cousin.

invited Rooney and young Robert Lee and one of their cousins, all of whom by this time were hard at work raising a crop of corn at the White House.

A great and sumptuous dinner Mrs. Braxton set for her guests in the old, over-bountiful Virginia style. The younger men ate with much heartiness and with no reflections on the waste. "We had been for so many years in the habit of being hungry," Bob Lee explained years after, "that it was not strange we continued to be so awhile yet." But General Lee noticed Mrs. Braxton's lavishness and though of course he did not refer to it while he was her guest, his mind dwelt on it as he drove back to Pampatike with Colonel Carter. "Thomas," said he, "there was enough dinner today for twenty people. All this now will have to be changed; you cannot afford it; we shall have to practise economy." [33]

The next day saw the end of his stay at Pampatike. When Traveller was brought around, he was not quite satisfied with the way the blanket was folded, so he had the servant take off the saddle, and kneeling on the ground he arranged the cloth as he thought it best fitted the animal's back. He kept a close eye on the girthing, also, and only when he was satisfied that his mount was comfortable did he say good-bye to his kinsfolk and start back to Richmond. On the way he stopped for a call at Ingleside, another Braxton home. "After this visit away from the city," wrote his son, ". . . he began looking about more than ever to find a country home." [34]

Lee's sojourn at Pampatike meant much more than rest. It marked the second great decision he reached after the war, a decision almost as important in its consequences as that to which he had come instinctively when he sat down at Arlington and wrote his resignation from the United States army. For it was at Pampatike that he saw for the first time President Johnson's proclamation of May 29. In this document, to all except fourteen designated classes of Confederates, amnesty and pardon were offered those who would take a specified oath to support the constitution and laws of the United States.[35] Full property rights, other than in slaves, were to be restored every man who took the oath. Those like Lee, in the excepted classes of the prominent, were privileged

[33] *R. E. Lee, Jr.,* p. 168.   [34] *R. E. Lee, Jr.,* 269.
[35] Text in II *O. R.,* 8, 578–80.

to make special application for individual pardon, with the assurance that "clemency will be liberally extended as may be consistent with the facts of the case and the peace and dignity of the United States."

This was a declaration of the sort for which Lee had told Meade he had been waiting before deciding whether he would take the oath. The statement of the President's intentions greatly relieved General Lee's mind. It opened a way, he thought, for the South's recovery. Her people realized the Confederacy was dissolved, and most of them were willing to accept the outcome. President Johnson's offer indicated that the administration was not to impose the harsh law of the conqueror and would not visit retribution upon the disarmed South, but, on the contrary, would respect the property and, by inference, the other rights of the great majority of those who had so recently been branded as "rebels" and "traitors." If Southerners embraced the offer in this proclamation, they might escape the worst horrors that had been threatened them when their cause was lost. And if, again, as a result of the President's amnesty and the South's acceptance, the states of the former Confederacy could regain the places they had held before 1861, they would be safe from rule by soldiers or by blacks. The future of the restored nation would then be bright. An early return to a union of all the states accordingly became in General Lee's eyes as desirable for the South as it was logical for people of a common stock who had settled the issues that divided them.

That was not all. Modest as he was, he knew that the men who had looked to him in battle were looking to him now. Once again he told himself that, as he had sought to set them an example during the life of the Confederacy, he must do no less in the hour of its death; and if there was no guarantee of personal security for them other than that of allegiance to the United States, he must show them so. Besides, he had some protection under his parole as a prisoner of war. Mr. Davis and all the other civil officers of the government lacked that. Were he to take the oath and recover his citizenship, he might be able to help them. He was not sure he could aid them, but he felt that perhaps a way would be found, and if so, he must be ready to follow it.

Would it be inconsistent in him to take this course? He prob-

ably answered then as he did the following October when he told
Beauregard: "True patriotism sometimes requires of men to act
exactly contrary, at one period, to that which it does at another,
and the motive which impels them—the desire to do right—is
precisely the same. The circumstances which govern their actions
change; and their conduct must conform to the new order of
things. History is full of illustrations of this. Washington himself
is an example. At one time he fought against the French under
Braddock, in the service of the King of Great Britain; at another,
he fought with the French at Yorktown, under the orders of the
Continental Congress of America, against him. He has not been
branded by the world with reproach for this; but his course has
been applauded." [36] Here Lee avowed a personal ideal as surely
as he drew an historical parallel. At Arlington, Washington had
been his model. After Appomattox he still looked for guidance to
the example of that majestic man.

But what of the special application that had to be made by all
those who were excepted from the amnesty proclamation? Was
that a humiliation that ought not to be borne? If this complica-
tion occurred to him, he disposed of it as he did, some months
later, in a letter to Josiah Tatnall. He told that officer: "Both
[those embraced in the amnesty proclamation and those excepted],
in order to be restored to their former rights and privileges, were
required to perform a certain act, and I do not see that an acknowledgment of fault is expressed in one more than the other." [37]

Reasoning in this way, Lee came back to Richmond to ascertain what he should do to comply with the President's proclamation, but when he arrived in the city he heard that District Judge
John C. Underwood had called on a Federal grand jury sitting in
Norfolk to indict him and other Confederates for treason against
the United States. [38] The threat of criminal proceedings did not
move him, for he was quite willing to meet any accusation that
might be brought against him, but it raised a question that puz-

[36] R. E. Lee to G. T. Beauregard, Oct. 3, 1865; Jones, *L. and L.,* 390.
[37] R. E. Lee to J. Tatnall, Sept. 7, 1865; *Jones,* 208. *Cf. Jones,* 218–19.
[38] Actually he had been indicted on June 7, 1865. For ascertaining the date of this
indictment, thanks are due the late Joseph P. Brady, the clerk of the United States Court
for the Eastern District of Virginia. After much search, Mr. Brady found this long-sought
entry in the criminal docket of the presiding judge. All the other records of the indictment have disappeared.

zled him: Would his decision to ask for a pardon be regarded as an effort to escape trial? Might it hurt the very people he wished to help? Would it mar the example he felt he should set? He reasoned that a trial was unlikely, inasmuch as he had been formally paroled, and he concluded that if the Federals did bring him into court, they might leave others alone.[39] So he adopted a direct expedient: he would enter his application for pardon, under the amnesty, but he would make it contingent on the non-prosecution of the charges against him. If he was to be brought to the bar he would not ask for pardon but would face the charge and accept the outcome. For the sake of the tens of thousands of Southern men who held paroles similar to his own, he would endeavor to have the terms of their surrender respected, and in dealing with the government he would assume this would be done. He would address his communication to General Grant, the officer who had taken his parole, and he would enclose in it his application to the President for pardon. There could then be no doubt that the application was not to be considered unless the authorities honored his parole and did not press a criminal prosecution. But how would General Grant view the matter? Sympathetically? His conduct at Appomattox certainly indicated that he would, but his views might have changed. Lee must find out. And through whom? On reflection, Lee decided to make verbal inquiry through his friend Reverdy Johnson, United States senator from Maryland, who had supported the Union cause yet was a firm advocate of reconciliation. Lee communicated with Senator Johnson, who consulted Colonel Adam Badeau, military secretary to General Grant. In a few days Lee learned that Grant would insist that the paroles be respected, and would endorse Lee's application for pardon, which he urged him to make.[40]

Apparently, Lee consulted no one else. Regarding the question as one of personal duty, he said nothing until he handed Custis Lee two papers, on June 13, and asked him to copy them.

[39] For this latter point, see *Fitz Lee*, 400. In the *Taylor MSS.* is a copy of the letter to Grant with this notation in the autograph of General Custis Lee: "When Gen. Lee requested me to make a copy of this letter to Presdt. Johnson, he remarked: It was but right for him to set an example of making formal submission to the Civil Authorities; and that he thought, by so doing, he might possibly be in a better position to be of use to the Confederates, who were not protected by Military paroles—especially Mr. Davis."
[40] Adam Badeau: *Grant in Peace*, 25–27.

This was the letter he wrote Grant:

Richmond, Virginia, June 13, 1865.

Lieutenant-General U. S. Grant, Commanding the Armies of the United States.

General: Upon reading the President's proclamation of the 29th ult., I came to Richmond to ascertain what was proper or required of me to do, when I learned that, with others, I was to be indicted for treason by the grand jury at Norfolk. I had supposed that the officers and men of the Army of Northern Virginia were, by the terms of their surrender, protected by the United States Government from molestation so long as they conformed to its conditions. I am ready to meet any charges that may be preferred against me, and do not wish to avoid trial; but, if I am correct as to the protection granted by my parole, and am not to be prosecuted, I desire to comply with the provisions of the President's proclamation, and, therefore, inclose the required application, which I request, in that event, may be acted on. I am, with great respect,

Your obedient servant,

R. E. LEE.

The enclosed application to the President was in this language:

Richmond, Virginia, June 13, 1865.

His Excellency Andrew Johnson,
    President of the United States.

Sir: Being excluded from the provisions of the amnesty and pardon contained in the proclamation of the 29th ult., I hereby apply for the benefits and full restoration of all rights and privileges extended to those included in its terms. I graduated at the Military Academy at West Point in June, 1829; resigned from the United States Army, April, 1861; was a general in the Confederate Army, and included in the surrender of the Army of Northern Virginia, April 9, 1865. I have the honor to be, very respectfully,

Your obedient servant,

R. E. LEE.[41]

[41] R. E. Lee, Jr., 164, 165; O. R., 46, part 3, pp. 1275–76. For Lee's view that no paroled prisoner should be required to take the oath as a condition of returning home, see his letter of April 25, 1865, to Grant, Jones, 204.

He did not subscribe to the oath and forward it with the letters, because no order requiring this had been received in Richmond when he wrote.[42]

To the decision represented by this application, General Lee adhered for the rest of his life. With him, mental opposition to the government was at an end. Submission to civil authority was real. In letters to his friends, he began to voice the sentiments that were to find fuller expression, six weeks thereafter, when he decided to take up, once again, the leadership of youth. "Tell [our returned soldiers]," he wrote Colonel Walter Taylor on June 17, four days after he addressed the President, "they must all set to work, and if they cannot do what they prefer, do what they can. Virginia wants all their aid, all their support, and the presence of all her sons to sustain and recuperate her. They must therefore put themselves in a position to take part in her government, and not to be deterred by obstacles in their way. There is much to be done which they only can do." [43]

News that General Lee had asked for a pardon soon became known. It had much the effect with the South that Grant and Halleck had predicted.[44] Many of those who had fought with General Lee reasoned that they could safely follow his leadership in this particular and could accept the President's amnesty. But there were die-hards who did not understand that Lee was taking this course to save the South from new anguish and to aid in the re-establishment of an equal union of all the states. Thinking he had acted both hastily and improperly, they criticised him accordingly and swore they would never follow his example. No single act of his career aroused so much antagonism. Twenty years after his death some of the "unreconstructed" Southerners were still insistent that Lee had erred, and, by asking a pardon, had admitted a fault. In the North his action was received with mild satisfaction as something in the nature of a dying sinner's repentance, but it was honestly applauded by Henry Ward Beecher.[45]

The possibility of Lee's trial for treason created as much talk as

---

[42] R. E. Lee, Jr., 165; O. R., 46, part 3, p. 1287.

[43] Taylor's General Lee, 298; Avary: Dixie After the War, 70–71; Barton H. Wise: Life of Henry A. Wise, 376, 377; D. H. Maury, 236.

[44] Halleck to Grant, May 5, 1865; II O. R., 8, 534, 535–36.

[45] "Of course we are full of complacency at Mr. Beecher's approval of Genl. Lee's course, but when he exalts Dalgren [sic] into a hero and martyr, we have less respect for

his application to Johnson. Offers of legal help came quickly, and were gratefully acknowledged.[46] "I have heard of the indictment . . . ," he said, "and made up my mind to let the authorities take their course. I have no wish to avoid any trial the government may order, and I cannot flee." [47] Holding to the view expressed in his letter to Grant—that paroled prisoners of war could not be brought to trial—he exerted himself chiefly to allay the resentment of his friends over the course the Federal authorities threatened to take in dealing with him. When one of a company of callers, a minister, declaimed bitterly against the indictment, Lee said simply: "Well! it matters little what they may do to me; I am old, and have but a short time to live anyway." And he turned the subject. A little later, when the clergyman was leaving, Lee followed him to the door and spoke with much earnestness. "Doctor," he said, "there is a good old book which I read and you preach from, which says, 'Love your enemies, bless them that curse you, do good to them that hate you, and pray for them which despitefully use you and persecute you.' Do you think your remarks this evening were quite in the spirit of that teaching?" The preacher apologized for his bitterness, whereupon General Lee concluded: "I have fought against the people of the North because I believed they were seeking to wrest from the South dearest rights. But I have never cherished toward them bitter or vindictive feelings, and have never seen the day when I did not pray for them." [48]

It could not have been long after this that Lee received General Grant's letter of June 20, in which the Federal commander upheld Lee's view that paroled prisoners of war could not be tried for treason so long as they observed their paroles. In endorsing and forwarding the application of General Lee to the President, General Grant went so far as to say: "I would ask that [Judge Underwood] be ordered to quash all indictments found against paroled prisoners of war, and to desist from the further prosecution of them." Grant also transcribed in his letter to Lee his "earnest

his judgment" (Mrs. R. E. Lee to Miss Emma Chilton, *MS.*, September n.d. [1865]— *Chilton Papers*). It is possible that Beecher's approval was given to Lee's decision to enter education rather than to his application for pardon.

[46] Among those who offered their services was Reverdy Johnson. See *Cooke*, 553.
[47] Jones, *L. and L.*, 383; *R. E. Lee, Jr.*, 175.   [48] *Jones*, 195-96.

recommendation" to the President that Lee's application for amnesty and pardon be allowed.[49]

No early action to quash the indictment was taken, despite Grant's letter, but Lee was not arrested and prosecution was not begun. When General Lee went away from Richmond, later in the month, he left a copy of Grant's letter with William H. Macfarlane, a lawyer and a friend, whom he authorized to show it to other officers who were in his condition. He declined to let the communication be printed, however, unless Grant's consent was procured.[50] By the end of July, Lee was about convinced that the treason indictment would not be pressed and that, on the other hand, he would not soon be granted a pardon. "I think . . .," he wrote Fitzhugh, "we may expect procrastination in measures of relief, denunciatory threats, etc. We must be patient, and let them take their course."[51] He was right. The individual pardon was never granted.

Pardon or no pardon, treason or no treason, Lee felt he should now set an example by going to work. Fitzhugh and Robert were progressing on their farms, but the General himself had no land. The lot in Washington which had been bequeathed him under the will of Mr. Custis, had been sold in 1864 for taxes.[52] He had lost $20,500 in Confederate and Carolina bonds. His holdings of $4000 in the Chesapeake and Ohio Canal Company had yielded nothing for years.[53] The return on his other securities was doubtful for the time being.[54] Arlington had shared the fate of the Washington property, and the $40,000 due his daughters from the estate of Mr. Custis could not be raised. The General did not even own the house in which his family was then sheltered. It belonged to John Stewart, a Scotch philanthropist of Richmond. With characteristic generosity and thoughtfulness, Mr. Stewart now offered the place to Mrs. Lee for as long as she was willing

[49] *O. R.*, 46, part 3, pp. 1286–87.
[50] *R. E. Lee, Jr.,* 175.   [51] *R. E. Lee, Jr.,* 178.
[52] Washington, D. C., *Liber N. C. T.,* 39, Folio 444; deed of July 11, 1864. This lot had never been transferred to General Lee. For establishing this fact, the writer's thanks are due Robert M. Lynn, of Washington, D. C.
[53] Inventory of the estate of Robert E. Lee, *Rockbridge County* (Va.) MS. *Records.*
[54] He had been able, however, to retain his bonds in the Erie Railroad and did not cash them until December, 1866 (*Markie Letters,* 71).

to stay there, and stipulated that if she insisted on paying for the use of the premises, he would take only Confederate money, in accordance with the terms of the original lease.[55] Appreciative as General Lee was of his landlord's kindness, he did not desire to remain in the city and did not feel that he could live on the bounty of Mr. Stewart.

Nor did he feel that he could accept any of the numerous other offers of hospitality that came to him—one to go to England as the life-guest of a generous nobleman. "I am deeply grateful," he wrote the Britisher. "I cannot desert my native state in the hour of her adversity. I must abide her fortunes, and share her fate." [56] Although General Meade had privately suggested him for governor of Virginia,[57] he would not consider entering politics. There is no evidence to show that he canvassed the outlook for his old specialty, engineering. As a man whose prime aim was to get away from the world, he clung to his idea of purchasing and working a small farm where Mrs. Lee and his daughters might live in quietness. Moreover, he believed that agriculture offered the best opportunity of the Southern soldier who had no profession and no money, and he often commended that vocation to his old soldiers. The suggestion that he undertake this new life on one of the Pamunkey properties he put aside at length because, as Mrs. Lee explained, he "seemed to think it would be difficult for us to obtain supplies down there or to get servants to remain, and that it would be better for us to go higher up the country." [58] He considered Clarke County, which Colonel Carter had praised, and at length he became interested in a tract in Orange County, near the railroad bridge over the Rapidan, in a beautiful section close to the scene of some of his campaigns.[59] He withheld a final decision about buying the place, however, probably in view of his uncertainty as to the treason proceedings.[60]

[55] R. E. Lee, Jr., 170.
[56] R. E. Lee, Jr., 170, quoting Long. Names and dates connected with this offer are missing, but the incident itself has verisimilitude. De Leon in Belles, Beaux and Brains of the 60's, 427, stated that Lee was offered also the command of the Rumanian army.
[57] Moncure D. Conway in 17 Mag. of American History, 469.
[58] Mrs. R. E. Lee to Mrs. W. Hartwell Macon, MS., June 23, 1865, Johnston MSS. graciously made available to the writer by J. Ambler Johnston of Richmond. Mrs. Macon had offered the Lees the hospitality of her home.
[59] Fitz Lee, 402.
[60] Cf. R. E. Lee to R. E. Lee, Jr., undated. R. E. Lee, Jr., 174; "I can do nothing until I learn what decision in my case is made in Washington."

While he waited, there came a letter from Mrs. Elizabeth Randolph Cocke, a widow of wealth and station, who resided at Oakland, a fine estate in Cumberland and Powhatan Counties, on the south side of the James River, some fifty-five miles above Richmond. She had a vacant cottage on a quiet part of her Powhatan property; would the General and his family use it, and the land that went with it, at their pleasure? Her letter may have been written in some understanding of Lee's needs and wishes, and it was followed by a visit to Mrs. Lee from Mrs. Cocke. Her desire to entertain them was so manifest and her tone so cordial that the family accepted,[61] the more readily because Mrs. Lee, who could not travel far, would be able to make most of the journey by canal boat.[62]

Prior to June 9—probably at the time he first contemplated moving into the country—General Lee had inquired of the provost-marshal whether he would need a passport for leaving Richmond, and had been assured that he would not, but as there had been a change in the office, he took pains to write again.[63] Encountering no obstacle, he proceeded to case up the domestic goods, which was no small task for a large household that had been refugees in Richmond for nearly two years.

The General's spirits were visibly raised at the near prospect of getting away from crowds and callers, bustle, and bluecoats. While he was packing his own trunk, with some desultory feminine assistance, he passed several times into the adjoining room to show to his girls and to their guest, a minister's daughter, odd belongings of interest that he chanced upon. Presently he appeared with a wide-brimmed, drab, felt hat, flat-crowned. "Miss Josie," he said, "has your father a good hat?"

As the young woman, Miss Josephine Stiles, had not seen her father for some time, she could not answer for his wardrobe.

"Well," said he, "I have two good hats, and I don't think a good rebel ought to have two good articles of one kind in these hard times. This was my dress-parade hat"—it probably was the one he

---

[61] R. E. Lee, Jr., 171; Mrs. R. E. Lee to Mrs. W. Hartwell Macon, MS., June 23, 1865, loc. cit.
[62] Markie Letters, 62.
[63] R. E. Lee, Jr., 173; O. R., 46, part 3, p. 1267.

had worn at Appomattox. "Take it, please, and if your father has not a good hat, give him this one from me." [64]

He similarly bestowed quite a number of the buttons off his uniform coats, along with photographs[65] and other souvenirs, on girl friends of his daughters, who begged them when they came to say good-bye; but after the Federals issued an order requiring all Confederate buttons to be covered or removed, he parted with no more of them, lest he get some young beskirted rebel into trouble with the provost-marshal.[66]

Finally, the preparations for departure were complete. Custis journeyed ahead as courier, riding Traveller, who, of course, had to go wherever his master rusticated. The rest of the family, one afternoon between June 26 and June 30, went down to "the Basin," a few squares below their home, and took the packet-boat, which started up the James River and Kanawha Canal a little before sunset.[67]

The ladies soon went below, into the long saloon that was divided, after supper, into one compartment for men and another for women. There they retired. The captain of the packet busied himself and made ready for the General the best bed his boat could provide. But Lee would not accept special favors. Instead, he spread his military cloak over him and slept on deck—the last night that he ever spent under the open sky. In moderate weather it was not usually an unpleasant journey, with the boat moving slowly along the canal, pulled by the stout horse on the tow-path, while the water swished against the sides of the laden craft, and the driver's horn sounded musically every few miles to warn the lock-keeper of the vessel's approach. Worse travel there was,

[64] *Stiles,* 357. The hat is now in the Confederate Museum, Richmond, Va.

[65] One of the most beautiful and characteristic of his letters, sending photographs to his young admirers, was that of May 9, 1865, to Miss Belle Stewart of Brook Hill: "I am surprized Miss Belle that you should want the likeness of an old man when you can get that of so many young ones, but as Keith says such is the case, I send you the last I have. I hope it may serve to recall sometimes one who will never forget you" (*Bryan MSS.*). He was constantly asked for autographs and pictures and gave them freely. *Cf Markie Letters,* 69–70; Lee to Miss Annie W. Owens, *MSS.,* March 22, 1866, Nov. 29, 1869, June 18, 1870, for copies of which the writer is indebted to Mrs. Frank Screven of Savannah, Ga.

[66] *Brock,* 341.

[67] The date of departure cannot be fixed with certainty, but as Mrs. Lee sat for a photograph, on which the cancelled stamps are marked "June 28," it is probable that this is the date of their delivery in Richmond. This would indicate that the family left on June 29 or 30, though it is possible, of course, that the pictures were mailed to her at Derwent. The picture in question is by Vannerson and Jones and is reproduced in Volume III, opposite p. 210.

surely, than that of a June night on the "Jeems River and Kanaw'y Canal"!

About sunrise the boat reached Pemberton, the landing nearest Oakland. Custis Lee and Edmund Cocke, a veteran of the Army of Northern Virginia, were waiting for the packet and helped get the party across the ferry and up to the mansion, where breakfast was ready.[68] It must have been a relief past words to the General to be in the country again, with his family, in an atmosphere reminiscent of the old days at Arlington.

A week at Oakland[69] and then to Derwent, two miles away, the property Mrs. Cocke had placed at his disposal. It was a plain tenant's house, with two rooms above and two below, and had an "office" in the yard. Mrs. Cocke had equipped it with furniture from Oakland and had given it a simple air of comfort, which was heightened by a fine grove of trees.[70] The neighborhood was secluded, the land was poor, and the summer was hot, but the large, hard-working family of Palmores, who surrounded Derwent,[71] supplied butter and vegetables to supplement frequent baskets from Oakland. Lee was more than content. He had what he most desired—quiet and an opportunity to rest. For a while he travelled nowhere except to church. Then he began to ride about the neighborhood. One of his first visits was to Palmore's store, where he discussed crops with the owner. Turning at last, he found that virtually the whole countryside had flocked into the place to see him and to hear him talk. He apologized with dignity, when he saw the crowd, for having kept Mr. Palmore from waiting on his "numerous customers." [72] Ere long, he went to

---

[68] *R. E. Lee, Jr.*, 171, quoting Captain E. R. Cocke.

[69] While he was there, Mrs. Preston's butler entered the dining room, where family and guests were seated at a meal. The Negro came to say farewell as he was leaving to try his fortune as a freedman. "I well remember," Mrs. Preston wrote, "the kindness with which the General rose from his seat, and, shaking the old servant cordially by the hand, gave him some good advice and asked Heaven to bless him" (*Mrs. Preston*, 272).

[70] G. M. Graves in *Richmond Times-Dispatch*, Jan. 20, 1907; *Mrs. Preston*, 272.

[71] *Cf.* Mrs. R. E. Lee to Miss Mason [Sept. 14, 1865], quoted in Avary: *Dixie After the War*, 159: "The settlement of Palmore's surrounding us does not suffer us to want for anything their gardens or farms can furnish." Mrs. Lee had Mrs. Spencer Palmore make a new pair of trousers for the General and, when they had been delivered, thriftily sent for the scraps, so that she could patch the garment when it had worn thin (Mrs. R. E. Lee to Mrs. Spencer Palmore, *MS. n.d.*, 1865—*Palmore MSS.*). In acknowledgment of the kindness of the family she gave Miss Willie Hooper Palmore a photograph of herself and one of the General and sent the boys some tracts and religious poems (*Palmore Papers*).

[72] *Mrs. Preston*, 272.

General Cocke's old mansion at Bremo, visited his brother **Carter** Lee, and when he had no mission, rode his gray daily for exercise.[73] The only one of his military family whom he met during these first weeks was Major Giles B. Cooke, who was visiting at Belmead.[74] "We have a quiet time, which is delightful to me," he cheerfully wrote Robert.[75] "Our neighbors are kind," he told Rooney, "and do everything in the world to promote our comfort."[76]

There is no way of measuring the strain on General Lee's nerves and self-control during the weeks before he came to this retreat. He had been upheld not only by the power of his will, but also by his deep spirituality, which seemed, somehow, never to be touched by the emotions of the warrior. Always able to pray for his enemies throughout the war, he could forgive them now. But the calm bearing must have been bought at a heavy price, for there was no stoppage, no check, in the rapid degeneration of heart and arteries that had been going on since the spring of 1863, at least. He aged as much, each year after the war, as he did during any twelve months of the struggle.

His social nature he commanded as usual at Derwent, and he could send cheery messages to Norvell Caskie about the suitors of the neighborhood.[77] He could so exercise his self-mastery that he read nothing about the war and felt no desire to do so. But he was acutely conscious of the sufferings of the Southern people, he agonized over the mistreatment of President Davis, and, willingly or not, he dwelt in memory on the achievements of his soldiers. He reflected, in particular, on the odds they had faced, of men and material, and he felt impelled to set before the world the truth about the scanty numbers of those who had been proud to style themselves "Lee's Miserables." Although he urged his principal

---

[73] *R. E. Lee, Jr.,* 174, 175, 176, 177.
[74] G. B. Cooke: *Just Before and After Lee Surrendered to Grant,* 7.
[75] *R. E. Lee, Jr.,* 177.   [76] *R. E. Lee, Jr.,* 178.
[77] "Tell [Miss Norvell] that Miss Anna Logan was driven ovei here yesterday in a buggy by Captain Owens of Louis'—I fear these Louisianians think our Virginia girls belong to them. I met Capt. Bridges at Belmead the other day, where he had been refreshing himself since the war. None of them shall bear her off, I assure her" (R. E. Lee to James H. Caskie, *MS.,* July 29, 1865. *Caskie MSS.*). In this letter Lee asked Caskie to transfer to his nephew, Louis H. Marshall, certain stock in the Bank of Virginia and in the Farmers' Bank that Lee had held as trustee for his sister, Mrs. Wm. L. Marshall, of Baltimore. Mrs. Marshall had died without a will but she had always told General Lee she wished the stock to go to her only child, and Judge Marshall, her husband, had acquiesced in this.

lieutenants to write their memoirs,[78] he was not interested in pondering his own mistakes or in reviewing the strategy of his opponents. Seemingly he held no military post mortems. His one thought was of the men who had fought under him, and his sole purpose in planning a history of his campaigns was that their "bravery and devotion" might "be correctly transmitted to posterity." Said he: "This is the only tribute that can now be paid to the worth of [the army's] noble officers and soldiers." He declined, however, to make the book a commercial undertaking and rejected proposals to that end.[79]

His materials for the history were meagre. He had copies of his reports through the Gettysburg campaign, but most of the later reports, along with much correspondence and other documents, had been burned by headquarters' clerks, it will be recalled, on the retreat from Petersburg. The archives of the Confederate War Department had of course been seized. His one hope was that he could recover from other sources something of what had been lost. On July 31, in a circular letter to a number of his general officers, he set forth his purpose to record the story of his men's valor, and asked for any reports, orders, or returns his comrades might have or might be able to procure for him.[80] The subject continued to be a theme of considerable correspondence during the months that followed. He was not moved to undertake early composition of the book and may even have been deterred by the later remark of his brother Carter that "everybody says the copyright of Lee's History of the War would bring $100,000." [81] To make money by capitalizing the story of American strife would have seemed monstrous to him.

This work apart, the contention that was rising again as ominously as in 1861 he desired to avoid. He had hoped in the year of secession that he would not be compelled to share in the strife that was then in the making. Equally was he anxious now to live a retired life. But just as there had been brought to Arlington Judge Robertson's message from Governor Letcher that had

---

[78] Cf. Lee to Longstreet, March 9, 1866. 5 S. H. S. P., 268.

[79] Jones, 180, 221. Cf. R. E. Lee to J. A. Early, Nov. 22, 1865, ibid., 181. Cf. Markie Letters, 66.

[80] Letter in Jones, 180. He wrote a special letter to Walter H. Taylor, who had handled the returns of the army. Taylor's General Lee, 309. Cf. Irvine Walker, 199.

[81] Quoted in Winston, 367.

thrown him into the struggle for Southern independence, so now one day in August there came up the road to Derwent, unannounced and unexpected, a tall and bulky gentleman with another summons to service for Virginia and the South.

7ª Apl '65

Genl
I have rec'd your note of this date. Though not entertaining the opinion you express of the hopelessness of further resistance on the part of the Army of N. Va — I reciprocate your desire to avoid useless effusion of blood, & therefore before Considering your proposition ask the terms you will offer on Condition of its Surrender.

Very respy your Obdt

R E Lee
Genl

Lt Genl U. S. Grant —
Commdg Armies of the U States

LEE'S FIRST NOTE ON THE SURRENDER

This note, dated April 7, 1865, was written by General Lee in response to one addressed him on the same day from Farmville, by General Grant, who stated that further Confederate resistance was hopeless and that he desired to shift from himself "the responsibility of any further effusion of blood, by asking . . . the surrender" of the Army of Northern Virginia. Lee personally wrote the answer so that the news of negotiations for surrender might not become known to the troops.

After the original in the U. S. War Department.

THE McLEAN HOUSE AT APPOMATTOX COURTHOUSE, WHERE, ON APRIL 9, 1865, THE ARMY OF NORTHERN VIRGINIA WAS SURRENDERED

After a photograph made the same month.

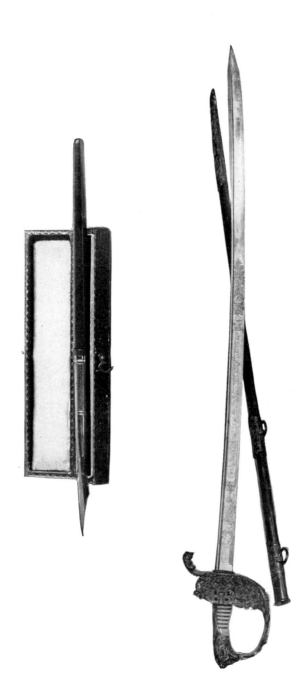

THE PEN WITH WHICH THE SURRENDER OF THE ARMY OF NORTHERN VIRGINIA WAS SIGNED, AND THE SWORD GENERAL LEE WORE AT THE TIME

The pen is the property of Sydney Smith Lee, and the sword belongs to Mrs. Hunter DeButts and Mrs. Hanson Ely, daughters of Captain R. E. Lee. Both pen and sword are in the Confederate Museum, Richmond.

We, the undersigned Prisoners of War, belonging to the Army of Northern Virginia, having been this day surrendered by General Robert E. Lee, C. S. A., Commanding said Army, to Lieut. Genl. U. S. Grant, Commanding Armies of United States, do hereby give our solemn parole of honor that we will not hereafter serve in the armies of the Confederate States, or in any military capacity whatever, against the United States of America, or render aid to the enemies of the latter, until properly exchanged, in such manner as shall be mutually approved by the respective authorities.

Done at Appomattox Court House, Va., this 9th day of April, 1865.

GENERAL LEE'S PAROLE, SIGNED ALSO BY CERTAIN OF HIS STAFF OFFICERS

The fifth name, almost illegible, is that of Colonel Charles Marshall.

After the original in the Confederate Museum, reproduced by permission of its owner, Mrs. Madge Ould Powers, daughter of the late Judge Robert Ould.

LEE BEFORE THE FIRE OF BATTLE HAD FADED FROM HIS EYES

A photograph taken by Brady in rear of the Lee House, Richmond, a few days after the General's return from Appomattox. The officers with him are (left) General Custis Lee and (right) Colonel Walter Taylor.

PAMPATIKE, RESIDENCE OF COLONEL THOMAS H. CARTER, KING WILLIAM COUNTY, VIRGINIA, THE FIRST HOME VISITED BY GENERAL LEE, BEYOND THE CONFINES OF RICHMOND, AFTER HIS RETURN FROM APPOMATTOX

It probably was at Pampatike that Lee decided to apply for the return of civil rights under the first amnesty proclamation.

After a photograph reproduced by courtesy of Spencer L. Carter of Richmond.

DERWENT, THE COTTAGE IN CUMBERLAND COUNTY, VIRGINIA, LENT TO GENERAL LEE IN JUNE, 1865, BY MRS. ELIZABETH RANDOLPH COCKE OF OAKLAND

This humble place was the home of the Lee family in the summer of 1865.

THE "OLD" PRESIDENT'S HOUSE AT WASHINGTON COLLEGE, OCCUPIED BY GENERAL LEE AND HIS FAMILY FROM DECEMBER 2, 1865, TO APPROXIMATELY THE END OF MAY, 1869

"Stonewall" Jackson, whose first wife had been a daughter of President Junkin of Washington College, had at one time resided here.

THE "NEW" PRESIDENT'S HOUSE AT WASHINGTON COLLEGE, OCCUPIED BY GENERAL LEE DURING THE LAST SIXTEEN MONTHS OF HIS LIFE

Some of the older trees around the house were planted by him.

LEE—THE LAST PHASE

One of the last photographs of General Lee, taken in Lexington in 1870.

GENERAL LEE'S OFFICE IN THE BASEMENT OF THE CHAPEL AT WASHINGTON COLLEGE

The room remains today precisely as it was when he left it on the afternoon before his last illness began, September 28, 1870.

VIEW FROM THE PARLOR OF THE "NEW" PRESIDENT'S HOUSE INTO THE DINING-ROOM WHERE GENERAL LEE DIED

This picture, taken at Washington College during the presidency of General Custis Lee, shows the house more elaborately furnished than during the lifetime of his father.

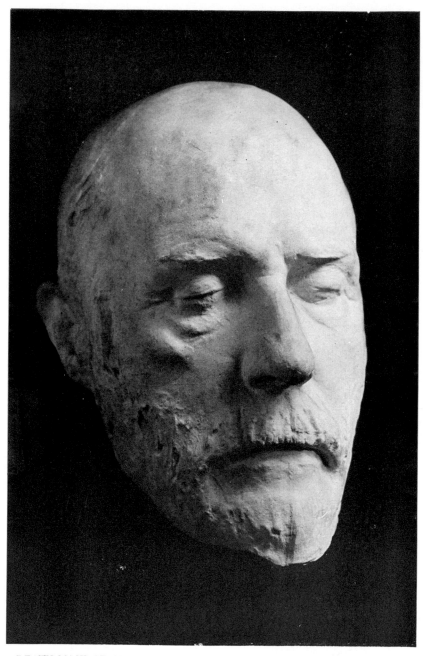

DEATH MASK OF GENERAL LEE, TAKEN AT LEXINGTON, OCTOBER, 1870
After a plaster cast in the Confederate Museum, Richmond.

THE CHAPEL AND CAMPUS OF WASHINGTON COLLEGE DURING THE FUNERAL OF GENERAL LEE, OCTOBER 15, 1870

The men in uniform are the cadets of the Virginia Military Institute.

THE RECUMBENT STATUE OF LEE IN THE CHAPEL OF WASHINGTON AND LEE UNIVERSITY

The artist was the late Edward V. Valentine, who had taken measurements and had modeled a bust of Lee during the lifetime of the General.

CHAPTER XIII

A Third Decision

THE visitor proved to be John W. Brockenbrough, rector of Washington College, Lexington, Va., and teacher of a private school of law in that town. To the complete surprise of General Lee, who had not been approached in any way, he stated that on August 4 the trustees of Washington College had unanimously elected the General president of the institution, and wished to know if he would accept. Judge Brockenbrough presented a letter from the committee of the board in which the invitation was extended formally. The salary was to be $1500 per annum, plus a house and garden and one-fifth of the tuition fees of the students, which were raised to $75 each. It was customary for the president, in return for this compensation, not only to administer the affairs of the college but also to teach philosophy.[1]

The conversation between General Lee and Judge Brockenbrough unfortunately was not reported by either of them. There is no way of telling to what extent General Lee familiarized himself with the extreme poverty and distressful outlook of the college. All that is known is that when the judge started back to Lexington he had the General's promise to consider the call.[2] Lee had never contemplated accepting a college presidency, though General Scott before the war had observed how well suited Lee was for such a post.[3] As he canvassed the idea, however, it seemed

---

[1] Judge Brockenbrough brought a letter from John Letcher, in which the former governor said: "The salary now increased to $1,500 and fees, will provide the means of support in a country like this, where everything is usually abundant and easily to be obtained."—*Statement of H. D. Campbell.* See *Riley,* 4, 23; *R. E. Lee, Jr.,* 179; MS. *Minutes of the Trustees of Washington College* (cited hereafter as *Trustees' Minutes*), Aug. 3–4, 1865; J. W. Brockenbrough *et al.* to Robert E. Lee, MS., Aug. 5, 1865, *Archives of Washington and Lee University,* made available through the kindness of Doctor H. D. Campbell, former dean and later historian of that institution. For copies of the *Trustees' Minutes* and of General Lee's *Letter Books* while president of Washington College, the writer is indebted to Doctor William Moseley Brown, as is set forth in more detail in the appendix of acknowledgments.

[2] *Riley,* 4.   [3] E. C. Gordon, in *Riley,* 75.

to Lee that the summons was providential, in that it both offered him a livelihood and an opportunity of service to his people.[4] The spiritual aspect of the work appealed to him strongly. In a time of heightened passions and lowered morals, he was being asked to take part in training the youth of the South, his former soldiers and their sons and younger brothers. The labor was one for religion and for the country, but was he qualified for it? He had never taught since he had been a cadet-assistant at West Point, and he did not feel that he had strength for conducting classes in addition to discharging executive duties. If it could be arranged that he had no instruction to do, was he competent to be president?

There were other considerations, also. Should he assume the direction of a college that was Presbyterian in fact, regardless of its name and charter? And what of the hostility that would be aroused against the college because of him? He was excepted from the President's amnesty and was a prisoner on parole. The North hated him, he felt, and looked on him as a traitor and a rebel. Would the college suffer by reason of his connection with it? Would animosity toward him be visited on it? These were the questions he argued with himself after Judge Brockenbrough's visit.

While he was debating, he received a letter from his old chief of artillery, Brigadier General W. N. Pendleton, who was rector of the Episcopal church in Lexington. Pendleton urged General Lee's acceptance and assured him that the institution thereafter would be wholly undenominational. That removed one obstacle. "If I thought I could be of any benefit to our noble youth I would not hesitate to give my services," Lee told General Pendleton.[5]

Before he decided finally, Lee rode to Albemarle County to consult his old friend Reverend Joseph P. B. Wilmer, an Episcopal clergyman whose judgment he much respected. When he told him of the invitation, the General found the cleric distressed to think that a man of Lee's achievements and ability was willing to consider the presidency of a small, wholly inconspicuous college. If Lee inclined to educational work, there were other institutions

---

[4] *Cf.* Mrs. Lee to Miss Mason [Sept. 14, 1865]: "I do not think he is very fond of teaching, but he is willing to do anything that will give him an honorable support" (Avary: *Dixie After the War*, 159).

[5] *Riley*, 5 n.; *Jones*, 146.

of greater fame and standing, Wilmer argued, any one of which would be glad to have him as its head. Lee brushed this objection aside; the cause gave dignity to the institution. It seemed that Providence had opened this, and not another, door to him. Was he competent to undertake the work? That was what he wanted to know. If he was, he would assume the task in the hope that what was left of his life would be a blessing to others and to the South. Mr. Wilmer's chagrin faded away at Lee's avowal. He reassured the General and congratulated him on feeling disposed to give his life and testimony to the cause of education. Wilmer fell to talking, then, about Christian influence in education, and Lee responded with much feeling—with eloquence, Wilmer later affirmed.[6] Perhaps, in his conversation with Mr. Wilmer, the General renewed the arguments he had advanced to Captain Scheibert that day at Chancellorsville when, as battle approached its furious climax, Lee had discussed with the German observer the future of education in the South. Perhaps, too, in brushing aside quickly the suggestion that he might find a more exalted academic office, Lee was influenced by the fact that the college to which he had been called bore the name of Washington, and had received from his model and hero a part of its early endowment.

It must have been very soon after this conversation that General Lee wrote his conditional acceptance in this letter:[7]

Powhatan County, August 24, 1865.

Gentlemen: I have delayed for some days replying to your letter of the 5th inst. informing me of my election by the Board of Trustees to the Presidency of Washington College, from a desire to give the subject due consideration. Fully impressed with the responsibilities of the office, I have feared that I should be unable to discharge its duties to the satisfaction of the trustees or to the benefit of the Country. The proper education of youth requires not only great ability, but I fear more strength than I now possess, for I do not feel able to undergo the labour of conducting classes

[6] Wilmer's familiar account (*Riley*, 9; *R. E. Lee, Jr.*, 182, and in many other places) was first given in an address delivered at Sewanee, October, 1870, when a memorial service for General Lee was held. Reverend J. P. B. Wilmer, who was named Protestant Episcopal Bishop of Louisiana in 1866, is not to be confused with his first cousin, Right Reverend Richard H. Wilmer, Protestant Episcopal Bishop of Alabama.
[7] Facsimile in *Riley*, 8.

in regular courses of instruction. I could not, therefore, undertake more than the general administration and supervision of the institution. There is another subject which has caused me serious reflection, and is, I think, worthy of the consideration of the Board. Being excluded from the terms of amnesty in the proclamation of the President of the U. S., of the 29th May last, and an object of censure to a portion of the Country, I have thought it probable that my occupation of the position of President might draw upon the College a feeling of hostility; and I should, therefore, cause injury to an Institution which it would be my highest desire to advance. I think it the duty of every citizen, in the present condition of the Country, to do all in his power to aid in the restoration of peace and harmony, and in no way to oppose the policy of the State or General Government directed to that object. It is particularly incumbent on those charged with the instruction of the young to set them an example of submission to authority, and I could not consent to be the cause of animadversion upon the College.

Should you, however, take a different view, and think that my services in the position tendered to me by the Board will be advantageous to the College and Country, I will yield to your judgment and accept it; otherwise, I must most respectfully decline the office.

Begging you to express to the trustees of the College my heartfelt gratitude for the honour conferred upon me, and requesting you to accept my cordial thanks for the kind manner in which you have communicated their decision,

I am, gentlemen, with great respect,

Your most obt servt.,

R. E. LEE.

Messrs. John W. Brockenbourgh [sic], Rector, S. McD. Reid, Alfred Leyburn, Horatio Thompson, D.D., Bolivar Christian, T. J. Kirkpatrick, Committee.

As the trustees promptly relieved General Lee of all instructional duty, and expressed their agreement with his views, the question of his future work was quickly settled.[8] The effect on

[8] *Trustees' Minutes,* Aug. 31, 1865.

Lee was immediate. Idleness and uncertainty were at an end. He had a task and he would discharge it. In his correspondence he began to set even more vigorously than before the example he thought the South required. He may have been prompted also to a more positive course because he saw the gloomy portents of the troubled times. A reaction was under way in the country. The North, being misled by partisans, was turning towards a policy of repression and revenge, of treason trials and of Negro rule. By this, the South was stirred to a bitterness worse than that of war. More men were talking of emigrating. Others were hopeless, and still others were affirming they would never take the oath of allegiance to the United States.

Were these feelings to continue, the future was dark, indeed. Were they allayed, and unity and good-will substituted for them, prosperity and happiness would come again to the South. So General Lee reasoned. He still believed that public activity on his part, which was in itself distasteful to him, might react against the cause he wished to aid. "I am unfortunately so situated," he often said, "that I can do no good; and as I am anxious to do as little harm as possible, I deem it wisest for me to keep silent." [9] Especially as the head of a college, he should avoid controversy and submit to constituted authority. But in the distress of the day he saw his duty. This much he could and should do: on all those who asked his counsel, in person or by letter, he would continue to urge patience in repression, diligence in adversity, justice in judgment, and courageous acceptance of the consequences of war. To this he turned himself more fully. Lee the warrior became Lee the conciliator. Within less than five months from the time he had said he would rather die a thousand deaths than go to General Grant, he was telling Southern men to abandon all opposition, to regard the United States as their country, and to labor for harmony and better understanding. Seldom had a famous man so completely reversed himself in so brief a time, and never more sincerely. In the stormiest of the days that followed he was not to shift a foot. The stern asperities of congressional reconstruction might cause him to fear that reconciliation would be long delayed, but they were not to make him despair. "I look forward to better

[9] *Jones,* 199.

days, and trust that time and experience, the great teachers of men, under the guidance of an ever-merciful God, may save us from destruction, and restore to us the bright hopes and prospects of the past" [10]—that was the foundation of all his political faith during the reconstruction, and it was a foundation that stood. From quiet Derwent, as soon as he had decided conditionally to take the presidency of the college, letters went out in answer to one and another of his old associates who sought his advice. In these letters Lee's state of mind is mirrored. "It should be the object of all," he wrote in declining to contribute to a magazine that A. M. Keiley was planning to publish in the interest of better relations between North and South, "to avoid controversy, to allay passion, give full scope to reason and every kindly feeling. By doing this and encouraging our citizens to engage in the duties of life with all their heart and mind, with a determination not to be turned aside by thoughts of the past and fears of the future, our country will not only be restored in material prosperity, but will be advanced in science, in virtue and in religion." [11]

More in detail he wrote former Governor Letcher:

"The questions which for years were in dispute between the State and General Government, and which unhappily were not decided by the dictates of reason, but referred to the decision of war, having been decided against us, it is the part of wisdom to acquiesce in the result, and of candor to recognize the fact.

"The interests of the State are therefore the same as those of the United States. Its prosperity will rise or fall with the welfare of the country. The duty of its citizens, then, appears to me too plain to admit of doubt. All should unite in honest efforts to obliterate the effects of war, and to restore the blessings of peace. They should remain, if possible, in the country; promote harmony and good feeling; qualify themselves to vote; and elect to the State and general Legislatures wise and patriotic men, who will devote their abilities to the interests of the country, and the healing of all dissensions. I have invariably recommended this course since the cessation of hostilities, and have endeavored to practice it myself." [12]

[10] R. E. Lee to M. F. Maury, Sept. 8, 1865; *Jones*, 206.
[11] R. E. Lee to A. M. Keiley, Sept. 4, 1865; *Jones*, 204.
[12] R. E. Lee to John Letcher, Aug. 28, 1865; *Jones*, 202.

Captain Josiah Tatnall of the Confederate navy, who wrote him about taking the oath, and of the possible bad effects of such action on Mr. Davis's defense against the charge of treason, was sent a copy of Lee's application for pardon, a statement of Lee's reasons for filing it, and a few words about the future: "The war being at an end, the Southern States having laid down their arms, and the questions at issue between them and the Northern States having been decided, I believe it to be the duty of every one to unite in the restoration of the country, and the reestablishment of peace and harmony. . . . It appears to me that the allayment of passion, the dissipation of prejudice, and the restoration of reason, will alone enable the people of the country to acquire a true knowledge and form a correct judgment of the events of the past four years. . . . I have too exalted an opinion of the American people to believe that they will consent to injustice; and it is only necessary, in my opinion, that truth should be known, for the rights of every one to be secured." [13]

The optimism of the concluding sentence of this message to Tatnall appeared in many of his messages to discouraged Confederates. These letters were not meant for the newspapers and were not published, but copies were passed from hand to hand, no doubt, and the sentiments of General Lee became well known. Necessity forced Southern men to set their jaws and to strengthen their hearts for the black vigil of reconstruction; General Lee's example made it easier to do so. General Wise had said, on the retreat to Appomattox, that General Lee was the Confederacy in the eyes of his army: Lee's advice now became the law of public conduct for men of moderate mind in the South. They were the quicker, also, to enter upon hard, unremunerative employment, when they heard that he had accepted, at a salary of $1500 per annum, the presidency of a small college.

The South was inspired by his choice, and so were the men who had elected him.[14] They had acted in the first instance on a remark attributed to one of General Lee's daughters, Mary—that the people of the South were willing to give her father everything he might need but that no offer had been made of any position in which he could earn a living for himself and his family.[15] After

13 R. E. Lee to Josiah Tatnall, Sept. 7, 1865; *Jones*, 205–6.
14 Professor E. S. Joynes, in *R. E. Lee, Jr.*, 180.   15 *Mrs. Preston*, 272.

they had voted unanimously on August 5 to offer the presidency to General Lee, they had sat for a few minutes as if stunned by their own temerity.[16] Now that they had his acceptance, they prepared to work with him and to raise funds for the restoration of the college.

At the same time they may well have felt that their new president was out of scale with their institution. Washington College at that time was a name, a site, a small body of faithful men, and little besides. Established in 1749, at Greenville, Augusta County, as the Augusta Academy, it had been the pioneer classical school in the Valley of Virginia. At the first meeting of the trustees after the battle of Lexington,[17] the name of the institution was changed to Liberty Hall. Its principal at that time was William Graham, who had been a Princeton classmate and friend of Henry Lee's, soon thereafter distinguished as "Light-Horse Harry."

Under Graham and his early successors, several changes in the site of Liberty Hall were made, and its fortunes varied with the times, but it enjoyed the support and patronage of the Presbyterian Church in the Shenandoah Valley and thereby was kept alive through the Revolution. In 1796, on representation by the trustees, George Washington gave the school the hundred shares of stock in the James River Company which the general assembly of Virginia had voted him. In gratitude, the trustees thereupon resolved to call the institution Washington Academy.[18] Following a fire in 1802, it was moved to Lexington, and on January 2, 1813, it was chartered as Washington College. Built on the old frontier, the college always looked westward and trained many youths from Tennessee and Kentucky, though most of its students came from the Valley of Virginia. On April 18, 1861, the day following the secession of Virginia, the Unionist president of the college, Doctor George Junkin, tendered his resignation.[19] Before his successor could be chosen, the war broke out. The students of 1861 volunteered as a unit, joined Jackson at Winchester, and fought through the war, many of them in the Stonewall brigade. The plant of the

---

[16] *Riley*, 1–3. [17] May 13, 1776.

[18] "The name Washington Academy appears for the first time in the Trustees' Minutes, March 9, 1798, but the General Assembly of Virginia on Jan. 19, 1798, changed the name from Liberty Hall Academy to Washington Academy."—*Statement of Doctor H. D. Campbell.*

[19] Doctor Junkin died in Philadelphia, May 20, 1868.

school suffered in the struggles. When David Hunter's raiders reached Lexington in 1864, they looted Washington College and burned the Virginia Military Institute, where Jackson had taught. The college library was scattered past recovery. Even the books of the literary societies did not escape. The laboratory equipment was broken up or carried away. During the last winter of the war, though the professors remained at their posts and taught the forty-five students who offered, chiefly in the preparatory department, the work of the institution was virtually suspended.[20] The end of the war found the buildings in such disrepair that some of them were scarcely habitable. Others were commandeered and used by the Federal garrison of the town.[21] Part of the campus was under cultivation.[22] In the summer of 1865 so dire was the plight of the college that the faculty, which consisted of four professors, was authorized to borrow money to repair the buildings. The trustees undertook to see that a sufficient number of rooms to house prospective students were put in order.[23] Even after these efforts, it was necessary to negotiate a loan of $5000 with which to meet salaries, buy apparatus, and pay interest on previous indebtedness.[24] The institution, in a word, was as nearly dead as it could be, without causing its supporters to abandon it altogether.

Prospects for attendance in the fall of 1865 were as gloomy as for everything else. Few had the money to pay for college training and some of those who had the means had been touched by the turbulence of the times and had no desire to settle down to the quiet of academic life.[25] But with Lee as their leader, the trustees were willing to carry on. Following the meeting of

[20] Faculty report, June 20, 1865, quoted by *Riley*. The early history of the college and the roster of the alumni were published as *Catalogue of the Alumni of Washington College, Virginia, for the Year 1869*. For conditions generally at the college, see *R. E. Lee, Jr.*, 180; *Riley*, 38–39; *Jones*, 80–81.

[21] *Trustees' Minutes*, Aug. 3–4, 1865.

[22] *Trustees' Minutes*, Aug. 4, 1865.   [23] *Trustees' Minutes*, June 21, 1865.

[24] *Trustees' Minutes*, Aug. 4, 1865. This poverty was not shaken off quickly. As late as February, 1866, when place had to be provided for the geological specimens, the faculty had to make the erection of the necessary shelves conditional on the carpenter's willingness to wait seven months for his money (*Riley*, 7 n.). In April, 1866, the water rent of the college for 1863 and 1864 was still unpaid (*Trustees' Minutes*, April 26, 1866).

[25] *Cf. Jones*, 95, quoting Doctor J. L. Kirkpatrick. Besides the regular fee of $75 (*Trustees' Minutes*, Aug. 4, 1865) every student was charged $10 for each modern language. This included lodging but not board. Indigent, worthy students, unable to pay these fees, could give bond that they would do so (*ibid.*).

August 31 the rector issued a public announcement that the General would be president of the college. This read as follows:

"The gratifying duty of announcing to the country the acceptance by Gen. Robert E. Lee of the Presidency of Washington College has been devolved upon the undersigned by the Board of Trustees of that institution. The accession of this distinguished gentleman to the faculty of this venerable college, and as its honored chief, is destined, we trust, to mark the commencement of a new era in its history, and most cordially do we congratulate its numerous friends on this most auspicious event. The high, noble and patriotic motives which impelled our beloved chief, in accepting the honorable, but comparatively humble, position tendered to him by the authorities of the college, must win for him a new title to the admiration and love of his countrymen. The college, under the administration and supervision of Gen. Lee will resume its exercises on the 14th inst.

"At a meeting of the Board of Trustees of the college, convened at Lexington on Thursday, the 31st ult., the following resolution was unanimously passed, the publication of which is demanded, as an act of justice alike to Gen. Lee and themselves:

"*Resolved,* That the board heartily concurs in and fully indorses, the sentiments so well expressed by Gen. Lee in his letter of acceptance of the Presidency of Washington College, that 'it is the duty of every citizen, in the present condition of the country, to do all in his power to aid in the restoration of peace and harmony, and in no way to oppose the policy of the State or General Government directed to that object'; and that 'it is particularly incumbent on those charged with the instruction of the young to set an example of submission to authority'; sentiments that cannot fail to commend themselves to the approval of the President of the United States, and to the unqualified assent of all sensible and virtuous citizens.

"In dedicating his future life to the holy work of educating the youth of his country, Gen. Lee presents a new and interesting phase of his grand and heroic character—a character than which no more perfect model exists among living men. ' 'Tis a solid fabric, and will well support the laurels that adorn it.' Let the young men of the country, North as well as South, be wise, and profit not less by his precepts than by his great example.

JOHN W. BROCKENBROUGH,

Rector of Washington College.

"Lexington, Va., Sept. 1, 1865." [26]

This document was widely printed. Despite its moderate tone, it aroused the antagonism of some rabid individuals who thought President Johnson should forbid Lee's acceptance of the office.[27] Little of this comment, however, found its way into the press. Apparently the country did not realize the significance of what General Lee had done. It seemed to most editors, from their silence, that the former Confederate general-in-chief simply had "found a position."

[26] *New York Times,* Sept. 7, 1865, quoting *The Lexington Gazette Special.*

[27] *Cf.* Bright to Sumner, Oct. 20, 1865: "Now nobody is punished. Lee is allowed to become Principal of a College to teach loyalty to your young men, and I suppose bye and bye Davis will be free" (*Proc. Mass. Hist. Soc.,* 1912, p. 145). *Cf.* also "M. Le B." to President Johnson: "Aren't you ashamed to give Lee the privilege of being a President of a college? Satan wouldn't have him to open the door for fresh arrivals . . ." (Fleming: *Documentary History of Reconstruction,* 34).

CHAPTER XIV

The Road from Appomattox to Lexington

On September 15, 1865, General Lee started for Lexington on Traveller.[1] He sent his baggage up the canal and went alone, for it was not yet certain what accommodations could be found for Mrs. Lee and his daughters.

It was a departure that symbolized not for himself only but likewise for the entire South a turning from war and politics to peace and education. Yet he took "the road from Appomattox to Lexington"[2] as unostentatiously as if he had been the humblest dominie of the countryside, bound for a backwoods school. He rode slowly, for the way was long and the weather was hot. Early in the afternoon he stopped at the house of a friend and remained there overnight. The next day, the temperature still oppressive, he kept the same schedule. On the third afternoon, he reached the crest of the Blue Ridge, beyond which lay his future home.[3] As he looked over into the Valley, was he thinking of Jackson and of Thoroughfare Gap, of Sharpsburg and of Harpers Ferry . . . or

[1] *Cf.* Mrs. Lee to Miss Mason [Sept. 14, 1865]: "He starts tomorrow *en cheval* for Lexington. He prefers that way, and, besides, does not like to part even for a time from his beloved steed, the companion of many a hard-fought battle" (Avary: *Dixie After the War*, 159).

[2] This phrase originated, as far as the writer knows, with Professor S. C. Mitchell of the University of Richmond.

[3] General Lee's stopping places on the journey to Lexington cannot be established in order. Inquiry generously made by G. M. Dillard and by Jackson Beal of Scottsville, Va., make it reasonably certain that he spent one night at Stony Point, the home of the Reverend Philip Slaughter. There is also a tradition in Albemarle that he stayed at Plain Dealing, the home of Bishop Wilmer, but this tradition probably confuses his visit to Wilmer in August with his ride to Lexington in September. In 3 *Confederate Veteran*, 321, the statement is made that he came one evening on his journey to a house from which the master was absent. Without introducing himself, he asked if he might spend the night there. The mistress of the home hospitably agreed and made her unknown guest welcome. When the farmer returned, he was delighted to recognize the General. This probably occurred on the evening when Lee was near the crest of the Blue Ridge, as it is stated that Lee had previously sought shelter at several other places where hospitality had been declined. This could hardly have happened on any of the larger estates east of the mountains, where he would almost certainly have been known and welcomed.

of the college up among the hills, and of a peaceful union of all the states that religion and education would insure against a renewal of war? None can answer, but as he had put all his self-discipline into a determination to close his mind to the irrevocable past, is it not probable that his thought was of the future?

At 3 P.M. on September 18 as quietly as he had left Derwent, General Lee rode into Lexington and ended his journey of 108 miles. Astride Traveller, he was dressed in a uniform of gray, from which all the insignia and the Confederate buttons had been submissively removed as the Federals had commanded.[4] No escort or companion attended him. He had been invited to be the guest of Colonel S. McD. Reid, senior member of the board of trustees, but as his host was not looking for him until the next day, he rode on toward the town inn, intending to lodge there that night. People at once recognized him. In answer to their salutations, he bowed and took off his hat.[5] Some of his former soldiers were loitering in the street—they were to be found everywhere then—and when they saw their old commander approach the hotel, they came up to assist him in dismounting. Professor James J. White, Reid's son-in-law and a member of the college faculty, happened to turn into the street at the moment and realized that the man on the gray charger must be General Lee. Hurrying forward, he introduced himself and insisted that the General go with him to Colonel Reid's, where everything was ready for him. Lee acquiesced and went off with Professor White—Captain White, as he always called him, for White had borne that title in Confederate service. Lee quickly "broke the ice" by his attention to the children of the household[6] and he spent the afternoon and evening socially. The next morning he arose early, wrote a letter to Mrs.

---

[4] Mrs. Preston (*loc. cit.*, 272–73) stated on the authority of Professor J. J. White that Lee was dressed in white linens, but this account is second-hand. In her reminiscences, Mrs. Angus McDonald, who saw General Lee as he passed her door, affirmed that he wore gray, which would seem more appropriate for a dusty journey. Mrs. McDonald's recollections, which are a prime historical source for many incidents of Lee's residence in Lexington, were published in part in *General Lee After Appomattox*, by Hunter McDonald. His article appeared originally in 9 *Tenn. Hist. Mag.*, 87–101, and was reprinted as a pamphlet, cited hereafter as *McDonald*. References are to the pagination of the reprint, not of the original publication. Mention of General Lee's appearance on his arrival is in *McDonald*, 5.

[5] *McDonald*, 5.

[6] So observed Reverend H. M. Field, a guest in the house at the time, quoted in *R. E. Lee*, 423.

Lee before breakfast, and soon was ready to inspect the college he was to direct. He had never before seen it.[7]

The trustees met on September 20, the second day after General Lee's arrival, with a much larger attendance than usual. A committee was at once appointed to wait on the General and to escort him to the meeting place. On his arrival he was welcomed by the rector and was introduced to the members. After he retired, the trustees discussed a number of measures for his comfort. The president's residence on the campus was occupied in part by a physician of the town, Doctor R. L. Madison, about whose lease there was some contention. One committee was designated to proceed for the recovery of the property, and another was authorized to put the house in habitable condition. The treasurer was instructed to pay immediately to the president one-half of his salary of $1500 that was not due until January. Still other committeemen were to confer with him and to arrange the details of his inauguration. Resolutions were presented for making a public appeal to procure a sufficient endowment to assure the president's salary, regardless of contingency.[8] These acts exhibited the trustees' sense of obligation to General Lee. They felt that they owed him the best they could give him because he had been willing to take the presidency, but they felt, at the same time, that they were acting for the whole South in doing him honor. They never relaxed in their consideration for him. Their first concern, after the welfare of the institution, always was for his happiness. The minutes of the board are a continuing record of unremitting kindness.

Use of the president's house could not be regained immediately, and the premises had to be repaired when vacated. Lee did not wish to impose on the hospitality of the Reids, meantime. He was suffering, too, from rheumatism, and he did not like to stir about the town because, when he had ridden quietly down Main Street, a few days after his arrival, the citizens had cheered him loudly. Every impulse prompted him to avoid a repetition of this.[9] So, these circumstances all combining and the opening of the college having been postponed in order to give the carpenters

[7] The details of the journey to Lexington are given in this letter to Mrs. Lee, Sept. 19, 1865; *R. E. Lee, Jr.*, 184.
[8] *Trustees' Minutes*, Sept. 20-21, 1865.   [9] *Riley*, 67; 3 *Confederate Veteran*, 321.

228

more time, the General decided to spend a few days at the Rockbridge Baths, a resort eleven miles from Lexington.

He found there Mrs. Chapman Leigh and Miss Belle Harrison, of Brandon, two of his cousins of whom he was very fond. He played with Mrs. Leigh's children, enjoyed the company of the young women and went on several rides with them. Daily he took the baths, which he found delightful, but he wrote Mrs. Lee: "I feel very solitary and miss you dreadfully."[10] Mrs. Leigh and Miss Harrison were his only companions. "I could not trespass on them always," he confided to his wife.[11] He must have had evenings of solitude when he had to muster all his self-control "not to be turned aside by thoughts of the past and fears of the future."[12]

Returning to Lexington on September 30, and taking lodgings at the hotel, General Lee was ready for his inauguration. Of this event, arranged for October 2, the trustees had planned to make a great occasion, by which the college and General Lee's connection with it would be advertised to the country. But the General did not desire the ceremonies to be elaborate, and out of deference to his wishes, unpretentious exercises were held. Faculty, guests, and students assembled a little before 9 A.M. in the physics classroom, on the second floor of the college building next the south dormitory.[13] On the hour, the trustees entered with the General. The little company of spectators rose for a moment. Prayer was offered by Reverend W. S. White, the oldest minister of the city, who did not omit to invoke divine guidance for the President of the United States. Then Judge Brockenbrough spoke briefly on the satisfaction of the college at the acceptance of General Lee, whom he eulogized in a few words. Much more he could say, the judge went on, had it not been decided there would be no speech-making. He concluded by calling on a justice of the peace to administer the presidential oath to Lee. The General, who was dressed in gray, had been standing meantime with folded arms, looking at Judge Brockenbrough. Silently he now attached his name to the oath, which had come down from the early days of the school in this odd language: "I do swear that I will, to the best of my skill and judgment, faithfully and truly discharge the duties

[10] R. E. Lee to Mrs Lee Sept. 25, 1865, *R. E. Lee, Jr.,* 185–86.
[11] R. E. Lee to Mrs. Lee, Oct 3, 1865, *R. E. Lee, Jr.,* 188.
[12] See *supra,* p. 220. [13] F. A. Berlin, in *Riley,* 42.

required of me by an act entitled, 'An act for incorporating the rector and trustees of Liberty Hall Academy,' without favor, affection or partiality." The signed document was forthwith committed to the waiting county clerk to be made a matter of record. This done, Judge Brockenbrough turned over the college keys to General Lee, who said nothing during the short proceedings. A brief handshaking followed, and the General passed with the trustees into his office.[14] This was a nearby room which the ladies of Lexington had furnished for him with "new carpet from Baltimore, curtains, etc.," to use Lee's own vague masculine description.[15]

"I have entered upon the duties of my new office," he wrote, "in the hope of being of some service; but I should prefer, as far as my predilections are concerned to be on a small farm, where I could make my daily bread."[16] He quickly established a routine of duty. Rising early at the Lexington Hotel, where he resided until the arrival of his family, he proceeded afoot to the college. Before 7:45 he was at chapel for the fifteen-minute services, which he invited the ministers of the principal Lexington churches to hold in rotation. If the minister failed to appear, Lee waited until a few minutes to the hour and then quietly got up and went to his office. From 8 until 1 or 2 P.M. he usually worked there,[17] or attended to other labors on the campus. The afternoons were generally given over to social duties or to exercise, chiefly rides out of town on Traveller. Unless there were religious or academic exercises that he felt called upon to attend, he remained in his room at the hotel after supper. He sometimes found the evenings immoderately long, though he usually retired at 10. In his bantering letters to his daughters there was an undertone of the loneliness he always felt when separated from his family.

Having no clerk in his office and very little help on the campus, he was forced to transact in person even the least important matters of college business. To endless, close economies, he was compelled to give direct, continuing attention. On him fell, likewise,

---

[14] *New York Herald,* Oct. 7, 1865, p. 1, col. 5.

[15] R. E. Lee to Mrs. Lee, Oct. 3, 1865; *R. E. Lee, Jr.,* 187.

[16] R. E. Lee to R. H. Chilton, *MS.,* Oct. 6, 1865; *Chilton Papers.*

[17] This schedule was an hour later in December, January, and February (*Jones, 99,* 104, 1?1, 123, 124; Joynes in *Cent. U. S. C.,* 26).

the supervision of all improvements to the grounds and of all repairs to the buildings, which were in dire dilapidation. He regularly visited the classes during recitation, listened for ten or fifteen minutes and then bowed his way out. During examinations he sat for at least an hour with each class of struggling students. Accessible to all callers, he conferred regularly with the professors every week in faculty meetings.

It was vastly different from army days, when he had the indefatigable Taylor and four or five clerks to assist in the "paper work," that was always irksome and occasionally exasperating to him. He probably had not lost his old antipathy for handling documents, but in none of the many accounts of his daily life at Lexington is there so much as a hint that he ever complained. Hard, unpleasant work was part of the burden of the times. He accepted it and simplified it as much as he could by a system of reports, "weekly and monthly—almost military in their exactness —which he required" of every one of the teachers.[18] "When the members of the faculty assembled in his office to lay before him the reports for the week just closed, he was invariably found prepared to receive them, having disposed of all the business which those of the week before had imposed on him, and being now in full and cheerful readiness for any work, though much of it was sheer drudgery, which the new reports might require."[19]

After the faculty came to know him better, some of the members would protest against the amount of work the General performed. The trustees were equally solicitous. He always insisted, in reply, that he owed it to the boys at the most critical time of their lives, and to their parents, also, to give the students the closest care. Besides, he argued, daily administration was required for the success of the discipline he established when he came to the college,[20] discipline that centred around what is now styled the "honor system." So far as is known, General Lee had no plans for enlarging the curriculum when he assumed charge of the college, but his own training, his long experience in construction, his four years of hourly grappling with the harsh realities of war, and his knowledge of the needs of the South, com-

18 Joynes, *Cent. U. S. C.*, 24. 19 J. L. Kirkpatrick in *Jones*, 104.
20 Kirkpatrick, in *Jones*, 104; see *infra*, pp. 278 ff.

bined, very soon, to give him definite opinions concerning the instruction the college should offer. Prior to his presidency the curriculum had covered six subjects. The head of the college had instructed in political economy as well as in philosophy. One professor had Latin, another Greek, a third mathematics, and the fourth "natural philosophy," that is, chemistry and physics. Lee did not frown on any of these subjects. On the contrary, as will appear when the details of his educational policy are fully explained, he was a believer both in the classics and in the pure sciences. But he did not think that these of themselves sufficed to meet the needs of the impoverished South, whose first problems were those of economic recovery and enlarged trade. Accordingly, Lee acquiesced without reservation in a plan that had been under consideration to provide wider training for the students by the immediate creation of five additional departments, two of which represented, in effect, a division of "natural philosophy." The five proposed chairs were in addition to that of "mental and moral science and political economy," which was to be entrusted to a separate instructor, in accordance with the understanding reached when Lee agreed to become president. The new professorships recommended at the first meeting of the trustees after his inauguration were probably designed in part, also, to qualify the college for participation in the "land-grant fund" set up for agricultural and mechanical education under the Federal act of 1862. They were:

1. Practical chemistry, including metallurgy and agricultural chemistry, so that the teaching of chemistry would be entirely separated from that of physics.
2. Experimental philosophy and practical mechanics, including mechanics, mechanical drawing and architecture. This became, in substance, the chair of physics.
3. Applied mathematics, including analytical mechanics, astronomy, civil engineering and building.
4. Modern languages, including French, German, Spanish, and Italian.
5. History and literature, including modern history, English literature and rhetoric, philosophical grammar and comparative philology.[21]

[21] *Trustees' Minutes,* Oct. 24, 1865.

Funds for the establishment of these chairs were not available. Part of the endowment was yielding nothing. Only some fifty students had registered on the day the session was scheduled to open,[22] and though the number was increasing fast, there was no assurance that the tuition fees they paid would suffice to provide new salaries. Still, with General Lee as their leader, the trustees were ready to undertake expansion, and if they could not have immediately all the desired new chairs, they would fill three forthwith and would wait for better times. Physics, or natural philosophy, was set up as a distinct department, and chemistry was given the same independent status. This meant a net increase of one. A professor of applied mathematics was named, to inaugurate what later became the school of engineering. Instruction in modern languages was extended, and philology was linked temporarily with them in a new department.[23] General Lee was especially anxious that Spanish should be taught at the college. He had not forgotten what he had learned of that language in Mexico,[24] and he was convinced that the relations of the United States with Spanish-speaking countries were destined soon to become much closer.[25]

To help in meeting the expense of the new departments and to insure the future of the college, the trustees promptly began the endowment solicitation that had been authorized the previous summer. General Lee wrote several letters to support this undertaking[26] but otherwise he apparently had little to do with it, and by present-day standards he would not be accounted a good "academic beggar." The trustees had their own endowment committee, which named the financial agents and directed their work. These representatives began a widespread quest for funds, and, considering the poverty of the times, they gathered in sizable sums. Most Southerners who possessed any means were certain to listen when an appeal was made for "General Lee's College," as it soon was called.

An effort was made, also, to prevail upon the state to appropriate to the college some of the land-grant funds from the Federal

[22] Riley (op. cit., 39 n.) mistook the enrollment of 1864–65 for that of 1865–66 and wrongly gave the number as twenty-two. For the correct figure, see Lee to Mrs. Lee, Oct. 3, 1865, R. E. Lee, Jr., 187.

[23] Jones, 89.

[24] D. Gardiner Tyler in Riley, 130.

[25] Joynes in Cent. U. S. C., 29

[26] See infra, pp. 247, 258.

Government. General Lee furthered this, as much as he could,[27] but his particular duty was to see that available monies were spent economically so as to yield the last cent of return.

It was gray, unpleasant work and it consumed many, many hours. If an old fence was torn down, General Lee saw to it that the timber was preserved. Even worn-out tools he would not permit to be thrown away. When a faculty member started to open a new, wrapped catalogue, in order to look up some disputed point, Lee interposed and handed him one that had been used before. Even after the college had passed the worst poverty of 1865–66, Lee was incensed to find that a maul had been made of a part of a felled locust tree he had intended for use as a gate post. Sometimes his wrath overflowed at stupid carelessness and small waste. He might spare the immediate offender, but the next comer was certain to find him in bad humor, though he always made subsequent amends for being savage.[28]

Taxing as was this new life, General Lee found time to answer the multitude of letters that reached him on subjects unrelated to the affairs of the college. Punctilious in his correspondence, he never left a letter unanswered when he thought the writer would expect a reply. Some solicited help, some sought positions, and some asked for letters of recommendation. In a typical instance, a former officer inquired if there was any prospect of getting a professorship at Washington College. The General replied sympathetically: "I am very sorry to hear of the difficulties which surround you and of the losses you have sustained. It adds another to the long list of those in whose welfare and happiness I take deep interest. It will always give me pleasure to serve you, and should I find any opportunity of securing an eligible position, will at once act and let you know. In the meantime you must work zealously at what offers and not be discouraged at disappointments which beset us all. The country is full of good men seeking employment, which adds to the difficulty of securing it, and the objections made by the authorities to all who have been engaged

---

[27] *Trustees' Minutes,* Oct. 24, 1865; R. E. Lee to John B. Baldwin, *MS.,* Nov. 22, 1865, *Archives of Washington and Lee University.* For these two references and for a careful review of General Lee's connection with the new curriculum, the writer is indebted to the late Dean H. D. Campbell.

[28] E. C. Gordon in *Riley,* 79 ff. Gordon cited (p. 80) a characteristic example.

in the war add further obstacles. Agriculture therefore at present, seems to offer the only pursuit for obtaining a living, and it is this fact which has turned the attention of so many to it. I am sorry to say there is no position at Washington College, to be filled. . . . I will write at once to Mahone, who I believe has again charge of the S[outh] Side R. R. to know if there are any vacancies with him. . . . I send you the paper you desire, which I hope will answer your purpose." [29] To another he mailed a desired statement of service in the Army of Northern Virginia and added: "I hope it may answer your purpose. But I think an old engineer-officer ought to make a good farmer; and I advise you not to abandon such an honorable and independent pursuit, until you are very sure you can do better." [30] Letters asking for help continued to reach him from all parts of the South, until the very end of his life.[31]

Many of his former comrades wrote him in answer to his request for material to be used in his projected book on the Army of Northern Virginia. "I hope both you and Johnston," he told Beauregard, "will write the history of your campaigns. Everyone should do all in his power to collect and disseminate the truth in the hope that it may find a place in history, and descend to posterity." [32] The assembling of material was not to be an easy task, soon finished, because, as he wrote a Northern publishing house, "It will be some time before the truth can be known, and I do not think that period has yet arrived." [33] Despite difficulties, he held to his undertaking during 1866, because he believed he owed it to his men to chronicle their deeds. He is reported to have said to some of his friends, "I shall write this history, not to vindicate

[29] R. E. Lee to R. H. Chilton, Oct. 6, 1865. *Chilton Papers.*
[30] R. E. Lee to unnamed correspondent, May 25, 1866, *Jones,* 252. For other endorsements by Lee of former officers, see that of Colonel J. R. Hagood in *Mixson,* 122; that of Major H. B. McClellan, *MS.,* Aug. 29, 1865, *H. B. McClellan MSS.;* and that of Major George Duffey, *MS.,* July 21, 1870, for copy of which last paper the writer makes grateful acknowledgment to Mrs. Thomas P. Bryan, of Richmond. In every instance Lee shaped the terms of his endorsement to his knowledge of the man's qualifications and character. He gave no "blanket endorsements."
[31] *Cf.* R. E. Lee to Walter H. Taylor, March 26, 1868; *Taylor's General Lee,* 311. For an interesting case of assistance to a woman who claimed a kinship of which Lee knew nothing, see R. E. Lee to Hill Carter, *MS.,* April 17, April 25, May 18, May 29, 1868; *Shirley MSS.*
[32] R. E. Lee to G. T. Beauregard, Oct. 3, 1865; *Jones,* 207. For other letters on the same theme, see *ibid.,* 181, 208.
[33] R. E. Lee to Scranton and Burr. Oct. 25, 1865: *Jones,* 245.

myself, or to promote my own reputation. I want that the world shall know what my poor boys, with their small numbers and scant resources, succeeded in doing." [34] Whenever he learned of their new achievements in spite of dark adversity his admiration for them increased. An associate at Washington College told the General one day that he had seen a maimed and once-affluent veteran at work ploughing a field in cheerful spirit, grateful that he had one arm left and a chance to use it. "What a noble fellow!" said Lee. "But it is just like one of our soldiers! The world has never seen nobler men than those who belonged to the Army of Northern Virginia." Hearing, again, of a young former officer who had accepted work as an express-porter and was toiling good-humoredly under a man who had been his subordinate in military service, Lee exclaimed: "He deserves more credit for that than for anything he ever did in the army!" [35] When one of his old lieutenants reported to the General that he was winning the battle against poverty, Lee always answered with enthusiasm. "I am much gratified at the reception of your letter," he wrote Major George Duffey, "and greatly pleased to learn your success and prosperity in the prosecution of your business. I hope all of our friends may go to work as zealously as you have done and labor as diligently." [36] Later, when one of his chaplains started to make a tour of several Southern states, Lee told him: "You will meet many of my old soldiers during your trip, and I wish you to tell them that I often think of them, try every day to pray for them, and am always gratified to hear of their prosperity." [37]

In all these letters to former associates, if the occasion permitted, Lee preached his doctrine of conciliation, nor did he allow the mounting hostility of Northern politicians to discourage him. He wrote General Cadmus Wilcox: "I fear the South has yet to suffer many evils, and it will require time, patience, and fortitude, to heal her affliction." [38] But, facing that, he kept straight on, with

[34] *Jones*, 180.

[35] 1 *Macrae*, 185. It was perhaps typical of the spirit of the times that the express-porter's new superior was as deferential to his employee as if the two had still been in the army at their old grades.

[36] Lee to Major George Duffey, *MS.*, June 14, 1867, loaned the writer by Mrs. Thomas P. Bryan of Richmond.

[37] *Jones*, 322, 323.

[38] R. E. Lee to G. T. Beauregard, Oct. 3, 1865; R. E. Lee to C. M. Wilcox, Dec. 23, 1865; *Jones*, 207–8.

hope in his heart and with moderation his unfailing counsel. "I would suggest that you leave out all the bitter expressions against the North and the United States government," he once remarked to a minister who was reporting a fiery speech delivered at the college. "They will do us no good under our present circumstances, and I think such expressions undignified and unbecoming." [39] Similar sentiments, not so plainly put, appeared in many earnest letters to his friends. They were voiced, also, in the conversations that turned, in spite of him, to the war and its outcome.

One such conversation was with Herbert C. Saunders, a British literary traveller who came to Lexington in November, 1865, and spent an evening with him at the hotel. Lee had a deep admiration for the achievements of the Anglo-Saxon race[40] and had always been appreciative of English sympathy.[41] He received Saunders cordially, and in the course of their talk explained freely, as he always would, the treatment that had been accorded the prisoners of war he had taken, for he regarded the charges of cruelty to these men as a reflection on his personal honor.[42] The discussion then turned to the Southern view of slavery, to the attitude of neutrals toward the Confederacy, and to the disparity of numbers in the principal engagements fought in Virginia.

Lee told why such scant results sometimes followed his victories. "The force which the Confederates brought to bear," Saunders reported, "was so often inferior to that of the Yankees that the more they followed up the victory against one portion of the enemy's line the more did they lay themselves open to being surrounded by the remainder of the enemy. He likened the operation to a man breasting a wave of the sea, who, as rapidly as he clears a way before him, is enveloped by the very water he has displaced."

Saunders must have been most tactful in his questioning, for he prevailed upon the General to talk of Appomattox: "He spoke of

---

[39] Jones, 197.

[40] R. E. Lee to W. H. Nettleton, May 21, 1866: ". . . to no race are we more indebted for the virtues which constitute a great people than to the Anglo-Saxon" (Jones, 251).

[41] Cf. R. E. Lee to C. W. Law, Sept. 27, 1866: "The good opinion of the English people as to the justice of that cause, constitutional government, is highly appreciated by the people of the South . . ." (Jones, 220).

[42] Jones, 192. Cf. R. E. Lee to Mrs. Jefferson Davis, Jan. 23, 1866; Jones, 212.

the final surrender as inevitable, owing to the superiority in numbers of the enemy. His own army had, during the last few weeks, suffered materially from defection in its ranks, and, discouraged by failures and worn out by hardships, had at the time of the surrender only 7892 men under arms, and this little army was almost surrounded by one of 100,000. They might, the General said with an air piteous to behold, have cut their way out as they had done before, but, looking upon the struggle as hopeless, I was not surprised to hear him say that he thought it cruel to prolong it." When Saunders rose to go, at 11 o'clock, "he begged me to stay on, as he found the nights full long."

Subsequently, Saunders sent Lee an account of this interview and requested permission to publish it. As Lee read over the manuscript[43] he noted that the Britisher had been in some doubt as to Lee's opinion of the right of secession. Regarding this, opposite the appropriate paragraph, Saunders had written: "Query C'd you frame this so as to represent yr real views? . . ." Lee read on:

"This right [of secession][44] he [Lee] told me he always held as a constitutional maxim and I believe I am not doing injustice to him when I say that the conviction that one man cannot, for many years together, hold his own against four or five, [(] a conclusion which recent events have brought forcibly to his mind)[45] has not by any means persuaded him that his interpretation of the Constitution was a wrong one. As to the policy of secession on the part of the South he was at first distinctly opposed to it and it was not until Lincoln issued a proclamation for 75,000 men to invade the South which he deemed so clearly unconstitutional that he had no longer any doubt what course his loyalty to the Constitution and to his State required of him."

This, of course, was not accurate. It indicated, first of all, that Lee in 1861 had hesitated between adhering to the Union and accepting the action of his state in withdrawing from it. He could not let that stand. Saunders was wrong, also, in stating that Lee had "always" held the right of secession as a "constitutional maxim." On the contrary, at the approach of the conflict, as he had plainly said at the time, Lee had regarded secession simply as

[43] In August, 1867; R. E. Lee, Jr., 229.
[44] This does not begin a paragraph in the original.
[45] The beginning of this parenthesis does not appear in the text.

revolution, and he had believed that if moderation had been exercised on both sides, there would have been no occasion to exercise
the right of revolution. Saunders must be assured of this. Besides, the Englishman's parenthetical remarks were a bit flam-
boyant, and his reference laid too much emphasis on Lee's personal views, and, inferentially, on the divergence between those
views and the theory of secession that had been held in 1861 by
many Southerners. Lee accordingly took his pen and, precisely
as he had edited Marshall's drafts of military reports, he eliminated
Saunder's flourishes and made the references to himself as nearly
impersonal as he could. His corrected version of the passage read:

"This right he told me was always held as a constitutional
maxim at the South. As to its exercise at the time on the part of
the South he was distinctly opposed, and it was not until Lincoln
issued a proclamation for 75,000 men to invade the South which
was deemed clearly unconstitutional that Virginia withdrew from
the U. States."

This statement was literally correct, was not ostentatiously personal, and was not calculated to revive old differences or to bring
Lee unpleasantly before the public.[46] A few other errors of no
great consequence in Saunders's interview he noted and corrected,
but, at the end, he decided to withhold consent to the publication.
He wrote the author: "I have an objection to the publication of
my private conversations, which are never intended but for those
to whom they are addressed. I cannot, therefore, without an entire
disregard of the rule which I have followed in other cases, and in
violation of my own sense of propriety, assent to what you propose. I hope, therefore, you will excuse me. . . . In the hasty

[46] Judge R. W. Winston, who found at Washington and Lee University this interesting document, put upon it in his *Robert E. Lee,* 392 ff., a different interpretation than
that here given. Judge Winston held that Lee never believed in secession at any time. To
escape the charge of a contradiction between this theory and Lee's argument on secession
in the "Acton letter" (see *infra,* p. 302) the judge suggested that perhaps Lee did not
compose the communication to Sir John Acton. It will be pointed out in a note on p. 304
that some of the material used in the "Acton letter" was in General Lee's desk at the
time of his death, and apparently had been studied by him. This would seem to dispose
of the theory of a different authorship, though Lee may have received assistance from
some constitutional lawyer in preparing the paper. Apart from that, however, it suf-
fices to say that even if Lee had not himself written the "Acton letter" he would not have
signed a statement that misrepresented his views of a vital constitutional question. Lee
corrected Saunders for averring that he believed in secession before the war. If a literary
assistant had been wrong in stating after the war that Lee then believed secession had been
a constitutional right, Lee would certainly have corrected him, too.

perusal which I have been obliged to give the manuscript inclosed to me, I perceive many inaccuracies, resulting as much from my imperfect narrative as from misapprehension on your part. Though fully appreciating your kind wish to correct certain erroneous statements as regards myself, I prefer remaining silent to doing anything that might excite angry discussion at this time, when strong efforts are being made by conservative men, North and South, to sustain President Johnson in his policy, which, I think, offers the only means of healing the lamentable divisions of the country, and which the result of the late convention at Philadelphia gives great promise of doing." [47]

Not all his correspondence was in serious strain. General David Hunter wrote General Lee to ask his opinion on two points: The raid he had made in 1864, Hunter explained—it was the raid during which Washington College was looted—had been undertaken to prevent the dispatch of 40,000 men with whom the Federals had been told General Lee was preparing to reinforce General Johnston. Had the raid served that purpose? And further, did not Lee think Hunter had adopted the most feasible line of retreat when he had gone westward through the mountains, instead of northward, down the Shenandoah Valley?

It was an opportunity General Lee could not resist, for Hunter had been one of the most incompetent of generals and the most inveterate of partisans, and his raid had been a classic in military mismanagement. Lee replied very courteously that Hunter's information had been erroneous. "I had no troops to spare General Johnston, and no intention of sending him any—certainly not forty thousand, as that would have taken about all I had. As to the second point, I would say that I am not advised as to the motives which induced you to adopt the line of retreat which you took, and am not, perhaps, competent to judge of the question; but I certainly expected you to retreat by way of the Shenandoah

---

[47] R. E. Lee to Herbert C. Saunders, Aug. 22, 1866: *R. E. Lee, Jr.,* 230–31. The date, it will be noted, was nine months after the interview. The "late convention at Philadelphia" met on Aug. 14, 1866, and organized a new party to support the conservative and conciliatory policy of the President in opposition to the radicals (Dunning: *Reconstruction, Political and Economic,* 75). Lee persisted in his refusal to appear in the public eye, whether through newspapers, magazines, or books. He repeatedly declined to assist prospective biographers (*Jones,* 165, 166, 246) and he never gave an interview to a reporter (see, as typical, the incident in *Jones,* 283; see also, *infra,* p. 405).

Valley, and was gratified at the time that you preferred the route through the mountains to the Ohio—leaving the Valley open for General Early's advance into Maryland."[48]

Still more of humor appeared in his answer to a spiritualist who asked his opinion on some military question. He replied that soldiers might differ as to the answer. His own judgment was poor at best, and as the spiritualists had the power to communicate with all the great captains of the past, he could not obtrude his opinion in such company.[49]

The hardest letter Lee had to write that winter was one in answer to Mrs. "Stonewall" Jackson. On a visit to Lexington she brought for his perusal the manuscript of a *Life* of her dead husband, written by his former chief of staff, Major R. L. Dabney. Lee read it over, as he said, for the delight of the narrative, but had neither the heart nor the time to review critically the long text; yet when Mrs. Jackson asked for its return, Lee could not wholly overlook the fact that in his zeal for the fame of his chief, Major Dabney had unintentionally made some claims that were at variance with Lee's knowledge or his recollection of the facts. This was true of the proposed attack after Malvern Hill and of the operations against the Federals who had attempted to capture the reserve artillery when the army had recrossed from Maryland to Virginia at the end of the Sharpsburg operations. Still more was Dabney mistaken in his representation of the incidents leading to Jackson's march around the right flank of Hooker in the greatest of all his achievements. Lee had the task of correcting error without seeming in any wise to discredit his beloved Jackson. With great care, on January 25, 1866, he wrote a tactful correction, but the very circumstances of its composition made the letter seem vague to those unfamiliar with the operations.[50]

In correspondence, college duties, and a very simply social life, the autumn of 1865 wore away and the winter came. Custis was with the General at the hotel now, having been elected professor

---

[48] Quoted, in part, in *Jones*, 240–41.

[49] *Jones*, 239. For other examples of Lee's miscellaneous correspondence, see *Jones*, 254; Lee to unnamed correspondent, *MS.*, March 11, 1867, Library of Congress; Lee to F. Johnston, Salem, Va., *MS.*, March 4, 1869; *Draper MSS.*, 5ZZ, 99, State Hist. Soc. of Wisconsin, kindness of Miss Iva A. Welch.

[50] 2 *Henderson*, 472–73. For the questions in controversy, see *supra*, vol. II, pp. 407–8 and vol. II, Appendix 5, p. 587.

of civil engineering at the Virginia Military Institute,[51] but Mrs. Lee and her daughters had not yet come,[52] as their house was still unready. Lee pushed the repairs as rapidly as he could, watching every detail and reporting regularly to Mrs. Lee. Carpets and curtains rescued from Arlington by Mrs. Britannia Kennon of Tudor Place were sent down to Lexington. As no furniture was available in Lexington, a little, a very little, was purchased in Baltimore. A piano was presented by its admiring manufacturer. Mrs. Edmund Randolph Cocke asked the privilege of equipping Mrs. Lee's room. Servants of a sort were procured. Some of the ladies of Lexington put on the "last touches" of domesticity.

On the morning of December 2, 1865, after one disappointment, General Lee had the pleasure of welcoming his wife and his daughters at the packet landing, a mile and a quarter from the town. They arrived aboard the private boat of the president of the canal, and were accompanied by Robert E. Lee, Jr., who was recuperating from malaria, contracted while he was raising a fabulously fine crop of corn at the White House.[53] Riding on Traveller, with the family in a carriage, General Lee escorted them to the house, where the thoughtful wife of a member of the faculty had arranged breakfast.

With great interest the young people went over the old residence. Mrs. Lee's quarters were both comfortable and attractive, for Mrs. Margaret Preston, a poet of some distinction, had designed the furniture, which a one-armed Confederate veteran had made with much skill. The new Stieff piano stood almost alone in its glory in the parlor. Some of the other rooms were embarrassingly bare. The Arlington carpets, made for more spacious rooms, had all been tucked in around the walls. Although the best had been made of scant materials, the effect of the extemporized furnishings was, on the whole, somewhat odd.

In a few hours the house was made more intimate. The family silver had been sent to Lexington for safe-keeping during the war,

[51] R. E. Lee to Mrs. Lee, Oct. 3, 1865; *R. E. Lee, Jr.,* 187; same to same, Nov. 30, 1865; *ibid.,* 202.

[52] Lee to C. G. Memminger, Nov. 27, 1865, Capers: *Life of C. G. Memminger,* 377–78.

[53] General Lee had offered to assist Robert with his education, after the war, and if his son did not desire that, he urged him to start farming for himself at the White House on a moderate scale (*R. E. Lee, Jr.,* 191).

and on the approach of Hunter's raiders had been buried by a sergeant at the Virginia Military Institute. Robert was now sent over to assist in digging up the cutlery and urns the young people had known since infancy. He returned with them, quickly enough, but when he opened the two chests, the contents were found to be much blackened and for the time could not be used. General Lee was not to be outdone; he opened his old camp chest and brought out the pewter plates and the knives and the forks with which he and his headquarters mess had eaten their scant fare. A shortage of chairs developing, he produced his old camp stools.[54]

These reminders of the war were not out of place: the house itself had associations with the struggle. Prior to the war it had been occupied by the then president, Reverend George Junkin, D.D. One of his daughters had married a sombre religious professor in the Virginia Military Institute across the hill, and he had come to live with his wife's parents.[55] The sentimental no doubt felt that something of the spirit of that soldier, Thomas Jonathan Jackson, abode where Lee dwelt. In the building where Jackson had dwelt Lee thought often of his brilliant lieutenant. "It is as pleasant as profitable to contemplate his character, to recall his patriotism, his piety, and his unselfish nature," he wrote a preceptor of Jackson's youth.[56]

The spirit of the stern Jackson might linger in the house, and his old chieftain might be the tenant at law, but from the first it was apparent that the real commander-in-chief on that front was Mrs. Lee. She asserted her authority with promptness. Nearly all Lexington flocked to the house to welcome the family and to pay tribute to General Lee. One evening, when the place was thronged and Lee was in animated conversation with a distinguished guest, Mrs. Lee broke in with a command from the rolling chair. "Robert," she said, "Herbert Preston has lost his cap; will you go into the back parlor and see if he has left it

[54] All the details are from *R. E. Lee. Jr.*, 189 *ff.*

[55] C. A. Graves in *Riley,* 24. Another of Doctor Junkin's daughters had married Colonel J. T. L. Preston of Virginia Military Institute.

[56] *Jones,* 158. *Cf.* Lee's letter of Aug. 21, 1869, to Q. D. Julio of St. Louis, declining to accept a picture of the last meeting of Lee and Jackson, because he wished the painter to have all the profit from his work (*Jones,* 275). See *Jones,* 157, for a lettter from Lee to Mrs. Jackson, forwarding Jackson's overcoat.

there?" Obediently he who had sent 70,000 men a-marching broke off his talk and left the room to search for the head covering which the youngster, in strict accordance with the habit of small boys, had put down and had forgotten. The spectators were shocked at Mrs. Lee's temerity; the General said nothing. In fact, he submitted as cheerfully to domestic authority as ever he had to Congress and President. With his family about, his spirits rose visibly. "My father appeared bright and even gay," wrote Robert E. Lee, Jr., who had not seen him since the day at Pampatike. The General went to work vigorously to make the house attractive for his family. As soon as the weather permitted, he planted shrubs and roses, set out trees, repaired the stable, built walks, and prepared a vegetable garden. "In a short time," chronicled the son, "we were quite comfortable and very happy." [57] There were no regrets in the family because he had declined an offer of $10,000 a year to act as titular head of an insurance company, while remaining at the college.[58]

[57] *R. E. Lee, Jr.*, 204, 205.

[58] "Excuse me, sir," he had said, when he found that the company's representative simply wanted the use of his name, "I cannot consent to receive pay for services I do not render" (*Jones,* 174). See also R. E. Lee to unnamed correspondent, May 21, 1866 (*Jones,* 175). For another insurance offer, see *Winston,* 367.

CHAPTER XV

First Fruits at Washington College

CHRISTMAS came and passed, a very different Christmas from that dreadful season in the Petersburg trenches twelve months before. With the New Year, Lee had to make a hard trip to Richmond. On December 4, 1865, the general assembly of Virginia had met, undisturbed as yet by a hostile Congress. Friends of education decided to make an appeal to it on behalf of the colleges. Several of these institutions had bonds guaranteed by the state and were dependent on the interest for a part of their support. This interest had stopped with the collapse of the Confederacy: the schools were anxious that the legislature make good the arrears and resume payment. A demonstration before the committee of the house of delegates on schools and colleges was arranged, and General Lee was asked to appear with Colonel Bolivar Christian, of the board of trustees, in behalf of Washington College, which owned $88,000 of the bonds.[1]

It was a mission of a sort from which every sensibility of Lee's nature shrank, but with the college's welfare at stake, it had to be performed. The General travelled to Staunton and thence went by railroad to Richmond, where he arrived on January 11, 1866. The legislators expected to give him audience that evening, but on a statement by Colonel Christian that the General was wearied by his journey, his hearing was deferred until the next day. At 9:30 Lee went with Christian before the committee, which was assembled in the office of the first auditor, in the basement of the Capitol. Christian was to present a formal memorial from the college, setting forth its former resources and financial distresses, and General Lee was to speak briefly on this paper. Except for his broken remarks to the men at Appomattox it was the third speech, however condensed, he had ever undertaken to make. The

[1] *Trustees' Minutes*, Dec. 28, 1865; 17 *S. H. S. P.*, 358 ff.

first had been delivered only a hundred feet away, on the next
floor of the Capitol, that day when he had been received by the
Virginia convention as commanding general of her army of defense. The second had been the warning he had given the overconfident people of Orange in the summer of 1861 on his return
from his inspection of the Manassas defenses.

After his associate had explained the plight of the institution,
Lee arose. He had little to add, he said, to what Mr. Christian
had told the committee. There were about one hundred students
at the school. The buildings had been repaired, though the Federal army had left nothing but the walls. All the philosophical
and chemical apparatus had been destroyed[2] but had been replaced
by the trustees. The money used in repairing the buildings and
restoring the equipment had been borrowed in the expectation
of receiving the interest with which to repay it.

That was his whole speech. Perhaps it did not matter at all
what he said: the members of the committee heard him with
their hearts, rather than with their ears. He was still their chieftain, not to be denied, and they took a short recess in order that
they might greet him.[3]

As Agnes Lee was then in Richmond, the General had a pleasant time with her and with Richmond friends, though he took
pains to avoid functions and public appearances. He remained in
Richmond for about a week, helping to make friends for the bill
to aid the colleges, and left for home, at last, on a day when the
snow was sifting ominously down. The weather grew worse as
he approached the mountains. Darkness had fallen when he
reached Staunton. He remained there all night, and the next
morning, despite gloomy prognostications by his friends, he went
on to Goshen, which was the nearest point to Lexington on the
railroad. Arriving there at 10 o'clock, he found the road to Rockbridge Baths unbroken and the stage driver not anxious to keep
his schedule, but Lee coaxed him into starting, and covered the
distance in safety. As the North River was past fording, he was

---

[2] The newspaper account reads that "all the philosophical and chemical apparatus had
been destroyed by the same party, but," etc. It is not certain this language is Lee's.
[3] *Richmond Inquirer*, Jan. 11, 12, 1866. *Cf.* H. K. Beale, *The Critical Year*, quoting
J. W. Sharp to Thaddeus Stevens (from the *Stevens MSS.*): "When Genl. Lee's name
was mentioned in the House of Delegates . . . it was received with cheers on all sides."

ferried across. On the opposite bank he was lucky enough to find a delayed stage bound for Lexington.[4]

It was a rough, perhaps a dangerous, journey, but it was not in vain. The general assembly passed an act for the relief of the institutions, by which some $28,000 of interest was distributed among them.[5] This measure was fathered by the senator from the Lexington district, David S. G. Cabell.

Other financial assistance was at hand, also. Even before General Lee had gone to Richmond, Reverend S. D. Stuart, one of the agents of the school, had returned from Baltimore, where he had raised $9000 toward the endowment of the presidency. Reverend Doctor W. S. White simultaneously collected $8000 from friends of the institution in the Valley of Virginia.[6] Still another representative, Reverend E. P. Walton, had established headquarters at Memphis, Tenn., and was meeting with liberal responses to his appeal for the school. About the same time, as a result of one of the few letters of direct solicitation that Lee had written,[7] Cyrus H. McCormick became interested in the college. He was a native of Rockbridge County, in which the institution was located, and he had made the first grain reaper in a shop not many miles from Lexington. On January 6, 1866, the board was told that Mr. McCormick had given $10,000 to the endowment fund. This was a great donation for the times, and was received with the thanks of the college. In appreciation of gift and benefactor, the trustees resolved to elect a professor to the McCormick chair of Experimental Philosophy and Practical Mechanics,[8] later styled the Mr. McCormick chair of Natural Philosophy. The gift was the more encouraging because McCormick stated that if others made corresponding contributions he might present more money to the college.

These funds relieved somewhat a dark financial situation. Increasing fees paid by the students, who were coming in ever-larger

[4] R. E. Lee to Agnes Lee, Jan. 29, 1866; *R. E. Lee, Jr.*, 208; R. E. Lee to Reverdy Johnson, Jan. 27, 1866; *Jones*, 210–11.

[5] *Acts of the General Assembly of Virginia*, 1865–66, pp. 73, 438. The bill passed the senate unanimously but barely escaped defeat in the house (*Journal of the House of Delegates*, 1865–66, 340, 386–87).

[6] *Richmond Dispatch* of Jan. 5, 1866, quoting *The Staunton Spectator; Richmond Dispatch*, Jan. 11, 1866, quoting *The Central Presbyterian*.

[7] Cf. *supra*, p. 233 and *infra*, p. 258; *Winston*, 374.

[8] *Trustees' Minutes*, Jan. 6, 1866; *Richmond Dispatch*, Jan. 11, 1866.

number, also eased somewhat the school's distress. Before the end of the session the total enrollment had reached 146, of whom 59 came from other Southern states than Virginia.[9] A balanced budget, however, was by no means assured. Borrowing had to be continued. At some period of his administration—it is not possible to say when—General Lee himself made a loan of $6000 to the college. He had its bond for that amount at the time of his death.[10]

During the winter of 1865–66 distresses came with satisfactions. Mistreatment of President Davis was a load on Lee's heart.[11] The politicians had taken the saddle in Washington. Federal soldiers who had fought against the South and had come to respect the Confederates no longer spoke for the government. Thaddeus Stevens's voice was becoming more powerful than that of any other man in the Union. The moderate policy of President Johnson was bringing upon him the wrath of those who deserved B. H. Hill's withering denunciation as "invisible in war and invincible in peace." Stern "reconstruction" legislation was in the making. A "test oath" was being devised to keep out of office all those who had fought or had enacted laws for the South. The stage was set to make President Davis a shining victim.

This change gave General Lee deep concern. He could not believe that Congress would hold to the policy of repression displayed in the test oath. "I have hoped," he wrote Reverdy Johnson, "that congress would have thought proper to have repealed the acts imposing [the 'ironclad' oath], and all similar tests. To pursue a policy which will continue the prostration of one-half the country, alienate the affections of its inhabitants from the Government, and which must eventually result in injury to the country and the American people, appears to me so manifestly injudicious that I do not see how those responsible can tolerate it."[12] Lee did not see, however, that he could personally do any-

---

[9] *Catalogue of Washington College . . . for the Collegiate Year Ending June, 1866. Published by Order of the Board of Trustees* (cited hereafter as *1865–66 Catalogue*), 12.

[10] Inventory attached to the will of Robert E. Lee, *Rockbridge County (Va.) MS. Records.* Lee, of course, may have taken this bond at a time when the college was unable to pay his salary, or he may have advanced the money toward the construction of the chapel. Dean Campbell stated that $1000 of the total was advanced toward the building of the "new" president's house.

[11] R. E. Lee to Walter H. Taylor, May 25, 1866; *Taylor's General Lee*, 310.

[12] R. E. Lee to Reverdy Johnson, Jan. 27, 1866; *Jones*, 211.

thing to prevent the passage of this hard legislation. "I am not in a position to make it proper for me to take a public part in the affairs of the country," he wrote. "I have done and continue to do, in my private capacity, all in my power to encourage our people to set manfully to work to restore the country, to rebuild their homes and churches, to educate their children, and to remain with their states, their friends and countrymen. But as a prisoner on parole, I cannot do more; nor do I believe it would be advantageous for me to do so." [13]

Contrary to his wishes, and in a manner most obnoxious to him, the General was now unexpectedly brought into contact with the men who were shaping laws against the South. On December 13, 1865, Congress had agreed on the appointment of a joint committee to "inquire into the condition of the states which formed the so-called Confederate States of America, and report whether they, or any of them, are entitled to be represented in either house of congress." Sub-committees had been named for the various geographical divisions of the South. That on Virginia, North Carolina, and South Carolina had Senator Jacob M. Howard of Michigan as its chief inquisitor. He and his associate began taking testimony on January 23, 1866, and continued at intervals until April 19. They examined all manner of witnesses— Southern legislators, ante-bellum politicians, demagogues, a few Confederate soldiers and sympathizers, some native Unionists of the South and a considerable number of Northerners residing in the subjugated states. Senator Howard's questions, as a rule, were civil but not always *apropos*. He spent much time in eliciting the opinion of his witnesses on such matters as the disposition of the South to pay taxes, the probability of its supporting a foreign country in case of a war involving the United States, and the willingness of the Southern people to receive Northern people socially.

General Lee's name had frequently come into the testimony of the committee. Judge John C. Underwood had testified that, in his opinion, eleven in twelve of any jury that could be drawn in Virginia "would say that Lee was almost equal to Washington, and was the noblest man in the State." John Minor Botts had

13 R. E. Lee to J. W. Brockenbrough, Jan. 23, 1866; *Jones*, 179.

informed the committee of plans to make General Lee governor of Virginia. Colonel Orlando Brown, assistant commissioner in the bureau of freedmen, refugees, and abandoned lands, had stated of Lee, "I know of no man who has more fully the hearts of a people than he has the hearts of Virginians." [14]

The committee could not resist the temptation to summon and examine at first hand the man whom Botts with venom had said was "at the head of the rebellion." Lee was accordingly called as a witness. He went by way of the Orange and Alexandria Railroad, arrived during the afternoon of February 16, and drove direct to the Metropolitan Hotel, where he registered. It was the first time he had been in Washington since April 18, 1861, when he had gone home with Blair's offer and Scott's exhortation ringing in his ears. He denied himself to callers, where practicable, as he did not wish to make himself conspicuous. Some of Lee's younger friends organized an impromptu force of ushers, a "staff" they called it from military habit, and they tried to keep the boorish and the importunate from Lee. He was overwhelmed, however, with callers and could not combat the curiosity of the public. His box was soon overflowing with cards and notes. [15]

Most of those who thronged about him were content to shake his hand or to seek autographs and souvenirs, but there was one embarrassing moment. An ex-Confederate persistently wheedled an usher with requests to be presented, until at last the former officer thought the quickest way to end the bother was to take the man to Lee, let him shake the General's hand, and then hustle him off. No sooner was the veteran before Lee than he took the floor. "General," he began, "I have always thought that if I ever had the honor of meeting you face to face, and there was an opportunity allowed me, I would like to ask you a question which nobody but you can answer. I seem to have that opportunity now. This is what I want to know: What was the reason that you failed to gain the victory at the battle of Gettysburg?" Lee's ushers, of course, were aghast, and the other auditors were outraged at such presumption. But Lee did not frown or redden or turn aside. Advancing straight to the man, he took him by the hand. "My

[14] *Reports of the Reconstruction Committee,* 39th Congress; Part II, pp. 7, 121, 126. Cf. also testimony of J. M. Wood of Lynchburg, *ibid.,* 87.
[15] *Richmond Dispatch,* Feb. 21, 1866; *Mrs. Clay,* 368.

dear sir," he said quietly, "that would be a long story, and would require more time than you see I can possibly command at present; so we will have to defer the matter to another occasion." To the credit of ushers and admirers it may be added that they did not commit homicide on the person of the inquirer.[16]

On February 17, Lee was called before the committee, was sworn, and then was examined by Senator Howard. The interrogation occupied two hours. General Lee did not want to testify, and though he was resolved to lose neither his dignity nor his temper, he was determined to say no more than was demanded of him. Explaining at the first opening that he lived "very retired" and had little communication with politicians, he gave only the most general, cautious answers to Senator Howard's inquiries about the sentiment of the people on reunion, the payment of taxes, and the treatment of the Negro.

Senator Howard thereupon asked one of his favorite questions: "In the event of a war between the United States and any foreign power," said he, "such as England or France, if there should be held out to the secession portion of the people of Virginia, or the other recently rebel states, a fair prospect of gaining their independence, and shaking off the government of the United States, is it, or is it not, your opinion that they would avail themselves of the opportunity?"

"I cannot speak with any certainty on that point," answered General Lee. "I do not know how far they might be actuated by their feelings. I have nothing whatever to base an opinion upon. So far as I know, they contemplate nothing of the kind now. What may happen in the future I cannot say."

Howard pressed him: "Do you not frequently hear, in your intercourse with secessionists in Virginia, expressions of a hope that such a war may break out?"

The General did not like the reference to secessionists. "I cannot say I have heard it," he answered. "On the contrary, I have heard people (I do not know whether you would call them secessionists or not—I mean those people in Virginia with whom I associate) express a hope that the country may not be led into a war."

Still Howard hung on: "In such an event, do you not think

16 *Mrs. Preston*, 274.

that many of that class of persons whom I call secessionists would join the common enemy?"

"It is possible. It depends upon the feelings of the individual."

"If it is a fair question," asked Howard, "—you may answer it, or not, as you choose—what, in such an event, might be your own choice."

"I have no disposition now to do it, and I never have had."

Howard was not content to let that simple answer suffice: "And you cannot foresee that such would be your inclination in such an event?"

"No," said Lee, evidently not pleased with so needless a catechizing. "I can only judge by the past. I do not know what circumstances may produce. I cannot pretend to foresee events. So far as I know the feeling of the people of Virginia, they want peace."

Howard then asked something about the Confederacy's plan of foreign alliances, and inquired: "The question I am about to put to you you may answer, or not, as you choose: Did you take any oath of fidelity or allegiance to the Confederate Government?"

Lee replied with simple dignity: "I do not recollect having done so; but it is possible that, when I was commissioned, I did. I do not recollect whether it was required. If it was required, I took it; or, if it had been required, I would have taken it; but I do not recollect whether it was or not."

Henry T. Blow, a Republican member of the House of Representatives from Missouri, next started a line of inquiry regarding industrial conditions in Virginia and the South's opinion of President Johnson's reconstruction policy.

"You do not feel down there," Mr. Blow said, "that while you accept the result, that we are as generous as we ought to be under the circumstances?"

"They think that the North can afford to be generous."

"That is the feeling down there?" Blow went on.

"Yes, and they think it is the best policy—those who reflect upon the subject and are able to judge."

"I understand it to be your opinion," Blow next said, "that generosity and liberality toward the entire South would be the surest means of regaining their good opinion?"

"Yes, and the speediest," answered the General.

Howard then returned to the attack with more hypothetical questions about the South's attitude in case a President like Buchanan should again recognize the right of secession; and when he had exhausted that theme, he proceeded to quiz Lee concerning the willingness of Southerners to convict Jefferson Davis of crime because of his action during the war.

"They do not generally suppose that it was treason against the United States, do they?" Howard asked.

"I do not think that they so consider it," General Lee replied.

"In what light would they view it? What would be their excuse or justification? How would they escape in their own mind? I refer to the past."

"I am referring to the past and as to the feelings they would have. So far as I know, they look upon the action of the state, in withdrawing itself from the government of the United States, as carrying the individuals of the state along with it; that the state was responsible for the act, not the individual."

"And that the ordinance of secession, so-called, or those acts of the state which recognized a condition of war between the state and the general government, stood as their justification for their bearing arms against the government of the United States?" Howard elaborated.

"Yes, sir," General Lee answered. "I think they considered the act of the state as legitimate; that they were merely using the reserved right which they had a right to do."

Once again Mr. Howard made the case personal to the witness: "State, if you please—and if you are disinclined to answer the question you need not do so—what your own personal views on that question were."

"That was my view," replied Lee in an even voice, without attempting to justify secession; "that the act of Virginia in withdrawing herself from the United States carried me along as a citizen of Virginia, and that her laws and her acts were binding on me."

"I have been told, General," said Howard after a minute, "that you have remarked to some friends in conversation that you were wheedled or cheated into that course by politicians."

"I do not recollect making any such remark. I do not think I ever made it."

"If there be any other matter about which you wish to speak on this occasion," said the Michigan senator, "do so freely."

"Only in reference to that last question you put to me," Lee answered. "I may have said, and I may have believed, that the position of the two sections which they held to each other was brought about by the politicians of the country; that the great masses of the people, if they understood the real question would have avoided it; but not that I had been individually wheedled by the politicians."

"That is probably the origin of the whole thing?"

"I may have said that; but I do not even recollect that. But I did believe at the time that it was an unnecessary condition of affairs, and might have been avoided if forbearance and wisdom had been practiced on both sides."

The sub-committee then turned the inquiry to the enfranchisement of the Negro and asked Lee's judgment of the South's attitude. He avoided the political aspects of the subject and said he thought the South would decide primarily on whether it considered the Negroes qualified for the ballot. "My own opinion," said he, "is that, at this time, they cannot vote intelligently, and that giving them the right of suffrage would open the door to a great deal of demagogism, and lead to embarrassments in various ways. What the future may prove, how intelligent they may become, with what eyes they may look upon the interests of the state in which they may reside, I cannot say more than you can."

Next came questions about Lee's knowledge of "cruelties practiced towards the Union prisoners at Libby prison and Belle Isle." Lee told the sub-committee that he was unaware of any, and had no reason to suppose that any had been practised, though he believed that privation had been suffered by prisoners for whom the South could not provide food and shelter. "I never had any control over the prisoners," he said, "except those that were captured on the field of battle. Them it was my business to send to Richmond to the proper officer, who was then the provost marshal general. In regard to their disposition afterwards, I had no control. I never gave an order about it. It was entirely in the hands of the War Department." He was unacquainted, he explained, with commanders and with conditions at Andersonville and at Salisbury.

"And of course," said Mr. Howard, "you knew nothing of the scenes of cruelty, about which complaints have been made, at those places."

"Nothing in the world," insisted the General. "As I said before, I suppose they suffered from the want of ability on the part of the Confederate states to supply their wants. At the very beginning of the war I knew there were sufferings of prisoners on both sides, but, as far as I could, I did everything in my power to relieve them, and urged the establishment of the cartel, which was established."

He returned to this point a little later: "I made several efforts to exchange the prisoners after the cartel was suspended; I do not know why it was suspended; I do not know to this day which side took the initiative; I know that there were constant complaints made on both sides; I merely know it from public rumor. I offered to General Grant, around Richmond, that we should ourselves exchange all the prisoners in our hands. There was a committee from the Christian Association, I think, which reached Petersburg and made application to me for a passport to visit all the prisons in the South. My letter to them I suppose they have. I told them that I had not the authority; that it could only be obtained from the War Department at Richmond, but that neither they nor I could relieve the sufferings of the prisoners; that the only thing to be done for them was to exchange them; and to show that I would do whatever was in my power, I offered then to send to City Point all the prisoners in Virginia and North Carolina, over which my command extended, provided they returned an equal number of mine, man for man. I reported this to the War Department, and received an answer that they would place at my command all the prisoners at the South, if the proposition was accepted. I heard nothing more on the subject."

"Has there been any considerable change in the number of the Negro population in Virginia during the last four years?" asked Mr. Blow, in a manifest desire to change the subject.

Lee answered this calmly, and after a few more questions about the Negro, was allowed to leave the stand.[17]

His testimony was not of a sort to charge editorial bombs, and it received no more than casual mention in the news columns.[18] If the committee had any other motive than curiosity in summoning him as a witness, it failed to accomplish its purpose.

There is a story that after he had been excused by the committee, General Lee went over to Arlington in the late afternoon and gazed long at the old mansion that never again was to be his home. Already it was taking on the appearance of a cemetery. New roads had been cut through it. The old spirit of the place was gone.[19] The story of a visit is, however, apocryphal. "I did not approach Arlington nearer than the railway. I know very well how things are there"—so Lee wrote.[20]

The next day General Lee attended church in Washington, but is said to have entered very quietly and to have seated himself in the last pew in the auditorium. The following morning, February 20, he started home by the same route over which he had come.[21]

So far as is known, Lee penned no account of this journey or

[17] Lee's testimony, verbatim, is in *Report of the Reconstruction Committee*, 39th Congress, part II, pp. 129 *ff.*

[18] *New York Tribune*, Feb. 19, 1866, p. 1, col. 1; *Philadelphia Inquirer*, Feb. 19, 1866, p. 1, col. 4.

[19] The story that he went to Arlington rests on the authority of the Washington correspondent of *The New York Tribune*, whose article on the subject was reprinted in *The National Intelligencer* of Feb. 22 (p. 2, col. 2) and read as follows: "General Lee at Arlington.—A gentleman of this city having occasion to pass through Arlington at dusk on Saturday saw a lonely figure standing with folded arms at the foot of a tree. Struck with the sorrowful attitude of the person, he walked past him, and saw that it was Robert E. Lee standing in the street that passes through the middle of his old estate. Mrs. Lee had applied to the President for a restoration of this estate, which has virtually become a National Union soldiers' cemetery. The expectation is general that the President will order its restoration."

[20] *Markie Letters*, 68–69.

[21] *The National Intelligencer* of Feb. 22 (p. 2, col. 6) wrongly credited this report to *The Alexandria Gazette* of "Monday" (Feb. 19). The correct date is given in *The Alexandria Gazette* of Tuesday, Feb. 20, 1866. *The Richmond Dispatch* of Feb. 14, 1866, stated, on the alleged authority of *The Baltimore Sun*, that General Lee had been in Baltimore the preceding Sunday, Feb. 11, but as he was in Lexington on Feb. 10 (*R. E. Lee, Jr.*, 213), this report seems based on error. All the evidence is that he arrived in Washington direct from Virginia. *Cf. National Intelligencer*, Feb. 17 (p. 3, col. 3). The files of *The Baltimore Sun* do not show the item *The Richmond Dispatch* published. There seems no foundation for the report in *The Philadelphia Inquirer* (Feb. 19, 1866, p. 1, col. 1) that while Lee was in Washington he was "the recipient of a large dinner party, tendered him by Rebel sympathizers who have been trying to get him into Washington for the four years of the war."

his impressions of it except to Markie Williams. He wrote her,
April 7, 1866:

"In my late visit to Washington, knowing how our God mixes
in the cup he gives us to drink in this World, the sweet with the
bitter, I had hoped I might have found you there. But you were
far beyond my reach. The changed times and circumstances did
recall sad thoughts, but I rejoiced to think, that those who were
so prominent in my thoughts, at former periods when returning
from long and distant excursions, and whose welcome was so
grateful, were now above all human influences and enjoying
eternal peace and rest. I saw however other friends, whose kind
reception gave me much pleasure, yet I am now considered such
a monster, that I hesitate to darken with my shadow, the doors
of those I love best lest I should bring upon them misfortune." [22]

If the journey had any other effect than this on Lee, it was to
deepen his tactiturnity on public questions. "I have thought from
the time of the cessation of hostilities," he wrote Mrs. Davis,
shortly after his return to Lexington, "that silence and patience on
the part of the South was the true course; and I think so still.
Controversies of all kinds will, in my opinion, only serve to continue excitement and passion, and will prevent the public mind
from acknowledgment and acceptance of the truth." [23] And to
General Early he wrote the next month, "We shall have to be
patient, and suffer for a while at least; and all controversy, I think,
will only serve to prolong angry and bitter feelings, and postpone
the period when reason and charity may resume their sway. At
present the public mind is not prepared to receive the truth." [24]
Even at the college, he never talked of war or of politics, except
in the presence of his most intimate friends, otherwise than
with the greatest reserve.[25]
Silence was his rule in the face of accusations brought against
himself, as well as in dealing with those directed at the cause for
which he had fought. "The statement is not true," he wrote that

[22] *Markie Letters*, 68.
[23] R. E. Lee to Mrs. Jefferson Davis, Feb. 23, 1866; *R. E. Lee, Jr.*, 223.
[24] R. E. Lee to J. A. Early, March 15, 1866; *Jones*, 215.
[25] Joynes in *Cent. U. S. C.*, 31.

same spring, regarding the familiar libel of his mistreatment of slaves, which was revived in *The Baltimore American,* "but I have not thought proper to publish a contradiction, being unwilling to be drawn into a newspaper discussion, believing that those who know me would not credit it and those who do not would care nothing about it. . . . It is so easy to make accusations against the people at the South upon similar testimony that those so disposed, should one be refuted, will immediately create another; and thus you would be led into endless controversy. I think it better to leave their correction to the return of reason and good feeling." [26]

College duties and correspondence alike grew heavier with the spring. Lee's interest in his work was increasing and his zeal for education was becoming more pronounced. The previous October he had written his son Robert, "If I find I can accomplish no good here, I will then endeavor to pursue the course to which my inclinations point," that of procuring a small farm.[27] He wrote after his return from Washington:

"I consider the proper education of [the South's] youth one of the most important objects now to be attained, and one from which the greatest benefits may be expected. Nothing will compensate us for the depression of the standard of our moral and intellectual culture, and each state should take the most energetic measures to revive its schools and colleges, and, if possible, to increase the facilities of instruction, and to elevate the standard of living." [28]

Some of this heavy correspondence during the winter of 1865–66 was with those who contributed to the endowment of the college. Lee was loath to write "begging letters," and he much resented the action of one of the college's financial agents in seeking to collect funds with which to raise his salary as president;[29] but he

[26] R. E. Lee to "a gentleman in Baltimore," April 13, 1866; *R. E. Lee, Jr.,* 224–25. *Cf.* R. E. Lee to E. J. Quirk, March 1, 1866, *Jones,* 213. For the original charge, see vol. I, pp. 390 *ff.*
[27] R. E. Lee to R. E. Lee, Jr., Oct. 30, 1865; *Jones,* 404.
[28] R. E. Lee to G. W. Leyburn, *MS.,* March 20, 1866; *Lee's MS. Letter Book.* Apparently Mr. Leyburn wanted to use this letter in soliciting contributions for Washington College.
[29] *Jones,* 178–179; see *infra,* p. 368.

had to struggle daily with the financial distress of the school, and he was greatly pleased when gifts were received. Not long after Lee came back from Washington, Warren Newcomb of New York donated $10,000 with which to endow ten scholarships.[30] General Lee acknowledged the benefaction with unwonted warmth: "In presenting you [the trustees'] grateful thanks for your generous aid in behalf of the college, I beg leave to express my sense of your liberality to the cause of education, now so essential to the prosperity of the South. The re-establishment of her colleges upon a broad and enlightened basis, calculated to provide for the proper instruction of her people, and to develop her dormant resources, is one of the greatest benefits that can be conferred upon the country. Those contributing to this great result will be ranked by posterity among the most meritorious citizens." [31] A gift of books he acknowledged with the assurance that "they form the most valuable collection in the library, will do much for the advancement of science, give an impulse to the spread and development of that knowledge so highly valued by your esteemed brother, and cause his memory to be revered and cherished by the wise and good." [32]

Personal gifts came with those for the college and were acknowledged painstakingly. If it was a dressing gown from a fair in Baltimore, he valued it the more highly "in remembrance of [the] munificent bounty bestowed on thousands of destitute women and children by the 'Association for the Relief of Southern Sufferers,' the fruits of which shall live long after those who have received it have mouldered into dust." [33] If it was membership in a Petersburg literary society that bore the name of the great "Stonewall," he accepted it and praised the "laudable design of self-improvement, in accomplishing which I can commend them to no more worthy example than his whose name they have adopted." [34] Of a saddle and bridle sent by admirers in Maryland, he wrote, "Were I not reminded at every point to which I

[30] *Trustees' Minutes*, March 10, 1866.

[31] R. E. Lee to Warren Newcomb, *MS.*, March 22, 1866; *Lee's MS. Letter Book.* This was the same Newcomb whose widow established H. Sophie Newcomb Memorial College, now a unit of Tulane University, New Orleans.

[32] R. E. Lee to Rathmell Wilson, March 26, 1866; *Jones*, 245.

[33] R. E. Lee to unnamed Baltimore woman, May 3, 1866; *Jones*, 250.

[34] R. E. Lee to C. R. Bishop. Jr., May 5, 1866; *Jones*, 250.

turn, at the South, of their benevolent labors for its relief, their gift would serve to keep me in mind of their sympathy and generosity." [35] An autographed copy of Worsley's translation of the *Iliad* with a fine dedicatory poem, he praised discriminately and in a different tone: "Its perusal has been my evening's recreation, and I have never enjoyed the beauty and grandeur of the poem more than as recited by you. The translation is as truthful as powerful, and faithfully reproduces the imagery and rhythm of the bold original. The undeserved compliment to myself in prose and verse, on the first leaves of the volume, I receive as your tribute to the merit of my countrymen who struggled for constitutional liberty." [36]

During the spring of 1866 a tragedy far closer to his daily life than Homer's line was prevented by General Lee. A horse thief who had been troubling the countryside was caught and brought to Lexington. No sooner was word of his incarceration received than farmers from Rockbridge began to ride into town. Soon

---

[35] R. E. Lee to the Ladies of the Southern Relief Fair, May 12, 1866; *Jones, 251.*

[36] R. E. Lee to P. S. Worsley, Feb. 10, 1866; *Jones,* 248. On hearing that Worsley was ill, he invited him to Lexington (*ibid.*). The poem to Lee appears in *Jones,* 78, and reads as follows:

. . . . οἷος γὰρ ἐρύετο Ἴλιον Ἕκτωρ

Iliad, VI, 403.

The grand old bard that never dies,
  Receive him in our English tongue!
I send thee, but with weeping eyes,
  The story that he sung.

Thy Troy is fallen, thy dear land
  Is marred beneath the spoiler's heel.
I cannot trust my trembling hand
  To write the things I feel.

Ah, realm of tombs!—but let her bear
  This blazon to the last of times:
No nation rose so white and fair,
  Or fell so pure of crimes.

The widow's moan, the orphan's wail,
  Come round thee; yet in truth be strong!
Eternal right, though all else fail,
  Can never be made wrong.

An angel's heart, an angel's mouth,
  Not Homer's, could alone for me
Hymn well the great Confederate South,
  Virginia first, and Lee.

there was a crowd in front of the jail, and talk of lynching the thief, whose name was Jonathan Hughes. Word of this reached General Lee—for rumor quickly covered the little town—and he went at once to the scene of the trouble. He found the old jailer on the steps of the prison doggedly facing the crowd, and holding the keys high above his head. Either from respect for the man's years or else from admiration of his courage, the mob hesitated to rush him and take the keys. That gave Lee his opportunity. Moving about quickly and quietly, he urged each knot of men not to attempt violence but to let the law take its course. Most of those in the gathering had fought under General Lee, and in answer to his appeal, they began to leave. Soon the danger of violence was past. Then, as inconspicuously as he had come, Lee walked away. Hughes was convicted and sent to prison for eighteen years.[37]

It was during this period of great college activity that Lee first began to doubt whether he could write the history he had projected the previous summer.[38] He continued to collect material and to urge his old comrades to gather it. From Walter Taylor he received some careful estimates of the army's strength,[39] but from most other sources Lee found the haul very scanty. "It will be difficult to get the world to understand the odds against which we fought," he wrote Early, "and the destruction, or loss, of all the returns from the army embarrasses me very much." [40] To a prospective German translator he wrote, "It has been my desire to write a history of the campaigns in Virginia; but I have not yet been able to commence it, and it is so uncertain that I shall be able to accomplish my purpose, that I think it unnecessary to make any arrangements for its translation into a foreign language. Should circumstances hereafter render such a course proper, I shall not forget your kind proposition." [41] This letter was written within a day or two of the first anniversary of his return to Richmond from Appomattox. How far the tides of time had carried him in those twelve months!

[37] C. A. Graves, an eye-witness, in *Riley*, 28–30.

[38] It was during this period, also, that Lee had the interview with the Marquess of Lorne described on pp. 300 *ff*.

[39] R. E. Lee to C. A. White, Oct. 4, 1867; *Jones*, 264.

[40] R. E. Lee to J. A. Early, March 15, 1866; *Jones*, 214, *cf. ibid.*, 219, 221.

[41] R. E. Lee to Lieutenant von Clausenitz [*sic*], April 16, 1866; *Jones*, 249. The name may have been Clausewitz and the addressed perhaps a kinsman of the great writer on strategy.

On April 26–28 the trustees held a most important three-day session, during which they debated and endorsed a revision of the course of study. The plan was drafted by the faculty and was approved by General Lee. In some part, it may have been his own creation. The old curriculum was abolished, and in its place an elective system was introduced, with nine separate "Schools" from which the student might choose.

The first three were Latin, Greek, and Mathematics, in each of which three years of instruction were to be given. In the fourth school, Moral Philosophy, two years were to be provided. In Chemistry, Natural Philosophy, and Practical Chemistry, only one course each was to be offered. The ninth school, Modern Languages, was to embrace French, German, Spanish, and Italian, and, temporarily, English, Philology, and Modern History, arranged in such classes as the professor thought necessary. In each school students who attained a fixed minimum were to be declared proficients. Those who fulfilled special requirements set in each instance by the faculty were to be recognized as graduates.

While matriculates were free to consult their personal needs and to follow their own desires in selecting their classes, they were, of course, to be admitted only to those for which their preparation equipped them, and all of them had to have at least fifteen recitations a week. Those who wished to proceed to the degree of Bachelor of Arts must be proficient in Latin, Greek, Mathematics, Chemistry, Moral Philosophy, and Natural Philosophy. For the degree of Master of Arts, graduation was necessary in Greek, Latin, Mathematics, Chemistry, Moral Philosophy, Applied Mathematics, English Philology, and two of the modern languages. A distinctly scientific course was to be offered, leading to baccalaureate in philosophy. This would be awarded those proficient in Chemistry, Mathematics, Practical Chemistry, Natural Philosophy, Applied Mathematics, Modern History, and two of the modern languages. The classics and moral philosophy could be omitted altogether.[42]

The action taken in April by the trustees was supplemented at two meetings in June and at a special sitting in July. As fully developed at that time for the session 1866–67, the new curriculum

[42] *Trustees' Minutes,* April 26, 27, 1866.

offered in the academic departments a considerable range of study.

The preparatory course, which General Lee had found in existence when he came to Lexington, was continued. "This course," the catalogue read, "has been temporarily organized to meet the wants of applicants for admission, who, though in many cases grown young men, are unprepared to enter the regular classes. In many instances the backwardness of the applicant is due not to incapacity or want of diligence but to the almost entire suspension of preparatory schools during the late war, and to the fact that many of these young men were themselves during those years in the military service. As the want of good preparatory schools still exists, and will probably continue for some time in many parts of the Southern states, and as young men are likely to make more rapid and satisfactory progress when associated, as here, with those of their own age, than when classed with boys in the preparatory schools—it is believed that this department meets a real need of the country as at present situated. . . . A student may find it convenient to study some subjects, in this department, while pursuing others in the regular course." [43]

Admission to the school of Latin presupposed the declensions and conjugations and Cæsar, Sallust, and Ovid. The first year covered composition and grammar, Cæsar, Nepos, and Ciccro. The senior class read Horace, Virgil, Terence, Juvenal, and Persius, with exercises in Latin composition and some study of Roman literature and institutions.

Greek was taught from the foundations, the Anabasis and Memorabilia being read in the first year. In the senior of the three classes, the reading was Thucydides, Æschylus, Aristophanes, and Homer.

As the School of Modern Languages and English Philology was new, its curriculum was not set forth in detail, though due warning was given that Anglo-Saxon would be taught.

The course in Moral Philosophy was to cover Mental Philosophy, Logic, Rhetoric, and "belles-lettres" in the first year, and "Moral Philosophy with Evidences of Christianity and Political Economy" in the second.

[43] *1865–66 Catalogue.* 14.

In Mathematics the preliminary requirements were only arithmetic, though it was "very desirable" that students should have studied algebra, at least to equations of the second degree, and that they should have some knowledge of plane geometry. The regular instruction began with algebra and plane and solid geometry. The other classes followed the usual progression, with differential and integral calculus and the calculus of variations in the senior class.

The new School of Applied Mathematics covered civil engineering and analytical mechanics. For civil engineering the second-year mathematics was prerequisite, and for analytical mechanics, the third class in mathematics. In physics, the course covered a wide range in a single session.

The School of Chemistry included general instruction for one year, with some semblance of laboratory work. "Three days [a week]," read the department's announcement, "are devoted to lectures, illustrated by elaborate experiments; the other two days to recitations on the lectures and text-book. At each recitation some members of the class are required to repeat experiments previously given in connection with lectures. The laboratory is also accessible at convenient hours for students to practice manipulations privately." The senior class studied mineralogy and geology. A School of Practical Chemistry was described in the catalogue and was to cover "metallurgy and the application of the principles of chemistry to agriculture, mining, manufacturing, and the mechanic arts, together with vegetable and animal physiology." But this instruction, for the time, was to be distributed among the teachers in the other scientific schools. The same arrangement was announced for the School of History and Literature, which was to include "Modern History, English Literature and Criticism; Rhetoric, Elocution, Philosophical Grammar, and Comparative Philology."

The Schools of Applied Mathematics, Natural Philosophy, Chemistry and Practical Chemistry, according to the new plan, "embraced a complete course of civil engineering." The catalogue announced: "Young men wishing to become 'professional engineers' will be allowed to confine themselves to such branches of study in these schools, as are requisite to make them accomplished

264

in their profession. To such as become proficient in the studies of this department a certificate to that effect will be awarded." That was equivalent to the definite establishment of a department of engineering as distinguished from the courses in the liberal arts.[44]

This was not the only extension. The law school long conducted in Lexington by Judge John W. Brockenbrough, rector of the college, had attracted desirable students and had won no little reputation. At a special meeting in June, 1866, a committee was named to confer with Judge Brockenbrough and to report a plan by which the "Lexington Law School," as it was called, should become connected with the college.[45] This was arranged at a meeting in July, and the affiliated School of Law and Equity was duly announced.[46] It was to include junior and senior courses, in both of which three recitations of three hours each were to be given weekly. Seemingly, the college assumed no financial responsibility for the Law School and exercised no authority over it.

Before the end of the session, Cyrus W. McCormick gave another $5000 for the establishment of the chair of Experimental Philosophy and Practical Mechanics.[47] A gift of approximately $1000 of desirable books was also received.[48] Three excellent men were chosen to the faculty—Richard S. McCulloh, as McCormick Professor of Experimental Philosophy and Practical Mechanics, Colonel William Allan as professor of Applied Mathematics, and E. S. Joynes as professor of Modern Languages.[49] Colonel Allan had been Jackson's ordnance officer and subsequently wrote an admirable study of the Valley Campaign of 1862. He later conducted a very successful boys' school near Baltimore. McCulloh had been in Confederate service and had devised an elaborate plan for the destruction of Federal shipping. After the war he had been temporarily imprisoned by the Federals. Joynes had

---

[44] All these details are from *1865–66 Catalogue*, 15 *ff.*
[45] *Trustees' Minutes*, June 9, 1866.
[46] *Trustees' Minutes*, July 18, 1866; *1865–66 Catalogue*, 23.
[47] *Trustees' Minutes*, June 27, 1866. [48] *Trustees' Minutes*, June 28, 1866.
[49] *Trustees' Minutes*, April 26, 1866. Reverend J. A. Lefevre was elected professor of Moral Philosophy but declined (*Trustees' Minutes*, April 26, June 27, 1866). Reverend John L. Kirkpatrick of Davidson College was elected in his stead (*Trustees' Minutes*, July, 17, 1866).

been in the War Department. General Lee made it his rule, in choosing among men of equal qualifications, to give preference to Confederate veterans.[50]

All these circumstances combined to round out a session that marked a definite advance. A struggling college that opened with four professors and a thin platoon of students was able to print a catalogue that listed 146 matriculates and a faculty for the next year of 14 members, exclusive of the president. In scope, its curriculum had been virtually doubled. Schools of Engineering and of Law had been established. For the inquiring student, the library had been partially restored. The election of courses had been made the privilege of every one, and the honor system in its fullness had been established.

Interest on the $88,000 of the pre-war endowment had again been made available. The financial campaign had been vigorously prosecuted. Mr. McCormick's gifts and the activities of Doctor W. S. White and Reverend S. D. Stuart had yielded cash or pledges amounting to $42,000. Reverend E. P. Walton of Baltimore, one of the endowment agents, as already noted, had gone to Memphis and from that base had visited Mississippi, Arkansas, Louisiana, and Texas. He had appointed numerous local agents, and seems to have known his business thoroughly. Very carefully, he kept two subscription books, one for gifts of $100 or more and the other for smaller contributions. In the second book he subdivided the donations of $1 from those of a greater size, and when he made the mistake of having the book opened with a subscription of $10, he carefully pinned up that page and started a new "because $10," in his pencilled note, "was deemed too small an amount to open this book with." In the first year, Mr. Walton procured subscriptions of $45,280 to the endowment fund. No gifts below $100 were included in this total. In addition, two friends had contributed 640 acres of Texas land. Most of these subscriptions were represented by notes, rather than by cash, for the times were hard, but in nearly every case interest was promised. Apparently Mr. Walton had met with some skepticism as to General Lee's intention of remaining at the head of Washington College, for in one of the cities he had visited, probably

50 *Jones*, 322.

Memphis, he had written a vigorous newspaper letter in which he insisted that though Virginia would "lavish her treasures" on Lee, the General would not dissolve his connection with Washington College "to preside over the University or Military Institute, or any other institution." [51]

The trustees proceeded to expand and improve the college plant as the endowment increased. Provision for the enclosure of the college grounds was made. [52] A superintendent of grounds and buildings was chosen, as was a clerk to the faculty. [53] Without the president's knowledge, his salary was doubled and was put at $3000. [54] Fifteen hundred dollars were appropriated for new scientific equipment. [55] Ambitious plans were made for the erection of a new dormitory for 100 men, [56] though subsequently it was found that facilities at the college and in the town were ample to house the students. [57] A new chapel was authorized, at a cost not to exceed $10,000. [58] Appropriation was made for gymnastic apparatus, [59] repairs to the professors' houses were ordered, [60] and a resolution was adopted for the construction of "a mansion" for the president, as soon as the funds were available. [61] To find the money for all these enlargements, without encroaching on the principal of recent donations, the college named Colonel William Allan the general agent of endowment, [62] and resolved to make another effort to procure part of the sum voted to the states by Congress for the promotion of agricultural and mechanical training. [63] A college that had been very near death was to live again with a vigor it never had known.

The summer passed very quietly. Building and repairs at the

---

[51] *Subscription Books of Rev. E. P. Walton:* Treasurer's Records, Washington and Lee University. For locating these interesting documents, the author is indebted to Professor W. M. Brown, formerly of the department of education, Washington and Lee University. The letter to the "Editors *Commercial,*" regarding Lee's intention to remain at Lexington, is conspicuously pasted in the front of Mr. Walton's subscription book of larger gifts.

[52] *Trustees' Minutes,* April 28, June 8, 1866.

[53] *Trustees' Minutes,* June 27, 1866. [54] *Trustees' Minutes,* June 27, 1866.

[55] *Trustees' Minutes,* June 28, 1866. [56] *Trustees' Minutes,* June 28, 1866.

[57] *Trustees' Minutes,* July 17–18, 1866. See *infra,* p. 255, note 58, and p. 318.

[58] *Trustees' Minutes,* July 18, 1866. It is quite possible that General Lee advanced part of the $6000 which the trustees resolved the college might spend at once on the chapel if thereby it might be advanced to the stage where it could be used. See *supra,* p. 248, note 10.

[59] *Trustees' Minutes,* July 18, 1866.

[60] *Trustees' Minutes,* July 18, 1866. [61] *Trustees' Minutes,* July 18, 1866.

[62] *Trustees' Minutes,* June 28, 1866. [63] *Trustees' Minutes,* July 18, 1866.

college occupied much of the General's time. He felt he should supervise the construction in person, because he wished to economize, and also because he held no high opinion of some of those engaged in this sort of work. "You will have to attend to your contractors," he wrote Robert the next fall. "They will generally bear great attention, and then circumvent you." [64]

Although remaining in Lexington himself, he sent Mrs. Lee to the Rockbridge Baths, eleven miles from the town, and as often as he could, he rode over to see her.[65] In this way he came very soon to know most of the people who lived by the roadside, especially the children. When he saw them, his eyes would light up and he would begin to smile. Almost always he would draw rein and chat with them. Soon they came to look on him as peculiarly their own.

It was the same way in Lexington. Every Christmas he had presents for all the children of his acquaintance[66] and often he let them ride Traveller.[67] One of his small sweethearts met him on the street while she was trying to escape from a tiny sister who insisted on following her. "Oh, General!" she said in exasperation. "Fanny won't go home—please make her!" Obediently and diplomatically the General prevailed on both of them to reverse their runaway steps, and with one on either hand he led them back home. Another young friend of five, a boy who had been fired by his pastor to go in quest of Sunday-school recruits, hurried to Lee one Sabbath morning and besought the General to be his "new scholar." Seeing the lad was disappointed because he could not attend, and observing that some college boys had stopped to listen to his colloquy with the young evangelist, Lee delivered himself for the benefit of the students: "Ah, C——, we must all try to be good Christians—that is the most important thing. I can't go to your Sunday-school to be your new scholar

---

[64] R. E. Lee to R. E. Lee, Jr., Oct. 18, 1866; *R. E. Lee, Jr.,* 243.

[65] Long, *op. cit.,* 467, quoted a charming little story of Lee's courtesy to a friend of the family who came to the house one day in the absence of Mrs. Lee to do some canning for her.

[66] *Mrs. Preston,* 273.

[67] One of the most pleasant memories of the late Doctor Henry van Dyke was that of being permitted by General Lee to ride Traveller while at one of the Virginia springs, probably in 1867. "Gen. Lee," van Dyke wrote, "was a hero of my boyish admiration" (Henry van Dyke to Thomas Smyth, July 20, 1912, in Thomas Smyth: *Autobiographical Notes, Letters and Reflections,* 595).

today, but I am very glad that you asked me. It shows that you are zealous in a good cause, and I hope that you will continue to be so as you grow up. And I don't want you to think that I consider myself too old to be a Sunday-school scholar"—this was especially addressed to the listening college boys. "No one ever becomes too old to study the precious truths of the Bible!" [68] This five-year-old may have been the same youngster who slipped away from his mother during the college commencement exercises and calmly trotted up on the platform to be with General Lee. He sat down on the floor at Lee's feet, leaned over, put his head against the General's knee and soon went to sleep. Lee continued immobile and in an uncomfortable position for the remainder of the meeting, so as not to disturb the little sleeper. [69] Another time, as he was starting out for his ride, the General met the tiny daughters of two of his professors. Both of them were wearing sunbonnets and were cautiously riding a slow and sleepy old horse up a back street. Lee promptly invited them to go with him and escorted them out on one of his favorite rambles. They had high converse and much sport as well, for one of the little girls was just recovering from mumps and had her jaws covered up. Lee professed great concern lest she give the disease to Traveller. [70]

Occasionally the General encountered a timid child whose reserve was not easily overcome. One small miss visited in his house for days and would not come to him or even talk to him, being afraid, perhaps, of his beard. While Lee was in his chamber one morning she tiptoed to the door and paused. He invited her to enter, but she declined. She condescended, however, to glance about the room and happened to spy a little stuffed penwiper in the figure of a man that some female member of the household had stuck on the wall. "Is that your doll-baby?" the child inquired. "Yes," said Lee, delighted to find a ground of common understanding. From that hour the girl was his friend: possession of a doll made youth and age akin. [71]

If General Lee triumphed in this instance over diffidence, he

---

[68] *Jones,* 412–13.

[69] *Jones,* 413. In Mrs. Preston's version of this incident (*loc. cit.,* 272), it is stated that the General beckoned to the child, who had lost his parents in the crowded auditorium and was running in fright up and down the aisles looking for them.

[70] *R. E. Lee, Jr.,* 372–73.   [71] *McDonald,* 7.

was thwarted once in dealing with juvenile pugnacity. Stopping one afternoon during a thunderstorm at the house of acquaintances, he found both the master and the mistress away from home and only the youngsters there, busily playing marbles on the floor. He insisted that they continue their game as he sat and waited for the storm to end. Finally, two of the boys fell to quarrelling and soon came to blows. Lee at once intervened, but in vain. "I argued," he said in recounting the episode, "I remonstrated, I commanded; but they were like two young mastiffs, and never in all my military service had I to own myself so perfectly powerless. I retired beaten from the field, and let the little fellows fight it out." [72]

Lee made many young friends through his mail. A correspondent from Georgia announced to the General the existence of a proud young namesake and probably asked Lee to write him a letter of counsel. The General carefully penned it in kindly paragraphs, concluding with the admonition: "Above all things, learn at once to worship your Creator and to do His will as revealed in His Holy Book." [73]

Often, on his rambles, Lee met and talked with his former soldiers. The oddest of all his encounters, and one that he related in much amusement to his family, occurred in a dense forest, where he met a man who had served in the ranks. The veteran at once recognized his former commander and stopped his horse. "General Lee," he said, "I am powerful glad to see you, and I feel like cheering you." Lee expostulated: they were alone in the woods and there was no reason for such a salutation. But the soldier insisted, and until distance drowned the sound, Lee could hear the loyal warrior crying "Hurrah for General Lee"—doubtless with a rebel yell following it. [74]

At the end of his rides to visit his wife, the General usually found Mrs. Lee temporarily benefited by the baths. In August she sustained a fall that was thought to retard her progress, [75] but

---

[72] *Mrs. Preston,* 273.

[73] R. E. Lee to A. P. M. ——, May 29, 1866; *Jones,* 411. For a somewhat similar acknowledgment of a namesake, see *ibid.,* R. E. Lee to Mrs. Robert W. ——, Aug. 29, 1866; *Jones,* 411.

[74] *R. E. Lee, Jr.,* 372.

[75] On Aug. 9, Mrs. Lee's crutch slipped on a wet floor and she was thrown off a low porch. Her eye and face were much bruised (R. E. Lee to R. H. Chilton, *MS.,* Aug. 13, 1866; *Chilton Papers; R. E. Lee, Jr.,* 238).

this accident apart, it was a pleasant and busy summer. Lee's only complaint—if it might be so styled—was over the weight of his correspondence. "I have about a bushel of letters to answer and other things to do," he wrote Mrs. Lee.[76] Appeals of every imaginable sort came to him almost every day. One writer wanted him to find an orphan child for her to adopt; the head of a convent sought through him to get ten or twelve fatherless girls to be educated; another asked him to locate a lost lover who had "belonged" either to "Mr. Lee's" or to "Mr. Johnston's" army; soldiers invoked his counsel; widows implored his help; newspaper editors solicited interviews; lecturers offered their services— the load was heavy, month after month, from the time he returned to Richmond after Appomattox until his death.[77]

"I hope," Mrs. Margaret Preston once said to him, "you do not feel obliged to reply to all these letters."

"I certainly do," he answered. "Think of these poor people! It is a great deal of trouble for them to write; why should I not be willing to take the trouble to answer them? And as that is all I can give most of them, I give it ungrudgingly."[78]

In addition, he had a more personal correspondence his feelings and his sense of duty would not permit him to neglect. Marriages were occurring frequently in the wide circle of his acquaintance-ship, and deaths came often. Old friends entered new business or met with ill-fortune. Lee wrote to all of them.[79] Once he confessed he did not have the heart to offer consolation to a minister on the loss of his young wife, but he did it nonetheless,[80] and to many a Southern widow he addressed a message of sympathy on the passing of her husband. When boys died in the college, his letters had a special note of personal distress.[81]

The letter he wrote William F. Wickham, father of General

---

[76] R. E. Lee to Mrs. Lee, Aug. 2, 1866; *R. E. Lee, Jr.*, 241; *cf. ibid.*, 237 *ff.*
[77] *Long*, 468; *Jones*, 238. *Cf.* R. E. Lee to Colonel F. R. Farrar, *MS.*, Feb. 12, 1869; *Lee's MS. Letter Book.*
[78] *Mrs. Preston*, 275.
[79] *Cf.* R. E. Lee to W. T. Sherman, March 27, 1867, *Lee's MS. Letter Book,* regarding an insane man who was threatening an appeal to the military authorities.
[80] *Jones*, 439; P. H. Hoge: *M. D. Hoge*, 256.
[81] *Cf.* R. E. Lee to Mrs. Elliott, Feb. 21, 1867; *Jones*, 434; R. E. Lee to Mrs. G. W. Randolph, April 11, 1867; *Jones*, 434; R. E. Lee to Samuel Boykin, Nov. 7, 1868, regarding the death of Howell Cobb; *Jones*, 264; R. E. Lee to Mrs. ——, April 6, 1868, on the demise of her student-son; *Jones*, 433; R. E. Lee to Samuel R. Gordon, Feb. 28, 1870; *Jones*, 435.

Williams C. Wickham, on the demise of his venerable wife, a niece of General Lee's mother, deserves to be quoted in full. It was written when William Lloyd Garrison, *The Independent,* and their supporters were assailing the college because of an affair presently to be described.[82]

My dear Mr. Wickham   Lexington 4 March 1868

I grieve most deeply over the great sorrow that has fallen upon you and your house.

Death in its silent, sure march is fast gathering those whom I have longest loved, so that when he shall knock at my door I will more willingly follow. She whom we mourn is among those whom I have longest and most dearly loved. She was the favorite of my mother, the object of my boyish affection and admiration, and has been cherished, fondly cherished, in the long years of manhood. She will always live in my memory, and the farthest recollection of her brings me nothing but pleasure.

May He who has dealt the blow in mercy temper its affliction, and enable us to say, His will be done.

Yours in true friendship

Mr. Wm. F. Wickham   R. E. LEE[83]

His letters to girls who were about to embark on matrimony were cordially written, but in some of them there seems to be a note of farewell, as if marriage in those hard times meant an end of visits and of jests. It was in this spirit he wrote Laura Chilton, daughter of his old friend and one-time chief of staff, General Chilton. She was about to marry Colonel Peyton Wise.

My dear Miss Laura—   Lexington Va., 22 Nov. 1869.

Your invitation to your wedding has carried me back to the pleasant days when you were a little girl in Texas, when you and Emmie gave me so much pleasure, the purest if not the greatest I enjoyed while there. Ever since that time I have entertained for you both the truest affection & have watched with much anxiety

---

[82] See *infra*, pp. 345 *ff.*

[83] *Wickham MSS.*, placed at the writer's disposal, along with much invaluable critical assistance, by Honorable H. T. Wickham.

your progress in life. You will not be surprised then at the interest I feel in your approaching marriage, & at my sincere prayer that the Great God of Mercy may shower upon you his richest blessing & so direct your course in this world that you may enjoy his peace, his blessed peace, here & life eternal hereafter. My thoughts will be with you though I cannot be present on the day of your wedding, & I cordially sympathize with your father & mother in all their feelings, to whom & to Miss Emmie, you must give my affectionate love, & must tell them they had better send the latter to me now, or that they will soon lose her.

. . . .

And now with the most sincere affection for yourself & my cordial regards for Col. Wise

I remain truly & as ever
Your friend
R. E. LEE

Miss Laura Mason Chilton[84]

Letters of felicitation went, likewise, to friends embarking on new business ventures. This one went to a firm with which was associated a man who had received hundreds of dispatches from Lee, written in far different strain:

Gentⁿ   Lexington, Va: 26 Jan. '66

I am much obliged to you for your business card and the pleasure it has afforded me, to know that you have entered into partnership. I know you will do your work well, I please myself therefore with the prospect of your great success.

I wrote to your Senior, a few days since at 'Mason Mississippi,' and hope he will receive my letter. I do not consider my partnership with him yet dissolved, and shall not let him go during life.

Wishing you all happiness and prosperity, I am with great affect'n

Your ob't ser't

Longstreet, Owen & Co.
New Orleans.[85]

---

[84] *Chilton Papers.* The omitted paragraph contained merely an unimportant message to friends.

[85] Original *MS.* belonging to Professor Wm. Warner Moss, Jr., of New York, who graciously placed a copy at the writer's disposal.

Lee's correspondence of this sort must have run to thousands of letters, which are cherished by their owners but are now unduly scattered. The General kept copies of comparatively few of them.

So busy was Lee with his correspondence, this particular summer of 1866, and so far was his mind turned to the work of peace that he did not follow closely the operations of the world's newest conflict, the Seven Weeks' War between Austria and Prussia.[86] As for the accumulating literature of the struggle in which he had been engaged, he continued to leave it alone and still had no inclination to read any of it.[87]

[86] R. E. Lee to A. T. Bledsoe, Oct. 28, 1867; *Jones*, 158. Lee noted, however, "at the time of the occurrence, I thought I saw the mistake committed by the Austrians; but I did not know all the facts, and you are aware that, though it is easy to write on such a subject, it is difficult to elucidate the truth."

[87] *Ibid. Cf.* also R. E. Lee to Charles Carter, April 17, 1867, *Jones*, 193; R. E. Lee to J. M. Mason, March 3, 1870; *Jones*, 233.

CHAPTER XVI

"My Boys"

ONE day that September (1866), while General Lee was riding out on the road to the Rockbridge Baths, he stopped at a roadside spring. He found some young men there who recognized him instantly, handed him a drink of water, and then told him about themselves. They were from Tennessee, they explained, and were prospective students at Washington College. Might they give him their introductions from General Ewell and others of his former officers? Lee read the letters—how often and in scenes how different had he opened messages from Ewell!—and inquired of the boys whither they were bound. To Rockbridge Baths, they said, to spend part of the time before the opening of college. Lee forthwith wrote and delivered them a line to the proprietor of the springs, John A. Harmon. "My dear Major," it read, "These are some of my new boys. Please take care of them." [1]

That note did more than win for the Tennesseans the most cordial of welcomes at the baths; it displayed as well the spirit in which General Lee regarded the students of Washington College. He held them as his "boys" in his labor with them and in his hopes for them. His "boys" they were in the disciplinary system he had developed to such an extent by the beginning of his second session that its details may now be reviewed. [2]

His "boys" were not all boys. In fact he never called them "boys" to their faces. In private conversation as in official dealings, each of them was "Mister." [3] Many of them were veterans of his own campaigns and wore beards. [4] A few of them were reckless and violent, hardened by their experience in war and loose in their habits. College to them was a minor adventure, endurable only

---

[1] J. W. Ewing in *Riley*, 70.
[2] It will be understood, of course, that in this topical chapter the illustrative incidents did not all occur in the first two years of General Lee's administration.
[3] S. M. Yonge's *MS. Recollections of Washington College under General Lee* (cited here after as *S. M. Yonge MS.*).
[4] *McDonald*, 10.

275

because it offered opportunities for wassailing in the bars of the town and for hunting the defiant fox in the hills around Lexington. Other ex-soldiers, serious-minded, were typified by a young man who tramped all the way to the campus from Alabama, bringing with him his father's gold watch and three hundred dollars, all the family could raise for his schooling.[5] These students worked with a zeal that set a standard for the college, and as they had obeyed General Lee's orders during the war, they cheerfully submitted themselves to his discipline now. They were indifferent to dress, had no money to waste, and were anxious to equip themselves as rapidly as possible for their careers.[6] The third group consisted of boys who were just coming of the age to enter college and had not seen service in the army—"yearlings" they were styled by the veterans.[7] Sons of rich men and of poor, they differed little, except in preparation, from those who crowd the registrars' offices today. Some of them had been spoiled at home and were sent to Lexington in the belief that the discipline and influence of General Lee would undo parental mistakes.[8]

For the well-being of a student-body so diversified and so difficult to handle, General Lee felt an obligation that sometimes weighted him down. Especially when he saw them together, in assembly, did their care hang heavily on him. Coming out of chapel one morning he was seen to be so much affected that he was asked if anything was wrong. "I was thinking," he answered simply, "of my responsibility to Almighty God for these hundreds of young men." [9] He was mindful of every one of them, as will presently appear, but doubtless in his heart he was most moved by the struggles of his former soldiers, and by the persistence of those who bore the shackles of poverty. Yet he would not permit his veterans to lament the years during which they had worn the Southern uniform. A favorite and brilliant pupil he called to him one day and cautioned against overwork. The student defended himself. "I am so impatient," said he, "to make up for the time I lost in the army—." Lee flushed instantly. "Mr. Humphreys," he exclaimed in a tone but one pitch removed from

---

[5] *Riley*, 131.   [6] *Riley*, 55.   [7] *McDonald*, 10.
[8] For conditions generally in the student-body, see *Jones*, 123, quoting J. L. Kirkpatrick.
[9] *Riley*, 107.

anger, "however long you live and whatever you accomplish, you will find that the time you spent in the Confederate army was the most profitably spent portion of your life. Never again speak of having lost time in the army!"[10] So far as he could, he helped these former soldiers and the poorer students.[11] To Humphreys he awarded a scholarship the donor had left to his nomination, and in Humphreys's interest he wrote a commendatory letter which that student, later a savant of distinction, cherished to the day of his death.[12] Lee almost wept when the boy who had covered the long road from Alabama told him of his hopes and ambitions, and he arranged it that the stout-hearted youth should board cheaply in the country and should have employment, though it was only as a farm laborer, during the long vacation.[13] He discovered that another lad from the far South, who was residing in the country to save expense, had no place to study between classes. Making a place for the boy in his office, he insisted that he work there, and when he missed him one day, he rode out to see if his young companion was sick.[14]

By diligent correspondence, he solicited work in summer for boys who needed money with which to complete their college course. Regarding an engineering student who sought a temporary position, he wrote the president of the James River and Kanawha Canal Company, "He is a very promising young man, of great energy & integrity of character & is willing to take any position in which he can make himself useful & earn his subsistence for the time. You may probably have known his father Col. Angus McDonald, who died during the war and left a widow & seven children, of whom H. is the eldest, six others are to be educated."[15] Some students who could not get summer work or raise money among their friends were accepted, as already recorded, on credit, evidenced solely by their notes of hand.[16]

[10] *Riley*, 39.
[11] *Cf.* R. E. Lee to M. D. Hoge, *MSS.*, Jan. 23 and Feb. 27, 1869; *Lee's MS. Letter Book*.
[12] R. E. Lee to W. L. Ewing, Feb. 13, 1867; *Lee's MS. Letter Book*.
[13] *Riley*, 131, quoting J. J. Allen.   [14] 62 *Harpers Weekly*, 412.
[15] R. E. Lee to Major Chas. S. Carrington, *MS.*, July 2, 1867; *Freeman MSS*. This letter was given the writer by R. M. Lynn of Washington, D. C.
[16] *Trustees' Minutes*, Aug. 4, 1865; R. E. Lee to Rudolph Kliberg, *MS.*, Feb. 19, 1870, *Lee's MS. Letter Book*. *Cf.* also Committee on Loan Fund, *MS. Faculty Minutes*, Sept. 29, 1870. In one instance, the college received a student in return for a portrait of Chief Justice Marshall (R. E. Lee to Mrs. A. L. J.; *MS.*, March 24, 1870, *Lee's MS. Letter Book*).

General Lee initiated the honor system very soon after he came to Lexington, and made it the basis on which all students were received. Faculty visitation of dormitories and all forms of espionage were abolished. If any breach of discipline occurred or any injury was done to college property, he expected the students who were involved in it to report to him. "We have no printed rules," Lee told a new matriculate who asked for a copy. "We have but one rule here, and it is that every student must be a gentleman." [17] The first and the final appeal was to the student's sense of honor.[18] "As a general principle," he told a young professor, "you should not force young men to do their duty, but let them do it voluntarily and thereby develop their characters. The great mistake of my life was taking a military education." [19] The code of the college, as Lee developed it, was positive though unprinted. The regulations, though few, were always enforced. "Make no needless rules," he admonished the faculty. And again, "We must never make a rule that we cannot enforce." [20]

Except in a few particulars, he did not attempt any compromise with the system he had inherited at West Point and had employed there. He turned away from it altogether,[21] with the explanation that he was not training men for the army but for civil life. The discipline fitted to make soldiers was not the best to qualify men for the duties of citizenship or for success in life. "For many years," said he, "I have observed the failure in business pursuits of men who have resigned from the army. It is very rare that any one of them has achieved success." He may even have gone so far as to emphasize by his own movements in the company of military men that he was no longer a soldier and was not disciplining cadets. It was noticed in Lexington that on occasions when the faculty and students of Washington College appeared with the staff and corps of the Virginia Military Institute, General Lee never marched in time with the drum-beat or kept step with the head of the other school.[22] But though he put all the past behind him and administered the college as if he had never

[17] Collyar in *Riley,* 66. As a matter of fact, the college had an ancient set of rules that covered, in some respects, the conduct of students, but not in the sense this inquirer and General Lee meant.
[18] Ewing, in *Riley,* 71.   [19] Humphreys, in *Riley,* 38.
[20] Joynes, in *Cent. U. S. C.,* 33; *cf. infra,* p. 289.
[21] Gordon, in *Riley,* 84.   [22] Humphreys, in *Riley,* 35.

exercised authority as a commanding general in the field, he drew a clear and constant distinction between military rule and self-controlled obedience to constituted authority. One of his oft-repeated maxims was, "Obedience to lawful authority is the foundation of manly character." [23]

The first application of the great fundamental—"be a gentleman"—was to the students' habits of study. The General countenanced no idleness. Even under the elective system, all students had to take at least fifteen hours of classroom work each week, and every man was required to belong to one or the other of the two literary societies.[24] Although he was himself believed to prefer mathematics,[25] Lee urged no particular courses on the boys, but he insisted that they attend regularly the classes in which they were registered.[26] General holidays were few.[27] At Christmas the men got only one day's intermission, or at most two. When the students threatened to "cut" classes because Lee would not allow them a long Christmas recess, he calmly warned them he would close the college if they did so.[28] In partial compensation, the length of the session was reduced to a flat nine months. All requests for leaves of absence, even for a day, had to be passed upon personally by the president.[29] He knew that the presence of most of the students represented some one's sacrifice in those difficult times, and he was determined that students should not waste what others had sweated to provide. A Georgia student absented himself from classes in order to share in the fine skating that a long and heavy freeze on North River offered. Very soon there came a summons to the president's office.

"Mr. ——," said Lee in kindly tones, "I notice you have been absent for a number of recitations."

"Yes, sir," the boy answered truthfully, "I was skating on North River."

"Mr. ——, if you had asked for permission to go skating, your work is very good, and I would have given you permission with

---

[23] *Riley,* 18, 20; Kirkpatrick in *Jones,* 94.
[24] *Riley,* 26, 61; *cf. ibid.,* 136.   [25] *Riley,* 134.
[26] Joynes, *Cent. U. S. C.,* 23; *Riley,* 136.
[27] *Cf. Jones,* 107; *Riley,* 143. *Cf.* also *Lexington Gazette,* Dec. 16, 1868: "Last Monday the students of Washington College asked General Lee for a holiday, that they might enjoy the skating on the River. The General let them *slide.*"
[28] Gordon in *Riley,* 84.
[29] *Cf. MS. Faculty Minutes,* Dec. 14, 1869.

pleasure. And now, Mr. ——, you know our Southern people are very poor, and to send you to college, your parents must be forced to economize, and deprive themselves of many things."

The boy choked up. "Stop, General Lee," he said, "you will never see me in your office again." And thereafter, to the end of General Lee's life, that student gave no cause for complaint. One reminder of his parents' sacrifices was enough.[30]

A new matriculate from North Carolina disdained both books and class attendance for his first month in college. When the reports came in, Lee sent for the boy and went over all his grades, asking if a mistake had been made in recording them. The student admitted that his marks were as good as he deserved. He had no excuse to make for his absences from class. Lee happened to be acquainted with the boy's parents and explained that he knew so poor a report would cause them great sorrow. If, again, the report was printed in the catalogue, it would humiliate them. "I do not know what to do," he said, and sat for a moment. Then, without another word, he quietly tore up the paper. The boy broke down and wept and, after a few words from Lee, promised to do his utmost. He redeemed his pledge in every particular.[31]

As with these two young men, so with many. In their awe of him, and in their affection for him, students rarely neglected the study they knew he valued so greatly. The standard of attainment at the college went higher and higher. Both from faculty and from students, the best was elicited.[32]

Lee's second application of the code of a gentleman was to the general deportment of the students. Unostentatiously and with few preachments, but hourly and earnestly, Lee sought the elevation of the boys' morals rather than the mere repression of vice, in the words of one of the members of his faculty.[33] At the same time he waged active war on liquor. One day, while he was walking in Lexington, he saw a young man stagger from a bar-room, and he fired up instantly. "I wish," he said to his com-

---

[30] MS. Memoir of J. F. Minis, Savannah, Ga., kindly supplied the author.

[31] 16 Confederate Veteran, 455–56. Sometimes he would tell indifferent students, "I have a way of estimating young men which does not often fail me. I cannot note the conduct of any one, for even a brief period, without finding out what sort of a mother he had. You all honor your mothers: need I tell you that I know you will have that honor in reverent keeping?" (Mrs. Preston, 274).

[32] Joynes, in Jones, 126. [33] Jones, 122, quoting Joynes.

panion, "that these military gentlemen, while they are doing so many things which they have no right to do, would close up all of these grog-shops, which are luring our young men to destruction." [34] He had seen too much of the ill-effects of alcohol in the army not to make him regard it as a dangerous enemy. "My experience through life," he wrote a temperance society among the students, "has convinced me that, while moderation and temperance in all things are commendable and beneficial, abstinence from spirituous liquors is the best safeguard of morals and health." [35] There was little hard drinking among the majority of the students,[36] but those who fell deeply into their cups were expelled from the college. Lee was meticulous, however, in his insistence that guilt be beyond doubt.[37] In one case, all the faculty were for sending a student home for frequenting bar-rooms and getting drunk. "Have any of you *seen* this young man intoxicated?" Lee asked. Nobody had. "Have any of you seen him entering bar-rooms?" None of them could affirm it. "We must be very careful how we are influenced by hearsay," the General concluded, in substance. "During the war at a time when my physical and mental strain was intense, I was reported to the executive as being habitually intoxicated and unfit for the discharge of my duties." [38]

More than one boy who slipped into imprudent drinking probably had much the same experience as the lad who was summoned to the president's office after the General had seen him a bit uncertain on his legs in the street.

"Mr. ——," said Lee, when the student appeared, "I had occasion to write to your mother some time ago and it gave me great pleasure to tell her how well you were getting along in college."

The young man, thrown off his guard, could only answer

[34] *Jones,* 169–70.

[35] R. E. Lee to S. G. M. Miller et als., Dec. 9, 1869; *Jones,* 170. It was in talking with some of his students that Lee told how he had been able to dispense with spirits. He said: "When I went into the field, at the beginning of the war, a good lady friend of mine gave me two sealed bottles of very superb French brandy. I carried them with me through the entire campaign; and when I met my friend again, I gave her back both her bottles of brandy, with the seals unbroken. It may have been some comfort to me to know that I had them in case of sudden emergency, but the moment never came when I needed to use them." He prefaced this story by saying: "Men need no stimulant; it is something, I am persuaded, that they can do without" (*Mrs. Preston,* 273–74).

[36] S. M. Yonge MS.

[37] *E.g., MS. Faculty Minutes,* Jan. 28, 1869.   [38] *Riley,* 36, quoting Humphreys.

rhetorically, "I trust I may ever live worthy of your commendation."

Looking squarely at him, Lee went on, "Mr. ——, did it ever occur to you that when you reach middle life, you may need a stimulant, and if you have accustomed yourself to taking stimulants in your early life it will require so much more to have the desired effect at a time when you may need it?" How much better it would be, the General concluded, if the young man would leave intoxicants alone in his student days. The boy did.[39]

Good habits of worship Lee ranked with those of study and of general deportment. Compulsory chapel attendance he abolished at the close of his first year at the college, but he was always anxious that the students should be present and he sought various ways of assuring this.[40] He always was at chapel himself, sitting in the same place, next the wall on the north side of the new building, in the second pew from the front.[41] The college Y. M. C. A., which he did much to organize, always had his encouragement, his contribution, and his praise in his annual report.[42] He invited the ministers of the town to act in turn as chaplain, and jointly to meet the students at the opening of the session. Painstakingly he prepared and sent each Lexington pastor a list of the matriculates of his faith, and he encouraged the clergymen to keep in touch with them.[43]

The General understood the ways of boys in church-going, however, and he was not mystified when his old chief of artillery, General Pendleton, the Episcopal rector, complained that many of the collegians of that denomination were attending the Presbyterian church, drawn no doubt, the old gunner gamely admitted, by the eloquence of the minister, Doctor Pratt. As Lee well knew,

[39] *Riley*, 114–15.

[40] The late Professor C. A. Graves, who was in the college at the time, was authority for the statement that compulsory attendance was abolished after Lee's first year in Lexington. The collateral evidence is to the same effect. The catalogues continued, through inadvertence on the part of some one, to carry a notice that attendance on chapel and on one church service on Sunday was obligatory (*Riley*, 24–25; MS. *Faculty Minutes*, Sept. 16, 1868; Sept. 8, 1867; Sept. 12, 1870. *Cf. Jones*, 111, 441. MS. *note of C. A. Graves* to the writer, Dec. 9, 1927).

[41] *Riley*, 99 n.

[42] *Riley*, 25; *Jones*, 441. He gave it $50 per annum during the first part of his administration (*Riley*, 194), and during the last year $100 (*Jones*, 432).

[43] *Riley*, 66; see also C. A. Graves in *ibid.*, 22–31; *Jones*, 121–22, 123, 286, 440. *Trustees' Minutes*, July 17, 1866.

Doctor Pratt had a very charming daughter, Grace, whom the young men of the dormitories much admired. So, when General Pendleton voiced his distress that Episcopal boys were flocking to the church of the Presbyterian orator, General Lee had the answer. "I rather think," said he, "that the attraction is not so much Doctor Pratt's eloquence as it is Doctor Pratt's Grace." [44]

Although he jested about this with Doctor Pendleton and took care never to preach to the boys, General Lee was in nothing more serious than in his concern for their spiritual well-being. "If I could only know that all the young men in the college were good Christians," he said on one occasion, "I should have nothing more to desire. I dread the thought of any student going away from the college without becoming a sincere Christian." [45] He was careful to place in Christian homes the boys who boarded in town, and he frowned on anything, excursions in particular, that interfered with their Sabbath-day worship. [46]

To keep the peace was the last of the four simple requirements General Lee made of "his boys" in obedience to the first law of being a gentleman. Respect for good order meant something in the late sixties. For Lexington presented a field of more serious contention than the customary clashes between town and gown, or between the college boys and the "tooth picks," as the students for some obscure reason styled the local youths. [47] The town had a Federal garrison part of the time, and was not always fortunate in the commander of the troops. To assist the Negroes, the freedmen's bureau was active. Agitators appeared frequently. Several times it seemed that issues were made by the military authorities simply to embarrass Lee. [48] The students flashed with wrath whenever they thought that this was happening or that the General was being assailed. To protect him, they would balk at nothing. Lee, therefore, had constantly to keep the students in hand. In two instances, as will appear in course, matters grew serious. On all other occasions, Lee was able to forestall trouble. Sometimes he made formal written appeals to the students, [49] as

---

[44] *Riley*, 62.

[45] *Riley*, 25. See *Jones*, 440, for a somewhat similar statement so rhetorical as not to sound like General Lee.

[46] *Riley*, 133.

[47] *McDonald*, 10.

[48] Jones, *L. and L.*, 428.

[49] *Jones*, 104–5.

on a rather exciting day when word got around that a radical who was to address a political meeting that night intended to abuse General Lee. Students averred they would break up the gathering, and made plans to do so. Hearing of this, the General summoned about a dozen of the student-leaders to his office and told them he desired the college people to stay away from the meeting. Although it was then after 3 o'clock, his wishes were communicated quickly to all the boys, and none of them went.[50]

Occasionally the students organized what they styled "callithumps," which consisted of a march into the town, and a tin-pan serenade. If there was no particular reason why they should not do so, the General occasionally let the boys satisfy in this fashion the primal urge to make a noise. But when there was danger of a clash with the military, or when the sick were likely to be disturbed, or when the "callithumps" were designed to annoy some "carpet-bagger" or "scallywag," the General exercised a veto, mild but firm. Sometimes he posted a formal request, which the young men dubbed "general orders." [51] As often, he communicated with them through their own representatives. In every instance it was sufficient for him to say that he did not want them to make a disturbance. His wish was their law.[52] A "monster callithumps," planned with enthusiasm, was unprotestingly abandoned when the president of one of the literary societies arose and announced, "Gentlemen, nothing doing tonight, Marse Robert says not." [53] At his request, "callithumps" were completely abandoned in 1868.[54]

In administering this code of honor, General Lee was cognizant of the importance of what is now termed "college spirit." It was the academic equivalent of the *esprit de corps* that had made the Army of Northern Virginia terrible in battle. The only approach he ever made to a speech at the college, except when he conducted the closing exercises of the session, had to do with this quality. It was one night at a joint meeting of the literary societies, when he was standing on the floor, thronged by the members. He told

[50] *Riley*, 85.
[51] Joynes, in *Cent. U. S. C.*, 25. For a detailed description of the callithumps, see **14** *Confederate Veteran*, 177.
[52] *Riley*, 61, 122, 137.
[53] *Riley*, 111.   [54] *S. M. Yonge MS.*

them then, briefly, that it was "the duty of the students to do all in their power to add *éclat* to the exercises of the approaching commencement." [55]

These, then, were the things he required of "his boys"—that they be gentlemen in all things, that they study faithfully, that they hold to high moral standards, that they "remember their Creator," and that they keep the peace.

What he required of himself in his dealings with them was not so simple. He put his emphasis, first of all, on the individual. "We must not respect persons," a professor once contended in the course of a faculty argument. Lee answered quickly, "I always respect persons, and care little for precedent." [56] The weak or the inexperienced boy who was making an effort was always sure of his understanding sympathy. "May I give you one piece of advice, sir?" he said to one of his younger teachers. . . . "Well, sir, always observe the stage-driver's rule. . . . Always take care of the poor horses." [57]

When a boy came to college for the first time, and entered his office to report, the General always rose to welcome him and greeted him with a graciousness that made the strange lad comfortable. He usually asked the newcomer what course of study he intended to follow, and though he never interfered with a matriculate's free election of his course, he sometimes would commend those who he thought had chosen wisely. In a few moments the student had been bowed out. If he was young, he was usually sent to board at a selected private home in the town.[58] The older boys lived in the dormitory. In either case, for months, the boy might not see General Lee again, except at chapel or on

---

[55] *Riley*, 26, quoting C. A. Graves.
[56] Joynes, in *Cent. U. S. C.*, 33. [57] *Riley*, 28, quoting C. A. Graves.
[58] *Cf.* Lee to Captain A. P. Pfifer, *MS.*, June 15, 1869: "The regulation of Washington College, which allows and encourages young men to reside in the town of Lexington is considered by us to be very advantageous to the students themselves. It separates them into small groups, where they are removed from the temptations that may be incident to the residence of large bodies of young men in the same building, and it brings [them] under the influence of family life and associations, which we regard as very useful both to their morals and their manners. The policy of the Faculty is rather to encourage students, especially the younger ones, to board in this way, and the result we think has been very favorable. Board and lodging can be had for students in the most respectable families of Lexington, where they will receive the best influences. On the other hand, also, the opportunity is afforded of rooming in the College, and boarding at the College Hotel, at a lower rate, so far as the accommodations of the College will permit" (*Lee's MS. Letter Book*).

the walks. But he was not forgotten, and when he met the president, he was always addressed by name. For Lee always made it a point to identify every student. One boy came to the college from Baltimore, where he had been presented to the General at a reception, along with a host of others. As soon as he entered the General's office in Lexington, he was recognized by Lee and was greeted by name, with a recountal of the circumstances of their previous meeting.[59] At a faculty meeting, when the roster was being read to see that all the students were taking sufficient work, General Lee repeated a name, emphasizing each syllable as if he were trying to recall the individual. Then, half-reproachfully, he exclaimed: "I have no recollection of a student of that name, it is very strange that I have forgotten him. I thought I knew every one in the college. How long has he been here?" He pursued the question until he was convinced that he had never seen the boy, who was a newcomer and had entered the college during his absence.[60]

General Lee knew the men's standing, too. "He is a very quiet, orderly young man," he said one day to a caller who inquired about a student's progress, "but seems very careful not to injure the health of his father's son. He got last month"—he spoke without consulting the records—"only forty on his Greek, thirty-five on his Mathematics, forty-seven on his Latin, and fifty on his English, which is a very low stand, as 100 is our maximum. Now, I do not want our young men to really injure their health; but I wish them to come as near it as possible." [61] In another instance, he expressed regret, when a student's name was mentioned at faculty meeting, "that he has fallen back so far in his mathematics." The professor assured him he was mistaken: the

[59] *Riley*, 106.

[60] *Jones*, 99; *Mrs. Preston*, 273. Only once in Lexington was it recorded of Lee that he did not recognize a man he had previously met. In that case, after Lee had found out the visitor's name, he was much ashamed that he had not recalled him. "I ought to have recognized him at once," the General said. "He spent at least an hour in my quarters in the city of Mexico just after its occupation by the American army, and although I have never seen him since"—there had been but one interview—"he made a very agreeable impression upon me, and I ought not to have forgotten him" (*Jones*, 237). H. M. Field (*Bright Skies and Dark Shadows*, 301) stated that Professor White told him that when the two were walking together and approached students, Lee would ask White the boys' names so that he might call them; but if this was so, it was because the General could not identify their features at a distance. It is certain, from a great variety of evidence, that he knew all the student-body.

[61] *Jones*, 129.

boy was one of the best in his class. "He got only fifty-four last month," Lee insisted. An appeal to the report proved him right. An error had been made in copying the student's standing.[62] In both these cases, no doubt, Lee spoke with precision because he had the students on his mental list of those who needed special attention, but he always kept in mind the general level of a boy's performance. When the old-fashioned, all-day examinations were held, he would sit for an hour or two as the pupils wrestled with their questions.[63] He judged results not by the number of new matriculates but by the number of old students who returned. "That," he said, "is the measure of the success with which we have performed our duty."[64] Even the more personal affairs of students were of concern to him. If they were extravagant in money matters he knew it.[65] If their health was impaired, he investigated and counselled.[66]

The faculty met every week and reported those who were derelict. The General summoned them soon thereafter, through notes circulated by the college janitor, Lewis.[67] At the end of each month, when fuller records of standing were filed by the professors, Lee put on the bulletin board a list of those whom he wished to see.[68] In his office, alone, he received these delinquents, who usually were loath to discuss afterwards what happened between them and the General. The treatment probably was fitted to the patient, and usually it was administered in a few sentences, with a gentleness that impressed the student more than sternness would have done. Boys frequently came out in tears. Seldom did they have to go a second time into that drab room under the new chapel.[69] Some of the things told them there

---

[62] Jones, 130.

[63] Riley, 27. Occasionally the students' struggle with their examinations provoked Lee's secret mirth instead of his sympathy. Observing one boy who gazed and gazed at his examiner without uttering a word, Lee laughed and whispered, "He is trying to absorb it from Mr. Humphreys," the teacher (M. W. Humphreys in Richmond Times-Dispatch, Jan. 20, 1907).

[64] Humphreys, loc. cit.

[65] Riley, 32; R. E. Lee to W. A. Patrick, MS., Feb. 10, 1870; Lee's MS. Letter Book.

[66] R. E. Lee to A. Lessums, MS., May 16, 1867; Lee's MS. Letter Book; H. M. Field: Bright Skies and Dark Shadows, 300; Humphreys, loc. cit. Lee gave Humphreys some flannel undershirts that Mrs. Lee had made for the General from goods that had run the blockade.

[67] Riley, 126.   [68] Riley, 61.

[69] Jones, 100–101, 284; Riley, 44, 47, 51, 57. 110.

might be maxims for the guidance of youth in every age. For a youngster who was in rebellion against authority, he put a life-rule in a single sentence: "You cannot be a true man until you learn to obey." [70] Occasionally, very occasionally, some boy would carry his defiance with him into the president's office. Then an explosion might occur, as in the case of a Kentuckian who kept chewing tobacco during a disciplinary interview. "Mr. ——," said Lee, "chewing is particularly obnoxious to me. Go out and remove that quid, and never appear before me again chewing tobacco." Shortly afterwards the young man was before the president once more—and was chewing as vigorously as ever. Lee stopped for a moment and wrote a line or two on a sheet of paper. Then he turned quietly to the boy: "Mr. ——, here is a note for you. It will be posted on the college bulletin in ten minutes." The youngster, between chews, took the paper and read: "Mr. —— is dismissed from Washington College for disrespect to the President." That was all. One who was in the school at the time observes: "Within three or four days the man went home, and during the interim of his remaining in Lexington, not a student would speak to him, and he left without a man of them going to see him off." [71]

Serious or persistent breaches were referred to General Lee by the faculty, or were brought up by him at the weekly meeting in order to get the professors' advice.[72] The offender was interviewed and, if need be, his parent was notified. Here is a typical letter:

Lexington, Va., December 12, 1867.

My dear Sir:—

I am glad to inform you that —— has made more progress in his studies during the month of November than he did in October, and, as far as I can judge from the reports of his professors, he is fully capable of acquiring a sound education, provided he will faithfully apply himself. I am sorry, however, to state that he has been absent several times from his lectures in

[70] Joynes, in *Cent. U. S. C.,* 35.   [71] *MS. Memoir of J. F. Minis.*
[72] "On motion of Prof. Allan it was resolved that Messrs. [five students] be sent for by the President and admonished because of their conduct in the public streets of Lexington on Saturday Feb. 22nd, which consisted in riding at full speed up and down the streets and was so disorderly as to attract general attention" (*MS. Faculty Minutes,* Feb. 24, 1868).

the month of November. Thirteen times he tells me he was prevented from attending by sickness, but five times, he says, he intentionally absented himself. He absented himself in the same way several times in October; and I then explained to him the necessity of punctual and regular attendance in his classes, which he promised to observe.

I have again impressed upon him this necessity, and again he promises amendment; but I have thought it proper to write to you on the subject, that you might use your authority with him; for I have been obliged to give him to understand that, if this conduct is repeated, I shall be obliged to return him to you.

Hoping I may be spared the necessity, I remain,

With great respect, your obedient servant,

R. E. Lee.[73]

All other expedients failing, the General would direct a student to "withdraw." When this happened, reconsideration seldom followed, for a rule that Lee commended to his faculty was, "Never raise an issue which you are not prepared to maintain at all hazards." [74] This form of "withdrawal" was accounted far less discreditable than expulsion, and was almost always accompanied by as sympathetic a letter to the parent or guardian as General Lee felt the facts warranted. "Under the circumstances," he wrote the father of one boy, "the Faculty deemed his longer connection with the College disadvantageous to him, and not beneficial to the Institution, and therefore required his withdrawal from college. I hope he may have reached home before you receive this, and that his experience here may be so far beneficial to him, as to teach him the necessity of steady application and untiring industry in whatever he undertakes." [75]

To a parent who asked that his son be readmitted after he had been ordered to leave the school, he wrote: "Notwithstanding their sympathies for him, his youth and sense of error, [the faculty] came to the resolution that they could not with propriety reverse their first decision, without the risk of encouraging the

---

[73] *Jones,* 102; *cf. ibid.,* 253.
[74] Joynes, in *Cent. U. S. C.,* 33. *Cf. supra,* p. 278.
[75] *Lee's MS. Letter Book,* Jan. 28, 1867, to unnamed gentleman.

other students to do the same thing under the expectation of like immunity, by which not only the lives of others, but of themselves, might be involved." [76]

He addressed this to a man in public life: "It is with extreme regret that I inform you that it has become necessary for your son, Mr. ——, to leave College. In consequence of his frank acknowledgment and written promise of future good behavior, his misconduct on a former occasion was overlooked by the Faculty, and he was restored to his classes; but he has been unable to keep the pledge then given; and even if he could be permitted, he is unwilling to remain under the circumstances. I have therefore authorized him to return home and his connection with the College is dissolved. I hope this severe lesson will teach him the self-command he so much needs, and enable him to refrain from a vice, which, if it becomes a habit, may prove his ruin. He is a youth of good capacity, candor and truth. These qualities have endeared him to the members of the Faculty, and I trust his future course will reinstate him in their good opinion, and in the confidence of his comrades." [77]

In February, 1869, a lad got into some scrape and left college. His mother wrote to the General asking about the affair. He replied painstakingly and concluded: "On the first arrival of your son at College I was agreeably impressed by his appearance and manners and was anxious that he should be favorably located. Until the occurrence which caused him to leave College, I had remarked nothing objectionable in his conduct, but what might be attributed to youthful indiscretion and thoughtlessness and as one of these instances was calculated to teach him to what such conduct might reasonably lead, I was in hopes his own good sense would correct it. I however hope that this last occurrence will teach him a lesson that he will never forget, and save him and you from any future distress. I hope that he has safely reached you before this and that his contrition and conduct will relieve you from further anxiety." [78]

Still again, in January, 1870, he had to write a minister that three protégés of his had decided to leave college. The rest of

[76] R. E. Lee to H. S. M.——, MS., Jan. 31, 1867; *Lee's MS. Letter Book.*
[77] R. E. Lee to ——; MS., March 8, 1867; *Lee's MS. Letter Book.*
[78] R. E. Lee to Mrs. ——; MS., Feb. 12, 1869; *Lee's MS. Letter Book.*

his letter so well illustrates his methods of dealing with the eternal problem of youth that it is worth quoting *in extenso:*

"Impressed by their appearance and manners and the high character they brought with them, I caused them to be introduced into the family of one of the most worthy gentlemen of the city, Mr. David E. Moore, where I hoped they would find many of the comforts of home, with the social and family influences to which they were accustomed. For the first two months of the session their progress was good, and attention to their lectures and studies regular, but during the latter part of December their attendance has been irregular and their studies have been neglected. I have from week to week during this time called their attention to the impropriety of this course, as far as the Messrs. —— were concerned, and urged upon them the necessity of strict and regular attendance upon their classes. Mr. —— always gave indisposition as the reason for his absences which of course I gave credit to. From facts that have come to the knowledge of the Faculty, it is their opinion that the neglect of their studies by these young gentlemen, especially the Messrs. —— has been caused by their frequenting the public billiard room in Lexington where they have wasted much of their time and money the past month. The cause whatever it may be is much to be regretted for I had hoped that they would have derived all the benefits of the instruction of the College and have laid the foundation for a solid education. As I know the great interest you take in these young gentlemen and as you did me the kindness to give them a letter to me I have thought I ought to make you the foregoing statement, lest you attribute their leaving College to graver causes." [79]

These were not easy letters to write or pleasant letters to receive. Answers to them were not always indited in a considerate spirit. The father of one boy who had been guilty of a serious violation of the college code provoked the General greatly by a long apology. "Now it is evident to my mind," said Lee to a member of the faculty, "that this is a disingenuous letter. He does not

[79] R. E. Lee to Reverend B. B. Blair, *MS.,* Jan. 17, 1870; *Lee's MS. Letter Book.*

fairly represent the facts, and will completely ruin his son, as well as seriously interfere with our discipline. Now, sir, I will show you what I have written him in reply." It was a very keen, flawlessly polite rebuke, but the professor, who was acquainted with the man to whom the letter was addressed, knew that its point would be entirely lost on its recipient. He told General Lee so. The General was perplexed. "Well, sir," he said at length, "I cannot help it; if a gentleman can't understand the language of a gentleman, he must remain in ignorance, for a gentleman cannot write in any other way." [80]

When students' shortcomings were not serious enough to justify expulsion, Lee occasionally suspended them. In such case it was his custom to exact a written pledge that the offensive conduct would not be repeated. In at least one instance it seems that the giving of such a pledge and the lifting of the suspension were made a matter of collegiate record and probably were announced on the bulletin board.[81]

Further down the list were cases of indolence, of mistakes in courses, of discouragement, and of restlessness. All these General Lee handled personally. He conferred with every man who wanted to attend another school[82] or quit college,[83] with all those who desired to make changes in their classes,[84] and even with those who sought temporary leaves of absence.[85] The lazy lad he sometimes prodded with a spur of humor. "How is your mother?" he asked one boy. "I am sure you must be devoted to her; you are so careful of the health of her son." [86] The overconfident he took down quickly. "This young man is going to graduate in one

---

[80] *Jones*, 285–86.   [81] MS. *Faculty Minutes*, Feb. 26 and March 1, 1870.

[82] *Cf.* Lee to Reverend B. T. Lacy (*MS.*, Oct. 9, 1865), who had been one of Jackson's chaplains and most useful in the Chancellorsville campaign: "Mr. Henson seemed to prefer attending a classical school. . . . I did not attempt to influence him as the great object is for him to receive the best education. I need not tell you the advantages of a college course over all academies. The benefits of instruction from specific Professors in each branch of learning, and the emulation and encouragement derived from intercourse with a number of young men engaged in the same pursuit, and all striving for preeminence. The future of our country depends upon our youth. Whatever we may have lost, I hope our moral and intellectual culture may be preserved. It is therefore of primary importance that all should use to the best advantage the means at their disposal" (*Original in New York Historical Society*). For Lacy, see *supra*, vol. II, pp. 521 ff.

[83] MS. *Faculty Minutes*, Jan. 6, Jan. 13, Feb. 10, March 2, June 1, Nov. 3, 1868; Jan. 5, 1869; Feb. 1, 1870.

[84] *Riley*, 33, 117; MS. *Faculty Minutes*, Jan. 6, Jan. 13, March 30, Nov. 24, 1868.

[85] MS. *Faculty Minutes*, March 2, May 18, 1868.

[86] Joynes in *Cent. U. S. C.*, 35.

session," he said as he introduced a cocksure youngster to one of the professors. The boy expostulated: he had been misunderstood. He meant two years, not one. "Ah," said the General, "he has concluded to postpone it for a session. Well, sir, I wish you the full realization of your hopes; but I must tell you that you will have no time to play baseball." [87] The student who failed in a final examination, he sometimes allowed another trial.[88]

Those who got in trouble because of a prank that had no hurtful intent were sure of a merciful hearing. In the winter of 1866–67, John M. Graham, a matriculate from Tennessee, found his supply of wood diminishing with rapidity. Suspecting that one of the Negro janitors was helping himself to the hickory, Graham loaded a stick with gunpowder and left it temptingly on the pile in his room. Next morning the stove in Professor Joynes's classroom blew up, and the place was set afire. The flames were quickly put out and small damage was done, but there was a first-class sensation, for Joynes insisted that the act was malicious. General Lee brought up the matter at chapel the following day and asked that any student who knew anything about the affair would report at his office that morning. Reasoning that the janitor had stolen his wood to feed Professor Joynes's fire, rather than go through the snow to the college woodpile, Graham took a companion with him, to bear him witness, and went to see the General. He related his story and explained how he had set the trap for the thief. "But, General," he had the wit to conclude, "I didn't know it was Professor Joynes." Lee laughed. "Well, Mr. Graham, your plan to find out who was taking your wood was a good one, but your powder charge was too heavy. Next time use less powder." [89] There the matter ended.

Another youngster, who absented himself too frequently from class, was called to give an account of his wasted hours. Terror-stricken in the presence of the old chieftain, the boy stammered out something about an illness and then, realizing that he looked perfectly healthy, he started to tell about having left his boots at the shoemaker's. "Stop, Mr. ——, stop, sir! One good reason is enough," said Lee. The student added, years later, in telling the

[87] *Jones*, 244.
[88] MS. *Faculty Minutes*, June 15, 1870.   [89] *Riley*, 71–72.

story: "I could not be mistaken about the twinkle in the old hero's eyes." [90] Such calls to the General's office, whatever the outcome, were not relished. When a student emerged from the ordeal, his fellow-collegians often asked, "Who said 'Good-morning' first," or, in other words, did the victim know when the General was through with him? [91]

Lee did not wait until a boy was in trouble to counsel him. When a lad needed encouragement, he called him in.[92] If a student had made a mistake of taste in a public speech and had abused the "Yankees," Lee counselled him in moderation.[93] Once a year he wrote to the parents of every boy who had done well a letter in which the student was commended;[94] and at the end of the session he often added an autographed line of approbation to the student's final report.[95] In addition, during the later years of his administration, he kept a list of "distinguished undergraduates," [96] one of the few echoes of West Point.

The General did not mingle with the students, as a rule,[97] but he made them feel that he had a personal interest in them. Meeting a small group of his "boys" in the street, he would omit none of them in his greeting.[98] Whether in public or in private, his tone of voice in speaking to them was low, but his enunciation was so clear that every word was distinct.[99] When students came to ask him to autograph pictures he did so cheerfully and without protest.[100] Those who had bereavement at home were excused from classes without red tape. Many were received by his daughters in his home, though he firmly manœuvred to see that they respected the law of the parlor by leaving at 10 o'clock.[101] When students' parents came to Lexington, he always called on them, much to their satisfaction and vastly to the enlargement of the students' pride.[102] The timid boy he never overlooked. At commencement, in 1869, a stage carrying a group of students to the railroad stopped in front of the president's residence for one

[90] R. E. Lee, 332.   [91] Mrs. Preston, 300.

[92] Riley, 124.   [93] Riley, 82.

[94] Cf. R. E. Lee to Boaz Ford, Cartersville, Va., MS., June 28, 1870, for a copy of which the writer is indebted to Jackson Davis, LL.D.

[95] Riley, 60, 116, 117.   [96] Riley, 127.

[97] Riley, 142.   [98] Riley, 140.

[99] 13 Confederate Veteran, 359-60.   [100] Riley, 46, 57, 113.

[101] Riley, 72, 92, 109 118; R. E. Lee Jr., 245.

[102] Joynes in Cent. U. S. C., 31.

of the Misses Lee. While the vehicle was waiting, all except a retiring youngster piled out and went into the house to say good-bye to the General. He chatted with them awhile, and then, learning there was one boy still on the stage, he went out and talked to him until the vehicle started.[103]

They felt his influence, did those boys of his, from the first time they went into his office to register. Although not actually afraid of him, they were most anxious not to offend him. Standing in awe of him, they yet had an exalted affection for him. Some of them thought they saw in his face the whole tragedy of the war, but the discerning knew he had kindness and humor of a kind. One student's sharpest recollection of the General was of the manner in which he "laughed inwardly" at a lecturer's jokes.[104]

Few as were the evidences of Lee's discipline, it was effective with the students.[105] He "had the power to bring out," wrote one of his boys, years after, "and did bring out, the very best that there was in every student."[106] "No college in the land," asserted one of the ministers who served at the chapel, "had a harder-working Faculty or a better-behaved, more orderly set of students."[107] Said one of his professors: "We doubt . . . whether at any other college in the world so many young men could have been found as free from misconduct, or marked by as high a tone of feeling and opinion, as were the students of Washington College during these latter years of General Lee's life."[108]

Once, however, Lee met with defeat in his dealings with the students; once they rebelled successfully. That was toward the end of the session of 1865–66, when General Pendleton undertook on Friday afternoons to give a course in declamation. The students either resented having to take what they considered a class better suited to the preparatory school than to the college, or else they disliked the oratorical style of the old artillerist. In their first protest, they adroitly pinned papers to the tail of Pendleton's coat as he went up the aisle, applauded him noisily before he said anything, and then bombarded him with wads of paper. The

[103] *Riley,* 63. [104] *Riley,* 50.
[105] *Riley,* 51, 61, 122; Joynes in *Cent. U. S. C.,* 25.
[106] Judge Robert Ewing, in *Riley,* 58.
[107] *Jones,* 284. Cf. *ibid.,* 122. During the session of 1869–70, only 6 students in a body of nearly 350 had to be disciplined (*Trustees' Minutes,* June 22, 1870).
[108] Joynes, in *Jones,* 123.

General indignantly lectured them on bad manners and managed
to finish the hour, but he complained to General Lee. At the next
recitation, when Lee himself sat in the classroom, all, of course,
was peaceful. But the following week, when Pendleton again
essayed to face the boys alone, the members of the class enlisted
some confederates who stood outside the windows and yelled and
blew horns. Then, when the minister refused to capitulate, some
one threw into the room a dog with a tin can tied to his tail.
The mad flight of the animal completed the chaos. Indignantly,
General Pendleton denounced such rudeness and quit—to come
no more.[109] For that one time, Lee was powerless, and all the influence he had built up did not avail to force the students to listen
to Pendleton's discourses on how to recite Rienzi to the Romans,
or Mark Antony's oration, or Patrick Henry's cry, "Give me Liberty or give me death!"

It was never so in anything else, either while the boys were in
college or thereafter. For Lee's influence over his students did not
end when he handed them their degrees and declared them graduates of Washington College. It followed them and helped to
shape their lives through the difficult years of poverty that preceded the South's recovery. To this day there remains a thinning
company whose proudest boast is that its members were General
Lee's "boys" at Lexington. They have not forgotten that he said
of them: "My only object is to endeavor to make them see their
true interest, to teach them to labor diligently for their improvement, and to prepare themselves for the great work of life." [110]
And again: "I have a self-imposed task, which I must accomplish. I
have led the young men of the South in battle; I have seen many
of them fall under my standard. I shall devote all my life now to
training young men to do their duty in life." [111]

It was not easy to watch the welfare of nearly 400 boys, and it
was not always pleasant to keep in hand all the small details and
close economies of a poor, overcrowded college. The weight of
his people's sorrow lay on his heart, all the while, and in his mind
he sometimes had to do battle with many memories. He was

---

[109] M. W. Humphreys in *Richmond Times-Dispatch*, Jan. 20, 1907; 14 *Confederate Veteran*, 177–78.
[110] R. E. Lee to C. F. Deems, Aug. 4, 1866; *Jones*, 247.
[111] H. W. Hilliard at the Augusta, Ga., Memorial Meeting, *Jones*, 120–21, 476.

sustained in it all by the self-mastery that was, in large sense, one expression of his religion. Belief in God's mercy and submission to His will, in a faith that never seemed to be troubled by doubt, were stronger after Appomattox, if that were possible, than before. There was little of the personal evangelist in his make-up. "I find it so hard," said he, "to keep one poor sinner's heart in the right way that it seems presumptuous to try to keep others," but he did speak of religion when he thought he could help,[112] and he was deeply interested in religious revivals, such as that which swept the V. M. I. in May, 1869.[113] He was not an ascetic. Discussing Lent, he said: "The best way for most of us is to fast from our sins and to eat what is good for us." [114] His sense of the practical showed itself in his religion, as in everything else. When a minister at chapel fell into the habit of praying so long that classes were delayed, Lee asked a member of the faculty, "Would it be wrong for me to suggest that he confine his morning prayers to us poor sinners at the college, and pray for the Turks, the Jews, the Chinese, and the other heathen some other time?" [115] He believed in regular church attendance, and usually when his own church was open for service he was to be seen in his pew, the second from the pulpit and directly in front of the chancel. Always he knelt during the prayers, and loyally he listened to Doctor Pendleton's sermon.[116] Sometimes attention was bought at a price. Under the gallery, perpendicular to the other seats, ran a long bench on which sat some of the McDonald boys, who were too numerous to get into the family pew that adjoined General Lee's. Often, during the rector's discourse, which was not among the briefest of human utterances, one or another of the McDonald lads would go to sleep and would fall to the floor with a thud. It must have been very diverting to most of the congregation, which doubtless looked forward to it, but it never caused the General even to change expression.[117]

The General had family prayers every morning before breakfast,[118] but his own spiritual life was bound up with the daily Bible reading and with special seasons of private devotions. The Bible

112 *Jones*, 433.
113 *R. E. Lee, Jr.*, 352.
115 *Jones*, 426.
117 *McDonald*, 9.

114 *Riley*, 100.
116 *Jones*, 425.
118 Cf. *Jones*, 480.

was to him the book of books—"a book," he wrote, "which supplies the place of all others, and . . . cannot be replaced by any other." [119] He received various copies of the Bible, both for himself and for the college,[120] but the one he used was a pocket edition he had carried with him in all his campaigning since he had been a lieutenant colonel in the United States army.[121] He was interested deeply in the work of Bible societies and served as president of the Rockbridge organization.[122] Even for the circulation of small religious newspapers he was willing to make a personal effort.[123]

Thus far it is easy to proceed in analyzing Lee's religion in after-war days. Beyond this it is not possible to go. Simple as was his soul, he had "meat to eat that ye know not of."

[119] R. E. Lee to F. R. Farrar, Sept. 19, 1867, *Jones,* 114–15. He told J. William Jones: "There are many things in the old Book which I may never be able to explain, but I accept it as the infallible word of God, and receive its teachings as inspired by the Holy Ghost" (*Richmond Times-Dispatch,* Jan. 20, 1907). *Cf.* to Markie Williams, Dec. 20, 1865: "I prefer the Bible to any other book. There is enough in that, to satisfy the most ardent thirst for knowledge; to open the way to true wisdom; and to teach the only road to salvation and eternal happiness. It is not above human comprehension, and is sufficient to satisfy all its desires" (*Markie Letters,* 65).

[120] *Cf.* R. E. Lee to A. W. Beresford Hope, April 16, 1866; *Jones,* 431; and R. E. Lee to A. B. Grosart, April 30, 1866; *Jones,* 250.

[121] *Jones,* 427; *Riley,* 189.

[122] *Jones,* 427; *cf.* R. E. Lee to Reverend George Woodbridge, April 5, 1866; *Jones,* 431. *Cf. ibid.,* 256, for a letter regarding a Bible alleged to have belonged to him that had been stolen from Arlington. "If the lady who has it will use it as I hope she will, she will herself seek to restore it to its rightful owner. I will, therefore, leave the decision of the question to her and her conscience."

[123] R. E. Lee to Miss Fauntleroy, *MS.,* Jan. 19, 1869, *Lee's MS. Letter Book,* apropos of the distribution of *The Little Gleaner.*

CHAPTER XVII

LEE AND THE RECONSTRUCTION ACTS

THE session of 1866–67 opened on September 13 with a greatly increased registration.[1] Before the end of March the enrollment had risen to 345,[2] and by commencement it was 399. Of these, only 139 matriculates came from Virginia. Tennessee sent 60, Kentucky 44, and Texas 33. Every Southern state was represented.[3] It was a very large student body for those pinching times. In comparison, the University of Virginia had 490 that year, the University of North Carolina, 128, Yale, 709, and Harvard, 961. The students were, also, perhaps a more serious company, in the main, than had come to Lexington the previous autumn. Except for some disturbances on the nights of November 23–24, the behavior of the boys gave General Lee little concern until early spring.[4] In caring for the fuller classes, the faculty was worked hard but was recruited during the winter. Colonel William Preston Johnston, son of General Albert Sidney Johnston, was named Professor of History and Literature, to take his chair on February 1, 1867.[5] Besides authorizing the appointment of an assistant professor of Latin and Mathematics,[6] the trustees relieved Lee of some of his duties by the choice of a young superintendent of grounds and buildings.[7] However, there was enough outdoor duty, and to spare, because the trustees, at General Lee's instance, had put first among the construction projects of the college the erection of a new chapel. It was to cost not more than $10,000 when completed. As already explained, $6000 might be spent at once if this would carry the work far enough to make the edifice serviceable.[8] Gen-

---

[1] This is the date set in the 1866 Catalogue.
[2] *Lexington Gazette*, March 20, 1867. [3] *1866–67 Catalogue*, 18.
[4] For his appeal to the boys not to repeat the offense, see *Jones*, 106.
[5] This action was taken despite fear that funds might not be available for paying his salary (*Trustees' Minutes*, Oct. 12, Nov. 15, 1866).
[6] *Trustees' Minutes*, Nov. 15, 1866.
[7] *Riley*, 89. This position had been created the previous June. See *supra*, p. 267.
[8] *Trustees' Minutes*, July 18, 1866. See *supra*, 267, note 58.

eral Lee was most anxious to have a larger, more appropriate place of worship, because of its anticipated influence on the spiritual life of the students. He devoted himself to building the structure economically and within the allowed appropriation. With Custis's assistance,[9] he gave to it daily supervision and the experience gained in dealing with labor when he had been an army engineer.[10] The slow progress of the construction and the strait limits of his available funds seemed only to make him the more determined to complete it. He had personally selected the location for it, conspicuously opposite the line of older buildings on the hill, and he intended it to be the centre of college life.

Autumn slipped away and with the darker skies of winter came a gloomier outlook for Virginia and the rest of the South. Congress and the President had disagreed bitterly over reconstruction. The committee that had heard General Lee and a host of witnesses had reported in April. On the basis of its findings, an elaborate plan was being built up to force the Southern states to acquiesce in the enfranchisement of the Negroes as a condition of readmission to the Union. The government that had been functioning reasonably well in Virginia, its difficulties considered, was now threatened with overthrow.

General Lee of course saw the trend of all this. In May, 1866, a short time after the committee made its report, he gave an interview to the young Marquess of Lorne, later the ninth Duke of Argyll, who married Princess Louise, daughter of Queen Victoria.[11] During their conversation, which was unrestrained, Lee

[9] Henry Louis Smith in *Washington and Lee Alumni Magazine*, November, 1927, p. 28.

[10] *Jones*, 107–8. The old chapel was to be turned over to the department of experimental philosophy and applied science, provided the cost did not exceed $900 (*Trustees' Minutes*, July 18, 1866).

[11] R. E. Lee, Jr., related (*op. cit.*, 244) that the marquess and his companion called at a time when no servant was at hand. General Lee met them himself but not having on his glasses could not read their cards. He ushered them into the parlor and presented them to Mrs. Lee without calling their names. Mrs. Lee, observing that the young man was thin and mistaking him for a prospective student, began to caution him to be mindful of his health in the stern winter climate of Lexington. This led to explanations, whereupon all laughed at the mistake. Argyll did not mention this in his *Passages from the Past*, but stated, on the contrary, that he called at Lee's house in the evening by appointment. It is possible that the incident and the person have been confused in the account by R. E. Lee, Jr. J. W. Ewing, in *Riley*, 71, stated that Sir Garnett Wolseley also visited Lee at Lexington, but as there is no reference in Wolseley's letters to this, Mr. Ewing probably misunderstood the name.

displayed deep concern over the prospect. It would be long, he said, before there is any improvement in the condition of the people. "The Radical party are likely to do a great deal of harm, for we wish now for good feeling to grow up between North and South, and the President, Mr. Johnson, has been doing much to strengthen the feeling in favor of the Union among us. The relations between the Negroes and the whites were friendly formerly, and would remain so if legislation be not passed in favor of the blacks, in a way that will only do them harm."

Lee went on in a voice that Lorne thought very sorrowful, though there was not a touch of bitterness in it: "We [They?] do not seem to see that they are raising up feelings of race—and if a bad feeling is raised in consequence of unfair laws being passed against the weaker party it must yield. The blacks must always here be the weaker; the whites are so much stronger that there is no chance for the black, if the Radical party passes the laws it wants against us. They are working as though they wished to keep alive by their proposals in Congress the bad blood in the South against the North. If left alone the hostility which must be felt after such a war would rapidly decrease, but it may be continued by incessant provocation. The Southerners took up arms honestly: surely it is to be desired that the good-will of our people be encouraged, and that there should be no inciting them against the North. To the minds of the Southern men the idea of 'Union' was ridiculous when the states that made the Union did not desire it to continue; but the North fought for the Union, and now, if what appears to be the most powerful party among them is to have its own way, they are doing their best to destroy all real union. If they succeed, 'Union' can only be a mere name."

The young marquess, who had recently been in Washington, remarked that he had met many who approved of the President's course and would work for reconciliation.

"Yes," said Lee, "but none seem to be courageous enough to oppose the Radicals, who are therefore able to do what they like, and no one stands fairly up to them to hinder them. Surely if the Union be worth preserving, they should try to conciliate the whole nation, and not do all they can against the Southern part of it." In this there was an echo of his statement before the re-

301

construction committee, that it was good policy, in his opinion, for the North to conciliate the South.[12]

Lorne replied that he thought the great majority repudiated the extreme utterance of Thaddeus Stevens. He did not believe that the proposals of the reconstruction committee for confiscating Southern property and for disfranchising the whites would be acted upon favorably.

Lee politely refrained from comment on this prophecy.[13]

As the debate in Congress and in the country progressed during 1866, Lee followed the newspapers with more care than usual and cut from them a number of articles that stated the Southern point of view in its historical bearings. These clippings he put away in a drawer of his table-desk for future use.[14] The scope and content of Federal legislation were still undetermined in the early winter of 1866-67, but it was manifest that the vindictive spirit of Thaddeus Stevens and his radical followers was triumphing over the wise policy of reconciliation that Lincoln had devised and Johnson had sought to apply. Twenty months after Appomattox, the political prospect of the South was far gloomier than it had been at the time of the amnesty proclamation, issued before the paroled Southern soldiers had all found their way home.

These were the conditions in which General Lee received, during December, 1866, a letter from Sir John Dalberg Acton, later Lord Acton. In this letter, the British historian asked for an expression of Lee's views on the constitutional issues involved in secession and on the longer political outlook, in order that he might counsel wisely the editors of a new British review. General Lee took pains with his answer.[15] Apparently, he procured from the library of one of the literary societies a volume on the American Constitution, in order that he might speak by the book,[16] and he referred to several of the newspaper articles he had gathered

---

[12] See *supra*, p. 252. [13] Argyll: *Passages from the Past*, I, 165 ff.

[14] They are still (1934) there, in his office at Washington and Lee, which has not been disturbed since the day he left it.

[15] Original in archives of Washington and Lee University. Acton's letter is so interesting and throws so much light on his character as well as on British estimates of the Southern cause that it is printed as Appendix IV—4. To the late Dean H. D. Campbell, who discovered it in the archives of Washington and Lee, the writer's thanks are due for a copy of this document.

[16] *Riley*, 168.

during the year. He wrote his reply to Acton on December 15, 1866, but as the communication was not published at the time, the existence of the paper was not generally known until the appearance of Lord Acton's *Correspondence* in 1917. Lee's letter, therefore, cannot be said to have had any appreciable influence on the South or on the determination of the questions with which it dealt, but it is very much the fullest expression of Lee's views and, when read with certain passages from some of his other correspondence, it shows clearly what he thought of the political prospect and how he viewed in retrospect the constitutional issue for which he had fought.

It will be remembered that in 1861 Lee knew little about the constitutional involvements of secession. In one of his few known references to the subject, he confused the preamble of the Articles of Confederation with that of the Constitution of 1787. He went with Virginia on her secession because his whole background, his training, and his social and family ties led him to feel instinctively that his first allegiance, at a time of tragic but inescapable choice, was to her.[17] He held that in her secession Virginia carried him with her. As he fought for the Southern cause, however, he came to see its meaning. Sacrifice clarified it. One cannot say when or how—whether it was by his own reading, or through the debates in winter quarters, or from the contagion of political belief—but Lee absorbed the Southern constitutional argument and was convinced by it. "All that the South has ever desired," he wrote in January, 1866, "was that the Union, as established by our forefathers, should be preserved; and that the government, as originally organized, should be administered in purity and truth."[18] Speaking of his own course, he wrote: "I had no other guide, nor had I any other object than the defense of those principles of American liberty upon which the constitutions of the several States were originally founded."[19] To a friend in the West he wrote in 1869 what in 1866 undoubtedly was his opinion: "I was not in favor of secession, and was opposed to war; in fact . . . I was for the Constitution and the Union established by our forefathers. No one now is more in

[17] See *supra*, vol. I, p. 440.
[18] R. E. Lee to Chauncey Burr, Jan. 5, 1866; *Jones*, 210.
[19] R. E. Lee to Captain James May, July 9, 1866; *Jones*, 217–18.

favor of that Constitution and that Union; and, as far as I know, it is that for which the South has all along contended. . . ." [20]

In the fuller statement to Acton he now brought the state's rights argument to bear on the immediate question of the status of the seceded states. ". . . While I have considered the preservation of the constitutional power of the General Government to be the foundation of our peace and safety at home and abroad, I yet believe that the maintenance of the rights and authority reserved in the states and to the people, [is] not only essential to the adjustment and balance of the general system, but the safeguard to the continuance of a free government. I consider it as the chief source of stability to our present system, whereas the consolidation of the states into one vast republic, sure to be aggressive abroad and despotic at home, will be the certain precursor of that ruin which has overwhelmed all those that have preceded it."

He cited then the various historic warnings in America against centralization of power, and argued, by reference to the Hartford convention and the constitution of Massachusetts, that secession was conceded to be a right by two of the states that subsequently most opposed it. "Judge Chase, the present chief justice of the U. S.," he went on, "as late as 1850, is reported to have stated in the Senate, of which he was a member, that he 'knew of no remedy in case of the refusal of a state to perform its stipulation,' thereby acknowledging the sovereignty and independence of state action." [21]

Here Lee dropped the argument from the past and turned to the outlook:

"But I will not weary you with this unprofitable discussion. Unprofitable because the judgment of reason has been displaced by the arbitrament of war, waged for the purpose as avowed of maintaining the union of the states. If, therefore, the result of the war is to be considered as having decided that the union of the states is inviolable and perpetual under the constitution, it nat-

[20] R. E. Lee to Geo. W. Jones, March 22, 1869; *Jones*, 273–74.

[21] This item about Chase was gleaned by Lee from one of the newspaper clippings he preserved and in itself seems to negative the suggestion of Judge Winston that the "Acton letter" was not written by Lee but may have been prepared at his request by some lawyer friend. It is possible, of course, as stated *supra*, p. 239, note 46, that Lee had some legal assistance in drawing up this paper.

urally follows that it is as incompetent for the general government to impair its integrity by the exclusion of a state, as for the
states to do so by secession; and that the existence and rights of
a state by the constitution are as indestructible as the union itself.
The legitimate consequence then must be the perfect equality of
rights of all the states; the exclusive right of each to regulate its
internal affairs under rules established by the constitution, and
the right of each state to prescribe for itself the qualification of
suffrage. The South has contended only for the supremacy of
the constitution, and the just administration of the laws made
in pursuance of it. Virginia to the last made great efforts to save
the union, and urged harmony and compromise. Senator Douglas,
in his remarks upon the compromise bill recommended by the
committee of thirteen in 1861, stated that every member from
the South, including Messrs. Toombs and Davis, expressed their
willingness to accept the proposition of Senator Crittenden from
Kentucky, as a final settlement of the controversy, if sustained by
the Republican party, and that the only difficulty in the way of
an amicable adjustment was with the Republican party. Who
then is responsible for the war? Although the South would have
preferred any honorable compromise to the fratricidal war which
has taken place, she now accepts in good faith its constitutional
results, and receives without reserve the amendment which has
already been made to the Constitution for the extinction of slavery. That is an event that has long been sought, though in a
different way, and by none has it been more earnestly desired
than by citizens of Virginia. In other respects I trust that the
constitution may undergo no change, but that it may be handed
down to succeeding generations in the form we received it from
our forefathers." [22]

In summary, then, General Lee believed that the rights of the
states must be preserved, though the right of secession admittedly
was no longer among them. He did not think the Federal Government had the authority under the Constitution to dictate
suffrage requirements to the states, though he was entirely willing
that the prohibition of slavery should be written into the Con-

---

[22] *Lord Acton's Correspondence*, I, 302–5. Apparently, Lord Acton made no use of
this letter in any of his writings.

stitution. He held that the Southern states could not be denied their civil rights and their places in Congress under the theory of an indestructible Union, a theory which the North itself supported.

Like most Southerners, Lee supported President Johnson and of course opposed the program of the Radicals. In July, 1866, he had written: "Everyone approves of the policy of President Johnson, gives him his cordial support, and would, I believe, confer on him the presidency for another term, if it was in his power." [23] In October, 1867, he told Longstreet, who seemingly desired his endorsement of some move in support of the Republicans, "While I think we should act under the law and according to the law imposed upon us, I cannot think the course pursued by the dominant political party the one best for the interests of the country, and therefore cannot say so, or give them my approval." [24] When Longstreet took a contrary course, and joined the Republicans, Lee said "General Longstreet has made a great mistake." [25] Lee saw the temptation to which his old lieutenant yielded, and he frankly told General Chilton the South could expect no part in the administration of national affairs for many years. For that reason, among others, the South should turn her energies to the development of her industries. [26]

Despite the gloom of the political outlook, Christmas, 1866, was a pleasant season for the Lees. Not long before it, the General had a welcome visit from the old teacher of his youth, William B. Leary, to whom he gave a warm letter of personal endorsement. [27] Rooney did not come up for the holidays, [28] and Mildred was with friends in Maryland, but the other girls and Custis were at home, and Robert arrived on December 20.

Young Lee brought a familiar friend with him—none other than the sorrel mare, Lucy Long, that Jeb Stuart in the fall of 1862 had given his chief. From that time until the spring of 1864 the General had used her alternately with Traveller. Broken

[23] R. E. Lee to James May, July 9, 1866; *Jones*, 217.
[24] R. E. Lee to James Longstreet, Oct. 29, 1867; *Jones*, 227.
[25] 5 *S. H. S. P.*, 176.
[26] R. E. Lee to R. H. Chilton, *MS.*, Jan. 10, 1867; *Chilton Papers*.
[27] *R. E. Lee, Jr.*, 417.
[28] R. E. Lee to R. H. Chilton, *MS.*, Jan. 10, 1867, "Fitzhugh was detained . . . in an effort to procure the necessary labor to cultivate his farm" (*Chilton Papers*).

down then by hard riding and scanty feed, the mare had been sent out to Henry County, Virginia, to recuperate. Lee recalled her before the opening of the Appomattox campaign, but never received her. She got into a stable of government horses and was sent to Danville, where she either was stolen or else was carried off by some soldier when the Confederacy collapsed. In some way she reached Essex County, Virginia, where she was sold to an honest man. Her resemblance to the General's war-time mare having been noted, Lee learned of her whereabouts, proved her identity, and paid for her out of consideration for Stuart's memory.[29] The horse was brought to young Robert Lee's during the autumn and was kept there until nearly Christmas. Then she was shipped by rail to Staunton, at which point Robert met her. "I found there Colonel William Allan," wrote the junior Lee, "who had a buggy and no horse, and as I had a horse and no buggy, we joined forces and I drove him over to Lexington, 'Lucy Long' carrying us with great ease to herself and comfort to us. My father was glad to get her, as he was very fond of her. When he heard how she came over, he was really shocked, as he thought she had never been broken to harness."[30]

Lee gave Lucy Long good care, of course, employing her chiefly as a riding horse for his daughters, but personally he almost always used Traveller. That silent veteran of his campaigns had a place in the General's heart next after his God, his country, his family, his veterans, and his boys. Much as he disliked having his own photograph taken,[31] he was glad to suggest a picture of Traveller at the Rockbridge Baths,[32] and when Markie Williams proposed to paint a picture of the horse, he wrote the detailed description already quoted,[33] and was anxious to know how her work was progressing.[34] The charger spent much of his time in the front yard of Lee's house, and he always received his

---

[29] R. E. Lee, Jr., 250.   [30] R. E. Lee, Jr., 251.

[31] Cf. R. E. Lee, Jr.: "My father never could bear to have his picture taken, and there are no likenesses of him that really give his sweet expression" (25 Confederate Veteran, 50).

[32] This is the familiar picture showing Lee, in half-profile, astride the quiet horse. It was taken by A. H. Plecker of Lynchburg. See his account of the incident in 30 Confederate Veteran, 117.

[33] See supra, vol. I, pp. 645–46 and Markie Letters, 73–75.

[34] Cf. Lee to Markie Williams, Jan. 1, 1868: "How are you progressing with Traveller[']s portrait[,] Markie? He is getting old like his master, and looks to your pencil to hand him down to posterity" (Markie Letters, 80).

master with the same toss of the head that had acknowledged the soldiers' cheers during the war. Lee often had sugar for the horse and sometimes was seen gazing silently at him as though recalling the scenes they had shared.

Traveller enjoyed the easy, honored life he led at Lexington, but, like other heroes, he found that he had to pay a price for fame. In his case, the souvenir hunters were his bane. They stole so much of his mane and tail that he became suspicious of all strangers, and would never let any of them get behind him without exhibiting nervousness.[35] However, he preserved docility with his master, and if he broke away, a whistle from Lee would halt him. Lee insisted that he could not see how any man could ride a horse for any length of time unless there developed a perfect understanding between rider and mount.

Until 1869, in the course of an afternoon, the General frequently rode Traveller to Rockbridge Baths and back, a distance of twenty miles, and on the way he would often give him a stiff run, a "breather," as he called it.[36] Another favorite ride was to Colonel Ross's, where he would talk of farming.[37] When he was away from Lexington, Lee sent messages to the horse just as he did to the members of his family. "How is Traveller?" he inquired. "Tell him I miss him dreadfully and have repented of our separation but once and that is the whole time since we parted." And again, "I hope Traveller is well and wants for nothing. I want him more than ever now that I shall be alone." During a season when he boarded the animal in the country outside Lexington, he visited him every week, and when he was absent and a stranger was attending the horses, he left minute instructions for their care. On days when his mount had to be shod, the General stood by him during the ordeal. "Have patience with Traveller," he urged the blacksmith as the horse danced about, "he was made nervous by the bursting of bombs around him during the war."[38] Members of the family who had gone from home on visits were regaled occasionally with news about the favorite steed. To Mildred he wrote that winter, "Traveller and

---

[35] *McDonald*, 5. Lee wrote Mary, Oct. 29, 1865: "The boys are plucking out his tail, and he is presenting the appearance of a plucked chicken" (*R. E. Lee, Jr.*, 193).
[36] *R. E. Lee, Jr.*, 371.   [37] *Riley*, 81.
[38] *Riley*, 68, 68 n., 74, 93, 93 n., 112, 136; *cf. R. E. Lee, Jr.*, 428.

Custis are both well, and pursue their usual dignified gait and habits, and are not led away by the frivolous entertainments of lectures and concerts."[39] Such was his loyalty to Traveller that it was an ominous sign of his approaching end when Lee had to admit that the trot of his steed was getting harder. Rightly enough, on the day that Lee was buried, the horse followed directly behind the hearse.[40]

Other animals, too, shared the General's love during the years at Lexington, as they had during the period of the war. He kept a cow, after the manner of most village people in those days of open spaces, and he was distressed on his departure for the Hot Springs in the last summer of his life to leave the faithful milker sick. "You do not mention the cow," he wrote back, "she is of more interest to me than the cats, and is equally destructive of rats." A few days later he said: "I am glad the cow is better. She stands next in my affections to Traveller." The news of her death drew this sorrowful comment: "Our good cow will be a loss to us, but her troubles are all over now, and I am grateful to her for what she has done for us. I hope that we did our duty to her."[41]

Dogs he esteemed somewhat less than in the days at Fort Hamilton, but he had frequent mention of at least one canine. That was "Duckie," a very small, helpless creature that Mr. and Mrs. Edward Childe brought with them from France when they came on a visit. "He had crossed the Atlantic in fear and trembling," Robert Lee recorded, "and did not apparently enjoy the new world. His utter helplessness and the great care taken of him by his mistress, his ill health and the unutterable woe of his countenance greatly excited my father's pity. After he went away, he often spoke of him, and referred to him, I find, in one of his letters."[42]

Near the end of his life, when Lee could not enjoy Traveller, because of the condition of his heart, he sought a dog. Writing to Fitz Lee, not a month before he died, the General said: "Your letter on the dog question has been unavoidably delayed. I thank you very sincerely for recollecting my wishes on the subject and

[39] R. E. Lee to Mildred Lee, Dec. 21, 1866; *R. E. Lee, Jr.*, 249.
[40] *R. E. Lee, Jr.*, 374; Jones, in *Riley*, 218.
[41] *R. E. Lee, Jr.*, 424, 426, 427–28. [42] *R. E. Lee, Jr.*, 370–71.

[for] your steps to comply with them. First I must inform you that it is not my purpose to put my dog to towing canal boats or hauling dirt carts, but want him to play the part of a friend and protector. His disposition is therefore of vital importance—he ought not to be too old to contract a friendship for me—neither is his size so important to me as a perfect form." [43] Cats, of course, the women of the house had about them always, more numerously perhaps than Lee desired, but he made no protest.[44] Whether Lee liked some species of animals or not, their suffering pained him deeply. One winter, not far from Lexington, a forest fire added great beauty to the night. But when some one praised it to Lee, he could not wholly agree. "It is beautiful," he admitted, "but I have been thinking of the poor animals which must perish in the flames." [45]

The new year, 1867, brought a call. There still was hope that Congress would leave President Johnson free to permit Virginia to elect a governor without military interference. Several possible conservative nominees were suggested. General Lee was the most conspicuous of them.[46] It was not a new proposal. Besides the suggestion General Meade had made, John B. Baldwin the previous year had put forward Lee's name at a public meeting, when it had met with much applause. Some of the Radicals who had testified before the reconstruction committee were convinced that a plan was under way to name the General.[47] By the end of January, 1867, sentiment for Lee was so strong that Judge Robert Ould wrote to know if he would accept the nomination. The General was sick when Ould's letter arrived, but he replied at once. He was appreciative, he wrote the judge, but he preferred private life, which he thought was better suited to his condition and age. He believed there were many more capable of filling the position and of promoting the interests of the people. He went on:

"I think it most important, in selecting a Chief Magistrate of

[43] *New York Times,* April 16, 1930, quoting the letter, then on exhibit, from the collection of Henry Woodhouse.
[44] *Cf.* Mrs. R. E. Lee to Mildred Lee, MS., Dec. 25, 1866, *Duke Univ. MSS.*
[45] *Jones,* 163–64. [46] *Lexington Gazette* of Jan. 9, 1867, quoting *Richmond Whig.*
[47] *Reports of the Reconstruction Committee,* 121, 151.

the Commonwealth, for the citizens to choose one capable of fulfilling its high trust, and at the same time not liable to the misconstruction which their choice of one objectionable to the General Government would be sure to create, and thereby increase the evils under which the State at present labors.

"I have no means of knowing, other than are apparent to you, whether my election as Governor of Virginia would be personally injurious to me or not, and therefore the consideration of that question in your letter has not been embraced in my reply. But I believe it would be used by the dominant party to excite hostility toward the State, and to injure the people in the eyes of the country; and I therefore cannot consent to become the instrument of bringing distress upon those whose prosperity and happiness are so dear to me. If *my* disfranchisement and privation of civil rights would secure to the citizens of the State the enjoyment of civil liberty and equal rights under the Constitution, I would willingly accept them in their stead.

"What I have written is intended only for your own information. . . ." [48]

To State Senator Cabell he said: "As regards the mention of my name for the next Governor, that has been finally settled by the late Bill of Congress. But I expressed my views on the subject some time since to Mr Ould of Richmond, who will no doubt disclose them to you if you desire. I believe my election would be injurious to Virginia, & I cannot therefore consent to become a candidate." [49]

Both these were serious answers, written at a serious time, and the tone is quite different from that of the polite but impersonal letters in which he so often rejected business offers. Evidently he gave thought to the proposal. Although he had told Ben. Hill during the war that his talents were military, not civil,[50] he might, in other circumstances have looked favorably on Judge Ould's suggestion. He may have been influenced unconsciously by the fact that his father had been governor of Virginia after the

[48] R. E. Lee to Robert Ould, Feb. 4, 1867; *Jones*, 222.
[49] Lee to David S. G. Cabell, *MS.*, Feb. 25, 1867: *Library of Congress*.
[50] *Jones*, 224.

Revolution. One of Mrs. Lee's ambitions for him was that he should end his career with the same honor.[51]

Very shortly after General Lee answered Judge Ould, the political outlook changed grimly for the worse. The Radicals in Congress triumphed decisively over President Johnson, and in the face of his veto, passed the First Reconstruction Act on March 2, 1867. In a supplementary law of March 23 this was elaborated.[52]

These two statutes subordinated to army officers the government of ten Southern states, Virginia among them. The states themselves ceased to exist for the time, in the eyes of the Federal Government, and became military districts. Before they could be relieved of this armed rule and allowed representation in Congress again, each of the ten states must elect a constitutional convention on the basis of manhood suffrage, Negroes included. Further, this convention had to draft a constitution giving the ballot to all male adults. The people were thereupon to ratify the new constitution, and Congress, if it saw fit, was to approve. Then a legislature, chosen as required by the modified organic law, was to meet and accept the Fourteenth Amendment to the Federal Constitution. This amendment contained a section disqualifying for office virtually all those who had held official position and had thrown in their lot with the Confederacy.

On March 13, 1867, the First Reconstruction Act was proclaimed in Virginia. On that day, the proud Old Dominion became Military District No. 1. Dictatorial power to remove functionaries, to make appointments, to hold a general registration, and to initiate all the steps required under the new Federal law was vested in the soldier who had for some time been in charge of the Union forces garrisoning Virginia, Major General John M. Schofield.[53]

What should Virginians do about this harsh legislation? Should they passively resist? Should they refrain from participating in the elections, or should they save what they might? In a bitterness of spirit they had not felt in 1865 people asked these questions. It was one thing to be defeated in war; it was quite another

[51] Mrs. Mary Custis Lee to R. H. Chilton, *MS.*, Dec. 12, 1870; *Chilton Papers.*
[52] 14 *U. S. Statutes at Large*, 428; 15 *U. S. Statutes at Large*, 2.
[53] H. J. Eckenrode: *Political History of Virginia during the Reconstruction* (cited hereafter as *Eckenrode*), 52.

to see Congress enact laws avowedly designed to disfranchise white men and to subject them to the political domination of their former slaves. "It is bad enough," Mrs. Lee indignantly wrote Mrs. Chilton, "to be the victims of tyranny, but when it is wielded by such cowards and base men as Butler, Thaddeus & Turner it is indeed intolerable. The country that allows such scum to rule them must be fast going to destruction and we shall care little if we are not involved in the crash." And again, "They still desire to grind [the South] to dust & wish to effect this purpose by working on the feelings of the low & ignorant negroes many of whom do not even comprehend what *a vote* means[.] My indignation cannot be controlled and I wonder our people, helpless and disarmed as they are[,] can bear it. Oh God how long?" [54]

These were the sentiments of thousands who looked to Lee for guidance. He had followed the newspapers the previous year but as the climax approached, he avoided reading the attacks delivered in Congress on the South.[55] Nor would he now permit himself to be brought into the controversy through the public prints. In three private letters, however, he set forth his opinions freely, and in at least one instance, an accurate though unauthorized statement of his views was printed in a newspaper,[56] very soon after the passage of the Reconstruction Act.

It was this public statement that prompted him, in answer to an inquiry from his friend Judge Robert Ould of Richmond, to express his opinion of Virginia's duty. Under date of March 29, 1867, he wrote as follows:

"My dear Sir

"I recd this mo[ng] your letter of the 26th Inst: & do not know on what authority my opinions have been announced in the public papers. It was certainly not by mine, & from what I am told remarks are attributed to me of which I have no knowledge. When the Sherman bill became a law & its execution imperative, I considered it right & just to the people of the State, that it should

---

[54] Mrs. R. E. Lee to Mrs. R. H. Chilton, *MS.*, March 10 and May 6, 1867; *Chilton Papers.*
[55] Mrs. R. E. Lee to Mrs. R. H. Chilton, *MS.*, March 10, 1867; *loc. cit.*
[56] *Lexington Gazette,* March 27, 1867.

be submitted as required for their action, & that the call for a convention should be legitimately & properly made. I have never read the bill passed by the Senate of Virginia for that purpose, & do not know its provisions; but if there was then a difference of opinion as to the proper mode, there can be none since the passage of the supplemental bill; & I think all persons entitled to vote should attend the polls & endeavour to elect the best available men to represent them in the convention, to whose decision every one should submit. The preservation of harmony & kind feelings is of the utmost importance, & all good citizens should exert themselves to secure it & to prevent the division of the people into parties. The interests of all are inseparably connected & can only be preserved by our united wisdom & strength. I think it useless to offer arguments to show the propriety of this course. Its advantages are too manifest.

"It is extremely unpleasant to me, for reasons which I think will occur to you, that my name should be unnecessarily brought before the public, and I do not see that any good can result from it. I hope therefore you will not publish my letter, but that you will try & allay the strife that I fear may arise in the State.

"With great regard your obt Servt   R. E. LEE." [57]

As the wrath of the South rose in resentmen⟨t⟩ ⟨o⟩f the Federal legislation, Lee had to urge his view with tact⟨.⟩ The South, he wrote General Dabney H. Maury, was acting under compulsion. Each state should consult its best interests as far as it could. The Reconstruction Act would be carried out: a convention would be called and a constitution drafted. As that was certain, "the question, then, is, shall the members of the convention be selected from the best available men in the State, or the worst?" The Radicals would be well pleased, he presumed, if they and the Negroes were left to make the new organic law of the commonwealth. In the circumstances, he thought it the duty of all citizens who were not disfranchised to qualify and to vote for the best men they could get to be candidates for the convention. When

[57] *Ould MSS.*, courteously made available to the writer by Colonel and Mrs. W. Frank Powers of Richmond. The original of this letter has been given the Virginia Historical Society.

that body met, it should determine what should be done, and in its decision the whole white population should acquiesce. He did not so state in plain words, but he left it to be inferred that if the convention decided it should enfranchise the Negroes, in order to procure the readmission of Virginia into the Union, the people should endorse this action.[58] "Although [the convention's] decision may not be considered at the time the most advantageous," he said in his other letter on the Reconstruction Acts, "it should be recollected that it can be improved as opportunity offers, and in the end I trust all things will work together for our good."[59]

He refused to despair of the future, though "greater calamity," in his opinion, might yet result from the misunderstanding between the sections.[60] "The dominant party cannot reign forever," he had written one of his sons in February, "and truth and justice will at last prevail."[61] "The present condition of affairs," he told an unnamed Petersburg lady, "is, as you state, calculated to cause much anxiety, but not enough, in my opinion, to cause us to despond, or to cease in our efforts to direct events to a favorable issue."[62] And in June he wrote Rooney, in language curiously rhetorical for him, "Although the future is still dark, and the prospects gloomy, I am confident that, if we all unite in doing our duty, and earnestly work to extract what good we can out of the evil that now hangs over our dear land, the time is not distant when the angry cloud will be lifted from our horizon and the sun in his pristine brightness again shine forth."[63]

Within the college, the session of 1866–67 passed quickly, amid the exactions of a thousand duties. Visitors came in the usual numbers. Among them was William Swinton, author of *The Campaigns of the Army of the Potomac*, who was then travelling through the South, collecting from Confederate leaders some of the historical material he used in his *Twelve Decisive Battles of the War*. "He seems to be gentlemanly," Lee confided to Rooney,

[58] R. E. Lee to D. H. Maury, May 23, 1867; *Jones*, 226–27.
[59] R. E. Lee to Mrs. —— of Petersburg, Va., May 21, 1867; *Jones*, 225.
[60] R. E. Lee to Frank Fuller, April 20, 1867; *Jones*, 224.
[61] R. E. Lee to W. H. F. Lee, Feb. 26, 1867; *R. E. Lee, Jr.*, 258.
[62] *Jones*, 225.
[63] R. E. Lee to W. H. F. Lee, June 8, 1867; *R. E. Lee, Jr.*, 260.

in manifest relief, after Swinton's departure, "but I derive no pleasure from my interviews with book-makers. I have either to appear uncivil or run the risk of being dragged before the public." [64]

The intermediate examinations were stiff. "The ordeal through which the higher classes passed," Lee wrote his still-absent daughter, "was as severe as any I ever witnessed." [65] The general level of performance was high,[66] and the students were serious. Lee himself seems to have shared in the general pursuit of knowledge, for he took from the library a volume on calculus and presumably regaled himself in the realm of his favorite mathematics.[67] He found time, too, to think once again of the history of his campaigns he still hoped to write,[68] though he had told Acton he was progressing slowly "in the collection of the necessary documents." [69]

In March occurred the session's gravest breach of discipline. Some of the students heard there was to be a speech-making to the Negroes on the evening of the 22d and, boy-like, five of them determined to attend. One of the group foolishly took a pistol with him. They went to the Freedmen's Church and, finding it dark, decided that the meeting must be at the schoolhouse, so they tramped thither. On their arrival, the student who carried the pistol approached a window to see if there was a gathering within. Immediately a Negro accosted him, cursed him, and made a motion as if to draw a weapon. The student took out his own firearm and started to beat the Negro, but presently desisted and went away with his companions. In some manner he eluded arrest, but the four others were brought before the mayor and were tried. As soon as General Lee heard of the affair, he summoned the quartet who had been in court. When they came, the student who had been engaged in the altercation also appeared. In accordance with the honor system of the college, he explained the circumstances, and assumed the entire blame. He was promptly expelled and the others were reprimanded. Three weeks later the assistant superintendent of the Freedmen's Bureau

---

[64] R. E. Lee to W. H. F. Lee, June 8, 1867; *R. E. Lee, Jr.,* 261.
[65] R. E. Lee to Mildred Lee, Feb. 16, 1867; *R. E. Lee, Jr.,* 254.
[66] *Ibid.*
[67] *Riley,* 169.
[68] *R. E. Lee, Jr.,* 259.
[69] *Lord Acton's Correspondence,* I, 305.

wrote General Lee on the subject, apparently determined to make an issue of it, but he dropped the matter, it seems, after Lee wrote him the facts in the case.[70]

A month before commencement, President Davis was released on bail from his long confinement at Fort Monroe, Virginia. General Lee had felt from the first the injustice of making the Confederate President a scapegoat,[71] and he had consulted with friends to see if anything could be done in Mr. Davis's behalf. He had carried his war-time chief on his heart and in his prayers, confident of his acquittal if brought to trial, yet sensitive to Mr. Davis's sufferings.[72] The news that Davis was at last free from prison, General Lee received with relief and thankfulness. He wrote the former executive: "You can conceive better than I can express the misery which your friends have suffered from your long imprisonment, and the other afflictions incident thereto. To none has this been more painful than to me, and the impossibility of affording relief has added to my distress. Your release has lifted a load from my heart which I have not words to tell, and my daily prayer to the great Ruler of the world is, that He may shield you from all future harm, guard you from all evil, and give you the peace which the world cannot take away. That the rest of your days may be triumphantly happy is the sincere and earnest wish of your most obedient, faithful friend

[70] R. E. Lee to J. W. Sharp, *MS.*, April 13, 1867; *Lee's MS. Letter Book*. It was about this time that General Lee is alleged to have set the seal of his approval on the Ku Klux Klan. According to Susan Lawrence Davis (*Authentic History of the Ku Klux Klan*, 81) just prior to the first convention of the K. K. K. at Nashville, in May, 1867, the Pulaski, Georgia, or Tennessee Klan sent members to General Lee to ascertain if the continuance of the order met with his approval. The tradition is that he answered: "I would like to assist you in any plan that offers relief. I cannot be with you in person but I will follow you but must be invisible; and my advice is to keep it as you have it, a protective organization." From this remark it is claimed that the Klan got its name, "the invisible empire." Miss Davis, who based her history on personal conversations with many of the early members of the Klan, thinks there can be no doubt that this story of General Lee's affiliation with the Klan was generally credited, but she has not been able to find any mention of it in any of the records of the Klan she has thus far examined. No sort of reference to the incident, or to the Klan, appears in any of General Lee's papers that have come under the eye of the author of this work. He is not disposed to accept the story, though satisfied, of course, that Miss Davis recorded it precisely as it was given to her by some of the early members of the Klan.

[71] On May 13, 1867, President Davis was admitted to bail (7 *Rowland*, 175-76). *Cf.* R. E. Lee to Josiah Tatnall, Sept. 7, 1865: "It will, I think, be admitted that Mr. Davis has done nothing more than all the citizens of the Southern States, and should not be held accountable for acts performed by them in the exercise of what had been considered by them unquestionable right" (*Jones*, 205).

[72] R. E. Lee to Mrs. Jefferson Davis, Jan. 23, 1866; *Jones*, 212.

and servant." [73] Doubtless the feelings expressed in this letter brightened the commencement for General Lee.[74]

During the final exercises, when the trustees met, they had no report of large gifts to the endowment during the year, except for one donation from the Ladies Association of Louisville, Ky.[75] Some of the subscriptions previously made had not been met.[76] The solicitors of the college, however, had gathered many small pledges and some cash during the year. Reverend E. P. Walton returned $27,950, exclusive of gifts under $100, as compared with $45,280 in 1865–66.[77] As students had paid $22,000 for tuition, the trustees had some latitude in making appropriations at their June meeting. A "boarding house," or commons, to cost $5000 was authorized, though this action was later rescinded. Certain needed land was purchased. Laboratory apparatus costing $7600 was ordered, to be paid for over a period of three years. A thousand dollars were set aside for advertising. Commutation of $300 was allowed each of the professors to whom the college did not supply a house. Even the expense of a band to enliven the commencement exercises was approved.

Nor were these the only outlays sanctioned. It was General Lee's custom, during the meetings of the trustees, to report and then to retire in order that the board might be under no restraint in debating his recommendations.[78] While he was absent from the room at the June meeting, the building committee was instructed to contract at once for the erection of a new house for the president at a cost of $12,000, later raised to $15,000. General Lee did not think this should be done, and argued that other improvements should have precedence, but there was no gainsaying the trustees.[79]

[73] R. E. Lee to Jefferson Davis, June 1, 1867; *Jones*, 258–59.

[74] *R. E. Lee, Jr.*, 262–63. The baccalaureate sermon was preached by Reverend John A. Broadus (*Trustees' Minutes*, June 20, 1867; Robertson's *John A. Broadus*, 224, 227).

[75] R. E. Lee to Mrs. Susan Preston Hepburn, *MS.*, May 31, 1867; *Lee's MS. Letter Book*.

[76] *Trustees' Minutes*, June 20, 1867.

[77] *Walton's subscription books*, Treasurer's Records, Washington and Lee University.

[78] Joynes in *Cent. U. S. C.*, 32.

[79] *Trustees' Minutes*, June 19, 20, 1867; for the President's house, see *ibid.*, and Aug. 20, 1867; also *Jones*, 177. To meet the immediate financial drain of these expenditures, the trustees authorized the borrowing of $10,000. Tuition and other college fees were raised slightly to make the total $105, exclusive of board, or $115 with a modern language (*Trustees' Minutes*, June 20, 1867).

No new professors were elected, because funds for the endowment of the additional chairs had not been raised. The only
change in duties was the creation of the combined office of clerk
and librarian, at a salary of $600 per annum.[80] Arrangements
with Judge Brockenbrough for the operation of the law school
were continued another year.[81] The committee on instruction
expressed its gratification at the work of the session and had no
reforms to suggest.[82]

If the second year offered no such dazzling comparisons as
could have been made at the end of the session of 1865–66, it was
because the transformation had already occurred. Everything
now depended on enlarged endowment. The assets of the college, as of January, 1867, were estimated by General Lee as follows: Buildings, $40,000; grounds, $10,000; apparatus, exclusive
of prospective purchases, $1000; endowment, including securities
not paying interest, $190,000. Salaries were $11,000 per annum,
and tuition receipts, as already noted, were $22,000.[83] The school,
Lee had written in March, was progressing as well as could be expected.[84] He believed at the time that in another year he would
have done all he could at the college and that he could retire to
"some quiet spot" east of the mountains where he could prepare
a home for Mrs. Lee and his daughters.[85] Confinement, he had
told an old friend, "agrees less with me even than labour in the
field."[86] To Markie Williams he had written a year before: "I
am easily wearied now, and look forward with joy to the time,
which is fast approaching, that I can lay [sic] down and rest."[87]

[80] *Trustees' Minutes*, June 19, 1867.
[81] *Trustees' Minutes*, June 19, 1867.   [82] *Trustees' Minutes*, June 20, 1867.
[83] R. E. Lee to unnamed correspondent, Jan. 26, 1867; *Lee's MS. Letter Book*.
[84] *Lexington Gazette*, March 20, 1867.
[85] R. E. Lee to W. H. F. Lee, June 8, 1867; *R. E. Lee*, 260.
[86] R. E. Lee to R. H. Chilton, Jan. 10, 1867; *Chilton MSS.*
[87] April 7, 1866; *Markie Letters*, 70.

CHAPTER XVIII

A Social Conciliator

As college work at the end of the session of 1866–67 was better organized than it had been the previous summer, the General could take a vacation, a needed one, for he had been almost continuously at work since he had moved to Lexington, nearly two years before.

First there came a trip to a lovely mountain, the Peaks of Otter, about thirty miles away, in Bedford County. It was undertaken on horseback, with his daughter Mildred, who had at last returned home after her lengthy visit in Maryland. The road led through a thinly settled, picturesque country, the beauty of which, in the verdure of late June, appealed profoundly to General Lee.[1] His spirits were high and Traveller was prancing, as they made their way over the hills, with Mildred at his side on Lucy Long. Lunching by the road, they came in the afternoon to the James River, where the ferryman proved to be a veteran of the Army of Northern Virginia. He refused to accept anything for conveying his old commander across the stream.

Up the valley of the James the two riders climbed, past mountain cabins and occasional prosperous homes. Out where the road was the steepest, they came upon a group of dirty-faced youngsters at play. The General spoke to them—he never passed children without doing so—and asked jestingly if they did not think some water would help their countenances. The children gaped and ran away. Presently the riders made a turn in the winding road, and down from a cabin, now visible for the first time, trooped the same youngsters, in clean aprons, their faces hurriedly but surely washed, and their hair combed. "We know you are General Lee," cried one of the group. "We have got your picture." Their toilet was in his honor.

[1] Whether the trip began on June 21 or June 28, it is not possible to determine.

320

The hotel at the Peaks of Otter nestles unassumingly in the high gap that leads over the mountain. The eminence that visitors are wont to climb lies directly above. On horseback one may get within 700 yards of the crest, which is 4000 feet above sea level —a high mountain for that friendly range. Walking from the hotel, the distance to the summit by the difficult track is a mile and a quarter, and by the easy route, two miles and a half. The General and his daughter arrived at the hotel about 9 o'clock in the evening, spent the night there, and very early the next morning set out for the mountain top under the escort of the proprietor. They rode in Indian file as far as the horses could scramble and then they went on afoot. When the crest was reached, the General sat down on one of the rocks and studied the far-sweeping landscape below him. He had little to say and seemed very sad. Was it that the magnificence of the blue panorama stirred him deeply, as noble scenery often did,[2] or was he wondering about the future of the people of Military District No. 1 whose homes were spread out there before his vision?

Down from the mountain and straight on toward Liberty, county seat of Bedford, father and daughter rode. On the way a sudden thundershower overtook them and forced them to gallop back to the nearest cabin. The General lifted the girl off the horse and hurried her into the house, while he led the animals to the shed. When he came back the atmosphere in the tiny dwelling was uncomfortable: the reticent mountain woman had not been pleased that a stranger of her sex had come dripping into her house, forming pools of water wherever she paused on the clean floor. Still less, now, did she relish the arrival of a booted man, who was tramping mud on the boards she had laboriously scoured white. The General sensed her indignation and almost in the breath that he asked permission to remain until the rain had passed, he apologized for marring the beauty of a floor he gallantly extolled. Somewhat mollified, the housewife invited her guests into her best room, which her absent husband, a veteran of the Army of Northern Virginia, had adorned with pictures of Lee and Jackson, Davis and Johnston. She did not associate the

---

[2] "No words can express the intense enjoyment he would get out of a brilliant sunset" (Mrs. Preston, *loc. cit.*, 276, quoting "one of his daughters").

man before her, in the wet coat, with the soldier whose likeness was on her wall, but she was measurably appeased, as is the way of mortals, with the continuing praise of the bearded cavalier. After a while, when the thunder-cloud had gone over, the General bowed his way out and went for the horses. In his absence, Mildred obligingly told her hostess who he was. "The woman seemed stunned," the General's daughter wrote, and her startled mind ran on to the return of her husband to whom she would break the incredible news that his old commander had been under his roof. "What will Joey say, what will Joey say?" she kept repeating.

That afternoon the General and Mildred reached Avenel, in the little town of Liberty,[3] the home of William M. Burwell, a connection of theirs. Back among the people of her own sort, Mildred sought to dress appropriately. When she came downstairs for the evening, her father was surprised to see her glorified in crinoline—her own crinoline at that! How was it done, when she had brought no luggage with her, other than her saddle-bag? The General had to be advised, in his masculine ignorance, that a resourceful young lady of fashion could contrive to roll up her hoops until she was able to squeeze them into the saddle-bags, and, in due season, to be ready for suitors or for ceremonies. The General was greatly amused.

That night and the next day, Sunday, were spent at Avenel. Monday morning the two rode westward again, paralleling the line of the Virginia and Tennessee Railroad[4] for about twelve miles, until they reached the home of Captain Pascal Buford, at the site of the present Montvale.[5] The captain was a successful old farmer whose extensive property had been little injured by moving armies and roving commissaries. He had entertained Mrs. Lee, Mary, and Agnes for a short time during the war, and he was delighted now to see the General and another of his daughters. They spent the afternoon going over the Buford farm, and at night they sat down to a supper so bountiful that it almost overflowed the table.

[3] Liberty later became known as Bedford City. Avenel was subsequently the residence of J. W. Ballard.
[4] Now the Norfolk and Western.
[5] The railroad station was then called Buford'e

When the meal and the evening chat were over, and Mr. Buford was showing his guests to their rooms, the General thoughtfully inquired at what time they should be ready for breakfast.

"Well, General," said Buford indulgently, "as you have been riding hard, and as you are company, we will not have breakfast tomorrow till sunup."

The General, of course, did not allow himself to smile, and doubtless he was ready to sit down at table on Tuesday morning the very minute the rim of the sun shone over the horizon, but in the Lee family circle, for many a day thereafter, he delighted to tell of the kindly host whose consideration for his guests prompted him to defer breakfast until four-thirty!

That fifth day away from home was pleasantly passed at Captain Buford's. On Wednesday the General and Mildred covered the forty-one miles back to Lexington, by way of Buchanan and Natural Bridge. It was a pleasant excursion after so long a period of all-consuming labor.[6]

Mrs. Lee's condition had not been favorable during the spring, for she had worried over the course of the reconstruction. Often she made herself indignant by reading the newspapers, but she could hardly leave them alone, because, as she explained, few books were available, and she had no employment if she did not read.[7] "I know you long sometimes for the banks of the Potomac and James," she confided to an old friend. "I confess I do[.] These mountains seem to shut out all I used to know and love[,] yet I am thankful we have found an asylum here and such kind people."[8] Her invalidism was so confirmed that she wrote, "The greatest feat I can expect to accomplish will be to walk across my room without crutches & even that I have no hope of accomplishing."[9] The General felt, as he had in peaceful years before the war, that a change of scene would do her good and that the mineral waters of some popular "springs" might relieve her rheumatism. He left the choice of a resort to her, and she selected the Greenbrier White Sulphur, "merely on the ground, I believe,"

[6] The only account of this trip to the Peaks was written many years later by Miss Mildred Lee and was printed in *R. E. Lee, Jr.*, 271–73.
[7] Mrs. R. E. Lee to Mrs. R. H. Chilton, *MS.*, March 10, 1867; *Chilton Papers*.
[8] Same to same, March 10, 1867; *loc. cit.*   [9] Same to same, May 6, 1867; *loc. cit.*

the General wrote Rooney, "that she has never tried those waters, and, therefore, they might be of service to her."[10] As soon as he got back from the Peaks of Otter, he began to make his preparation to take her to the spa—a long, bone-breaking journey by railroad and conveyance over the mountains.

Some time in July the party set out, Mrs. Lee, Agnes, Miss Mary Pendleton, and Custis. They were to go by the stage to Goshen, thence by train to Covington, and on from that town by horse-drawn vehicles to the springs, which were across the new state line in Greenbrier County, West Virginia. General Lee rode ahead on Traveller, accompanied by Captain-Professor J. J. White, who was becoming a close friend.[11] After a night at Covington, the adventurers climbed into the clumsy old four-wheelers and made ready for the last struggle with the mountain roads. The hotel proprietor had reserved a special coach for the Lees, and now sent out lunch with his compliments. When the drivers were about to give the word, the General discovered that the other vehicles were overcrowded, while there were vacant seats in the one assigned his party. He insisted that some of those who were uncomfortably placed should travel with Mrs. Lee—an invitation he did not have to repeat.[12] Off rumbled the carriages, with Lee and White still on horseback.

Traveller and his companion soon outdistanced the coaches and brought their riders in good time to the half-way house, where it was customary to break the journey with a wash, a lunch, and a rest in a quiet, darkened room, after the noise and dust of the road. The General had quarters reserved for Mrs. Lee and happened to be on the stairs when, below him, he heard some young girls from Maryland trying to coax the maid into finding them a chamber in the crowded little tavern. She apologized volubly but kept explaining that all the space had been taken. When the

[10] R. E. Lee to W. H. F. Lee, June 8, 1867; R. E. Lee, Jr., 260.

[11] R. E. Lee, Jr., 274. It is impossible to give precise dates for Lee's arrival and departure from the springs. His letters during the summer were few. The hotel registers are no longer in existence. The only available supplementary check is afforded by The Lexington Gazette, which chronicled his movements but unfortunately gave conflicting dates. See its files, July 24, Aug. 11, and Aug. 26, 1867. R. E. Lee, Jr., said the family went "about the first of July," and remained there three weeks, but this is manifestly an error, unless General Lee subsequently returned, for there appears in R. E. Lee, Jr., 277, a letter written from the White Sulphur, dated Aug. 5.

[12] R. E. Lee, Jr., 274.

General smiled at the colloquy, the girls for the first time became conscious of his presence. They looked up at him and, though they had never seen him before, they identified him on the instant. Nearly sixty years after, one of the two recalled her impressions of that moment:

"The man who stood before us, the embodiment of a Lost Cause, was the realized King Arthur. The soul that looked out of his eyes was as honest and fearless as when it first looked on life. One saw the character, as clear as crystal, without complications or seals, and the heart, as tender as that of ideal womanhood. The years which have passed since that time have dimmed many enthusiasms and destroyed many illusions, but have caused no blush at the memory of the swift thrill of recognition and reverence which ran like an electric flash through one's whole body."

At once the General insisted that the young ladies, who also were on their way to the White Sulphur, should refresh themselves in Mrs. Lee's room. They were mortified that he had overheard their complaints, but they accepted his courtesy with blushing thanks. For a few moments they talked with him, and that day they laid the foundation of a friendship to which history owes one of the most interesting accounts of the social life of General Lee.[13]

Ending a hard journey, the family reached White Sulphur that afternoon. At the time, and for forty years thereafter, this resort consisted of a rambling central hotel, a huge wooden structure with long, wide porches, beyond which were rows of small cottages, each of them usually occupied by a single family. General Lee had the Harrison Cottage in Baltimore Row, and around him he found many whom he had known in the old days before the Potomac had become a chasm. He ate in the main dining room, at a table with W. W. Corcoran of Washington, Mildred Lee, Miss Pendleton, and Custis. Mrs. Lee's meals, of course, were served in her cottage.

The social impulse of the General was always strong, and now, in renewed contact with long-separated friends, it asserted itself vigorously. For such another period in his life one has to go

---

[13] Christiana Bond: *Memories of General Robert E. Lee* (cited hereafter as *Miss Bond*), 18.

back to the years at Fort Monroe. He did not write of social happenings as exuberantly in 1867 as he did in 1833—he left to the women of the family the chronicling of arrivals and departures—but he unmistakably enjoyed the company.

Young gallants at the springs admired him, of course, but kept at a distance, for he overawed them. The older men, in some instances, he purposely avoided, because they were forever talking of the war and of politics, two subjects he considered it his duty to leave alone. With the women guests, particularly the girls, he seemed less reserved. "Apparently," Miss Bond concluded, "he felt among the maidens a safety from intrusion which he could not have among those to whom his personality, and the great issues which he represented, were uppermost thoughts." [14]

The centre of the social life of "The White" was the parlor of the main hotel. It was a vast place, nearly always thronged. "Here," writes Miss Bond, "everyone took part in a promenade up and down the great uncarpeted space, not usually in couples but in lines of three or four. Here introductions took place, here engagements were made, and this was the stranger's opportunity to be absorbed into the strenuous stream of life. . . ." [15] On the evening of his arrival, it was expected that the General would come into the parlor, and there was some hurried consultation as to how he should be received. Some honor, of course, must be shown him, but would applause embarrass him? Before the question could be answered, Lee entered. There was a moment's hush, and then, as if by common impulse, every one rose and remained silent and standing until he took a seat.[16]

After that, assured that no demonstration would be made, he went regularly into the parlor, and as often as he did so, he was surrounded by groups of young women, with whom he talked, half-seriously, half-jestingly. If new girls came to the hotel, he saw that they were made to feel at home. The homeliest and least known were as sure to receive his courteous attention as the fairest or the most aristocratic. When flirtations developed—and they were many—the General followed them with interest. Not a few love-affairs had their origin in his introductions.

He kept to his old habit of pretending to seek sweethearts for

[14] *Miss Bond*, 27.   [15] *Miss Bond*, 24.
[16] 21 *Confederate Veteran*, 53; Alderman and Gordon: *I. I. M. Curry*, 213–14.

his sons, and while Custis remained at the White that summer with the family, the General pledged him to at least one of his young favorites. Custis was as modest as his father, and self-conscious besides, and was not at all willing to be delivered. For a long time he refused to share in the promenade. When at last he consented and was introduced, he became a resigned attendant on the salons, but usually he stood silently by the young lady to whom the General had promised him as a cavalier. "General Custis," she said, one morning, "why do you not sit down?" He answered, "I am a modest man, and for a modest man to have his hands and his feet on his mind at the same time is too much; when I stand, my feet are off my mind and I have only my hands to attend to."

But Custis Lee was not always silent or embarrassed. He found, in some fashion, that a freckled-faced young girl, with a dumpy figure, had a father who had shown kindness to Confederate prisoners, among whom had been soldiers of his own command. Forthwith Custis decided that the girl, who up to that time had received no attention at the resort, should be a belle. He called in the Confederate veterans and asked them to aid him. They gallantly consented. From that day on, never had a girl a more attentive following. "How she danced and walked and flirted! What famous men contended for the honor of her hand! How she was encircled by a brilliant group, all bent upon doing her honor! No doubt her children proudly cherish yet the memory of the time when their quiet, plain little mother was the belle of the White!" [17] General Lee was greatly delighted at the girl's pleasure and at the device his retiring son had hit upon for repaying, as far as he might, the generous action of her father.

Lee's quiet participation in the promenades and his talk with guests occupied only a small part of the long summer days. "There are some 500 people here," he wrote Robert in August, "very pleasant and kind, but most of my time is passed alone with Traveller in the mountains." [18] Sometimes he had companions or found them. One day two of his feminine friends made a bargain to ascend the mountain behind the hotel. It was a remote, rough place, where he did not think women should venture

[17] *Miss Bond*, 37–38.
[18] R. E. Lee to R. E. Lee, Jr., Aug. 5, 1867; *R. E. Lee, Jr.,* 278.

alone. So, after they had started, he rode Traveller up the steep grade until he came upon them. "I overheard you this morning planning to climb the mountain," he said very simply, "and I could not suffer you to go unattended. With your permission I will accompany you." He offered a seat on his steed to each of them in turn, but as neither would accept a lift, he led the horse by the bridle-rein and walked up with them. He did not leave them until they were safely back in sight of the hotel.[19] Often his entire ramble was in solitude, but not in loneliness, for it was a rule with him always to occupy his hours of exercise with pleasant meditations and with a study of whatever beauty he might find. "When I was with the army," he once told a nephew, "I had to take daily rides in order to obtain the exercise that was necessary for me. When I got on my horse . . . no matter what battle or movement was impending, and no matter what my cares or troubles were, I put all such things out of my mind and thought only of my ride, of the scenery around me, or of other pleasant things, and so returned to my work refreshed and relieved and in a better and stronger condition. If it had not been for . . . power [to do this], I do not see how I could have stood what I had to go through with." [20]

Those weeks at the White were not entirely made up of restful rides and light talk. Northern people were beginning to visit the springs again: they did not always show the spirit of reconciliation, nor were they received with it. The women were more resentful than the men, and as they were much more numerous, any vindictiveness on the part of the Northerners was met with something akin to social ostracism. Against every manifestation of this spirit General Lee felt he should exert himself publicly. If former Federal officers avoided him, through consideration for his sensibilities, he quite subordinated the past to the present in a desire to see Southern hospitality vindicated and the strangers put at ease. He was thoughtful, too, in dealing with the Northern ladies, also, and sought, as far as he could, to break up the ice of animosity.

One Northern family group, though bearing a noted name,

[19] *Miss Bond*, 41–42.
[20] George Taylor Lee: "Reminiscences of General Robert E. Lee, 1865–68"; 26 *South Atlantic Quarterly*, 244.

was so forbidding in manner that not a single member of General Lee's circle made the acquaintance of any of them. When the General discovered this, while he was chatting in the parlor, he reminded his girl friends of their duty to be hospitable, and said that as nobody could present him, he would introduce himself to the austere guests. Would any of the young people go across the room with him for that purpose?

Only one was willing. "I will go, General Lee," she said, "under your orders."

"Not under my orders," he answered, "but it will gratify me deeply to have your assistance."

As they started, he told her of his grief at finding Southern young people so bitter.

"But, General Lee," the girl broke out, "did you never feel resentment toward the North?"

He stopped and in a low voice answered: "I believe I may say, looking into my own heart, and speaking as in the presence of God, that I have never known one moment of bitterness or resentment."

Then, after a pause, he told her: "When you go home I want you to take a message to your friends. Tell them from me that it is unworthy of them as women, and especially as Christian women, to cherish feelings of resentment against the North. Tell them that it grieves me inexpressibly to know that such a state of things exists, and that I implore them to do their part to heal our country's wounds."

With that he went on and, after introducing himself and presenting his youthful companion, sat down with the group whom the young girls, in his presence, did not dare call Yankees. "The invisible restraint which had existed in social intercourse between the representatives of the different sections still remained, but the example and influence of the illustrious leader modified its expression and led to exchanges of courtesies"—so, years after, wrote the woman who had crossed the floor with him and had braved the frigid bearing of the strangers.[21]

A rumor passed around the piazza one day that General Grant was to visit "The White." Every one began to speculate on what

[21] *Miss Bond*, 32–34.

would happen when the two former adversaries met. One young girl ("Some of us would gladly have slain her on the spot," wrote Miss Bond) had the hardihood to inquire: "Well, General Lee, they say General Grant is coming here next week; what will you do then?"

A faraway look came into his eyes. He passed by the bad taste of the question. "If General Grant comes," he said, "I shall welcome him to my home, show him all the courtesy which is due from one gentleman to another, and try to do everything in my power to make his stay here agreeable." [22]

Despite the good manners of most of the guests, Lee had to contend with some fire-eaters and, what was worse, with some rhetorical admirers. One man of this type kept asking for an introduction to the General. He was so bombastic in his speech that the friend of the Lees to whom he made the request hesitated to present him. However, one evening, as they were in front of the Lee cottage, there seemed no way of avoiding an introduction, though the General and Mrs. Lee were at the time entertaining some callers. No sooner was the man's name pronounced than he began: "Do I behold the honored roof that shelters the head of him before whose name the luster of Napoleon's pales into a shadow? Do I see the walls within which sits the most adored of men? Dare I tread the floor which she who is a scion of the patriotic house of the revered Washington condescends to hallow with her presence? Is this the portico that trails its vines over the noble pair——"

The General was bewildered and the guests were aghast, but Mrs. Lee, as always, was mistress of her own home. Calmly and with a kind look she interrupted the flow of nonsense. "Yes," she said, "this is our cabin; will you take a seat upon the bench?" [23]

Before the time came to leave "The White," at the end of a three weeks' sojourn, General Lee was taken sick.[24] In a short while, he recovered sufficiently to ride over to the Old Sweet, whither the family then moved, for it was the fashion of the day to go to at least two or even three springs in a season. After his arrival, his physical distress grew into a real illness, superinduced,

[22] Grant did not come; *Miss Bond*, 39–40.
[23] *Mrs. Preston*, 274–75.   [24] *Miss Bond*, 43.

as Lee thought, by a cold. "It seems to me," he wrote later, "if all the sickness I ever had in my life was put together, it would not equal the attack I experienced." [25] His recovery was slow, and the seizure, whatever its nature, left him feeble. Fortunately, the quarters were quite comfortable. One of the parlors on the first floor was made into a bedroom so that Mrs. Lee could be rolled about on the porch and into the ballroom to watch the dancers.

While the General was slowly getting better, some of the mountaineers came to the hotel with fruit for sale. When they saw their old commander—for they were survivors of his army—they forgot their trade and raised the rebel yell. And after the General acknowledged their tribute by shaking hands with each of them, they insisted that he accept the contents of their baskets.[26] Such incidents were of frequent occurrence: wherever he went he met men who had served under him. Whether they had saved something from their country's wreck or were fighting with black poverty, they wanted to do what they could and to give him what they had, to show their affection for him.[27]

Early in September it was arranged that Custis should escort home his mother, his sister, and Miss Pendleton, and that the General should return by a more leisurely journey, halting for his health at three resorts on the way. He reached Healing Springs on September 10, and was still so much indisposed that he had to remain there until the 13th or 14th. He then went on by easy stages and reached Lexington on the 17th.[28]

He had been away from the college almost continuously since its close the previous June. As he had rested he should have been re-established in health; but there had begun to creep more fre-

[25] Lee to Martha Williams, Oct. 4, 1867, *Markie Letters*, 76; Lee to Mrs. Andrew Talcott, *MS.*, Oct. 14, 1867, *Talcott MSS.* (*VHS*).

[26] R. E. Lee, Jr., 276–77. Jones, 323–24, recounts how two veterans in homespun tramped down from the mountains to see him at the White Sulphur and went to him in the parlor, where the usual throng surrounded him. Lee received them cordially and talked pleasantly with them, while the rest of the company stood and watched and listened.

[27] Cf. R. E. Lee, Jr., 276, the story of the mountaineer who was found opening the blinds of Lee's room at the Warm Springs. "Go away," commanded Miss Pendleton, "that is General Lee's room." The man obeyed but said mournfully, "I only wanted to see him."

[28] This is the date given in *The Lexington Gazette* of Sept. 18, 1867. His letter of Sept. 12 to Mrs. Lee (*R. E. Lee, Jr.*, 279) indicated that he hoped to get home on Sept. 16. Cf. *Markie Letters*, 76. An incident of Lee's stay at one of these resorts, probably apocryphal as to place and details, appears in 21 *Confederate Veteran*, 53.

quently into his letters an occasional sentence indicating his belief that he was getting old and that the end was not far distant. A sense of weakness and perhaps a note of weariness, too, appear in his family correspondence. "I am still so feeble," he wrote Rooney on September 20, "that I cannot attend to the pressing business connected with the college." [29] Again, in contrast to his old-time gaiety, he wrote the "Beautiful Talcott," who was still beautiful despite war and time, "Trouble and distress seem to pervade every part of the world, and peace and happiness are secure in none." [30]

[29] *R. E. Lee, Jr.*, 283. *Cf.* his letter of Feb. 4, 1867, to Judge Robert Ould, *Jones,* 222, and his letter of Aug. 5, 1867, to his son Robert; *R. E. Lee, Jr.,* 277.

[30] Lee to Mrs. Andrew Talcott, *MS.,* Oct. 14, 1867, *Talcott MSS. (VHS).*

CHAPTER XIX

THE RETURN TO PETERSBURG

ROONEY LEE, it will be remembered, had lost his high-born young wife, Charlotte Wickham, during December, 1863, while he was a prisoner of war. In 1867, when he was thirty, Rooney—Fitzhugh now in the General's correspondence—began to pay attention to another girl of fine station, Miss Mary Tabb Bolling, a daughter of G. M. Bolling of Petersburg, Va. By August of that year it was known in the Lee family that Rooney hoped to marry her. His father heard the news with interest, for he had met her during the siege of Petersburg and he liked her. After the General had returned from the springs in September, 1867, word came that the charming lady had capitulated to the cavalryman. The General promptly wrote Rooney his unqualified congratulations. "I have the most pleasant recollection of 'Miss Tabb,'" he said, "and of her kindness to me, and now that she has consented to be my daughter the measure of my gratitude is filled to overflowing. I hope she will not delay the consummation, for I want to see her very much, and I fear she will not come to see me until then. You must present her my warm love, and you both must accept my earnest prayers and most fervent wishes for your future happiness and prosperity." [1]

As soon as the approximate date for the wedding was set, the General was most warmly urged to attend the ceremonies. His mind was reluctant. He had not yet entirely recovered from the illness of the summer,[2] and, in the second place, he told himself he would have little opportunity of seeing his son and the bride in the rush of a great affair. But his chief reason for declining, though he may not have realized it, lay very much deeper, in his most personal and most profound reactions to the outcome of the war. He had never been disturbed about his own fate and he had never pitied himself. Broken-hearted and despairing he never

---

[1] R. E. Lee to W. H. F. Lee, Sept. 20, 1867; *R. E. Lee, Jr.*, 283–84.
[2] R. E. Lee to James Longstreet, Oct. 29, 1867; *Jones*, 227.

had been. He had agonized, however, over the plight of the Southern people, so many of whom, in person or by letter, had poured out their sorrows to him. The grief that many saw in his face after the war, it may be repeated, was wholly theirs, grief for the maimed men who were losing their battle to earn a living, grief for the women who were trying to rear children without a father, and grief for a land that had lost its power and wealth and now lay shackled and prostrate. For none was that grief keener than for the people of Petersburg, that stout-souled city of grim memory. In them he saw the suffering of the whole South. Never did he think of them otherwise than with the deepest sorrow, and he dreaded to visit again the scenes of his travail of soul during the last winter of the war.[3]

But what would be the wedding of a Lee if the General were not present? How, indeed, could there be fitting nuptials without him? Fitzhugh must have felt sharply the point of the question, for he journeyed to Lexington and so persuasively pleaded his case that the General consented to attend. Lee's first plan was to visit his sons on their farms and then to go on to Petersburg, but he abandoned this idea and prepared to proceed by way of Richmond only. He ordered in the old capital a new suit of broadcloth for the occasion,[4] perhaps the first clothes he had bought since the war, except the trousers made near Derwent. From necessary economy he had been wearing his old gray coats.[5]

While the arrangements for the wedding were being matured, General Lee was served with a *subpoena* to appear as a witness on November 26 at the Federal circuit court in Richmond. Custis was summoned, also. It was assumed, though not certainly known, that some new step was to be taken in the trial of President Davis. Either by chance or else to save the cost and trouble of a second trip, the ceremonies were definitely set for November 28, during the week the General was to appear in Richmond. Consequently, when he left Lexington it was on a double mission, half joyful, half sad, half social, half legal.

[3] R. E. Lee to Mrs. ———, May 21, 1867; *Jones, 225*; R. E. Lee to W. H. F. Lee, Dec. 21, 1867; *R. E. Lee, Jr.,* 293.

[4] R. E. Lee to Mrs. Lee, Nov. 26, 1867; *R. E. Lee, Jr.,* 287.

[5] When the Marquess of Lorne was in Virginia, the previous year, he noted that virtually all the men still wore gray. A black coat, he said, was most unusual.

Accompanied by Custis, he reached Richmond on the afternoon of November 25, and went to the Exchange Hotel, where
Rooney was awaiting him.[6] Lee had been to the city only once
since he had left for Oakland, late in June, 1865, and on that
single visit, in the interest of the college, he had kept very much
in retirement. Now he felt he could allow himself social pleasure
without making himself conspicuous. Some activity would have
been forced on him, perhaps, even if he had been unwilling.
After supper, on his first evening at the hotel, when he attempted
to go through the lobby, he was at once surrounded by men who
knew him and had served under him. All of them greeted him
with great cordiality. Strangers and Northerners joined the crowd
that sought to shake his hand.[7] It was the first time since the war
that a promiscuous crowd in any Southern city had the opportunity of showing its affection for him, and its admiration of the
course he had pursued after Appomattox. He may have been
surprised and moved by this spontaneous warmth of welcome,
but he was destined to discover that every other city of the South
had the same feeling for him.

When he could escape from the hotel he started on a round of
visits. One was to the Caskies', at the southeast corner of Eleventh
and Clay,[8] which had been one Richmond home of his family
before they had moved to the Stewart house on Franklin Street.
Mildred was now visiting Norvell Caskie and was very happy,
her father wrote, because she had a train "about two yards longer"
than her young hostess's.[9]

During the course of the evening, General Lee went also to
Judge Ould's, and there, for the first time since that black March
of 1865, he saw Jefferson Davis. The former President had come
to Richmond to appear before the Federal court on the treason
charge. Neither of the two leaders of the Confederacy nor any
one who witnessed the meeting left any record of what they said

---

[6] *Richmond Dispatch,* Nov. 26, 1867.   [7] *Richmond Whig,* Nov. 26, 1867.

[8] There is some confusion regarding the Caskie homes. This one, the home of James
Kerr Caskie, is on the site noted in the text and is the house associated with Lee. Directly
across from it, at the northeast corner of Eleventh and Clay, was the mansion of John
Caskie, father of James K. Caskie. This was subsequently the Virginia Hospital. So far
as is known, General Lee never stayed there. For this information the writer is indebted
to Miss Nannie H. Jones, daughter of Mrs. Seddon Jones, *née* Norvell Caskie.

[9] R. E. Lee to Mrs. Lee, Nov. 26, 1867: *R. E. Lee, Jr.,* 286-87.

or how they looked as they faced each other, both of them under indictment, there in the old capital, now a part of Military District No. 1, garrisoned by their one-time adversaries. Probably the conversation was deliberately social and casual, for a number of people were present. "[He] looks astonishingly well," General Lee wrote Mrs. Lee, "and is quite cheerful. He inquired particularly after you all." [10]

The next day, November 26, obedient to the summons of the court, General Lee presented himself at the Federal building, whither he had gone so often during the war to confer with the chief executive. He found Mr. Davis there once again, ready to be tried if the government chose, and he had a long and pleasant chat with his former chief as they waited. The expectation had been that the chief justice would come down from Washington and sit with Judge Underwood, but as Chase did not appear, all that could be done was to impanel a grand jury. Though the reason for this was not announced, it was with an eye to drawing a new and fuller indictment against Mr. Davis.[11]

The jury was "mixed," white men and Negroes, and it was harangued at length by the judge.[12] Upon its retirement, the clerk read the list of witnesses. Lee's name came first. Spectators grew silent, awaiting his answer. They were disappointed, for the General was in another room at the moment and did not hear the crier. The district attorney rose immediately and explained obligingly that Lee was in the city and would be ready at any time to go before the grand jury. Other witnesses were thereupon called. For the remainder of November 26, Lee was overwhelmed with visitors. Every one knew he was in Richmond; every one, it seemed, was anxious to call on him.[13] He spent an exceedingly busy ten hours and must have been as weary as he was gratified.

The grand jury took its time and did not summon the General again until the next day. Ushered in at 2 P.M., he was subjected

[10] R. E. Lee to Mrs. Lee, Nov. 26, 1867; *R. E. Lee, Jr.,* 287.

[11] *Southern Opinion,* Nov. 30, 1867.

[12] Lee rarely referred to the antics of Judge Underwood, but Mrs. Lee had an opinion she did not hesitate to express: "Have you read Underwood's charge to his grand jury 5 of whom are negroes? It is the most remarkable piece of composition I ever read, the most *false* & *vindictive* & that such a creature should be allowed to dispense justice is a perfect *farce.* I think his meanness and wickedness have affected his brain" (Mrs. R. E. Lee to Mrs. R. H. Chilton, *MS.,* May 6, 1867, *Chilton Papers*).

[13] *Richmond Dispatch,* Nov. 27, 1867.

to the jury's inquisition.[14] He was, of course, an unwilling witness. Judging from the indictment returned on March 26, 1868,
the evidence he was required to give the jurors had to do solely
with known military movements, which the grand jury presented
as proof of armed insurrection against the authority of the United
States.[15] Apparently there was no effort to probe into the personal relations of President Davis and General Lee, and no attempt
to bring out any of the inner history of the Confederacy. The
whole of the treason proceedings, in fact, dealt with facts familiar
to every American of the time. After his two hours in the jury
room, General Lee was excused from further attendance.[16]

The following afternoon, November 28, he joined the large
wedding party that was to go over to Petersburg, a distance of
twenty-two miles, on a special car attached to the regular train.

Perhaps the restraint of the jury room was still upon him.
Doubtless memories, as bitter as brave, had been aroused by the
questioning of the grand jury. All these were revived as the train
made its way southward. The wedding guests were chattering
and laughing, as youth has a right to do; the General sat silent
and sad-faced. In spite of his rule to think of the past as little
as he could, he must have been pondering all the black yesterdays
brought up as he passed places of bloody contest and familiar
name—Drewry's Bluff, the Howlett Line, Bermuda Hundred, and
Port Walthall Junction, where Whiting had failed Beauregard.
A little more and Lee would approach the bridges over which
part of the army had passed that dreadful night of April 2, 1865.
On the left, close to the river, would be Fort Stedman. To the right
and westward, scarcely out of range, would be old Blandford
Church, the Crater, Fort Mahone, and, farther away, the Boydton
plank road, Fort Gregg, the Turnbull house and Hatcher's Run.
Every one of these must have brought back a pang: Peters-
burg . . . Petersburg . . . how he had suffered in body and in

---

[14] If any minutes of his testimony were preserved, they have never come to light, despite the writer's search for them, with the experienced aid of the late Jos. P. Brady.

[15] 7 *Rowland*, 179.

[16] *Richmond Enquirer and Examiner*, Nov. 29, 1867; *Richmond Dispatch*, Nov. 29,
1867. Some passages in these references would indicate that General Lee appeared before
the grand jury on Nov. 28, but the 27th seems to be the correct date. It is of record that
General Lee was with the jurors from 2 to 4 P.M. As he told Mrs. Lee in his letter of
Nov. 29 (*R. E. Lee, Jr.*, 288) that he arrived in Petersburg at 3 P.M. on the afternoon of
Nov. 28, he obviously could not have been in court at the hour mentioned.

mind over its people! How he had been tortured that night when he had been compelled to turn his back on them and leave them, their women and their children, to the mercy of the Federals, whose challenging guns had followed him over the same Appomattox to which he now had come.

The brakes were grinding, the train was stopping: it was Pocahontas, a scattered settlement on the north bank of the river. The moment the wheels ceased turning there came a crash of sound—music, a band, the notes of the Marseillaise. The performers had come over to do him honor and had been waiting in the station. They played through the French anthem the Southern soldiers had loved, and then they climbed aboard the train. Slowly over the river and through the town the train was pulled to the Washington Street Station, which was crowded. The windows of Jarratt's Hotel nearby and the streets and roadway around it were jammed. People started cheering the moment General Lee appeared, and they opened their applauding, smiling ranks as he walked to the curb, where his host, General William Mahone, had a carriage with four white horses awaiting him. Around the vehicle surged the throng, acclaiming him, rejoicing to see once more the man whose thin line had so long kept their city safe. The final defeat was forgotten in the memory of the victories won against odds so commanding. Some of the men wished to take the horses from the traces and to drag the carriage themselves, but Lee insisted that if they did this, he would have to get out and help them, so they desisted. The band began to play again, tune after tune beloved of the South, but its notes were almost drowned in the applauding roar of the multitude. The crowd would not let the carriage continue on its way until the General had risen in his seat, had taken off his hat, and had bowed to his well-wishers. This first phase of his reception must have relieved him: very different were these smiling, appreciative, and confident people from the pinched victims of disaster he had been picturing to himself half an hour before. With them the war was over, and they had buried most of its sorrows.[17]

[17] The Negroes of the town chanced to have a parade on the day of General Lee's arrival. A stranger inquired what it was all about, as if the Negroes waited, in those days, for a reason to march the streets. A wag of the town answered that the Negroes were the former slaves of General Lee and had turned out to welcome him to Petersburg (*Richmond Enquirer and Examiner*, Dec. 2, 1867, quoting *The Petersburg Express*).

Upon his arrival at the Mahone residence, on the corner of Sycamore and Marshall Streets,[18] the General found a note from Miss Bolling, in which she invited him to call on her that afternoon. It was not for him to refuse so gentle a request. Promptly and gallantly he went across the street to Mr. Bolling's home, Poplar Lawn, nearly opposite the park where the Federal wounded from the battle of the Crater had been brought.[19] Ushered in, he saw the majestic young lady in the full flush of the excitement that preceded the wedding, and he presented her a necklace that Mrs. Lee and he had chosen. The bride-to-be was pleased to express her delight with it.

Then, for memory's sake and old affection, Lee went to Chelsea, the Banister home, where on his Sunday visits during the siege he had eaten many a Spartan dinner. Those of the family who had survived the horrors of the war were there to greet him, among them Anne Banister, who was now sixteen and very lovely to behold. "Remember, my dear," Lee said to her, after he had chatted awhile, "I am to have the honor of taking you in to supper. Ask your escort to lend you to me. Your aunt, Mrs. Bolling, is sick and will not come down, so I want to take you in." Anne danced for joy.[20]

Three hours before the time set for the ceremony, the good people of Petersburg began to gather at the church, more perhaps to see General Lee than to witness the ceremony, though that was draped with all the dignity the proud city could command.[21] The crowd far overflowed the edifice and thronged the street. At last the guests began to arrive—first of all, General Lee in his new broadcloth suit, escorting Mrs. Carr.[22] In the doorway he stooped for a moment to kiss a little girl who smiled up at him.[23] Behind General Lee were General and Mrs. Mahone. Presently came Miss Bolling and her ten bridesmaids. A like num-

[18] Now the site of the Wm. R. McKenney Free Library.
[19] This was later the home of Samuel W. Zimmer, former mayor of Petersburg.
[20] *Mrs. Campbell Pryor's MS. Memoirs.*
[21] *Cf. The Richmond Whig* of Dec. 2, 1867: "We are not invidious when we say that no matrimonial pair in this or any other Commonwealth have fathers purer, better, or representing a higher degree of Virginia gentility than the twain to whose union we have alluded."
[22] The author has not been able positively to identify Mrs. Carr. She probably was a lady from northern Virginia, an old-time friend of the Lees, who had married a Petersburg druggist.
[23] *MS. Note of Miss Virginia Mason.*

ber of the friends of Rooney were at hand to support him in his happy ordeal.[24] It was a gathering of the Lee clan, for besides the General, the groom, and Mildred, there were in attendance Custis, Robert, and Fitz Lee, the nephew. Nearly all the notables of that part of Virginia were present, also. President Davis himself would have been a spectator, but for the death of his mother-in-law, Mrs. Howell.

After the wedding came the supper, in the most lavish style of the old Dominion. Anne Banister was there, true to her commitment, and proudly entered the dining-room on the arm of General Lee. Doubtless her pride was heightened by the fact that she wore a long dress for the very first time.[25] Dutifully the next morning, before any of the Mahones had descended to breakfast, the General penned a lengthy letter to his wife. He described the happy event to her, as fully as a man could be expected to do, though he did not essay the precious details of the apparel of the bride and her maids. All he could say to satisfy the curiosity of Mrs. Lee and the stay-at-homes was the vague and masculine: "The bride looked lovely, and was in every way captivating. . . . Mildred was all life, in white and curls." [26]

The morning meal completed, Lee went on an odd mission. While he had maintained his headquarters at the Turnbull house, an old woman of the neighborhood had frequently sent him eggs and butter in a time of universal want. He had not forgotten her, and now that he was back in Petersburg he went to call on her. It must have cost him an effort, even after the welcome the city had given him, for there at Turnbulls' the heart-breaking crisis of April 2, 1865, had begun. The house itself was gone, destroyed by fire that fatal morning, but all around were the ghastly reminders of the siege, the *chevaux-de-frise* scarcely rotted away, the earthworks grim and red, and not yet softened in line by crabgrass or ragweed.

Back from this visit, he lunched with the Bollings. They had passed word that their friends might call on the General that afternoon, and those who revered him came by scores. In the evening an affair was given in honor of the bride at the home of

[24] *Richmond Enquirer and Examiner*, Dec. 2, 1867, quoting *The Petersburg Express*.
[25] *Mrs. Campbell Pryor's MS. Memoirs.*
[26] R. E. Lee to Mrs. Lee, Nov. 29, 1867; *R. E. Lee, Jr.*, 287–88.

Wm. R. Johnson, who resided on the corner of Washington and Davis Streets.[27] The General attended—he did not absent himself from any of the entertainments—and he seemed to enjoy himself greatly. "He was delighted," his son recorded, "to find the people so prosperous, and to observe that they had it in their hearts to be gay and happy." [28]

Every one knew, apparently, that the General was to journey back to Richmond on Saturday, November 30. As he went to the station they crowded the highways of Petersburg once again to bid him farewell. The train conveying him to Richmond pulled out amid a roar of cheers. He was as loath to go as he had been unwilling to come. "In consequence of being told that the new couple were to leave Petersburg the morning after the wedding, I had made my arrangements to return [to Richmond] Saturday. If I had known that they would remain till Monday, as it is now their intention, I should have made my arrangements to stay"— thus he wrote Mrs. Lee after he had reached Richmond.[29]

Custis, Robert, and Fitz Lee journeyed back with him to his old capital. After they had their supper at the hotel, the General started out to make some calls on old friends. He took Robert with him and made a wide circuit—Mrs. Caskie's, where both the elders were sick abed, Mrs. Triplett's, Mrs. Peebles', Mrs. Brander's, Mrs. J. R. Anderson's. "There were many others he went to see," Robert wrote, "for I remember going with him. He sat only a few minutes at each place—'called just to shake hands,' he would say. All were delighted to see him. From some places where he was well known he could hardly get away. He had a kind word for all, and his excuse for hurrying on was that he must try to see so and so, as Mrs. Lee had told him to be sure to do so. He was bright and cheerful, and was pleased with the great affection shown him on all sides." [30]

He spent Sunday quietly in Richmond—it was a cold day with much ice in evidence—and on the morning of December 2, with Custis and Robert he went down James River to Brandon, home

[27] Mr. Johnson was a son of the noted turfman. Davis Street at that time was known as Folly Street. For the identification of Petersburg names and sites the writer is indebted to Doctor W. F. Drewry and to Captain Carter Bishop.

[28] *R. E. Lee, Jr.*, 289.

[29] R. E. Lee to Mrs. Lee, Dec. 1, 1867; *R. E. Lee, Jr.*, 290.

[30] *R. E. Lee, Jr.*, 291.

of his cousins, the Harrisons. In all his years he had never been to that gracious mansion, and as he had promised at the Rockbridge Baths in 1865 to visit the place the next time he came to Richmond, he took this opportunity. The brief voyage carried him down the channel between Drewry's and Chaffin's Bluff and past City Point, where Grant had headquarters for nearly ten months. But Lee did not talk of war and apparently he made an effort to avoid thinking of it. He did not converse much, and what he had to say to his sons dealt with the old river plantations, places dear to him from many associations. "I passed Shirley twice . . . with a heavy heart," he subsequently wrote Hill Carter, ". . . I took a long look each time at the House, the grounds and the farm from the hurricane deck of the Steamer, hoping to see some of the family to no purpose. I thought if I could only see your 'white eyebrows' as our Uncle Randolph described them, I would have been content." [31]

An all-too-brief night and part of a day were pleasantly passed at Brandon. Then he came back to Richmond by steamer, spent Thursday, December 5, at Hickory Hill, the Wickham home in Hanover County,[32] and on December 6 started for home, which he reached on December 7. He had missed two faculty meetings in succession,[33] but he was at his post again on December 9.

It was the longest absence from college Lee thus far had allowed himself during the session, and it marked a definite transition in his state of mind. He was far happier after this visit and more willing to travel and to mingle with his people again. Prior to the journey to Petersburg he had been oppressed by the poverty, losses, and misery of the Southern people. He had travelled little after he had come to Lexington and he did not know how the South was reviving, or in what spirit it was adjusting itself to the reconstruction. To the Marquess of Lorne he had said that it would be many years before the South could recover, and he had daily carried its sorrows on his heart. Then, almost over-

---

[31] R. E. Lee to Hill Carter, *MS.,* April 17, 1868, *Shirley MSS.*

[32] "I am so glad now that I stopped at Hickory Hill on my return to Lexington. It has given me pleasant thoughts for the rest of my life, and the last look at one the like of whom I shall never see again." *Ibid.* The reference is to the venerable William F. Wickham, one of the noblest men of his generation in Virginia.

[33] Those of Nov. 25 and Dec. 2.

night, he found himself in a new atmosphere. Instead of distress, idleness, and vain regret, he found good cheer, industry, and a courageous acceptance of the outcome of the war, along with pride in the old cause and affection for those who had led it. The people were not sitting in the ashes, lamenting their losses and bewailing their subjection to military rule. Rather were they rebuilding the wastes, accepting the inevitable with patient courage, and exhibiting the very quality that Lee had praised in writing to A. M. Keiley, a Petersburg man—the "determination not to be turned aside by thoughts of the past and fears of the future."[34] Lee saw all this and in a self-revealing passage of a letter to Rooney gave expression to a sense of relief that was reflected in all his correspondence and counsel thereafter:

"My visit to Petersburg was extremely pleasant. Besides the pleasure of seeing my daughter and being with you, which was very great, I was gratified in seeing many friends. In addition, when our armies were in front of Petersburg, I suffered so much in body and mind on account of the good townspeople, especially on that gloomy night when I was forced to abandon them, that I have always reverted to them in sadness and sorrow. My old feelings returned to me, as I passed well-remembered spots and recalled the ravages of the hostile shells. But when I saw the cheerfulness with which the people were working to restore their condition, and witnessed the comforts with which they were surrounded, a load of sorrow which had been pressing upon me for years was lifted from my heart."[35]

[34] See *supra*, p. 220.
[35] R. E. Lee to W. H. F. Lee, Dec. 21, 1867; *R. E. Lee, Jr.*, 293.

CHAPTER XX

The Johnston Affair and Old Animosities

The college, meantime, had opened auspiciously and uneventfully for the session of 1867–68, with an enrollment that exceeded 400 by October 4 and climbed before June to a total of 410,[1] eleven more than had been registered the previous session, and nearly three times as many as in 1865–66. Attendance from Virginia and from Tennessee was slightly lower than during the term preceding, but there were more boys from other states, of which eighteen were represented.[2] All the former professors were again in service, reinforced by a number of young assistants. As in 1866, the full membership of the faculty, including the president, was twenty-two.

Lee was kept busy with his administrative duties, which continued so heavy that he protested every absence from his office involved an accumulation of work.[3] Agnes and Mary were both away in Maryland for the greater part of the winter. Mildred, the one-time absentee, not only kept house, but had in addition the care of another Mildred, daughter of General Lee's brother, Charles Carter Lee. To distinguish his daughter from this little niece, who had come to Lexington to go to school, General Lee dubbed the younger Mildred "Powhattie," after the name of her native county. Besides "Powhattie," two of her brothers, the General's nephews, took their meals with the family that winter while rooming elsewhere and attending college.[4] Custis continued to live with his parents and taught in the Virginia Military Institute adjoining the college. Mildred took seriously the man-

---

[1] Lee to Martha Williams, Oct. 4, 1867; *Markie Letters*, 78.

[2] This total of eighteen does not include Virginia and Tennessee. For the list see *1867–68 Catalogue*, 16.

[3] R. E. Lee to Mrs. W. H. F. Lee, May 29, 1868; *R. E. Lee, Jr.*, 313.

[4] They were George Taylor Lee and Henry Lee (Lee to Hill Carter, *MS.*, April 25, 1868; *Shirley MSS.*). The previous winter George Taylor Lee and Robert Carter Lee, son of Sidney Smith Lee, had been the General's guests on the same basis (Mrs. R. E. Lee to Mrs. R. H. Chilton, *MSS.*, March 10 and May 6, 1867; *Chilton Papers*).

agement of this sizeable household and ruled with an autocracy that amused her father. "'Life' has it all her own way now," the General wrote Robert in January, 1868, "and expends her energy in regulating her brother and putting your mother's drawers and presses to rights."[5] To his new daughter-in-law he confided that Mildred "has . . . had her hands full, and considers herself now a great character. She rules her brother and my nephews with an iron rod, and scatters her advice broadcast among the young men of the college. I hope that it may yield an abundant harvest. The young mothers of Lexington ought to be extremely grateful to her for her suggestions to them as to the proper mode of rearing their children, and though she finds many unable to appreciate her system, she is nothing daunted by their obtuseness of vision, but takes advantage of every opportunity to enlighten them as to its benefits."[6]

Mildred was so busy that she had little time to go out with the General, who consequently had to take his exercise alone. "My only pleasure," he wrote Mrs. Rooney Lee, "is in my solitary evening rides, which give me abundant opportunity for quiet thought."[7] Christmas passed quietly, with Robert up from Tide-water for the season. January opened sadly for Lee. For a time, a brief time fortunately, he lost some of the cheerfulness he had gleaned from the Petersburg visit. "My interest in Time and its concerns," he wrote, "is daily fading away and I try to keep my eyes and thoughts fixed on those eternal shores to which I am fast hastening."[8]

The gloom of a dark, wet winter was deepened early in February by the most unpleasant happening of General Lee's entire administration of the college. On North River, flowing directly by Lexington, there was a dam, above which was a long stretch that froze readily and afforded excellent skating in cold weather. Students and townspeople thronged it. On the afternoon of February 4, one E. C. Johnston, a former Federal soldier, went down to the river to enjoy the ice. He had come to Lexington in the autumn of 1865 as an agent of the American Missionary Associa-

[5] R. E. Lee to R. E. Lee, Jr., Jan. 23, 1868; *R. E. Lee, Jr.,* 302.
[6] R. E. Lee to Mrs. W. H. F. Lee, March 10, 1868; *R. E. Lee, Jr.,* 304.
[7] *Ibid.*
[8] Lee to Martha Williams, Jan. 1, 1868; *Markie Letters,* 78.

tion and had established some schools for the instruction of freed-men. From this work, apparently, he had turned to store-keep-ing, but his affiliations with the Negroes made him somewhat notorious and distinctly unpopular. He was accustomed to carry a pistol and had it with him that day, explaining later that he did so at the instance of friends who considered his life was in danger.

Soon after Johnston got on the ice he noticed that other skaters shunned him. So he determined to skate down the river, away from those who objected to his presence. He went on for some-thing more than a mile and then, turning a bend, came in view of a crowd that included town boys of various ages and a number of students from the college. Some of them knew the reputation of Johnston as one who consorted with the blacks, and they com-menced to hoot and to yell at him—"just as the rebels used to yell when making a charge in the army," Johnston subsequently narrated. The object of this contempt skated past the crowd, without a word on his part or any act of violence on theirs. He went on to the dam, where he rested awhile, in sight of the young men, and then he started back up the river. His tormentors re-sumed their jibes at once, as boys always will, when they see their victim is harassed. Johnston kept on toward them, swinging from side to side of the river. At one crossing, a lad of about twelve came close to him and hurled the most insulting of epi-thets at him.

Then Johnston lost his head. He caught hold of the youngster, drew his pistol and threatened to shoot him if he repeated the words. The boy's older brother and probably some others came up immediately. Johnston thereupon released his grip and started off, pursued by the crowd, which began to abuse him hotly. The Northerner foolishly tried to dispute with them and thereby sharpened their language. In the excitement, some of the youths cried "Hang him" and "Drown him." According to one version of the affair, Johnston was told he had to leave town within ten days, and was warned that if he said anything about the affair, the townsmen would come to his store and lynch him. He finally got off the river. Pelted with ice and clods as he went away, he reached shelter in safety, with sundry bruises and bumps, but with no serious injuries to show for his misadventure. That night a group of unidentified men, in disputed numbers—one version says five, Johnston insisted it was "a crowd"—came to his place of business, beat upon the door, rattled the shutters, and shouted insults. After a while, arousing no one, they went away. Johnston, as it happened, was not in the building at the time.

If General Lee heard anything of the episode, it probably was no more than that a Northern radical had drawn a pistol on a little boy and had been driven from the ice. And that was the way the college community looked at it. Johnston, however, was out for revenge. He went forthwith to the mayor of the town, J. M. Ruff, and gave his version of the affair, insisting that the boy who insulted him was "at least sixteen or seventeen years old." His assumption apparently was that all those he had encountered on the river were students. He demanded protection and called upon the mayor to punish the guilty. In the absence of specific charges against any named student, the mayor told Johnston that he could not control the college boys. Johnston then reported the matter to the military authorities. Word of it reached Brigadier General Douglas Frazer, the assistant military commissioner for the district. He, too, went to see the mayor and came away with an exaggerated picture of the lawlessness of the students. General Frazer thereupon communicated with his superior, Brevet Major General O. B. Willcox, commanding the sub-district of Lynchburg.[9] General Willcox came at once to Lexington and investigated. He talked with Johnston and with various witnesses to the affray, and also with the mayor, whom he thought "lacking in energy and determination but . . . well disposed."[10] Then he went to see General Lee and, for the first time, acquainted him with the fact that Johnston considered he had been insulted by members of the student-body because he was a Northerner. General Willcox supplied the names of three students who were alleged to have been involved. General Lee expressed his deep regret and immediately began an inquiry into the facts. Finding that two of the accused boys had been engaged

[9] There is a possibility, here, that the order of these various conferences and appeals may be confused, as the accounts do not agree.
[10] O. B. Willcox to S. F. Chalfin, A. A. G., MS., Feb. 15, 1868; *Adjutant General's Office, U. S. A.*

in the affair, he directed one of them to withdraw immediately, and wrote the parents of the other to remove him from college. The third young man, who had been present but had not participated in the row, applied for permission to leave the institution and was allowed to do so. This action was taken by General Lee without calling the faculty together and while General Willcox was still in town. It was coupled with assurance to the Federal commander that he would expel any student guilty of disorderly conduct.[11] General Willcox went back to Lynchburg well satisfied. "Mr. Johns[t]on is partly to blame himself," he reported, "as he threatened to shoot one of the small boys when they first set on him. . . . As Johns[t]on had not complained of any particular person to the mayor he had made no arrests or other progress in the case, the parties being wholly unknown, but I saw no signs of any disposition to screen disturbers of the peace."[12]

A few days after General Willcox's departure, word was alleged to have been sent to Johnston that he had better leave town, as the students were preparing to give him a "callithumps."[13] The Northerner had already planned to remove his business elsewhere and he soon departed for Covington.[14] Here the matter might have ended, but for the feeling of Johnston and some of his friends that he had been badly treated. They endeavored to strike back—at General Lee, at the school and at General Willcox, whose refusal to take extreme measures had incensed them.

Washington College that winter had boldly launched in the North a promising campaign for financial support. Reverend E. P. Walton had charge of the solicitation and tactfully prevailed upon more than thirty New Yorkers of prominence to unite in a call for a meeting on the evening of March 3 in the principal hall of Cooper Institute. The signers included Henry Ward Beecher, Bishop Potter, Charles F. Deems, W. E. Dodge, Peter Cooper, and A. A. Low. Despite inclement weather, the assem-

---

[11] Willcox to Chalfin, loc. cit.; MS. Faculty Minutes, Feb. 17, 1868.

[12] Willcox to Chalfin, loc. cit.

[13] For the nature of these callithumps, see supra, p. 284.

[14] The first version of this affair, written by a sympathizer with Johnston, appeared in The New York Independent, April 2, 1868, page 2, col. 5. Johnston's own account is in ibid., May 21, 1868, page 6, col. 1. Willcox's views were reflected in a letter signed "L," published in The New York Tribune, April 20, 1868, reprinted in The Independent of April 30, 1868. Willcox's brief official report has already been cited.

blage included some 500 persons. It was one of the first gatherings that came together in the North after the war to assist a Southern college directed by former Confederates, and for that reason its proceedings have a place not only in the life of Lee but also in the history of Southern education.

Officers for the meeting were chosen and letters were read from a number of prominent people, who expressed their willingness to help. Among them were Governor R. E. Fenton, James T. Brady, a lawyer who appeared in the case of Jefferson Davis, Horace Greeley, Gerrit Smith, and George William Curtis.

Governor Fenton expressed his pleasure that "practical business education" was to be given in Southern colleges. "I need not say," he wrote Mr. Walton, "that I sympathize with the patriotic and benevolent features of the institution which you represent."

Gerrit Smith's letter contained a check for $200 for the Lexington school. "I wish our wealthy men of the North could give that college a couple of hundred thousand," he wrote, and went on: "Sufficient cause why the North should give large help to the South is that the one is rich and the other poor. 'But the South is a sinner,' say thousands. True, she is; but sinners should be helped as well as saints. What, however, is the North but her fellow-sinner? England cursed us both with Slavery. Then we cursed ourselves with it—the North as well as the South upholding it. And then came on the war. The South, no less brave than the North, yet being by far the weaker party, fell under. Now it only remains for us to forgive each other, to love each other, and to do all the good we can to each other. So shall we become a united people; and, profiting by our great mistakes in the past, we shall enter upon a new and happy national life."

George William Curtis wrote: "I should most gladly do anything in my power to show that the most radical men in this part of the country cherish no unkind, much less any vindictive feeling, toward the people of any State or section as a class, and that the true Radical policy is merely the security of fair play and equal opportunities for all. Prompt and universal education in the Southern States is the truest and most enduring reconstruction. Every word spoken for it, every dollar given to it, is the sincerest peace-offering."

After the letters had been read, Henry Ward Beecher introduced a series of resolutions, one of which is as applicable now as it was in 1868. It was this:

"Resolved, that while we rejoice in the earnest labor which has lately been bestowed upon the primary education of the most ignorant classes of the South, we believe that this labor should be accompanied with equal zeal for instruction in the higher walks of learning, so that the college may furnish an abundant supply of teachers for the people, and by its example of higher education continually raise the standard and ideal of the common school."

Then Professor Roswell Dwight Hitchcock of New York Union Theological Seminary addressed the audience. Washington College, he said, "was doing a noble work and required aid. The cause of education in the South appeals not to the prejudices of men but to the patriotism of the people. Of General Lee, who led the armies of the Rebellion, he could only speak as of a brave man, who, when he found that the cause he had espoused was a lost one, at Appomattox Courthouse, behaved himself as a gentleman and a Christian. Of Robert E. Lee he could say, that since the war he had acted the part of the gentleman, the patriot, and the scholar, sedulously keeping himself secluded from the public gaze; and laboring now at the head of the institution . . . he was entitled to all honor."

Henry Ward Beecher closed the meeting with a characteristic speech in which he urged the cause of education. He pleaded for Washington College, because it was in Virginia and because Lee was its president. He would not withhold his support from any Southern school, but for this one his sympathies were strong. No one regretted the course which General Lee had chosen in former days more than he, the speaker, did. But if he had been born in Virginia, brought up amid her institutions, educated in a Southern college, he might have been prompted to take a course just as bad or erratic, as did Lee or Johnston. Lee was now pleading for mental bread for his students. Whatever his error in war, Lee had now devoted himself to the sacred cause of education. Did men ask if Lee might not pervert the minds of youth? No! Lee would not fail to instill patriotism and love of country in the minds of all his students. Mr. Beecher spoke with great earnestness and was much applauded.[15]

Apparently, no collection was taken before adjournment, but the meeting was altogether as good an introduction to the people of New York as could have been asked. If it had been followed by similar endorsements from a few other leading men of the North it might have meant much to Washington College. The gathering, however, aroused the wrath of some of the old abolitionists who at that time knew nothing of the Johnston incident. *The New York Independent* of March 12 made the rally at Cooper Institute the text for an editorial article on "Education at the South."

It was the duty of the North, said the paper, to forget all ill-will and to help the South in education, but when it came to "supporting a college of which the late commander of the Confederate army is the president, we must respectfully decline." *The Independent* went on in this strain:

"We do not think that a man who broke his solemn oath of allegiance to the United States, who imbrued his hands in the blood of tens of thousands of his country's noblest men, for the purpose of perpetuating human slavery, and who was largely responsible for the cruelties and horrors of Libby, Salisbury and Andersonville, is fitted to be a teacher of young men."

At this point in the article, an asterisk was inserted and a footnote was added to this effect:

"We have been reminded, since this article was in type, that the last thing which Gen. Lee did, as an officer of the American Army, was to hold an interview with Gen. Scott at his request; and, when Gen. Scott, trusting to his loyalty, showed him his maps and drawings of the defences of Washington, he took them with him to Arlington, upon the pretense that he wished to examine them more particularly and then, without returning them, went over to the rebel side![16] We have also been reminded of the fact that slaves found on his plantation at Arlington averred that he had treated them with atrocious cruelty."

[15] This account is epitomized and in part is quoted directly from *The New York Tribune* and from *The New York Times* of March 3, 1868.

[16] This unfounded story, in a slightly different guise, was revived by *Harpers Weekly* in the summer of 1870 (*cf.* R. E. Lee to Sidney Herbert, June 29. 1870; *Alexandria Gazette*, July 14, 1870).

Such a man, the article continued, must give evidence of re-pentance and some guarantee that students would not be taught to honor and to imitate his example. "We wish to be assured, moreover, before contributing money to Gen. Lee's college, or any other similar institution at the South, that it does not tolerate the hell-born spirit of caste, by turning from its doors students of a dark complexion."

After more in this tone, *The Independent* proceeded to show what it was pleased to call "the spirit that prevails in Gen. Lee's college" by quoting the following from a letter written by "a loyal clergyman of Tennessee."

" 'In passing over the East Tennessee and Virginia Railroad, I occasionally meet with young men dressed in a singular uni-form. Upon inquiry, they tell you they belong to Gen. Lee's school at Lexington, Va. I remarked on one occasion that I was not aware that that institution was a military school.

" 'Oh! well, it isn't exactly. But we wear uniforms, and drill," was the reply.

" 'What do you call your uniform?'

" 'Officers' gray.'

" 'Do you like it?'

" 'Yes; we won't have anything else. We won't wear the d—d Yankee blue at Gen. Lee's school.' "

"Is this the sort of college to which the Christian loyalists of the North should make contributions?" indignantly asked *The Independent,* wholly unconscious that the Virginia Military In-stitute, as well as Washington College, was located at Lexington, and that some of the uniformed cadets of the institute evidently had been joking with the worthy "loyal clergyman of Tennessee."

Not content with the testimony of one minister, *The Inde-pendent* quoted another, who had written in a letter:

"As I told you before, it is out of the question for our children to go in any peace to the rebel schools. They are neglected, in-sulted, and finally driven out of the school; and we want to have a position where they can be treated as they deserve."

On this *The Independent* commented: "Is there any evidence that Washington College, under the presidency of Gen. Lee, is anything else than a rebel school, in which a loyal student would be subjected to insult and persecution? The friends of freedom at the North will be likely, we think, to demand an answer to this question before contributing to its support." If believers in education wanted to promote that cause in the South, let them help Berea College, Kentucky, where instruction was given "last year [to] more than three hundred students—of whom something over half were colored, the most advanced class in the South." [17]

When the issue containing this article reached Lexington, one of Johnston's friends, who signed himself "A Resident of Lexington," wrote a very bitter letter to the periodical, instancing the treatment of that young man as further proof of what *The Independent* had charged. The letter began in this fashion:

"Residing in Lexington, and having seen more or less of the students and professors of Washington College daily since Lee assumed the presidency of the institution, I feel it my duty to give to the people a few facts, which will, I trust, show the philanthropists of the North the animus of the institution to which they are contributing. The professors are, without a single exception, thoroughly rebel in sentiment, and act accordingly. . . . No student can remain in the college who is not a rebel; not, I suppose, from any law of the institution to that effect, but from the universal sentiment of those connected with the school."

Then followed a partisan view of Johnston's encounter and of his efforts to procure redress.

The Independent printed with this a statement that as efforts were being made in the North to collect money for Washington College, it felt called upon to print the letter, "showing how rampant is the spirit of rebellion, proscription and mobocratic violence in that institution." The editor appended to the communication a paragraph in kindred spirit: "In view of facts like these, which come to us from a responsible source, we should

[17] *New York Independent*, March 12, 1868.

think that every man who has given a cent to Gen. Lee's college would see and feel that he has been imposed upon, and that his money has been worse than thrown away." [18]

In the same issue appeared an article by William Lloyd Garrison, protesting against donations to Washington College. "What of the patriotism of General Lee or Washington College?" he demanded. "Is the vanquished leader of the rebel armies now a patriot, or disposed to teach the rebel sons of rebel parents lessons of patriotism? . . . Who is more dumb, or, apparently, more obdurate than himself? *He* at the head of a patriotic institution, teaching loyalty to the Constitution, and the duty of maintaining that Union which he so lately attempted to destroy!"

The incidents related by the "Resident of Lexington" and those quoted in *The Independent* were exceedingly bad advertising for the college in the eyes of those who knew nothing of the facts. In another letter, which *The Independent* printed on April 16, 1868, more of the same sort of publicity was given. This was written by Miss J. A. Shearman, a Northern woman, who recounted how she had gone South to teach school in the fall of 1865, "with a heart full of forgiving pity and yearning sympathy." She was soon disillusioned, she said.

"My first year in the South took me to Lexington, Va. I traveled one entire day in the company of Gen. Lee; and, being confirmed by his external deportment in my preconceived belief that he was what the world is accustomed to call a gentleman, I took heart as regards my novel position. My first excursion in Lexington, which was simply to a hardware store, on a shopping errand, was the occasion of my first insult from the students of Washington College. A group of them followed me into the store, and then beckoned to their comrades outside to come and take a look at the Yankees, at the price of twenty-five cents a look. I wrote to Gen. Lee, saying that I had come there with kind and peaceable intentions; that it was my purpose to conduct myself as a lady; and that, while I did so, I claimed the right to be treated as such. To this I received no reply; and I soon decided that to expect protection from that quarter would be vain.

[18] *New York Independent*, April 2, 1868, p. 4, col. 5.

Thenceforth I met every insult in silence and patience. Never did I walk the streets of Lexington without rudeness, in one form or another. Ladies glorified in compelling the Yankee woman, in her good nature, to step into the mud for their accommodation; the boys of the aristocratic school of the place hooted every time I passed them; and the students sneered and cursed alternately. From one set of students, whose boarding-house I was compelled constantly to pass, I habitually received the polite salutation of '—— Yankee —— of a nigger teacher,'[19] with the occasional addition of an admonition to take up my abode in the infernal regions. I have been awakened from my sleep, in the dead of night, by horrible serenades, performed under my window, by these same gentlemanly young men. I have taught an evening school while brickbats were being thrown by them at the windows. And, finally, I came near being driven out, with my companions, in consequence of a statement, made by the ex-mayor of the place, that the students were planning to burn the school property in which we were living."[20]

It would have been hard for General Lee to have combated hostility to the college based on his failure to answer the complaint of an unknown woman that she had been ridiculed in a Lexington hardware store by unidentified young men whom she took to be students of Washington College. Fortunately for the college, however, its anonymous critic, the "Resident of Lexington," had trod on the toes of General Willcox, and had hinted that the Federal commander had been much too lenient in the Johnston case. This aroused "L," one of Willcox's admirers, "L," probably Captain Lacey of his staff, who had accompanied him to Lexington in February.[21] This officer wrote *The New York Tribune*[22] a correct account of the affair, which *The Independent* had the grace to reproduce. "This correction," wrote "L," "will, I trust, be sufficient to exonerate General Lee, but for whom and

19 The lady spelled out the plain words in her letter.
20 *New York Independent*, April 16, 1868.
21 This assumption is based upon the fact that the letter was signed "L," was dated at Lynchburg, Willcox's headquarters, was shaped in much the same language as Willcox's report, was said by General Lee (*infra*, p. 357) to have been written "by an officer of the army," and manifestly was composed by some one who had investigated the facts.
22 April 20, 1868.

the cause of education, so essential to the welfare of the South, I should not notice the letter and article referred to. As to the slur which was sought to be cast upon General Willcox in the letter 'for consulting with Lee and other notable rebels,' instead of making military arrests, his duty and orders first required him to confer with and demand redress at the hands of the town and college authorities; and, as all was done that could be properly demanded, no military interference was called for. . . . I can assure you that General Willcox is not the man to slight his duty, or to refuse redress and protection when required; and, in this case, where the offenders were promptly punished by General Lee, and where the attack on the part of the boys was invited by Johnston's threat of shooting a little boy, and the presentation of pistol, he does not, certainly, deserve censure for not further prosecuting it. No further complaints have been received from Lexington which is as quiet as any college town in the United States." [23]

Johnston saw this letter, after he had taken up his residence in Covington, and he returned to the charge in a long argumentative communication to *The Independent*.[24] He denied that proper efforts had been made to identify the boys who had attacked him. "*The Tribune* correspondent," he went on, "says three have been expelled. Now I don't know but they have. But this I do know, that every time I have been in Lexington since that time I have seen some students going to and from college who were foremost in the riot; and why are they not expelled? Not merely because I could not identify them; for Gen. Lee kept the matter in his own hands, and I was not allowed an opportunity to identify them—for reasons known to himself, I suppose. At that time examinations were going on at the college, and some were being expelled because they could not pass examination [*sic*]. Is it possible that these three were of the number that could not pass examination?"

Again, he argued, in the latter part of his letter, "*The Tribune* correspondent says 'Lexington is as quiet as any college-town in the United States.' I have been in a good many college-towns,

23 This letter, *loc. cit.*, is dated April 10, 1868.
24 *New York Independent*, May 21, 1868.

and I have never been in a place where the students were in the habit of getting drunk and going through the town, two or three nights a week, firing pistols and threatening to shoot people; and this certainly is the case in Lexington."

He aimed his parting blow at the college: "The following will show you how much they regard Mr. Beecher. A few days since, a gentleman stepped into the office of one of the trustees with a check of $5000 from Northern men to get the signature of the trustee upon it. This remark was made: 'Why, this is from Beecher's party, isn't it? Well, if Beecher and the Devil were to draw straws, I don't know who would get the longest.' 'Well, but we are getting money from them,' said he with the check. 'Yes,' was the reply, 'their money is as good as anybody's, I suppose.' This is a fact which cannot be controverted."

While Johnston's final defense apparently did not circulate beyond the columns of *The Independent,* the first letter from Lexington and the accompanying editorial comment of the periodical were copied widely. Other publications joined in denunciation of the college.[25] Among others, the Yale College weekly, *The Courant,* reproduced the initial article from *The Independent.* Until that time General Lee had taken no notice of the attacks, no doubt feeling that it was futile to argue with publications that printed absurd lies as sober fact, but he did write the New Haven paper. "I regret," said he, "that such an accusation against any literary institution in the country should have been copied in *The Yale Courant.* The statements of the 'Resident of Lexington' have been repeatedly denied, and I had hoped that a letter from an officer of the army, published in *The New York Tribune* of 20th April, would have satisfied all fair-minded persons of their injustice. As it gives all the facts in the case, and will have more weight than anything I could say, I enclose a slip from *The Lexington Gazette,* which republished it. Very respectfully, your obedient servant." *The Courant* promptly and generously made the *amende honorable.*[26] Similar letters were written several

---

[25] *Lexington Gazette,* May 6, 1868.

[26] *Yale Courant,* June 3, 1868, which quoted Lee's letter. The next autumn *The Boston Traveler* assailed the college as lawless and denounced Lee's administration as perfunctory, but it commanded no such audience as listened to the old abolitionists, speaking through *The Independent* (*Lexington Gazette,* Nov. 11, 1868).

individuals who inquired directly of Lee for the facts in the case.[27]

Mr. Walton got pledges and cash amounting to $4300 in New York, including $1000 from Henry Ward Beecher, Gerrit Smith's $200, and $100 each from John A. Griscom, Samuel J. Tilden, and Jas. W. McCulloh.[28] But it is quite likely that the vehemence of the attacks prompted the college to withdraw its agent and to abandon the canvass. The agitation exhibits, moreover, one reason why General Lee avoided all public appearances and every act that might lead to controversy. The temper of the time was not suited to co-operation between North and South. Every effort to that end, no matter how honestly planned or how sincerely undertaken, was certain to spur extremists, North and South.

Before the Johnston affair had been forgotten, there came another episode that might easily have had troublesome results. In an altercation one Friday evening, May 8, 1868, near the gate leading to his home, Francis H. Brockenbrough, a younger son of Judge Brockenbrough, was shot by a Negro youth named Cæsar Griffin. The injury did not result from any organized clash nor did it concern the college directly, for Francis was too young to be a student there, though two of his brothers were. But as the boy's wound threatened to cause his death, excitement was high.

The students organized a man-hunt, and when the Negro was found, they put a rope around his neck and marched him to the courthouse square. Some spectators thought they intended to lynch him then and there, but that was not their intention. At General Lee's instance they turned the miscreant over to the officers of the law, and went back up the hill to college.[29]

Two days later a rumor got afloat that the students intended to storm the jail and to kill the black in case young Brockenbrough died. This rumor came to the ears of the military commissioner of Lexington, Lieutenant Jacob Wagner of the Twenty-ninth Infantry, and he passed it on to General Lee. The General not infrequently received complaints which some of his friends

---

[27] Cf. Lee to F. B. Lewis, MS., May 18, 1868; Lee's MS. Letter Book.

[28] Walton's Subscription Books, Treasurer's MS. Records, Washington and Lee University.

[29] Cf. D. Gardiner Tyler, in Riley, 129–30, and R. E. Lee, Jr., 300.

thought were preferred against the students by people seeking notoriety, but whenever these were officially presented, he always investigated them.[30] In this instance, as the day was Sunday and the academic body was scattered, the only way the General could reach the boys was through the Y. M. C. A. So he immediately wrote the president of that organization, a former captain in the Confederate army, telling him of the commissioner's apprehension. Lee expressed his confidence that the students contemplated no such action as Wagner feared, but he concluded, "I earnestly invoke the students to abstain from any violation of law, and to unite in preserving quiet and order on this and every occasion." [31] Finding the next day that there was no foundation for the report that the college boys planned to lynch the Negro, General Lee so advised Lieutenant Wagner.[32] But that officer had become alarmed for the good order of the town under his charge, and at some stage of the affair called on General Willcox for troops. A company arrived promptly, but its patrol of the streets did not relieve the commissioner's concern. He feared the soldiers were so few in number that a conflict with the citizens was likely, and he appealed for reinforcements. General Willcox was cooler and more experienced and decided to wait for further demonstration before putting more armed men into the town. His judgment was vindicated. In a short while order was fully restored, without any violence beyond that of language and the harmless discharge of a few pistols in the air.[33]

Fortunately, the college was not hurt by this incident, which, however, became historic. Cæsar Griffin was tried before Judge Hugh W. Sheffey in the circuit court of Rockbridge County at the November term, 1868, and as Francis Brockenbrough had recovered by that time, the assailant was given a penitentiary term of only two years. Federal Judge J. C. Underwood forthwith issued a writ of habeas corpus, and soon released the culprit on the grounds that Sheffey was not a duly-constituted judge but a mere usurper, and that there was, in reality, no legal machinery for the punishment of crime in Virginia. This was a virtual dec-

---

[30] Kirkpatrick in *Jones.* 97–98.
[31] R. E. Lee to G. B. Strickler. *MS.,* May 10, 1868; *Lee's MS. Letter Book.*
[32] R. E. Lee to Jacob Wagner, *MS.,* May 11, 1868; *Lee's MS. Letter Book.*
[33] *Lexington Gazette,* May 27, 1868.

Iaration of anarchy, and might have had the direst consequences had not General Bradley Johnson interested Judge Salmon Chase in the situation. The chief justice came to Richmond, heard the case in the United States circuit court in May, 1869, and promptly reversed Underwood.[34]

A third unpleasant occurrence took place that winter. In time it antedated the others. In importance it ranked below them. The Senate of the United States had before it the credentials of Philip F. Thomas, duly-elected junior senator from Maryland. Thomas had been Secretary of the Treasury during part of the administration of Buchanan and had been accused by the radicals of consorting with "traitors," on the eve of the war. He also had a son in the Confederate army. His admission to the Senate was challenged for these reasons. On February 19, 1868, when the resolution to seat Thomas was about to come to a vote, Reverdy Johnson, the other senator from Maryland, made a final appeal for his colleague. In the course of his argument, he contended that attempts at compromise, and official failure to take extreme measures early in 1861, did not constitute treason or display sympathy with rebellion, as was alleged against Thomas. Instancing Senator Cameron, who had been Secretary of War at the beginning of Lincoln's first term, Johnson maintained that Cameron's action in not arresting Lee when he came to tender his resignation did not carry with it any imputation of disloyalty on the secretary's part.

Cameron, who was slow to understand what Johnson was talking about, at length explained the circumstances of Lee's resignation, as he understood them.

"I will tell you why he was not arrested," said he. "General Lee called on a gentleman who had my entire confidence, and intimated that he would like to have the command of the Army. He assured that gentleman, who was a man in the confidence of the administration, of his entire loyalty, and his devotion to the interests of the administration and of the country. I consulted with General Scott, and General Scott approved of placing him at the head of the Army. The place was offered to him unoffi-

---

[34] *Chase's Circuit Court Decisions,* 364. For this reference and a scholarly review of this extraordinary case, the writer is indebted to State Senator Henry T. Wickham.

cially, with my approbation, and with the approbation of General Scott. It was accepted by him verbally, with the promise that he would go into Virginia and settle his business and then come back to take command. He never gave us an opportunity to arrest him; he deserted under false pretenses. . . ."

Johnson inquired: "Did I understand the honorable member to say that General Lee made the statement which he now mentions to him, or that he got it through a third party?"

"Through a gentleman who had my confidence and in whom I relied entirely."

"That is another matter," Johnson insisted. "The statement was not made to the honorable member."

"I have no doubt of its truth," Cameron retorted.

"That I am equally sure of," said the Marylander, "but I doubt very much its truth. It is not in keeping with the character of Lee."

At this point he was interrupted by laughter, led by Senator Conness of California. Johnson fired.

"Gentlemen may laugh," he retorted, "but I say to the honorable member from California, who indulges in merriment, that General Lee is as honorable a man as any man to be found in the State of California. He has offended; that I admit."

The argument veered away from Lee and ended presently in a vote to refuse to seat Thomas.[35]

Cameron's charge, which of course went into the record, soon came to General Lee's eyes. Never did he reply to attacks on his strategy or on his conduct of campaigns. He had ceased to answer the oft-repeated old lie that he had been cruel to the Arlington Negroes. But Cameron's allegation, like the charge that he starved prisoners of war,[36] Lee regarded as a reflection on his personal honor, and he met it on February 25 in a letter he wrote Senator Johnson. This read as follows:

"My attention has been called to the official report of the debate in the Senate of the United States, on the 19th instant, in which

[35] *Congressional Globe*, 2d Session, 40th Congress, 1270–71; B. C. Steiner: *Life of Reverdy Johnson*, 214–15.
[36] For two of Lee's letters denying the charges of cruelty, see 1 S. H. S. P., 121–22, 178.

you did me the kindness to doubt the correctness of the statement made by Honorable Simon Cameron, in regard to myself. I desire that you may feel certain of my conduct on the occasion referred to, so far as my individual statement can make you. I never intimated to any one that I desired the command of the United States Army; nor did I ever have a conversation with but one gentleman, Mr. Francis Preston Blair, on the subject, which was at his invitation, and, I understood, at the instance of President Lincoln. After listening to his remarks, I declined the offer he made me, to take command of the army that was to be brought into the field; stating, as candidly and as courteously as I could, that, though opposed to secession and deprecating war, I could take no part in an invasion of the Southern States. I went directly from the interview with Mr. Blair to the office of General Scott; told him of the proposition that had been made to me, and my decision. Upon reflection after returning to my home, I concluded that I ought no longer to retain the commission I held in the United States Army; and on the second morning thereafter I forwarded my resignation to General Scott. At the time, I hoped that peace would have been preserved; that some way would have been found to save the country from the calamities of war; and I then had no other intention than to pass the remainder of my life as a private citizen. Two days afterward, upon the invitation of the Governor of Virginia, I repaired to Richmond; found that the convention then in session had passed the ordinance withdrawing the State from the Union; and accepted the commission of commander of its forces, which was tendered me.

"These are the ample [simple?] facts of the case, and they show that Mr. Cameron has been misinformed." [37]

He never again wrote of the details of his resignation from the army.

The hard, wet winter that had just ended at the time of the Brockenbrough shooting was accompanied by much sickness in Lexington. Two of the cadets of the V. M. I. died of pneumonia. Mrs. Lee suffered more than usual, and "Powhattie" did not escape. The General took such exercise as he could get and he

[37] *R. E. Lee, Jr.*, 27–28

found much satisfaction, one March day, in following the ploughs of a neighboring farmer around the circuit of his fields.[38] He caught cold, however, and had to admit, when the rough weather was past, that he had "not been as well . . . as usual," [39] but he still delighted in his occasional rides on Traveller.[40] The depression of January vanished; he had pleasure in his work. "I much enjoy the charms of civil life," he wrote General Ewell about this time, "and find too late that I have wasted the best years of my existence." [41]

Perhaps the prospect that detracted most from the "charms of civil life" was the approaching trial of President Davis. Going to Richmond as an unwilling witness in the proceedings was a "painful errand" for General Lee, even though it held out the prospect of meeting with his sons.[42] To Agnes, who had seen Mr. Davis as he passed through Baltimore, Lee wrote: "It is a terrible thing to have the prosecution hanging over him, and to be unable to fix his thoughts on a course of life or apply his hands to the support of his family. But I hope a kind Providence will shield and guide him." [43] As the time for the expected trial drew on, his tone was even more serious. "God grant," said he, "that, like the impeachment of Mr. Johnson, it may be dismissed." [44] On May 1, 1868,[45] Lee went to Richmond, under summons, only to find the proceedings deferred until June. He took advantage of his proximity to his sons, and paid them a brief visit.

The coming of spring had already reawakened the General's love of agriculture and had increased his faith in the South's recovery through hard labor, particularly by the men who had fought sterner battles. "Work is what we now require," he had written Hill Carter in earnest strain, "work by everybody and work especially by *white* hands. Labour and economy will carry us through. We must spend less . . . than we formerly did. We

[38] R. E. Lee to R. E. Lee, Jr., March 12, 1868; *R. E. Lee, Jr.,* 306.
[39] R. E. Lee to Agnes Lee, March 28, 1868; R. E. Lee to R. E. Lee, Jr., April 25, 1868; *R. E. Lee, Jr.,* 308, 311.
[40] *R. E. Lee, Jr.,* 311.
[41] R. E. Lee to R. S. Ewell, March 3, 1868; *Jones,* 118.
[42] R. E. Lee to Mrs. W. H. F. Lee, March 10, 1868; *R. E. Lee, Jr.,* 303.
[43] March 28, 1868; *R. E. Lee, Jr.,* 307–8.
[44] R. E. Lee to Mrs. W. H. F. Lee, May 29, 1868; *R. E. Lee, Jr.,* 312.
[45] *Richmond Enquirer and Examiner,* May 2, 1868; *Richmond Dispatch,* May 2, 1868.

require very little and we must use that little sparingly. By this course the good old times of former days which you speak of will return again. We may not see them but our children will, and we will live over again in them. I hope they may imitate the virtues and avoid the errors of their ancestors, and maintain the moral and literary standards which they practiced." [46] He went to his sons' plantations in a cheerful spirit and found them doing better with their farms than he had anticipated.[47] Rooney had built a new house, which Lee praised as "convenient, well-arranged and well-built." [48] Robert was living in an old and dilapidated structure which his father did not visit at the time but described as "scarcely habitable." [49] The stay was all too brief, but as the General had laid out a schedule he was soon back in Lexington.[50]

While Lee was away, Colonel R. E. Withers wrote for *The Lynchburg News* a statement of the General's political views. It was not directly attributed to Lee but it reflected certain of his opinions with measurable accuracy. It read as follows: "General Lee deprecates the acerbity of political feeling now so rife in the land, and is disposed to believe that more moderation and prudence in the expression of opinion, and less bitterness in the denunciation of political opponents, would conduce more to the speedy settlement of the vexed questions which now agitate the country. He, however, studiously avoids political discussions, and, with rare discretion, affords no room for cavil to the enemies of the South." [51]

[46] R. E. Lee to Hill Carter, *MS.*, April 25, 1868; *Shirley MSS.* Lee believed in a wise immigration policy to supply Southern farms with white labor. On Dec. 30, 1869, he wrote: "The question of supplying labour to the South is one of vital importance in which all classes are concerned and particularly the agriculturist, inasmuch as regular and constant work is more necessary to his prosperity than in most of the other industrial pursuits. I believe this can only be secured by the introduction of a respectable class of labourers from Europe, for although a temporary benefit might be derived from importation of the Chinese and Japanese, it would result I fear in eventual injury to the country and her institutions. We not only want reliable labourers, but good citizens, whose interests and feelings would be in unison with our own . . ." (R. E. Lee to Thos. H. Ellis, *MS.*, copy of which has been generously supplied the writer by James R. Gilliam, Jr., of Lynchburg, Va.).

[47] R. E. Lee to Hill Carter, *MS.*, May 18, 1868; *Shirley MSS.*

[48] R. E. Lee to the architect, Albert L. West, *MS.*, May 14, 1868; kindly placed at the writer's disposal by Miss Georgia West, daughter of the addressee.

[49] Lee to Martha Williams, April 14, 1868; *Markie Letters,* 81–82.

[50] *R. E. Lee, Jr.,* 312.

[51] Reprinted in *Richmond Dispatch.* May 6, 1868.

Lee was in Richmond again on June 3 when Mr. Davis's case was due to be called and Chief Justice Chase was expected to be present. While the General was waiting in a room opposite that set aside for the judges, he was unexpectedly and somewhat unwillingly forced to hold an informal reception. H. H. Wells, a New Yorker who held the office of Governor of Virginia by military appointment,[52] was in court as a spectator, and came forward for an introduction. The General chatted with Wells for only a few minutes and then was interrupted by friends, most of them Richmond lawyers, who gathered about him to shake hands. Lee greeted all of them cordially but did not engage in much conversation.

By agreement, when the Davis case was reached on the docket it was postponed to November 30, and General Lee and the other witnesses were recognized in the sum of $5000 each for their appearance at that time. As Rooney was one of his fellow-witnesses, the General had opportunity of seeing him while he was in the old capital,[53] but once again he hastened back to Lexington, this time in order to be present during the examinations. He left Eastern Virginia somewhat unwillingly because he had wanted to spend a day at Shirley. "It was the loved home of my mother," he wrote rather wistfully, "and a spot where I have passed many happy days in early life, and one that probably I may never visit again." [54]

In gratifying contrast to the two calls to Richmond, and coming between them, was a mission to Lynchburg, on May 20, 1868, to attend the annual council of the Protestant Episcopal Church of Virginia, as a lay delegate from Grace Church, Lexington. Lee was present when the body met in Saint Paul's Church, Lynchburg, and he doubtless heard the sermon of Reverend J. A. Latané of Staunton from the text: "Sow to yourselves in righteousness, reap according to kindness; break up your fallow ground; for it is time to seek the Lord, till he come and rain righteousness upon you" [55]—a discourse intended to show the

---

52 *Eckenrode*, 104.
53 *Richmond Dispatch, Richmond Whig, Richmond Enquirer and Examiner*, June 4, 1868; for the departure from home, *Lexington Gazette*, June 3, 1868; for the proceedings in court, 7 *Rowland*, 195–96.
54 R. E. Lee to Mrs. W. H. F. Lee, May 29, 1868; *R. E. Lee, Jr.*, 213.
55 Hosea 10: 12.

special need of the Church at that time. Following the sermon, Bishop Johns made an appeal for the diocesan missionary society and took up a collection. Then the holy communion was administered. At the afternoon session, which began at 2:20 o'clock, the General was again in his place.[56]

The next two days must have been busy, for Lee was named a member of three committees, that on the state of the Church, that on Church salaries, and that on a memorial to his old friend, Bishop William Meade.[57] On the last day of the council meeting, the General was nominated a delegate to the general convention of the Protestant Episcopal Church, the highest honor the council could pay one of its members, but he was not elected, doubtless because he did not feel he could attend. He made no speeches on the floor of the council: "He was a constant but silent attendant," according to a newspaper report.

The guest of John William Murrell, he received as much attention from the citizens of Lynchburg as his regular presence at the council meetings permitted. An odd incident happened while he was at Mr. Murrell's. One night he was awakened by sounds as of some one gasping in pain. He waited awhile, listening for some member of the family to come to the relief of the sufferer. Hearing no one, he got up, put on his clothes and went to his host's door. He awoke Mr. Murrell with a tap and explained. Mr. Murrell made the rounds of the house but was unable to find anything amiss. The family concluded that the General had been dreaming of a battlefield.[58] Perhaps General Lee decided that some one had been snoring.

In all other respects, the session of the council passed without incident, and on the afternoon of May 22, the General took the packet-boat up the James River and Kanawha Canal for home.[59]

Examinations crowded the days that followed Lee's June trip to Richmond, which occurred soon after the council meeting. Then came commencement. The college had a graduating class

[56] *Lynchburg Virginian,* May 20, May 21, 1868. For all these references to Lee's visit to Lynchburg, the writer is indebted to Miss J. M. Campbell, librarian of the Jones Memorial Library, Lynchburg, Va.

[57] *Lynchburg Virginian,* May 22, 1868.

[58] MS. Memoirs of John W. Murrell, most courteously lent by Doctor Thomas W. Murrell of Richmond.

[59] *Lynchburg Virginian,* May 23, 1868.

of fourteen—two in civil engineering, seven bachelors of law, five bachelors of arts—and it staged for them the most elaborate ceremonies that had been held since the war. The chapel was formally dedicated on June 14, much to General Lee's satisfaction, and the baccalaureate sermon was preached in the Presbyterian church by the president's former Richmond rector, a courageous German refugee, Doctor Charles Minnigerode.

General Wade Hampton was another commencement guest, as orator before the literary societies,[60] and he of course met his old commander. Lee was busy with the board of trustees, but he arranged his engagements so that he could entertain the South Carolinian at dinner, and with him he talked frankly of the war. It was one of the few occasions after 1865 on which he did so.[61] Their exchange ranged far—back to the beginning of the struggle and to their decision to share the fortunes of the South. Then it was that Lee made the simple observation that is the surest answer to all those who have contended that he hesitated before resigning from the United States army in 1861: "I did only what my duty demanded," he said. "I could have taken no other course without dishonor. And if all were to be done over again, I should act in precisely the same manner."[62]

The conversation turned, ere long, to Early's last campaign in the Shenandoah Valley. "When everything is known," said General Lee, "I don't think that General Early will be blamed as much as he has been." Presently Stuart's name was mentioned. Instantly the voice of Lee, which had been low, became clear and warm. "General Stuart was my ideal of a soldier. He was always cheerful under all circumstances, always ready for any work and always reliable. He was able to stand any amount of fatigue and privation. When he stopped for a night's rest, he could throw himself on the ground, and, with his saddle or a log for a pillow, he would fall asleep almost immediately, and sleep as if in a bed. Then, if I sent an officer to him with an order, he was awake at the first call or touch. When his eyes opened his mind became fully awake. He did not have to yawn or stretch

[60] *Richmond Dispatch*, May 27, 1868; *Washington College, Virginia: Commencement Week* (one-sheet program); Washington and Lee Library.
[61] The only other men with whom he talked as freely of hostilities were his brother, Charles Carter Lee, his cousin, Cassius Lee, and Custis Lee.
[62] *Jones*, 142, on the authority of General Hampton.

to get himself awake, but his mind and body seemed to awake at the same time and to become active and alert. Before any other officer that I ever had could get himself and his men awake, Stuart would be in the saddle, with his men in line, and be ready to move." [63]

The trustees were in session three days, June 16–18, inclusive, and heard the usual reports, including that on the endowment campaign. Reverend E. P. Walton, who had conducted the canvass in New York, had been able to gather only $9200 in large gifts during 1867–68 as compared with $45,280 in 1865–66, and $27,950 in 1866–67. His total for the three years, including $5278 of small gifts, had been approximately $88,848 and 640 acres of land. Mr. Walton had opened a separate account for "Contributions to the Building Fund for Genl. R. E. Lee's residence as Prest. of Washington College," but as he listed only six subscriptions, it is likely that Lee insisted this form of solicitation should be stopped. The same thing probably applies to Mr. Walton's proposed "Annual Subscriptions to Gen. R. E. Lee's salary," for only one pledge is listed under this heading.[64] Undeterred by the small increase in endowment, the trustees outlined new plans for interesting friends of education in the college, and authorized the expenditure of $600 for the employment of canvassers the following year.[65]

Numerous appropriations were made, including one of $500 for clerical assistance to General Lee, to be expended as he pleased.[66] A great volume of minor business was transacted. As the college still lacked funds for the establishment of a law school of its own, the arrangement with Judge Brockenbrough was continued, though a new committee was named to devise a plan for the permanent connection of a law school with the college.[67]

The important decisions of the trustees had to do with the course of study. The department of English was taken from the

[63] General Lee's nephew, then a student at the college, overheard this part of the conversation. See G. T. Lee: "Reminiscences of General Robert E. Lee," *South Atlantic Quarterly,* July, 1927, pp. 249–50.

[64] This was of $60 per annum, by R. A. Lancaster, of Richmond. For General Lee's protest against this form of solicitation, see *supra,* p. 258 and Jones, 178–79.

[65] *Trustees' Minutes,* June 17, 1868.   [66] *Trustees' Minutes,* June 17, 1868.

[67] *Trustees' Minutes,* June 16–17, 1868.

School of Modern Languages and added to the School of History and English Literature. New courses in natural history and geology were authorized. The faculty was instructed to proceed with plans for enlarging the scientific department, a work that subsequently took on large importance. A "survey board" also was established. This was to consist of the president and the professors of mathematics, applied mathematics, natural philosophy, and chemistry. It was intended to prepare maps and to make geological surveys.[68]

Twenty-five new scholarships were approved, five of them to go to selected students already in college, and twenty to promising young men in academies and high schools selected by the faculty. Finally, in a commendable determination to raise the standards of the college, the trustees decided to change the requirements for the degree of master of arts. Up to this time that degree represented satisfactory graduation in nine schools, five of which had to be completed with "distinguished attainments" that justified the award of the "certificate of distinguished proficiency." It was now provided that after the session of 1868–69, the master of arts would have to win this distinction in seven instead of five schools. In only two schools was he to be allowed merely to "pass." [69] The suggestions for all these improvements were made in the president's report and in faculty papers transmitted to the board by him.

So ended the third session at Lexington under Lee's presidency. It had brought its vexations and its disappointments, and it had witnessed the only serious attack made on General Lee and the college during his administration. Although the endowment had not been increased largely, the year, financially, had not been very difficult, and scholastically it had been the best since the war. To Lee, along with some sorrows and sickness, it had brought new satisfactions. He made no move to resign as he had

---

[68] Lee interested himself in this work and helped to collect data for a map of the area thirty miles around Richmond (Lee to Robert Carter, MS., Feb. 16, 1870; *Shirley MSS.*).

[69] *Trustees' Minutes,* June 17, 1868; for the degree requirements, see *1867–68 Catalogue,* 39. At this meeting the trustees dismissed the committee previously appointed to consider that part of the president's report for 1866–67 relating to a "National System of Military Education." The institution's records do not show where this proposal originated, but it probably was devised elsewhere than at Washington College (*Trustees' Minutes,* June 16, 1868).

intimated the previous year he might do when the session of 1867–68 closed. Instead, as his devoted associates saw, his love for the college increased with each year.[70] He showed that feeling very positively when he received a call to accept the vice-chancellorship and active administration of the University of the South. This invitation was based on a report that Lee was dissatisfied at Washington College and would be glad to make a change. Lee answered that he appreciated the honor the trustees of Sewanee had done him. "They have, however," he wrote, "been misinformed as to my feelings concerning my present position, and even if they were as represented, I could not now resign with propriety unless I saw it was for the benefit of the college." With a few more polite words he declined the offer.[71]

[70] Joynes, in *Jones,* 121.
[71] R. E. Lee to Right Reverend William M. Green, Sept. 23, 1868, *Dr. Quintard,* 179.

CHAPTER XXI

Salvaging the Wrecked Family Fortunes

If there had been anything in auguries, the summer of 1868 should have been the happiest of seasons for the Lees, for it began with the suggestion of a high honor—nothing less than that General Lee be made the Democratic nominee for the presidency of the United States. It was a qualified proposal, to be sure, for it was postulated on the assumption that the Democrats had to name a soldier to defeat General Grant, the Republican choice. *The New York Herald* put Lee's name forward in an editorial that read in part as follows:

"But if the Democratic Committee must nominate a soldier— if it must have a name identified with the glories of the war—we will recommend a candidate for its favors. Let it nominate General R. E. Lee. Let it boldly take over the best of all its soldiers, making no palaver or apology. He is a better soldier than any of those they have thought upon and a greater man. He is one in whom the military genius of this nation finds its fullest development. Here the inequality will be in favor of the Democrats for this soldier, with a handful of men whom he had moulded into an army, baffled our greater Northern armies for four years; and when opposed by Grant was only worn down by that solid strategy of stupidity that accomplishes its object by mere weight. With one quarter the men Grant had this soldier fought magnificently across the territory of his native State, and fought his army to a stump. There never was such an army or such a campaign, or such a General for illustrating the military genius and possibilities of our people; and this General is the best of all for a Democratic candidate. It is certain that with half as many men as Grant he would have beaten him from the field in Virginia, and he affords the best promise of any soldier for beating him again." [1]

[1] *New York Herald*, quoted in *The Lexington Gazette*, July 1, 1868.

Lee must have smiled at this article, if, indeed, he saw it, but the auguries were not fulfilled. He had little time and perhaps little heart for smiling that summer. Sickness dogged the family. Mrs. Lee had become nervous and had been brooding so much over the plight of the South under military rule that her husband had feared she would aggravate her physical condition. Agnes had been sick while in Maryland, and though she had not yet come home, was said to be looking very unwell. The General planned to take all of them away, and after he had comfortably established them at the springs Mrs. Lee preferred, he intended to go on with Mildred to the White Sulphur and to drink its waters for his rheumatism.[2]

It was July 14 before the first stage of this journey could be undertaken and the family moved to the Warm Springs.[3] There it was assigned to the Brockenbrough Cottage, with Mrs. Lee on the first floor and her daughters in the rooms above. All might have gone well had not Mildred contracted a low, debilitating fever which the doctor diagnosed as typhoid. Her mother, of course, could not nurse her. The burden fell on the General and on Agnes. In her sickness, Mildred developed whimsies, and insisted that she could not sleep unless her father sat by her and held her hand. He did not try to argue her out of this or to substitute some one else for the vigils. Night after night he stayed there, in the little upstairs chamber of the cottage, until the dance was over and the chatter ceased on the lawn and the lamps went out. What was he thinking about through those long hours, he who had commanded tens of thousands of men in the bloodiest battles of the continent, and yet had spent so many of his days as nurse to mother, to invalid wife, and to children?

It was August 14 before Mildred was pronounced convalescent, and even then she was so weak she could not speak.[4] When she recovered sufficiently to travel, the General took her and the rest of the family from the Warm to the Hot Springs, and, after a few days, went on with Mildred to the White Sulphur.

He found a large gathering of former Confederates there, including many of his old generals and not a few of the civil

---

[2] R. E. Lee to W. H. F. Lee, July 1, 1868; *R. E. Lee, Jr.*, 318.
[3] *R. E. Lee, Jr.*, 320.
[4] R. E. Lee to W. H. F. Lee, Aug. 14, 1868; *R. E. Lee, Jr.*, 322–23.

officials of the dead government. Nearly all of them were talking politics. Grant and Schuyler Colfax had been nominated by the Republicans. Against them the Democrats had entered Governor Horatio Seymour and Francis P. Blair. Recent as was the war, some of the Democrats believed that they had a chance of electing their candidates, and certain of those at the springs were busily devising ways and means to that end. Already the alarmed Republicans were warning the North that the South was unreconciled, and that the Negroes were being unfairly treated, and that the election of Seymour and Blair would undo the victory won at the cost of so much blood. General Lee, of course, had little part in these discussions. In fact, he avoided politics so sedulously that more than one of his comrades complained privately that he was distinctly cool to them.[5]

Unexpectedly, however, he found himself involved in the controversy. General W. S. Rosecrans, one of the managers of the Democratic campaign, knew that some of the leading Southerners visited "The White" every summer, and he came down from New York to see if he could procure from them a statement of their acceptance of the results of the war, and of their willingness to deal justly with the Negroes. This, in General Rosecrans's opinion, might offset the Republican propaganda and help the Democratic ticket.[6] Naturally, Rosecrans consulted Lee first of all upon his arrival, and explained that as Lee was a representative Southerner, his assurance of the South's loyalty to the Union would carry weight in the North. Lee demurred. He could not assume to speak for the South, he said; if Rosecrans wished to know the feeling of the former Confederacy, he could inquire of the public men who were at the springs.

Being willing to ask in the name of politics what he would not have sought for himself personally, Rosecrans requested Lee to bring these gentlemen together that he might meet them. Lee's politeness and his desire to help in the restoration of good feeling prompted him to accede and to invite a number of former soldiers and publicists to his cottage. There, while Lee was noticeably quiet, General Rosecrans exchanged opinions with

[5] John S. Mosby, quoted in Watson's *Notes on Southside Virginia*, 248.
[6] R. E. Lee to Wade Hampton, *MS.*, Aug. 29, 1868; *Lee's MS. Letter Book*.

373

Beauregard, Alexander H. Stephens, and others. Nearly all of them assured him of the willingness of the people to support the Union and to deal justly with the Negro. Only the last man to be asked for his views, ex-Governor F. W. Stockdale of Texas, spoke out bluntly and said that the South would keep the peace but was not a dog to lick the hand of the man that kicked it. Lee then rose and brought the conference to an end.[7]

Rosecrans was not through. On August 26 he addressed Lee a formal letter asking that the Southerners with whom he had conferred at the cottage unite in a formal statement of their views.[8] Anxious as Lee was to allay ill-feeling and to heal the wounds of war, such a request was embarrassing. He had never written a line on politics for publication since the war, and he hesitated to break his rule, especially as he was unfamiliar with the language of political discussion.

What, then, should he do? Among the guests at the springs was Alexander H. H. Stuart, a Virginia lawyer of much sagacity and judgment, who had been Secretary of the Interior under Fillmore. Stuart's good sense showed him that Virginia had to pay a price for a return of her rights of statehood and he was working quietly but skillfully to that end. He was the man Lee needed to help him, for he could be relied upon to show conservatism along with candor. Through General John Echols, Lee sent Rosecrans's letter to Stuart and asked him to write an

---

[7] T. C. Johnson: *Life and Letters of Robert Lewis Dabney,* 498 ff. Doctor Dabney was not present and received his account of the meeting from Governor Stockdale. The latter told Dabney that he was the last to leave the room, and that as he was saying good-bye, Lee closed the door, thanked him for what he had said and added: "Governor, if I had foreseen the use these people desired to make of their victory, there would have been no surrender at Appomattox, no, sir, not by me. Had I foreseen these results of subjugation, I would have preferred to die at Appomattox with my brave men, my sword in this right hand." This, of course, is second-hand testimony. There is nothing in Lee's own writings and nothing in direct quotation by first-hand witness that accords with such an expression on his part. The nearest approach to it is the claim by H. Gerald Smythe that "Major Talcott"—presumably Colonel T. M. R. Talcott—told him Lee stated he would never have surrendered the army if he had known how the South would have been treated. Mr. Smythe stated that Colonel Talcott replied, "Well, General, you have only to blow the bugle," whereupon Lee is alleged to have answered, "It is too late now" (29 *Confederate Veteran,* 7). Here again the evidence is not direct. The writer of this biography, talking often with Colonel Talcott, never heard him narrate this incident or suggest in any way that Lee accepted the results of the radical policy otherwise than with indignation, yet in the belief that the extremists would not always remain in office. For these reasons the writer is unwilling to quote this doubtful testimony in the text.

[8] Text lost but easily reconstructed from Lee to Rosecrans, *MS.,* Aug. 26, 1868; *Lee's MS. Letter Book.*

374

answer. In a short time Stuart brought a draft which Lee read over carefully and slowly in the lawyer's presence. It was to this effect:

"General:

"I have the honor to receive your letter of this date, and, in accordance with your suggestion, I have conferred with a number of gentlemen from the South, in whose judgment I have confidence, and who are well acquainted with the public sentiment of their respective States.

"They have kindly consented to unite with me in replying to your communication, and their names will be found, with my own, appended to this answer.

"With this explanation, we proceed to give you a candid statement of what we believe to be the sentiment of the Southern people in regard to the subjects to which you refer.

"Whatever opinions may have prevailed in the past with regard to African slavery or the right of a State to secede from the Union, we believe we express the almost unanimous judgment of the Southern people when we declare that they consider these questions were decided by the war, and that it is their intention in good faith to abide by that decision. At the close of the war, the Southern people laid down their arms and sought to resume their former relations to the government of the United States. Through their State conventions, they abolished slavery and annulled their ordinances of secession; and they returned to their peaceful pursuits with a sincere purpose to fulfil all their duties under the Constitution of the United States which they had sworn to support. If their action in these particulars had been met in a spirit of frankness and cordiality, we believe that, ere this, old irritations would have passed away, and the wounds inflicted by the war would have been, in a large measure, healed. As far as we are advised, the people of the South entertain no unfriendly feeling towards the government of the United States, but they complain that their rights under the Constitution are withheld from them in the administration thereof. The idea that the Southern people are hostile to the negroes and would oppress them, if it were in their power to do so, is entirely unfounded.

375

They have grown up in our midst, and we have been accustomed from childhood to look upon them with kindness. The change in the relations of the two races has brought no change in our feelings towards them. They still constitute an important part of our laboring population. Without their labor, the lands of the South would be comparatively unproductive; without the employment which Southern agriculture affords, they would be destitute of the means of subsistence and become paupers, dependent upon public bounty. Self-interest, if there were no higher motive, would therefore prompt the whites of the South to extend to the negro care and protection.

"The important fact that the two races are, under existing circumstances, necessary to each other is gradually becoming apparent to both, and we believe that but for malign influences exerted to stir up the passions of the negroes, the relations of the two races would soon adjust themselves on a basis of mutual kindness and advantage.

"It is true that the people of the South, in common with a large majority of the people of the North and West, are, for obvious reasons, inflexibly opposed to any system of laws that would place the political power of the country in the hands of the negro race. But this opposition springs from no feeling of enmity, but from a deep-seated conviction that, at present, the negroes have neither the intelligence nor the other qualifications which are necessary to make them safe depositories of political power. They would inevitably become the victims of demagogues, who, for selfish purposes, would mislead them to the serious injury of the public.

"The great want of the South is peace. The people earnestly desire tranquillity and restoration of the Union. They deplore disorder and excitement as the most serious obstacle to their prosperity. They ask a restoration of their rights under the Constitution. They desire relief from oppressive misrule. Above all, they would appeal to their countrymen for the re-establishment, in the Southern States, of that which has been justly regarded as the birth-right of every American, the right of self-government. Establish these on a firm basis, and we can safely promise, on behalf of the Southern people, that they will faithfully obey the Constitution and laws of the United States, treat the negro populations with kindness and humanity and fulfil every duty incumbent on peaceful citizens, loyal to the Constitution of their country." [9]

All this was what Lee had been thinking and saying ever since May, 1865. The language was slightly more rhetorical than he would have employed, but the sentiments were precisely his. A single change was all Lee thought necessary. Stuart, in speaking of the development of better relations between the races, had said, "but for malign influences exerted to stir up the passions of the negroes," etc. That grated on Lee. "Mr. Stuart," he said, "there is one word I would like to strike out if you have no objection. You have used the word *malign*. I think that is rather a harsh word, and"—he smiled as he went on, "I never did like adjectives."

Mr. Stuart immediately erased the offending word, and the letter was approved. Lee signed it, as did thirty-one other leading Southerners at the springs. It was forwarded to Rosecrans and was soon published. Its reception varied with the feelings and political opinions of those who read it.[10] Lee followed it up by suggesting to Wade Hampton that, if he approved the letter, he get other Southern leaders to add their signatures and forward them to him or to General Rosecrans.[11] And at Rosecrans's request Lee gave him the names of some Southern generals residing in New York.[12]

Whether it was that the air was too heavily surcharged with politics, or whether it was that Lee was exhausted by his long nursing of Mildred, he did not enjoy the social life of "The White" so much as he had the previous summer. He tried to be enthusiastic about the place and the company,[13] but he left early in September for the Hot Springs, and by September 14 was back home.[14]

[9] A. F. Robertson: *Alexander Hugh Holmes Stuart*, 261–63.
[10] A. F. Robertson, *op. cit.*, 263; full text in *Lee's MS. Letter Book*.
[11] *Lee's MS. Letter Book*, Aug. 29, 1868.
[12] Lee to Rosecrans, MS., Aug. 29, 1868; *Lee's MS. Letter Book*.
[13] R. E. Lee, Jr., 324.
[14] *Faculty Minutes* of that date show him present. See also *Lexington Gazette*, Sept. 16, 1868.

He found at Lexington at least two more letters from Rosecrans, in which the Northerner urged Lee to call public meetings
throughout the South to ratify the "White Sulphur Letter."
With an eye to effective publicity, Rosecrans recommended that
these gatherings be held at intervals so that the proceedings of all
of them would find a place in the newspapers. He enclosed, also,
a political program which had been drawn up by some of Seymour's advisers. In short, his old opponent of Sewell's Mountain
was enthusiastically initiating Lee into the secrets of the campaign and was trying to make a politician of him. But Lee
would have none of it. He felt that he had gone as far as he
should in making a single exception to his rule of complete
public silence on political questions; so he turned the letters over
to General Echols with the request that he ask Mr. Stuart to
answer them. Echols explained to Stuart that Lee "did not
desire to be connected any further, in any way, with the political
questions or canvass of the day." Lee himself repeated this to
Rosecrans. "When I united with the gentlemen, at the White
Sulphur Springs," he said, "in the reply to your letter addressed
to me there, I went as far as I thought it was proper for me to
do under the circumstances of the case, and did not intend to
connect myself with the political questions of the Country, or to
depart from the course I had adopted on entering upon my
present vocation."[15] He had little time for outside activity, even
if he had felt the inclination, for he was soon deep in the heavy
work incident to the registration of the students and the reopen-
ing of the college on September 17.

Attendance was not so large as during the previous session.
The total enrollment for the session of 1868–69 was 348 as against
410 the previous year. The decline, which was chiefly in students
from Virginia, Tennessee, and Kentucky, probably reflected

---

[15] John Echols to A. H. H. Stuart, Sept. 16, 1868; A. F. Robertson, *op. cit.*, 264. Lee
to Rosecrans, *MS.*, Sept. 18, 1868; *Lee's MS. Letter Book*. The writer's friend, Colonel
Jennings C. Wise, is of opinion that General Lee was the moving spirit in a general plan
to organize the conservatives of the South for a just restoration of the Union, and in an
article in *The Tidewater Tribune* (Hampton, Va., October, 1929) he stated that General
Lee "summoned General Longstreet [and others] to the White Sulphur to join with him
in proclaiming the terms upon which the South would return to the Union." The writer
has found no confirmation of this, but believes, on the contrary, that Lee had no part in
the campaign beyond that set forth in the text. In the absence of any positive evidence to
the contrary, it is impossible to reconcile any theory of political activity on the part of
General Lee with the statement made in the letters quoted above.

economic conditions and the improvement of institutions available nearer the homes of young men ready for college.[16] As a whole, the students settled down to their work promptly enough, but the memory of the disturbances of the previous winter had not died in the minds of the military authorities. On November 19 Lee received a letter in which the commanding officer of the troops in Lexington advised him that the Negroes planned to have a meeting at the fair-grounds the next evening and were fearful that the students would interfere. The General had heard nothing of the proposed gathering. Neither had any of those with whom he talked. Nevertheless, he issued a warning. Stating his belief that the boys had no intention of troubling the Negroes, he requested that those who might be led by curiosity to go to the place of meeting would refrain from doing so. "From past experience," he concluded, "they may feel certain that, should any disturbance occur, efforts will be made to fix the blame on Washington College. It therefore behooves every student to keep away from all such assemblies." He wrote, also, to the commander of the Federal garrison and told him he did not think the students purposed to obstruct the exercises. He added: "Everything, however, in our power will be done by the Faculty as well as myself to prevent any of the students attending; and I heartily concur with you in the hope that the peace of the community may at all times be preserved."[17] The meeting was held without interference. Not a student was there. It was the last time any charge was made that the students were conspiring against the free assembly of the Negroes.

Except for a trip of two days to the fair at Staunton in October,[18] Lee did not leave Lexington during the whole of the fall and winter. From the beginning of the session to the second week in April, 1869, he missed only one faculty meeting. In contrast to the hard, unhappy summer, it was a pleasant time, broken by the coming and going of kinspeople. The General's

---

[16] *1868–69 Catalogue*, p. 16.

[17] *Jones*, 104–5.

[18] *R. E. Lee, Jr.*, 330. A woman who saw him at the fair remembered that he rode into the grounds on Traveller, attended by a number of gentlemen. She wrote: "The women's booths stood beside the gate. All were waiting to see our idolized hero. Cheers arose from the crowd as he entered. He lifted his hat and looked upward. So, plainly, he gave to his God the glory" (*MS.* note to the writer, Jan. 21, 1930, from "A Lover of Lee," Grottoes, Va.).

nephew, Edward Lee Childe, journeyed over from Paris and was a welcome guest in October.[19] Rooney and his wife, coming in November, were much entertained. The young Mrs. Lee had been coached by her husband in the ways of the family and had been told, in particular, that the General would expect her to be present punctually at family prayers, which were always held before breakfast. She met the test and had a perfect attendance, during a stay of three weeks, with not a single tardiness over which to blush. The General's estimate of her, already high, was raised by this *tour de force*. For her part, she confided to other members of the household that she did not believe even George Washington himself, if the father of his country had been late at family prayers, would have the unqualified good opinion of General Lee.[20]

At Christmas, Robert arrived for a stay of two weeks, and all the girls were at home. Only Rooney, of the six children, was absent. It was the last time as many as five of them were together during Lee's lifetime. The General had much delight in their company. Christmas morning he had remembrances for them all, and for Mildred a pile of treasures. It developed that sometime previously she had mentioned in his hearing the presents she wanted, and he had bought everything she had mentioned, instead of selecting one gift from the list. As the father of numerous daughters, he should have known better. However, the family historian did not record that the other Misses Lee were jealous at this show of partiality. Perhaps they regarded it as the crowning bit of "spoiling" to which Mildred was entitled because of her long illness.[21]

Robert and his father were much together during this visit. They frequently inspected the new "president's house" that was now nearing completion on the same ridge with the old resi-

[19] *R. E. Lee, Jr.*, 327.

[20] *R. E. Lee, Jr.*, 330. Winston, *op. cit.*, 411–12, quoted a contrary Lexington tradition that Mrs. Rooney Lee was late at prayers her first two mornings. On the second, Lee remarked that "no day should be lived unless it was begun with a prayer of thankfulness and an intercession for guidance." Then he said: "And now, my child, unless you get down to morning prayers, your old father will give you no more kisses." The writer has followed the version of the Lee family both because it is first-hand and also because it accords better with Lee's known treatment of women. He was always the courtier in his manners.

[21] *R. E. Lee, Jr.*, 324.

dence. They rode out together, too, Lee on Traveller and Robert on Lucy Long. The General's health for the time seemed excellent and his spirits were high. "He also took me around with him visiting," Robert records, "and in the mild festivities of the neighbors he joined with evident pleasure." [22]

Shortly after the Christmas parties broke up, the last word was written in the treason proceedings that had been initiated almost four years before. President Davis had never been brought to trial because of legal difficulties that Chief Justice Chase saw in the way of the prosecution. The technical ground on which proceedings were halted was that Mr. Davis had been punished already under the Fourteenth Amendment to the Constitution, which barred him from office, and that he could not be tried again for any act of war against the United States during the struggle with the South. This contention was embodied in a motion to quash the indictment, and on this the court divided. Chase was for sustaining the motion, Underwood was for denying it. On December 5, 1868, the division of the judges was certified to the Supreme Court of the United States. The general amnesty proclamation of December 25 followed in less than three weeks and of course operated to stop the prosecution of any former Confederate for treason.[23] On February 15, 1869, the indictments against General Lee, Rooney, Custis, and Fitz Lee, fourteen other general officers of the Confederacy, and nineteen other persons, were nolle prossed.[24]

Coming after the general amnesty proclamation, this formal dismissal of the indictments passed almost unnoticed. There is no reference to it, or to the December amnesty proclamation, in General Lee's correspondence. The outcome of the proceedings did not lead him to change in any respect the rule he had imposed upon himself to refrain from the public discussion of questions apt to arouse political or sectional antagonisms. Nor did the amnesty proclamation in a material way change Lee's status, though he could no longer be accounted a paroled prisoner

---

[22] *R. E. Lee, Jr.*, 333.

[23] 6 Richardson's *Messages and Papers of the Presidents*, 708.

[24] *MS. Records U. S. Circuit Court*, Richmond, Va. For the establishment of the facts regarding the indictment of General Lee and the *nolle pros.*, the late Jos. P. Brady, clerk of the United States Court for the Eastern District of Virginia, was due the writer's warmest thanks.

of war. In one respect the adoption of the Fourteenth Amendment offset the amnesty in that it barred him from state or Federal office of any sort. As a soldier, he had taken oath to support the Constitution, and, consequently, under the third paragraph of the new amendment, a two-thirds vote of Congress would be required to restore to him the right to hold office. When the new constitution of the state was ratified and the test-oath was eliminated[25] he could have qualified to vote, but he did not do so. He did not die disfranchised, in the strict sense of the word, nor as a paroled prisoner of war, often as this has been asserted, but he did end his days disbarred from office.

The only effect of the amnesty proclamation on Lee was to make it possible for him to undertake the recovery of property seized at Arlington. The silver, as already noted, had been sent to Lexington and, after it had been dug up and cleaned, was in daily use. Through the efforts of Mrs. Britannia Kennon, virtually all the portraits at the Custis mansion had been removed to Tudor Place, Georgetown, and after the war had been forwarded. The boat carrying them was sunk in the canal below Lexington, but when it was raised the pictures were salvaged and were restored so skillfully in Baltimore that they seemed undamaged.[26]

But the Washington relics had been left at Arlington in 1861. Some of them were stolen and carried away by individuals, as were the small personal belongings of the Lees, found in the house by marauding Federal soldiers. When General McDowell took over Arlington as a Federal post, the servant in charge told him of the depredations that had occurred. To save the remaining effects of Washington from theft and to safeguard them for Mrs. Lee, General McDowell removed them across the Potomac to the Department of the Interior. Placed on exhibit at the Patent Office, with the legend "Captured at Arlington," they constituted a rather pitiful display—a pair of candelabra, part of a set of china that Lafayette had given Mrs. Washington, a punch bowl, a looking-glass, a washstand, a "dressing bureau," a few of

---

[25] See *infra*, pp. 414–15.

[26] *R. E. Lee, Jr.*, 190, 354. Mrs. Rufus King had also been active in trying to preserve some of Mrs. Lee's belongings (5 *Wisconsin Magazine of History*, 371–72).

Washington's tent poles and pins, a little of his bed clothing and a pair of his breeches, with a waistcoat—nothing that had any value apart from its association with the first President.

In the winter of 1868–69, Captain James May, of Illinois, a long-time friend of the Lees, saw the relics, thought they should be returned, and consulted some of his friends in the administration. All of them agreed that it was proper to restore the articles to Mrs. Lee. The President had power to take this action, under existing law, and was sounded out. Although he declined to commit himself until the matter came before him in some definite form, Captain May was satisfied Johnson would not withhold his consent. Captain May accordingly wrote Mrs. Lee on February 9, 1869, suggesting that she apply for the relics. Mrs. Lee of course sought the counsel of the General, and he, knowing her natural interest in the property, and believing that the return could be arranged without contention, approved of her proceeding as Captain May suggested. So she addressed a brief application to the President on February 10, under cover to Captain May.[27] He delivered it to Secretary O. H. Browning of the Department of the Interior, who brought it to the President's attention at a cabinet meeting. The chief executive and all his advisers were unanimously for complying with Mrs. Lee's request, and the Secretary of the Interior was authorized to deliver the goods to Mrs. Lee upon proper identification. Mr. Browning communicated promptly with Lee, under date of February 24, whereupon the General replied that Mrs. Lee had designated Mrs. Beverly Kennon to identify the articles and to receipt for them.[28] Browning was a native Kentuckian, though a staunch Republican and a resident of Illinois, and in antebellum days he had known the Lees. His part in facilitating the return of Mrs. Lee's property was personal and friendly.

As there was no effort at concealment, the news of the prospective restoration of the relics was printed on February 26, 1869, in *The Washington Evening Express*. Unfortunately, it was erroneously stated that General Lee had made the application, that the relics had been taken from "the Arlington House, Gen-

[27] Mrs. Lee to President Johnson, *MS.*, Feb. 10, 1869; *MS. Dept. Interior*, P. and M. File, Box 144.
[28] R. E. Lee to O. H. Browning, *MS.*, Feb. 26, 1869; *Lee's MS. Letter Book*.

eral Lee's estate," and that they were to be placed in the hands of some person deputized by the General to receive them.

On the basis of this publication, General John A. Logan, of Illinois, introduced into the United States House of Representatives on March 1, 1869, a resolution calling on the committee on public buildings and grounds to ascertain "by what right the Secretary of the Interior surrenders these articles so cherished as once the property of the Father of his Country to the rebel general-in-chief." Pending inquiry and report, the Secretary of the Interior was requested not to permit the delivery of the property.[29] The Radicals who controlled the House permitted no debate on the resolution, but rushed it through at once.

The committee held a hurried hearing, with Captain May and Secretary Browning as the principal witnesses.[30] On March 3, a few hours before the Congress adjourned *sine die,* the committee reported a resolution that the Washington relics were the property of the United States and that any attempt on the part of the administration "to deliver the same to the rebel General Robert E. Lee is an insult to the loyal people of the United States." The articles should remain in the Patent Office, the resolution concluded, and should not be delivered to any one without the consent of Congress.[31]

Thomas L. Jones of Kentucky offered a minority report, asserting that the articles were the property of Mrs. Lee, and that as they had been taken from Arlington without authority of the United States, and were of little value except as family heirlooms, they should be returned to her. Jones's attempt to discuss his recommendation was cut off by a call for the previous question. His resolution was then voted down: ayes, 34; nays, 92; not voting, 96. The majority resolution was thereupon passed, and the Kentuckian could do no more than print his remarks in the appendix to *The Congressional Globe.*[32]

General Lee must have felt keenly this action by Congress, but

[29] *Congressional Globe,* 3d Session, 40th Congress, March 1, 1869, pp. 1742–43.
[30] R. E. Lee to Captain May, March 12, 1869; *Mason,* 342.
[31] *Globe,* as above, p. 1895.
[32] *Globe,* as above, pp. 1895–96; Jones's undelivered address (*ibid.,* Appendix, 295–97) is the chief source of information about the proceedings. Mr. Jones tried to make it plain that Lee himself was not involved. "That distinguished and noble gentleman and hero," he boldly wrote, "has had nothing whatever to do with this transaction, but, in regard to it has maintained the delicacy and dignity which have characterized him

his observations upon it were brief. "[The relics] were valuable to [Mrs. Lee]," he wrote, "as having belonged to her great-grandmother,[33] and having been bequeathed to her by her father. But as the country desires them, she must give them up. I hope their presence at the capital will keep in the remembrance of all Americans the principles and virtues of Washington."[34] In a letter of thanks to Jones he said: "It may be a question with some whether the retention of these articles is more 'an insult,' in the language of the Committee on Public Buildings, 'to the loyal people of the United States' than their restoration; but of this I am willing that they should be the judge, and since Congress has decided to keep them, [Mrs. Lee] must submit."[35] He was even more philosophical about the property that had been carried away from Arlington by private persons. "From what I have learned," said he, "a great many things formerly belonging to General Washington . . . in the shape of books, furniture, camp equipage, etc., were carried away by individuals and are now scattered over the land. I hope the possessors appreciate them and may imitate the example of their original owners, whose conduct must at times be brought to their recollection by these silent monitors. In this way, they will accomplish good to the country."[36]

A more serious matter occupying General Lee's attention that winter was the settlement of the Custis estate, of which he was still active executor. It will be remembered that Lee had liberated the slaves of his father-in-law during the winter of 1862–63, when, despite the demands of the aftermath of the Fredericksburg campaign, he had found time to check the list of Negroes and to have the deed of manumission recorded in the Hustings Court of the City of Richmond.[37] The other requirements of the

through life, and which now especially challenge the admiration of every unprejudiced and manly heart. These articles were the property of Mrs. Lee, and hers only, for her natural life. . . ." The writer is much indebted to Enoch A. Chase of Washington for information regarding the effort of the Lees to recover Arlington and its relics.

[33] Mrs. General Washington.

[34] R. E. Lee to Geo. W. Jones, n.d.; *R. E. Lee, Jr.,* 337.

[35] R. E. Lee to T. L. Jones, March 29, 1869; *R E. Lee, Jr.,* 338.

[36] *R. E. Lee, Jr.,* 337; *cf. Jones,* 220.

[37] *R. E. Lee, Jr.,* 89–90. See also R. E. Lee to Amanda Parks, March 9, 1866; *Jones,* 404. The original deed, from the records of the Hustings Court of Richmond, is now in the Confederate Museum, Richmond. It was acknowledged before Benj. S. Cason, J. P. of Spotsylvania County, Va., Dec. 29, 1862, and was recorded in Richmond, Jan. 2, 1863.

will General Lee had not been able to carry out. Arlington, which had been sold for delinquent taxes on January 11, 1864, was now the property of the United States and had been set aside as a soldiers' cemetery. The price paid was $26,860,[38] but the money was merely transferred from one government account to another. The "Four-Mile" tract had similarly passed out of the hands of the family. At the end of the war, General Lee had been of opinion that Smith's Island had shared the fate of Arlington and the "Four-Mile" property.[39] He therefore considered that the only realty left to the estate was Romancoke,[40] which Mr. Custis had left to Robert, and the White House, which had been bequeathed to Rooney. Each of these farms contained 4000 acres and, it will be recalled, had been given subject to the condition that if the sale of certain other real estate and the labor of the slaves did not yield enough to pay the legacies to the granddaughters, these two farms were to be worked and part of the proceeds set aside until the full amount of $40,000 had been realized.

It was an odd situation. Two of the sons were in possession of their full share of the estate, thanks to the fact that the land left them had been within the Confederate lines, but Custis had been deprived of virtually the whole of his prospective inheritance by the tax sales, and the daughters, it then appeared, had no prospect of receiving the cash bequests their grandfather had devised for them.

General Lee's first impulse after the war had been to wait, trusting that his civil rights would be restored and that he could proceed to clear the estate, though, meantime, he asked a friendly attorney to investigate the case.[41] As the prospect of a pardon faded out, he still hoped that he might redeem Arlington, which he assumed the government had sold in the belief that the estate was his. "I should have thought," he told a Northern friend,

[38] Decker and McSween: *Historic Arlington*, 79–84. R. E. Lee to W. H. Hope, April 3, 1866; *Jones*, 247. Decker and McSween put the price at $26,100.

[39] R. E. Lee to Reverdy Johnson, Jan. 27, 1866; *Jones*, 211; Moore: *The Family Life of Washington*, 190.

[40] After the war, in the Lee correspondence, *Romancock* became *Romancoke*.

[41] Letter to Reverdy Johnson, *loc. cit.;* Lee to Francis S. Smith, *MS.,* April 5, 1866, for a copy of which the writer wishes to acknowlege the kindness of Mrs. Thomas P. Bryan of Richmond.

"that the use of the grounds, the large amount of wood on the place, the teams, etc., and the sale of the furniture of the house, would have been sufficient to have paid the taxes. I do not know whether the Secretary of War would relinquish possession of the estate, or permit its redemption under the Virginia laws. If he did, and should require $26,860 stated to have been bid for it by the United States, to be refunded, it would be out of my power to redeem it." [42] In the circumstances, Lee could do nothing to prevent the award to the government of a tax-sale title, which was allowed on September 26, 1866. [43]

That same year General Lee told Robert to regard Romancoke as his own, subject to such a charge as might be necessary to make up the bequests to the Misses Lee. The General felt that deduction in the amount of these gifts should be made in view of the shrinkage of the estate. [44] A similar understanding doubtless was reached with Rooney.

Lee had strong attachment to the soil, and though he did not complain because the misfortunes of war had fallen heavily on his wife and children, he had lasting interest in the old family properties and a deep love for them. In April, 1866, some one in New York had tried to sell him a painting of the White House as it had been before the Federals burned it. Lee replied that he was unable to purchase works of art. He added: "The White House of Pamunkey, as it lives in my memory, must suffice for my purposes." [45] To a woman who sent him photographs of a painting of Stratford, he wrote: "Your picture vividly recalls scenes of my earliest recollection and happiest days. Though unseen for years, every feature of the house is familiar to me." [46]

Cherishing these feelings, he was only deterred from an active effort to recover Arlington by his failure to find any practical means of attaining his result, though there was a general feeling in the spring of 1868 that the property would be returned. [47] In January, 1869, J. S. Black of Washington, a lawyer and publicist of high position, volunteered his services in proceedings for the

[42] R. E. Lee to W. H. Hope, April 5, 1866; *Jones*, 246.
[43] Decker and McSween, *op. cit.*, 79–84.
[44] R. E. Lee to R. E. Lee, Jr., May 26, 1866; *R. E. Lee, Jr.*, 236.
[45] R. E. Lee to unnamed correspondent, April 17, 1866; *Jones*, 249.
[46] R. E. Lee to Miss Mattie Ward, May 28, 1866; *Jones*, 364.
[47] 1 *Macrae*, 225.

restoration of the former Custis property. The case demanded abilities as distinguished as those of Black, because in addition to the involvements of the tax sale, there were prospective complications owing to the fact that Custis Lee had not taken, and did not propose to take, his grandfather's "name and arms," as required under the Custis will.

Lee acknowledged and accepted Mr. Black's offer with a hearty "I thank you." He explained that he had no personal property interest in Arlington and that his desire simply was to turn it over to the rightful heir. "I have not as yet taken any steps in the matter," he wrote Black, "under the belief that I could accomplish no good, nor do I wish to do so, unless in your opinion some benefit would result from it."[48] He was willing to go to law for Mrs. Lee's and Custis's sake, but he did not wish to enter into litigation that would arouse dark passions, to no good purpose.

Meantime, it was discovered that though Smith's Island had been sold for delinquent taxes on June 15, 1864,[49] it could be recovered under Virginia law. Action was accordingly instituted, and on April 23, 1868, the court returned the property to the Custis estate.[50] Rooney became interested in this land, which the General was anxious to make productive for the estate. The place contained 4038 acres, was in the Atlantic, off Cape Charles, and had never appeared to Lee to be so valuable as Mr. Custis had thought it was.[51] Lee now suggested that Rooney and Robert visit the island and devise some plan for its use or disposition. Whatever they recommended, he would approve. They might find it desirable, he said, to buy the freehold themselves.[52] Rooney went there and found that except for the small government reservation and lighthouse, the property had been much neglected and misused. Wild cattle were roving over it, and its value was declining. Good business dictated that unless a better

---

[48] R. E. Lee to J. S. Black, Jan. 13, 1869; *Jones,* 229–30.

[49] R. E. Lee to Francis S. Smith, *MS.,* Nov. 2, 1867, a copy of which was given the writer by Mrs. Thomas P. Bryan of Richmond.

[50] *Chancery Order Book* No. 2, pp. 70 and 127; Northampton County court; *Abstract of title to Smith's Island,* prepared for the Lawyers' Title Ins. Co. by Reuben J. Martin, for use of which the writer is indebted to Judge T. C. Fletcher.

[51] When Lee had been at Old Point in 1832, he had visited Smith's Island and had reported on it to Mr. Custis (Lee to Custis, *MS.,* May 22, 1832; *Duke Univ. MSS.*).

[52] R. E. Lee to W. H. F. Lee, Aug. 14, 1868; *R. E. Lee, Jr.,* 323.

offer could be had, the two sons should take the island in hand and should make what they could from it. "I should like this whole matter arranged as soon as possible," the General concluded, "for my life is very uncertain, and its settlement now may avoid future difficulties." [53] A friendly agent, Hamilton S. Neale, accordingly advertised the property, and on December 22, 1868, receiving no higher bid, sold it for $9000 to W. H. F. and R. E. Lee, Jr.[54] The General took the note of his sons for the principal, payable without interest in thirteen years.[55] From his own funds he took an equivalent amount and transferred it to his daughters, as part of the legacy due from their grandfather's estate. This was invested for them in railroad bonds.[56] To raise the money with which to pay the Misses Lee he evidently had to sell a sizeable block of securities, for soon after making the settlement he reinvested something more than $8000 of his own funds.[57] The net result of the sale of the island to his sons was that the daughters received a third of their legacy, the boys got the island and the General lost the interest on $9000.[58]

With the sale of Smith's Island, General Lee had proceeded as far as he could in settlement of the estate.[59] Nothing more

[53] R. E. Lee to W. H. F. Lee, Sept. 28, 1868; *R. E. Lee, Jr.,* 326–27.

[54] This is the date mentioned in R. E. Lee to W. H. F. Lee, Oct. 19, 1868; *R. E. Lee, Jr.,* 328. The price is given in *Northampton Co. Deed Book* No. 37, p. 689. For this and other references to Smith's Island, the author is indebted, through Senator G. Walter Mapp, to George T. Tyson, clerk of Northampton County. Although the agent declined to accept the full commissions, the cost of the sale and transfer was $950 (R. E. Lee to Hamilton S. Neal[e], *MS.,* Feb. 9, 1869; *Lee's MS. Letter Book;* same to same, *MS.,* Feb. 23, 1869, *ibid.*).

[55] This note appears among the assets listed in the appraisal of General Lee's will, Nov. 7, 1870; *Will Book* 19, p. 361, *Rockbridge Co. (Va.) Court Records. Cf. R. E. Lee, Jr.,* 378.

[56] R. E. Lee to R. H. Maury, *MS.,* Feb. 19, 1869; *Lee's MS. Letter Book.*

[57] R. E. Lee to R. H. Maury, *MS.,* Feb. 27, 1869; *Lee's MS. Letter Book.*

[58] *Cf.* R. E. Lee to Walter H. Taylor, Dec. 2, 1869; *Taylor's General Lee,* 312: "Smith's Island has been bought by my sons Fitzhugh and Robert. They will sell it, but I do not know whether they will lease it."

[59] Owing to the commendable reticence of the Lees in all that concerned their financial affairs, the sale of Smith's Island and the subsequent settlements constitute a chapter that presents many difficulties. The following is believed to be an accurate summary of what happened but it is subject to correction: After General Lee's death, Mrs. Lee and the other heirs made a friendly agreement with Robert and Rooney by which Smith's Island was conveyed to them in fee (Nov. 30, 1871; Jan. 15, 1872; *Deed Book* 37, p. 689; *Northampton Co. Court Records*). In return, the two sons waived their part of their father's estate (*Will of Mary Custis Lee, Rockbridge County Will Book* 21, p. 179), so that the legacies due the daughters might be paid and White House and Romancoke relieved of the lien put on them under that part of Mr. Custis's will which made the bequests for his granddaughters a charge on those two estates and on Smith's Island. Nine thousand dollars was much less than the value of Smith's Island. Consequently, when Mrs. Lee died and the note of Rooney and Robert became part of the joint assets of the

could be done about Arlington or about the "Four-Mile tract," though, as late as the summer of 1870, hopes were maintained and a conference with his lawyer was held by General Lee.[60]

The family, of course, had never been able to live after the beginning of the war as it had lived in the sumptuous, earlier years. Simplicity had been a virtue during the days of the Confederacy; thereafter it was a necessity. When the Confederacy fell, $20,000 of Lee's securities, about one-fourth of his estate, became worthless.[61] The family had only the interest on his other investments, which yielded not more than $3600 a year. During the months immediately after the surrender he may not have been able to collect on that basis.[62] For the first year of his presidency, living had been most spartan, with no luxuries and little travel.

Parents and children had taken their condition philosophically. They made no pretenses when they went abroad and they offered no excuses when they entertained friends at plain dinners.[63] Lee "was fond of elegance of every sort; fine houses, furniture, plate, clothing, ornaments, horses, equipage," wrote a young assistant who observed him closely during his presidency. "But he could and did deny himself and his family the enjoyment of such things when he did not have the money to buy them. I have seen him in garments which many men of smaller income and far less reputation would have been unwilling to wear. . . . He impressed these ideas and habits on his family. Mrs. Lee's usual occupation in the dining room . . . during the evenings was

estate, they reconveyed three-fifths of Smith's Island to their surviving sisters and brother, so that all of them became tenants in common (*Deed Book* 38, p. 498, *loc. cit.*). The survivors and their heirs retained the property until Nov. 1, 1911, when it was sold to Samuel Oliver Campbell of New York (*Deed Book* 66, p. 72, *loc. cit.*). He built a handsome club-house on the island and on Oct. 21, 1926, transferred it, for $90,000, to Smith's Island Corporation, Richmond, Va. (*Deed Book* 84, p. 380; *loc. cit.*). The United States Government meantime had added to its reservation on the island and had erected thereon a powerful lighthouse and a coastguard station (*Deed Book* 46, pp. 224–28, *loc. cit.*).

[60] R. E. Lee to Mrs. Lee, April 11, 1870; *R. E. Lee, Jr.,* 396; same to same, July 15, 1870; *R. E. Lee, Jr.,* 414. For the circumstances attending the payment of $150,000 to Custis Lee for Arlington by the United States in 1883, see Decker and McSween, *op. cit.,* 83–84; Memorial of G. W. C. Lee, *Sen. Doc.* 96, 1st sess., 43d Congress; U. S. *vs.* Lee, 106 *U. S.,* 196.

[61] Appraisal of estate, will of R. E. Lee, *loc. cit.*

[62] This estimate is based on the assumption that approximately $48,000 of his holdings represented pre-war investments.

[63] E. C. Gordon, in *Riley,* 95.

mending her husband's and son's underclothing. . . . I met one of his daughters at a railway station. She had a basket of very fine pears, on the beauty of which I commented. 'Yes,' she said, 'they are nice and I would offer you one; but I have just enough for my dessert tomorrow.' She then laughed and said: 'I want this inscribed on my tombstone:

> " ' "Although on pleasure she was bent,
>   She had a frugal mind." ' " [64]

After the first session at Lexington the increase in General Lee's salary from $1500 to $3000, plus his share of tuition fees, of course relieved his finances somewhat. For 1866–67 the college paid him a total of $4756,[65] but he did not change his style of living. The only difference was in his provision of more extensive summer vacations for his family. He was able, also, to offer financial help to Robert in stocking his farm and in building a new house, though he stated downrightly that the money he might lend Robert for the erection of a better residence would be taken from the sum he was putting aside for the purchase of a home for Mrs. Lee.[66] Robert declined to touch this fund.

Speaking generally, and for the whole of General Lee's life, the dollar mark was a symbol that occurred seldom in his correspondence. So large a household, with fortune so changeful, had its financial problems, of course, but it was not dominated or depressed by them. The General had a horror of debt[67] and he prudently avoided it by living within his income, however small it was. Nothing is more impressive, in the intimate annals of the family, than the absence of complaints about hard living or lack of money. They were frank in their family conversation. The General teased all his daughters.[68] Jesting among themselves of

---

[64] E. C. Gordon, in *Riley*, 95–96.

[65] *MS. Treasurer's Records*, Washington and Lee Univ., for which entry the writer is indebted to the late Dean H. D. Campbell.

[66] R. E. Lee to R. E. Lee, Jr., March 21, 1869; *R. E. Lee, Jr.*, 342.

[67] *Riley*, 95.

[68] See, as typical, *R. E. Lee, Jr.*, 193, 194, 195, 253. Custis, too, came in for a certain measure of bantering, particularly because of his continued bachelorhood. In 1869, Lee reverted to his favorite jest (see *supra*, p. 327 and vol. I, p. 136) and bespoke the daughter of Colonel Walter Taylor—a tiny tot—for Custis (R. E. Lee to W. H. Taylor, Dec. 2, 1869; *Taylor's General Lee*, 313). General Lee was glad for his sons to marry, and urged them to do so, but he was never anxious for his daughters to wed. None of them ever did.

I. Robert E Lee of the U.S. Army do make ordain
& declare this instrument to be my last will & testament
revoking all others.

1. All my debts, whatever they may be, & of which they are
but few, are to be punctually & speedily paid.

2. To my dearly beloved wife Mary Custis Lee I give &
bequeath the use profit & benefit of my whole estate reals &
personal, for the term of her natural life, in full confidence
that she will use it to the best advantage in the education &
care of my children.

3. Upon the decease of my wife it is my will & desire that
my estate be divided among my children, in such proportion
to each, as their situations & necessities in life may require,
& as may be designated by her; & I particularly request that
my second daughter Anne Carter, who from an accident she
has met in one of her eyes, may be more in want of aid than the
rest may, if necessary, be particularly provided for.

Lastly. I constitute & appoint my dearly beloved wife
Mary Custis Lee, & my eldest son George Washington Custis
Lee (when he shall have arrived at the age of twenty one years)
executrix & executor of this my last will & testament, in the
construction of which I hope & trust no dispute will arise.

Witness   In witness of which I have set my hand & seal
Fred. A. Smith this thirty first day of August in the year one thousand
Capt. Engs.   eight hundred & forty six   R E Lee   {Seal}
R Cruickshank

The will of General Lee, drawn twenty-four years before his death, while an officer in

392

Schedule of Property

100 Shares of the Stock of the Bank of Virginia — Richmond $10,000.00
39 Shares of the Stock of the Valley of Virginia, Winchester..   3,900.00
$6100 of Jas: R. & Kanawha Comp[superscript] Bonds — — — — — — —   6,100.00
$2000 Virginia 6 per ct State Bonds — — — — — — —   2,000.00
$2000 Phila Wil: & Baltimore R.R. 6 per ct Loan   2,000.
$2000 Bonds of Kentucky 6 per cts — — — — — — —   2,000.
6 per cts Bonds of the State of Ohio — — — — — — —   5,000.
Bond of John Hyde & wife — — — —   8,000.
Bonds of Workman & Rice & of Louis Vogel, St Louis Miss   4,500.
1 Share of Nat. theatre, Washington City   250
                                                                      _____
                                                                      $38,750,000

Nancy, & her Children at the White House, New Kent,
all of whom I wish liberated, so soon as it can be done to their
advantage & that of others.
An undivided third part of the tract of land in Floyd,[superscript: va] devised
to me by my Mother, of which I am negociating a Sale with Dr H.
Burwell for $2.500.
Any Share of the property in Hardy [Va] belonging to the estate of
my father.
Any Share of a claim of the property, leased to the Government
by my father at Harpers ferry, & believed to belong to his Estate
My Share, or 1/3 of 200 acres of land in Fairfax Co. Va:
                                                                    R. Lee

the United States Army, and never superseded; after the original in the records of
Rockbridge County, Virginia.

many things, they wrote one another reams about the details of marriages, visits, and journeyings, for all of them except Custis were strongly social in nature. But money was a theme they tacitly avoided.[69] The repeated business offers that came to him seem to have awakened no yearnings. Nothing appears in his correspondence to show any desire on the part of any member of the family that he accept the post of supervisor of agencies of the Knickerbocker Life Insurance Company, a position pressed on him in the winter of 1868–69 at the then dazzling salary of $10,000. Not a flutter was aroused in the president's house, so far as one may now judge, by rumors that he might be named president of the Chesapeake and Ohio Railroad.[70] When he rejected a subsequent proposal that he remove to New York and, at a large salary, represent Southern commerce[71] his girls did not even hint that life in New York would be interesting. The household was content to live modestly and to share the hardships of the time, and Lee himself was even more determined than before 1861 to save all he could. For the protection of his wife and daughters he spent no more than necessity and duty claimed of him. He was successful in his thrift and invested wisely in good securities. Never so poor a man as he was supposed to be after the war, he died worth some $88,000, not counting the $20,500 he had put into Southern war-time issues or the $4000 he had in bonds of the Chesapeake and Ohio Canal Company.[72]

[69] He did not permit himself to be imposed upon in money matters. At Longstreet's instance, in 1866, he accepted position as non-resident director of the Great Southern and Western Life, Accident and Insurance Co. Three years later, when the concern went into receivership, he was called upon to pay a stock subscription of $500 he had never made. He wrote General John B. Hood, asking him to see what should be done and authorizing him to get counsel, if need be, to represent him.

[70] *Lexington Gazette,* Nov. 18, 1868; R. E. Lee to H. J. Ferber, *MS.,* Feb. 8, 1869; *Lee's MS. Letter Book.*

[71] Reverend T. V. Moore, in *Jones,* 476.

[72] Inventory of the estate of Robert E. Lee, attached to his will, *loc. cit.*

CHAPTER XXII

The General Revisits Familiar Scenes

To only one business enterprise, during the whole of his residence in Lexington, did General Lee give his active support. That was to the Valley Railroad Company. And then he was induced to participate, not for financial benefit to himself, but because he thought the undertaking would help the college and the town.

Lexington was without railroad connection. The nearest station was Goshen, on the Chesapeake and Ohio, twenty-three miles distant, over a nightmare of a road. As an alternative, the traveller had nothing except the James River and Kanawha Canal, along which the canal boat crept for twelve hours to Lynchburg, fifty miles away. Lexington people were divided in the opinion as to which route was the worse. Once, when asked by a visitor to recommend the best way from Lexington to the outer world, Lee replied: "It makes but little difference, for whichever route you select, you will wish you had taken the other." [1] Lexington had long dreamed of a railroad up the Shenandoah Valley, and after the close of the war actively agitated it. The Baltimore and Ohio, which was interested in the possibilities of the territory, had Colonel James Randolph make a survey in 1866, from Harrisonburg, Rockingham County, southward to Salem, Roanoke County. North of Harrisonburg there already were two stretches of railroad that could easily be joined together and connected with the main line of the Baltimore and Ohio. At Salem the Virginia-Tennessee, now the Norfolk and Western, would be reached. Valley people argued that the construction of a railway from Mount Jackson to Salem, southward by Harrisonburg, Staunton, and Lexington, would open a new and useful north-and-south route.

[1] R. E. Lee, Jr., 346; 1 Macrae, 220 ff.

The counties along the proposed line were willing, despite their poverty, to market $1,200,000 of securities and to subscribe the proceeds to stock of the corporation. For the purchase of a railroad bond issue, sufficient to cover the rest of the construction cost, the promoters looked hopefully to Baltimore, Md., a sympathetic city enriched by the war and linked already with the Shenandoah Valley by the ties of trade. The leaders of the enterprise arranged, at length, to appear before the business men and council of that city and to present the project formally. They appealed insistently to General Lee to accompany them. He had been suffering from a cold that had kept him indoors for a week,[2] his duties at home and at the college were heavy,[3] and he did not feel he was suited for this sort of undertaking, but he was so importuned that he thought it would appear "ill-mannered and unkind to refuse."[4] So, on April 20, 1869, he set out for Baltimore with a delegation that included most of the notables of that part of Virginia.

They reached Baltimore on the evening of April 21,[5] and were received with much cordiality. General Lee went to the home of Samuel Tagart, a friend he had met at the White Sulphur. Most of the delegates, of whom there were ten from General Lee's county alone, stopped at the Eutaw House,[6] at Fayette and Eutaw Streets. Inevitably, the visit took on something of a public nature. Aside from those who were curious to see a celebrity, numerous Lee and Custis kinsfolk resided in Baltimore, as did many friends who had been cherished since the days of his residence there in 1849–52. All of them wanted to greet the General again and many of them attended a reception given in his honor by the Tagarts. Lee was anxious, if possible, to avoid a public appearance and to escape all speech-making, and he asked if he might not be excused from attending the gathering of business men and merchants, which was to be one of the main events of the visit. His request was referred to John W. Garrett, president of the Baltimore and Ohio, whose co-operation was more essen-

---

[2] R. E. Lee to John Woodbridge, MS., April 5, 1869; Lee's MS. Letter Book; R. E. Lee to R. E. Lee, Jr., April 17, 1869; R. E. Lee, Jr., 344–45.

[3] Cf. Lee to Robert R. Carter, MS., April 7, 1869: "I can rarely leave here, so much am I occupied with my helpless wife and large college duties" (Shirley MSS.).

[4] R. E. Lee to W. H. F. Lee, April 17, 1869; R. E. Lee, Jr., 345.

[5] Baltimore American, April 22, 1869.   [6] Baltimore Sun, April 23, 1869.

tial to the success of the enterprise than that of any one else. Mr. Garrett, doubtless realizing that Lee's presence would attract many who would not come otherwise, urged that the General be at the meeting.

On the morning of April 22 the delegation organized by electing General Lee chairman. The mayor and councilmen were introduced, and arrangements were made for two gatherings the next day. Shortly after noon on the 23d, the General went to the Corn and Flour Exchange. Another Virginia delegation, which was urging an extension of the Alexandria, Orange and Virginia road southward from Lynchburg to Danville, was due a hearing that day, also, and had arrived before the spokesman for the Shenandoah. When Lee entered with Albert Schumacker and the members of the reception committee, he was welcomed with handclapping and cheers and was given a seat facing the president's chair. The meeting was duly opened, the visitors were assured a friendly hearing, and General Lee was called upon. But he did not make a speech. Instead, he simply announced that Colonel M. G. Harmon, president of the Valley Railroad, would address the meeting in behalf of that line. Colonel Harmon spoke, the merchants voted a resolution of endorsement, the other committee was heard, its appeal to the city council was similarly approved, and the meeting adjourned. The Baltimore hosts, regardless of their political view, greeted Lee and the Virginians with much cordiality and escorted the General from the room.[7] Just eight years before, on that very day, and almost at that very hour, Lee had been ushered out of another crowded hall, in the excited city of Richmond, where he had been given command of the Virginia forces.

That afternoon at 4 o'clock the delegation appeared before the city council, convened for the purpose in the Western Female High School, on Fayette Street, between Paca and Green. Admission was by card, but the building was jammed with an interested audience, of whom a fourth were women. Before this assemblage General Lee had to endure the ordeal of a laudatory

---

[7] *Baltimore Sun* and *Baltimore American*, April 24, 1869. For these references to *The Baltimore Sun* and for other information regarding General Lee's visit to Baltimore, the author is indebted to Doctor Milton Offutt of Johns Hopkins University. See also *Baltimore Gazette*, quoted in *Richmond Dispatch*, April 26, 1869.

introduction—an ordeal he always faced without moving a muscle or showing the least touch of emotion, though inwardly he writhed. When the eulogium was ended, the General read a memorial which he had prepared with care before he left Lexington.[8] If the reading was to be accounted a speech, it was much the longest General Lee ever made.

The formal presentation of this paper being the only business before the meeting, the councilman who had introduced the General obligingly announced that opportunity would be given for the ladies to meet him by crossing the platform on which he stood. Then began a gruelling half-hour, the worst, no doubt, that Lee had passed since Appomattox itself. He shook hands with each of the ladies cordially, but he had to listen to all their compliments, and by many of them he was saluted with a kiss. Fond as he was of the company of women, he would have preferred not to meet them in cohorts. The end of the line was reached at last, however, and Mayor Banks escorted Lee to the street, where another throng greeted him with high huzzahs.[9]

Cheers did not build railroads. "The delegates have had a pleasant time in Baltimore," said the hostile *American,* "and will probably go away with plenty of fair promises, of which those made upon the part of the Council are not likely to be fulfilled; certainly not until the banks cease to protest the notes of the city, and it has some money in its treasury." [10] A later article in the same paper was even more critical: "The affair was a very successful one if regarded simply as an ovation in honor of General Robert E. Lee, but as a business operation it has been a conspicuous failure. The General of the late 'so-called' Southern Confederacy has been feted and smiled upon, and banqueted, toasted, and hurrahed over to an extent that would have satisfied even Andrew Johnson, and as Mr. Lee has a reputation for personal modesty, must have greatly disgusted him. In fact the whole demonstration was in every particular feature a social and

[8] Text in Appendix IV—5. The original is in *Lee's MS. Letter Book,* undated, but follows a letter of April 5, 1869.

[9] *Baltimore Sun,* April 24, 1869. *The Gazette* is quoted in *The Richmond Dispatch* of April 26, 1869, as stating that these ceremonies occurred at the Corn Exchange, but this may have been due to misreading on the part of the man who clipped the item. The account in *The Sun* doubtless is correct.

[10] *Baltimore American,* April 24, 1869.

political rather than a business operation. There were crowds everywhere, but they were sympathizers with the Chief of the late rebellion, and not subscribers to Virginia railroads; they bestowed cheers liberally, but will button their pockets tightly when the demand for actual aid is made." The paper went on to argue that Baltimore was not financially in condition to subscribe, and that if she were, Virginia as yet gave no assurance that the investment would be secure.[11]

General Lee remained in Baltimore a few days after the hearing in order to attend the further meetings of the Virginia committee.[12] Besides, there were friends whom he wished to see and, in addition, a particular mission he had to perform: he wanted to purchase Mrs. Lee a small carriage, in which she could be placed easily and driven comfortably. He found what he desired and wrote her of it with manifest pleasure.[13] On Sunday, April 25, he went with his host to Saint Paul's Episcopal Church, on the corner of Saint Paul and Saratoga Streets. Word of his presence in the church spread about that part of the town and brought a great crowd to the door. When he left the building, at the close of the service, all hats were off and he had to walk for a long distance between lines of sympathizing people.[14] On Wednesday, April 28, he journeyed out to the country place of his cousin, Mrs. Samuel George, near Ellicott City. Thence he went for a short visit at the nearby home of Washington Peter, a first cousin of Mrs. Lee's and also his own intimate friend.

Before he left for this visit, Reverend John Leyburn called and, in the name of Cyrus H. McCormick, invited Lee to New York to see the inventor. Doctor Leyburn pointed out the advantages to the college from a closer relationship with Mr. McCormick and argued so persuasively that though Lee was anxious to return to Lexington, he agreed to defer a decision until he had been to see Mr. Peter. When the General reached Baltimore again, Doctor Leyburn called to hear his decision. Lee told him that he was grateful for Mr. McCormick's invitation but could not then attempt the journey.

---

11 *Baltimore American*, April 26, 1869, p. 1.
12 *Baltimore Sun*, April 27 and April 28, 1869.
13 R. E. Lee to Mrs. Lee, April 27, 1869; *R. E. Lee, Jr.*, 348.
14 *R. E. Lee, Jr.*, 347.

"I think I see, General," said Leyburn, "that the real difficulty lies in your shrinking from the conspicuity of a visit to New York. I can readily understand that this would be unpleasant. But you need not be exposed to any publicity whatever; my friend has given me *carte blanche* to make all arrangements for your coming. I will engage a compartment in the palace-car of the night train, and will telegraph my friend to meet you with his carriage on your arrival in New York."

Lee replied quickly and with deep feeling: "Oh, Doctor, I couldn't go sneaking into New York in that way. When I go there, I'll go in daylight, and go like a man."

Leyburn, of course, had no answer to this and accepted Lee's refusal as final. But the interview did not end here. The minister was a very interesting man, a very able one, a native of Lexington, long a pastor in the North. He had gone South during the war and after its close had moved to Baltimore, where he had charge of an independent Presbyterian church. Feeling that Leyburn could be trusted and might be able to help the South, Lee continued the conversation and described some of the conditions in the South. He told how the Confederate states had lost much of their best blood. The North had sent some of its finest youths to the front, but had been able to draw so heavily from the immigrant population and from the slums of the city that its losses had not been proportionately so great.

Then the conversation turned to the attitude of the Northern press. Lee expressed his regret that Northern newspapers continued to assert that the object of the war had been to perpetuate slavery. "On this point," wrote Doctor Leyburn in a subsequent report of the interview, "he seemed not only indignant but hurt. He said it was not true. He declared that, for himself, he had emancipated most of his slaves years before the war, and had sent to Liberia those that were willing to go; that the latter were writing back most affectionate letters to him, some of which he received through the lines during the war. He said, also, as an evidence that the colored people did not consider him hostile to their race, that during this visit to Baltimore some of them who had known him when he was stationed there had come up in the most affectionate manner and put their hands into the carriage window to shake hands with him. They would hardly have received him in this way, he thought, had they looked upon him as fresh from a war intended for their oppression and injury."

"So far," said Lee, "from engaging in a war to perpetuate slavery, I am rejoiced that slavery is abolished. I believe it will be greatly for the interests of the South. So fully am I satisfied of this, as regards Virginia especially, that I would cheerfully have lost all I have lost by the war, and have suffered all I have suffered, to have this object attained."

Again he spoke of the misrepresentation of the South by Northern writers, and said, "Doctor, I think some of you gentlemen that use the pen should see that justice is done us." The conversation was ended only when Rooney Lee, who had just arrived in Baltimore, entered the room.[15]

Lee's pleasant stay in Baltimore came to a close on May 1, when he travelled with Mr. and Mrs. Tagart to Washington in order to pay his respects to President Grant. This was done on suggestion from the White House. It had been proposed to Lee the previous winter that he invite General Grant to Lexington—doubtless because a visit from the President-elect and a meeting between the two adversaries would win favorable publicity for the college. General Lee had declined. "I should be very glad if General Grant would visit Washington College, when I would endeavor to treat him with the courtesy and respect due the President of the United States. But if I were to invite him to do so, it might not be agreeable to him, and I fear, at this time, my motives might be misunderstood, both by himself and others, and that evil would result, instead of good. I will, however, bear your suggestion in mind, and, should a favorable opportunity offer, will be glad to take advantage of it."[16] Now that he knew Grant desired to see him, he went without any questionings, and without any loss of equanimity. He had no apologies to make and he felt no embarrassment in meeting again the man to whom he had surrendered. Appomattox had put no stigma on his soul. "We failed," he wrote an old friend, not long before he called

[15] John Leyburn in 30 *Century*, 166–67. Doctor Leyburn wrote in 1885, sixteen years after the interview, but as he gave all the circumstances of General Lee's visit with absolute accuracy, there is no reason to doubt his direct quotations.

[16] R. E. Lee to unnamed correspondent, Jan. 8, 1869; *Jones*, 270.

on Grant, "we failed, but in the good providence of God apparent failure often proves a blessing." [17]

It was in this spirit, accompanied by Mr. and Mrs. Tagart, that he drove to the White House about 11 o'clock, and modestly introduced himself to Robert M. Douglas, Grant's secretary. John Lothrop Motley, the historian and diplomatist, was closeted with the President at the time, but he retired immediately. Grant and Lee shook hands and Grant presented his young secretary, who was a son of Stephen A. Douglas. The meeting was unceremonious and in keeping with the character of the two men, but Douglas saw it revived memories that saddened both of them.

Word of the expected call had leaked out, and rumor had it that the two were to discuss the policy the government was following in the South.[18] This was a wrong impression, of course, but as there exists no full account of the interview by an eyewitness or participant, the exact range of the conversation can only be surmised. It probably consisted only of a brief social exchange, with casual reference to the reasons for Lee's visit to Baltimore.[19] In fifteen minutes the two shook hands again and Lee left, to meet Grant no more. Bidding farewell to the friendly Tagarts, the General went to the home of Mrs. Britannia Kennon on Georgetown Heights.[20] He dined once with Mrs. Podestad, a kinswoman, wife of the secretary of the Spanish legation, and spent Sunday quietly with Mrs. Kennon.[21]

On Monday, May 3, or Tuesday, May 4,[22] the General went by

[17] R. E. Lee to Geo. W. Jones, March 22, 1869; *Jones*, 273–74. The "failure" in the context, was in "our struggle for States rights and constitutional government." He used somewhat the same phrase, in a letter of March 26, 1869, when he expressed sympathy with a man in Wyoming whose son fell fighting under Stuart "in the struggle of the Southern States for the right of constitutional government" (*Jones*, 275. *Cf*. R. E. Lee to C. W. Law, Sept. 27, 1866, *Jones*, 220, ". . . The justice of that cause, constitutional government." *Cf*. also R. E. Lee to C. F. Lee, June, 1870: ". . . their defence of the rights which they believed were guaranteed by the constitution," Page's *Robert E. Lee, Man and Soldier*, 668).

[18] *National Intelligencer*, April 29, 1869.

[19] For the various accounts of this interview, see Appendix IV—6.

[20] *National Intelligencer*, May 3, 1869; *Alexandria Gazette*, May 4, 1869. The latter paper noted that Mrs. Kennon's husband had been killed in the explosion on the *Princeton*. An excellent sketch of Mrs. Kennon is given in Moore: *The Family Life of Washington*.

[21] R. E. Lee, Jr., 349; *Alexandria Gazette, loc. cit.*

[22] *National Intelligencer* of May 3 said he would leave that day. On May 5 it said he had left on May 4. The more probable date is May 3.

steamer from Washington to Alexandria. He had passed through the city of his boyhood days on several occasions after the war, but he had never set foot on her streets from the time he left for Richmond in 1861 until he came ashore that day at the boat landing, on his homeward journey from Baltimore, and started to walk to the town house of Mrs. A. M. Fitzhugh of Ravensworth, widow of Mrs. Lee's maternal uncle. Recognized and warmly greeted as he went along, he found at Mrs. Fitzhugh's his sister-in-law, Mrs. Sydney Smith Lee, and his nephew Fitz, of the cavalry. His brother Sydney soon came up from his farm on the Potomac to meet him. It was the first time they had been together since they had left Richmond after the close of the war.[23]

Then followed three happy days. General Lee loved Alexandria. "There is no community," he said, "to which my affections more strongly cling than that of Alexandria, composed of my earliest and oldest friends, my kind school-fellows, and faithful neighbors." [24] The townspeople had equal regard for him, and when they heard that he was there, they began to call on him in such numbers that they almost swamped Mrs. Fitzhugh's house, which was located on the east side of Washington Street, near the corner of Queen. It became necessary to arrange a reception at a local hotel, Green's Mansion House, on the southeast corner of Cameron and Fairfax Streets.[25] Thither General Lee went on foot—the distance was only five squares—a little before 8 o'clock, on the evening of May 4, accompanied by two or three of his old personal friends. There were no flowers, no music, no ceremony. No announcement of the reception had been published, and no invitations had been sent out. The men who had walked with him from Mrs. Fitzhugh's simply arranged for the callers to file past the General as he stood in the hotel parlor.

[23] R. E. Lee, Jr., 350, 352.
[24] R. E. Lee to General M. D. Corse, et al., March 13, 1870; Jones, 176.
[25] The Fitzhugh house no longer exists. The old building and the grounds were bought by W. F. H. Finke, who built a new residence on the corner. The building was demolished, part of the site was utilized by Mr. Finke, and part was sold to C. C. Carlin, who made it the northern portion of his lawn. Directly opposite the Fitzhugh house was the home of Benjamin Hallowell, to whom General Lee had gone to school. Green's Mansion House was operated as a hotel for many years and later as apartments. It surrounds the Carlyle House, long famous and much visited by tourists. For the identification of these sites the author is indebted to Honorable C. C. Carlin of Alexandria, Va.

M. D. Corse, an Alexandrian who had commanded one of the brigades in Pickett's division, introduced those who had never met Lee.

Half the town came to greet him. For more than two hours the line was unbroken—old people who remembered his boyhood in the city and still called him "Robert," women whom he had known in his childhood, grizzling men who had been his schoolmates, hundreds who had followed him into battle, young mothers with their infants, girls who looked adoringly into his face and put up their cheeks to be kissed, boys who shook his hand shyly but never forgot that distinction to the end of their days, people of contrary political faith, Republicans, carpet-baggers, scalawags who wished to see the "chief of rebels," even a former slave from Arlington who was overjoyed to salute his one-time master. The callers must have numbered two or three thousand, and some of them, old acquaintances, were much changed. The war had not come visibly to spread fire and to shatter houses in the kindly old town, but it had bent shoulders and saddened hearts. The shadow of empty Arlington lay over all. Still, it was sweet to hear again the "dear, remembered names," to see that courage had not vanished, and to know that hope was not dead.[26]

Wherever he went on the street there was a joyful and sometimes a dramatic or amusing meeting. When he approached a corner a fat four-year-old boy stumbled and fell at the curbstone, as he ran to the General.

"Whose little boy was coming to see me?" Lee asked of him, as he picked up the little fellow.

"I am Robert E. Lee Johnston," replied the youngster proudly.

"And this is my little godson," the General said as he kissed him.

Soon afterwards he heard a voice calling, "Marse Robert, Marse Robert." Turning, he saw an old mulatto woman hurrying to him. "I am Eugenia," she said, when she came up, "one of the Arlington slaves."

---

[26] *Alexandria Gazette*, May 5, 1869. "It was more like a family meeting than anything else," this paper commented, "for we regard General Lee as one of our Alexandria boys. . . . We have never seen a more lovely exhibition of the grateful and unbought homage of the heart to worth and high character than was exhibited last evening."

Lee shook hands warmly. "I wonder if you would not like to have my picture, Eugenia?" he asked when they had talked for a few minutes.

" 'Deed I would, Marse Robert," she answered—and in due time received it by mail.[27]

Lee spent a night and part of a day at Mrs. Fitzhugh's and had a meeting with the venerable John Janney, who had presided over the Virginia convention when Lee had been made commander of the Virginia forces. These and other activities in the town were followed by a visit to the General's cousin, Cassius F. Lee, on Seminary Hill. He remained there for a night, called on Bishop Johns the next day and saw General Samuel Cooper again—a tragic figure now, an aristocrat in every impulse, brought down in fortune by the losses of the war. That evening, May 6, being Ascension Day, General Lee attended service at Christ Church, accompanied by his brother, Sydney Smith Lee. It was the last time the two ever knelt together.[28] He completed a dizzy twenty-four hours with a reception at the home of J. B. Daingerfield, where he had the pleasure of seeing still again some of his oldest personal friends. Here, as everywhere else during the Alexandria visit, the cordiality of the General's greeting was particularly remarked. He was "at home," and free of the reserve that sometimes was hard to distinguish from diffidence.[29]

The only distasteful personal incident of the visit, so far as is known, was the manner in which a reporter of *The New York Herald* dogged Lee for an interview, first in Baltimore and then in Alexandria. He finally got into the General's presence, but Lee received him standing and refused to talk. "I shall be glad to see you as a friend," he said, "but request that the visit may not be made in your professional capacity." Lee never talked to newspaper men, and, if he could avoid it, never permitted himself to be quoted in the press. He had been libelled often in the North, and in the South he had suffered many things during the war at the hands of editorial strategists.

On the morning of May 7, the General left for home by the

[27] *MS. Note* of the late Mrs. Mary G. Powell, graciously prepared for the writer, 1927.
[28] *Alexandria Gazette*, May 6, 1869; *R. E. Lee, Jr.*, 350–51.
[29] *Cf. Alexandria Gazette*, May 7, 1869.

Orange, Alexandria and Manassas Railroad, and arrived on the 8th, after an absence of eighteen days. From Staunton he brought Miss Peyton and his daughter Agnes over to Lexington with him. Had he enjoyed his visit? his family inquired. "Very much," he answered; "but they would make too much fuss over an old rebel." [30] More deliberately, he wrote Rooney: "I had, upon the whole, a pleasant visit, and was particularly glad to see again our old friends and neighbors in Alexandria and vicinity; though [I] should have preferred to enjoy their company in a more quiet way." [31] When one of his daughters protested that his hat was becoming disreputable, he replied half-grimly, half-jokingly: "You don't like this hat? Why, I have seen a whole cityful come out to admire it!" [32]

Scarcely was the General at home before he felt compelled to leave once more. The Lexington church had again named him as delegate to the council, which met that year in Fredericksburg, and though examinations were now close at hand, he did not think he should decline. [33] He doubtless made the trip down the Chesapeake and Ohio to Hanover Junction and thence up the Richmond, Fredericksburg and Potomac to Fredericksburg.

Word of his coming had spread. The brave little city turned out to do him honor. Although it was nearly midnight when his train arrived, the station was jammed, and as the moon was shining brightly, the people easily recognized the General. Instantly they raised the rebel yell as it had not been heard there since Sedgwick, in May, 1863, had been driven back across the Rappahannock.

A new barouche was in waiting to carry the General quickly to the home of his host, Major Thomas Barton. [34] Late as it was when he got there, Fredericksburg had no intention of letting his first hour in the town pass unobserved: the Veterans' Band

[30] *R. E. Lee, Jr.*, 348.
[31] R. E. Lee to W. H. F. Lee, May 11, 1869; *R. E. Lee, Jr.*, 352.
[32] *R. E. Lee, Jr.*, 348.
[33] He mistook the date and had to leave a week earlier than he had intended. He thought (*R. E. Lee, Jr.*, 353) that he had to be in Fredericksburg the first week in June, but the council actually met the last week in May.
[34] This house, V. M. Fleming informed the writer, was on the site of the present (1934) Princess Anne Hotel. The residence was built by James Maury (letter of V. M. Fleming, Dec. 14, 1927).

of the Thirtieth Virginia regiment—Corse's brigade, Pickett's division, the very name awakening echoes—turned out and serenaded him royally, before 1 o'clock. The General did not respond with a speech, after the way of politicians, but he sent out his thanks to the musicians, and Major Barton presented them with a bottle of something wherewith to console themselves for the General's silence.[35] It was noticeable that in the welcoming crowds the Negroes were as enthusiastic as Lee's own veterans.

A committee of the town's leading men called on the General the next day, when the council was due to open, and asked him if he would consent to hold a reception at the Exchange Hotel, in order that the people of the town might greet him. He declined. Having come to Fredericksburg to attend a religious meeting, he said, he did not think he should make any personal appearance. He would, he added, of course be glad to see any of his friends who called on him privately.[36] The people respected the General's wishes and allowed him to attend quietly the sessions of the council. The whole town chuckled, however, at the performance of a new settler, a Northern man, who wanted to see General Lee and had his own ideas of etiquette. He did not know General Lee's host and would not enter the Barton house unbidden, so he rode up with his wife and child and sent in a request that the General would "come out and see him." Lee left the house, walked down to the street, and greeted the trio in the vehicle.[37]

As usual, the General took no part in the debate of the council, though he was a member of the committee on the state of the church, and of the committee on clerical support.[38] He was not present at the session when the council debated the admission of delegates from a colored church, but he was understood to

[35] *Richmond Enquirer and Examiner*, May 28, 1869; *Richmond Whig*, May 31, 1869, quoting *The Fredericksburg News*.

[36] *Richmond Whig*, May 29, 1869. The committee included John L. Marye, J. Horace Lacy, J. H. Kelley, Elliott M. Braxton and others whose names were not given in the report.

[37] *Fredericksburg News*, quoted in *The Richmond Whig*, May 31, 1869. *Cf.* M. D. Conway in 17 *Magazine of American History*, 469.

[38] *Richmond Dispatch*, May 28, 1869, and information supplied, from the *Journal of the Council*, by Reverend George MacLaren Brydon, historiographer of the diocese of Virginia.

concur heartily in the decision that the representatives should be seated.[39]

From Fredericksburg, after the council ended on May 29, the General went to Richland, on the Potomac, and paid a two-day visit to his brother and intimate, Sydney Smith Lee, whom he had recently seen in Alexandria. Hurrying back, he reached Lexington late in the night of June 1 in time to attend the final examinations. He was rushing about faster than his heart would stand, but he made no complaint and, for the time, felt no ill-effects.

He returned in time for an event to which the family had long been looking forward: the new home—"the president's house," as General Lee always styled it to avoid the impression that it was his own[40]—at last, after many delays on account of the college's lack of funds, was finished and ready for occupancy.[41] Before going to Fredericksburg, the General had arranged all the details of the final cleaning and preparation.[42] On his return he had only to move in. The house had cost something more than the $15,000 originally appropriated for it.[43] A two-story building, with a wide centre hall, it was very comfortable though not architecturally impressive. Mrs. Lee's bedroom was on the first floor, so that she could go directly to the porch. Much to Lee's satisfaction, a commodious brick stable for Traveller adjoined the residence. It was gratifying, he said, to be under the same roof with his old friend.[44] Other convenient out-buildings and a small greenhouse were included. Water from a large cistern was pumped to a tank under the roof, whence it was distributed by gravity to the rooms below.

The house was occupied by General Lee for only sixteen months and a half, and, except for the sombre fact that he died there, it has fewer associations with him than is possessed by the "old president's house," the next residence on the hill. Although he manifestly was much interested in the new place, he certainly did not approve so large an outlay by the college, or any luxuries

[39] Richmond Dispatch, May 29, 1869.   [40] Jones, 177.
[41] The Lexington Gazette as long previously as Sept. 16, 1868, had reported the house completed.
[42] R. E. Lee to W. H. F. Lee, May 22, 1869; R. E. Lee, Jr., 353.
[43] Trustees' Minutes, June 24, Aug. 20, 1869.
[44] William and Mary Quarterly (new series), vol. 6, 283–84.

for himself, modest though they were. He probably had much less to do with the design and construction than has been generally supposed. His hand is most to be seen in the ample verandahs on three sides of the building, silent evidence, after sixty years, of his thought for Mrs. Lee's comfort in her invalidism.[45]

It was a place of pleasantness to the Lees. They had more space, larger convenience, and room for every member of the family. The General soon found the spot he liked best—the space in front of the large windows in the dining room, whence he could look across the campus and, in the other direction, over the fields to the mountains that always delighted his eyes.

The first impulse of the family was to share their new home with those friends whose hospitality they had not always been able to return in their first Lexington home. Invitations to their girl friends must have flowed freely from the pens of the Misses Lee. Shortly after commencement, Lee listed six young women guests, "all in the house, with others out of it." He added to Rooney, as one married man to another: The young ladies "are so much engaged with the collegiates that Custis and I see but little of them, but [Robert] could compete with the *yearlings*, which we cannot." [46]

One young friend there was whom Lee doubtless wished his daughters might entertain—the brilliant Norvell Caskie, to whom had come both happiness and sorrow, a sharp and sudden sorrow. In the late summer of 1868 her father, James H. Caskie, had died. When his affairs were settled it was discovered that he had met with ruinous losses and that his fortune, which had been large for the day, had been wiped out. Nothing was left for the invalid widow or for Norvell, the only child, who had just become engaged to A. Seddon Jones of Orange County. General Lee knew all these facts and grieved over the distress of Norvell and her mother. He rejoiced that she had found love, but he must have wondered how Norvell would fare on a lonely farm, she who had always lived in ease in a city home of rich culture. He wrote her this letter:

[45] *R. E. Lee, Jr.,* 357; *Richmond Whig,* May 31, 1869. The constructors were Messrs. Pole and Shields.

[46] R. E. Lee to W. H. F. Lee, June 30, 1869; *R. E. Lee, Jr.,* 359. The *yearlings*, it will be remembered, were the students who had not served in the army.

My dear Miss Norvell   Lexington Va: 14 Jany. 1869.

As the day of your nuptials approaches my thoughts revert to you more often & intensely, & I recall the manifold kindnesses of your dear father & Mother, & the affectionate consideration of yourself with increasing gratitude & pleasure

Your future happiness is therefore I assure you a matter of deep concern to me, & this most important event in your life one of great interest. May it prove as happy as I sincerely wish it; may the blessing of kind Heaven accompany you throughout your course on earth, & may a merciful Providence shield you from all evil, & lead you at the end to everlasting joy & peace.

Hoping that you will not forget us, but will sometimes give us the pleasure of your company   I am with true affection

Your constant friend

Miss Norvell Caskie[47]   R. E. Lee

The hospitality that Lee would gladly have shared with this fine girl was unostentatious, though occasionally he would serve wine that had somehow survived all the vicissitudes of the family since the days of "Light-Horse Harry." [48] The General himself participated in the entertainment of virtually all the guests and, his admirers observed, was able to adapt himself to any company. Even when a deaf old man called in the spring of 1869, the General was not outdone. He took a seat close to his visitor and devoted himself so patiently to conversation that the gentleman went away in high delight.[49]

If his house guests were girls, Lee always had a gentle raillery and gallant attentions for them, and if they were students from the college, he would sometimes sit for long evenings with them, when the ladies were away, and would talk of everything except the war. One frequent caller from among Lee's "boys" remembered that the General referred only once to the unhappy struggle, and then merely asked to what command the youth had belonged. The boy answered that he had enlisted in A. P. Hill's old regi-

---

[47] *Caskie MSS.* This friendship between Lee and Norvell Caskie is treated somewhat more fully in Freeman: "Lee and the Ladies," *Scribner's Magazine,* November, 1925.
[48] Joynes, in *Cent. U. S. C.,* 31.   [49] *Jones,* 236.

ment and then in the Black Horse Troop. Lee remarked that both had excellent records in the war, and changed the subject.[50] If Lee's guests were men, he gave them as much of his time as he could, looked closely after their comfort, and even blacked their boots himself when they left them at their door, thinking a servant would clean them.[51] He usually did the marketing for the household and was often to be seen with his basket on his arm. Never would he carry an umbrella on this or any other errand, even in the roughest weather. Scorn of such shelter was one mark of the soldier that he could not yield.[52]

It was in dealing with his own family that the deep affection of Lee's nature and his social graces most beautifully were displayed. "Once," wrote a former student of the college, "I was at the Lee home on the General's birthday, and was sitting with him when his son, General Custis Lee . . . entered the room. Memory of that meeting can never be effaced, the stately yet gracious greeting of the son and father, the familiar and fond aspiration that he might 'enjoy many happy returns of the day' brought tears to my eyes and brings them still." [53] Mrs. Preston, presenting the feminine point of view, recorded: "His tenderness to his children, especially his daughters, was mingled with a delicate courtesy which belonged to an older day than ours, a courtesy which recalls the *preux chevalier* of knightly times. He had a pretty way of addressing his daughters, in the presence of other people, with a prefix which would seem to belong to the age of lace ruffles and side swords. 'Where is my little Miss Mildred?' he would say on coming in from his ride or walk at dusk. 'She is my light-bearer; the house is never dark if she is in it.' " [54]

Toward Mrs. Lee his manner was always cheerful and affectionate, mingled now and then with a gentle jest or a polite dissent as her conversation justified. One day he was pacing the floor while Mrs. Lee was talking with a former student, himself an ex-soldier, on the vast difference between the ragged uniforms of the Confederates and the fine equipment of the Federals. "The

---

[50] *William and Mary Quarterly* (new series) vol. 6, 285.
[51] Mrs. Andrews: *Scraps of Paper*, 203–4.
[52] *MS. Memoirs of S. M. Yonge.*
[53] W. W. Scott in *William and Mary Quarterly* (new series) vol. 6, 285–86.
[54] *Mrs. Preston.* 286.

General . . . paused for a moment, his eyes lighting up, and at the conclusion of her remarks said, as he inclined forward with that superb grace, 'But, ah! Mistress Lee, we gave them some awful hard knocks, with all our rags.' "[55] Lee always claimed the honor of wheeling his wife into the dining room for meals, and frequently in the evening, as she sat knitting or mending, he would read aloud to her and to his daughters.[56]

His own reading was not wide during the years he was at Lexington. ". . . Having myself no library and those which were here having been scattered and broken up," as he wrote one inquirer, he could not consult even familiar books on the history of Virginia or of the American Revolution.[57] He made some researches while preparing the introduction to a new edition of his father's memoirs,[58] and he used a few printed authorities when writing his letter to Acton. In the spring of 1869 either he or some member of his family studied French history rather extensively.[59] As already noted, he read and enjoyed Worsley's translation of the Iliad, which was sent him by the author.[60] For the rest, he held principally to the two books that were his companions for more than twenty years, Holy Writ and the Protestant Episcopal prayer book. There was no pretense about his reading. Some books he did not intend to peruse and frankly said so.[61] Works on the war he purposely left alone. When David Macrae, a Scotch visitor, repeated a story that Lee and Grant had both read the proofs of a current history of the war, Lee immediately denied it for himself. He had never read a history of the war, he told Macrae, or the biography of any one engaged in it. "My own life has been written," he said, "but I have not looked into it. . . . I do not wish to awaken memories of the past." [62]

Outside his home, as in it, General Lee felt his social obligations, and without the least touch of the grand seigneur, he

[55] E. A. Moore, 219–20. [56] Jones, 402; Mrs. Preston, 276.
[57] R. E. Lee to Jeremiah Colburn, MS., April 2, 1867; Bryan MSS., placed at the writer's disposal, with characteristic courtesy, by John Stewart Bryan of Richmond, Va.
[58] See infra, p. 415.
[59] For an interesting analysis of Lee's reading at Lexington, see Riley, 157 ff.
[60] See supra, p. 260.
[61] Cf. the story (Jones, 283) of his answer to the agent who wanted him to recommend a book he had left with him. "You must excuse me, sir," said Lee, "I cannot recommend a book I have not read, and never expect to read."
[62] 1 Macrae, 220 ff. This material first appeared in The Glasgow Herald and was partially reprinted in The Savannah Daily Republican, April 9, 1870, p. 1, col. 2.

showed courtesies to virtually all those who came to Lexington. Besides calling on strangers or parents visiting their sons at college,[63] he often went to see the sick of the town, a lad with a broken leg[64] as surely as one of his own professors.[65] Regard for the ill was a part of his daily life, in the snows of winter and when the students were packing their trunks to go home.

As the session of 1868–69 closed, a wordy, angry campaign was being conducted over the new state constitution that had been drawn by a motley convention as one of the conditions of Virginia's readmission to the Union. Radicals and Negroes had controlled the convention and, after much wrangling, had drafted a document that provided universal suffrage and in almost the same clause disfranchised thousands of Confederates by paraphrasing the language of the Fourteenth Amendment to the United States Constitution. No person could vote or hold office in Virginia "who had been a senator or representative in congress, or elector of president or vice-president, or who held any office, civil or military, under the United States, or under any State, who having previously taken an oath as a member of Congress, or as an officer of the United States, or as a member of any state legislature, or as an executive or judicial officer of any State, shall have engaged in insurrection or rebellion against the same, or given aid or comfort to the enemies thereof." A three-fifths vote of the legislature was necessary to remove these disabilities. In addition, before any man could take office, the constitution stipulated that he must subscribe to a "test-oath," to the effect that he had not voluntarily aided the Confederacy or held office under it.[66]

These provisions were far milder than those the extreme radicals had originally adopted, but they would have kept from office in Virginia nearly all those best qualified to fill it. There was danger that conservative white men would vote against the constitution and thereby prolong military rule in Virginia, rather than submit to the enfranchisement of the Negroes and the disfranchisement of themselves. Fortunately, after the convention adjourned, this possibility was suggested: If Virginia would satisfy the first demand of the Radicals by granting the franchise to

[63] *Jones*, 236.
[65] Joynes, in *Cent. U. S. C.*, 22; *R. E. Lee, Jr.*, 324–25.
[64] *McDonald*, 6.
[66] *Eckenrode*, 101–2.

Negroes, might not Congress be prevailed upon to sanction a separate vote of the people on the offensive sections disfranchising Confederates and prescribing a test oath? If that were done, native white men might cast their ballots for the rest of the new constitution and assure its adoption. This would fulfill the last harsh requirement of the short-sighted Reconstruction Act. Then Virginia might be readmitted to the Union without being delivered for a generation into the hands of the Radicals and the enfranchised blacks. This proposal was duly formulated and was presented to General Grant, who regarded it favorably. Through the patient efforts of an able committee, a separate vote on the disfranchising sections of the new organic law was sanctioned by Congress and was authorized in an executive proclamation of May 14, 1869, which set July 6, 1869, as the date for the election of a governor and a legislature and for the rejection or ratification of the constitution.[67]

Was it the policy of wisdom for conservative white men to vote for the constitution, less the objectionable clauses, and thereby accept the Negro as a voter, in order to get rid of military rule? Or was it better to stand out against the enfranchisement of the Negro, and to take the chances of the termination of military rule and the restoration of statehood at a later time, in some other way?[68] The question was put to General Lee in the midst of the campaign and was answered directly: "I have great reluctance to speak on political subjects," he said, "because I am entirely withdrawn from their consideration, and therefore mistrust my own judgment. I have, however, said in conversation with friends, that, if I was entitled to vote, I should vote for the excision of the obnoxious clauses of the proposed constitution, and for the election of the most conservative eligible candidates for Congress and the legislature. I believe this course offers the best prospect for the solution of the difficulties in which the state is involved, accessible to us. I think all who can should register and vote." [69] This letter was not printed, but General Lee's opinion apparently became known and contributed to the desired

[67] *Eckenrode,* 121.
[68] Involved in the discussion, also, was the objection of conservatives to the over-elaborate and expensive plan of county government proposed in the constitution. Some thought this so bad as of itself to justify the electorate in rejecting the entire document.
[69] R. E. Lee to unnamed correspondent, June 11, 1869; *Jones,* 231.

result. The body of the constitution was ratified, and the two objectionable sections were rejected by approximately 40,000 votes. A governor of moderate views and a conservative legislature were elected.[70] On January 26, 1870, the President signed the bill re-admitting Virginia to the Union. The next day Military District No. 1 passed into the limbo of unhappy memories.

About the time the political campaign of 1869 was at its hottest, soon after General Lee returned from Fredericksburg, and on the eve of the college commencement, he completed a labor on which he had long been engaged—the editing of his father's *Memoirs of the War in the Southern Department.*

The first edition of this book, issued in 1812, had been in two well-printed volumes. In 1827, it will be remembered, a second edition, in one volume, badly printed on poor paper, had appeared. This contained some corrections and additions left in manuscript by "Light-Horse Harry" and many good notes by Major Harry Lee. In 1866 interest in the son created new interest in the sire. A third edition being demanded, Lee began to collect material for it and for a biographical sketch of his father with which he intended to preface the narrative. Charles Carter Lee, oldest living son of "Light-Horse Harry," sent copies of all the letters he had received from his father while he was at Harvard and "Light-Horse Harry" was in the West Indies.[71] William B. Reed of Pennsylvania, son of Governor Joseph Reed, gave Lee several letters written during the Revolution.[72] At that time Lee seems to have contemplated a general revision of the work and he discussed with Reed the details of a disputed chapter relating to the exploits of Sergeant Major John Champe,[73] but he soon gave up all ambitious editorial designs. That same winter he borrowed part of Marshall's *Washington* and of Sparks's *Correspondence of Washington* from the library of the Franklin Lit-

[70] *Eckenrode,* 125.
[71] C. C. Lee to R. E. Lee, July 25, 1866; *Henry Lee's Memoirs,* 56.
[72] R. E. Lee to Wm. B. Reed, Aug. 30, 1866; *Jones,* 254.
[73] Lee had some of the manuscript on his office desk one day when two of his professors began denouncing the iniquities of the Reconstruction Acts. The General turned to his papers and read a few lines of Hafiz on generosity and tolerance. He quoted the source, explained that Hafiz was a Mussulman, and asked: "Ought not we who profess to be guided by the principles of Christianity rise at least to the standard of this Mohammedan poet, and learn to forgive our enemies?" (*Jones,* 197–98). "Light-Horse Harry" Lee had quoted a very stilted translation of the original in the last letter he had written Carter (*Henry Lee's Memoirs,* 76).

erary Society,[74] and probably prepared the few unimportant references to these works that appear in the introductory sketch.[75] He had to put his task aside temporarily and seemingly he did not take it up again until the autumn of 1867, when once more he was consulting Marshall.[76] In the spring of 1869 he finished the new material for the book, though even then the concluding paragraphs show some signs of haste. The preface carries June 1, 1869, as the date of its completion. Later in the summer he was bothered by the publisher's insistence that a picture of Lee himself be inserted in the book. The General objected, but finally left the decision to Mrs. Lee, who sided with the publisher.[77] Late in 1869 the book was published, and in 1870 it was reissued. Lee's receipts from it were given his brother Carter, who had supplied most of the letters.[78]

Aside from a table of contents and descriptive headings at the beginning of each chapter, the body of the new edition received very little attention at the hands of General Lee or of any one else. "Light-Horse Harry" Lee's numerous notes to the first edition had been retained in the second, and Major Henry Lee's notes had been signed "Ed." General Lee reprinted both sets and also those that had been contributed to the second edition by Colonel Howard, but he did not explain this anywhere in the book. Shunning the controversy raised by Judge Johnson's *Greene*[79] and softening or omitting the asperities of some of the letters, he added only one note of consequence, that on Sergeant Major Champe.[80] This was not signed and might readily have been credited to "Light-Horse Harry" Lee but for the internal evidence. In one instance, a footnote from the second edition, citing an incident on another page, was republished without correcting the page number, which had been wrong when originally inserted. Instead of giving the proper page reference to the second edition, the note was based on the pagination of the first edition.[81]

74 *Riley*, 179.
75 *Henry Lee's Memoirs*, 17, 18, 38, 42, 45, etc.
76 *Riley*, 180.
77 *R. E. Lee, Jr.*, 365–66, 367.
78 *R. E. Lee, Jr.*, 398.
79 See *supra*, vol. I, p. 37.
80 *Henry Lee's Memoirs*, 411, *cf. ibid.*, 2d edition, 284.
81 *Henry Lee's Memoirs*, 292 n. The reference should be to page 284, not to p. 356. In the second edition this note occurred on p. 185, and the reference was to p. "356 ante," though the incident was given on p. 178.

The sketch of "Light-Horse Harry" Lee that preceded the text is the longest single composition from the pen of his most distinguished son. Occupying sixty-eight pages and containing nearly 34,000 words, from no point of view can it be accounted an effective piece of writing. The genealogy, which is adapted from that prepared by William Lee in 1771, is uncritical, confused, and laudatory and assumes the direct descent of the Virginia family from Launcelot Lee of London, who came to England with the Conqueror. It is very different in tone from anything General Lee ever wrote about himself. The career of Henry Lee from birth to his enlistment in the Revolutionary army is covered in some 500 words. Circumstances attending his retirement from the army are scarcely touched upon. The whole of his public service, except as it related to military appointments, is handled summarily. Not even the dates of Lee's tenure of office as governor of Virginia are put down. More than a fourth of the sketch is given over to extracts from the letters to Charles Carter Lee that overflow with preachments and pious exhortation. The picture one gets at the end does less than justice to the man and to his record. Reading the sketch, one can understand why Gamaliel Bradford, in citing another paper by Lee, admitted that it went a long way toward reconciling him to the General's failure to write a history of his campaigns.[82]

The shortcomings of this solitary venture into biography are the more remarkable in view of General Lee's conversation about his father, conversation that was most entertaining and rich in diverting anecdote. Lee's letters, it probably will be agreed, were nearly always smooth, and sometimes were written in a style that makes the reader's heart beat a trifle faster. But when he came to formal composition, most of the grace and all the spontaneity of his style disappeared. What he wrote became ponderous and dull.

Only twice in the outline of his father's life did Lee show his own feelings. In relating how his father went to Stratford a-wooing his cousin Matilda, he stopped to describe the place of his own birth, well-remembered in all its details, though he had not seen it in many years. "The approach to the house is on the south,

[82] Bradford: *Lee the American* (ed. of 1927), 151.

along the side of a lawn, several hundred acres in extent, adorned with cedars, oaks, and forest poplars. On ascending a hill not far from the gate, the traveller comes in full view of the mansion; when the road turns to the right and leads straight to a grove of sugar-maples, around which it sweeps to the house. . . ." Stratford had about it then, at the end of his life, the glamour that had hung over it when he had been packed into the carriage, with the rest of the family, and had been sent away from that paradise to Alexandria.

The other passage in which Lee the man showed himself through the work of Lee the author was in a quotation from a letter of "Light-Horse Harry" Lee's. His friend James Madison had written in 1792 to know whether Lee would consider the command that subsequently was given St. Clair, to subdue the Indians on the Miami and the Wabash. "Light-Horse Harry" had expressed willingness to go but had acknowledged regret at the prospect of leaving "my native country," as he styled Virginia. "No consideration on earth," he wrote, "could induce me to act a part, however gratifying to me, which could be construed into disregard or forgetfulness of this Commonwealth."[83] In republishing the letter General Lee italicized this sentence. Passing on to describe his father's efforts for a union of all the states, he concluded: "Although his correspondence at this time, as well as the course of his life, proves his devotion to the Federal government, yet he recognized a distinction between his 'native country' and that which he had labored to associate with it in the strictest bonds of union."[84] Like sire, like son!

Slow as was the preparation of this new edition of his father's *Memoirs,* General Lee's accumulation of material for a history of his own campaigns lagged still more.[85] In 1866 he was pleased at the prospect of getting copies of his correspondence with President Davis. "[They] will be of great use to me," he said, "and enable me to speak more fully of movements and their results."[86] He was disappointed in this hope, however,[87] and found much difficulty in locating other documents,[88] especially those relating

[83] *Henry Lee's Memoirs,* 45.   [84] *Henry Lee's Memoirs,* 46.
[85] For the early stages of Lee's efforts to gather data, see *supra,* pp. 212, 235.
[86] R. E. Lee to W. H. Taylor, May 25, 1866; *Taylor's General Lee,* 311.
[87] R. E. Lee to W. H. Taylor, Dec. 28, 1866; *Taylor's General Lee,* 311.
[88] 1 *Argyll,* 167; R. E. Lee to Sir J. D. Acton; 1 *Acton's Correspondence,* 304.

to the matter he most desired to establish accurately, namely, the comparative strength of the Union and Confederate armies. "If the truth were told just now," he said to Macrae in the spring of 1868, "it would not be credited." [89] He did not believe an impartial history could be written at so early a date,[90] and he was discouraging to biographers.[91] Sometimes when he was urged to undertake the book, he protested that he would be obliged to relate facts that would cause the conduct of others to be subjected to criticism and censure.[92] Although he never wholly abandoned his project, he accumulated few reports and returns after 1866 and made no start at composition.[93] His available letters contain nothing to confirm Jones's statement[94] that Lee applied to the War Department for copies of his official papers and met with a denial. It is certain that Lee had not done this as late as July, 1868.[95]

[89] 1 *Macrae*, 222.   [90] *Ibid.*

[91] *Cf.* R. E. Lee to unnamed correspondent, Dec. 7, 1869; Jones, *L. and L.*, 441; "The few incidents of interest in which I have been engaged are as well known to others as to myself, and I know of nothing I could say in addition." He wrote E. A. Pollard: ". . . There are but few who desire to read a true history of themselves" (Sept. 26, 1866; *Jones*, 165).

[92] *Jones*, 181.

[93] As late as June, 1870, he wrote to Cassius F. Lee in answer to a tender of information (Thomas Nelson Page: *Robert E. Lee, Man and Soldier*, 668–69).

[94] *Jones*, 181.

[95] R. E. Lee to General Wm. S. Smith, July 27, 1868: "I have understood that the Confederate military records are in one of the bureaus at Washington" (*Jones*, 268).

CHAPTER XXIII

Lee's Theory of Education

At the commencement of 1869, thirty-eight students were awarded degrees,[1] and some financial progress was recorded. General R. D. Lilley, the chief financial agent of the college, had worked with a zeal that won the fullest commendation of the trustees.[2] Miss Anne Upshur Jones of New York had donated a valuable assortment of personal effects during the winter.[3] On his election to the board of trustees, to fill the vacancy caused by the resignation of Colonel Samuel McD. Reid,[4] Cyrus H. McCormick had pledged an additional $5000 to the endowment.[5] To encourage small gifts, which had not always been paid when promised,[6] the trustees sanctioned a plan whereby endowment certificates with coupons were issued, each good for a year's tuition.[7] Vigor in furthering the campaign for funds was now urged once again by the trustees:[8] without it, golden plans for making the college more useful to the country could not be started.

These plans were set out for the approval of the trustees by the president and faculty in several papers that embody the fullest expression of General Lee's theory of education. The starting point was the deep conviction of General Lee that for all its poverty and distress, the South must promote general education. "Nothing," he said in 1866, "will compensate us for the depression of the standard of our moral and intellectual culture, and each

[1] *Trustees' Minutes,* June 23, 1869.   [2] *Trustees' Minutes,* June 23, 1869.
[3] *Jones,* 272; *R. E. Lee, Jr.,* 335 *ff.; Lee's MS. Letter Book,* Feb. 13, 1869, Feb. 26, 1869. This lady had intimated in 1867 that she intended to make the gift and that she was inclined to favor the Virginia Theological Seminary near Alexandria. General Lee had replied, answering her inquiries, but had assured her that he did not wish to divert any donation from the seminary, which he esteemed highly (*R. E. Lee, Jr., loc. cit.*).
[4] Colonel Reid, who retired because of age and ill-health, had been a member of the board since Feb. 20, 1819 (*Trustees' Minutes,* March 30, 1869).
[5] *Trustees' Minutes,* March 30, 1869, June 22, 1869.
[6] See *Trustees' Minutes,* June 23, 1869, for resolution on the collection of subscriptions then overdue. See also report of J. H. McLeary, *MS.,* June, 1871; Archives of Washington and Lee University.
[7] *Trustees' Minutes.* March 30, 1869.   [8] *Trustees' Minutes,* June 23, 1869.

420

state should take the most energetic measures to revive its schools and colleges, and, if possible, to increase the facilities of instruction, and to elevate the standard of learning." [9] To General John B. Gordon, he stated his premise more fundamentally: "The thorough education of all classes of the people is the most efficacious means, in my opinion, of promoting the prosperity of the South." [10] Education, he believed, was the best endowment of youth: "We must look to the rising generation for the restoration of the country." [11] He did not except the Negroes from the list of those whom education would help. [12]

While holding the deepest faith in education, and in the college as a means of promoting it, General Lee did not regard academic training as a finishing process. It was only the beginning. He had written one of his sons years before, "The education of a man or woman is never completed till they die." [13] Frequently in his correspondence with the parents of his students he spoke of a college as "laying the foundation of a solid education." [14]

Cultural studies he considered a most desirable element in this foundation, [15] and he was always pleased when a student selected them. But from the beginning of his work at Lexington, where he found Mathematics, Latin, and Greek well taught, he saw the South's need of better training in the sciences. With that in mind, he divided the School of Natural Philosophy, enlarged the instruction in chemistry, as already indicated, and built up a department of engineering.

As time passed he saw that the struggling South required men trained for the vocations as well as for the professions. His thought was given increasingly to what was styled "practical education," in the phrase of the day. "I agree with you fully," he wrote in 1867, "as to the importance of a more practical course of instruction in our schools and colleges, which, while it may call forth the genius and energies of our people will tend to develop the resources and promote the interests of the Country." [16]

[9] R. E. Lee to G. W. Leyburn, March 20, 1866; *Jones*, 214.
[10] R. E. Lee to John B. Gordon, Dec. 30, 1867; *Jones*, 91.
[11] R. E. Lee to R. S. Ewell, March 3, 1868; *Jones*, 117–18.
[12] *Jones*, 269.   [13] Jones, *L. and L.*, 317.
[14] *E.g.*, R. E. Lee to B. B. Blair, *MS.*, Jan. 17, 1870; *Lee MS. Letter Book*.
[15] Kirkpatrick in *Jones*, 90.
[16] R. E. Lee to unnamed correspondent, Jan. 18, 1867; *Lee's MS. Letter Book; Jones,* 91.

At their meeting in June, 1868,[17] the trustees had authorized the faculty to work out an extension of the scientific departments. The faculty, in turn, had named a committee to prepare a report, under the direction of Lee. This was presented and considered at a special meeting of the board in March, 1869, and was then made public.[18] At the annual meeting in June, 1869, the project was approved in most of its details and was given its final form.

"The great object of the whole plan," General Lee wrote in forwarding the report, "is to provide the facilities required by the large class of our young men, who, looking to an early entrance into the practical pursuits of life, need a more direct training to this end than the usual literary courses. The proposed departments will also derive great advantage from the literary Schools of the College, whose influence in the cultivation and enlargement of the mind is felt beyond their immediate limits." [19] In other words the plan proposed "practical education" in the cultural atmosphere of a university rather than in separate technical schools.[20]

Three new departments were projected—agriculture, commerce, and applied chemistry. The first-named was to supply the student with virtually everything he would require for the scientific management of a farm, from plant physiology to cost accounting or "rural economy." The school of commerce was to combine the modern "business-college course" with commercial geography, commercial law, and "commercial economy, or the administration and financial management of commercial enterprises, banks, insurance and joint stock companies, railroads, canals, ships, steamers, telegraphs, etc." [21] Applied chemistry was to cover mining and metallurgy and "chemistry applied to the arts"—industrial geology, botany, zoology and comparative anatomy, physiological chemistry, the use of the mouth blow-pipe, glass-blowing, "the use of tools practically taught," photography, "chemical technology, or the manufacture of acids, alkalies, salts, glass, pottery, illuminating gas and oils, soaps, paints, varnishes,

[17] *Trustees' Minutes*, June 17, 1868; see *supra*, p. 369.
[18] *Trustees' Minutes*, March 30, 1869; *New York Herald*, quoted in *Richmond Dispatch*, May 1, 1869.
[19] *1868–69 Catalogue*, 57.
[20] Joynes in *Jones*, 127, also in *Cent. U. S. C.*, 28.
[21] *Cf.* C. S. Marsh in 34 *Journal of Political Economy*, 657–59.

dyes, drugs, fermented and distilled liquors, vinegar, sugar, starch, bread, gelatine, leather, etc.," and, finally, "economy and the management of chemical manufactures."

In addition, the report recommended the development of the engineering schools to include training in mechanical engineering. With the proposed department of applied chemistry, this would so broaden the instruction that three branches would be taught—civil engineering, mechanical engineering, and mining engineering and applied chemistry.[22] English and French were to be taught with all the engineering courses. "In the mechanical studies," the report concluded, "a large portion of time should be given to the neat and exact execution of working drawings of machines, masonry, carpentry, &c.: without skill in which essential labour no one is qualified to take charge of works of construction, or superintend industrial establishments, in such a manner as is called for by the present advanced state of the arts."

"Laboratory methods," though not given precisely that name, were emphasized. "It is very important," read the report, "that the instruction in these professional courses be made as practical as possible; and, to that end, that there be annexed to those Departments a farm and garden, a mechanical workshop and a laboratory or workshop for metallurgic and chemical operations." All these might be remunerative, or at least should support themselves, the committee contended. "Even the laboratory, if judiciously conducted, may be self-sustaining, instead of requiring heavy appropriations and fees to pay for costly experiments and destroyed apparatus; which has been the difficulty generally encountered in imparting instruction in practical chemistry to young and unskillful beginners—a difficulty, which has often compelled this method of instruction, confessedly the best, to be reluctantly abandoned, even in institutions amply endowed."[23]

Along with the extension of the scientific departments, the faculty report of March 30, 1869, recommended the establishment of "press scholarships," not exceeding fifty, to "young men intending to make practical printing and journalism their business

---

[22] In the technical lay-out presented in the report, agriculture was considered one "course," commerce another, civil and mechanical engineering a third, and mining engineering and metallurgy a fourth.

[23] For the complete report, see *1868–69 Catalogue*, 56 *ff.*

in life; such scholarships to be free from tuition and College fees, on condition that when required by the Faculty, they shall perform such disciplinary duties as may be assigned them in a printing office or in the line of their professions to a time equal to one hour in each working day." The faculty suggested, further, that the trustees either make some agreement with a printing office, or else provide a plant at the college, where students could receive instruction and, as far as practicable, be compensated for their labor. To establish desirable contacts and to simplify the entry of young printers and journalists into the college, the faculty suggested, moreover, that it be authorized to buy $5000 of advertising and to pay for it in tuition and college fees.

The trustees had promptly approved the general idea and the proposal to supply tuition in return for newspaper advertising, but they had called on the faculty to see what arrangements could be made outside the college for practical instruction in typographical art.[24] Faculty members duly did this and reported in June that a limited number of boys could receive instruction in the plant of Lafferty & Company, in Lexington, without cost to the college. This expedient was approved in the hope that some larger or better plan would be developed from it.[25] Pursuant to this authority, the college on August 9, 1869, circularized the typographical unions of the South, inviting them to nominate candidates, over fifteen years of age, for scholarships that were to be good for a term of two years. Each holder of a scholarship was to labor one hour a day at his calling.[26]

This school, it must be remembered, was projected at a time when most of the country weeklies and many of the journals in small towns were owned and operated by practical printers, who usually conducted a job-printing business as well. These papers generally afforded a living for only one man, and perforce were "edited" by their owners. Often the editorials were "written at the case." That is, they were not penned and then put in type but were composed as the "editor" stood in front of his type case with his "stick," and "set" them. Printers of this sort, their sons

[24] *Trustees' Minutes*, March 30, 1869.   [25] *Trustees' Minutes*, June 23, 1869.
[26] Roscoe Ellard: "Robert E. Lee and Journalism" (*Washington and Lee University Bulletin*, vol. 25, no. 11, p. 7), quoting Augustus Maverick: *Raymond and New York Journalism*, 355.

and helpers, were those for whom the "press scholarships" were intended. Apparently the aim was to train the printer to be an editor rather than to qualify the prospective editor in the art of printing. "The reason we propose giving these press scholarships is this," Professor William Preston Johnston told a reporter of *The New York Sun*, ". . . Printing is one of the arts which diffuse education and we should therefore seek to qualify printers for the task of educating as far as possible. We do not hope to make men fit for the editorial chair *at once,* but we do hope to give them as thorough a training as possible in the ways of their profession and to give them as good an education as possible that they may make better and more cultivated *editors*." [27]

Along with the extension of the scientific schools and the establishment of the press scholarships, the faculty recommended and the trustees approved the establishment of a separate chair of English Language and Literature, as soon as funds were available. History and Political Economy were to be taken from that chair and, with International Law, were to constitute a separate school.[28]

At the same time the trustees authorized the selection of six "resident masters," who corresponded, in a sense, to the fellows of more recent appointment in American universities. Three men were to be named annually, for terms of two years, from among the graduating masters of arts of the college. They were to pursue at least one study in the college, were to teach one hour a day, were to have exemption from all college fees, and were each to receive $200 annually from the college. Efforts were to be made to endow these masterships at $3000 each.[29]

Finally, in this enlarged program, a summer school was projected. It was to be under the care of an executive committee consisting of three members of the faculty and was to be taught by the assistant professors or by others specially licensed for the purpose. Students who passed the course of this summer school could be admitted to the regular college classes.[30] Apparently the purpose of this school was to supply the deficiencies in preparation that were then hampering the work of the college.

[27] Ellard, *op. cit.,* 9–10, quoting *New York Sun.*
[28] *Trustees' Minutes,* March 30, 1869.
[29] *Trustees' Minutes,* March 30, 1869.   [30] *Trustees' Minutes,* June 23, 1869.

These plans, like those General Lee had received when he came to Lexington, were pervaded with the ideals of Christianity. Taught in no school, religion was to be inculcated through all of them. Lee had come to Lexington as much a missionary as an educator. When he had told Pendleton in 1865 that he would not hesitate to give his services to the college, if he thought he could be of any "benefit" to the youth of the South, he had used the word as much in its moral as in its educational sense.[31] He meant precisely what he said in an oft-quoted remark: "If I could only know that all the young men in the college were good Christians, I should have nothing more to desire. I dread the thought of any student going away from college without becoming a sincere Christian."[32] His first conversation about the college, that with Reverend Mr. Wilmer, had turned to the part religion should have in his work there. The same purpose dominated to the last. Yet he rarely employed the term *"Christian* education": he did not believe there was any other kind worthy of the name.

If General Lee had lived longer and the funds had been found, still other educational ideals doubtless would have been developed at Washington College. As it was, the program of 1869 represents the scene at its widest before the curtain dropped. To summarize, General Lee took a college whose president and four professors, prior to his coming, had been teaching Greek, Latin, "Natural Philosophy," Mathematics, and "Moral Philosophy" to a handful of boys, and he either enlarged, or planned to enlarge this institution to this general plan:

I. A classical college, with a Christian atmosphere, elective courses, and high standards, presenting the cultural studies as the "foundation of a solid education."

II. A group of scientific schools, with special emphasis on chemistry and engineering, civil, mining, and mechanical, and with laboratory facilities for all the sciences. In these scientific schools, as in the classical courses, the elective system prevailed, but a fixed minimum of work was required.

III. In the classical college and for the schools of science, adequate training was to be provided in modern languages, includ-

[31] *Jones,* 146.　　　[32] See *supra,* p. 283.

ing Spanish, which General Lee himself insisted was of special importance because the relations of the United States with Latin America were destined to be much closer.

IV. A school of commerce, similar in many respects to those established in recent years in the United States. It did not cover economic theory, however, so fully as do modern courses in commerce, and it was intended to give students practical knowledge of subjects among which were some now relegated to business colleges, namely, office-methods, including penmanship, book-keeping, and stenography.

V. A school of agriculture, with what would now be styled a "demonstration farm."

VI. A system of press scholarships, designed primarily to acquaint young printers with editorial methods and to enlarge their education.

VII. A school of law as an integral part of the college.[33]

VIII. A summer school to assure the better preparation of students entering the regular courses.

IX. The encouragement of advanced study through the establishment of "resident masterships," corresponding to modern university fellowships.

X. The conduct of research, for the public welfare, by members of the faculty, or persons appointed for the purpose. In the particular circumstances of the college, the investigations undertaken were in topography.

XI. Provision, by scholarship, for bringing selected young men to the college from the high schools and private academies of the South.

XII. Frequent and rigid examination of all students in all departments.[34]

[33] Almost every year during General Lee's administration some proposal was made for a more intimate connection between the college and the law school operated by Judge Brockenbrough, rector of the college since 1865. The usual condition, lack of money, prevented any extension of the law course and led the trustees to continue the annual agreement with Judge Brockenbrough. In 1869, General John C. Breckinridge visited the college to see his student-son (*R. E. Lee, Jr.,* 341) and made so favorable an impression that the trustees decided to sound him out and to see whether he would accept a law professorship. If he were willing to do so, the college planned to associate him with Judge Brockenbrough in a formal department of law. Otherwise, the existing arrangement was to be continued (*Trustees' Minutes,* March 30, and June 24, 1869). Breckinridge would not accept, and the college took no further action until 1870, when J. Randolph Tucker was chosen second professor of law.

[34] *Cf.* report of committee on the president's report, *Trustees' Minutes,* June 23, 1869.

XIII. In all the activities of the college, the honor system in its fullness to prevail.

Poverty prevented the full attainment of this ideal in General Lee's time. Work in commerce did not develop beyond the modest proportions of a "Students' Business School," which had been privately established some years before[35] and subsequently was affiliated with the college.[36] The department of agriculture was not opened, nor were the press scholarships used. Nevertheless, Lee's plan was definite and advanced. It attracted much attention at the time, particularly in the emphasis placed on "practical education." *The New York Herald* predicted that the movement was "likely to make as great an impression upon our old fogy schools and colleges as [General Lee] did in military tactics upon our old fogy commanders in the palmy days of the rebellion." [37]

The educational ideal of Washington College was not expressed solely in a formal curriculum and in the development of a more extended range of study. The college believed, also, in the physical training of youth. At a time when the trustees were searching for money with which to establish new departments, they considered the purchase of a playground, an "athletic field" in modern collegiate phraseology. And when they scarcely were able to provide money for needed laboratory equipment, the trustees cheerfully appropriated $1100 to equip a students' boat club.[38] The literary societies were equally esteemed. "There is scarcely a feature in the organization of the college," wrote General Lee, "more improving or beneficial to the students than the exercises and influence of the societies. . . ." [39]

The alumni took their place, too, in the academic order that came into being during General Lee's administration. They had been organized for many years,[40] but their society was vitalized and their part in the commencement exercises was magnified. In 1868–69 a general catalogue of the alumni was prepared and was printed by order of the trustees.[41] It contained a sketch

[35] *1867–68 Catalogue*, 37.
[36] *1869–70 Catalogue*, 44. Cf. MS. *Faculty Minutes*, Oct. 5, Oct. 12, 1869.
[37] Quoted in *Richmond Dispatch*, May 1, 1869.
[38] *Trustees' Minutes*, June 22–23, 1869.
[39] R. E. Lee to unnamed correspondent, March 27, 1866; *Jones*, 246.
[40] *1865–66 Catalogue*, 27.   [41] *Trustees' Minutes*, March 30, 1869.

of the history of the college, a list of all the known officials and teachers and a roster of some hundreds of graduates and former students. Under many of the names were notes of service in the Confederate army, and not a few were followed by the grim phrase, "Killed at Manassas" or at Chancellorsville or "Died in Service." Alumni were proud of their connection with the college and conscious of their responsibility toward it. "The objects of this association," read the second article of the constitution, "are, to keep fresh the pleasant memories of College life; to preserve and strengthen the ties of friendship there formed; and to exercise a filial care over the interests and welfare of *Alma Mater,* to whom we acknowledge a debt of gratitude never to be forgotten." [42]

Such was the college envisioned at Lexington as Lee's five-year administration was drawing to its close. The question now to be answered is, How much of the ideal was directly contributed by General Lee? To what extent was he the author of the projects, many of them novel, presented for the approval of the trustees?

The new professorships were established in 1865 with his consent and warm approval but probably not on his initiative. Plans for the extension of the scientific schools were prepared under his direction, and the section relating to instruction in agriculture probably originated with Professor Campbell and with him. [43]

Beyond this it is difficult to go. Nothing was put forward that was not approved by Lee or, at the least, acceptable to him, yet his authorship of specific proposals cannot be established. Many of the advances undoubtedly were suggested by his able colleagues. The press scholarships, for instance, were an advanced conception, yet it is far more likely that William Preston Johnston suggested them than that General Lee did. Johnston was interested in public affairs and was professor of English. He was a member of the committee that drew up the plan for the extension of the scientific courses. When a representative of *The New York Sun* journeyed to Lexington to know what the press scholarships were designed to do, Johnston and not Lee was the man

[42] *Catalogue of The Alumni of Washington College, Virginia,* 71.
[43] *MS. Faculty Minutes,* June 7, 1870.

who explained them to him.[44] General Lee's connection with the plan probably was limited to endorsing it. From his own unpleasant experience with newspapers he probably felt there was abundant need for the training Johnston advocated.

The adoption of new methods and courses by members of the faculty was made easy by the nature of Lee's relations with the professors. He was president: none of his associates ever was in any sort of doubt about that, though he was often an elder brother to them and never an autocratic executive.[45] He counselled them in their problems and visited them in their distress,[46] but he required them to be at their posts and he insisted on prompt and accurate reports.[47] In the only instance when he had to take disciplinary measures against a member of the faculty, an assistant professor, he promptly dismissed him and paid no heed to a students' petition for the reinstatement of the offender.

The teachers had a certain awe of Lee. Humphreys found it easy to start a conversation with him but sometimes embarrassing to continue it.[48] On one of their long rides together, General Lee and Captain White were overtaken by darkness and had to spend the night at a farmhouse, where there was only one vacant room and only one bed in that room. To White's dismay, he had to share the General's couch, but he spent the night on the rail and slept not at all, for fear of disturbing his chief. Privately, the professor admitted afterwards that he "would as soon have thought of sleeping with the Archangel Gabriel as with General Lee."[49] Outside the family, White was the General's closest friend in Lexington. That he was Lee's intimate, White insistently denied. "No man," said he, "was great enough to be intimate with General Lee."[50] The other professors shared his feeling toward the General, and they would not have thought of crossing him or of presuming upon him.

[44] Supra, p. 425.
[45] Joynes, in ,ones, 121.
[46] Professor Joynes recorded (Cent. U. S. C., 22), that when he was sick one winter in Lexington, General Lee came every day through a deep snow and climbed high steps to inquire about him and to encourage Mrs. Joynes.
[47] Professor C. A. Graves (Riley, 27) described how General Lee rebuked an assistant professor who had absented himself from college without asking leave of the president. When Lee met him on his return, he said: "Good morning, Captain, I am glad to see you back again. It was by accident, sir, that I learned that you were away."
[48] M. W. Humphreys in Richmond Times-Dispatch, Jan. 20, 1907.
[49] Valentine, quoting White, in Riley, 153–54.
[50] Riley, 66 n.

But in conferring with the instructors and in planning for the college, Lee encouraged free expression of opinion and the largest initiative. In matters of departmental control he gave the teachers the maximum liberty of action. "In his intercourse with his faculty," wrote Professor William Preston Johnston, "he was courteous, kind, and often rather playful in manner. We all thought he deferred entirely too much to the expression of opinion on the part of the faculty, when we would have preferred that he should simply indicate his own views or desire." [51] In Professor Joynes's eyes, Lee seemed deliberately to minimize himself. If an associate had a new idea, he could present it without fear that it would be frowned upon or regarded as an act of insubordination. Lee never pretended to educational omniscience. In one of the most illuminating of all the observations on the relations of General Lee with his faculty, Doctor Gordon wrote: "One proof of [Lee's] wisdom was his unwillingness to express his opinion on a subject which he had not carefully considered. On subjects which he had considered he was the most dogmatic of men. But not infrequently at the meetings of the faculty he would say: 'Gentlemen, this is a new question to me; I cannot venture an opinion. I prefer to hear what Doctor K[irkpatrick] or Colonel A[llan] or Professor M[cCulloh] has to say about it.' In every case he would name the man who ought to have been, and who generally was, most familiar with, and best informed on, the subject under discussion." [52]

Lee never made a speech before the professors, though he quieted many a brewing storm.[53] Faculty meetings, one imagines, had much the atmosphere of General Lee's headquarters mess during the quiet periods of the War between the States. But when his professors faced problems of instruction or of organization, he treated them much as he did his corps commanders in action: he gave them the warmest moral support and he brought to the scene all his resources for their use, but he let them make their own dispositions. Under this system the best qualities of his faculty were aroused. Their ambition was to please him. They considered it an honor to work in a college he directed, and they

[51] R. E. Lee, Jr., 315.
[52] E. C. Gordon, in Riley, 83.   [53] Cent. U. S. C., 33.

felt that they were making educational history. Complete harmony and the utmost energy, in Joynes's phrase, pervaded the college.[54] The faculty did not labor in vain or follow to no purpose the leadership of the president. Washington College became a mighty force in Southern education and, through its engineering school, was largely the inspiration of the men who developed the steel industry in the South.[55] Defeated in war, Lee triumphed in his labor to upbuild the South.

[54] *Cent. U. S. C.*, 28, 33.
[55] Robert Ewing in *Tenn. Hist. Mag.*, January, 1926, pp. 214 *ff.*

CHAPTER XXIV

THE BEGINNING OF THE END

THE general decline in Lee's health had become so serious by June, 1869, that he seems even to have thought that the strain of commencement might prove fatal to him.[1] After that ordeal was behind him, he had to consider his physical condition in making his plans for the summer.[2] He hoped that he might visit Rooney and Robert after the college closed and still be able to return to Lexington in time for the annual meeting on July 13 of the Educational Association of Virginia. Although he was a member of that body, he had never attended any of its conventions, and he felt that if he absented himself when the organization met at his own town, he would be considered inimical to it.[3] By shortening his stay with his sons he might have gone down to the Pamunkey and have been back by the date of the meeting, but for the fact that new college officers were to begin their duties on July 1 and

[1] R. E. Lee to R. E. Lee, Jr., June 19, 1869; *R. E. Lee, Jr.*, 358: "If I live through the coming week, I wish to pay you and F—— a visit. . . ."

[2] R. E. Lee to W. H. F. Lee, June 30, 1869; *R. E. Lee, Jr.*, 359.

[3] General Lee was always sympathetic with the other educational institutions of Virginia. It will be recalled that when Miss Anne Upshur Jones wrote him she intended to make a gift to some school, and was interested in the Episcopal Seminary near Alexandria but wished to know something of Washington College, he warmly praised the seminary (see *supra*, p. 420, note 3). On Jan. 21, 1867, answering a letter from Mrs. Coleman of Williamsburg on the future of the College of William and Mary, he expressed affectionate interest in the recovery of that old foundation from the effects of the war: "Your beautiful appeal in behalf of William and Mary was not needed to excite in me an interest in its welfare; for that I have felt all my life, and I have watched with anxiety the prospects of its resuscitation. . . . It must necessarily suffer under the depression incident to the calamities which oppress the state, but they will pass away, and William and Mary will again resume her place in the front rank of the colleges of the country. Time, which brings a cure to all things, will, I trust, remove the difficulties in the way of her progress and her restoration. Although without the influence you ascribe to me, it will give me pleasure to do all in my power for her advancement and prosperity" (*Richmond Times-Dispatch*, Oct. 17, 1921, p. 1). From the list of educational institutions in Virginia, published by the Educational Association of Virginia at the end of 1868, the name of Washington College was inadvertently omitted. The secretary wrote Lee an explanation, which Lee immediately accepted, urging the secretary to give himself no concern about it (R. E. Lee to W. R. Abbot, MS., Jan. 21, 1869; *Lee's MS. Letter Book*). Dean Campbell of Washington and Lee told the writer in 1933 that General Lee believed the University of Virginia should be essentially a graduate school and that Lee outlined to Professor John B. Minor a detailed plan of secondary education.

would require some coaching. He accordingly gave up his plan and stayed in Lexington, which he found so quiet and pleasant, with the students away, that he wished he could remain there all summer.[4] The Educational Association duly convened at the college[5] with some of the most eminent teachers of the state in attendance, John B. Minor, Basil L. Gildersleeve, Matthew Fontaine Maury, Charles L. Cocke, and John P. McGuire among them. General Lee doubtless was present but he made no address and served on none of the committees.[6]

Very soon after the convention closed, the General took Mrs. Lee to the Rockbridge Baths, where she had decided she would spend the summer. Scarcely had Lee reached the springs, however, when he received the unexpected news that his brother Sydney Smith Lee had died at Richland, his home on the Potomac. The General set out immediately, but had to contend, as usual, with very poor transportation. When he arrived at Alexandria, on the evening of July 24, it was to find that the funeral had occurred late the previous afternoon.[7] Lee was much shaken by the sudden taking of a brother he had loved to the end of his life as warmly as in the days of their boyhood in that same old city. He wrote Mrs. Lee: "May God bless us all and preserve us for the time when we, too, must part, the one from the other, which is now close at hand, and may we all meet again at the footstool of a merciful God, to be joined by His eternal love never more to separate."[8]

In melancholy mood, he went from the Mansion House, Alexandria, to Ravensworth, rested a day or two in its pleasant shade, and wandered about the well-beloved old house. At the door of the room in which his mother had died, he paused, almost overwhelmed by memories. "Forty years ago," he said, "I stood in this room by my mother's death-bed! It seems now but yesterday!"[9]

Robert was with him, having come up to attend the funeral,

---

[4] R. E. Lee to unnamed correspondent, July 9, 1869; *R. E. Lee, Jr.,* 360.

[5] Lee had been mistaken as to the time of the opening meeting. It was July 13, not July 15, as he had thought.

[6] *Minutes of the Educational Association of Virginia;* Fourth Annual Session . . . Lynchburg . . . 1870.

[7] *Alexandria Gazette,* July 24, 1869. The body was placed in a vault in the Methodist Episcopal cemetery, to await the family's decision concerning the place of final interment.

[8] R. E. Lee to Mrs. Lee, July 25, 1869; *R. E. Lee, Jr.,* 362.   [9] *R. E. Lee, Jr.,* 363.

and he now prevailed on the General to return home by way of the White House. Lee reached there on July 30 and on August 1 he attended Saint Peter's Church in New Kent County, a place precious to the family because of the tradition that George Washington had married within its walls the "Widow Custis" from whom Mrs. Lee was descended.[10]

The General did not think his daughter-in-law was looking well and he believed that her baby, his namesake, would be the better for a trip to the mountains. So he prevailed on young Mrs. Lee to go to the springs with him. He was pleased at the prospect of having the young mother and her child in his care, and he hastened to write his excuses to a friend at whose home he had promised to stop on his way back. ". . . I shall travel up," he wrote, "in a capacity that I have not undertaken for many years— as escort to a young mother and her infant, and it will require the concentration of all my faculties to perform my duties even with tolerable comfort to my charge. . . ."[11] On August 2 the mother went to Petersburg, to see her family for a day, while the General and Rooney awaited her in Richmond.[12] As always happened now, whenever he was away from Lexington, visitors began to pour in on Lee in such numbers that he was compelled to hold an impromptu reception in the parlors of his stopping-place, the Exchange Hotel.[13] The next day, August 3, he set out for the springs, and after a long railroad trip and a wearying drive from Goshen to Rockbridge Baths, safely delivered the mother and the youngster to Mrs. Lee. It was a tedious journey and it may not have been altogether prudent, for the youthful object of the General's care was just recovering from a severe attack of whooping-cough. Obedient to his doctor's order, the General departed in a few days for the White Sulphur, in the hope that its waters would benefit his health. He took with him Mildred and Agnes, who found a gay season in progress.[14]

---

[10] *Cf.* R. E. Lee to Miss Virginia Ritchie, *MS.*, Oct. 23, 1869.

[11] R. E. Lee to unnamed correspondent, Aug. 1, 1869; *R. E. Lee, Jr.*, 364–65.

[12] *Richmond Whig*, Aug. 3; *Richmond Dispatch*, Aug. 4; *Richmond Enquirer and Examiner*, Aug. 3, 1869.

[13] *R. E. Lee, Jr.*, 365.

[14] The General's correspondence at The White seems to have been heavier than during most of his vacations. While there he received a business offer of some sort, or a tender of money, that he acknowledged feelingly, but declined at once (R. E. Lee to R. W. ——; Aug. 26, 1869; *Jones*, 175). The details are not known.

George Peabody was among the guests, as was the General's table-mate of the summer of 1867, W. W. Corcoran of Washington.[15]

It probably was while Lee was at this resort that Reverend W. F. Broaddus began to talk of a meeting there in behalf of his project to establish an orphanage for the children of Virginia soldiers killed during the war. Jones stated[16] that General Lee frequently wrote Mr. Broaddus about this and conferred in person with him regarding it. Lee's sympathies were of course with the enterprise, and his contributions to it were frequent.[17] But when it was planned to hold a gathering at the springs, where inflammatory eloquence probably would have been applied for the extraction of gifts, he declined to attend.

General Lee desired, in fact, "to avoid all public gatherings that had anything to do with the war." [18] On two or three occasions he wrote as though he would have gone, if he could, to meetings held to memorialize the dead or to dedicate Confederate burial grounds,[19] but in actual fact after the war he never was present at a single assembly of any sort related in any way to the struggle between the states. "I think it wisest," he wrote, "not to keep open the sores of war, but to follow the example of those nations who endeavored to obliterate the marks of civil strife, and to commit to oblivion the feelings it engendered." [20] He even held, in 1866, that it was unwise at that time to attempt to raise Confederate monuments. He wrote General Rosser, "All, I think, that can now be done is to aid our noble and generous women in their efforts to protect the graves and mark the last resting-places of those who have fallen, and wait for better times." [21] Every such effort to care for the tombs of Southern soldiers had his instant endorsement. "The graves of the Confederate dead will always be green in my memory, and their deeds be hallowed in my recollection"—thus he wrote the chairman of a memorial

[15] Lee had been exchanging letters with Corcoran since 1867 in the interest of the college (7 *S. H. S. P.*, 152 *ff.*).

[16] *Jones*, 233–34.

[17] During the last year of his life he gave $100 toward the education of soldiers' orphans (*Jones*, 432).

[18] The quotation is Jones's language, not Lee's.

[19] *Cf.* R. E. Lee to W. H. Travers, June 23, 1866; *Jones*, 324. *Cf.* also R. E. Lee to Mrs. William Coulling, March 5, 1866; *Jones*, 325.

[20] R. E. Lee to unnamed correspondent, apropos of the "Gettysburg Identification Meeting," *Jones*, 234.

[21] R. E. Lee to T. L. Rosser, Dec. 13, 1866; *Jones*, 257.

association in Richmond.[22] When the proposal was first made in 1866 to bring back to their native states the bones of the Confederates slain at Gettysburg, he expressed the belief that the Gettysburg Association would not be lacking in respect for the Southern men buried there. In any case, he said, it would be time enough to talk of moving them when a reason for it arose: "I am not in favor of disturbing the ashes of the dead, unless for a worthy object, and I know of no fitter resting-place for a soldier than the field on which he has nobly laid down his life." [23] Hearing, four years later, that what had been feared by many had come to pass and that the graves of the Confederates were being neglected at Gettysburg, General Lee was for restoring to Virginia soil the ashes of the men who at his command had charged the ridge. He set aside in this instance his rule against the publication of his letters of endorsement, and both he and his family contributed generously to the fund being raised for the reinterment.[24] But his opposition to fervid meetings remained unchanged. They aroused old passions and they might stir up ill-will against the South. It was in this spirit, no doubt, that he discouraged Mr. Broaddus's plan, and it was in this same spirit that he declined to read books on the war. They kept alive feelings it was better to bury for the country's good.

Late in arriving, he had but a short stay at the springs, and before the end of August he was back in Lexington, preparing for the family's return. He did not leave again until spring, though he received many invitations to visit different parts of the South. One of the most pressing was to attend a commercial convention in Louisville on October 12. He sent in reply an optimistic letter in which he affirmed that if the people cherished the principles of their fathers and practised their virtues, they would find it easy to revive the South. "Every man must, however, do his part in this great work. He must carry into the administration of his affairs industry, fidelity, and economy, and

[22] R. E. Lee to Mrs. Wm. Coulling, March 5, 1866; *Jones*, 325. *Cf.* R. E. Lee to Mrs. V. S. Knox, August, 1866; *Jones*, 324. He was equally earnest in his support of the various efforts to raise funds for the relief of the needy in the South (*cf.* R. E. Lee to Mrs. Miles Lells, Sept. 26, 1866; *Jones*, 256. See also *Jones*, 228).
[23] R. E. Lee to Fitz Lee, Dec. 15, 1866; *Jones*, 325.
[24] R. E. Lee to Mrs. Mary E. (Geo. W.) Randolph, March 8 and 17, 1870; *Jones*, 280, 281; *Richmond Dispatch*, March 30, 1870; *cf.* R. E. Lee to Thomas Martin, March 15, 1870; *Jones*, 280.

apply the knowledge taught by science to the promotion of agriculture, manufactures, and all industrial pursuits. . . . In my particular sphere I have to attend to my proper business, which occupies so much of my attention that I have but little time to devote to other things." [25]

His "proper business" was heavy enough after September 16, when the college opened. The attendance was slightly less than that of the previous session,[26] but the geographical distribution of the student-body was wider. As other colleges in Virginia were now somewhat restored, the students from the Old Dominion, who had numbered 130 in 1867-68, and 111 in 1868-69, dropped to 77. The boys from Kentucky, Tennessee, and Texas also formed a somewhat smaller contingent, but there were larger groups from most of the other parts of the South. All the states of the Confederacy were represented by at least ten men each. Twenty came from the North.[27] All these young men had to be assigned to their classes and adjusted to the life of the college—a troublesome task, though one soon discharged.

The session got smoothly underway and passed with few incidents. Its chief feature was the vigorous continuance of the campaign for endowment. George Peabody had assigned the college a claim he had against the commonwealth of Virginia, and was indirectly in correspondence with the college regarding it at the time of his death.[28] Expectations were raised also by reports that Missourians had given $10,000 to support the chair of Applied Chemistry, and that General W. S. Harney of the United States

[25] R. E. Lee to Blanton Duncan, Sept. 14, 1869; *Jones*, 231. He wrote a somewhat similar letter on May 11, 1869, to Colonel Lawrence S. Marye, regretfully declining an invitation to a commercial convention in Memphis: "It would afford me great gratification," he said, "to aid in every way in my power the efforts that [they?] are making to restore the prosperity of the country" (*Lee's MS. Letter Book; Richmond Dispatch*, May 21, 1869).

[26] The total enrollment in 1868–69 was 384; in 1869–70, it was 344; *1869–70 Catalogue*, 17.

[27] *1869–70 Catalogue*, 17.

[28] R. E. Lee to G. P. Russell, Sept. 27, Nov. 10, 1869; *Jones*, 276, 437; *MS. Faculty Minutes*, Nov. 16, 1869; R. E. Lee to Lewis Allen, Jan. 7, 1870; *Jones*, 278. In this last letter General Lee expressed regret that indisposition had prevented his attending Mr. Peabody's funeral. The trustees later named a committee to prosecute the claim (*Trustees' Minutes*, June 23, 1870). Mrs. Lee had not been impressed by the gift to the South in 1867 of the "Peabody fund." She wrote Mrs. Chilton, "I cannot hear how Mr. Peabody's munificent donation is to be applied[.] I fear it will benefit the South but little if it is to found schools with Yankee teachers" (Mrs. R. E. Lee to Mrs. R. H. Chilton, *MS.*, March 10, 1867; *Chilton Papers*).

army had donated $1000 toward the endowment of the "presidential chair" in the college.[29] General Lee was much gratified by the benevolence of Harney and wrote him personally, recalling kindnesses done him by that Federal officer in the years preceding the war.[30]

Along with these satisfactions came distress in November at the fate of Professor Frank Preston. He had been graduated a bachelor of arts in 1860, had been a volunteer in the Rockbridge Artillery, and had been captain in the cadet corps at the Virginia Military Institute. Chosen assistant professor of Greek in Washington College, he resigned in 1869 to accept the professorship of Greek and German in the College of William and Mary. Scarcely had he entered upon his duties when he sickened and died. Lee was much attached to the young artillery Hellenist. He issued a sorrowful announcement to the student-body and suspended classes for the day—a rare occurrence at Washington College.[31]

The life of the family was very pleasant that fall. Mrs. Rooney Lee and the General's little grandson, Robert, remained in Lexington for some time after they left the springs. Edward Childe paid another visit at the end of September and brought with him not only a wife but also the little dog of woeful countenance that aroused the General's pity.[32] Mrs. Lee's health was no better but she was able to ride out with the General, on sunny autumn afternoons, in the carriage he had purchased for her the previous spring in Baltimore. These were their last rides together. She was not with him, however, the afternoon he had trouble with the strong-limbed Lucy Long. He used her to pull the carriage— Traveller disdained such employment—and that day he had driven her down the river, with Mrs. Rooney Lee and the baby, to call on the William Preston Johnstons. They made the trip comfortably, and the General was driving the mare up the stiff grade to the front of the house when she stumbled and fell as if dead. Lee jumped out, began to unfasten her harness and soon discovered that she had been choked by a tight collar. The General was acutely distressed and reproached himself hotly for

---

[29] *Lexington Gazette*, Feb. 18, 1870, quoting *Richmond Dispatch*.
[30] R. E. Lee to W. S. Harney, Feb. 26, 1870; *Jones*, 279.
[31] *MS. Faculty Minutes*, Nov. 23, 1869; *Jones*, 438; *R. E. Lee, Jr.*, 374–75.
[32] See *supra*, p. 309.

having permitted such a thing to happen. He caressed the animal and told her he was ashamed of himself for mistreating her in this wise after all her fidelity to him.[33]

It is quite within the possibilities that the excitement of this incident contributed to the illness that marked the beginning of the end. The symptoms commenced about October 22, 1869, and at first were simply those of another severe cold, which kept Lee indoors and forced him to be absent from the faculty meeting of October 26.[34] He was better within a week and on November 2 was able to take a ride on Traveller and to confer with the faculty,[35] but he was again confined to the house for a few days,[36] and when he was allowed to go out once more, his weakness was pronounced and he felt a certain depression of spirits. ". . . Traveller's trot is harder to me than it used to be and fatigues me very much," he had to admit to his son at the beginning of December.[37] Truth was, his doctors by this time had diagnosed his malady as the same "inflammation of the heart-sac" from which in 1863 he had suffered much. This was attended now by rheumatism of the back, right side, and arms. Rapid exercise, afoot or on horseback, caused difficulty in breathing. Apparently the physicians did not explain to him the nature of his trouble, but he knew his heart was affected. He confided this to Custis, and told his eldest son that he considered himself doomed, but he said nothing of it to any other member of the family.[38]

As Christmas approached he wrote cheerfully to Rooney, who could not come to Lexington for the holidays, and he sent a message to Robert in the same spirit. On New Year's Day he kept open house to his friends and had much satisfaction in serving them oysters procured in Norfolk through Colonel Walter Taylor.[39] He still had strength for his correspondence and he did not miss another faculty meeting until the end of March, 1870.[40] He was able, too, to see visitors, bidden and unbidden. One after-

[33] R. E. Lee, Jr., 371.
[34] MS. Faculty Minutes, Oct. 26, 1869; Lexington Gazette, Oct. 27, 1869.
[35] MS. Faculty Minutes, Nov. 2, 1869; Lexington Gazette, Nov. 3, 1869.
[36] He was absent from the faculty meeting of Nov. 9.
[37] R. E. Lee to W. H. F. Lee, Dec. 2, 1869; R. E. Lee, Jr., 374.
[38] Cf. R. E. Lee, Jr., 379.
[39] Taylor's General Lee, 313, 314. For Lee's feast on oysters at Easter, 1868, see ibid., 311.
[40] See MS. Faculty Minutes.

noon, during the autumn, a stranger accosted him at the gate of his house, talked with him for a few moments, and had just gone off, well-pleased, when Reverend J. William Jones, pastor of the Baptist church and a chaplain of the college, walked up for a chat. After they had exchanged greetings, Lee remarked of the man who had just left, "That is one of our old soldiers who is in necessitous circumstances." Jones, who was already something of an historian and was wholly unreconstructed, inquired to what command the veteran belonged. "He fought on the other side," said Lee, very simply, "but we must not remember that against him now." Jones subsequently learned from the man that General Lee had given him money to help him on his way.[41]

As the winter wore along, the General's free movement was greatly hampered by his physical condition. He rode out when the weather was favorable and he could do so with somewhat less discomfort, once he mounted his horse, but he could not walk much farther than to his office. Constantly in pain, he was unable to attend to anything beyond his college duties and his necessary correspondence.[42] He insisted he was better, as February passed, but by the middle of March he was less optimistic and had reached the conclusion that if the spring brought no improvement, he would resign. "I am admonished by my feelings," he said, "that my years of labor are nearly over, and my inclinations point to private life."[43] He did not come readily to this belief that he would soon have to leave the college. As recently as the previous December, in declining the presidency of the Southern Life Insurance Company, he had written that he felt he should not abandon the position he held, so long as he could be of service to the college.[44]

The professors of the college, seeing him almost daily, realized

[41] *Jones,* 196–97.

[42] R. E. Lee to Agnes Lee, Feb. 2, 1870; *R. E. Lee, Jr.,* 383; R. E. Lee to W. H. F. Lee, Feb. 14, 1870; *R. E. Lee, Jr.,* 384.

[43] R. E. Lee to Robert H. Miller, *MS.,* March 22, 1870; R. E. Lee to M. D. Corse *et al.,* March 18, 1870; *Jones,* 176. These letters to Miller and Corse were in answer to a proposal that he accept a place, corresponding to that of a managing director of a modern chamber of commerce, for the development of the trade of Alexandria. It was probably about this time that Lee said: "I am too old for the work that I am trying to do" (M. W. Humphreys in *Richmond Times-Dispatch,* Jan. 20, 1907).

[44] R. E. Lee to J. B. Gordon, Dec. 14. 1869; *Jones,* 277. The impairment of his health was not generally known. There had never been a time when he received more business offers, or offers with larger promised compensation (R. E. Lee to unnamed correspondent, Aug. 26, 1869; *Jones,* 175; *cf.* also *R. E. Lee, Jr.,* 376).

how serious his condition had become. Individually, from time to time, they urged him to take a long rest. He met every such appeal with a courteous "No." Feeling that it was his sense of duty and his unwillingness to burden them that kept him from going away, they arranged among themselves a division of his college work and wrote him a letter in which they asked him to take a vacation and to spend it in travel for his health. In order that he might not be embarrassed by any nomination of their own, they proposed that he select one of their number to be titular acting president in his absence.[45] It is quite likely that the suggestion of travel was made after conference with his physicians, who were very anxious for him to seek a climate where he would be less liable to contract colds.[46]

Upon the delivery of this communication from the faculty, Lee's doctor and his family united with the professors in new importunities. Lee yielded. "I think I should do better here," he wrote, "and am very reluctant to leave my home in my present condition; but they seem so interested in my recovery and so persuasive in their uneasiness that I should appear obstinate, if not perverse, if I resisted longer."[47] On March 22, 1870, he formally notified the faculty that he had decided to take their suggestion and that he would name Professor Kirkpatrick to act as president in his absence.[48] The selection evidently was made with care, for Doctor Kirkpatrick, professor of moral philosophy, was a mature man of wide educational experience.

Lee very promptly decided where he would go. He had long desired to visit the grave of his daughter, Annie, near the White Sulphur Springs, Warren County, North Carolina, for he had been unable to make the trip when, in August, 1866, the friendly people of the neighborhood had unveiled a simple monument to her memory.[49] ". . . I have always promised myself to go [there]," he told Rooney, "and I think, if I am to accomplish it, I have no time to lose. I wish to witness her quiet sleep, with

45 MS. *Faculty Minutes*, March 20, 1870; *cf. Jones*, 115–16.
46 "This is a terrible climate in winter and spring," Mrs. Lee had confided to Mrs. R. H. Chilton, March 10, 1867 (*Chilton Papers*).
47 R. E. Lee to Mildred Lee, March 21, 1870; *R. E. Lee, Jr.*, 384–85.
48 MS. *Faculty Minutes*, March 22, 1870.
49 R. E. Lee to Mrs. Jos. S. Jones, *et al.*, July 25, 1866; *Jones*, 394–95. *Cf.* also *R. E. Lee, Jr.*, 241–42.

her dear hands crossed over her breast, as it were in mute prayer, undisturbed by her distance from us, and to feel that her pure spirit is waiting in bliss in the land of the blessed." [50] From Warrenton he purposed to go either to Norfolk or to Savannah, and on his return journey he intended to stop and see his sons. His daughter Agnes, who had nursed him during his sickness, was to accompany him now.

[50] R. E. Lee to W. H. F. Lee, March 22, 1870; *R. E. Lee, Jr.,* 305.

CHAPTER XXV

THE FINAL REVIEW

ON the afternoon of Thursday, March 24, looking very badly,[1] General Lee left Lexington on the canal packet-boat for Lynchburg, to begin a tour for his health,[2] as his father had done at the end of his career. If it had been a quiet journey on which he set out, it might have benefited him greatly and might perhaps have prolonged his life. As it was, his two months of travel probably hastened his death. Much of his time had to be spent on the railroads, and many of his days were crowded with all the incidents of a triumphant progress, full of excitement and most injurious to an impaired heart. Still, if his sands were running out so swiftly that a few months were of no great moment, there could not have been a more fitting close. Was he preparing to face his Maker? Did he ask himself if he had walked humbly in the ways of God's appointing? Had he chosen rightly and counselled with prudence after the war? If, on his knees in prayer, he put these heart-searching questions, the South was ready to answer them for him. The last and most beautiful chapter of his life was opening.

In its initial stage his travel was retired. After a wearying night on the canal and a tedious day on the railroad, he reached Richmond on the afternoon of Friday, March 25, and went to the Exchange and Ballard House.[3] Too weak to go visiting or even to attend to some purchases Mrs. Lee had asked him to make, he remained quietly at the hotel and saw only the personal friends who called. The senate of Virginia, however, as soon as it learned he was in Richmond, unanimously extended him the privileges of the floor and would have been pleased to accord him a formal reception, an honor he declined in a characteristic letter.[4] On

---

[1] *Riley*, 130–31. [2] *Lexington Gazette*, March 25. 1870.
[3] *Richmond Enquirer*, March 26, 1870.
[4] *Journal of the Senate of Virginia*, 1869–70, pp. 227, 230.

444

Saturday he had a two-hour examination by three of the leading physicians of the city, who told him they would study his case further and would report their findings to his doctor in Lexington. "I think I feel better than when I left Lexington, certainly stronger, but am a little feverish. Whether it is produced by the journey, or the toddies that Agnes administers, I do not know"— thus he reported himself to Mrs. Lee.[5]

The hotel at which he stopped in Richmond consisted of two buildings on opposite sides of Franklin Street, connected by an overhead bridge. The General was crossing this bridge with Agnes, one day during his visit, when he encountered the familiar figure of Colonel John S. Mosby, he of the renowned partisan rangers. "The General was pale and haggard," Mosby subsequently wrote, "and did not look like the Apollo I had known in the army." They exchanged greetings, and a little later Colonel Mosby called at the General's room for a social chat. "I felt oppressed by the great memories that his presence revived," Mosby wrote, "and while both of us were thinking about the war, neither of us referred to it."

Mosby left ere long, but soon was back again, bringing with him a man whose presence recalled the tragedy of Gettysburg and the dread day of Five Forks—General George E. Pickett. Mosby had met Pickett, by chance, just after he had left the room, and when he had remarked that he had called on their old commander, Pickett had said that he would pay his respects if Mosby would return with him, but that he did not want to be alone with Lee.

The General had not seen Pickett since Appomattox, if, indeed, he saw him then, and he had conducted no correspondence with him after the war. From Mosby's account it would seem that General Lee received Pickett with his full reserve, a reserve that could be icy and killing though coupled always with perfect courtesy. Sensing the unpleasantness of the meeting, Mosby got up in a few moments and Pickett followed him. Once outside the room, Pickett broke out bitterly against "that old man" who,

[5] R. E. Lee to Mrs. Lee, March 29, 1870. This letter (*R. E. Lee, Jr.*, 388–89) was written from Richmond and is misdated. It obviously was penned on March 27, for it referred to the fact that Agnes had gone to church. Agnes's letter of April 3, to her mother (*ibid.*, 391), shows that the General left Richmond on March 28. Lee's autograph "7's" and "9's" looked very much alike.

he said, "had my division massacred at Gettysburg." [6] As far as is known, General Lee never afterwards referred to the meeting or to General Pickett, but this was not an experience to be coveted for a man with heart-disease.

A much more welcome visitor was Colonel J. L. Corley, who had been Lee's chief quartermaster, an able and devoted man. Without hinting that he thought General Lee needed an escort, Colonel Corley decided he should accompany his old chieftain on his projected journey, and by one device or another, diplomatically prevailed upon the General to let him make the arrangements to attend him southward from Charlotte, where he offered to meet him on an agreed date. It was a service of the most considerate sort, unobtrusively rendered from love of his old leader, and it contributed immeasurably to lessen the discomfort of the trip.

On the afternoon of Monday, March 28, at 2 o'clock, the General and his daughter left Richmond for Warrenton, N. C. They reached their objective at 10 o'clock the same night and received warm welcome at Ingleside, the home of Mr. and Mrs. John White, who were known to Agnes, as were many others in the neighborhood, from her stay among them in the second year of the war. The next morning, March 29, the Whites supplied the General and his daughter with masses of white hyacinths, and Captain William J. White, John White's son, placed a team and vehicle at their disposal that they might go unaccompanied to the cemetery. "My visit . . . was mournful, yet soothing to my feelings," the General wrote Mrs. Lee. From the graveyard they drove to the home of Joseph Jones, where they were entertained at dinner, and then they returned to Captain White's house.[7] A number of people called during the evening. "I was glad," Lee told his wife, "to have the opportunity of thanking the kind friends for their care of [Annie] while living and their attention to her since her death. I saw most of the ladies of the committee who undertook the preparation of the monument and the enclosure

---

[6] *Memoirs of Col. John S. Mosby,* 380–81.

[7] For the initials of the Messrs. White and for interesting facts regarding them, the writer is indebted to Mrs. Catherine Pendleton Arrington, of Warrenton, N. C. Captain White purchased for North Carolina, from John Key of Kinghorn, Scotland, husband of his aunt, the swift India steamer *Lord Clyde,* which subsequently was rechristened *Advance.* This vessel, which Mr. Key fitted out at his own expense, became the most successful of the Wilmington blockade runners. See P. M. Wilson: *Southern Exposures,* 57–58.

of the cemetery. . . ."[8] Perhaps this kindness disposed him to yield to the importunities of Mr. White's daughters, and to give them a lock of his hair, which is to this day one of the treasures of the family.[9]

Now began the public part of the tour—public not because Lee desired it so, but because the people heard of his coming and insisted on honoring him. The General left Warrenton that night, March 29, with Agnes, aboard a sleeping-car, the first on which he had ever ridden, but he was rendered wakeful by the novelty and the interruptions. At Raleigh, which was some sixty miles distant, via the Raleigh and Gaston Railroad, scores were waiting in the station. "Lee, Lee," they cried, and cheered him again and again. But he had retired and no doubt was glad to escape an appearance.[10] At another station on the way the same sounds of affectionate welcome reached Lee's ears.

The journey continued all the next day, by way of Salisbury, Charlotte, and Columbia. As the presence of the General on the train soon was known, word was dispatched ahead by the railroad telegraphers. Former Confederates sent in fruit from the other cars. At every place where the train stopped for meals the proprietors of the restaurants served lunches and coffee on his car as soon as they learned the General would not alight. Salisbury had a band and a multitude to do him honor. So had Charlotte, where the faithful Colonel Corley reported himself. "Namesakes appeared on the way, of all sizes. Old ladies stretched their heads into the windows at way-stations and then drew back and said, 'He is mighty like his pictures' "—so Agnes wrote her mother. Columbia, S. C., was reached in a pouring rain, but presented a great crowd. Most of the stores had been closed. All the Confederate veterans had been mustered and, with a large number of other citizens, had been marched in procession to the station of the Charlotte, Columbia and Augusta Railroad. Colonel Alexander Haskell was master of ceremonies, he who had commanded the Seventh South Carolina Cavalry and in October,

---

[8] R. E. Lee to Mrs. Lee, April 2, 1870; *R. E. Lee, Jr.,* 390; Agnes Lee to Mrs. R. E. Lee, April 3, 1870; *ibid.,* 391–92.

[9] Letter of Mrs. Catherine Pendleton Arrington to the writer, Jan. 19, 1928.

[10] The people of Raleigh were under the impression that the General intended to stop there (*Richmond Enquirer,* March 28, 1870, quoting the *Raleigh Sentinel*).

447

1864, had been wounded in battle with Butler. In the crowd, also, was General E. Porter Alexander, Longstreet's chief of artillery and the man who had conducted the bombardment that had preceded Pickett's charge. But there were no war reminiscences now, only smiles and handshakes and cheers. General Lee was forced to go to the platform, where he was introduced by Colonel Haskell and was met with a roar. He bowed his acknowledgments but made no speech.[11]

Finally, at 9:30 on the evening of March 30, nearly twenty-four hours after the General had left Warrenton, he reached Augusta, Ga., where he expected to spend the night, before going on to Savannah.[12] Mayor Allen and a committee of citizens were at the station to receive him. The guest was placed in a carriage with the mayor, Miss Russell, and Alderman Stovall. Agnes and Colonel Corley rode in a second carriage with General McLaws, Colonel Rains, and Major T. P. Branch. The party was escorted to the Planter's Hotel, where others gathered to pay their respects.[13] Lee was weary, for the journey had been exhausting,[14] and he yielded to the appeal that he remain in Augusta a day and not attempt to go on to Savannah the next morning.

But if it was rest he sought, he did not find it. He had to hold a reception nearly the whole of the forenoon. "Crowds came," Agnes wrote her mother. "Wounded soldiers, servants, and workingmen even. The sweetest little children—namesakes—dressed to their eyes, with bouquets of japonica—or tiny cards in their little fat hands—with their names." [15] Among the callers were friends of other days, and several of Lee's old generals, among them A. R. Wright and W. M. Gardner,[16] as well as McLaws. The people must have thronged Lee, for it is recorded that a boy of thirteen, who wished to see him, had to worm his way through the crowd until, at length, he stood by the side of

---

[11] *Columbia Phœnix,* quoted in *Savannah Republican,* April 2, 1870.

[12] The sources for this part of the journey are R. E. Lee to Mrs. Lee, April 2, 1870, and Agnes Lee to Mrs. R. E. Lee, April 3–4, 1870; *R. E. Lee, Jr.,* 390–94. From this point on, newspaper reports supplement the family letters.

[13] *Constitutionalist,* quoted in *Richmond Dispatch,* April 4, 1870; *Augusta Chronicle,* quoted in *Savannah Republican,* April 1, 1870.

[14] *R. E. Lee, Jr.,* 390.

[15] Agnes Lee to Mrs. R. E. Lee, April 3, 1870; *R. E. Lee, Jr.,* 393.

[16] General Gardner had been under Lee's command only for a short time, see 6 *C. M. H.,* 417–18.

the General and looked up at him in wondering reverence. This lad's name was Woodrow Wilson.[17]

That evening there was a serenade and another crowd. It was far too fast a pace for a man in Lee's condition. But what was he to do? How was he to deny himself to the women who had prayed for him, to the men who had fought with him, or to the parents of those who had fallen in his ranks?

The next day, April 1, the General and his daughter left the hotel with Colonel Corley for Savannah.[18] A swift team carried him in a carriage to the station; his veterans mustered once again and gave him a rebel yell. He bowed and retired into the private car that had been attached to the train. But he was not quite through with generous Augusta. A boy of fourteen, who had climbed aboard, opened the door, rushed impulsively in and offered him a white rose he had plucked that morning and had brought into town with him. "General Lee," wrote the "boy" when he was past seventy, "laid aside his paper, rose from his seat, bowed with the grace of a Chesterfield, took the rose and said: 'I thank you, my son, and now with your permission I will present it to my daughter.' Miss Lee herself gave a gracious smile. General Lee then continued: 'I see by the books under your arm that you are a schoolboy. Study hard and make a man of yourself.' "[19]

At some point on the journey of 160 miles to the familiar city of Lee's first engineering labors, a reception committee came aboard. It included former Quartermaster General Lawton, General J. F. Gilmer, who had been chief engineer of the War Department, Andrew Lowe, and others. In their company, a little after six, the General left the train at Savannah to face one of the largest crowds that ever assembled to welcome him. The people had been disappointed by his non-arrival the previous day[20] and now they overflowed the train shed. His escort had difficulty in making a way for him to the open barouche that was

[17] Woodrow Wilson: *Robert E. Lee, An Interpretation*, 11–12.

[18] Lee, prior to this time, had twice been invited warmly to Savannah and, in declining, had said it would have afforded him much pleasure to visit the city (R. E. Lee to unnamed correspondent, Dec. 5, 1868; *Jones*, 270).

[19] William H. Fleming in *The Augusta Herald*, Sept. 14, 1930, quoting *The Atlanta Journal*.

[20] *Savannah Republican*, April 1, 1870.

in waiting for him.[21] Cheer followed cheer, until the General had to rise and bow his acknowledgments. The Negroes of the city and some of the Federal garrison joined cheerfully in the demonstration.

As soon as the cheering crowd would permit, Lee was driven to the home of General Lawton, at the corner of York and Lincoln Streets. Later in the evening he was taken to the residence of Andrew Lowe, where he was to sleep. "With the exception of an appearance of weariness, General Lee looks better than we expected to find him," *The Savannah Republican* reported, "yet, it appeared to us that an inexpressible sadness was visible in his features, momentarily, no doubt, and caused by the demonstrations of filial love and devotion thus shown him by a people whom he had striven in vain to liberate from political bondage."[22]

After the General had left, the Washington Comet Band and the Saxe Horn Band appeared in front of the Lawton house to serenade him. A crowd gathered quickly, and the bands alternated with selections. When "Dixie" was played, it seemed from the shouts as if the days of the Confederacy had come back again. In answer to the calls for the city's guest, General Lawton came out and thanked the people but asked them to excuse the old commander on account of weariness. He tactfully refrained from saying that General Lee was at Mr. Lowe's, as that, of course, would have started the crowd thither. The bands then struck up "The Bonnie Blue Flag" and presently marched off to serenade General Joseph E. Johnston, who was then residing in Savannah.[23]

A drive about the town the next morning, April 2, was followed by calls on the families he knew. After that came a dinner at Mr. Lowe's with a number of his comrades, among them General Joseph E. Johnston, General Lawton, and General Gilmer. It was the first time Lee had seen Johnston since the war. In his correspondence there is no reference to this fact or to the char-

---

[21] Lee rode with General Lawton. The young son and namesake of the Georgian was on a small seat in the same vehicle.

[22] *Savannah Republican*, April 2, 1870.

[23] *Savannah Republican*, April 2, 1870. Agnes Lee's letter of April 3, *loc. cit.*, gave the added information that the bands alternated with their music.

acter of their conversation, but it doubtless was cordial. During this visit to Savannah, the two were photographed together in the familiar picture that shows them, grizzled and old and feeble, seated on opposite sides of a small table.

The Confederate officers Lee saw in Savannah were more numerous and better circumstanced than any he had met. He felt justified in presenting to them the plight and the needs of one of the most loyal and distressed of their comrades, General Samuel Cooper. Having learned on his last visit to Alexandria that Cooper was overtaxing his strength at hard, uncongenial work, in an effort to earn a living for his family, Lee proposed that his old associates raise a fund for General Cooper's relief. General Lawton and others quickly agreed. They collected some $300, after General Lee's departure. He added $100 on his own account and sent the whole to Cooper on August 4. "You must pardon me for moving in this matter," Lee then wrote his long-time companion-in-arms.[24]

Lee was happy to greet old friends and to make new. Particularly was he pleased when the Mackays got back to town and reopened their familiar house in Broughton Street.[25] But he found the pace too hard, and in his letters home expressed regret that he had undertaken the long journey. "I wish I were back," he said, though he much appreciated the hospitality shown him.[26]

Declining an invitation from General Chilton to visit Columbus, Ga.,[27] he planned to go down into Florida on April 8, and on the way to visit Cumberland Island, where his father was buried, but Agnes fell sick and that prevented his departure until Tuesday, April 12. He set out then aboard the steamer *Nick King,* which ran leisurely between Savannah and Palatka on the Saint John's River.[28] With him and his daughter went his Savannah host, Andrew Lowe, "thinking Agnes and I were unable to take care of ourselves," as the General confided to Mrs. Lee. At Brunswick, where the people turned out to see him,[29] the party

[24] *R. E. Lee, Jr.,* 421.
[25] Miss Katharine Stiles related (*Richmond Times-Dispatch,* Jan. 20, 1907) that Lee told her to write the absent Mackays that "the old man" was not able to go to the mountains for a visit and that they must come back to town in order that he might see them once again.
[26] R. E. Lee to Mrs. Lee, April 2 and 7; *R. E. Lee, Jr.,* 390 and 394–95.
[27] R. E. Lee to R. H. Chilton, *MS.,* April 7, 1870; *Chilton Papers.*
[28] *Savannah Republican,* April 14, 1870.
[29] *Brunswick Appeal* of April 15, quoted in *Savannah Republican,* April 17, 1870.

was joined by William Nightingale, grandson of General Nathanael Greene and successor to the ownership of Dungeness, the estate on which "Light-Horse Harry" Lee had died. When the boat tied up at Cumberland Island they went ashore to the burial ground. ". . . Agnes decorated my father's grave with beautiful fresh flowers," Lee wrote, and added simply: "I presume it is the last time I shall be able to pay to it my tribute of respect. The cemetery is unharmed and the grave is in good order, though the house of Dungeness has been burned and the island devastated." [30]

Entering historic Saint John's River, Lee and his daughter about 4 o'clock on the afternoon of Wednesday, April 13, touched at Jacksonville, Fla. As soon as the gang-plank was lowered, a committee from the city[31] came aboard to greet the General in the upper saloon of the vessel. People streamed aboard until the *Nick King* was almost swamped. One by one, duly introduced, they passed and joyfully shook hands with Lee. As many more remained disappointed on shore, unable to get on the ship. To satisfy them, the General was asked to go on deck. When he walked out and stood where he could be seen, a strange thing happened: a complete silence fell on the throng, a silence of admiring reverence, as if the people thought it would be worse than discourtesy to applaud the old chieftain who embodied in their eyes the cause for which they had fought. ". . . The very silence of the multitude," reported *The Jacksonville Union,* "spoke a deeper feeling than the loudest huzzas could have expressed." [32]

Jacksonville people were anxious for the General to stop there, but he had made his plans to go on to Palatka aboard the same vessel, and, as usual, he held to his schedule. So, after half an hour, the crowd left with tears and a "God-bless-you" and the *Nick King* continued southward up the broad river, past a landscape that delighted the General.

The boat was to remain for the night of April 13 at Palatka, before beginning its return trip, and there it was met by another

---

30 R. E. Lee to Mrs. Lee, April 18, 1870; *R. E. Lee, Jr.,* 398.

31 It consisted of Colonel Sanderson, Colonel Daniels, Colonel Fleming, Doctor Maxwell, and H. T. Boyd.

32 Quoted in *The Savannah Republican,* April 16, 1870.

old friend, whom Lee probably had not seen since he had sorrowfully said good-bye at Appomattox—Colonel R. G. Cole, chief commissary of the Army of Northern Virginia. He lived on a plantation near Palatka, and, of course, insisted on entertaining his old chief. As it was a pleasant, warm day, Lee could walk out of doors among Colonel Cole's orange-trees and pluck fruit from them. He enjoyed, also, the abundant, inviting fish.

The return voyage was quieter. About 4 P.M., April 14, the boat tied up at Jacksonville. As it was not to sail until 3 o'clock the next morning, the General and his party were escorted ashore, were driven about the town, and were entertained by Colonel Sanderson. From Jacksonville they went on to Savannah, where they arrived during the forenoon of Saturday, April 16.[33]

Lee then determined not to return home by the most direct route, but to come up the coast, so as to visit Charleston, S. C., and friends in Tidewater Virginia. On the morning of April 25 he left Savannah for Charleston,[34] accompanied now only by Agnes, whose health was giving her father some concern. The political situation in South Carolina was tense at this time, and General Lee was anxious to escape all demonstrations that might heat blood and provoke a clash. Accordingly, he hoped that word of his coming might not precede him, but a telegram was sent by some admirer a short time before the train was due to reach the Carolina city, and a company of his friends met him at the station. They respected his wishes, however, and permitted him to be driven quietly to the home of W. Jefferson Bennett, who was to be his host.[35] Major H. E. Young, the Charleston member of his staff, had planned to entertain him, but had bereavement in his family.[36] Mr. Bennett was a citizen of wealth and standing, with two sons at Washington College. He had six attractive young people in his household, at 60 Montague Street, when General Lee arrived. All of them welcomed their guest with much awe and trembling, but were soon put at ease by his manner toward them.[37]

---

[33] *Savannah Republican*, April 17, 1870.   [34] *Savannah Republican*, April 26, 1870.
[35] *Charleston Courier*, April 26, 1870.
[36] *Letter of A. R. Young to the writer*, Nov. 8, 1927.
[37] *Letter of A. B. Murray to the writer*, Nov. 17, 1927. Mr. Murray, who has kindly supplied details of this part of the General's visit, was one of the young members of the Bennett household.

Within a few hours the whole city began to clamor for a glimpse of him. That evening the Post Band serenaded. The next morning his old friends began to call. A delegation came to ask if he would not agree to hold a reception at one of the hotels, in order to give the public an opportunity of greeting him. He excused himself,[38] but he could not escape the admiring homage of the people. Mr. Bennett thereupon announced a reception to the Confederate officers of Charleston, in honor of General Lee, and designated A. B. Murray to receive the guests at the door and to present them. Among others came Major Hutson Lee, who during General Lee's service in the Carolinas, early in 1862, had been quartermaster in the Charleston district. As soon as the major entered the room, Lee said: "I have a crow to pick with you, Major." The former quartermaster at once inquired why. Lee challenged him: Had not the major been in Richmond on such-and-such a date, and had he not gone to witness a review beyond the city? Lee thought he had seen him at that time. The major answered in astonishment that he had been there. "Then, why," concluded Lee, "did you not come up and speak to me?" Major Lee excused himself by saying he had not presumed to approach the commanding general, but he left the reception in amazement. He had met the General only two or perhaps three times, yet Lee had noticed him among the thousands at the review in the summer of 1862, and now, eight years after, instantly recalled both the man and the incident.[39]

The fire units of the town had a parade on the afternoon of April 27, and when they were dismissed the white companies assembled in Meeting Street, procured a band, and marched to the Bennett house. Their cheers brought the General to the portico, where he bowed his acknowledgments. This would not suffice. Introductions were demanded and much brief speech-making was staged. At General Lee's request, C. G. Memminger, former Confederate Secretary of the Treasury, expressed the General's appreciation of the compliment paid him. Still the firemen held on. "Just one word," they kept crying until, at last, the General thanked them in a few sentences and pleaded his indisposition as the reason for his silence. It was the nearest he was

[38] *Charleston Courier*, April 27.   [39] A. B. Murray, *loc. cit.*

brought to the embarrassment of a public address during the whole of his tour.[40]

Mr. Bennett had planned a general reception for the evening of the 27th, but had realized that many women and children would not venture on the streets at night, and consequently he invited some to call between 1 and 3 P.M., while those who had escorts were bidden for the evening. Between the two affairs a very notable dinner was served.[41] The guests were as much surprised at the General's memory for names as Major Lee had been. He chatted for a few moments with all who were presented to him, and then, when they came to go, he shook hands with each again and called every one of them by name. To a little girl who had given him a flower, he said as she was leaving with her mother, "See, Rosa, I have not lost your flower!" [42]

It was, altogether, a great event, which *The Charleston Courier* grew eloquent in describing: "Old and young, the gray beards and sages of the country, the noble, pure, honorable, poor and wealthy, with hardly an exception, were present, and glad to do him honor. Stately dames of the old school, grandmothers of seventy, and a long train of granddaughters, all flocked around the noble old chief, glad of a smile, of a shake of the hand; and happy was the girl of twelve, or fourteen, who carried away on her lips the parting kiss of the grand old soldier." General Lee seemed feeble and weary that evening, but he was pleased to observe the good cheer of the people. "It is so grateful," he said, "to see so much elasticity among your people; and I am astonished to see Charleston so wondrously recuperated after all her disasters." [43]

So far as the records show, General Lee did not revisit in Charleston any of the scenes of his labors in the first winter of the war. He kept away purposely from the places that revived the memories of the war, not only in the South Carolina port, but wherever he travelled. After 1865 he went to five cities only

---

[40] *Charleston Courier*, April 28, 1870.

[41] Mrs. R. E. Lee to Mildred or Mary Lee, May 9, 1870; *R. E. Lee, Jr.*, 405; A. B. Murray, *loc. cit.*

[42] A. B. Murray, *loc. cit.*

[43] *Charleston Courier*, April 29, 1870. Captain F. W. Dawson (*op. cit.*, 169) noted that busy as Lee was, he arranged a private interview in order that young Mrs. Dawson might be presented to him.

that were connected closely with his own military operations—Richmond, Petersburg, Fredericksburg, Charleston, and Savannah. Aboard train or on steamer he passed by the Richmond-Petersburg defenses, and several times he used the railroad that crossed the old battleground of Culpeper, but on horseback he never rode over any of the fields where his troops had been engaged, except for his journey to Pampatike, soon after the surrender. All this was deliberate. Had he been able to do so he would have ploughed up the trenches and would have followed the example he applauded "of those nations who endeavored to obliterate the marks of civil strife." [44]

On April 28 the General left Charleston for Wilmington, where he had been invited to stop.[45] The northward route was by way of Florence to Meares Bluff.[46] There, when the cars stopped, a committee came to Lee's seat and asked him if he would go aboard a special train that had been sent out from Wilmington and would precede the regular locomotive to that city. The General consented, perforce, and left his coach to make the transfer. As he stepped to the platform, there was a word of command, the roll of a drum, and a line of boys in gray uniforms presented arms as their band started to play. They were the cadets of Cape Fear Academy, under charge of one of Lee's old brigadiers, R. E. Colston, but they must have seemed tragically like the thousands Lee had beheld during the early days of the war, before their uniforms of gray had become bloody rags. If the General was affected by the sight of these cadets, he said nothing. He passed the cadets in silence and went aboard the special train, into a car where only a few passengers were seated. They received him, according to a chronicler of the times, with "a suppressed whisper of admiration, respectfully restrained," but when those who had clambered down to get a first glimpse of him came back into the coach, they began to crowd about him, to his evident embarrassment. In answer to questions, he said he would stop at Wilmington, probably for a day, but he begged that there be no further demonstration.

Arriving at the brave old town that must have revived dark

[44] See *supra*, p. 436.
[45] *Charleston Courier*, April 30, 1870; *Wilmington Journal*, March 27, 1870.
[46] This appears as Mars Bluff on the map in *O. R. Atlas*, Plate 139.

memories of Fort Fisher, he was escorted by the cadets to the home of George Davis, who had been attorney general in the Confederate cabinet.[47] There, at last, was privacy, and with it, old acquaintanceship. For Mrs. Davis was an Alexandria woman, daughter of Doctor Orlando Fairfax, whose family had been friends of the Lees and Custises back in the peaceful old days before the politicians had revived the slavery question.[48]

A night of quiet, and then another day of crowds and receptions. Friends by the score called on him at the Davis house. The whole corps of the Cape Fear Academy came at his request, probably because he did not want them to feel that he was unappreciative of the honor they had sought to do him the previous evening. A dinner given by Mr. Davis brought to the house other friends and the celebrities of the town. Despite the crowded day, the General found time to call on Bishop Thomas Atkinson, who had been rector of a church in Baltimore when Lee had been stationed in that city.[49]

On April 30 Lee left Wilmington and went by way of Weldon to Portsmouth, Va., where he was to take the ferry across the Elizabeth River to Norfolk. As usual, word of his coming had preceded him and had brought a vast throng to the station. When he left the train a new surprise awaited him: Wilmington had welcomed him with a line of cadets; Portsmouth received him with a roaring salute. Some of the young men of the town had borrowed from one of the fire companies a cannon bearing the name of a contemporary journalist of passing fame, "Brick" Pomeroy, whom General Lee had met in Richmond at the beginning of his tour.[50] With this gun they fired rounds in the General's honor. And, as a fitting companion when artillery was barking, there in the van of the crowd, waiting to greet his old chief, was Colonel Walter H. Taylor. With him, General Lee walked to the ferry, while the crowd outdid "Brick" Pomeroy in noisy greeting. ". . . Those shouts," noted the veracious annalist of Norfolk, "were not of the measured 'hip-hip-hurrah'

[47] *Wilmington Journal*, April 29, 1870. For this and other references to General Lee's visit to Wilmington, the author is indebted to Miss Emma Woodward, head of the public library of Wilmington, N. C. For Davis, see 1 *C. M. H.*, 601.
[48] *R. E. Lee, Jr.*, 401.
[49] *Wilmington Journal*, April 30, 1870; *R. E. Lee, Jr.*, 401.
[50] *R. E. Lee, Jr.*, 389.

kind now in vogue, but were the genuine old-fashioned Confederate yells. . . ."[51] Behind Lee, as he slowly went aboard the ferry boat, were some hundreds of admiring Portsmouth people, anxious to have a sight of him or to share his company. He went into a cabin for the brief run across the river, and there he might have been overrun by enthusiastic admirers had not some of his friends guarded the door. Outside, Roman candles and rockets were being fired to notify the waiting multitude on the Norfolk side that the General was aboard. Before the boat was across the stream, the United Fire Company of Norfolk opened in salute with its cannon and continued to fire until the ferry was in the slip. When Lee stepped ashore, the great throng began to cheer as loudly as had their neighbors on the other side of the Elizabeth. Amid the din of their welcoming shouts, with the rebel yell as a sharp, continuing accompaniment, the General was escorted to a carriage and was driven off quickly with Colonel Taylor.[52] His Norfolk stopping-place was the fine, quiet home of Doctor William Selden, bounded by Freemason Street, Botetourt Street, and the river.[53]

Faithful to long habit, Lee insisted on attending Sunday morning worship the day after his arrival, and he invited one of his host's daughters, Miss Caroline Selden, to go with him. ". . . The street was lined with adoring crowds," Miss Selden wrote. "For one block before reaching Christ Church we had almost to force our way through a narrow pathway they seemed to have left for him. Every hat was in the air, but being Sunday the homage was very quiet, and I well remember that he held his hat in his hand all the way."[54]

When Sunday was passed, William E. Taylor, who was no kin to Walter H. Taylor, gave a very elaborate dinner, at which a number of Norfolk men were invited to meet the General. The Taylors were an old family, with a wealth of silver, china, and

[51] Burton: *History of Norfolk*, 133.

[52] *Norfolk Journal*, May 2, 1870. For this and other references to this visit, the writer is indebted to the Carnegie Library of Norfolk.

[53] Now the residence of C. W. Grandy, to whom, and to whose aunt, Miss Caroline Selden, daughter of Doctor Selden, the author is indebted for information regarding the General's stay in Norfolk. Louis Jaffé, editor of *The Norfolk Virginian-Pilot*, also most generously supplied data.

[54] Letter of Miss Caroline Selden to C. W. Grandy, *MS.*, Aug. 2, 1926.

glass, and they did their utmost to provide an evening of honor for the man whom Colonel Taylor so loyally had served.[55]

The Seldens tendered Lee a reception on the night of May 4, when many of his old soldiers came to shake his hand and to gaze once more—and for the last time—on his calm countenance. They represented every station in life and many units of the Army of Northern Virginia. It probably was at this time that "Bryan" called to see him, the faithful "Bryan" of war-time head-quarters. Another caller was a man who linked Lee with an earlier captain after whom many of his officers had sought to model: Emanuel J. Myers, eighty-nine and feeble, was brought to the Seldens' and was introduced to General Lee. On his coat he wore the cross of the Legion of Honor which he had received as a member of the Old Guard from the hands of Napoleon him-self.[56]

This dinner, the reception, and a professional conference with Doctor Selden, who was a physician of high standing, consumed nearly all the General's strength. Rain kept him from making at least one anticipated call. On May 5 he bade farewell to his host's family and quietly left the city on the steamer that ran up the James to the river plantations he intended to visit.[57] His one regret was that so many residents of Norfolk were leaving their city to get work. "Virginia needs her young men," he said.[58]

First he stopped again at the lower of the three Harrison estates called Brandon. The mistress of Lower Brandon, Mrs. Isabella Ritchie Harrison, and her kin were people he had known long and affectionately. The atmosphere was that he loved best. There were no crowds to cheer him, no receptions to tire him. He could relax—almost for the first time since March 24, when he had left Lexington. He drove to the other Brandons, saw all his friends and connections in the neighborhood, went to church on Sunday, May 8,[59] wrote a few family letters and enjoyed the delights of the place. "Brandon is looking very beautiful," he told Mrs. Lee, "and it is refreshing to look at the river. The garden is filled with flowers and abounds in roses. The yellow jasmine is

---

[55] Miss Selden, *loc. cit.*
[56] Miss Selden, *loc. cit.*; R. E. Lee, Jr., 402; *Norfolk Journal,* May 6, 1870.
[57] *Norfolk Landmark,* Jan. 18, 1911.   [58] *Ibid.*
[59] This statement that he attended church rests on oral tradition in the community.

still in bloom and perfumes the atmosphere." He was beginning now to talk of returning to Lexington and methodically set the tentative date for May 24, precisely two months from the time he had left home.[60]

From Brandon, Lee went to Shirley, by pre-arrangement with Hill Carter.[61] He arrived with Agnes on Tuesday, May 10, and spent there the better part of two days, in calm like that of Brandon, and doubtless in much happiness of soul. In 1868, it will be remembered, he had expressed a desire to go once more to Shirley, and had questioned whether he ever would do so again: now he was there, with a surer premonition that he was looking for the last time on the garden, on the fine old house, and on Peale's famous portrait of his hero, Washington. No record of his stay at Shirley remains except the epigram of "one of the daughters of the house," who has since died. She recalled "the great dignity and kindness of General Lee's bearing," his willingness to autograph his pictures for them, and his old fondness for having his hands tickled. "We regarded him with the greatest veneration." She concluded: "We had heard of God, but here was General Lee!"[62]

While the General had been in Savannah, Mrs. Lee had carried out a long-cherished plan of visiting Rooney at the White House. The General had not believed she would go,[63] and when he had urged her in March to begin her preparations for the journey, she had replied, rather disdainfully, she had "none to make; they have been made years ago."[64] On April 20 she had arrived in Richmond by the James River and Kanawha Canal[65] and had then taken the railroad to the White House.[66] General Lee planned to join her there and to visit his sons on their farms, and he would have driven directly across country from Shirley had not Agnes decided to accompany him. As her baggage would have required a wagon, which would have had to cover twenty-five

---

[60] R. E. Lee, Jr., 404.
[61] R. E. Lee to Hill Carter, MS., May 4, 1870; Shirley MSS.
[62] R. E. Lee, Jr., 405.   [63] R. E. Lee, Jr., 378.
[64] R. E. Lee to W. H. F. Lee, March 22, 1870; R. E. Lee, Jr., 386.
[65] Richmond Enquirer, Richmond Dispatch, April 21, 1870.
[66] While there, Mrs. Lee received some boxes of old letters, "with some other debris," as she said, "of what the Yankees had left of a once happy and well-filled house." She destroyed the whole (Mrs. R. E. Lee to Mrs. W. Hartwell Macon, MS., June, n.d., 1870; Johnston MSS.).

miles of bad roads, the General decided to go on to Richmond by steamer and to finish the journey by rail. He accordingly left the old Carter plantation on Thursday, May 12, and arrived at Rooney's home that evening.

Aside from a few familiars, there were no other guests at the White House. The General was free to rest and to play with his small grandson and namesake, to whom he was much attached. During his stay he rode over alone to spend a brief time with his bachelor son Robert at his plantation. The General knew, of course, that Robert lived in the former overseer's house at Romancoke while planning to build a home. He knew, too, that men who were struggling with the land and "keeping bach," in the Virginia phrase, did not live elaborately. But he was not prepared for what he saw when Robert drove him up to the entrance. The house was small and crude in design, was seventy-five years old, and had a roof that because of disrepair sagged in the middle. The interior was even worse. "My father," wrote Robert, "always dignified and self-contained, rarely gave any evidence of being astonished or startled. His self-control was great and his emotions were not on the surface, but when he entered and looked around my bachelor quarters he appeared really much shocked." [67] Robert was so much better off at the time than he had been in the early days of his venture at Romancoke that he had some pride in his advancement, and consequently he was not, perhaps, altogether prepared for his father's dismay. However, with his usual tact, the General relieved all possible embarrassment by making a jest of Robert's surroundings. When, however, they sat down at table, supplied with a scant store of battered and nondescript china and cutlery, the father could not withhold suggestion that the son might advantageously lay out a small sum to improve the equipment of the "mansion." [68]

Lee's only other visit was to White Marsh, the home of Doctor Prosser Tabb, in Gloucester County. Mrs. Tabb was "Cousin Rebecca" to the whole Lee family and had been a favorite with General Lee for forty years. She had been most urgent that he come to see her and permit the young people of the household to get acquainted with him. He and Robert drove to West Point,

[67] R. E. Lee, Jr., 407.   [68] R. E. Lee, Jr., 407.

put their conveyance aboard the Baltimore steamer, and went very comfortably to Cappahoosic Wharf. When the boat reached the landing the passengers crowded in such numbers to the port side, in order to see the General, that the gangway was below the level of the wharf. The captain had to order all of them to starboard so as to right the ship, whereupon Robert got his vehicle ashore. It was late afternoon by this time, and as it was getting chilly, the younger man drove rapidly to save his father from exposure to the night air. The General made no comment, but he did not fail to observe the hard treatment of the horse. So much was he distressed by it that he told several people, "I think Rob drives unnecessarily fast," a remark that youth in every generation has heard.

Hearty welcome and a large company of kinsfolk and friends awaited Lee at the Tabb homestead. A pleasant evening was followed by a long night's rest, with Robert and his father sleeping in the same bed, because of the crowded house. It was the first time this had happened in many years, and the General remarked the fact, recalling affectionately that when Robert had been a little lad he had begged to sleep with him.

After breakfast the next morning the General walked through the gardens and then went for a drive with Doctor Tabb and Robert, under the care of the doctor's overseer, Graves by name. Lee praised Graves's husbandry and wholly won his heart, whereupon Doctor Tabb told the General that the man was one of the old soldiers of the Army of Northern Virginia and had fought to the end at Appomattox. Lee, of course, proceeded to extol him the more.

The overseer made no pretenses. "Yes, General," he said, "I stuck to the army, but if you had in your entire command a greater coward than I was, you ought to have had him shot."

Lee was much amused and repeated the answer when he got back to the house. "That sort of coward makes a good soldier," he said.

Declining the reception the Tabbs wished to give him, the General rested as much as he could, had dinner with some special guests, and enjoyed talk with his young cousins. It was while chatting with one of them that Lee made the remark that has

462

beers, in some sense, the slogan of Virginia ever since. The youthful kinswoman had asked despairingly what fate held for "us poor Virginians." Earnestly the General answered:

"You can work for Virginia, to build her up again, to make her great again. You can teach your children to love and cherish her."

After a night made restless by his fear that he might oversleep himself, Lee caught the steamer early the next morning and went back up the river with his son. Robert left the boat at West Point, in order to take his horse home, and the General went on to the White House, where the steamer stopped and Rooney met him. Another period of rest at Fitzhugh's, and then, with many farewells, he took the train for Richmond on the morning of May 22, ten days after his arrival at the White House.[69] Mrs. Lee remained, but Agnes accompanied him, and Robert went up for the day as a filial guard of honor.[70]

From May 22 to May 26 the General remained in Richmond. He went shopping at least once and bought a set of heavily plated knives and forks, which he sent to Robert. Much of his time was given over to medical examination by the Richmond doctors who had gone over him before he began his Southern tour. "I am to have a great medicine talk tomorrow," he wrote rather grimly on the day of his arrival.[71]

He had to endure, also, what must have seemed, in prospect, equally distasteful—measurement for a bust that was to be made of him. But the young artist who did the work was gentle, deft, and considerate, a cultured man and a good conversationalist. The General and he soon understood each other. When the

---

69 The account of Lee's visit, particularly of his stay at Romancoke and White Marsh, is paraphrased from *R. E. Lee, Jr.*, 406 ff. Captain Lee had excellent memory and a strong sense of humor, and for the events of his father's career that he witnessed he is the most intimate and delightful of biographers. If he had spent more time with his father during and after the war, the world probably would have received from him an admirable life of General Lee.

70 R. E. Lee to G. W. C. Lee, *MS.*, May 20, 1870; *Duke Univ. MSS.*; Mrs. R. E. Lee to Mrs. W. Hartwell Macon, *MS.*, c. May 25, 1870, *Johnston MSS.*

71 R. E. Lee to Mildred Lee, May 23, 1870; *R. E. Lee, Jr.*, 411. Doctor M. H. Houston, one of the examining physicians, on June 10, 1870, addressed a letter to Doctor S. M. Bemiss of New Orleans, who in 1863 had attended General Lee. Doctor Houston wished to know something of General Lee's previous illness, and in discussing the case gave the fullest available account of General Lee's symptoms. "The diagnosis is obscure," Doctor Houston wrote, "but the symptoms point to chronic pericarditis" (*Bemiss MSS.*, courteously placed at the writer's disposal by S. M. Bemiss, of Richmond).

sculptor, E. V. Valentine, remarked that the war had greatly altered his fortunes, General Lee answered quietly—his humor was never boisterous—that "an artist ought not to have too much money." [72] Later, as the conversation turned again to adversity, Lee observed, "Misfortune nobly borne is good fortune." Valentine at the time thought this was original with General Lee, but subsequently, in reading the *Meditations of Marcus Aurelius,* he found the sentence there. ". . . No more appropriate epitaph," wrote Mr. Valentine, "could be carved on the tomb of the great Virginian." The sculptor could not have known at the time, of course, that Lee got his admiration for Marcus Aurelius from his father, who placed that emperor high among his venerated immortals.

The artist at length completed his measurements, and explained that he would have to go to Lexington to do the modelling, and could do so either immediately or in the autumn. Lee replied that he would have more leisure later on but that Valentine had better make the visit at once. He gave no reasons, but the young statuary understood that Lee thought his end was near at hand.

On May 26, Lee left Richmond for the last time. He had remained as quiet as possible during his stay in the city and had acquainted few of his friends with his presence. It is likely that on his final departure from the capital he had defended for three years, there were few at the station to bid him farewell. He passed from the central scene of his life's drama as though he had been the humblest actor on its stage.

Apparently the route he took was to Charlottesville by the old Virginia Central, thence to Lynchburg by the Orange and Alexandria, now the Southern, and on to Lexington by the packet.[73] He reached home on the morning of May 28, two months and four days from the time he had left.

Physically, he was little the better for the tour. The day after his arrival in Savannah the General had written Mrs. Lee, "I

[72] E. V. Valentine, in *Riley,* 147. This is an expansion of an article printed originally in *The Outlook* of Dec. 22, 1906.

[73] *Richmond Enquirer,* May 27, 1870; *Richmond Dispatch,* May 30, 1870, quoting *The Lynchburg Republican.* Before he left Richmond, Lee wrote Mildred: "If Sam [one of his servants] is well enough, and it should be otherwise convenient, he could meet me with Lucy and the carriage or with Traveller. If not, I will get a seat up in the omnibus" (*R. E. Lee, Jr.,* 411).

think I am stronger than when I left Lexington, but otherwise can see no difference." [74] Five days later he had said, "I hope I am a little better. I seem to be stronger and to walk with less difficulty, but it may be owing to the better streets of Savannah. I presume if any change takes place it will be gradual and slow. . . . I do not think travelling in this way procures me much quiet and repose." [75] Again, on April 11 he had written, "The warm weather has dispelled some of the rheumatic pains in my back, but I perceive no change in the stricture in my chest. If I attempt to walk beyond a very slow gait, the pain is always there. It is all true what the doctors say about its being aggravated by any fresh cold, but how to avoid taking cold is the question. It seems with me to be impossible. Everything and anything seems to give me one. I meet with much kindness and consideration, but fear that nothing will relieve my complaint, which is fixed and old. I must bear it." [76]

He had enjoyed his trip up the Saint John's River more than any other part of his tour, and when he had returned to Savannah he had felt improvement, but he found some of his symptoms aggravated. "I hope I am better," he had repeated on April 18, "I know I am stronger, but I still have the pain in my chest whenever I walk. I have felt it also occasionally of late when quiescent, but not badly, which is new." [77] He had continued under heavy strain, with calls, receptions, much letter-writing in answer to invitations, and endless interruptions by visitors. Savannah physicians who had examined him for about an hour on April 18, at the instance of friends, had confirmed the previous diagnosis but had been somewhat encouraging in their agreement that the heart had not been injured, and that the pericardium might not be involved. Lee had not tied to the hope they had held out. ". . . Perhaps their opinion is not fully matured," he had said. [78]

The visits to Charleston and Wilmington had been particularly wearing, because so many social events had been crowded into so

[74] R. E. Lee to Mrs. Lee, April 2, 1870; *R. E. Lee, Jr.,* 390.

[75] R. E. Lee to Mrs. Lee, April 7, 1870; *R. E. Lee, Jr.,* 394–95. This letter is wrongly dated April 17 in Captain Lee's book, but it appears in its proper place chronologically.

[76] R. E. Lee to Mrs. Lee, April 11, 1870; *R. E. Lee, Jr.,* 397.

[77] R. E. Lee to Mrs. Lee, April 18, 1870; *R. E. Lee, Jr.,* 399.

[78] R. E. Lee to Mrs. Lee, April 18, 1870; *R. E. Lee, Jr.,* 399.

brief a time. He probably had been at his lowest ebb when he had reached Norfolk and had found some rest at Doctor Selden's. Reports that he had heart disease had now become public property,[79] and at Wilmington he had told friends that he was sure his ailment was of the heart and that it was incurable.[80]

He had begun to gain some ground from the time he had gone to Brandon.[81] In fact, if he had not sought quiet when he did, it is altogether probable that he would have died on the road. When he had reached the White House, Mrs. Lee had been disturbed at his appearance. "He looks fatter," she had observed, "but I do not like his complexion, and he seems still very stiff." [82] Now that he was home, though he seemed buoyed up for the time, there was no real improvement: his malady was progressive.

Precisely what that malady was, his physicians were neither agreed nor positive. The diagnosis of simple pericarditis tentatively made in 1870 did not adequately explain his symptoms then and does not satisfy the present-day clinician. The illness of 1863, from which his trouble dated, may have been an acute pericarditis secondary to his throat infection. Later, he probably had a combination of maladies. His serious heart condition was almost certainly angina pectoris rather than "rheumatism," as he thought. This angina, his principal malady, may have been accompanied by a chronic adhesive pericarditis. In addition he had some arthritis and a hardening of the arteries, which was rapid after 1866, if the changes shown in his photographs may be accepted as evidence. These two major conditions, the angina and the arteriosclerosis, evidenced the effects of the war and of the reconstruction on a system that had originally been very strong.[83]

The psychological effect of the southern tour on Lee himself is not easily determined, because he said very little about it. He must have felt deep satisfaction, of course, that the South was looking courageously to the future and was laboring to recover

[79] *Savannah Republican,* April 29, 1870. [80] *R. E. Lee, Jr.,* 401.
[81] R. E. Lee to Mildred Lee, May 7, 1870; *R. E. Lee, Jr.,* 403; R. E. Lee to Mrs. Lee, May 7, 1870; *ibid.,* 401.
[82] Mrs. R. E. Lee to Mary or Mildred Lee, May 9–13, 1870; *R. E. Lee, Jr.,* 405.
[83] For a critique of the available data on General Lee's maladies, the writer is indebted, through Doctor Allen W. Freeman, to the kindness of Doctor Lewellys F. Barker, the distinguished emeritus professor of medicine in Johns Hopkins University. The detailed findings of Doctor Barker are given in Appendix IV—7.

what had been lost during the war. Personally, it was not his nature to indulge any pride in the affection the people displayed, though he was gratefully appreciative of their kindness to him. In general, the effects were cumulative of those that followed his visit to Petersburg in November, 1867, when, for the first time, he had seen how the Southern people were shaking off the war. The only difference was that he now felt his end was at hand. He had paid his final visit of respect to the grave of his daughter and to the burial-place of his father and the early home of his mother. For the last time he had greeted many of those who had executed his orders and had fought his battles. He had consciously said farewell.

The impressions made on the public by the tour were all favorable and in many ways helpful. It meant much to the generation of Woodrow Wilson to have seen General Lee. So it was, also, with those elders who had read of his campaigns but had never looked upon him. As for his old soldiers, the memories of their days of triumph overcame, in his presence, the hard realities of life. Their cause was personified and glorified in him and they felt themselves enriched by their association with him. Even in the North, among people of liberal mind, his avoidance on his travels of everything that would keep alive the old animosities aroused a measure of admiration. "It will be seen," *The New York World* commented, "that the 'Southern heart' is still fired by emotions that kindled the late civil strife, and it is pleasant to witness the dignified and temperate course of General Lee in the midst of these heart-felt orations [ovations?]. The name of Lee is identified with the most heroic deeds of the war for independence, and it is pleasant in these latter days to find it connected with words and acts of fraternal reconciliation and pacification." [84]

[84] *New York World*, quoted in *Richmond Enquirer*, May 4, 1870.

CHAPTER XXVI

FAREWELL TO NORTHERN VIRGINIA

ON his return to Lexington, General Lee found that instruction at the college had progressed without particular incident during his absence.[1] The trustees had met on April 19, as they had a reason for wishing to be in session when he was not present. They had at that time approved the action of the faculty in urging Lee to take a rest, had recommended that his leave be extended until the end of the session, at least, and had designated Professor White to act as the president's confidential secretary and aide in case Lee returned before commencement. This had accorded with an earlier resolution of the faculty that had contemplated a plan for relieving the General of part of his work.[2] The trustees had gone much farther than this: "In order that the president's mind be relieved of any concern for the support and comfort of his family," they determined to convey to Mrs. Lee the use of the president's house for life, and to pay her an annuity of $3000 a year in case the General died or suffered disability.[3] This was done, the board insisted, because part of the gifts for the president's house had been made to provide for Mrs. Lee, and also because much of the new endowment of the college had been donated as a tribute to General Lee.

The whole resolution had been conceived in the friendliest spirit and was in keeping with the consideration shown General Lee during the whole of his administration by the appreciative trustees. It was consonant, also, with the facts attending many of the donations to the college. General Ewell, for example, had given $500 for the endowment, on condition that the interest go to Lee's salary, and admirers at the White Sulphur one summer had proposed to raise $50,000 "to be used by the college for his benefit during his life, and to revert to his family at his death."

[1] *Richmond Dispatch*, May 30, 1870.   [2] *MS. Faculty Minutes*, March 29, 1870.
[3] *Trustees' Minutes*, April 19, 1870.

468

In both instances, Lee had urged that the money be dedicated to permanent endowment,[4] and he would not now consent to the proposal of the trustees. On the very day he got home he wrote his acknowledgments to the board and said: "Though fully sensible of the kindness of the Board, and justly appreciating the manner in which they sought to administer to my relief, I am unwilling that my family should become a tax to the college, but desire that all its funds should be devoted to the purposes of education. I know that my wishes on this subject are equally shared by my wife,[5] and I therefore request that the provisions of the fourth and fifth resolutions [covering the conveyance of the house and the annuity] . . . may not be carried into effect. I feel full assurance that, in case a competency should not be left to my wife, her children would not suffer her to want."[6] Despite the General's wishes, the board quietly had the life-term lease recorded, and adhered to its resolution regarding the annuity.[7] The election of Custis Lee as head of the college in succession to his father carried with it the occupancy of the president's house and thereby removed Mrs. Lee's objections to the continued use of that property after the death of the General. Mrs. Lee steadfastly declined, however, to accept the annuity.[8]

Scarcely had the General settled himself at home than Valentine made his promised visit to model the bust. Lee showed him the family pictures and offered him one of the first-floor rooms of his residence as a temporary studio, but the sculptor preferred not to disturb the family, and after much searching found a vacant store under the hotel that he could utilize. There, on a low platform, Lee sat for Valentine, with the understanding that nobody but Custis or Professor White was to be admitted. Lee was not comfortable during this ordeal. Often, unconsciously, he would put his hand to his heart, as if in pain, but he made no complaint. The nearest he came to it was when he asked if Custis might not come and sit in his stead, as there was said to be a resemblance between them. Veteran and artist talked of many

---

[4] *Jones*, 117–18, 178.

[5] Mrs. Lee had not then returned from her visit to her son.

[6] R. E. Lee to J. W. Brockenbrough, May 28, 1870; *Jones*, 116; *Trustees' Minutes* June 23, 1870.

[7] *Trustees' Minutes.* June 21, 1870.   [8] *Jones.* 116–17, 178.

things—of the days of Lee's boyhood, of his swims in the Potomac, of his years at West Point, of his experience in the Mexican War, and of the themes of the day. Once Lee asked Valentine if he knew a certain sculptress, whose name he did not recall with precision. When Valentine identified her, Lee said: "Oh, that is the name! Well, the lady wrote me a very polite letter in which she asked if I would give her sittings for a bust, at the same time enclosing photographs of some of her works which were not too profusely draped. In her letter she also asked when she could come to make the bust, and a friend, who had been looking at the pictures, suggested July or August, as the most of her works seemed to have been done in the summer time."

Valentine had jokes of his own. He much wanted a pair of the General's boots for a statue he intended to design, and he very adroitly asked for them in this wise: An office-seeker, he said, besought Andrew Jackson to make him minister to England, and when told that post was filled, asked if he might not be secretary of legation. Advised that no vacancy was in prospect there, he appealed to be made vice-consul. Jackson gave the same answer. "Well, then, Mr. President," said the ambitious seeker after fame, "would you give me a pair of old boots!" Valentine added: "That is what I would like to have you do for me, General."

"I think there is a pair at the house that you can have," Lee answered, after he had smiled at Valentine's jest and at his finesse. The next day General Lee delivered them in person—a pair of dress boots, size 4½C, that bore on the lining the words, "R. E. Lee, U. S. A." [9]

One day during the course of Valentine's work, the sitter heard a noise in the room. Looking up, he saw a student of the college who had learned that the General was sitting for a bust, and had determined, boy-like, to see what it was all about. General Lee showed no impatience at this intrusion. "How would you like to be in my place, Mr. Carlton?" he inquired. The student, much abashed, made a speedy exit. [10]

At last the modelling was done, and as Mrs. Lee could not come to look at the bust it was carried to her home in order that she might criticise it and, if she liked it, give it the approval

---

[9] These boots are now in Richmond.   [10] *MS. note of H. G. Carlton,* Jan. 17, 1923.

without which she would permit neither a portrait of the General, a photograph, nor a work of plastic art to go forth officially. A bad fifteen minutes for her husband followed. Several of Mrs. Lee's friends had gathered to serve as her advisers. Valentine turned the bust repeatedly, so as to afford the best views; and at the direction of his wife the General moved likewise, and stood now in profile, now with full face towards them. It was an ordeal as bad as battle, but it brought no protest from his lips. Was it not the first duty of an old soldier to obey the orders of superior authority?

One more visit and Valentine was gone. On his call to say good-bye, he found Lee chatting in the parlor. "I feel that I have an incurable disease coming on—old age," Valentine heard him say. "I would like to go to some quiet place in the country and rest." [11]

But there was little time for rest. The date for the college commencement was approaching. Final examinations kept the president for long hours. Then followed the formal exercises and the meeting of the trustees, a rather important meeting, at that. Lee reported at length on the work of the year.[12] Only one student had been dismissed, two had been suspended, and three had been withdrawn by parents at the request of the faculty. Religiously the life of the college had been active. The Y. M. C. A. had erected a Sunday-school building near House Mountain and had organized a like school near Thorn Hill. Fifty students were teaching classes on the Sabbath. One hundred and twenty-nine were church members, and nineteen of these had joined during the session. The advancement of the students was noticeable. Their knowledge was declared to be larger and more precise. Classes had been divided into sections of convenient size. The School of English Language and Literature had been organized and its work apportioned among three professors of other departments. Instruction in the School of Applied Chemistry also had been given but required a regular professor.

Plans for the future included the closing of the preparatory department, which was no longer necessary, the reorganization of the business school, and the adoption of definite curricula for

[11] Valentine, in *Riley*, 148 *ff*.   [12] *Lee's MS. Letter Book*, June 21, 1870.

the Schools of Agriculture and Commerce. The trustees approved most of these recommendations and, in addition, provided that the law department should become one of the regular schools of the college, with Judge Brockenbrough as its head. It was at this time that John Randolph Tucker was elected second professor.[13] A junior law course was authorized, with the proviso that if a student followed only this course in law, he would be required to take work in one of the other departments of the college.[14] Temporary instruction was arranged for the schools that did not have full professors, and an adjunct professor of ancient languages was named in the person of a Confederate veteran and recent graduate of the college, Milton W. Humphreys.[15] No large gifts to the college were reported, but there were whispers that a great astronomical observatory was soon to be erected in Virginia and that it might be procured for Washington College.[16] Finally, the trustees repeated their resolutions regarding provision for Mrs. Lee and urged the General to take all possible measures for the protection of his health, even if this involved travel in the United States or abroad. Professor White was continued as confidential secretary and aide to the president. The commencement itself was brilliant. Twenty-eight degrees were conferred. Reverend W. T. Brantly of Atlanta, Ga., a minister of much distinction, delivered the baccalaureate sermon.[17] and Hugh Blair Grigsby told of the achievements of the trustees of Liberty Hall Academy.[18]

Lee must have been heartily tired of doctors' examinations by this time, for he had been thumped and quizzed in Richmond, in Savannah, and in Richmond again, to say nothing of his consultation with Doctor Selden in Norfolk and his regular sieges at the hands of Doctors Barton and Madison in Lexington. But adherence to professional advice was part of his creed of obedience to constituted authority,[19] and he yielded now to a new

---

[13] See *supra*, p. 427, note 33.   [14] *Trustees' Minutes*, June 22, 1870.
[15] *Trustees' Minutes*, June 23, 1870.
[16] *Trustees' Minutes*, June 21, June 22, 1870.
[17] His observations on Lee's Christian life appear in *Jones*, 480.
[18] *Trustees' Minutes*, June 22, June 23, 1870.
[19] *Cf.* his letter from Savannah to Mrs. Lee, April 7, 1870: "Please say to Dr. Barton that I have received his letter and am obliged to him for his kind advice. I shall begin today with his new prescriptions and will follow them strictly" (*R. E. Lee*, 395).

request that he go to Baltimore and consult Doctor Thomas Hepburn Buckler, a physician of high standing who had gone to Paris after the War between the States and had come back to the United States on a visit

On June 30, 1870, just a week after the trustees adjourned, General Lee set out for Baltimore alone.[20] He went by canal boat to Lynchburg and thence by rail past Orange and Culpeper, scene of many a week's encampment, to his own city of Alexandria. "We arrived at Alexandria at 5:00 P.M. [July 1]," he duly chronicled for Mrs. Lee, "and were taken to Washington and kept in the cars till 7:45, when we were sent on. It was the hottest day I ever experienced, or I was in the hottest position I ever occupied, both on board the packet and in the railroad cars, or I was less able to stand it, for I never recollect having suffered so much." [21]

He was met at the train by Mr. and Mrs. Tagart and was driven to their home. So exhausted was he by the journey that he stayed abed the next morning until 8 o'clock—something almost without precedent. It was a rainy day and it brought confinement to the house and a two-hour physical examination at the hands of Doctor Buckler, who was more encouraging than some of the other physicians had been. "He says he finds my lungs working well, the action of the heart a little too much diffused, but nothing to injure. He is inclined to think my whole difficulty arises from rheumatic excitement, both the first attack in front of Fredericksburg and the second last winter. Says I appear to have a rheumatic constitution, must guard against cold, keep out in the air, exercise, etc., as the other physicians prescribe. . . . In the meantime, he has told me to try lemon-juice and watch the effect." [22]

Neither the weather, the heat, nor the doctor's examination quite daunted the General. In the very letter in which he recounted all this, he teased Mrs. Lee for her familiar tardiness by holding high the example of Mrs. Tagart, who had come with Mr. Tagart to the station more than an hour before the arrival of the train bearing Lee. His host, the General admiringly avowed,

---

[20] R. E. Lee, Jr. (op. cit., 412) said the General left on July 1, but from the itinerary given in the General's letter of July 2 (ibid., 412–13) it is obvious that the journey could not have been made in a single day.

[21] R. E. Lee to Mrs. Lee, July 2, 1870; R. E. Lee, Jr., 413.

[22] R. E. Lee to Mrs. Lee, July 2, 1870; R. E. Lee, Jr., 413.

had "a punctual wife, who regulates everything for him, so that he had plenty of time for reflection." [23] Nor did his physical condition dim Lee's love of the pleasant company of his kin. He paid a visit, probably on July 4, to Washington Peter, and after a second examination by Doctor Buckler he went for a leisured stay at Goodwood, near Ellicott City, the home of his cousin, Charles Henry Carter.

In that friendly atmosphere he remained considerably more than a week. Then, on July 14, he crossed the Potomac for the last time, southward bound. Perhaps he gazed at the pillars of Arlington, gleaming in the sunlight, as he had seen them so often when he had ridden home from Washington. But if they moved his heart, he said nothing of it to Mrs. Lee. He wrote, instead, that he had caught cold and that he found it "piping hot" at the Mansion House in Alexandria, where he put up for the night. On the 15th he had a conference with his old attorney, Francis L. Smith, about the possible recovery of Arlington, but he got little encouragement.[24] At the instance of Mr. Smith, Lee removed from the hotel to the lawyer's residence, where many of his friends came to "pay their respects," in the good old phrase of the times. Among them was Colonel John S. Mosby. Lee talked with him and, as they were about to part, said to him, "Colonel, I hope we shall have no more wars." [25]

That afternoon, if his plans worked out according to his schedule, he went to Cassius Lee's home, which was his headquarters for a round of visits—parting calls in the most sombre sense—to old friends in the neighborhood of Arlington.[26] In the company of Cassius Lee, whom he had known all his life in closest intimacy, the General felt none of the restraint he usually displayed in talking about the past. Together, with no audience except Cassius Lee's silently attentive sons, they ranged the years. When they came to the dark era of blood, Cassius Lee questioned and the General explained. They talked of Jackson, and Lee told how the failure of "Stonewall" to get on McClellan's

---

[23] R. E. Lee to Mrs. Lee, July 2, 1870; *R. E. Lee, Jr.,* 412–13.
[24] R. E. Lee to G. W. C. Lee, MS., July 22, 1870; *Duke Univ. MSS.*
[25] *John S. Mosby's Memoirs,* 380; *Watson's Notes on Southside Virginia,* 247. *The Alexandria Gazette* of July 18, 1870, recorded that Lee was Smith's guest.
[26] Packard (*op. cit.,* 158) noted that Lee, from young manhood, was always meticulous in visiting his kinspeople.

flank had forced him to fight the battle of Mechanicsville, lest the Federals on the other side of the Chickahominy sweep into Richmond. But he must have had ample praise for Jackson, for he expressed the belief that if his great lieutenant had been with him at Gettysburg that battle would have been a Confederate victory. "Jackson," said he, "would have held the heights which Ewell took on the first day." Ewell he accounted a good officer, but one who would never exceed his orders. Directed to go to Gettysburg, Ewell would not occupy a position beyond the town.

Cassius Lee asked him why he had not moved on Washington after the second battle of Manassas. The General answered: "Because my men had nothing to eat. I could not tell my men to take that fort"—pointing to the nearby ramparts of Fort Wade— "when they had nothing to eat for three days. I went to Maryland to feed my army." That led him to describe the mismanagement of the Confederate commissary.

The Southern press came in for stern criticism. Patriotism, the General said, seemed to have no weight with the newspapers. They would print troop movements regardless of the effect on the plans of the army. Lee explained to his cousin that when Longstreet was sent south in the summer of 1863 every effort was made to keep the facts from the enemy, but the papers told all about it.

Who was the ablest Federal general he had opposed? He did not hesitate a moment for the answer. "McClellan, by all odds," he said emphatically.[27]

This was the fullest conversation on military matters that General Lee ever had after the war, and is the only one of which a measurably adequate record exists. The talk with Wade Hampton was brief and, it will be remembered, was but partially reported.[28] Lee's reticence in discussing the war was always noticeable and extended to his correspondence.[29] Concerning the in-

[27] Cazenove Lee, quoted in *R. E. Lee, Jr.,* 415–16. Lee was never ungenerous in praising Federal officers. He told D. H. Maury (*op. cit.,* 239) that he did not see why Sherman should have been so much praised for his march to the sea "when the only question before him to decide was whether he could feed his army by consuming all the people had to eat"; but in conversation with David Macrae he spoke highly of the abilities of Sherman who, he said, "had always been a good soldier."
[28] See *supra,* p. 367.
[29] Jones recorded only one instance in which Lee talked with him of the war, and that was to procure confirmation of his memory—for the use of some correspondent— that he had never asked for a truce in which to bury his dead (*Jones,* 239).

475

cidents of his resignation in 1861, he seems to have written only two letters—the familiar one to Reverdy Johnson[30] and another to Sidney Herbert in which he denied the oft-repeated story that he remained "on the staff of General Scott" to the last possible hour in order that he might discover the military secrets of the Federal Government.[31]

So far as is known, he wrote only two general letters on his campaigns. The more lengthy of the two was in answer to some inquiries from W. M. McDonald, who was writing a school history. In this letter, dated April 15, 1868, Lee explained why he went into Maryland in 1862, and why he chose to stand on the hills behind Fredericksburg rather than to dispute Burnside's crossing. In describing the strategy of these operations, he wrote with the same clear and direct logic displayed in so many of his letters to President Davis. "As to the battle of Gettysburg," he went on, "I must again refer you to my official accounts. Its loss was occasioned by a combination of circumstances. It was commenced in the absence of correct intelligence. It was continued in the effort to overcome the difficulties by which we were surrounded, and it would have been gained could one determined and united blow have been delivered by our whole line. As it was, victory trembled in the balance for three days, and the battle resulted in the infliction of as great amount of injury as was received, and in frustrating Federal plans for the season." [32]

Lee used somewhat the same language, though he was more reserved, in replying to questions from B. H. Wright of Rome, N. Y., a West Pointer and an engineer. "The failure of the Confederate army at Gettysburg," Lee told Wright, "was owing to a combination of circumstances, but from which success might have been reasonably expected." [33] In the remainder of this letter, Lee answered queries from Wright regarding Burnside's movements to Fredericksburg, and the feasibility, after the campaign of 1862, of an alternative plan of Federal operations devised by

30 Printed in full, *supra,* pp. 361–62.

31 This yarn, generally believed during the war, had been printed in *Harpers Weekly* during the summer of 1870 (*Alexandria Gazette,* July 14, 1870, quoting Lee's letter of June 29, 1870).

32 *Jones,* 266.

33 R. E. Lee to B. H. Wright, Jan. 18, 1869; Jones, *L. and L.,* 452–53, the name and address being supplied from *Lee's MS. Letter Book.*

Wright. "As regards General McClellan," said Lee, "I have always entertained a high opinion of his capacity, and have no reason to think that he omitted to do anything that was in his power." This letter to Wright was so cautiously written that publication would have done no harm. The answers to McDonald concluded with the request, "I must ask that you will consider what I have said as intended solely for yourself."

Comment on particular campaigns was rare. Lee twice gave his estimate of the strength of his army at the Wilderness-Spotsylvania campaign.[34] He confirmed as substantially correct a narrative of "Lee to the rear," [35] and he wrote Doctor A. T. Bledsoe the well-known letter regarding responsibility for Jackson's movement at Chancellorsville—a letter that exhibits alike his candor and his respect for the fame of his dead lieutenant.[36] Beyond this, he held to the silence he imposed upon himself when he returned home from Appomattox. Perhaps in those two days with Cassius Lee, in the summer of 1870, he talked more of his battles than in all the rest of his post-bellum career. And it was with less heaviness of heart.

Five days were spent in the pleasant company of Alexandria friends; then on the morning of July 19[37] the General went to Ravensworth. The weather continued uncomfortably hot. Coupled with his pain, it kept him close to the house and compelled him to forego anticipated visits to his sons and to his sister-in-law, the widow of Sydney Smith Lee. He remained at Ravensworth until July 25 and then returned home.

Despite the heat, his trip of nearly four weeks had done him temporary good. He had moved slowly, had rested much, had avoided all crowds, and had enjoyed the fellowship of his own kin, fellowship always precious to him. In thanking Doctor Buckler for his treatment and for an invitation to go back with him to Paris, General Lee reported himself improved. "I shall endeavor to be well by the fall," he wrote. His spirits were said to be "fine," and he was reported to be looking better.[38]

[34] R. E. Lee to Colonel J. A. White, Oct. 4, 1867; *Jones*, 264; R. E. Lee to W. S, Smith, July 27, 1868; *Jones*, 268.
[35] R. E. Lee to J. T. Mason, Dec. 7, 1865; *Jones*, 318.
[36] See *supra*, vol. II, Appendix 5, p. 587; *Jones*, 158–59.
[37] *Alexandria Gazette*, July 19, 1870.   [38] *Lexington Gazette*, July 29, 1870.

In June, 1870, Leander J. McCormick had confirmed rumors that he contemplated the erection of a large astronomical observatory in Virginia. As he belonged to the inventor's family, long resident in the neighborhood of Lexington, the trustees had hoped that he might be prevailed upon to establish the observatory in connection with Washington College. A committee had been named at that time to correspond with Mr. McCormick on the subject. Soon after General Lee returned from his trip to Baltimore and Alexandria, the project was thought to be nearer realization, and further steps to procure the observatory for the school were considered necessary. General Lee accordingly asked for a special meeting of the trustees on August 6, at which time the committee was instructed to inquire of McCormick on what terms he would permit the institution to co-operate. If he would agree to put the observatory there, the trustees pledged themselves to keep it in order, to appoint a professor of astronomy, and to raise an endowment of $100,000.[39] That offer epitomized the progress the college had made during General Lee's administration. In 1865, when he came to Lexington, talk of raising $100,000 for the endowment of a single new department would have seemed madness. Now the trustees spoke of it confidently.

General Lee was named chairman of the committee to report the board's action to the philanthropist. Subsequently Mr. McCormick came to Lexington, and, in conference with members of the faculty and of the board, reasserted his purpose to finance the observatory. He said he was not committed to any location, but was determined to have it under the control of some Virginia college of established position. A movement forthwith was launched in Lexington to support the trustees' plan and to raise funds. On October 1, after General Lee had been stricken, the trustees in special meeting had renewed their previous offer and guaranteed an appropriation of $6000 a year, pledging $100,000 of the endowment to that purpose.[40] Had General Lee lived, it is quite probable that the observatory, which was ultimately placed at the University of Virginia, would have been erected at Lexington.

General Lee's doctors were determined that his duties should

[39] *Trustees' Minutes,* Aug. 6, 1870.   [40] *Trustees' Minutes,* Oct. 1, 1870.

not exhaust him; so, on August 9, about two weeks after his return home from Northern Virginia, they packed him off to the Hot Springs. He started alone with Captain White, and determined to go as far as he could by railway, but after he had taken the train at Goshen the pleasures of the mountains allured him. The two companions quit the railroad and rode to the Bath Alum Springs, where they spent the night. "[We] were in luck," he announced to Mrs. Lee, "in finding several schools or parts of them rusticating on alum-water. . . . They presented a gay and happy appearance." Early the next morning, he and Professor White went on to the Warm Springs. There they had breakfast and met a number of the General's friends—"small company but select," as he described it. From "The Warm" it was but a short ride to the Hot Springs, which they reached at 9:30.

Lee forthwith, as in duty bound, consulted the resident physician, who prescribed thermal treatment and predicted that, if the patient stayed long enough, the results would be good. "I hope I may be benefited," Lee wrote, "but it is a tedious prospect." In the letter reporting this to Mrs. Lee,[41] there is discernible a temporary change in Lee's epistolary style. Its smoothness was lost. His sentences became short and abrupt, as if they had been spoken aloud by a man who found it difficult to catch his breath. A week of this, and then, as he grew better, he returned to his usual manner of writing.

The General held faithfully to the "spouts" and "broilers" that were supposed to benefit rheumatism, but he did not enjoy them. Nor did he find much solace in the company at the springs. "Society has a rather solemn appearance," he told Mrs. Lee, "and conversation runs mostly on personal ailments, baths and damp weather. . . . I am having a merry time with my old cronies, tell Mildred. I am getting too heavy for them now. They soon drop me." [42] And again: "It is very wearying at these public places and the benefit hardly worth the cost. I do not think I can even stand Lexington long. . . . A Mr. and Mrs. Leeds, from New Orleans [have arrived], with ten children, mostly little girls. The latter are a great addition to my comfort." [43]

41 R. E. Lee to Mrs. Lee, Aug. 10, 1870; R. E. Lee, Jr., 421.
42 R. E. Lee to Mrs. Lee, Aug. 14, 1870; R. E. Lee, Jr., 424, 425.
43 R. E. Lee to Mrs. Lee, Aug. 23, 1870; R. E. Lee, Jr., 428, 429.

The General felt somewhat improved as his stay was prolonged,[44] but on August 29 he left the springs for Staunton, to attend a meeting of the stockholders of the Valley Railroad. The project for the construction of this line was now slowly taking shape. Although Baltimore had subscribed nothing, the town of Staunton had bought 1000 shares, Botetourt County had subscribed for 2000, and Rockbridge County had taken up 4000. The general feeling was that the rest of the money could be raised for the road, and that if the enterprise got the support of individuals of means in the territory it was to serve, construction could be commenced. Colonel M. G. Harmon, the president of the company, had done much, but when the stockholders met in Staunton on the morning of August 30 he announced that he could not stand for re-election and that he desired General Lee be named his successor. Lee's name, influence, and management, in the opinion of Colonel Harmon, were precisely what was needed to carry the railroad into the realm of reality.

Lee, of course, had no wish to take on new burdens and, from his knowledge of the poverty of the people, he had no great faith in the enterprise. "It seems to me," he wrote Cyrus H. McCormick, "that I have already led enough forlorn hopes."[45] At another time he would have reasoned that it was not prudent for a struggling railroad to have a president whose death might come any day. When, however, old friends and associates insisted that he and he alone could make a success of a carrier that would serve the Valley, help the town of Lexington, and benefit the college, he accepted the post. His salary, which had not been fixed, and may not even have been mentioned until after he consented to take the place, was put at $5000 a year. This money was hardly a consideration, for it is said, though on vague authority, that he declined, the same summer, a business offer of $50,000 per annum.[46]

Upon the conclusion of the stockholders' meeting, General Lee returned to Lexington. It was his last journey. The session was

---

[44] R. E. Lee to Mrs. Lee, Aug. 27, 1870; *R. E. Lee, Jr.*, 431.

[45] *McCormick MSS.*, cited in *Winston*, 407.

[46] *Jones*, 176–77; *Valley Virginian*, Aug. 25 and Sept. 1, 1870. For the latter reference, which for the first time gives the date of General Lee's acceptance of the presidency of the railroad, the author is indebted to General H. L. Opie, publisher of *The Staunton News-Leader*.

scheduled to be opened shortly, and many preliminaries had to be arranged. On September 5 the faculty met and discussed, among other things, the means of procuring a better representation of students at chapel, a subject that had concerned the trustees. Professors were of opinion that if a clock and a bell were put in the chapel tower, to give the boys notice of the hour, more of them might come. Installation of an organ, the staff also decided, would help.[47] The faculty met again on the 10th, and still again on the 13th, for preliminary conferences.[48] On the same days the trustees assembled for a variety of miscellaneous business—a discussion of chapel attendance, debate on whether Professor Campbell should be permitted to act as county superintendent of schools, and consideration of the act of Judge Brockenbrough in resigning as trustee and rector because he had become a regular professor of law in the college.[49] All these meetings required General Lee's direct attendance, or his accessibility in case the trustees wished to consult him. Despite the strain, he began to feel stronger and soon accounted himself definitely better.[50] The members of the faculty were much encouraged by the evidences of his zeal and energy.[51]

On Thursday, September 15, came the formal opening of the college session. The entire student body gathered in the chapel, where General Pendleton conducted the usual brief worship. The president was there, of course, and had much in mind the deliberations of trustees and of faculty on the attendance of students on the morning services; so, when the acting chaplain had finished, the General arose, made a number of announcements regarding the organization of the classes, and then "expressed his earnest hope that both professors and students would attend regularly the daily prayers at the chapel." It was a short appeal but was remarked as perhaps the longest "speech" the General had ever made at the college.[52]

[47] *Trustees' Minutes,* Sept. 13, 1870.　　[48] *MS. Faculty Minutes.*
[49] *Trustees' Minutes,* Sept. 10 and 13, 1870.
[50] R. E. Lee to S. H. Tagart, Sept. 28, 1870; *R. E. Lee, Jr.,* 433.
[51] W. P. Johnston in *Riley,* 207.
[52] *Richmond Dispatch,* Sept. 24, 1870, quoting a letter from Lexington.

CHAPTER XXVII

"Strike the Tent!"

THREE days after the opening of the session of 1870–71, un-observed by formal ceremonies and perhaps unnoticed, the fifth anniversary of General Lee's arrival in Lexington occurred. He had changed greatly in appearance since that September afternoon of 1865 when he had drawn rein on Traveller in front of the hotel. His hair was entirely white now and his gait was slow. Once the most erect of men, he was beginning to stoop in the shoulders. The nervous strain of the war and the difficult exercise of a stern self-control during reconstruction had proved too much for even his stout system. Although he was only sixty-three, he was an old man.

Yet none of the work he had done since the summer of 1865 had the shadow of senescence upon it. On the contrary, nothing more surely exhibits the strength of his intellect than the sustained quality of his labors and the continued sureness of his judgment during years when a similar physical condition would have been accompanied, in the case of most men, by a progressive mental decline. He had taken a feeble, old-fashioned college and had made it a vigorous pioneer in education, the admiration of the South. Although that had demanded hourly thought and many months of grinding labor, it had not been his chief contribution to his country since the close of the war. His example had been more important than his administration. He had meant less to education than to reconciliation. Denounced and lied about, in a time more difficult than any America had ever known except in the most baffling period of the Revolution, he had preached this gospel of silence and good-will, of patience and hard work:

"If the result of the war is to be considered as having decided that the union of the states is inviolable and perpetual under the constitution, it . . . is as incompetent for the general government to impair its integrity by the exclusion of a state, as for the states to do so by secession; . . . the existence and rights of a state by the constitution are as indestructible as the union itself. The legitimate consequence then must be the perfect equality of rights of all the states."

"The war being over . . . and the questions at issue . . . having been decided, I believe it to be the duty of every one to unite in the restoration of the country, and the reestablishment of peace and harmony."

"I think it wisest not to keep open the sores of war, but to follow the example of those nations who endeavored to obliterate the marks of civil strife, and to commit to oblivion the feelings it engendered."

"All should unite in honest efforts to obliterate the effects of the war, and to restore the blessing of peace. They should remain, if possible, in the country; promote harmony and good feeling; qualify themselves to vote; and elect to the state and general Legislatures wise and patriotic men, who will devote their abilities to the interests of the country, and the healing of all dissensions."

"The dominant party cannot reign forever, and truth and justice will at last prevail."

"It should be the object of all to avoid controversy, to allay passion, [and] give full scope to reason and every kindly feeling. By doing this and encouraging our citizens to engage in the duties of life with all their heart and mind, with a determination not to be turned aside by thoughts of the past and fears of the future, our country will not only be restored in material prosperity, but will be advanced in science, in virtue and in religion."

"You can work for Virginia, to build her up again, to make her great again. You can teach your children to love and cherish her."

"I look forward to better days, and trust that time and experience, the great teachers of men, under the guidance of an ever-merciful God, may save us from destruction and restore to us the bright hopes and prospects of the past."

"We failed, but in the good providence of God, apparent failure often proves a blessing."

"My experience of men has neither disposed me to think worse of them nor indisposed me to serve them; nor, in spite of failures which I lament, of errors which I now see and acknowledge, or of the present aspect of affairs, do I despair of the future. The truth is this: The march of Providence is so slow and our desires so impatient; the work of progress is so immense and our means of aiding it so feeble; the life of humanity is so long, that of the individual so brief, that we often see only the ebb of the advancing wave and are thus discouraged. It is history that teaches us to hope." [1]

This was the counsel of a man who not only was capable of accurate observation and precise reason, but who also was absolute master of his own soul. Had he left Virginia in 1865 many of the best men of the South might have emigrated with him, and those who remained might have been under the domination of Negroes and carpet-baggers for a generation. The South might have become an American Poland. Instead, to repeat, the Confederates came to consider it as much the course of patriotism to emulate General Lee in peace as it had been to follow him in war. More than any other American, General Lee kept the tragedy of the war from being a continuing national calamity. He did not survive to behold the industrialism he foresaw for a South rid forever of the burden of slavery, but he lived to witness the readmission of the last of the former Confederate States to the Union, despite a thousand obstacles. From five such years of passion as 1865–70, what more could any man have hoped? Who would not have been willing, when that was consummated, to say *Nunc dimittis?*

Like a soldier in action, General Lee regarded his taking off as probable at any time, but he had no special premonitions and he made no deliberate preparations for the great adventure. He worked on from September 18 to September 27 in accordance with a precise and busy schedule. He saw students between 8:45 and 10:30 A.M.[2] Then, until dinner, which came after 2 o'clock, he attended to the routine of the college. Then he had a brief nap, and, later, if the weather was fair, he took a short ride on Traveller over the hills around Lexington, in the strange companionship that had existed for eight years between master and mount.

[1] The source of these separate quotations already has been given, except that of the last. It is from R. E. Lee to Charles Marshall, n.d., 17 *S. H. S. P.*, 245; 35 *Confederate Veteran*, 364.

[2] These new hours were provided under resolution of June 27, 1870 (*MS. Faculty Minutes*, that date).

Returning home, the General spent his evenings quietly there. He read, during his last days, of the Franco-Prussian War, and all his sympathies in that contest were with the French. "No," he wrote a kinswoman, not long before Sedan, "I am not 'glad that the Prussians are succeeding.' They are prompted by ambition and a thirst for power. The French are defending their homes and country." In that he saw the struggle of his own Southland.[3]

On September 27 he attended faculty meeting as usual. The attendance was thin, and the business was of no great importance: three students wished indulgence in the payment of their tuition fees, and one wanted to withdraw on account of ill-health; a committee reported the names of ministerial students who should be admitted without charge; rules were presented to govern the award of literary medals offered by Joseph Santini of New Orleans. The teachers who were seeking to stimulate attendance on chapel services were directed to consider the purchase of hymn books. That was all. In the minutes of this meeting, the last that General Lee ever attended, his name does not appear. The only reference to him was in the line: ". . . present the President and Professors. . . ."[4]

The next morning, September 28, the General rose early and had morning prayers. If, as usual, he read the Psalter for the day, these were the words of Holy Writ with which the morning lesson ended:

"Praise the Lord, ye house of Israel: praise the Lord, ye house of Aaron.

"Praise the Lord, ye house of Levi: ye that fear the Lord, praise the Lord.

"Praised be the Lord out of Sion: who dwellest at Jerusalem."

And if he read on through the psalter for the evening he closed the Book on these lines:

"Though I walk in the midst of trouble, yet shalt thou refresh me: thou shalt stretch forth thy hand upon the furiousness of mine enemies, and thy right hand shall save me.

"The Lord shall make good his loving kindness toward me:

[3] Lee to Martha Williams, Aug. 27, 1870; *Markie Letters*, 90–91.
[4] *MS. Faculty Minutes*, Sept. 27, 1870. In some of the biographies of General Lee it is erroneously stated that this faculty meeting was held on Sept. 28, the day when Lee was stricken.

yea, thy mercy, O Lord, endureth for ever; despise not then the work of thine own hands."

Eight years before, on that very date, having concluded the Sharpsburg campaign, he had written President Davis from his camp on Washington River, "History records but few examples of a greater amount of labor and fighting than have been done by this army during the present campaign." [5] Six years before, on September 28, 1864, Ord had been preparing his surprise attack on Fort Harrison. Now, on a cloudy, chilly day, Lee had nothing on his calendar other than the routine of his office and a meeting of the vestry of Grace Church in the afternoon.

The first part of this schedule was rather heavy, for students were still being adjusted to their classes; but he found time, before dinner, to answer a letter he received that morning from Samuel H. Tagart, who, during July, had been his host in Baltimore. Mr. Tagart had written that he wanted to inveigle him into a correspondence. Lee responded cheerfully. "I am much better," he said in answer to a question from Tagart. "I do not know whether it is owing to having seen you and Doctor Buckler last summer or to my visit to the Hot Springs. Perhaps both. But my pains are less and my strength greater. In fact, I suppose I am as well as I shall be. I am still following Doctor B.'s directions, and in time I may improve still more." He concluded, as usual, with friendly messages: "Tell —— his brother is well and handsome, and I hope that he will study, or his sweethearts in Baltimore will not pine for him long. Captain —— is well and busy, and joins in my remembrances. . . ." [6]

He finished and sealed this letter, completed his morning's work, and was just stepping out from his office when he met Percy Davidson, a sophomore from Lexington, who had with him a small picture of Lee, which a girl had asked him to get the General to autograph. Davidson explained this and added that as Lee was leaving, he would come some other time. "No," said Lee, "I will go right back and do it now." He returned and signed his name for the last time. [7]

[5] O. R., 19, part 2, p. 633.
[6] R. E. Lee to S. H. Tagart, Sept. 28, 1870; R. E. Lee, Jr., 432–33.
[7] Washington and Lee Alumni Magazine, vol. 3, no. 1, January, 1927, p. 6. The picture, with the autograph, is now at Washington and Lee.

486

Then he went out again and shut the door behind him, to open it no more in life.[8] From the office he walked slowly home, ate his dinner, and slept for a short time in his arm-chair.[9]

It was chilly after dinner and rain began to fall steadily. Lee should have stayed at home to protect himself against a cold, but he did not feel he should miss the vestry meeting, which was to consider the perennial question of a new church building and was also to decide what could be done to increase the scanty salary of General Pendleton. Lee insisted on going, and took no precaution against the weather other than to put on his old military cape. He walked through the rain and went directly into the church auditorium. There was no heat in the building and no smaller room into which the vestrymen could conveniently retire. They had to sit in the pews, cold and damp.

Chatting a few minutes with his associates, the General gave an historical turn to his conversation and related several anecdotes of Chief Justice John Marshall and of his old friend Bishop Meade. Then, at 4 o'clock, he called the meeting to order. The discussion was close and tedious. Sitting with his cape about him, Lee presided, but, as usual, did not attempt to influence the deliberations. When all who would do so had expressed their views, Lee "gave his own opinion, as was his wont, briefly and without argument."

After they had decided what should be done about the church building, the vestrymen began to subscribe a fund to raise Doctor Pendleton's salary. Lee was tired by this time, and despite the chill of the place, his face was flushed, but he waited in patience. All the vestrymen contributed; the clerk cast the total and announced how much was still needed to reach the desired sum. It was $55, considerably more than the part of one who already had contributed generously, but Lee said quietly, "I will give that sum." [10]

Seven o'clock had struck, the hour at which, in so many of his battles, darkness had put an end to the fighting. The end had

---

[8] It is stated by some biographers that Lee left some unfinished letters on his table. This is improbable, for it was never General Lee's habit to leave today's work for tomorrow. No such letters are now on his table or are remembered by any of the older members of the staff of the college.

[9] Mrs. R. E. Lee to Miss Mary Meade, Oct. 12, 1870; *Va. Mag. of History and Biography,* January, 1927, pp. 23-26 (cited hereafter as *Meade Letter*).

[10] *Jones,* 432.

come now—not on a field of blood, but in the half-gloom of a bare little church, where the talk was of a larger house of prayer, and the only reminders of the days of strife were the cape and the weary, lined face of the old leader, and the military titles by which some of the vestrymen addressed one another. High command, great fame, heart-anguish, galling burdens had ended in this last service—to plan a little church in a mountain town, and to give of his substance to raise the pay of a parson who had been his loyal lieutenant in arms.

Bidding his associates good night, Lee walked home alone through the darkness and the rain, such a rain as had fallen that night when the army had crossed the Potomac on the retreat from Gettysburg. He climbed the steps. He entered the lighted house and turned into his chamber, as was his custom, to take off his damp covering and hat. Then he went to the dining room, where Mrs. Lee was waiting for him. She saw something unusual in his face and told him he looked chilly. "Thank you," he said in his normal voice, "I am warmly clothed."

It was rare that he, the promptest of men, should delay a meal half an hour, and as he often teased wife and daughters about their tardiness, Mrs. Lee from her rolling-chair smilingly challenged him: "You have kept us waiting a long time, where have you been?"

He made no reply. Taking his usual position in front of his chair, he opened his lips to say grace. But the familiar words would not come. Another instant and he sank back to his seat.

"Let me pour you out a cup of tea," said Mrs. Lee, "you look so tired."

He tried to answer but could make no intelligible sound. On the instant he must have realized that his summons had come, for a look of resignation lighted his eyes. Then he carefully and deliberately straightened up in his chair. If it was the "last enemy" he had to meet now, he would face him mindfully and erect, as if he were going into battle astride Traveller of the tossing neck.

Seeing that he was seriously ill, the family sent immediately for his physicians, Doctor H. T. Barton and Doctor R. L. Madison. Both of them had been at the vestry meeting with the General and as they lived farther from the church than Lee did, neither had reached home when the messenger arrived, but in a short time they hurried into the room. The General was placed on the couch that had been over by the windows. His outer garments were removed. "You hurt my arm," he said, and pointed to the shoulder that had long been paining him.

The physicians' examination showed no paralysis. He was very weak, had a tendency to doze, and was slightly impaired in consciousness. The doctors decided that he had what they termed "venous congestion," an impairment of the circulation that now would probably be termed a thrombosis. A bed was at once brought down from the second floor and was set up for him. Placed upon it, he turned over and went into a long and tranquil sleep, from which his physicians hoped he would awake much improved.

Their hopes were not altogether in vain. He was better the next day, though still very drowsy,[11] but manifestly required careful nursing and close watching. As the rain continued to pour down and the house became damp, a fire was lighted on the hearth. The dining table was removed and the room was turned into a sick-chamber. Friends and members of the faculty began a regular round of waiting at his side. He lay quietly, now awake, now asleep, always on the border-line of the unconscious. Ere long, he responded to the treatment the doctors prescribed, and physically he seemed to improve. Taking his medicine regularly and eating with some appetite, he soon was able to turn over in bed and could sit up to swallow. The attendants' questions he understood and would answer. His replies were monosyllables, but his family explained that he always was silent in sickness.[12]

Word spread, of course, that he was ill. The trustees had been called for September 29, the day after the General was stricken, and with their usual consideration for him they named a committee to express the board's regret at his absence and to consider the advisability of urging him to take a six-months' rest.[13] News-

[11] Meade Letter, loc. cit.
[12] Meade Letter, loc. cit., Johnston, in Riley, 208–10; R. E. Lee, Jr., 440; Childe, 334; Mrs. M. C. Lee to R. H. Chilton, MS., Dec. 12, 1870; Chilton Papers.
[13] Trustees' Minutes, Sept. 29, 1870; Cf. ibid., Oct. 1, for the trustees' letter of regret at his illness.

papers were quick to make inquiries and were able on September 30 to report him much improved.[14] Despite this, reports persisted that he was paralyzed and speechless.[15] In England, Disraeli's *Standard* was so certain his malady was fatal that a review of his career was made ready for publication.[16]

In Lexington apprehension battled with hope. The doctors remained confident, and Mrs. Lee talked of the time "when Robert gets well," [17] but in her heart she was haunted by the look that had come into his eyes when he had tried vainly to answer her at the supper table and then had sat upright. "I saw he had taken leave of earth," she afterwards wrote.[18] The superstitious whispered that his end was at hand because his picture had fallen down from the wall of his house;[19] and when a flashing aurora lighted the sky for several nights some saw in it a beckoning hand. One Lexington woman took down a copy of *The Lays of the Scottish Cavaliers* and pointed significantly to this quatrain:

> "All night long the northern streamers
> Shot across the trembling sky:
> Fearful lights, that never beckon
> Save when kings or heroes die." [20]

A week passed, and General Lee's improvement, though slight, was apparent and seemed to be progressive.[21] On October 8 a Richmond paper quoted his physicians as saying he would soon be out again. He still talked very little, and once, when Agnes started to give him his medicine, he said: "It is no use." But she prevailed upon him to take it. Conscious of nearly all that went on around him, he was manifestly glad to have the members of the family come in to see him. He did not smile during his whole illness, but he always met greetings of his wife and children with the pressure of his hand.[22]

[14] *Lexington Gazette*, Sept. 30, 1870; *Richmond Dispatch*, Oct. 7, 1870, quoting Lexington letter of Sept. 30, 1870.

[15] *Richmond Enquirer*, Oct. 4, 1870; *Richmond Whig* editorial, Oct. 4, 1870.

[16] *Richmond Dispatch*, Oct. 7, 1870, quoting *New York World*.   [17] *McDonald*, 7.

[18] Mrs. M. C. Lee to R. H. Chilton, *MS.*, Dec. 12, 1870; *Chilton Papers*.

[19] *McDonald*, 7.

[20] *McDonald*, 7. The lines were wrongly quoted by Mrs. McDonald and were said by her to be taken from the heading of a chapter in "an old romance, *The Scottish Cavalier*," but the lines evidently are from W. E. Aytoun's *Edinburgh After Flodden*.

[21] *Richmond Dispatch*, Oct. 6, Oct. 7, 1870.

[22] *R. E. Lee, Jr.*, 440.

On the morning of October 10, Doctor Madison thought his patient was mending. "How do you feel today, General?" he inquired.

"I . . . feel . . . better," said Lee, slowly but distinctly.

"You must make haste and get well; Traveller has been standing so long in the stable that he needs exercise."

The General shook his head deliberately and closed his eyes again. It had been much the same when Custis Lee had spoken of his recovery. Lee had then moved his head from side to side and had pointed upward.

That afternoon, without warning, his pulse began to flutter. His breathing became hurried. Exhaustion was apparent. The evening brought no improvement. At midnight he had a chill, and his condition was so serious that Doctor Barton had to warn the family.

One of his professors, son of his old comrade, Sidney Johnston, sat by him that night,[23] fully appreciative of the life that was ending. "Never," he recorded, "was more beautifully displayed how a long and severe education of mind and character enables the soul to pass with equal step through this supreme ordeal; never did the habits and qualities of a lifetime, solemnly gathered into a few last sad hours, more grandly maintain themselves amid the gloom and shadow of approaching death. The reticence, the self-contained composure, the obedience to proper authority, the magnanimity and Christian meekness that marked all his actions, preserved their sway, in spite of the inroads of disease, and the creeping lethargy that weighed down his faculties. As the old hero lay in the darkened room, or with the lamp and hearth fire casting shadows upon his calm, noble front, all the massive grandeur of his form, and face, and brow remained; and death seemed to lose its terrors, and to borrow a grace and dignity in sublime keeping with the life that was ebbing away. The great mind sank to its last repose, almost with the equal poise of health." [24]

Lee refused medicine and nourishment the next day, even from his daughters, but despite the confusion of his mind, self-dis-

---

[23] This is inferred from the particularity of the account Johnston gave of events during the evening and night of the 10th.

[24] W. P. Johnston, in *Riley*, 212, quoted from *Jones*, 450–51. This account appears also in *R. E. Lee, Jr.*, 438–39.

cipline still ruled, and when either of his doctors put physic to his mouth he would swallow it. During the morning he lapsed into a half-delirium of dreams and memories. ". . . His mind wandered to those dreadful battlefields." [25] He muttered unintelligible words—prayers, perhaps, or orders to his men. Sometimes his voice was distinct. "Tell Hill he *must* come up," he said, so plainly and emphatically that all who sat in the death-chamber understood him.

His symptoms now were aggravated. Mrs. Lee, in her rolling-chair, took her place by his bed for the last vigil and held his moist hand.[26] His pulse continued weak and feeble; his breathing was worse. By the end of the day the physicians admitted that the fight was lost: the General was dying. They could only wait, not daring to hope, as he lay there motionless, save for the rapid rise and fall of his chest. His eyes were closed. When he talked in his delirium he did not thresh about. The words, though now mingled past unravelling, were quietly spoken.

At last, on October 12, daylight came. The watchers stirred and stretched themselves and made ready to give place to those who had obtained a little sleep. Out of the windows, across the campus, the students began to move about, and after a while they straggled down to the chapel to pray for him. Now it was 9 o'clock, and a quarter past. His old opponent, Grant, was sitting down comfortably to breakfast in the White House. With axe or saw or plough or pen, the veterans of Lee's army were in the swing of another day's work. For him it was ended, the life of discipline, of sorrow, and of service. The clock was striking his last half-hour. In some corner of his mind, not wrecked by his malady, he must have heard his marching order. Was the enemy ahead? Had that bayoneted host of his been called up once again to march through Thoroughfare Gap or around Hooker's flank or over the Potomac into Maryland . . . moving . . . moving forward? Or was it that the war was over and that peace had come?

"Strike the tent," he said, and spoke no more.[27]

---

[25] Mrs. R. E. Lee to R. H. Chilton, *loc. cit.*   [26] *Meade Letter, loc. cit.*
[27] W. P. Johnston, in *Jones*, 450. For the details of the burial of General Lee see IV–8.

CHAPTER XXVIII

THE PATTERN OF A LIFE

THERE he lies, now that they have shrouded him, with his massive features so white against the lining of the casket that he seems already a marble statue for the veneration of the South. His cause died at Appomattox; now, in him, it is to have its apotheosis. Others survive who shared his battles and his vigils, but none who so completely embodies the glamour, the genius, and the graces with which the South has idealized a hideous war. His passing sets a period to the bloodiest chapter in the history of his country.

Yet even in the hour of his death there are omens that the future of the South is to be built not less on hope than on memory. The windows of the chamber do not look to the west but to the sunrise. He is not clad in the uniform of his army but in the wedding garment he bought when he went, all unwillingly, to the marriage feast in Petersburg and found the city of his last defense breathing with new life. Presently, the bells that are tolling his death will bring down from the highlands, like the clans at the sound of the pibroch, a host of those who had followed his standard. For the moment, the first mourners are the students of the college, younger brothers of his veterans, and the children of the schools of the town, abruptly dismissed from their classes when the first note from the church belfry announced his last battle ended.

Tomorrow a slow-footed procession will form to carry his body to the chapel of the college, and the press of the country will be praising his feats as a soldier and his high intellect as a leader, or else, once more, will be branding him a traitor. We who have followed his career through many pages have already discussed these things. Let us speak of them no more, but, ere the silent undertaker screws down the lid of the coffin, let us look at him

493

for the last time and read from his countenance the pattern of his life.

Because he was calm when others were frenzied, loving when they hated, and silent when they spoke with bitter tongue, they shook their heads and said he was a superman or a mysterious man. Beneath that untroubled exterior, they said, deep storms must rage; his dignity, his reserve, and his few words concealed sombre thoughts, repressed ambitions, livid resentments. They were mistaken. Robert Lee was one of the small company of great men in whom there is no inconsistency to be explained, no enigma to be solved. What he seemed, he was—a wholly human gentleman, the essential elements of whose positive character were two and only two, simplicity and spirituality.

When the nascent science of genetics is developed, Lee will be cited in the case-books along with those who appear in Galton's *Hereditary Genius*. For his most conspicuous qualities, it may be repeated, were derived in almost equal determinable proportions from his parents and from his grandparents. From his Grandfather Lee, came a sense of system, the power of critical analysis that kept him free of illusion, and, along with these, perhaps, his love of animals. His good looks were an endowment from his maternal grandmother, the "Lowland Beauty" at the sight of whom the grave eyes of George Washington are said to have lighted up. To his Grandfather Carter, Robert E. Lee owed much of the religion in his nature, something of his kindness, his love of family life and his devotion to his kin. "Light-Horse Harry" Lee passed on to his youngest son his fine physique, his aptitude for military affairs, his great intelligence, his daring, his sense of public duty, and the charm of manner that made him so readily a captain. The characteristics of his mother that reappear were her religion, her thrift, her self-control, her social sense, and her patience in adversity. If it seem unscientific, at first glance, to speak with so much assurance of Lee's inherited characteristics, it may be said that the celebrity of his forebears and the diligence of the family genealogists make the facts more apparent than in most cases. Were as much known of other great American families as of the Lees, as much might be said of their descendants.

Fortunate in his ancestors, Lee was fortunate most of all in that he inherited nearly all their nobler qualities and none of their worse. Geneticists will say, perhaps, that this is the explanation of genius—a chance combination of genes. Beyond the frontier that these pioneers have yet crossed lies the fact that at least four generations of the ancestors of Lee, prior to that of his immediate grandparents, had all married well. Back to Richard the immigrant, whose wife's family name is unknown, there was not one instance in which a direct progenitor of Lee mated with a woman of blood and of station below his own. His line was not crossed in a century and a half with one that was degenerating. If blood means anything, he was entitled to be what he fundamentally was, a gentleman.

The first reference to Robert E. Lee in an extant letter is the significant statement of his father that "Robert was always good and will be confirmed in his happy turn of mind by his ever-watchful and affectionate mother. Does he strengthen his native tendency?"[1] Penned when the boy was ten, this language registered the impression the absent father had formed when Robert was not more than seven years of age. The stamp of character must, then, have been upon him from childhood. When he emerges dimly as a personality, in the later days of his cadetship at West Point, many of his essential qualities are apparent. Thereafter, from the time he appears clearly at Cockspur Island and at Fort Monroe, he exhibits every characteristic that later distinguished him. Subsequent change in his character was negligible and is simply the development of the man by challenging circumstance. Of this there can be no question. So consistent is the description of the young lieutenant of engineers, in the early 1830's, alike by those who became his foes and by those who remained his friends, that one need not fear the picture is touched up with the later remembrance of qualities the grizzled General displayed when he had endured the hard ordeal of the War between the States.

This early development of character, like everything else that relates to Lee as an individual, is easily understood. Despite the ill-health of the mother and her unhappiness during her pregnancy, he had a strong and normal nervous system that was in-

[1] Henry Lee to Charles Carter Lee. Feb. 9, 1817, *Henry Lee's Memoirs*, 65.

495

vigorated by a simple outdoor life. Although there is no evidence that Mrs. Ann Lee had any secret dread that her son would develop the recklessness of his father, there is abundant proof that, with tactful wisdom, she inculcated in him from childhood the principles of self-control. From earliest adolescence he had upon him the care of his mother. George Washington, the embodiment of character, was his hero, made real and personal in the environment of Alexandria. At West Point his ambition to excel in his class led Lee to subject himself willingly and with a whole heart to a discipline that confirmed every excellence he had acquired at home. Physically more developed than most of the cadets, he had from the outset a better appreciation of what the training of the academy was intended to accomplish. All his early assignments to engineering duty were of a sort to impose responsibility. These circumstances did not destroy his sunny exuberance of spirit, but they set his character so early and so definitely that it did not change with years or woes.

Whether it was at the Des Moines Rapids, or during his superintendency of West Point, or in the president's house at Washington College—wherever he was in full four decades when the burden of battle was not on him—an old acquaintance would have observed little difference in his daily outlook, his nature, or his manners. Only in four particulars was the man who went to that last vestry meeting at the Episcopal church in Lexington unlike the lieutenant who bantered the "Beautiful Talcott" at Old Point in the moments he was not watching the contractors who might circumvent the government. His buoyant bearing had given place to a calmer cheerfulness, which might have been the case with any man who has bridged the chasm that divides the twenties of life from the sixties, even though no river of blood has flowed through the chasm. Again, the natural dignity of his person had settled into a more formal reserve, not because he had become less simple in heart or less approachable in manner, but because his conception of his duty to promote peace and national unity compelled him to put a wall between him and those who might have stirred unhappy memories and would certainly have kept open the old wounds of fratricidal war had he permitted them to talk of war. Even then it is quite likely that some of those who knew him after the war mistook their reverence for his reserve. He was changed, also, in that, after 1865, he put out of his heart the military career that long had fascinated him. All the misgivings he had felt before the war regarding the pursuit of arms were confirmed by five years at Lexington. He spoke his conviction, as always, when he told young Professor Humphreys that the great mistake of his life had been in pursuing the education of a soldier, and he was not jesting in his encomium to General Ewell on the delights of a civil life.[2] It was not by chance that he failed to keep step with the superintendent of V. M. I. when the two walked together at the head of the column of cadets.

These things apart, any one who had worked with him on the wharf at Saint Louis would have felt at home in his office in Lexington and would have found him the same man in the habits of life, in the steady routine, and in the simplicity of spirit that were his very ego. He rose early and cheerfully and had his private devotions. If he was away from home, he would write his domestic letters before breakfast. At the meal hour he would appear promptly, with greetings to all and with gentle, bantering reproaches for his always tardy wife. Were his food the sumptuous fare of bountiful Arlington, he would enjoy and praise each dish, eating with heartiness; but when he sat down to the plain diet of the first hard days at Lexington he showed the same relish and made no complaint.

Family worship over, he would go to work immediately, neatly dressed and with the whitest of linens, but never ostentatiously apparelled. In his labor he was swift and diligent, prompt and accurate, always systematic and instinctively thrifty. His ambition was in his labor, whatever its nature. He did not covet praise. Blushing to receive it, he assumed that others would blush when he bestowed it, and he spared what he thought were their feelings, though no man was quicker to appreciate and, at the proper time, to acknowledge the achievement of others. Place and advancement never lured him, except as promotion held out the hope of larger opportunity and better provision for his family. Even then he was meticulous regarding the methods he would employ to

[2] See *supra*, p. 363.

497

further himself financially, and he would never capitalize his name or draw drafts on the good opinion of friends or public. Yet he had all his life the desire to excel at the task assigned him. That was the urge alike of conscience, of obligation, of his regard for detail, and of his devotion to thoroughness as the prime constituent of all labor. He never said so in plain words, but he desired everything that he did, whether it was to plan a battle or to greet a visitor, to be as nearly perfect as he could make it. No man was more critical of his own performance because none demanded more of himself. The engineer's impulse in him was most gratified if something was to be created or organized, but if it concerned another's happiness or had a place in the large design of worth-while things, he considered the smallest task proper to perform. Only the useless was irksome.

He endured interruption of his work without vexation. Rarely was he embarrassed in his dealings with men. He met every visitor, every fellow-worker, with a smile and a bow, no matter what the other's station in life. Always he seemed to keep others at a judicious distance and did not invite their confidences, but he sought as a gentleman to make every right-minded person comfortable in his presence. With a tact so delicate that others scarcely noticed it, when he was busy he kept conversation to the question at issue, and he sought to make his interviews brief; but even so, his consideration for the sensibilities of others cost him many a precious hour. Wrangles he avoided, and disagreeable persons he usually treated with a cold and freezing courtesy. Should his self-control be overborne by stupidity or ill-temper, his eyes would flash and his neck would redden. His rebuke would be swift and terse, and it might be two hours or more before he was completely master of himself. Whoever visited him meantime would perhaps find him irascible, though sure to make amends. Exacting of his subordinates, he still reconciled himself often to working with clumsy human tools. Resentments he never cherished. When he found men unworthy of his confidence, he made it his practice to see them as little as possible and to talk to them not at all. Silence was one of his strongest weapons. During the war he summarized his code when he wrote these words on a scrap of paper that nobody saw until after his death:

"The forbearing use of power does not only form a touchstone, but the manner in which an individual enjoys certain advantages over others is a test of a true gentleman.

"The power which the strong have over the weak, the employer over the employed, the educated over the unlettered, the experienced over the confiding, even the clever over the silly—the forbearing or inoffensive use of all this power or authority, or a total abstinence from it when the case admits it, will show the gentleman in a plain light. The gentleman does not needlessly and unnecessarily remind an offender of a wrong he may have committed against him. He can not only forgive, he can forget; and he strives for that nobleness of self and mildness of character which impart sufficient strength to let the past be but the past. A true man of honor feels humbled himself when he cannot help humbling others." [3]

Lee sought to conclude his work by early afternoon, even if that compelled him to set a late hour for the meal. When dinner was done he was glad of a brief period of relaxation and sometimes of a little sleep, usually upright in his chair. Then he sought his daily exercise in a ride on his horse. He delighted to have a companion, and if he had one, he talked of pleasant topics. Riding alone, which he often did, he would close his mind to the difficulties of the day and to the problems of the morrow and would soothe himself with the discovered beauties of the countryside. Nothing of a physical nature gave him the same thrill as a glowing sunset. Usually, on these rides, he paid his calls on the sick and on strangers, as diligently as if he had been the parson of the town. This he regarded as one of his social duties, and he discharged it not only with willingness but also with satisfaction. Whether his ride included social calls or simply carried him to a given objective, he was always on the alert for the children and he never passed them without a greeting, and, usually, a chat.

His return home, like all his other movements, was according to a precise schedule. Unless a sudden storm detained him, he would be at his door promptly at dusk, and would soon be ready for his light evening meal—"tea" as the family called it. The

---

[3] *Jones,* 163. It is not known whether this and several other written notes in General Lee's military valise were original with him or had been copied from some little-known books that he had read.

hours then belonged to Mrs. Lee, to his children, and to his guests. He would read to them or converse cheerfully until bed-time, which was usually after 10 o'clock. When he retired to his own room he had his evening prayers and was soon asleep. His quarters at Lexington were always as neat as if he were still a cadet at West Point, but the only suggestion of the soldier was the army pistol that hung in its holster by the head of his bed. After Mrs. Lee's invalidism afflicted her, he rarely went out to social affairs. Before that time he sometimes attended her to parties or to dinners, where he preferred the company of women to that of men, and that of the daughters to the mothers'. Always his address was dignified, but to the young girls it was often bantering. Nothing delighted him more than gently to tease some blushing young beauty. He had neither high wit nor quick repartee, though occasionally he essayed a pun; but his smile, his manners, and his quick understanding made him socially irresist-ible. His conversation, however, never turned to forbidden topics, nor was there in it anything suggestive or of *double entente*. In all his letters, and there are several thousand of them, as in all his reported conversation, and there are countless anecdotes of him, no oath or vulgarism appears. He was clean-minded, though defi-nitely and unfeignedly attracted to intelligent, handsome women.

Leaves and furloughs during his army service and vacations after the war found him ready to travel, not to distant lands but to the spas of Virginia or, better still, to the houses of congenial friends. Most of all did he relish a round of visits to his own kin, with whom he delighted to talk of the doings of their rela-tives. Chatter of this sort never bored him. Naturally sociable and devoted to his countless cousins, he sympathized with all their distresses and rejoiced in their little triumphs. Rarely was he too busy, when time allowed of his writing at all, to chronicle every wedding, every birth, every journey, every sickness, for the information of his family correspondents. At home, in his earlier periods of leisure, he shared in the sports of his sons, and to the end of his life he gave to each of his daughters a measure of courtly attention fitted to the temperament and age of each of them.

At intervals his habitual cheerfulness was marred by a sense of

500

failure. This was most apt to overtake him when he was absent from home on long tours of military duty, for his simple nature made him dependent on his wife and children. Separated from them he often suffered loneliness and sometimes acute nostalgia. On occasion, and particularly during the difficult period when he was struggling to settle Mr. Custis's estate and to repair Arlington in 1857–59, this sense of frustration came upon him even at home. Then he would wonder why he did not advance more rapidly in the army and would puzzle himself to know how he could make adequate provision for his daughters, none of whom, in his heart of hearts, he wished to be married. These were the most unhappy times of his life, except perhaps those of his occasional illnesses. When sick, he would have few words even for his family, and was more than apt to lose his grip upon himself in dealing with others.

This was the pattern of his daily life. There is every reason to believe it was the mirror of his own soul. Those who look at him through the glamour of his victories or seek deep meaning in his silence will labor in vain to make him appear complicated. His language, his acts, and his personal life were simple for the unescapable reason that he was a simple gentleman.

Simple and spiritual—the two qualities which constitute the man cannot be separated. The strongest religious impulse in his life was that given him by his mother. After that, in youth, he probably came most under the indirect influence of Reverend William Meade, later bishop, the clergyman who did more than any one else to restore the Protestant Episcopal Church in Virginia from the ruin that had overtaken it during and after the American Revolution. Mr. Meade was rector in Alexandria for only eighteen months and then at a time when Robert was too young to heed his sermons; but he preached there often during Robert's youth and his spirit dominated the Episcopal Church in Virginia. He was a picturesque personality, one of the prophets of his generation. Holding to the beautiful forms of his faith, Mr. Meade breathed into its worship an evangelism as ardent as that of the younger American denominations. In his eyes, religion concerned itself equally with acts and with beliefs. No reformer was ever more uncompromising in his denunciation of cards or more unyielding in opposition to the old habit the barons of the Northern Neck had of staging races and of backing their horses with their dollars. None excoriated the stage with warnings more sulphurous than did Mr. Meade. Had he been sent to idolatrous Israel, he could not more solemnly have proclaimed the day of the vengeance of the Lord or have portrayed more darkly the fearsome punishment visited on the sinner for his hardness of heart. Yet he spoke "comfortably to Jerusalem." He gave the promise of forgiveness to the repentant, pictured glowingly to the faithful the bliss of a hard-won Heaven, and somehow planted in the hearts of the dominant class in that section of the Old Dominion a religion of simplicity, vigor, and sincerity.

It is a singular fact that young Robert Lee was not prompted by the exhortations of Mr. Meade or of like-minded clergymen to submit himself to confirmation. The reason cannot be surmised, unless it was that the theology of his youth had a vehemence and an emotionalism alien to his nature. He was content until he was past forty-five to hold to the code of a gentleman rather than to the formal creed of a church. The experiences of the Mexican War, the gentle piety of the Fitzhughs at Ravensworth, the example and death of Mrs. Custis, the simple faith of Mrs. Lee, and, more immediately, the purpose of his daughters to enter into the full fellowship of the church induced Lee in 1853 to renew his vows. After that time, first his sense of dependence on God for the uprearing of his boys during his long absences from home, and then the developing tragedy of the war, deepened every religious impulse of his soul.

And what did religion imply for him as he sent Pickett's men up Cemetery Ridge, as he rode to the McLean house, as he read of Military District No. 1, and as he looked down from the chapel platform at the scarred faces and patched garments of his students?

To answer that question is to employ the terms of a theology that now seems to some outworn and perhaps archaic. It was, however, the *credo* of a man who met the supreme tests of life in that he accepted fame without vanity and defeat without repining. To understand the faith of Robert E. Lee is to fill out the picture of him as a gentleman of simple soul. For him as for his grandfather, Charles Carter, religion blended with the code of *noblesse oblige* to which he had been reared. Together, these two forces resolved every problem of his life into right and wrong. The clear light of conscience and of social obligation left no zone of gray in his heart: everything was black or white. There cannot be said to have been a "secret" of his life, but this assuredly was the great, transparent truth, and this it was, primarily, that gave to his career its consistency and decision. Over his movements as a soldier he hesitated often, but over his acts as a man, never. There was but one question ever: What was his duty as a Christian and a gentleman? That he answered by the sure criterion of right and wrong, and, having answered, acted. Everywhere the two obligations went together; he never sought to expiate as a Christian for what he had failed to do as a gentleman, or to atone as a gentleman for what he had neglected as a Christian. He could not have conceived of a Christian who was not a gentleman.

Kindness was the first implication of religion in his mind—not the deliberate kindness of "good works" to pacify exacting Deity, but the instinctive kindness of a heart that had been schooled to regard others. His was not a nature to waste time in the perplexities of self-analysis; but if those about him at headquarters had understood him better they might often have asked themselves whether, when he brought a refreshing drink to a dusty lieutenant who called with dispatches, he was discharging the social duty of a host or was giving a "cup of cold water" in his Master's name. His manner in either case would have been precisely the same.

Equally was his religion expressed in his unquestioning response to duty. In his clear creed, right was duty and must be discharged. "There is," he wrote down privately for his own guidance, "a true glory and a true honor: the glory of duty done —the honor of the integrity of principle." [4] He probably never summed up this aspect of his religion more completely than in that self-revealing hour before he started to meet General Grant, when he answered all the appeals of his lieutenants with the simple statement: "The question is, is it right to surrender this

[4] *Jones*, 145.

army? If it is right, then I will take all the responsibility." [5] It was a high creed—right at all times and at all costs—but daily self-discipline and a clear sense of justice made him able to adhere to it.

Humility was another major implication of his religion. So lofty was his conception of man's duty to his Maker and to his neighbors, so completely did his ambition extend, all unconsciously, into the realm of the spirit, that he was never satisfied with what he was. Those who stood with him on the red field of Appomattox thought that his composure was due to his belief that he had discharged his full duty, and in this they were partially correct; but he always felt, with a sincerity no man can challenge, that he had fallen immeasurably short of his ideal of a servant of God. "So humble was he as a Christian," wrote Mrs. Lee on the day of his death, "that he said not long ago to me he wished he felt sure of his acceptance. I said all who love and trust in the Savior need not fear. He did not reply, but a more upright and conscientious Christian never lived." [6]

Born of this humility, this sense of unworthiness in the sight of God, was the submission to the Divine will that has so often been cited in these pages to explain his calmness in hours that would have wrecked the self-control of lesser men. There was nothing of blind fatalism in his faith. Resignation is scarcely the name for it. Believing that God was Infinite Wisdom and Eternal Love, he subjected himself to seeming ill-fortune in the confidence that God's will would work out for man's good. If it was a battle that had been won, to "Almighty God" he gave the glory; if it was a death that had brought grief to the family, he reminded his wife that their "Heavenly Father" knew better than they, and that there was eternal peace and sure reunion after life. Nothing of his serenity during the war or of his silent labor in defeat can be understood unless one realizes that he submitted himself in all things faithfully to the will of a Divinity which, in his simple faith, was directing wisely the fate of nations and the daily life of His children. This, and not the mere physical courage that defies danger, sustained him in battle; and this, at least equally with his sense of duty done, made him accept the

[5] See *supra*, p. 121.   [6] *Meade Letter*, loc. cit.

504

results of the war without even a single gesture of complaint.

Of humility and submission was born a spirit of self-denial that prepared him for the hardships of the war and, still more, for the dark destitution that followed it. This self-denial was, in some sense, the spiritual counterpart of the social self-control his mother had inculcated in his boyhood days, and it grew in power throughout his life. He loved the luxury that wealth commanded. Had he been as rich as his Grandfather Carter, he would have lived in a style as hospitable. Fine horses and handsome clothes and lavish entertainments would have been his; Arlington would have been adorned, and his daughters would have enjoyed travel and the richest comfort. But Arlington was confiscated, its treasures were scattered, each stage of his sacrifice for the South brought him lower and lower in fortune until he was living in a borrowed tenant house and his wife was husbanding the scraps from a pair of trousers a farmer's wife had made for him. His own misfortunes typified the fate of the Confederacy and of its adherents. Through it all, his spirit of self-denial met every demand upon it, and even after he went to Washington College and had an income on which he could live easily, he continued to deny himself as an example to his people. Had his life been epitomized in one sentence of the Book he read so often, it would have been in the words, "If any man will come after me, let him deny himself, and take up his cross daily, and follow me." And if one, only one, of all the myriad incidents of his stirring life had to be selected to typify his message, as a man, to the young Americans who stood in hushed awe that rainy October morning as their parents wept at the passing of the Southern Arthur, who would hesitate in selecting that incident? It occurred in Northern Virginia, probably on his last visit there. A young mother brought her baby to him to be blessed. He took the infant in his arms and looked at it and then at her and slowly said, "Teach him he must deny himself." [7]

That is all. There is no mystery in the coffin there in front of the windows that look to the sunrise.

[7] *Packard*, 158.

THE END OF THE LAST VALLEY CAMPAIGN

After his defeat at Waynesboro on March 2, 1865, Early was forced to flee the field, and, with difficulty, escaped to eastern Virginia. He visited Lee's headquarters about March 16,[1] and there received orders to return to his district and to reorganize what troops he could collect. As there was then no threat of any Federal advance into the Valley, which Sheridan had stripped and had left, Lee ordered what remained of Rosser's division of cavalry to join him for the spring campaign.[2] Before Early could reach the Valley, word came on March 21 that the Federals in east Tennessee were preparing for a raid on the Virginia and Tennessee Railroad, which, at Lynchburg, joined the Southside Railroad and brought Lee a considerable volume of supplies from the rich counties of southwest Virginia. General Lee's first purpose was to prevent this raid by dispatching cavalry against the Federal line of communications between Chattanooga and Nashville, and he called upon General Johnston to ascertain if this could be done.[3] If the Federal advance could not be prevented, he had to devise a way of meeting it. And that meant he must attempt a levy *en masse* to support the negligible organized units in the threatened district, which Lee even then was planning to reduce by one brigade of cavalry.[4] Was Early the commander to inspire the old men to come out, the leader to prevail on mothers to let their fourteen-year-old boys take the field? He had, Lee thought, "great intelligence, good judgment, and undoubted bravery," but his reverses in the lower Valley and his defeat at Waynesboro, Lee felt, had shaken the confidence of the troops and of the people. "If this feeling does exist," General Lee wrote the Secretary of War, who had formerly commanded in southwest Virginia, "a change of commanders would be advantageous, and so high an opinion have

---

[1] *Early*, 466. In *O. R.*, 46, part 3, p. 1317 the time of his arrival in Richmond is given as the night of March 14–15.

[2] *Early*, 466.

[3] *O. R.*, 49, part 2, p. 113. Actually, as Johnston advised Lee (*ibid.*, 1141), the troops that might be used for this purpose were in the district of Lieutenant General Richard Taylor, not in Johnston's.

[4] *O. R.*, 46, part 3, p. 1358.

I of General Early's integrity of purpose and devotion to his country, that should such be the case, I believe he would be the first to propose it." Would General Breckinridge give him his advice?[5] This was written on March 28, when Lee was watching the ominous movement of troops toward his right. The next day Lee had news that 4000 Federal cavalry were on a raid against southwest Virginia. He was impelled to act at once,[6] without waiting for an answer from Breckinridge, so he relieved Early, put in temporary command the senior officer on the ground and cast about for a successor. Hood occurred to mind or possibly was suggested by Breckinridge, but Lee feared that officer's physical condition, "and other considerations" which he did not specify, might "diminish his usefulness in that department." Beauregard might be the man.[7]

But Lee would not dismiss a loyal lieutenant with a formal order and a short dispatch. In his telegram to General Early[8] he said: "I will address you a letter to your house in Franklin County, to which you can return and await further orders," and the next day, March 30, though he needed every moment for the tasks on his own front, he took the time to write to Early in his own hand a lengthy and friendly letter, as considerate as ever was addressed to a soldier whom disaster had overtaken. Lee explained how essential it was to have the full support of the people and of the soldiers, and he told how he had reluctantly concluded that Early could not command the co-operation "essential to success," because of the reverses in the Valley, of which, he added tactfully, "the public and the army judge chiefly by the results." He went on: "While my own confidence in your ability, zeal, and devotion to the cause is unimpaired, I have nevertheless felt that I could not oppose what seems to be the current of opinion, without injustice to your reputation and injury to the service. I therefore felt constrained to endeavor to find a commander who would be more likely to develop the strength and resources of the country, and inspire the soldiers with confidence; and, to accomplish this purpose, I thought it proper to yield my own opinion, and to defer to that of those to whom alone we can look for support. I am sure that you will understand and appreciate my motives, and no one will be more ready than yourself to acquiesce in any measures which the interests of the country may seem to require, regardless of all personal considerations. Thanking you for the fidelity and energy with which you have always supported my efforts, and for the courage and devotion you have ever

[5] O. R., 46, part 2, p. 1166.
[6] O. R., 46, part 3, p. 1362 and O. R., 49, part 2, p. 1171.
[7] O. R., 49, part 2, p. 1171. [8] O. R., 49, part 2, p. 1171.

manifested in the service, I am, very respectfully and truly, your obedient servant." [9]

It was consideration in no sense unappreciated. General Early cherished the letter as his chiefest treasure, published it as an appendix to his useful *Memoir of the Last Year of the War for Independence,* defied the attempt of overzealous officials to take the original from him after the war on the ground that it was the property of the Federal Government, and included its text again in the *Autobiographical Sketch and Narrative of the War,* which was left in manuscript at the time of his death. He was one of General Lee's most faithful defenders, served as president of the Southern Historical Society, wrote a number of papers on Gettysburg, delivered an admirable memorial address on his old commander, and was active in planning a monument to him in Richmond.

APPENDIX IV—2

LEE'S FAILURE TO RECEIVE SUPPLIES AT AMELIA COURTHOUSE

The failure of General Lee to find supplies at Amelia Courthouse, when the Army of Northern Virginia arrived there on the morning of April 4, 1865, gave rise to various rumors.

Writing in 1866, James D. McCabe, Jr.,[1] charged specifically that "the trains which had been sent from Danville [to Lee at Amelia] had been ordered to Richmond to help carry off the government property, and that, through the inexcusable blundering of the Richmond authorities, the cars had been sent on to the Capital without unloading at the stores at Amelia Courthouse." Fitz Lee[2] quoted but did not altogether credit a report, of unstated origin, that "on that famous Sunday a train load of supplies arrived at Amelia Courthouse from Danville, but the officer in charge was met there by an order to bring the train to Richmond because the cars were needed for the transportation of the personal property of the Confederate authorities."

No foundation exists for that part of these stories alleging that supply trains were run past Amelia Courthouse after orders had been received to accumulate supplies there. Mr. Davis, however, thought it necessary, in his own defense, to show that his administration had not been guilty of neglect in failing to set up a depot at Amelia. In 3 *S. H. S. P.,* 97 *ff.,* he caused to be published a series of letters from

[9] *Early,* 468–69.
[1] *Op. cit.,* 617.   [2] *Op. cit.,* 383–84.

APPENDIX

General St. John and other officers denying that Lee had requested them to send supplies to Amelia Courthouse. These letters are convincing proof that no specific directions naming the village had ever been received.

On the other hand, in his final report General Lee stated: "*Not finding the supplies ordered to be placed there* [*i.e.,* at Amelia] twenty-four hours were lost," etc. In his appeal to the Amelia farmers,[3] he said he was expecting to find at Amelia "plenty of provisions, *which had been ordered to be placed here by the railroad several days since. . . .*"

There is, then, no doubt that Lee thought supplies had been ordered to Amelia, and no doubt that the commissary bureau received no direct instruction to place food and provender at that point. Was Lee mistaken, or were his orders misunderstood? There are no letters in the *Official Records* showing that General Lee requested prior to April 2 that supplies should be collected at Amelia Courthouse. Colonel W. H. Taylor is authority for saying that no such orders were sent from General Headquarters.[4] Whatever was done, then, in this particular, was done on April 2. Lee's first dispatch that day to the Secretary of War was received at 10:40 A.M. In it Lee said that he would withdraw to the north side of the Appomattox that night and could concentrate "near the Danville Railroad." He did not mention Amelia. "I advise," he said, "that all preparation be made for leaving Richmond tonight."[5] It can hardly be claimed that this was notice to the War Department to accumulate supplies on the Richmond and Danville Railroad, certainly not at Amelia. After the contents of this telegram had become known in Richmond, General St. John telegraphed Lee's chief commissary, Colonel R. G. Cole, asking what should be the destination of the reserve rations then in Richmond.[6] This message, of course, should have been delivered and answered at once; but it is a matter of record that the telegraph station at Edge Hill had then been abandoned,[7] and it probably was some time before a field station was opened elsewhere. Late in the day Lee telegraphed the Secretary of War that he would proceed to abandon his position that night. "I have given all the orders to officers on both sides the river. . . . Please give all orders that you find necessary in and about Richmond. The troops will all be directed to Amelia Courthouse."[8] This, needless to say, was indirect notice to the Secretary of War to provide supplies at Amelia. *But this message, whenever sent, was not*

3 See *supra,* p. 67.
5 *O. R.,* 46, part 3, p. 1378.
7 *Cf. supra,* pp. 49, 51.
4 See *infra,* p. 511.
6 St. John's report, *Lee MSS.—L.*
8 *O. R.,* 46, part 3, p. 1379.

received until 7 P.M.[9] Meantime, St. John had received no answer to his message to Cole. Not "until night" did it arrive. It read: "Send up the Danville Railroad if Richmond is not safe." [10] This language was, in itself, evidence of a long delay in transmission, for if Cole had written late in the day he would have known that Richmond was not safe.

Colonel Taylor may now be cited as a witness. In 1906 Captain W. Gordon McCabe wrote him for information regarding this incident. On December 9 Colonel Taylor replied as follows:

"I . . . will gladly do what I can in giving an answer to your inquiry 'whether (and where) there is extant the order of General Lee touching the collection of supplies for the Army of Northern Virginia at Amelia Court House in early April 1865.'

"I cannot say that any specific, written order for the collection of supplies at Amelia Court House is extant; nor do I assert that any such order was ever written.

"The presentation of the matter given in Mr. Davis's account would impress one with the idea that the several reports quoted were made in refutation of a charge that sometime previous to the 2nd April 1865, General Lee had given orders for the collection of supplies at Amelia Court House. I am sure that no such order was ever issued, but that is not the real question.

"On the second of April, however, a crisis in our affairs was reached. An emergency, not unexpected, compelled the immediate evacuation of Petersburg and Richmond and the retirement to the interior of General Lee's army.

"At that time large collections of supplies were at Richmond, Danville, Lynchburg and other points on the railroads, from which General Lee's army was supplied daily.

"When General Lee confronted the inevitable and notified the authorities at Richmond on April 2nd that he would have to evacuate his lines that night, he said in his telegram to the Secretary of War, 'Please give all orders that you find necessary in and about Richmond. The troops will all be directed to Amelia Court House.'

"What more did the War Department require in the matter of notice that rations would be required at Amelia Court House? The army was being supplied from day to day; in leaving its lines, it would for some days be necessarily cut off from the railroad; but its objective point on the railroad would be Amelia Court House; in the mean-

[9] It is marked "Received 7 o'clock," but the reference to the issuance of orders makes it clear that this was post meridian, as orders had not been given before 7 A.M.
[10] St. John's report, *Lee MSS.*—L.

time opportunity was given the Department to send supplies to that point.

"Was it necessary for General Lee to say specifically 'Have bread and meat ready for the troops on their arrival at Amelia Court House'? To the intelligent officers directing the operations of the Commissary Department was not the necessity for providing supplies for the troops at Amelia Court House apparent, when the Department was informed that that would be General Lee's objective point?

"Moreover, I am sure that General Lee gave verbal orders to the Chief Commissary and Chief Quarter-master of his army concerning supplies to the troops; and while I cannot say that each communicated with the head of his department at Richmond, yet, such is the estimate that I place upon their intelligence and efficiency, I am quite sure they must have done so.

"Of one thing I can speak positively and that is that General Lee thought that he had given all the orders necessary and expected to find supplies at Amelia Court House."

In quoting the request to Secretary Breckinridge to "give all orders that you find necessary in and around Richmond" Colonel Taylor evidently overlooked the hour of the receipt of the dispatch. He knew that orders—adequate in his opinion—had been given earlier in the day; it did not occur to him that their receipt had been delayed.

As Lee and Taylor, then, were both confident that the necessary orders had been issued, and as the internal evidence in Cole's despatch points to the fact that it was written hours before it was received, the conclusion is inescapable that there was a long delay on April 2 in forwarding some of the many telegraphic orders that must have been despatched. To that delay is doubtless due the misunderstanding and the apparent conflict of testimony. The commissary bureau, receiving no order, did not requisition the quartermaster-general for cars. Consequently, when the President asked for transportation for himself, his cabinet, the most indispensable records, and the government's bullion, he was told that it was available. When the despatch from Cole was at hand it was too late. St. John subsequently reported to Lee, "The transportation upon [the Richmond and Danville] road having been taken up by the treasury department and the personnel of the Confederate government officers. . . ." [11] Had Cole's answer come explicitly and earlier in the day the cars would have been used for food, of course, and the supplies could have been sent easily and in

[11] St. John's report, *Lee MSS.—L.*

reasonable abundance, for, it will be recalled, there were 350,000 **rations** of bread and meat in the capital.[12] If Lee's telegram had been received prior to 7 P.M., it, too, might have served every purpose. As it was, **on** a delay of a few hours in transmitting a message the immediate fate **of** the army may have hung.

APPENDIX IV—3

THE EXCHANGE OF NOTES ON APRIL 9, 1865

The principal sources for the exchange of notes on April 9, 1865, are: *Alexander,* 609; *Marshall's Appomattox,* 17–18; *Taylor's General Lee,* 289; *Humphreys,* 393–95; Meade's report, *O. R.,* 46, part 1, p. 605. The contradictions and confusion among these accounts and those based on them are many. Marshall stated that after Whittier went into the Federal lines he returned and brought Meade's promise of a truce for one hour. Marshall said nothing of the warnings Humphreys gave Lee to withdraw. The only mention of any request for a suspension of hostilities was by Marshall, who stated that after Lee and his attending officers rode to the apple orchard, a formal request for a suspension was made by Lee (*Appomattox,* 18). The reasons for shaping the narrative as it is in the text are these: Humphreys, who ought to know, says that Whittier carried the letter of Lee to Meade. If Whittier had received, also, the request for a suspension of hostilities, he would have carried that, too. Manifestly he did not carry it, because Meade at 10 A.M. forwarded Lee's letter to Grant (*O. R.,* 46, part 3, pp. 667–68), saying nothing of a request for a suspension of hostilities, and at noon (*O. R.,* 46, part 1, p. 666) mentioned a letter from Lee which he said he would forward to Grant. This letter could only have been the request for a truce. If Whittier carried the first letter and not the second, then the second either was sent by Taylor or Marshall into the Federal lines or else was given to the messenger whom Humphreys sent to Lee to warn him to retire. As neither Taylor nor Marshall mentioned delivering such a paper, the logical bearer would seem to be the courier or some unidentified officer from Humphreys. As this note reached Meade before noon, it could hardly have been sent after Lee returned to the Confederate lines and certainly not after Lee went to the apple orchard. Inasmuch as the original of this request for a suspension of hostilities is on the same paper as Lee's first note to Grant and is signed in the same

---

[12] St. John's report, *Lee MSS.—L.* As it was, St. John requisitioned all the wheeled transportation left in Richmond, loaded the wagons with food, and sent them after Lee.

way, it probably was written under the same conditions and very soon after the first message. The third letter of the day to Grant is on a different paper and seems to have been written under less pressure. It probably was composed at the apple orchard. If this is the correct chronology and sequence of the two notes to Grant, the only difficulties that remain are those presented by Meade's letter of noon and by his official report. In his letter of 12 M. he said nothing of any truce other than that of two hours which he then granted Lee. In his report, also, he spoke as though this were the only truce he made. On the other hand in writing Grant at 10 A.M. he referred to an answer he had written Lee. This naturally would be the letter consenting to one hour's truce, which Humphreys, Taylor, and Marshall all agree was allowed by Meade. Humphreys stated positively that this was the letter Whittier delivered between 11 and 12 o'clock. It therefore seems reasonable to suppose that Meade granted an informal truce for one hour, and after Forsyth's arrival (see *supra,* p. 131) agreed to a formal suspension of hostilities for two hours, satisfied that the surrender was near at hand. Perhaps Meade's failure to mention the earlier truce was due to the very informality of its character.

To accept literally the statement in Meade's report is (1) to reject all the evidence as to the truce of one hour, (2) to assume that no armistice on Meade's front had been allowed until the arrival at Lee's head-quarters of Colonel Forsyth, and (3) to assert that the letter of noon is in reality the dispatch of 10 A.M., with the hour changed and the reference to Forsyth added. This, in effect, arrays Meade against all the other witnesses, Federal and Confederate.

So far as Humphreys is concerned, the version adopted in the text accords fully with his narrative except that Humphreys did not mention Meade's letter of noon, of which it is possible that he knew nothing. The narrative here used does not disagree with Marshall, though he did not mention the warnings from Humphreys to withdraw. As for Taylor's narrative, it presents no obstacle to this chronology and helps little with it, because he was frankly confused in his memory as to what happened. It is worth noting that Alexander, who went over the evidence with some care, saw the inconsistency between the time the truce was supposed to begin and the time it actually covered. "This truce may have been prolonged," he stated (*op. cit.,* 608). Evidently he overlooked Meade's dispatch of noon which, it is believed, in reality extended a truce already agreed upon informally.

In Henry H. Humphreys's *Andrew Atkinson Humphreys: A Biography* (1924), the author took the view to which the present writer has come, though he differed slightly as to the time of the two truces. He said (pp. 306–7): "... General Lee withdrawing from the front of the II Corps, at about 11 A.M., the corps had come up with Longstreet's command. ... The corps was at once formed for attack, the VI Corps forming on the right of the II, when at the moment the attack was to begin, it was suspended by the arrival of General Meade. He had read General Lee's letter to General Grant, granted on his [Meade's] lines a truce for one hour, in view of negotiations for a surrender. The truce expired at 1 P.M. ... When the corps advanced at the expiration of the truce, the enemy's pickets or skirmishers had disappeared. ... The corps on reaching the fringe of timber was again halted by General Meade, with the information that the time of the truce had been extended. A staff officer of either General Ord's or General Sheridan's had ridden through the enemy's lines, bearing a message to General Meade that the truce with them was on."

APPENDIX IV—4

ACTON'S APPEAL TO LEE FOR THE SOUTHERN POINT OF VIEW

Bologna
November 4, 1866

Sir,

The very kind letter which Mrs. Lee wrote to my wife last winter encouraged me to hope that you will forgive my presuming to address you, and that you will not resent as an intrusion a letter from an earnest and passionate lover of the cause whose glory and whose strength you were.

I have been requested to furnish private counsel in American affairs for the guidance of the editors of a weekly Review which is to begin at the New Year, and which will be conducted by men who are followers of Mr. Gladstone. You are aware, no doubt, that Mr. Gladstone was in the minority of Lord Palmerston's cabinet who wished to accept the French Emperor's proposal to mediate in the American war.

The reason of the confidence shown in my advice is simply the fact that I formerly travelled in America, and that I afterwards followed the progress of the four years' contest as closely and as keenly as it was possible to do with the partial and unreliable information that reached us. In the momentous questions which have arisen since you sheathed the sword, I have endeavoured to conform my judgment to your own as well as I could ascertain it from the report of your evidence, from

515

the few English travellers who enjoyed the privilege of speaking with you, and especially from General Beauregard, who spoke, as I understood, your sentiments as well as his own. My travels in America never led me south of Maryland, and the only friends to whom I can look for instruction, are Northerners, mostly of Webster's school.

In my emergency, urged by the importance of the questions at issue in the United States, and by the peril of misguided public opinion between our two countries, I therefore seek to appeal to southern authorities, and venture at once to proceed to Headquarters.

If, Sir, you will consent to entertain my request, and will inform me of the light in which you would wish the current politics of America to be understood, I can pledge myself that the new Review shall follow the course which you prescribe and that any communication with which you may honour me shall be kept in strictest confidence, and highly treasured by me. Even should you dismiss my request as unwarranted, I trust you will remember it only as an attempt to break through the barrier of false reports and false sympathies which encloses the views of my countrymen.

It cannot have escaped you that much of the good will felt in England towards the South, so far as it was not simply the tribute of astonishment and admiration won by your campaigns, was neither unselfish nor sincere. It sprang partly from an exultant belief in the imminent decline and ruin of Democratic institutions, partly from the hope that America would be weakened by the separation, and from terror at the remote prospect of Farragut appearing in the channel and Sherman landing in Ireland.

I am anxious that you should distinguish the feeling which drew me toward your cause and your career, and which now guides my pen, from that thankless and unworthy sympathy.

Without presuming to decide the purely legal question, on which it seems evident to me from Madison's and Hamilton's papers that the Fathers of the Constitution were not agreed, I saw in State Rights the only availing check upon the absolutism of the sovereign will, and secession filled me with hope, not as the destruction but as the redemption of Democracy. The institutions of your Republic have not exercised on the old world the salutary and liberating influence which ought to have belonged to them, by reason of those defects and abuses of principle which the Confederate Constitution was expressly and wisely calculated to remedy. I believed that the example of that great Reform would have blessed all the races of mankind by establishing true freedom purged of the native dangers and disorders of Republics.

Therefore I deemed that you were fighting the battles of our liberty, our progress, and our civilization; and I mourn for the stake which was lost at Richmond more deeply than I rejoice over that which was saved at Waterloo.

General Beauregard confirmed to me a report which was in the papers, that you are preparing a narrative of your campaigns. I sincerely trust that it is true, and that the loss you were said to have sustained at the evacuation of Richmond has not deprived you of the requisite materials. European writers are trying to construct that terrible history with the information derived from one side only. I have before me an elaborate work by a Prussian officer named Sander. It is hardly possible that future publications can be more honourable to the reputation of your army and your own. His feelings are strongly Federal, his figures, especially in estimating your forces, are derived from Northern journals, and yet his book ends by becoming an enthusiastic panegyric on your military skill. It will impress you favourably towards the writer to know that he dwells with particular detail and pleasure on your operations against Meade when Longstreet was absent, in the autumn of 1863.

But I have heard the best Prussian military critics regret that they had not the exact data necessary for a scientific appreciation of your strategy, and certainly the credit due to the officers who served under you can be distributed and justified by no hand but your own.

If you will do me the honour to write to me, letters will reach me addressed Sir J. Acton, Hotel [Serry?], Rome. Meantime I remain, with sentiments stronger than respect, Sir,

Your faithful servant
JOHN DALBERG ACTON.

APPENDIX IV—5

MEMORIAL PRESENTED BY GENERAL ROBERT E. LEE TO THE MAYOR AND COUNCIL OF BALTIMORE, MD., IN THE INTEREST OF THE VALLEY RAILROAD, APRIL, 1869

To the Mayor and Council of the City of Baltimore, Md.

The committee appointed by the people of Rockbridge County, Va., to bring to the consideration of the City of Baltimore the advantage to be attained by the construction of the Valley Railroad, beg leave to make the following suggestions.

In 1866 a survey of the route from Harrisonburg in Rockingham

County, Va., to Salem in Roanoke (a distance of 113 miles) was made under the instructions of the President of the Baltimore and Ohio Railroad by Col. James Randolph.

The Report of this Survey, dated Jan. 15th, 1867, is so complete that it is scarcely necessary to repeat what has been there so well stated. It is commended to the people of Baltimore as worthy of their earnest consideration. The report is very full in regard to the through connections which this link established with the entire South-Western portions of the Country. It exhibits the advantages that Baltimore would derive, by forming a direct connection with this vast region, the wealth of which has been only but partially developed.

More than forty years ago, Baltimore offered a bonus to Virginia for the mere right of way through her domain. Now the right of way is not only freely granted, but in addition, the counties along the line have taxed themselves nearly a million of dollars to aid in the construction of the road, thus securing a strong and permanent local interest in its behalf.

It may be proper to urge a few reasons bearing upon the importance of the Valley Railroad as a link in the general Railroad system of the Country in addition to those that have been so well stated by Col. Randolph in his report. This road, connecting Harrisonburg with Salem, on the Va. and Tenn. Railroad, will complete the last link in the great chain from the Northern Cities to the South and South-west. From Salem to New York, Philadelphia and Baltimore by the Valley route, the distance is as short as by any route that is or can be constructed, and when this line is completed, it will afford a direct and favorite means of communication between the above mentioned cities and Memphis, Vicksburg, New Orleans and other points in the South West.

This link when filled will establish a continuous route from the Southwest to the Northeast, which will interest nearly all the main lines running from the West to the East. Starting from Salem on the line from Memphis to Norfolk, it will cross the James River and Kanawha Canal at Buchanan and Lexington, the Chesapeake and Ohio Railroad at Staunton (136 miles west of Richmond), the Manassas Gap and Loudoun and Hampshire Railroad at Strasburg and Winchester (about ninety miles from Washington) and thereby would constitute Baltimore a formidable competitor for the trade and travel of the great country, which these West and East routes command.

There is now partly under contract a railroad from Winchester to Hagerstown, and when that is completed there will be a direct line crossing the Baltimore and Ohio Railroad at Martinsburg (100 miles west of Baltimore), which then running northward will intersect the Pa. Central, the Erie, and New York Central Railroads and the Erie Canal. This route will afford the shortest line of travel from the large and populous portions of the North to much of the best part of the South. Such an intermediary line of road cannot fail to yield a paying stock.

So far the Valley R.R. has been regarded simply as a through line. Our purpose, however, is rather to call the attention of Baltimore to the less known, but scarcely less important local trade from the coun- ties (in the state) through which the road will pass. It runs through five of the most fertile counties in the Valley of Virginia—a valley, which in climate, soil, minerals and well distributed and continuous water power is believed not to be excelled in native wealth by any region of equal extent on this continent. The Counties referred to are Rockingham, Augusta, Rockbridge, Botetourt, and Roanoke. Four of these counties (omitting the county of Rockingham, one half of which the road crosses) had a population of 64,561, according to the census of 1860, which is now somewhat increased. They contain an area of improved farms of 498,156 acres and unimproved, 692,562 acres. This does not include the wild or mountain lands. Their gross prod- ucts in 1860, estimated at the present price would be worth $8,207,557 —whilst at present, the purchases from outside markets are estimated to amount to $2,150,000. This last estimate is probably greatly short of the real sum, since individual or mere personal purchases are not included.

The Valley Railroad would bring the City of Baltimore directly within the circle of competition, as a seller of these imports and as a purchaser of the surplus.

An inexhaustible supply of iron ore lies buried along the western base of the Blue Ridge mountains, parallel to the road from one ter- minus to the other—whilst a continuous forest of original growth covers the entire mountains. Charcoal iron of the best quality could be manufactured from these materials and almost without limit. Man- ganese, marble and other minerals exist in large quantities and are only undeveloped from want of an outlet to market. The numerous mineral springs, the public Institutions of Staunton, the literary insti- tutions of Lexington, the famous Natural Bridge of Rockbridge, the healthfulness of the climate and the picturesqueness of the scenery must always command a large pleasure-seeking travel when the coun- try is rendered accessible by railroad.

Such is a brief and unexaggerated statement of some of the characteristics of the counties which the Valley Railroad would traverse. With the tide of emigration now turning toward Virginia, should this region so favoured by Nature be brought in direct connection with such a market as Baltimore, it is almost impossible to overestimate the wealth a few years would produce.

Whether the Valley Railroad is considered as a link in the great chain uniting the Southwest with the Northeast or whether it be regarded as a mere local line sustained by the country which it traverses, the stock, should Baltimore subscribe, and thus give it assistance and patronage, will, without doubt, in a short time equal in value the stock of the Baltimore and Ohio Railroad—whilst at the same time the trade and profit that would be brought to the City of Baltimore must greatly increase its wealth and prosperity.

APPENDIX IV—6

LEE'S INTERVIEW WITH GRANT, MAY 1, 1869

Of the two most detailed contemporary published versions of Lee's interview with President Grant at the White House on May 1, 1869, one represented General Lee as saying too little, the other as talking too much. *The New York Herald*[1] reported the incident in this manner:

"The following conversation occurred between the President and General Lee, which lasted about five minutes:

"*General Lee:* Mr. President, I called today, in accordance with your kind invitation, with my friends here, Mr. and Mrs. Taggart [*sic*], of Baltimore, to thank you for the honor you have done me.

"*President:* I did wish, General, to have a somewhat lengthy conversation with you in regard to matters relating to your section of the country, if such will be agreeable to you.

"*General Lee:* Mr. President, I would much prefer that you should not take my opinions and views as representing those of the people of Virginia and the South, and I do not think I could give any useful information on that subject. If you will excuse me, Mr. President, I will repeat my thanks for your invitation, and bid you goodday."

All this may conceivably have been said, in substance, but it certainly is not all that was said. Lee would not have been so abrupt.

---

[1] Quoted in *The Richmond Dispatch,* May 8, 1869.

APPENDIX

The other extended version is that of *The New York Tribune*.[2] It described the interview as "polite and cordial," but marked by "a certain reserve." Nothing was said about the war, but Lee, at Grant's instance, is alleged to have "made several suggestions" on policies respecting Virginia and the South. He is credited, also, in this account, with opinions that hardly could be ascribed to him.

As neither of these accounts can be accepted, it probably is best to take the statements of Robert M. Douglas and of Robert E. Lee, Jr., as authentic, however much one might wish for something colorful, something dramatic: "The visit," Judge Douglas wrote long afterwards, "was merely one of courtesy, and did not last long."[3] Said Captain Lee, "this meeting was of no political significance whatever, but simply a call of courtesy. . . . The interview lasted about fifteen minutes, and neither General Lee nor the President spoke a word on political matters."[4]

General Badeau, who was not present, stated that his information came from Grant and from J. L. Motley. He wrote: "Motley said that both men were simple and dignified, but he thought there was a shade of constraint in the manner of Lee, who was indeed always inclined to be more formal than the Northern general. The former enemies shook hands; Grant asked Lee to be seated, and presented Motley. The interview was short, and all that Grant could remember afterwards was that they spoke of building railroads, and he said playfully to Lee, 'You and I, General, have had more to do with destroying railroads than building them.' But Lee refused to smile, or to recognize the raillery. He went on gravely with the conversation, and no other reference was made to the past. Lee soon arose, and the soldiers parted. . . ."[5]

APPENDIX IV—7

Available Data on the Illnesses of General Robert E. Lee

1863, end of March.—For the first time during the war, General Lee required medical attention. He was then aged fifty-six, florid, about 5 feet 10½ inches in height, and weighed about 165 pounds. His phys-

---

2 Reprinted in *The National Intelligencer*, May 4, 1869.
3 R. M. Douglas, in *The Youth's Companion*, Dec. 19, 1912, p. 700.
4 *R. E. Lee, Jr.*, 349.   5 Badeau, *Grant in Peace*, 26–27.

ical experience had been that of the average soldier. Periods of active campaigning had alternated with close occupation at a desk. As the commanding general of the army defending his country's capital, he carried heavy responsibilities. He was physically strong and athletic, capable of sustaining long hours without any evidence of fatigue. His teeth were good. There is no record of any serious illness before the war. His habits in all things were exemplary. He rode horseback regularly for exercise. His father had died of unknown cause, at the age of sixty-two. Ann Carter Lee, his mother, who lived to be only fifty-six, was long a semi-invalid, suffering probably from arthritis or perhaps from heart disease. General Lee's wife sustained a pelvic infection in childbirth and thereafter developed a general arthritis.

Upon examination, the diagnosis made was that of "inflammation of the heart-sac," following a throat infection. Lee was sufficiently sick to require treatment away from the army. He suffered a good deal of pain in chest, back, and arms. "It came on in paroxysms, was quite sharp," he wrote. Doctors examined "my lungs, my heart, circulation, etc. and I believe they pronounced me tolerable sound."

1863, April 10.—Lee was reported better and was expected soon to be well.[1]

1863, about April 15.—The patient resumed his military duties but was confined to his tent for a day or two at the end of the month.

1863, October.—An attack described variously as "sciatica," "rheumatism," and "lumbago," involving arm and back and making it impossible for Lee to ride for about a week.

1864, May–June.—A ten-day debilitating diarrhœa.

1865–67.—No recurrence of any acute symptoms, but occasional reference is made to trouble with "rheumatism" of the arms, shoulder, and back, with "sciatica" and with "lumbago." Lee showed an increased susceptibility to bad colds. After 1865 his photographs show him aging rapidly.

1866–68.—The General began to talk of getting old, and of having only a short span of life left him.

1869, October.—Lee had another illness which he mentioned in his letters as a "heavy cold," but from the importance attached to it by physicians in later discussion of the General's case, it is believed to have been very similar to the attack prior to the battle of Chancellorsville. He was not long in bed and began to go about in some two weeks.

1869, winter.—Following his illness, the General discovered that

[1] See *supra*, vol. II, p. 504.

rapid exercise produced pain and difficulty in breathing. He suffered from weariness and depression, and was almost constantly in pain while walking. It was reported among his friends that he had some serious trouble "about his heart." He began to look upon himself as virtually an invalid, and his appearance became somewhat haggard. In the opinion of his friends he "aged" greatly during this winter.

1870, February.—He hoped he was better and he felt stronger, but he could not walk with comfort much farther than 200 yards. When he got on his horse, however, he could ride with fair comfort.

1870, March.—His physicians were very anxious that he should visit a Southern climate as soon as possible.

1870, March–May.—He made an exhausting six weeks' tour through the Carolinas and Georgia and into Florida. Everywhere he went there were crowds, excitement, cheering, receptions, and dinners. At first he noticed that the warmer weather dispelled some of the rheumatic pains in his back, but he said: "I perceive no change in the stricture in my chest. If I attempt to go beyond a very slow gait, the pain is always there. It is all true what the doctors say about its being aggravated by any fresh cold, but how to avoid taking cold is the question. It seems to me to be impossible. . . . My complaint . . . is fixed and old." As the strain of the tour continued, he had the pain whenever he moved about, and he felt it occasionally even when he was quiet, though it was not so severe then as when he was walking. His rheumatic pains were less but his "pain along the breastbone always returns on making any exertion." During the tour he gained in weight and became more florid.

1870, April.—While in Savannah, Ga., he was examined by two physicians. He wrote: "They . . . think it pretty certain that my trouble arises from some adhesion of the parts, not from any injury of the lungs and heart, but that the pericardium may not be implicated, and the adhesion may be between the pleura and ——, I have forgotten the name."

1870, end of May.—On his return from this tour, and after two weeks of rest, the General was examined in Richmond. A brief letter from this physician, addressed to the army surgeon who treated the General in 1863, is the only direct medical testimony available. This physician said that the General's symptoms were obscure but indicated chronic pericarditis. He wished to know whether the General's trouble in 1863 had been an acute attack of that disease.

1870, July.—After a further period of rest, the General was able to travel alone and to ride horseback. He was somewhat stronger and attended to his regular duties. Examined in Baltimore in July by Doctor T. H. Buckler, then of Paris, he reported to his wife: "He [Doctor Buckler] says he finds my lungs working well, the action of the heart a little too much diffused, but nothing to injure. He is inclined to think that my whole difficulty arises from rheumatic excitement, both the first attack in front of Fredericksburg and the second last winter. Says I appear to have a rheumatic constitution, must guard against taking cold, keep out in the air, exercise, etc., as the other physicians prescribe. He will see me again. In the meantime, he has told me to try lemon juice and watch the effects."

1870, July 15.—He caught a fresh cold and was suffering very much from hot weather, to which he now seemed to have an added susceptibility.

1870, Aug. 5.—Having returned home, he felt better. The "rheumatic" pains continued but had diminished. The pain in his shoulders was lessened, he thought, "under the application of the blister." He told his physician, "I shall endeavor to be well by the fall."

1870, August.—He went to the springs, where he took the "broiler" and the "hot spout." For a while he noticed no change except a shift in the seat of his pains, but after ten days he felt somewhat better.

1870, Sept. 28, forenoon.—He wrote a friend, "I am much better. . . . My pains are less and strength greater."

1870, Sept. 28, afternoon.—His terminal illness began.[2]

1870, Oct. 12.—At 9:30 A.M. the General died quietly, fourteen days after he had been attacked. His physicians were quoted in the newspapers as saying that the immediate cause of his death was "mental and physical fatigue, inducing venous congestion of the brain, which, however, never proceeded so far as apoplexy or paralysis, but gradually caused cerebral exhaustion and death." No autopsy was performed.

GENERAL LEE'S MALADY AND THE PROBABLE CAUSES OF HIS DEATH

BY LEWELLYS F. BARKER, M.D., LL.D.

It is not possible, of course, to come to any certain conclusion regarding the nature of General Lee's illness and the cause of his death. There are, however, certain points in the history that are very suggestive.

[2] For the details, see *supra*, pp. 488 *ff*.

524

APPENDIX

First, the illness described at the end of March, 1863, of severe sore throat resulting in rheumatic inflammation of the sac enclosing the heart and accompanied by pain in the chest, back and arms occurring in paroxysms, may have been an acute pericarditis secondary to the throat infection.

In the absence of any definite statement with regard to pericardial friction sounds, the possibility of the so-called rheumatism affecting the arm, shoulder and back may not have been rheumatism but may have been angina pectoris.

Second, the probability that the General suffered from angina pectoris is indicated by the history in 1869 in which it is stated that exercise produced pain and difficulty in breathing. It is likely that there was some myocardial insufficiency at this time also.

Third, the fact that in 1870 he speaks of his symptoms as stricture in his chest and says that if he goes beyond a very slow gait the pain is always there strongly indicates the existence of angina pectoris. The fact that he felt the pain occasionally even when he was quiet would not nullify this idea. The statement that the pain along the breast bone always returned on making any exertion is almost pathognomonic of angina pectoris.

Fourth, the statement that in 1870 there may have been some adhesions of the parts though not of the pericardium may really mean that the doctors were puzzled as to why he should have pain there without signs of pericardial involvement. Of course angina pectoris would explain.

Fifth, if there was pain in both shoulders and in the back there may have been some real arthritis in the shoulder joints and in the joints of the spine in addition to the angina pectoris.

Sixth, the account of the terminal illness in 1870 suggests either an atherosclerotic cerebral process or a uræmic process secondary to cardiorenal changes. The possibility of a terminal pneumonia must, of course, be kept in mind though nothing is said of fever.

The General seems to have been a man of florid complexion. It was before the days of blood-pressure determinations and it is quite possible that he had a hypertension associated with arteriosclerosis.

Summing up then I think it is certain that the General had angina pectoris, that he probably had an atherosclerotic process that contributed to the terminal event, and that in all probability he had some arthritis, and possibly a chronic adhesive pericarditis secondary to a throat infection.

APPENDIX IV– 8

The Funeral of Lee

Word of Lee's death was passed quickly from the house to the campus and thence to the town, where the church bells soon were tolling. The stores closed. Students of all the schools left their classes.[1] The town was isolated at the time by flood, and the news did not reach Richmond or the rest of the country until late in the evening.[2] In nearly every Southern city public mourning began at once. Memorial meetings were planned and business was suspended on the day of the funeral. The general assembly of Virginia, which was then in session, recommended that the General's body be interred in Hollywood Cemetery, Richmond, at the expense of the state, and immediately dispatched a delegation to Lexington. If the family decided to bury Lee in Richmond, the delegation was instructed to escort the body to that city.[3] Students, faculty, and trustees met at once.[4] At the suggestion of the faculty, the trustees provided for the burial in a vault in the library, pending the erection of a permanent memorial to him. The trustees also decided that "Lee" should be linked with "Washington" in the name of the college and that the anniversary of the General's birth should always be a day of observance at the institution.[5] His office, by like agreement, was to remain as he left it. The trustees tendered Mrs. Lee a deed to the president's house and an annuity of $3000, as soon as the first shock of her grief had passed, but she declined both.[6]

At first no suitable coffin for the body could be found. Three caskets that an undertaker had ordered from Richmond, not long previously, had reached Lexington, but before they had been taken from the packet landing they had been washed away by the unprecedented floods that followed the long-continued, heavy rains. Fortunately two neighborhood boys, C. G. Chittum and Robert E. Hillis, found one of the coffins where it had been swept ashore. It was undamaged and was used for the General's body,[7] though it was a trifle short for him.[8]

[1] Jones, 452.   [2] Richmond Dispatch, Oct. 13, 1870.
[3] Richmond Whig, Oct. 14, 1870.   [4] Jones, 462.
[5] MS. Faculty Minutes, Oct. 12, Oct. 13, Oct. 14, Oct. 15, 1870; Trustees' Minutes, Oct. 13, Oct. 15, 1870.
[6] Trustees' Minutes, Oct. 28–29, 1870.
[7] Washington and Lee Alumni Magazine, January, 1927, p. 8; Petersburg (Va.) Progress-Index, Oct. 11, 1925; Statement to the writer by Geo. E. Hillis of Richmond. These circumstances are the origin of the myth that the coffin in which Lee was buried came floating mysteriously down the river.
[8] For this reason the body was buried without shoes.

At 9 A.M. on the morning of October 14, Reverend Doctor Pendleton, Reverend W. S. White, who had been Jackson's pastor, and Reverend J. William Jones, a former chaplain in the Confederate army, delivered eulogies. Doctor Pendleton, who made the principal address, based it on Psalm XXXVII, 8–11, 28–40, which he applied to the life of Lee.

Mrs. Lee having expressed her wish that the body be buried at Lexington[9]—any other arrangement being rendered impossible, in fact, by the flood—the remains, clad in plain, black, civilian clothes, were removed at 1:30 P.M. on October 14 from the president's house to the chapel, where they lay in state until 10 A.M. the next day, with selected students of the college as a guard of honor.

On the morning of October 15 a long procession of old soldiers, students, V. M. I. cadets, townspeople, and dignitaries formed in front of the president's house at 10 o'clock and moved through the principal streets of the town, with Traveller following directly behind the empty hearse. Every effort was made to avoid pageantry or the display of any spirit contrary to that which Lee had exhibited during the difficult days of the reconstruction. The veterans, who formed the guard of honor, did not wear their old gray uniforms: only a simple black ribbon in the lapel of the coat distinguished them. No flags were put on the coffin, none was carried in the procession, and few were flown anywhere in the town except at the V. M. I. From its turrets the banners of the fifteen Southern states were hung at half-mast. The only martial notes were supplied by the cadet corps and band, and by the booming of minute-guns from the parade ground of the institute. Through silent, crowded streets, past black-draped buildings, the procession returned to the college grounds and then moved to the chapel. The service for the dead was then read by General Pendleton, without eulogium of any sort, before a crowd that completely filled the building and banked in thousands outside it. Lee's sons and his daughters were there, as were Colonel Walter H. Taylor and Colonel Charles S. Venable of his staff.[10]

The service over, the body was carried to the vault, and the committal was read by the chaplain "from the bank on the southern side of the chapel, in front of the vault." The flood kept away many of Lee's famous lieutenants who wished to stand by his grave, but their place was taken by simple private soldiers, who had come down from

---

[9] *Cf.* G. W. C. Lee to W. H. Taylor, *MS.,* Dec. 6, 1870; *Taylor MSS.*

[10] Custis, Mildred, and Agnes Lee had been at home throughout the General's illness. Owing to the belief that the General would recover, W. H. F. Lee and R. E. Lee, Jr., and Mary Lee, who was visiting friends, were not summoned in time to reach Lexington through the high water until after the General was dead. Rooney and Robert arrived on the 14th.

the coves and from the mountains when they heard that he was dead. Some of them were in wornout shoes and battered hats and threadbare clothes, but they were men of the sort his leadership had made terrible in battle. They had cheered him at the Chancellor House. About him they had rallied after they had sullenly fallen back from Cemetery Ridge. They had cried "Lee to the rear" in the Wilderness and at the Bloody Angle. Theirs had been the tears that drew his own as they had tried to shake his hands or to touch his garments or to caress the flanks of his steed at Appomattox. And now, at the last, they compassed him about, a multitude on the hillsides. They had been silent as they had filed past in the chapel, for they were men of few words and reserved in their show of emotions, but when a solitary voice began "How Firm a Foundation"—they could sing! To the last bar they did him what honor they might in lines that seemed to echo the brave-hearted loyalty of the last days under his flag:

> "I will not, I will not desert to his foes;
> That soul, though all hell shall endeavor to shake,
> I'll never. no, never, no, never forsake." [11]

Memorial meetings were held throughout the South and in New York. They were addressed in different temper by speakers of varying ability, but they reflected the love of the whole South for General Lee. Mrs. Lee stated the simple fact when she wrote General Chilton: "If he had succeeded in gaining by his sword all the South expected and hoped for, he could not have been more honored and lamented." [12] Some of the addresses contained material that still serves the biographer of Lee.[13] President Davis spoke at the Richmond meeting,[14] and Colonel Charles Marshall in Baltimore.[15] A movement was at once organized to erect in the old Confederate capital a monument to General Lee. Out of the gatherings held in his honor sprang various associations to keep alive the two names with which this book may fittingly end, the names of Lee and of the Army of Northern Virginia.

---

[11] The most complete account of the funeral is in *Jones*, 455 *ff*. Some previously unpublished details appear in *McDonald*, 7–8. The list of pall-bearers appears in *Mason*, 357.

[12] Mrs. R. E. Lee to General R. H. Chilton, *MS.*, Dec. 12, 1870, *Chilton Papers*.

[13] Various memorial addresses were printed as pamphlets. A number are republished, in part, in *Jones*, 473 *ff*. and in *Mason*, 358 *ff*. For an account of the recumbent statue of Lee at Lexington, see Colonel William Allan in *Riley*, 226 *ff*.

[14] *Jones*, 339.

[15] *Jones*, 329.

ACKNOWLEDGMENTS

ACKNOWLEDGMENTS

At the head of the list of those to whom the writer would make acknowledgment must stand Inez Goddin Freeman, daughter of one of "Mosby's Men." Cheerfully sharing all the sacrifices that nineteen years' labor on this book entailed, she, more than any one else, made possible the untroubled leisure that composition required.

W. B. Freeman, a soldier of the Army of Northern Virginia, 1861–65, supplied much first-hand information and taught the writer from childhood to respect "the opposing army."

John Stewart Bryan, publisher of *The Richmond News Leader* and president of the College of William and Mary, not only gave access to the fine library at Laburnum, and to the Bryan MSS., but also helped in countless other ways. His encouragement was as constant as his judgment of historical values is sound.

Miss Henrietta Beverley Crump, the writer's secretary and chief copyist, contributed in a larger degree than can be realized to the accuracy of transcription and to the correct arrangement of footnotes, as well as to the quick assembly of needed books and papers. Miss Crump was assisted by Mrs. Marguerite Thaw Greene, Mrs. Margaret Barlow Williams, and Miss Mary Matthews.

Right Reverend Collins Denny, who combines wide historical knowledge with sound literary scholarship, aided the writer at every stage of the work and gave the final manuscript a critical reading.

H. J. Eckenrode was the writer's constant critic and principal historical adviser. His familiarity with Confederate literature and with the technique of research made him invaluable. During the early stages of the work he assembled many of the notes from published writings and calendared the Elliott MSS.

Wilmer L. Hall, state librarian of Virginia, was unfailingly helpful and resourceful in supplying books from the collection under his care, from the Library of Congress, and from other depositories.

Fairfax Harrison, son of Burton N. Harrison, private secretary to President Davis, and himself a brilliant inheritor of great traditions, gave encouragement at every stage of the work and critically read the MS. of the final operations of the war.

Miss Maud Sites was the writer's chief copyist in the archives of the War Department and in the manuscripts division of the Library of Congress. She was prompt, accurate, and indefatigable.

531

ACKNOWLEDGMENTS

Miss Mary Maury Fitzgerald, Gaston Lichtenstein, and Louis A. Burgess also served most acceptably in examining personal narratives of the war, in making a complete examination of the historical magazines, or in transcribing manuscripts.

Doctor William Moseley Brown, formerly professor of education in Washington and Lee University, collected for the writer a vast amount of material from the archives of that institution and consistently refused to accept any compensation, answering always that he was glad to contribute to a better understanding of General Lee.

Honorable Henry T. Wickham, from his great historical lore, explained many obscure points, read the MS. of the final volume of the work, made many helpful suggestions, and allowed the writer to copy the Wickham MSS.

In study of the terrain of Lee's operations the writer had the assistance of J. Ambler Johnston (who also read part of the manuscript and also granted access to the Johnston MSS.), of Harry M. Smith (who read the manuscript in its entirety), of Henry Taylor, of Archibald G. Robertson, of Brockenbrough Lamb, and of Allen J. Saville.

The following distinguished soldiers and publicists were of great assistance in these respects:

The Adjutant General, U. S. Army, readily permitted the use of all historical records under his care.

Colonel John Buchan, M. P., offered much encouragement in the early stages of the work.

Major Charles J. Calrow, formerly of G. H. Q., A. E. F., was most helpful in analyzing Second Cold Harbor and later operations north of the James.

The Chief Engineer, U. S. Army, courteously supplied maps and permitted free examination of the papers of that bureau.

Right Honorable Winston Churchill went over the ground of the Seven Days with the writer and made many helpful observations on the terrain.

Colonel Bryan Conrad, U. S. A., retired, read the entire MS., and was in every way one of the writer's most valued, discerning, and helpful critics.

Major General C. S. Farnsworth, U. S. A., retired, former chief of infantry, gave the writer the benefit of his judgment of the military difficulties presented at White Oak Swamp.

The late Marshal Ferdinand Foch supplied a discerning verbal critique of the Chickahominy battleground.

Major General Sir Robert Hutchison, British army, reviewed for the writer, from his wide experience in the World War, the factor of fatigue in the movements of Jackson's command during the Seven Days.

Colonel H. L. Landers, U. S. A., was immensely helpful. He allowed the writer to examine his full MS. narrative of the Seven Days Battles and supplied many admirable maps.

Right Honorable David Lloyd George, O. M., went over the ground of the Seven Days, advanced a most interesting theory of the delay of Jackson at White Oak Swamp, and discussed with acumen the comparative generalship of Lee and Jackson.

The late Captain W. Gordon McCabe, president of the Virginia Historical Society, and one of the best-furnished of all students of Confederate history, counselled the writer on many subjects relating to General Lee and, especially, to the siege of Petersburg and the personnel of the Confederate high command.

These staff officers of General Robert E. Lee, their descendants or kinsmen, as indicated, are due the writer's warmest thanks:

Major Giles B. Cooke furnished notes on Drewry's Bluff and extracts from his diary of the closing days of the war.

The late Colonel T. M. R. Talcott made many informative comments on Fredericksburg, on Chancellorsville, and on the relations of General Lee with his staff.

The late Colonel W. H. Taylor of Norfolk discussed freely General Lee's dealings with the War Department and answered many technical inquiries. His son, W. H. Taylor III, and his other descendants placed at the writer's disposal the invaluable Taylor MSS., a service not less notable in the manner than in the matter. Every possible courtesy that could be shown an investigator was received at the hands of this family, to which the writer is lastingly grateful.

The late A. R. Long of Lynchburg entrusted to the writer General A. L. Long's MS. narrative of the operations of the Army of Northern Virginia through the Gettysburg campaign.

To certain of the descendants of General Henry Lee the writer is indebted for many kindnesses. In particular:

Mrs. Hanson Ely and Mrs. Hunter DeButts, daughters of Captain R. E. Lee, permitted the writer to verify references in the Lee Papers at the Library of Congress.

Mrs. Hugh Antrim and the late Mrs. C. P. Cardwell, daughters of Major John Mason Lee, procured for the writer copies of two unpublished letters of Ann Carter Lee, directed other inquiries with much understanding sympathy, and loaned some valuable photographs.

ACKNOWLEDGMENTS

Miss Anne Mason Lee, daughter of Captain Henry Carter Lee, and William Floyd Lee and Sydney Smith Lee, her brothers, opened to the writer their rare Lee relics.

Doctor George Bolling Lee, son of General "Rooney" Lee, was most helpful in directing inquiries.

George Taylor Lee, nephew of General Lee, made numerous corrections of fact and supplied information on the domestic life of General Lee, which he shared during the Lexington period.

Robert R. Lee, also a nephew of General Lee, lent the family Bible of "Light-Horse Harry" Lee and furnished a valuable memorandum.

The following libraries, librarians, and historical societies contributed generously from their collections:

Brown University supplied an important MS. letter.

Carnegie Public Library of Norfolk gave information regarding General Lee's visit to that city in 1870.

The Confederate Museum, Richmond, made available all its rich stores, through the house regent, Miss Susan B. Harrison, who is the type of custodian the historical investigator delights to meet—informed, helpful, and co-operative.

Duke University allowed its useful collection of Lee manuscripts to be calendared. Its director of libraries, Doctor W. K. Boyd, put the writer in his debt for many kindnesses.

The Enoch Pratt Library, Baltimore, permitted a member of its staff, Miss Mary N. Barton, to collect for the writer information concerning General Lee's residence in that city.

The Jones Memorial Library, Lynchburg, thanks to its executive, Miss J. M. Campbell, kindly made extracts from Lynchburg newspapers for the period of General Lee's attendance on the Episcopal convention in that city.

The Library of Congress sent hundreds of books on inter-library loans and afforded every facility to the assistants of the writer who were examining its manuscripts. Doctor Herbert Putnam more than once saw to it personally that the needs of these research-workers were met.

The New York Historical Society promptly photostated all the Lee MSS. in its collection.

The New York Public Library, through its reference chief, H. M. Lydenberg, later its librarian, offered every facility. Mr. Lydenberg personally directed all necessary photostating.

The United States Military Academy Library was most helpful.

534

ACKNOWLEDGMENTS

Many of its officials—notably Miss Margery Bedinger, Major E. E. Farman, M. L. Samson, and Captain R. R. Neyland, former assistant adjutant—supplied copies of a multitude of needed documents.

Washington and Lee University supplied catalogues, pictures, and other items of importance.

The Valentine Museum permitted some of its rare newspapers to be copied.

The Virginia Historical Society was often consulted. Its former secretary, the late Doctor W. G. Stanard, never failed in response to scores of technical inquiries.

The Virginia Military Institute Library was generously searched by Colonel William Couper, who extended many courtesies.

The Virginia State Library, the writer's main recourse, was a model in helpful co-operation.

The State Historical Society of Wisconsin provided, with the kindness of Miss Iva A. Welch, a photostat of a useful MS.

The Wilmington, N. C., Public Library was freely opened. Its head, Miss Emma Woodward, transcribed much-needed items from Wilmington newspapers.

Other acknowledgments are made in the footnotes, but to the following the writer would like to express his thanks in more detail:

Matthew Page Andrews of Baltimore identified for the writer the church General Lee attended in Baltimore and also supplied a copy of an important letter written by Mrs. Lee after the war.

The descendants of the gallant General L. A. Armistead sent a copy of an interesting letter from General Lee to that officer.

Mrs. Catherine Pendleton Arrington filled many gaps in the writer's information regarding General Lee's visit to Warrenton, N. C., in 1870.

Doctor Lewellys F. Barker of Baltimore generously studied the data on General Lee's illnesses and wrote a memorandum on that subject.

Jackson Beal of Scottsville, Va., gave data on the route General Lee followed from Derwent to Lexington in 1865.

S. M. Bemiss, acting for himself and his brother and sisters, allowed the writer to examine the important Bemiss MSS., with their references to Lee's illness in 1863.

Captain Carter Bishop of Petersburg, Va., helped in the identification of sites in and around that city.

Thomas Boyd, biographer of "Light-Horse Harry" Lee, performed a very friendly service in directing the writer's attention to the Richard Bland Lee Papers in the Library of Congress.

ACKNOWLEDGMENTS

The late Gamaliel Bradford, the friend of every historical investigator, forwarded to the writer many letters that came to him containing information on Lee.

The late Joseph P. Brady graciously made an exhaustive search of the records of the United States district court at Richmond to establish the facts regarding the indictment of Lee in 1865.

Mrs. Thomas P. Bryan placed at the writer's disposal her useful collection of Lee letters.

Reverend George McL. Brydon, historiographer of the diocese of Virginia, supplied the initials and sketched the careers of several ministers whose names appear in General Lee's correspondence.

The late Dean H. D. Campbell of Washington and Lee graciously read the manuscript for the period covering General Lee's presidency of Washington College, saved the writer from a number of errors, and supplied many documents of 1865–70 to which the writer would not otherwise have had access.

Honorable C. C. Carlin of Alexandria kindly helped in the identification of sundry Alexandria sites associated with General Lee's life.

H. G. Carlton of Richmond gave the writer an interesting memoir of General Lee at Lexington.

W. S. Carroll of Memphis, Tenn., presented the writer with copies of an early letter of General Lee's and of several written by General Joseph E. Johnston.

Robert Hill Carter of Richmond greatly assisted the writer in procuring access to the papers of his family.

Spencer L. Carter of Richmond placed at the writer's disposal all the Carter MSS. in his collection.

B. E. Case of Hartford, Conn., through Doctor Lyon G. Tyler, gave the writer a soldier's interesting letter on the operations of June, 1864.

Miss Betty Cocke, University, Va., lent the writer in its entirety the large collection of the MSS. of her family—a most helpful service.

Carter S. Cole, New York City, gave a photostat of an unpublished letter, together with a new anecdote of Lee.

Mrs. W. A. Croffut, through Miss Maud Sites, kindly sent a copy of a pre-war letter from Lee to Major Ethan H. Hitchcock, her father.

The late R. E. Cunningham, Jr., gave the writer his notes of interviews with Colonel W. H. Palmer, together with a copy of a letter from General Lee commending General Harry Heth.

Doctor A. K. Davis of Petersburg helped in unravelling the confusion regarding some of the Petersburg sites, notably that involving the McIlwaine house.

ACKNOWLEDGMENTS

Honorable P. H. Drewry, M. C., gave the writer a copy of his excellent address on the Petersburg operations of June 9, 1864.

The late Doctor W. F. Drewry was most helpful in furnishing information regarding the Petersburg homes visited by General Lee in 1867.

Doctor T. Latané Driscoll cleared the doubts regarding General Lee's bivouacs on his return from Appomattox to Richmond.

Miss Stella Drumm of Saint Louis assisted most generously with information regarding Lee's work on the Mississippi.

The late Mrs. W. H. Elliott of Savannah, Ga., permitted the writer's investigator to abstract the Elliott Papers that are so important an item in the intimate life of Lee during the years following his graduation from West Point.

Mrs. Henry Fairfax allowed the writer, with characteristic kindness, full access to the papers of Colonel John W. Fairfax of the staff of General Longstreet.

The late V. M. Fleming of Fredericksburg conducted the writer over many of the scenes of the Spotsylvania operations, at the beginning of this research, and explained points that would otherwise have been obscure.

Judge T. C. Fletcher of Richmond painstakingly verified the names and ownership of many farms around Richmond that figured in Lee's operations in June, 1862, and also helped greatly to untangle the details of the sale of Smith's Island.

Doctor Allen W. Freeman of Baltimore was kind enough to elicit the co-operation of Doctor Lewellys F. Barker, whose service has already been acknowledged.

President F. P. Gaines of Washington and Lee University and his secretary, Miss Helen Webster, permitted no call, however hurried, to pass unheeded.

James R. Gilliam, Jr., of Lynchburg, Va., gave a copy of an important letter on immigration, written by General Lee.

Miss Mary F. Goodwin of Williamsburg, Va., contributed a copy of an ante-bellum letter of Mrs. Lee's.

C. W. Grandy of Norfolk was invaluable in procuring data on Lee's visit to that city in 1870.

William de Grange, former custodian of the records of the engineers bureau of the War Department, performed many kind services in assisting the writer's copyist, and himself unearthed many unknown Lee MSS.

ACKNOWLEDGMENTS

Mrs. Preston Hampton Haskell graciously copied for the writer an unique MS. letter to General Hampton from General Lee.

Former Governor D. C. Heyward of South Carolina helped to identify sites connected with Lee's tour of duty in South Carolina in the winter of 1861–62.

George S. Hillis supplied much desired information on the finding of the coffin in which General Lee was buried.

J. F. Howison was most helpful on the Fredericksburg operations and on the North Anna manœuvres of May 22–26, 1864.

R. M. Hughes of Norfolk, Va., biographer of General Johnston, gave much counsel from his ripe historical knowledge and saved the writer from several mistakes.

Miss C. S. Hunter of Winchester placed at the writer's disposal the interesting letters from General Lee to the Misses Margaret and Caroline Stuart.

The late Eppa Hunton, Jr., of Richmond, assisted the writer with many suggestions, based on his intimate knowledge of Confederate generals.

Miss Mary Jackson of Farmville, Va., collected for the writer much information on Lee's movements while in that town during the retreat to Appomattox.

Louis Jaffé, editor of *The Virginian Pilot* of Norfolk, aided the writer in establishing the facts of General Lee's visit to that city in 1870.

Miss Nannie H. Jones of Richmond was most kind in tracing Lee's relations with the Caskie family and in giving the writer copies of the letters Lee wrote her grandfather and her mother, Norvell Caskie, later Mrs. Seddon Jones.

A. R. Lawton, son of the distinguished quartermaster general of the Confederacy, gave his recollections of General Lee's visit to Savannah in 1870.

R. M. Lynn of Washington helped to examine the title of General Lee's property in that city.

The heirs of Major H. B. McClellan, in Chicago and at Biarritz, most generously gave the author a complete transcript of the McClellan papers.

Hunter McDonald of Nashville, Tenn., supplied much desired information on Lee's residence in Lexington.

Miss Anne V. Mann helped materially in the identification of Petersburg sites.

538

ACKNOWLEDGMENTS

Honorable G. Walter Mapp aided in developing the story of the Smith's Island property.

Miss Virginia Mason furnished a fine note on Lee's attendance at his son's wedding in 1867.

Mrs. Robert L. Mercer kindly lent the writer some welcome antebellum letters of Colonel and Mrs. Lee.

J. F. Minis of Savannah, Ga., gave much help in all that related to Lee's service in and around that city.

Miss Annie Minor of Richmond supplied several unpublished anecdotes and established for the writer new facts regarding the early schooling of Lee.

Reverend Wm. Jackson Morton of Alexandria verified facts as to the confirmation of Colonel Lee in 1853.

W. Warner Moss, Jr., sent a photostat of a post-bellum letter from Lee to Longstreet.

A. B. Murray of Charleston, S. C., was very helpful in assembling data on Lee's visit to that city in 1870.

Doctor Thomas W. Murrell lent the writer the MS. memoirs of his father, John W. Murrell, covering Lee's stay in Lynchburg after the war.

Doctor Milton Offutt of Johns Hopkins University transcribed for the writer the newspaper accounts of Lee's visit to Baltimore in 1869.

Mrs. Marian Carter Oliver graciously entrusted to the writer the precious collection of Lee letters at Shirley, and explained many puzzling aspects of the Carter genealogy.

General H. L. Opie of Staunton, Va., verified all the facts of Lee's acceptance of the presidency of the Valley Railroad.

Oliver Orr of Macon, Ga., the generous aide of all historical investigators, sent much useful material and suggested many sources of information.

The late Colonel W. H. Palmer, chief of staff to A. P. Hill, from his rich memory, clarified for the writer a number of confusing incidents.

John Pemberton of New York permitted the writer to examine the whole of the MSS. of his distinguished grandfather, Lieutenant General John C. Pemberton.

H. N. Phillips of Richmond lent the writer a very interesting memoir by R. W. Manson.

The late Mrs. Mary G. Powell, the historian of Alexandria, Va., did the writer uncounted kindnesses in collecting material on Lee's boyhood in that city.

ACKNOWLEDGMENTS

Mrs. Campbell Pryor, at the instance of M. R. Turner of Black-stone, Va., permitted the quotation of her rich MS. Memoirs.

Mrs. H. Pemberton Rhudy of New York and Philadelphia suggested a fruitful line of inquiry to the writer.

Judge Edgar J. Rich of Boston aided greatly in the solution of the question whether *Rawle* was used at West Point during Lee's cadetship.

Mrs. C. W. Schaadt gave the writer a copy of a most useful antebellum letter from General Lee to one of his daughters.

Mrs. Frank Screven of Savannah lent the writer a number of Lee MSS. and helped him to procure access to others.

Miss Caroline Selden of Norfolk, at the instance of C. W. Grandy, prepared a very charming account of General Lee's visit to Norfolk in 1870.

The late James Power Smith, aide to General Stonewall Jackson, advised the writer on many questions before the formal composition of this book began. His son, William B. Smith, suggested a number of channels of research in clearing up disputed items.

The late General Jo Lane Stern gave access to his MS. autobiography and solved many minor problems relating to operations on the North Anna River.

E. T. Stuart of Philadelphia placed his fine collection at the writer's disposal.

R. C. Taylor, Jr., of Norfolk, supplied an important missing link in the correspondence relating to the operations of June, 1864.

M. R. Turner of Blackstone, Va., helped in everything that relates to the retreat from Petersburg in 1865 and especially in the details of the withdrawal from Amelia courthouse.

Doctor Lyon G. Tyler forwarded a very helpful letter.

George T. Tyson traced the records in the sale of Smith's Island with much care.

Miss Georgia West permitted the writer to copy a letter General Lee wrote her father, a distinguished architect.

Miss Eliza M. Willis gave a copy of an unpublished letter of General Lee's.

S. M. Yonge, a student at Washington College under General Lee, permitted the quotation of interesting recollections.

To a multitude of others, some of them unknown, the writer's thanks are due for opening family papers, supplying old newspapers, and forwarding unpublished anecdotes of General Lee.

SHORT-TITLE INDEX

This Short-Title Index gives the names by which certain important sources mentioned once in the footnotes with the full title and the name of the author or editor are cited thereafter. Only to those manuscripts and publications that are the subject of frequent reference have short titles been assigned. The adopted short title appears on the left in italics, then the name of the author or editor, and, on the right, a longer, identifying title. In some instances these titles have been somewhat abbreviated, inasmuch as the Selected Bibliography contains full information.

Alexander. E. P. ALEXANDER. "Military Memoirs of a Confederate."

Anderson, C. C. ANDERSON. "Texas Before and on the Eve of the Rebellion."

Annals of the War. "The Annals of the War, Written by Leading Participants, North and South," originally published in The Philadelphia Weekly Times.

B. and L. "Battles and Leaders of the Civil War."

Battine. CECIL BATTINE. "The Crisis of the Confederacy."

Baylies. FRANCIS BAYLIES. "A Narrative of General Wool's Campaign in Mexico."

Beale, R. L. T. R. L. T. BEALE. "History of the Ninth Virginia Cavalry."

Bernard. GEORGE S. BERNARD. "War Talks of Confederate Veterans."

Bigelow. JOHN BIGELOW, JR. "Campaign of Chancellorsville."

Blackford. SUSAN LEIGH BLACKFORD, compiler. "Memoirs of Life in and out of the Army in Virginia . . ."

Bond. CHRISTIANA BOND. "Memories of General Robert E. Lee."

Boyd. THOMAS BOYD. "Light Horse Harry Lee."

Boynton. EDWARD C. BOYNTON. "History of West Point."

Bradford. GAMALIEL BRADFORD. "Lee the American."

Brock. R. A. BROCK. "General Robert Edward Lee."

Brock, Miss. SALLY BROCK. "Richmond During the War."

Cent. U. S. C. "Robert E. Lee: Centennial Celebration of His Birth—University of South Carolina."

Cent. U. S. M. A. "Centennial of the United States Military Academy."

Chamberlaine, W. W. W. W. CHAMBERLAINE. "Memoirs of the Civil War."

Childe. EDWARD LEE CHILDE. "The Life and Campaigns of Gen. Lee . . . translated from the French . . . by George Litting."

Chilton Papers. "MS. Papers of Gen. R. H. Chilton."

C. M. H. C. A. EVANS, editor. "Confederate Military History."

Cond. M. A. "Condition of the Military Academy, 1824, American State Papers, Military Affairs."

Conner. P. S. P. CONNER. "The Home Squadron Under Commodore Conner."

Cook, Joel. JOEL COOK. "The Siege of Richmond."

Cooke. J. E. COOKE. "Life of General Robert E. Lee."

Cullum. G. W. CULLUM. "Biographical Register of the United States Military Academy."

Dabney. R. L. DABNEY. "Life and Campaigns of Lieut.-Gen. Thomas J. Jackson."

Dame. W. W. DAME. "From the Rapidan to Richmond."

Darby. J. F. DARBY. "Personal Recollections."

Davis. JEFFERSON DAVIS. "The Rise and Fall of the Confederate Government."

Dawson, F. W. F. W. DAWSON. "Confederate Reminiscences."

De Leon. T. C. DE LEON. "Four Years in Rebel Capitals."

Drake's Hatton. J. V. DRAKE. "Life of General Robert Hatton."

Early. JUBAL A. EARLY. "Autobiographical Sketch and Narrative of the War Between the States."

Eckenrode. H. J. ECKENRODE. "Political History of Virginia During the Reconstruction."

Eggleston. GEORGE CARY EGGLESTON. "A Rebel's Recollections."

English Combatant. AN ENGLISH COMBATANT. "Battlefields of the South."

English Soldier. "Autobiography of an English Soldier with the U. S. Army.

Falling Flag. E. M. BOYKIN. "The Falling Flag."

Figg. ROYALL W. FIGG. "Where Men Only Dare to Go."

Fremantle. A. J. L. FREMANTLE. "Three Months in the Southern States."

French. S. G. FRENCH. "Two Wars."

Goolrick. JOHN T. GOOLRICK. "Historic Fredericksburg."

Gordon, Armistead. ARMISTEAD C. GORDON. "Memories and Memorials of W. Gordon McCabe."

Gordon. JOHN B. GORDON. "Reminiscences of the Civil War."

Gordon, G. H. G. H. GORDON. "History of the Campaign of the Army of Virginia."

Grayjackets. A CONFEDERATE (pseudonym). "The Grayjackets."

Grimes. PULASKI COWPER, compiler. "Extracts of Letters of Maj.-Gen. Bryan Grimes to His Wife."

Hagood. JOHNSON HAGOOD. "Memoirs of the War of Secession."

Hallowell. "Autobiography of Benjamin Hallowell."

Harrison, Mrs. Burton. MRS. BURTON HARRISON. "Recollections Grave and Gay."

Harrison, Walter. WALTER HARRISON. "Pickett's Men."

Head. T. A. HEAD. "Campaigns and Battles of the Sixteenth Regiment, Tennessee Volunteers."

Heintzelman's MS. Diary. "MS. Diary of Cadet S. P. Heintzelman."

Henderson. G. F. R. HENDERSON. "Stonewall Jackson and the American Civil War."

542

Henry. R. S. HENRY. "The Story of the Confederacy."

Hill, D. H. D. H. HILL. "North Carolina in the War Between the States, from Bethel to Sharpsburg."

History of McGowan's Brigade. J. F. J. CALDWELL. "History of . . . McGowan's Brigade."

Hitchcock. E. A. HITCHCOCK. "Fifty Years in Camp and Field."

Hoke. JACOB HOKE. "The Great Invasion of 1863."

Hood. J. B. HOOD. "Advance and Retreat."

Hotchkiss and Allan. JED HOTCHKISS AND WILLIAM ALLAN. "Chancellorsville."

Hughes. GEORGE W. HUGHES. "Memoir Descriptive of the March of a Division of the United States Army, under the command of Brigadier-General John E. Wool from San Antonio . . . to Saltillo . . . Senate Doc. 32, 1st sess., 31st Cong."

Humphreys. A. A. HUMPHREYS. "The Virginia Campaign of 1864 and 1865."

Jackson, Mrs. MRS. T. J. (MARY ANNA) JACKSON. "Memoirs of Stonewall Jackson."

Johnson's Greene. WILLIAM JOHNSON. "Sketches of the Life and Correspondence of Nathanael Greene."

Johnston's Bull Run. R. M. JOHNSTON. "Bull Run, Its Strategy and Tactics."

Johnston's Narrative. JOSEPH E. JOHNSTON. "Narrative of Military Operations."

Jones. J. WILLIAM JONES. "Personal Reminiscences, Anecdotes, and Letters of Gen. Robert E. Lee."

Jones, L. and L. J. WILLIAM JONES. "Life and Letters of Robert Edward Lee, Soldier and Man."

Kenley. J. R. KENLEY. "Memoirs of a Maryland Volunteer."

Keyes. E. D. KEYES. "Fifty Years' Observation of Men and Events."

La Bree. BENJAMIN LA BREE, ed. "Camp Fires of the Confederacy."

Lee, E. J. E. J. LEE. "Lee of Virginia."

Lee, Fitz. FITZ. LEE. "General Lee."

H. Lee's Carolinas. H. LEE. "Campaign of 1781 in the Carolinas."

Henry Lee's Memoirs. HENRY LEE. "Memoirs of the War in the Southern Department of the United States."

H. Lee's Observations. HENRY LEE. "Observations on the Writings of Thomas Jefferson."

R. E. Lee, Jr. R. E. LEE, JR. "Recollections and Letters of General Robert E. Lee."

Lee's Dispatches. D. S. FREEMAN, editor. "Lee's Dispatches."

Lewis, John H. JOHN H. LEWIS. "Recollections from 1860 to 1865."

Loehr. C. T. LOEHR. "War History of the Old First Virginia Infantry Regiment."

Long. A. L. LONG. "Memoirs of Robert E. Lee."

Longstreet. JAMES LONGSTREET. "From Manassas to Appomattox."

McCabe. JAMES D. MCCABE, JR. "The Life and Campaigns of General Robert E. Lee."

McClellan, H. B. H. B. MCCLELLAN. "The Life and Campaigns of . . . J. E. B. Stuart."

543

McClellan's Diary. W. S. MYERS, ed. "The Mexican War Diary of George B. McClellan."

McDaniel. J. J. McDANIEL. "Diary of Battles, Marches, and Incidents of the Seventh South Carolina Regiment."

McGuire, Mrs. MRS. JUDITH McGUIRE. "Diary of a Southern Refugee."

McIntosh. D. G. McINTOSH. "Review of the Gettysburg Campaign" in 37 S. H. S. P.

Macrae. DAVID MACRAE. "The American at Home."

Malone. W. W. PIERSON, JR., ed. "Diary of B. Y. Malone."

M. A. Regs. "Military Academy, Article 78 (Army Regulations) C. 1823."

Marginalia. "PERSONNE" (F. G. DE FONTAINE). "Marginalia."

Markie Letters. AVERY CRAVEN, ed. "To Markie, the Letters of Robert E. Lee to Martha Custis Williams."

Marks. JAMES J. MARKS. "The Peninsula Campaign in Virginia."

Marshall's Appomattox. CHARLES MARSHALL. "Appomattox. An Address . . . Jany. 19, 1894."

Marshall. CHARLES MARSHALL. "An Aide de Camp of Lee."

Mason. EMILY V. MASON. "Popular Life of General Robert Edward Lee."

Mason Report. "Senate Comm. Report No. 278, 1st. sess., 36th Cong."

Maury, D. H. D. H. MAURY. "Recollections of a Virginian."

Md. Doc. Y. "Maryland Senate Document Y, March 2, 1860."

Meade. GEORGE MEADE. "Life and Letters of George Gordon Meade."

Meade Letter. MRS. R. E. LEE TO MISS MARY MEADE, Oct. 12, 1870 Virginia Mag. of History and Biography, January, 1927.

Mexican Reports. "Exec. Doc. No. 1, 1st. sess., 30th Cong."

M. H. S. M. "Papers of the Military Historical Society of Massachusetts."

Mitchell, F. A. F. A. MITCHELL. "Ormsby MacKnight Mitchell."

Mixson. F. M. MIXSON. "Reminiscences of a Private."

Moncure. E. C. MONCURE. "Reminiscences of the Civil War."

Moore, E. A. E. A. MOORE. "The Story of a Cannoneer under Stonewall Jackson."

Morgan. W. H. MORGAN. "Personal Reminiscences."

Mosby, Stuart's Cavalry. J. S. MOSBY. "Stuart's Cavalry in the Gettysburg Campaign."

Myers, F. M. F. M. MYERS. "The Comanches."

Napier. B. NAPIER. "A Soldier's Story of the War."

Neese. G. M. NEESE. "Three Years in the Confederate Horse Artillery."

N. C. Regts. WALTER CLARK, ed. "History of the Several Regiments and Battalions from North Carolina in the Great War, 1861–65."

Nisbet. J. C. NISBET. "Four Years on the Firing Line."

N. O. R. "Official Records of the Union and Confederate Navies."

Northern Tour. H. D. GILPIN. "A Northern Tour; Being a Guide to Saratoga."

O. R. "Official Records of the Union and Confederate Armies."

Southern Generals. ANON. "Southern Generals, Who They Are and What They Have Done."

Stephens. A. H. STEPHENS. "A Constitutional View of the War Between the States."

Stiles. ROBERT STILES. "Four Years under Marse Robert."

Swinton. WILLIAM SWINTON. "Campaigns of the Army of the Potomac."

Talcott. T. R. M. TALCOTT. "General Lee's Strategy at the Battle of Chancellorsville in 34 S. H. S. P."

Talcott MSS. (F). "Talcott MSS. (Freeman)."

Talcott MSS. (VHS). "Talcott MSS. (Virginia Historical Society)."

Taylor, C. E. CHARLES E. TAYLOR. "Letters in Wake Forest Student, March, 1916."

Taylor, R. RICHARD TAYLOR. "Destruction and Reconstruction."

Taylor's Four Years. W. H. TAYLOR. "Four Years with General Lee."

Taylor's General Lee. W. H. TAYLOR. "General Lee."

Thomas. H. W. THOMAS. "History of the Doles-Cooke Brigade."

Thomason. JOHN W. THOMASON, JR. "Jeb Stuart."

Trustees' Minutes. "MS. Minutes of the Trustees of Washington College."

Villard. O. W. VILLARD. "John Brown, a Biography After Fifty Years."

von Borcke. HEROS VON BORCKE. "Memoirs of the Confederate War for Independence."

Walker, Irvine. C. IRVINE WALKER. "Life of General R. H. Anderson."

Warren. "Proceedings . . . of the Court of Inquiry . . . in the Case of Gouverneur K. Warren."

Webb. A. S. WEBB. "The Peninsula."

Welch. S. G. WELCH. "A Confederate Surgeon's Letters to His Wife."

Wells. E. L. WELLS. "Hampton and His Cavalry in '64."

West, J. C. J. C. WEST. "A Texan in Search of a Fight."

White. H. A. WHITE. "Robert E. Lee and the Southern Confederacy."

Wilcox's MS. Report. "MS. report of General C. M. Wilcox on the Operations of 1864." Among the Lee Military MSS.

Winston. R. W. WINSTON. "Robert E. Lee."

Wise. JENNINGS C. WISE. "The Long Arm of Lee."

Wise, G. G. WISE. "History of the Seventeenth Virginia Infantry."

Withers. R. E. WITHERS. "Autobiography of an Octogenarian."

Wolseley. G. WOLSELEY. "A Month's Visit to the Confederate Headquarters."

Wooten. D. G. WOOTEN. "Comprehensive History of Texas."

Worsham. JOHN H. WORSHAM. "One of Jackson's Foot Cavalry."

WPLB. "MS. Letter Book of the Superintendent of West Point."

Yonge MS. S. M. YONGE. MS. "Recollections of Washington College under General Lee."

SELECT CRITICAL BIBLIOGRAPHY

GENERAL PREFATORY NOTE

This bibliography is designed to be critical rather than comprehensive. It includes something less than half the works cited in the text, but it aims to bring together, under appropriate headings, those titles that are believed to be of value to the student of Lee's career. Readers who are reviewing particular incidents will find in the footnotes of the text many references that are not considered of sufficient importance to be listed here.

In the first general division of the bibliography, that devoted to Manuscripts, the various collections of Lee material are named, according to their location, in approximately the order of their use by the writer. The arrangement of the collateral manuscript material is alphabetical by the name of the owner or custodian. In addition to those manuscripts that can reasonably be regarded as collections, large or small, a multitude of single letters of General Lee's are extant. A few of these are in the hands of the descendants of Captain Smith Lee and have been assembled or copied by Mrs.

C. P. Cardwell. The remaining letters are so widely scattered that it has not seemed desirable to attempt to list them. Among the names in the Appendix of Acknowledgments will be found those of many persons who own and have given the writer access to particular letters written by General Lee.

The general arrangement within the various subdivisions of the section on Printed Sources and Authorities is alphabetical by authors or editors. To this, the only exception is the selected list of the biographies of General Lee.

In the subdivision on the War between the States, of the section devoted to Printed Sources and Authorities, will be found a heading Personal Narratives. Next to the *Southern Historical Society Papers,*[1] the items mentioned there contain, in the aggregate, more unfamiliar material on General Lee than perhaps any other classification. This list, which represents a winnowing of all the titles under this classification in the Library of Congress, in the New York Public Library and in the Virginia State Library, has, for convenience, been put under two captions—(1) Personal Narratives by Union and Confederate General Officers and by Officers of General Lee's Staff, and (2) Other Personal Narratives. Precedence for the entries under the former caption should not be taken to imply that the other narratives are of minor importance. In some instances their writers are the only known witnesses of important historical events. Along with these personal narratives, the reader may wish to consult the biographies in the subsection on the War between the States.

Special acknowledgment of assistance in the preparation of this bibliography must be made Wilmer L. Hall and his associates of the Virginia State Library.

MANUSCRIPT SOURCES—LEE MATERIAL

U. S. ADJUTANT GENERAL'S DEPARTMENT AND ENGINEER DEPARTMENT OF THE WAR DEPARTMENT, Washington, D. C. These official archives contain at least 90 per cent of all the extant military papers of Robert E. Lee. They cover the entire period from the date of his application for a cadetship to the time of his surrender at Appomattox Courthouse. The records of his service in the United States Army remain in the original files. The letters and documents for 1861–65 are principally from the captured archives of the Confederate War Department.

U. S. MILITARY ACADEMY, West Point, N. Y. Almost the only records left at West Point of Lee's cadetship are the reports of his official standing, the entries on the muster and pay-rolls, and the list of books he borrowed from the library. For his administration as superintendent, the records are abundant. Those of first importance for that period are included in the official letter books of the superintendent. These letter books were photostated in full for the writer.

UNITED CONFEDERATE VETERANS, TRUSTEES FOR THE GRAND CAMP OF VIRGINIA, Richmond, Va. This collection includes Lee's headquarters Letter Books and his Order Book, together with many miscellaneous papers covering the last fortnight of the war. Included are numerous reports on the Appomattox campaign and the reports of Maj.-Gen. C. M. Wilcox on operations from May 4, 1864, to the end of the war. The contents of the

1 These will be cited in this bibliography, as in the text, by the abbreviation *S. H. S. P.*

Letter Books and of the Order Book were copied for the Official Records, but the other material has been little used. A general description of this collection, prepared by the late Judge George L. Christian of Richmond appeared in 44 *S. H. S. P.*, 229–31. The papers are now in a bank vault in Richmond.

WASHINGTON AND LEE UNIVERSITY, Lexington, Va. Here are the Letter Books for most of Lee's administration as president, together with the minutes of the trustees and of the faculty, and much miscellaneous material accumulated chiefly through gift. The Letter Books missing from the archives of Washington and Lee are in Lee's private papers, next to be mentioned.

U. S. LIBRARY OF CONGRESS, Washington, D. C. Lee's private papers, used by Captain R. E. Lee in his Recollections and Letters of General Lee and by Jones in his Life and Letters, have been deposited in the Library of Congress. Although they were poorly transcribed in some instances and were often most unwarrantedly "edited" by Jones, most of these papers have been printed. With the permission of the owners, Mrs. Hanson Ely and Mrs. Hunter DeButts, daughters of Captain Lee, important quotations made in this book, from previously printed letters in this collection, have been verified by the originals.

C. C. LEE, Rocky Mount, Va. In the custody of C. C. Lee, Esq., trustee for the owners, are the originals of Lee's letters to his brother Charles Carter Lee. They relate almost exclusively to affairs of the family.

DUKE UNIVERSITY LIBRARY, Durham, N. C. In this library are letters and documents, more than fifty in number, that seem to have been, at one time, part of Lee's private papers, *supra*. They were purchased by Duke University and, in accordance with the best traditions of scholarship, were at once made accessible to students. Approximately two-thirds of the letters are printed, chiefly in Jones's Life and Letters.

VIRGINIA HISTORICAL SOCIETY LIBRARY, Richmond, Va. Here are some of the most important of the early letters of Lee. A few of them are in the bound manuscripts of the Lee family, but most of them are in the papers of Andrew Talcott. Other of Lee's letters to Talcott are in the collection immediately following.

D. S. FREEMAN, Richmond, Va. The Freeman Papers contain many copies and photostats of Lee MSS. and approximately half of Lee's known letters to Andrew Talcott. These Talcott letters were presented to the writer by Mr. and Mrs. John Stewart Bryan, who purchased them from the Talcott heirs.

HUNTINGTON LIBRARY, San Marino, California. In the Huntington Library are the originals of the thirty-nine letters written to Martha Custis Williams by Lee. They cover the period 1844 to 1870, but contain none for the years of the War between the States. These letters have been edited by Avery Craven and were issued in 1933 under the title "To Markie." They are interesting but not of major importance in the life of Lee. Other letters from Lee to Martha Custis Williams belong to George L. Upshur of New York.

MISS PHŒBE ELLIOTT, Savannah, Ga. Styled the Elliott MSS. in this biography, these are the letters written by Lee to "Jack" Mackay, his "chum"

549

at West Point, and they are among the most informative sources on Lee's life from 1831 to 1845.

CONFEDERATE MUSEUM, Richmond, Va. Here are numbers of miscellaneous papers of General Lee, all of which, except for late accessions, are mentioned in D. S. Freeman, ed.: A Calendar of Confederate Papers.

VIRGINIA STATE LIBRARY, Richmond, Va. Although sadly looted after the War between the States, the archives of Virginia, housed in the State Library, still contain some material on Lee's direction in 1861 of the mobilization of Virginia. Most of this material is printed or abstracted in H. W. Flournoy, ed.: Calendar of Virginia State Papers, v. 11.

MISSOURI HISTORICAL SOCIETY, St. Louis, Mo. This institution owns the letters of Lee to Henry S. Kayser, the engineer who took up the work of improving the harbor of St. Louis when the United States suspended appropriations. The society intends ultimately to print the papers and, meantime, denies access to them. A few extracts were given in Stella M. Drumm: Robert E. Lee and the Improvement of the Mississippi River (*Missouri Historical Society Collections,* vol. 6, no. 2, February, 1929).

MRS. FRANK SCREVEN, Savannah, Ga. Among the treasures of this patriotic lady are several of General Lee's letters, originally a part of his antebellum correspondence with the younger members of the Mackay family.

MRS. MARIAN CARTER OLIVER, Shirley, Va. The Shirley MSS. of the Carter family contain a few Lee letters. Most of them were written after the War between the States.

MISS NANNIE H. JONES, Richmond, Va. Miss Jones and other descendants of Norvell Caskie (Mrs. Seddon Jones) have in the Caskie Papers sundry letters addressed after 1861 by General Lee to members of the Caskie family.

JOHN STEWART BRYAN, Richmond, Va. The fine library of Laburnum, the Bryan home in Richmond, includes numbers of interesting Lee letters.

HENRY T. WICKHAM, Hickory Hill, Hanover County, Va. Although most of the great collection of Wickham Papers was destroyed by fire, some letters from members of the Lee family were saved.

J. AMBLER JOHNSTON, Richmond, Va. The Johnston MSS. list some unusual letters from Mrs. Lee and her daughters to their friends at Ingleside, the home of Doctor W. Hartwell Macon.

MANUSCRIPT SOURCES—COLLATERAL MATERIAL

BEMISS MSS., formerly of New Orleans, now of Richmond, Va. The important papers of the military surgeon who attended Lee during part of his illness in 1863. Here is the fullest account of Lee's symptoms at that time. The papers are in the hands of S. M. Bemiss, Richmond, Va.

CARTER MSS., Richmond, Va. Included are such of the papers of the Pampatike branch of the Carter family as escaped war and fire. They are few in number but precious, and are the property of Spencer L. Carter.

CHASE PAPERS, Washington, D. C. The Arlington Case: George Washington Custis Lee vs. U. S., a paper by Enoch A. Chase, read before Columbia Historical Society, Feb. 1, 1928, subsequently printed in *Virginia Law Review,* vol. 15, no. 3, January, 1929.

CHILTON PAPERS, Richmond, Va. Formerly the property of Brig. Gen. R. H. Chilton, chief of staff to General Lee, these papers are now in the Confederate Museum, Richmond, Va. They are of greater autographic than historical value but contain an important account of General Lee's death, written for Mrs. Chilton by Mrs. Lee.

COCKE PAPERS, University, Va. Miss Betty P. Cocke has preserved the large collection of papers of her distinguished grandfather, General P. St. George Cocke, defender of Manassas during the mobilization of 1861. These manuscripts are of high illustrative value, though they contain few direct references to Lee.

COOKE DIARY, Mathews, Va. This war-time diary of the last survivor of the staff of General Robert E. Lee is not in a form accessible to students, but Major Cooke graciously had the important sections copied for the writer. These copies are now among the Freeman Papers.

DENEALE PAPERS. Charles Deneale of Alexandria, Va., wrote a sketch of the early history of that city. A copy, generously made by the late Mrs. Mary G. Powell, is in the Freeman Papers.

FAIRFAX PAPERS, Richmond, Va. Chiefly of post-bellum date, these papers of Colonel John W. Fairfax, an officer of Longstreet's personal staff, contain numerous echoes of the Gettysburg controversy. The papers belong to Mrs. Henry Fairfax, widow of Colonel Henry Fairfax, son of the original owner.

LONG MS., Lynchburg, Va. Soon after his promotion to brigadier general and chief of artillery of the Second Corps, Army of Northern Virginia, A. L. Long, former military secretary to General Lee, wrote a brief account of the campaign of 1863. This Long MS., as it is cited in the text, is in the possession of the heirs of A. R. Long, of Lynchburg, Virginia. It contains a few items of minor importance not covered in Long's Memoirs of Robert E. Lee.

H. B. McCLELLAN MSS., Chicago and Biarritz. The capable adjutant general of "Jeb" Stuart's staff, Major H. B. McClellan, preserved a few interesting letters that passed between Lee and Stuart, and at some date after the war wrote an interesting memoir of his relations with General Lee. All these papers are now in the hands of the descendants of Major McClellan, who supplied the writer with full copies.

MAGILL PAPERS, Staunton, Va. The only papers of General A. P. Hill that remained in the hands of his family were a few odds and ends belonging to his daughter, Mrs. Lucy Hill Magill. On her death, they passed to her next of kin in Staunton. They are cited only once in the text and will be of little or no help to the biographer of Hill. At one time, the family possessed numbers of Hill's private letters, but gave virtually all of them to autograph collectors.

McGUIRE PAPERS, Richmond, Va. Doctor Hunter H. McGuire, medical director of the Second Corps, Army of Northern Virginia, was deeply interested in Confederate history. He kept many of his medical reports and, after the war, conducted a wide correspondence with other soldiers, chiefly of Jackson's staff. It was through him and through Major Jed Hotchkiss that Colonel G. F. R. Henderson collected much of the personal reminiscence that appears in his Stonewall Jackson. All these Mc-

Guire Papers have been carefully preserved and are in the Confederate Museum or in the possession of Mrs. Edward McGuire, Richmond, Va., as trustee for her brother and sisters, the children of Doctor H. H. McGuire.

PEMBERTON MSS., New York City. Lieutenant General John C. Pemberton left numerous unpublished manuscripts, which now belong to his grandson, John Pemberton of New York City. They include an unfinished defense of General Pemberton's conduct at Vicksburg. Among the papers is a letter from President Davis to General Pemberton, in which the attacks on Pemberton are compared with those directed against General Lee for his failure at Gettysburg.

MRS. CAMPBELL PRYOR MS., Washington, D. C. These delightful Incidents in the Life of a Civil War Child, by the former Anne A. Banister, contain some keen recollections of General Lee during the siege of Petersburg.

TAYLOR MSS., Norfolk, Va. These papers of Colonel Walter H. Taylor, Assistant Adjutant General, Army of Northern Virginia, constitute the most important source of collateral MS. material on the military career of General Lee. Their principal content is a series of letters written by Taylor from Lee's headquarters to his fiancée and to members of the Taylor family. These letters cover nearly the whole period of Lee's command of the Army of Northern Virginia. Only about half of them are printed, even partially, in Taylor's Four Years with General Lee. In addition to the war-time letters, which are frankness itself, there is among the Taylor MSS. a mass of post-bellum correspondence, newspaper clippings, etc. This is of high value because Colonel Taylor, knowing more of happenings at Confederate headquarters than any one else alive in 1900, and having an accurate and retentive memory, became an unofficial court of last resort in historical argument. These precious MSS. are in the custody of W. H. Taylor III.

YONGE MSS., Richmond Va. Included are Reminiscences of General Lee at Washington College, by S. H. Yonge.

PRINTED SOURCES AND AUTHORITIES

BIOGRAPHIES, APPRAISALS, CRITIQUES, AND COLLECTED LETTERS OF LEE

Biographies of General Lee number close to thirty and bear date from 1865 onward. Many of them were written before the publication of the Official Records, and are often inaccurate in military detail. Still others seem to have been based entirely on previous books of the same type and have no title whatever to authority. The following selected list cites certain of the more important of these biographies in what the writer believes to be the order of their relative historical importance.

LEE, ROBERT E. [JR.]. Recollections and Letters of General Robert E Lee; New York, 1905 (2nd edition, 1924, with unimportant addenda). The principal published collection of Lee letters from 1860 to the end of Lee's life, bound together with a pleasant narrative.

JONES. J. WILLIAM. Personal Reminiscences, Anecdotes and Letters of General Robert E. Lee; New York, 1874. Many score letters and countless anecdotes, a source-book rather than a biography. In using this work, caution must be exercised in citing Lee's words, as Doctor Jones was a very poor copyist.

JONES, J. WILLIAM. Life and Letters of Robert Edward Lee, Soldier and Man; Washington, 1906. Incomplete and padded with reports but containing more of Lee's ante-bellum letters than any other book.

MAURICE, SIR FREDERICK. Robert E. Lee the Soldier; Boston, 1925. The best brief study of Lee's strategy.

TAYLOR, WALTER H. Four Years with General Lee . . . New York, 1877. Written primarily to show the weakness of the Army of Northern Virginia at different stages of military operations, but containing many extracts from Taylor's letters, certain of the most significant anecdotes of Lee, and some very intelligent observations on Lee's strategy.

TAYLOR, WALTER H. General Lee: His Campaigns in Virginia, 1861–1865, with Personal Reminiscences; Norfolk, Va., 1906. An elaboration of the above with new material, a brief but analytical work of much importance.

BRADFORD, GAMALIEL. Lee the American; Boston, 1912. A scholarly, topical treatment, accurate in most details and charmingly written but fully appreciated only by those who possess some preliminary knowledge of Lee's career.

LONG, A. L. Memoirs of Robert E. Lee . . . New York, 1886. Diffuse, padded, and inaccurate in many particulars, having been written while Long was blind, but containing much material that is still highly valuable.

DAVIS, JEFFERSON. Robert E. Lee (North American Review, vol. 150, no. 398, January, 1890). An estimate of value.

LEE, FITZHUGH. General Lee; New York, 1894. Much solid narrative, interspersed with letters previously unpublished, but marred by many small inaccuracies and by poor proof-reading.

WHITE, HENRY A. Robert E. Lee and the Southern Confederacy . . . New York, 1897. Probably the best of the one-volume biographies, though published without footnotes.

PAGE, THOMAS NELSON. Robert E. Lee, Man and Soldier; New York, 1911. Probably second only to White among recent works.

SWIFT, EBEN. The Military Education of Robert E. Lee (Virginia Magazine of History and Biography, vol. 35, no. 2, April, 1927). A very valuable article, adequate except for lists of Lee's military reading brought to light subsequent to General Swift's inquiry.

WINSTON, ROBERT W. Robert E. Lee . . . New York, 1934. For the ante-bellum life of General Lee, the fullest of the one-volume biographies.

COOKE, JOHN E. A Life of Gen. Robert E. Lee; New York, 1875. Early and in many particulars inaccurate but possessing, in respect to certain incidents, the value of a narrative by a discerning eye-witness.

McCABE, JAMES D., JR. Life and Campaigns of General Robert E. Lee . . . New York, 1866. The earliest extensive biography. Grossly inaccurate in detail but useful for quotations from contemporary newspapers and for the estimate of Lee held by those closest to the events.

MASON, EMILY V. Popular Life of General Robert Edward Lee; Baltimore, 1872. Very crude but containing some material, doubtless procured from Mrs. Lee, available nowhere else.

BRUCE, P. A. Robert E. Lee; Philadelphia, 1907. A useful short work.

BROOKS, WILLIAM E. Lee of Virginia; Indianapolis, 1932. Contains the fullest exposition of the theory that Lee hesitated in 1861 whether he should join Virginia or remain with the Union.

YOUNG, JAMES C. Marse Robert, Knight of the Confederacy; New York, 1929. Includes some new material.

CRAVEN, AVERY, ed. "To Markie." The Letters of Robert E. Lee to Martha Custis Williams; Cambridge, Mass., 1933. See Manuscript Sources, Lee Material, supra, p. 545.

JOHNSTONE, W. J. Robert E. Lee the Christian; New York, 1933. A useful compilation.

BOOKS ON LEE'S ANCESTRY, YOUTH, AND CAREER PRIOR TO
APRIL 18, 1861

The lengthy study of the Lee genealogy by Doctor Edmund Jennings Lee: Lee of Virginia, 1642–1892 (Philadelphia, 1895) is so comprehensive that no other work on Lee's ancestry need be cited or consulted. A full bibliography of the United States Military Academy, as it was in Lee's cadetship and superintendency, is given in Centennial of the United States Military Academy (Washington, 1904, 2 vols.). Lee's published reports while an officer of the bureau of engineers appear as parts of the reports of the chief engineer, which are attached to those of the secretary of war. These last usually were printed as executive documents of the successive sessions of Congress. Full bibliographies of the general historical literature on the Mexican War of 1846–48 appear in J. H. SMITH: The War with Mexico (New York, 1919, 2 vols.) and in G. L. RIVES: The United States and Mexico, 1821–1848 (New York, 1913, 2 vols.). As so much is available elsewhere, the appended list includes only those books and articles that have special interest or importance for the period here covered.

ANDERSON, CHARLES. Texas Before and on the Eve of the Rebellion . . . Cincinnati, 1884. Invaluable on Lee's political views in the winter of 1860–61.

ANDERSON, ROBERT. An Artillery Officer in the Mexican War . . . New York, 1911.

ANDREWS, MARIETTA M. Scraps of Paper . . . New York, 1929. Contains an account of Lee's wedding, written by Mrs. Marietta Turner Powell, one of the bridesmaids.

BAYLIES, FRANCIS. A Narrative of Major General Wool's Campaign in Mexico in the Years 1846, 1847 and 1848 . . . Albany, 1851. Includes a reference to Lee's engineering service with Wool's column.

BOYD, THOMAS. Light-Horse Harry Lee; New York, 1931. The fullest study of the career of Lee's father.

CLAIBORNE, J. F. H. Life and Correspondence of John A. Quitman . . .
New York, 1860, 2 vols. Gives Quitman's version of the advice given
by Lee and the other engineers at a council of war called on September
11, 1847, to consider plans for attacking Mexico City.

DARBY, JOHN F. Personal Recollections . . . St. Louis, 1880. The autobiography of the man who was mayor of St. Louis during Lee's labor for
the improvement of the Mississippi.

DECKER, KARL and McSWEEN, ANGUS. Historic Arlington . . . Washington, 1904.

DRUMM, STELLA. Robert E. Lee and the Improvement of the Mississippi
River . . . (*Missouri Historical Society Collections,* vol. 6, no. 2, Febru-
ary, 1929). Quotes the KAYSER PAPERS, for which see Manuscript
Sources, Lee Material, supra, p. 546.

AN EXACT and Authentic Narrative of the Events which Took Place in
Baltimore on the 27th and 28th of July last [Baltimore (?) 1812]. Covers, though inadequately, the part of Henry Lee in the Baltimore riot.

GRAVES, CHARLES A. The Forged Letter of General Robert E. Lee (Reports
Va. State Bar Association, 1914, 1915, 1917–18 . . . [Richmond 1914?–
1918?]. A critical analysis of the forged letter in which Lee was alleged
to have told Custis Lee that "duty, then, is the sublimest word in our
language."

HALLOWELL, BENJAMIN. Autobiography of . . . Philadelphia, 1883. Includes recollections of Lee by one of his early teachers.

HITCHCOCK, ETHAN A. Fifty Years in Camp and Field; the Diary of . . .
edited by W. A. Croffut . . . New York, 1909. Contains more references than any like work to Lee's activities in Mexico.

HUGHES, GEORGE W. Memoir Descriptive of the March of a Division of the
United States Army under the Command of Brigadier-General John E.
Wool from San Antonio de Bexar, in Texas, to Saltillo, in Mexico . . .
(Sen. Doc. No. 32, 1st sess., 31st Congress).

JOHNSON, WILLIAM. Sketches of the Life and Correspondence of Nathanael
Greene . . . Charleston, S. C., 1822, 2 vols. The book that provoked
Major Henry Lee's Campaign of 1781 in the Carolinas. Contains much
of importance regarding "Light-Horse Harry" Lee.

LEE [GENERAL] HENRY. A Correct Account of the Conduct of the Baltimore
Mob . . . Winchester, Va., 1814. Not actually Lee's composition but
based on information supplied by him.

LEE [GENERAL] HENRY. Memoirs of the War in the Southern Department
of the United States . . . A New [Third] Edition, with Revisions, and
a Biography of the Author, by Robert E. Lee; New York, 1869. For a
critique of this see *supra,* vol. IV, pp. 415 ff.

LEE [MAJOR] HENRY. Observations on the Writings of Thomas Jefferson
with particular reference to the attack they contain on the memory of
the late General Henry Lee . . . New York, 1832; 2nd ed., Philadelphia, 1839. The second is the edition cited in the text.

LEE, [MAJOR] HENRY. The Campaign of 1781 in the Carolinas; Philadelphia, 1824.

McCLELLAN, GEORGE B. Mexican War Diary . . . edited by William Starr
Myers . . . Princeton, 1917.

MARYLAND SENATE. Correspondence Relating to the Insurrection at Harpers Ferry, 17th October, 1859; Annapolis, Md., 1860 (Maryland Senate Doc. Y, March, 1860).

MAURY, DABNEY H. Recollections of a Virginian in the Mexican, Indian and Civil Wars . . . New York, 1894. Includes the story of Lee's narrow escape from death in front of Vera Cruz.

PACKARD, JOSEPH. Recollections of a Long Life, edited by Thomas J. Packard . . . Washington, 1902. By an Alexandrian who knew Lee well.

PARKER, W. H. Recollections of a Naval Officer, 1841–1865 . . . New York, 1883. Contains a good description of the arrival of the U. S. fleet off Vera Cruz; gives the location of Smith Lee's battery.

POWELL, MRS. MARY G. History of Old Alexandria; Richmond [c. 1928]. Quoted many times, a repository of much useful information on the Alexandria of Lee's boyhood.

RHODES, CHARLES DUDLEY. Robert E. Lee, the West Pointer . . . Richmond, 1932.

RICHESON, VOORHEIS. History of the Fifth Cavalry; *Army Recruiting News,* vol. 11, no. 18, Sept. 15, 1929.

TAYLOR, ZACHARY. Letters from the Battlefields of the Mexican War; Reprinted from the Originals in the Collection of Mr. William K. Bixby of St. Louis, Mo. . . . Rochester, 1908. Shows that Lee and Taylor were fourth cousins.

U. S. CONGRESS, SENATE. Report of the Select Committee of the Senate Appointed to Inquire into the Late Invasion and Seizure of the Public Property at Harpers Ferry . . . (Sen. Comm. report No. 278, 1st sess., 36th Congress), Washington, 1860. Contains Lee's report, but no reference to the omitted paragraph regarding President Buchanan's suppressed proclamation. In the separately paged Testimony (pp. 46–47) appears Lee's evidence.

U. S. MILITARY ACADEMY. Article 78, Army Regulations—Regulations of the Military Academy. Undated, but approximately 1829; no title page; Library of Congress.

U. S. MILITARY ACADEMY. Official Register of the Officers and Cadets of the U. S. Military Academy . . . June, 1826, June, 1827, June, 1828, June, 1829. Official reprints of 1884.

U. S. MILITARY ACADEMY. Regulations for the . . . with an Appendix . . . New York, 1853. The regulations revised during Lee's superintendency and issued by his order.

U. S. MILITARY ACADEMY. Centennial of . . . Washington, 1904. See supra, p. 550.

U. S. PRESIDENT (POLK). Message from the President of the United States to the two houses of Congress . . . at the commencement of the first session of the Thirtieth Congress (Exec. Doc. No. 1, 1st sess., 30th Congress); Washington, 1847. Contains the reports by General Winfield Scott and his subordinates on the campaign from Vera Cruz to Mexico City.

VILLARD, OSWALD GARRISON. John Brown . . . a Biography Fifty Years After; Boston, 1911. The standard work, contains some important facts on Lee's part in suppressing the Harpers Ferry Insurrection; has an admirable bibliography.

VIRGINIA GENERAL ASSEMBLY. Report of the Committee Appointed . . . for the Purpose of Reinterring the Remains of General Henry Lee . . . at Lexington, Virginia . . . (Richmond, c. 1914).

WEST, DECCA LAMAR. Robert E. Lee in Texas; *Texas Monthly,* April, 1930.

LEE DURING THE WAR BETWEEN THE STATES

COLLECTIONS: SOURCES, NARRATIVES, ANECDOTES, SERIALS (EXCEPT NEWSPAPERS)

Annals of the War, Written by Leading Participants North and South . . . Philadelphia, 1879. Important for Gettysburg and the Wilderness.

Battles and Leaders of the Civil War . . . New York, [1887–88]. 4 vols. Next to the Official Records and the *Southern Historical Society Papers,* the most useful source on military operations, though its editorial footnotes are not without a Northern bias.

BERNARD, GEORGE S., ed. War Talks of Confederate Veterans . . . Petersburg, Va., 1892. Numerous narratives of the defense of Petersburg, with special reference to the battle of the Crater.

CANDLER, ALLEN D., comp. The Confederate Records of the State of Georgia; Atlanta, 1909–11, 6 vols. Contain some correspondence of Lee not elsewhere published.

CONFEDERATE, A [pseudonym]. The Grayjackets . . . Philadelphia, 1867. A depository of anecdote, much of which has real historical value.

CONFEDERATE STATES OF AMERICA, CONGRESS. Journal of the Congress of the Confederate States of America, 1861–1865; Washington, 1904–5, 7 vols. (Sen. Doc. No. 234, 2nd sess., 58th Congress).

CONFEDERATE VETERAN; Nashville, Tenn., 1893–1932, 40 vols. Along with much triviality, this magazine contains mines of personal narrative that have been ignored by historians.

[DE FONTAINE, F. G.] Marginalia, or Gleanings from an Army Note-book, by Personne, Army Correspondent of the Charleston Courier . . . Columbia, S. C., 1864. A very rich collection of contemporary anecdote.

FREEMAN, D. S., ed. A Calendar of Confederate Papers . . . Richmond, 1908. Covers the collection of the Confederate Museum, Richmond.

FREEMAN, D. S., ed. Lee's Dispatches . . . New York, 1915. The confidential correspondence of Lee with Davis, unavailable to the editors of the Official Records.

LA BREE, BENJAMIN, ed. Camp Fires of the Confederacy . . . Louisville, 1899. A miscellany that contains some useful material.

MILITARY HISTORICAL SOCIETY OF MASSACHUSETTS. Papers . . . Boston, 1895–1913, 13 vols. One of the most valuable and scientific of all collections of military narratives and studies of the War between the States.

MIILTARY ORDER OF THE LOYAL LEGION OF THE UNITED STATES. Military Essays and Recollections: Papers read before the commandery of the state of Illinois . . . Chicago, 1899, 3 vols.

MOORE, FRANK, ed. The Rebellion Record . . . New York, 1862–1871, 12 vols.

SELECT CRITICAL BIBLIOGRAPHY

OUR LIVING AND OUR DEAD. Official Organ, North Carolina Branch, Southern Historical Society . . . Raleigh, N. C., 1874–1876; 3 vols. and one no. of vol. 4. Contains some personal narratives of importance.

SOUTHERN HISTORICAL SOCIETY PAPERS; Richmond, Va., 1876–1930, 47 vols. Includes more valuable, unused data than any other unofficial repository of source material on the War between the States. A general index through vol. 38, compiled by Mrs. Kate Pleasants Minor, was issued as the July-October, 1913 number of the *Virginia State Library Bulletin*. This is now out of print. Perhaps the most notable of all the material in the *S. H. S. P.* is that covering the Gettysburg controversy, which crowded vols. 4–7 inclusive. For a history of this, see *ibid.*, vol. 5, pp. 88–89 and vol. 23, p. 342.

U. S. CONGRESS. Joint Committee on the Conduct of the War: Report of . . . in Three Parts . . . Washington, 1863. Federal post mortem on the Peninsular campaign, Second Manassas and Fredericksburg; interesting sidelights on Lee's generalship as seen from "the other side."

U. S. GENERAL STAFF SCHOOL, Fort Leavenworth, Kan. Source Book of the Peninsula Campaign in Virginia, April to July, 1862 . . . Fort Leavenworth, Kan., [1921]. A useful compilation.

U. S. WAR DEPARTMENT. The War of the Rebellion: A Compilation of the Official Records of the Union and Confederate Armies; Washington, 1880–1901, 70 vols. in 128. The volumes of this work to which were given the serial numbers 112 and 113 have never been printed. Concerning this, the prime source of all, it is only necessary to warn the investigator that some of the most important of Lee's dispatches were inaccessible to the editors, or else were received late and appear in vol. 51, part 2.

BIOGRAPHIES—COLLECTED

BRADFORD, GAMALIEL. Confederate Portraits; Boston, 1917. Includes studies of Longstreet and "Jeb" Stuart.

COOKE, JOHN E. Wearing of the Gray . . . Being Personal Portraits, Scenes and Adventures of the War . . . New York, 1867. Especially good for the sidelights it throws on the cavalry of the Army of Northern Virginia.

EVANS, CLEMENT A., ed. Confederate Military History, Atlanta, Ga., 1899, 12 vols. and a supplement, vol. 13. A work of uneven merits in its narrative sections but containing in the volume, or part of a volume, devoted to each state, a most useful collection of the biographies of the general officers born in or credited to that state.

PHILLIPS, U. B., ed. The Correspondence of Robert Toombs, Alexander H. Stephens and Howell Cobb . . . Washington, 1913. Includes numerous observations on Lee by Robert Toombs, one of his harshest contemporary critics.

[POLLARD, E. A.]. The Early Life, Campaigns, and Public Services of Robert E. Lee, with a Record of the Campaigns and Heroic Deeds of His Companions in Arms . . . by A Distinguished Southern Journalist . . . New York, 1870. First published in 1867 as Lee and His Lieutenants, but not exclusively a biography of Lee. Full of inaccuracies but containing many sketches of Confederate officers that give a fair view

SELECT CRITICAL BIBLIOGRAPHY

of the esteem in which various commanders were held by their immediate contemporaries. The tone throughout is laudatory.

SNOW, WILLIAM PARKER. Southern Generals, Who They Are, and What
They Have Done . . . New York, 1865. Published anonymously but
reissued in 1867 as Lee and His Generals and credited to Snow—a work
very similar to Pollard, *supra*.

BIOGRAPHIES—INDIVIDUAL

ARNOLD, THOMAS J. Early Life and Letters of General Thomas J. Jackson
. . . New York [1916].
BASSO, HAMILTON. Beauregard, the Great Creole; New York, 1933.
BUTLER, PIERCE. Judah P. Benjamin . . . Philadelphia, 1907.
CAPERS, H. D. Life of C. G. Memminger; Richmond, Va., 1893.
CLAIBORNE, J. H. Seventy Five Years in Old Virginia; Washington, 1904.
CLAY, MRS. CLEMENT C. A Belle of the Fifties; New York, 1904.
[COOKE, J. E.] The Life of Stonewall Jackson . . . by a Virginian . . .
Richmond, 1863. Much expanded in later editions.
COOLIDGE, LOUIS A. Ulysses S. Grant; Boston, 1917.
COX, WILLIAM E. Address on the Life and Character of General Stephen D.
Ramseur . . . Raleigh, N. C., 1921.
DABNEY, R. L. Life and Campaigns of Lieut-Gen. Thomas J. Jackson . . .
New York, 1866. Until Henderson the most dependable authority upon
Jackson and even now very useful.
Jefferson Davis, Constitutionalist, His Letters, Papers and Speeches, col-
lected and edited by Dunbar Rowland; Jackson, Miss., 1923, 10 vols.
Some material not printed elsewhere.
[DAVIS, VARINA HOWELL] Jefferson Davis . . . A Memoir by His Wife;
New York, 1890, 2 vols.
DRAKE, JAMES VAULX. Life of General Robert Hatton; Nashville, Tenn.,
1867. Hatton was a colonel in the West Virginia campaign of 1861; his
letters, here printed, are valuable.
FLEMING, FRANCIS P. Memoir of Capt. C. Seton Fleming of the Second
Florida Infantry, C. S. A. . . . Jacksonville, Fla., 1884. Contains some
useful letters on Rapidan-Cold Harbor operations of May–June, 1864.
FRENCH, SAMUEL G. Two Wars: An Autobiography; Nashville, Tenn.,
1901.
GARLAND, HAMLIN. Ulysses S. Grant; New York, 1920.
GOODE, JOHN. Recollections of a Lifetime . . . Washington, 1906. The au-
thor was a member of the Confederate Congress. His memoirs include
several anecdotes of Lee.
GRANT, ULYSSES S. Personal Memoirs; New York, 1885, 2 vols.
HENDERSON, G. F. R. Stonewall Jackson and the American Civil War; Lon-
don, New York, 1898, 2 vols. The standard work and one of the most
interesting of military biographies.
HOGE, P. H. Moses Drury Hoge; Richmond, 1899.
HOLLOWAY, L. C. [O. O.] Howard, the Christian Hero; New York, 1885.
HOWARD, O. O. Autobiography . . . New York, 1907, 2 vols.
HUDSON, JOSHUA H. Sketches and Reminiscences . . . Columbia, S. C.,

559

1904. The author was lieutenant colonel of the Twenty-sixth South Carolina infantry. His autobiography is a valuable source on the later stages of the investment of Petersburg.

HUGHES, ROBERT M. General [Joseph E.] Johnston; New York, 1893.

HUMPHREYS, H. H. A. A. Humphreys, A Biography; Philadelphia, 1924.

HUNTER, MARTHA T. A Memoir of R. M. T. Hunter; Washington, 1903. Includes an account of a long conference between Lee and Senator Hunter in the winter of 1864–65.

HUNTON, EPPA. Autobiography; Richmond, Va., 1933. Has several interesting incidents relating to Lee.

JACKSON, MARY ANNA. Memoirs of Stonewall Jackson . . . Louisville, Ky., 1895. By his widow.

JOHNSON, BRADLEY T. A Memoir of the Life and Public Service of Joseph E. Johnston . . . Baltimore, 1891.

JOHNSTON, T. CARY. Robert Lewis Dabney; Richmond, 1903. Besides some useful material on the war, this book contains a significant, though second-hand account of the "White Sulphur Letter."

JOHNSTON, WILLIAM PRESTON. The Life of General Albert Sidney Johnston . . . New York, 1878. Includes an incident of Lee's work as military adviser to the president.

KEYES, ERASMUS D. Fifty Years Observations of Men and Events; New York, 1884.

Life and Reminiscences of Jefferson Davis . . . by Distinguished Men of His Time . . . Baltimore, 1890.

McCLELLAN, H. B. The Life and Campaigns of Maj.-Gen. J. E. B. Stuart . . . Richmond, Va., 1885. By Stuart's A. A. G. The standard work.

McILWAINE, RICHARD. Memories of Three Score Years and Ten; Washington, 1909. Includes some sidelights on the retreat to Appomattox.

MEADE, GEORGE GORDON. The Life and Letters of . . ., by George Meade; edited by George Gordon Meade; New York, 1913, 2 vols. The fullest contemporary account of Lee's operations during 1863–65 by one of his principal opponents.

MERCER, PHILIP. The Life of the Gallant [John] Pelham; Macon, Ga., 1929. A sketch of the career of the gallant chief of the Stuart Horse Artillery.

MILES, NELSON A. Personal Recollections and Observations . . . Chicago, 1896.

NICOLAY, JOHN GEORGE, and HAY, JOHN. Abraham Lincoln. A History; New York, 1890, 10 vols.

NOLL, ARTHUR HOWARD, ed. Doctor Quintard, Chaplain C. S. A. and Second Bishop of Tennessee . . . Sewanee, Tenn., 1905. Contains memoirs of a chaplain in the West Virginia campaign.

NOLL, ARTHUR HOWARD. General Kirby Smith . . . Sewanee, Tenn., 1907.

O'FERRALL, CHARLES T. Forty Years of Active Service . . . Washington, 1904.

PEARSON, HENRY G. James S. Wadsworth of Geneseo; New York, 1913.

POLK, J. M. Memories of the Lost Cause and Ten Years in South America . . . Austin, Tex., 1907. A curious book, cited once for an episode at Gettysburg.

POLK, W. M. Leonidas Polk: Bishop and General; New York, 1893, 2 vols,
PRYOR, MRS. ROGER A. My Day; Reminiscences of a Long Life; New York, 1909.
PRYOR, MRS. ROGER A. Reminiscences of Peace and War; New York, 1904.
REAGAN, JOHN H. Memoirs with Special Reference to Secession and the Civil War . . . New York, 1906. Several incidents relate to Lee.
ROBERTSON, A. T. Life and Letters of John A. Broadus; Philadelphia, 1901.
ROMAN, ALFRED. The Military Operations of General Beauregard . . . New York, 1884, 2 vols.
ROYALL, WILLIAM L. Some Reminiscences . . . Washington, 1909. Especially important for a long letter on the battle of the Wilderness, written to Royall by Colonel W. H. Palmer.
SHOTWELL, RANDOLPH A. The Papers of . . . Edited by J. G. de R. Hamilton . . . Raleigh, 1929.
SLAUGHTER, PHILIP. A Sketch of the Life of Randolph Fairfax . . . Third edition; Baltimore, 1878. Contains Lee's letter to Doctor Orlando Fairfax on the death of Randolph Fairfax.
SMITH, WILLIAM ERNEST. The Francis Preston Blair Family in Politics; New York, 1933. 2 vols.
THOMASON, JOHN W., JR. Jeb Stuart; New York, 1930.
TYLER, LYON G. The Letters and Times of the Tylers; Richmond, 1884–1896, 3 vols. In vol. 2 are several references to Lee.
WALKER, C. IRVINE. The Life of Lieutenant-General Richard Heron Anderson . . . Charleston, S. C., 1917.
WISE, BARTON H. The Life of Henry A. Wise of Virginia; New York, 1899.
WITHERS, ROBERT E. Autobiography of an Octogenarian . . . Roanoke, Va., 1907.

HISTORIES AND STUDIES OF LEE'S BATTLES AND CAMPAIGNS

ALEXANDER, E. P. Lee at Appomattox (*Century Magazine,* vol. 63, no. 6, April, 1902).
ALLAN, WILLIAM. The Army of Northern Virginia in 1862 . . . Cambridge, 1892. Excellent as far as records were available at the time of publication.
BARNARD, J. G. The Peninsula Campaign and Its Antecedents . . . New York, 1864.
BATES, SAMUEL P. The Battle of Gettysburg . . . Philadelphia, 1875.
BATTINE, CECIL. The Crisis of the Confederacy . . . London, 1905. Evidently intended as a sequel to Henderson's Jackson; in some respects good but lacking the background of intimate knowledge of the ground and of the army.
[BENHAM, HENRY W.] Recollections of West Virginia Campaign . . . May, June and July, 1861 . . . Boston, 1873, from *Old and New,* June, 1873, and carrying the pagination of the magazine.
BIGELOW, JOHN, JR. The Campaign of Chancellorsville . . . New Haven, 1910. A model in the comprehensive treatment of a battle.
BORCKE, HEROS VON. Die grosse Reiterschlacht bei Brandy Station . . . Berlin, 1893. With Justus Scheibert as co-author. The fullest study of the action of June 9, 1863.

SELECT CRITICAL BIBLIOGRAPHY

BOYKIN, E. M. The Falling Flag: Evacuation of Richmond, Retreat and Surrender at Appomattox . . . New York, 1874. The writer was in Gary's cavalry brigade.

BROOKS, U. R. Butler and His Cavalry in the War of Secession . . . Columbia, S. C., 1909. Useful for the campaign of 1864.

BURNS, JAMES R. Battle of Williamsburgh . . . New York, 1865.

CHAMBERLAIN, JOSHUA L. Passing of the Armies . . . New York, 1915. Covers the surrender of the Army of Northern Virginia.

CHESNEY, C. C. Essays in Modern Military Biography; New York, 1874.

CHESNEY, C. C. A Military View of Recent Campaigns in Virginia and Maryland . . . London, 1863.

COOK, JOEL. The Siege of Richmond . . . Philadelphia, 1862. Indispensable on the preliminaries of the Seven Days.

CURTIS, NEWTON M. From Bull Run to Chancellorsville . . . New York, 1906. Clears up an obscure aspect of Gaines's Mill.

DODGE, THEODORE A. The Campaign of Chancellorsville . . . Boston, 1881.

DOUBLEDAY, ABNER. Chancellorsville and Gettysburg; New York, 1882 (Campaigns of the Civil War—VI).

DRAPER, J. W. History of the American Civil War . . . New York, 1867–1870; 3 vols.

ENGLISH COMBATANT, AN. Battle-fields of the South, from Bull Run to Fredericksburg . . . [Dedication signed T. E. C.] . . . New York, 1864, 1 vol. edition; London, 1863, 2 vol. edition.

FREMANTLE, LT. COL. A. J. L. Three Months in the Southern States, April–June, 1863; New York, 1864. The classic "foreign observer's" account of Gettysburg.

FULLER, J. F. C. Grant and Lee; New York, 1933. By one of Grant's admirers.

G., J. C. Lee's Last Campaign . . . Raleigh, 1866. Good material on events during and preceding the retreat to Appomattox.

GORDON, GEO. H. History of the Army of Virginia, under John Pope . . . Boston, 1880.

GORDON, GEO. H. A War Diary of Events in the War of the Great Rebellion, 1863–1865 . . . Boston, 1882.

GREEN, JACOB L. General William B. Franklin and the Operations of the Left Wing at the Battle of Fredericksburg . . . Hartford, Conn., 1900.

GUIDE to the Fortifications and Battlefields around Petersburg . . . Petersburg, 1866.

HALL, GRANVILLE D. Lee's Invasion of Northwest Virginia in 1861 . . . Chicago, 1911. Chiefly a reprint of official reports but includes some late comment by George A. Porterfield.

HENDERSON, G. F. R. The Science of War . . . London, 1905. Contains his excellent Campaign in the Wilderness.

HILL, D. H. A History of North Carolina in the War Between the States . . . Raleigh, N. C., 1926, 2 vols. By the son of Lieutenant General D. H. Hill. Covers only the period to Sharpsburg. Notable for its bibliographical footnotes.

HOKE, JACOB. The Great Invasion of 1863; Dayton, Ohio, 1887. A Pennsylvania view of the invading Confederate army of 1863.

SELECT CRITICAL BIBLIOGRAPHY

HOTCHKISS, JED and ALLAN, WILLIAM. The Battlefields of Virginia. Chancellorsville . . . New York, 1867. Especially useful on events of the late winter of 1862–63.

HUMPHREYS, A. A. The Virginia Campaign of 1864 and 1865; New York, 1883 (Campaigns of the Civil War—XII).

HYDE, THOMAS W. Following the Greek Cross, or Memories of the Sixth Army Corps; Boston, 1895.

JOHNSTON, R. M. Bull Run, Its Strategy and Tactics; Boston, 1913. Everything that such a book should be.

JONES, SAMUEL. The Siege of Charleston . . . New York, 1911. Against the background of Lee's previous labors there.

LAW, E. M. The Fight for Richmond in 1862 (Southern Bivouac, vol. 2, nos. 11 and 12, 1887). A good account of Gaines's Mill and Savage Station by a participant in the former battle.

MCCLELLAN, G. B. McClellan's Own Story; New York, 1887 [1886]. The narrative of Lee's adversary in the Seven Days' campaign and at Sharpsburg.

MARKS, REVEREND J. J. The Peninsula Campaign in Virginia . . . Philadelphia, 1864. By a minister who spent much time at Savage Station and observed McClellan's retreat to the James.

MARSHALL, CHARLES. Appomattox. An Address Delivered before the Society of the Army and Navy of the Confederate States in the State of Maryland on Jan. 19, 1894 . . . Baltimore, 1894. A major authority on the details of Appomattox.

MAURY, RICHARD L. The Battle of Williamsburg . . . Richmond, 1880.

MONTFORT, E. R. From Grafton to McDowell . . . Cincinnati, 1886. Contains some useful descriptions of Tygart's Valley.

MOSBY, JOHN S. Stuart's Cavalry in the Gettysburg Campaign; New York, 1908. A controversial document of uneven merit.

PAGE, CHARLES A. Letters of a War Correspondent . . . Boston, 1899. Gives some useful references to terrain, weather, etc.

PALFREY, F. W. The Antietam and Fredericksburg; New York, 1882 (Campaigns of the Civil War—V).

PORTER, FITZ JOHN (defendant). Proceedings and Report of the Board of Army Officers . . . in the Case of Fitz John Porter . . . Washington, 1879. Two editions, that in two volumes (Congressional Series No. 1871, 1872) contains the important maps.

ROBERTSON, LEIGH. The South before and at the Battle of the Wilderness . . . Richmond, 1878.

ROPES, JOHN C. The Story of the Civil War . . . New York, 1894–1913. 3 parts in 4 vols., completed by W. R. Livermore. An admirable study.

ROSS, FITZGERALD. A visit to the Cities and Camps of the Confederate States . . . Edinburgh and London . . . 1865. Reprinted from Blackwood's Edinburg Magazine.

SCALES, ALFRED M. The Battle of Fredericksburg . . . Washington, 1884.

SCHAFF, MORRIS. The Battle of the Wilderness; Boston, 1910. The fullest account of operations of May 4–7, 1864.

SCHAFF, MORRIS. The Sunset of the Confederacy; Boston, 1912. Narrative of the retreat to Appomattox, wordy and rhetorical but mustering many little-known facts.

SCHEIBERT, JUSTUS. Der Bürgerkrieg in dem Nordamerikanischen Staaten; Militärisch beleuchtet für den deutschen Offizier . . . Berlin, 1874. The summary by a Prussian observer of the military methods of the American armies; especially important for its statement of Lee's theory of the function of the high command; translated both into French and into English.

SMITH, GUSTAVUS W. Confederate War Papers; Fairfax Court House, New Orleans, Seven Pines, Richmond, and North Carolina . . . New York, 1884.

SMITH, GUSTAVUS W. The Battle of Seven Pines . . . New York, 1891.

U. S. WAR DEPARTMENT. Proceedings, Findings, and Opinions of the Court of Inquiry . . . in the case of Gouverneur K. Warren . . . Washington, 1883, 3 vols. Much material on Five Forks.

VENABLE, C. S., The Campaign from the Wilderness to Petersburg. Address . . . Before the Virginia Division of the Army of Northern Virginia . . . Richmond, 1879. Reprinted in 14 S. H. S. P. and quoted therefrom in the text of this work.

WEBB, W. S. The Peninsula; New York, 1882 (Campaigns of the Civil War —III).

WELLS, EDWARD L. [Wade] Hampton and His Cavalry in '64; Richmond, 1899.

WISE, GEORGE. Campaigns and Battles of the Army of Northern Virginia . . . New York, 1916.

WISE, JENNINGS C. The Long Arm of Lee . . . Lynchburg, Va., 1915, 2 vols. The fullest study of the artillery of the Army of Northern Virginia.

[WOLSELEY, GARNET, later VISCOUNT WOLSELEY.] A Month's Visit to the Confederate Headquarters . . . (*Blackwood's Edinburg Magazine,* vol. 93, no. 567, January, 1863). Visited the Army of Northern Virginia shortly after the Sharpsburg campaign.

YOUNG, JESSE BOWMAN. The Battle of Gettysburg . . . New York, 1913.

HISTORIES OF BRIGADES, REGIMENTS, AND OTHER UNITS OF THE CONFEDERATE
FORCES COMMANDED BY GENERAL LEE

The brigade and regimental histories of the Army of Northern Virginia are by no means as numerous as those of the Army of the Potomac. In addition to those here listed, some will be found in the *S. H. S. P.*

BAYLOR, GEORGE. Bull Run to Bull Run . . . Richmond, 1900. A history of Co. B., Twelfth Virginia Cavalry.

BEALE, R. L. T. History of the Ninth Virginia Cavalry . . . Richmond, 1899.

BLACKFORD, CHARLES M., JR. Annals of the Lynchburg Home Guard . . . Lynchburg, Va., 1891.

CALDWELL, J. F. J. The History of a Brigade of South Carolinians Known First as Gregg's and subsequently as McGowan's Brigade . . . Philadelphia, 1866. A most useful work.

SELECT CRITICAL BIBLIOGRAPHY

CLARK, WALTER, ed. Histories of the Several Regiments and Battalions from North Carolina in the Great War 1861–65; Written by Members of the Respective Commands . . . Raleigh and Goldsboro, N. C., 1901. Five invaluable volumes with many little-known references to General Lee.

DANIEL, FREDERICK S. Richmond Howitzers in the War . . . Richmond, 1891.

DAVIS, REVEREND NICHOLAS A. The Campaign from Texas to Maryland . . . Richmond, 1863. A history of the Fourth Texas through the battle of Fredericksburg.

DICKERT, D. AUGUSTUS. History of Kershaw's Brigade . . . Newberry, S. C., 1899. Most useful.

FIGG, ROYAL W. Where Men Only Dare to Go . . . Richmond, 1885. A history of the Parker Battery.

GOLDSBOROUGH, W. W. The Maryland Line in the Confederate States Army; Baltimore, 1869.

HACKLEY, WOODFORD B. The Little Fork Rangers . . . Richmond, 1927.

HARRISON, WALTER. Pickett's Men . . . New York, 1870. A brief history of the division.

HEAD, THOMAS A. Campaigns and Battles of the Sixteenth Regiment, Tennessee Volunteers . . . Nashville, Tenn., 1885. Invaluable on the Cheat Mountain campaign.

HERBERT, ARTHUR. Sketches and Incidents of Movements of the Seventeenth Virginia Infantry . . . n.p., n.d. Brief.

HURST, M. B. History of the Fourteenth . . . Alabama Volunteers . . . Richmond, 1863.

IRBY, RICHARD. Historical Sketch of the Nottoway Grays, Afterwards Co. G., Eighteenth Virginia Regiment . . . Richmond, 1878.

IZLAR, WILLIAM V. A Sketch of the War Record of the Edisto Rifles . . . Columbia, S. C., 1914. This unit belonged to Hagood's brigade.

LOEHR, CHARLES T. War History of the Old First Virginia Infantry Regiment . . . Richmond, 1884.

McCARTHY, CARLTON, ed. Contributions to a History of the Richmond Howitzer Battalion; Richmond, 1883–86, 4 pamphlets.

McDANIEL, J. J. Diary of Battles, Marches, and Incidents of the Seventh S. C. Regiment . . . n.p., 1862. Very brief.

MYERS, FRANK M. The Comanches: A History of White's Battalion, Virginia Cavalry, Laurel Brig., Hampton Div., . . . Baltimore, 1871. Good on the activities of the cavalry during the retreat to Appomattox.

NICHOLS, G. W. A Soldier's Story of His Regiment [61st Georgia] and Incidents of the Lawton-Gordon-Evans Brigade . . . n.p., 1898.

OWEN, WILLIAM M. In Camp and Battle with the Washington Artillery of New Orleans; Boston, 1885. Often quoted.

POLLEY, J. B. Hood's Texas Brigade . . . New York, 1910. A most informative work on a very famous brigade.

REID, J. W. History of the Fourth Regiment of S. C. Volunteers . . . Greenville, S. C., 1892.

SHAVER, LEWELLYN A. History of the Sixtieth Alabama Regiment . . . Montgomery, 1867. Exceptionally accurate.

SHOEMAKER, JOHN J. Shoemaker's Battery; Memphis, Tenn., n.d. This battery belonged to the Stuart Horse artillery.

SLOAN, JOHN A. Reminiscences of the Guildford Grays . . . Washington, 1883. Concerns Co. B, Twenty-seventh N. C. Regiment.

THOMAS, HENRY W. History of the Doles Cooke Brigade . . . Atlanta, 1903. Most informative.

WISE, GEORGE. History of the Seventeenth Virginia Infantry . . . Baltimore, 1870. Belonged to Pickett's division but was not at Gettysburg.

PERSONAL NARRATIVES BY UNION AND CONFEDERATE GENERAL OFFICERS
AND BY OFFICERS OF GENERAL LEE'S STAFF

ALEXANDER, E. P. Military Memoirs of a Confederate . . . New York, 1907. Occasionally overcritical but, on the whole, the most valuable single commentary on the operations of the Army of Northern Virginia.

BUTLER, BENJAMIN F. Private and Official Correspondence of . . . During the Period of the Civil War; Norwood, Mass., 1917.

COOKE, GILES B. Just Before and After Lee Surrendered to Grant . . . n.p., 1922. Reprinted in two editions from *The Houston* (Texas) *Chronicle*, Oct. 8, 1922.

EARLY, JUBAL A. A Memoir of the Last Year of the War for Independence in the Confederate States of America . . . Lynchburg, Va., 1867.

EARLY, JUBAL A. Autobiographical Sketch and Narrative of the War Between the States; with notes by R. H. Early . . . Philadelphia, 1912. This contains the whole text of the preceding item and much material on earlier operations. Early was also a prolific contributor to the Gettysburg controversy.

GIBBON, JOHN. Personal Recollections of the Civil War . . . New York, 1928. Completed in 1885 on the basis of war-time diaries and letters.

GORDON, JOHN B. Reminiscences of the Civil War . . . New York, 1903. Rich in incident but written late in life.

GRIMES, BRYAN. Extracts of Letters of . . . to His Wife. Written while in Active Service in the Army of Northern Virginia . . . Compiled by Pulaski Cowper . . . Raleigh, 1883. Excellent on operations witnessed by General Grimes.

HAGOOD, JOHNSON. Memoirs of the War of Secession from the Original Manuscripts of . . . Columbia, S. C., 1910. Useful material on operations of Hoke's division, May–December, 1864.

HOOD, JOHN B. Advance and Retreat . . . New Orleans, 1880. Comment on operations of the Army of Northern Virginia to the autumn of 1863, and thereafter concerned with the Army of Tennessee.

JOHNSTON, JOSEPH E. Narrative of Military Operations during the late War between the States . . . New York, 1872.

LONGSTREET, JAMES. From Manassas to Appomattox, Memoirs of the Civil War in America . . . Philadelphia, 1896. Important but inaccurate. For the various charges that Longstreet did not write some of the historical papers that appeared over his signature, and for his part in the Gettysburg controversy, see 4 *S. H. S. P.*, 4, and 5 *ibid.*, 273–74; *New Orleans Republican*, Feb. 27, 1876; *Philadelphia Weekly Times*, Feb.

23, 1878. Colonel Henderson's review of Longstreet's book, originally published in the *United Service Journal,* was reprinted in 39 *S. H. S. P.,* 104.

LONGSTREET, JAMES. General Longstreet as a Critic; *Washington Post,* June 11, 1893, p. 10, cols. 1 and 2. An important critique.

MARSHALL, CHARLES. An Aide-de-Camp of Lee, Being the Papers of Colonel Charles Marshall . . . Edited by Major General Sir Frederick Maurice . . . [Boston, 1927]. A major authority for the incidents covered but, unfortunately, incomplete.

PAXTON, ELISHA FRANKLIN. Memoir and Memorials . . . Composed of his Letters from Camp and Field . . . Collected and Arranged by his son, John Gallatin Paxton; Washington, 1907.

PICKETT, GEORGE E. Soldier of the South . . . Pickett's War Letters to His Wife . . . Boston, 1928. One of several editions of General Pickett's letters, edited by his wife. They are rarely quoted in these volumes.

SORREL, G. MOXLEY. Recollections of a Confederate Staff Officer; New York, 1917, 2d ed. One of the most charming of all books on the War between the States, with some candid character sketches.

TAYLOR, RICHARD. Destruction and Reconstruction: Personal Experiences of the Late War; New York, 1879. Excellent on the Valley campaign of 1862 and on the Seven Days; delightfully written.

OTHER PERSONAL NARRATIVES

ANDERSON, C. S. Train Running for the Confederacy (*Locomotive Engineering,* 1892, 1893, 1897, 1898). Contains much valuable data on the transportation of the Army of the Valley and the Army of Northern Virginia.

BEALE, G. W. A Lieutenant of Cavalry in Lee's Army; Boston, 1918.

BLACKFORD, MRS. SUSAN LEE (COLSTON). Memoirs of Life in and out of the Army in Virginia during the War between the States . . . Lynchburg, Va., 1894–96, 2 vols. Contains a noble account of Appomattox.

BORCKE, HEROS VON. Memoirs of the Confederate War for Independence . . . London, 1866, 2 vols. Not literally accurate in all particulars but useful on relations between Lee and Stuart.

BROCK, MISS SALLY [MRS. RICHARD PUTNAM]. Richmond During the War . . . New York, 1867.

BROWN, PHILIP F. Reminiscences of the War of 1861–1865 . . . Richmond, 1917. Good on Malvern Hill and Crampton Gap. The writer was in St. Paul's church, Richmond, on the day the city was evacuated.

CASLER, JOHN O. Four Years in the Stonewall Brigade . . . Guthrie, Okla., 1893.

CHAMBERLAINE, WILLIAM W. Memoirs of the Civil War . . . Washington, 1912. A most useful book by an officer often in contact with Lee.

CHAMBERLAYNE, C. G., ed. Ham Chamberlayne—Virginian . . Richmond, Va., 1933. Charming letters by a young artillerist.

CHESNUT, MARY BOYKIN. A Diary from Dixie . . . New York, 1905. A standard work on Southern society during the war, by the wife of James Chesnut, Jr.

CORBIN, RICHARD W. Letters of a Confederate Officer to His Family in Europe during the Last Year of the War of Secession . . . New York, 1913. By a member of General Field's staff; good on operations north of the James in 1864.

DAME, WILLIAM M. From the Rapidan to Richmond and the Spotsylvania Campaign; Baltimore, 1920. By a member of the Richmond Howitzers.

DAWSON, FRANCIS W. Reminiscences of Confederate Service . . . Charleston, 1882. Some first-hand views of Lee and of Longstreet.

DE LEON, T. C. Belles and Beaux and Brains of the 60's . . . New York, 1909.

DE LEON, T. C. Four Years in Rebel Capitals . . . Mobile, Ala., 1890.

DUNAWAY, WAYLAND F. Reminiscences of a Rebel . . . New York, 1913.

DUNLOP, W. S. Lee's Sharpshooters . . . Little Rock, Ark., 1899. Contains much information on the Spotsylvania campaign.

EGGLESTON, GEORGE CARY. A Rebel's Recollections . . . New York, 1875. A very sprightly and intelligent narrative.

FLETCHER, W. A. Rebel Private, Front and Rear . . . Beaumont, Texas, 1908. No direct references of importance to Lee but good on the morale of Hood's brigade; one of the most diverting of personal narratives.

GILL, JOHN. Reminiscences of Four Years as a Private Soldier in the Confederate Army . . . Baltimore, 1904. The author was one of Jackson's couriers during the Seven Days.

GILMORE, HARRY. Four Years in the Saddle; New York, 1866.

GRAHAM, JAMES A. The James A. Graham Papers; edited by H. M. Wagstaff . . . Chapel Hill, N. C. 1928. Excellent for the viewpoint of a young soldier of good education and social position.

HARRISON, MRS. BURTON. Recollections Grave and Gay . . . Richmond, 1911. Admirable picture of war-time Richmond, with a few glimpses of Lee.

HOPKINS, LUTHER W. From Bull Run to Appomattox, a Boy's View . . . Baltimore, 1908; 2d edition, 1911. The author belonged to the troop of cavalry that served as Lee's escort on entering Maryland in 1862.

HOWARD, MCHENRY. Recollections of a Maryland Soldier and Staff Officer . . . Baltimore, 1914. An excellent narrative.

HUSE, CALEB. The Supplies for the Confederate Army . . . Boston, 1904.

JOHNSTON, DAVID E. The Story of a Confederate Boy in the Civil War . . . Portland, 1914. One of the best of all the personal narratives, written by a member of the 7th Virginia Infantry, Kemper's Brigade.

JONES, J. B. A Rebel War Clerk's Diary . . . Philadelphia, 1866, 2 vols. Full of war-office gossip, much of it concerning Lee.

LEE, MISS S. L. War Time in Alexandria, Virginia (*South Atlantic Quarterly,* vol. 4, no. 3, July, 1905).

LEWIS, JOHN H. Recollections from 1860 to 1865 . . . Washington, 1895. By a lieutenant in Pickett's division.

LEWIS, RICHARD. Camp Life of a Confederate Boy of Bratton's Brigade . . . Charleston, S. C., 1883.

LIVERMORE, THOMAS L. Days and Events, 1860–66; Boston, 1920. A good picture of Lee, as he appeared to thoughtful men in the Army of the Potomac.

LYMAN, THEODORE. Meade's Headquarters, 1863–65; Letters of . . . from the Wilderness to Appomattox . . . Boston, 1922. Admirably edited by George R. Agassiz.

McCARTHY, CARLTON. Detailed Minutiæ of Soldier Life . . . Richmond, 1882. Very rich in its descriptions of army life.

McGUIRE, JUDITH W. [Mrs. JOHN P.] Diary of a Southern Refugee . . . Richmond, 1889, 3d edition. One of the best and most familiar accounts of Richmond during the war.

McKIM, RANDOLPH H. A Soldier's Recollections . . . New York, 1910. Excellent on Steuart's brigade at Gettysburg.

MALONE, BARTLETT Y. Diary of . . . edited by W. W. Pierson, Jr. . . . Chapel Hill, N. C., 1919. By a member of the 6th N. C. Infantry; a curious document but very useful for its notes on the weather.

MIXSON, FRANK M. Reminiscences of a Private . . . Columbia, S. C., 1910. One of the best and frankest narratives by a private soldier, a member of the 1st South Carolina Infantry, Jenkins's Brigade. Very full on the attempt to recover Fort Harrison, Sept. 30, 1864.

MONCURE, E. C. Reminiscences of the Civil War . . . n.p., [1914?] A thrilling account of the march from Spotsylvania to the North Anna, May, 1864; republished in Bulletin of the Virginia State Library, Nos. 2–3, July, 1927.

MONTEIRO, ARISTIDES. War Reminiscences of a Surgeon of Mosby's Command . . . Richmond, 1890.

MOORE, EDWARD A. The Story of a Cannoneer under Stonewall Jackson . . . New York, 1907. One of the half-dozen best; describes the career of the Rockbridge Artillery.

MORGAN, W. H. Personal Reminiscences of the War of 1861–65 . . . Lynchburg, Va., 1911.

MOSBY, JOHN S. Memoirs of [edited by Charles W. Russell]; Boston, 1917.

MOSBY, JOHN S. War Reminiscences . . . Boston, 1887.

NAPIER, BARTLETT. A Soldier's Story of the War . . . New Orleans, 1874.

NISBET, JAMES COOPER. Four Years on the Firing Line . . . Chattanooga, Tenn., 1914. By a captain in Trimble's old brigade.

PARKS, LEIGHTON. What a Boy Saw of the Civil War (Century Magazine, vol. 70, no. 2, June, 1905). Some fine incidents of Lee's two invasions of Maryland.

PECK, R. H. Reminiscences of a Confederate Soldier . . . Fincastle, Va., n.d. By a member of the 2d Virginia Cavalry.

POLLEY, J. B. A Soldier's Letter to Charming Nellie . . . New York, 1908. The author belonged to Hood's Texas brigade.

POTTS, FRANK. The Death of the Confederacy . . . edited by D. S. Freeman; Richmond, 1928. Published originally in The Palmetto Leaf, Cedar Springs, S. C., Dec. 25, 1926, Jan. 1 and 8, 1927. An important letter on the evacuation of Richmond and the surrender at Appomattox.

STEWART, WILLIAM H. A Pair of Blankets . . . New York, 1911. Many interesting references to Lee, especially in Pennsylvania and at the battle of the Crater.

STILES, ROBERT. Four Years under Marse Robert; Washington, 1903. Accurate and wholly delightful.

SELECT CRITICAL BIBLIOGRAPHY

STONEBRAKER, JOSEPH R. A Rebel of '61 . . . New York, 1899.

TAYLOR, CHARLES E. War Letters (*Wake Forest Student,* vol. 35, no. 6, March, 1916). The author was with Lee in western Virginia.

TONEY, MARCUS B. The Privations of a Private . . . Nashville, Tenn., 1905. This author, also, was with Lee in western Virginia.

WELCH, SPENCER G. A Confederate Surgeon's Letters to his Wife . . . Washington, 1911. This author, the surgeon of the 13th South Carolina, McGowan's brigade, wrote a series of letters that are to be rated among the very first sources of information on the health, morale, and food supply of the Army of Northern Virginia.

WEST, JOHN C. A Texan in Search of a Fight . . . Waco, Texas, 1901. Some good contemporary letters on the march into Pennsylvania and on Hood's charge, July 2, 1863.

WOOD, JAMES H. The War . . . Cumberland, Md., 1910. The author was a captain in the 37th Virginia.

WORSHAM, JOHN H. One of Jackson's Foot Cavalry . . . New York, 1912. Excellent in every way, especially for the campaigns in Western Virginia, 1861.

WRIGHT. MRS. D. GIRAUD. A Southern Girl in '61 . . . New York, 1905.

GENERAL AND MISCELLANEOUS

DAVIS, JEFFERSON. The Rise and Fall of the Confederate Government . . . New York, 1881, 2 vols. Indispensable but singularly reticent on Davis's dealings with General Lee.

HENRY, ROBERT S. The Story of the Confederacy; Indianapolis, 1931. The best short narrative of the war by a Southerner; graphic and dependable.

JONES, J. WILLIAM. Christ in the Camp or Religion in Lee's Army . . . Richmond, 1887.

LONN, ELLA. Desertion during the Civil War; New York, 1928.

MOORE, ALBERT BURTON. Conscription and Conflict in the Confederacy . . . New York, 1924. An excellent study of conscription and exemptions.

RAMSDELL, CHARLES W. The Confederate Government and the Railroads (*American Historical Review,* vol. 22, no. 4, July, 1917).

RAMSDELL, CHARLES W. General Robert E. Lee's Horse Supply, 1862–1865 (*American Historical Review,* vol. 35, no. 4, July, 1930).

RANDALL, JAMES G. The Newspaper Problem in its Bearing upon Military Secrecy during the Civil War (*American Historical Review,* vol. 23, no. 2, January, 1918).

SHANKS, H. T. The Secession Movement in Virginia, 1847–1861; Richmond [1934].

SMITH, EDWARD C. The Borderland in the Civil War . . . New York, 1927.

SMITH, FRANCIS H. The Virginia Military Institute . . . Lynchburg, 1912.

STEPHENS, ALEXANDER H. A Constitutional View of the Late War between the States; Philadelphia, 1868, 2 vols.

SWANTNER, EVA. Military Railroads during the Civil War (*Military Engineer,* vols. 21–22). Contains little on the South.

SELECT CRITICAL BIBLIOGRAPHY

BOOKS AND ARTICLES ON LEE'S CAREER
AFTER APPOMATTOX

The manuscript material and the works of R. E. LEE, JR., and of J. WIL-LIAM JONES are supplemented by a number of works, among which the following are of especial interest or importance:

ACTON, JOHN EMERICH EDWARD DALBERG ACTON, FIRST BARON. Selections from the Correspondence of . . . Edited with an Introduction by John Neville Figgis and Reginald Vere Laurence . . . London, 1917. Contains Lee's letter in answer to Acton's inquiry regarding secession and the attitude of the Southern States after the war.

AVARY, MYRTA L. Dixie After the War; New York, 1906. Some useful anecdotes.

BOND, CHRISTIANA. Memories of General Robert E. Lee; Baltimore, 1926, reprint of Recollections of General Robert E. Lee, originally published in *South Atlantic Quarterly*, vol. 24, 1925.

McDONALD, HUNTER. General Lee after Appomattox; originally printed in *Tennessee Historical Magazine*, vol. 9, no. 4, January, 1926.

MACRAE, DAVID. The Americans at Home: Pen-and-Ink Sketches of American Men, Manners and Institutions; Edinburgh, 1870, 2 vols. Contains (vol. 1) accounts of a visit to Lexington and of an interview with General Lee; includes, also, some incidents of Lee and the army. The first edition spells the name MacRae, the second Macrae. The latter form of the name is used in the text.

MARTIN, C. S. General Lee and a School of Commerce (*Journal of Political Economy*, vol. 34, 1926).

RILEY, FRANKLIN P. General Robert E. Lee After Appomattox; New York, 1922. Consists chiefly of memoirs by former students, together with several useful essays on Lee's career at Washington College.

SOUTH CAROLINA, UNIVERSITY OF. Robert E. Lee: Centennial Celebration of His Birth, Held under the Auspices of the . . . Columbia, S. C., 1907. Contains an address by Major H. E. Young of Lee's staff and an article on Lee as a college president by Doctor Edward S. Joynes of Lee's faculty, a paper in which the author supplemented the data published in the *University Monthly*, March, 1871.

U. S. CONGRESS. Report of the Joint Committee on Reconstruction, at the first session of the Thirty-ninth Congress; Washington, 1866. Bureau edition. Issued also as House report No. 30, 1st sess., 39th Congress. Contains Lee's testimony as a witness before the committee.

MAPS

Maps used by Lee during the Mexican War and a copy of one of those drawn by him are in the library of the Virginia Military Institute; those made by him personally or under his direction in Mexico are in the War Department, Washington.

The Atlas to Accompany the Official Records of the Union and Confederate Armies . . . Washington, 1891–95, is the great *vade mecum* for the study of Lee's campaigns, but it can be supplemented as follows:

Maps of the Seven Days Campaign, Prepared by LIEUTENANT COLONEL H. L. LANDERS, F. A., Historical Section, Army War College, Washington, D. C., August, 1929; drawn by DONALD E. WINDHAM. These maps have never been published.

Maps of Second Manassas contained in the two-volume edition of the Fitz John Porter Inquiry, *supra,* p. 559.

Atlas of the Battlefields of Antietam, Prepared under the direction of the Antietam Battlefield Board . . . Washington, 1904, the most detailed and accurate maps of any single battlefield on which the Army of Northern Virginia fought.

Topographic Map of Fredericksburg and Vicinity, Virginia, Showing Battlefields . . . Surveyed in 1931; issued by the Department of the Interior, Geological Survey.

Maps in JOHN BIGELOW, JR.: The Campaign of Chancellorsville; New Haven, 1910. These cover every phase of the operations.

Map[s] of the Battlefield of Gettysburg . . . Office of the Chief of Engineers, U. S. Army, 1876. These are the famous JOHN B. BACHELDER maps.

M. F. STEELE. American Campaigns; Washington, 1909, 2 vols. The second volume includes a convenient collection of maps, of virtually all the major operations of the War between the States.

For operations in Virginia, from the beginning of the campaign of 1864, there is available the series of maps prepared at the instance of General Grant and under the direction of Brevetted Brigadier General N. Micheler. These maps are reproduced in the Atlas of the Official Records but on a very small scale. The separate sheets, done in black and white, with the fortifications in color, are on a scale 3 inches to the mile or, for large sectors, 1½ inches to the mile. Although the names of residents and even of streams are often wretchedly misspelled, these maps are almost essential to close study of the terrain.

There are, in addition, some good maps in Battles and Leaders of the Civil War, and often, most unexpectedly, one finds valuable sketches in the Official Records. This is especially true of the reports of General G. K. Warren.

Before the historical student despairs of finding a map of a front he is studying, it is well to make direct inquiry not only to the Library of Congress but also to the War Department, where many maps not printed in the Atlas of the Official Records are in existence, and properly indexed. The Confederate Museum, Richmond, likewise contains some unpublished maps. Those available there in 1908 are listed in D. S. Freeman, ed. Calendar of Confederate Papers, 486 ff. A few rare maps have been added to the collection since that time. The map section of the Virginia State Library is also useful.

NEWSPAPERS

In the preparation of this biography, the files of all Richmond newspapers for the period of the War between the States have been searched, as have *The*

SELECT CRITICAL BIBLIOGRAPHY

Charleston Mercury and *The National Intelligencer* of Washington. *The New York Herald, The World, The New York Times,* and *The New York Evening Post* have been examined for special periods of the war. For events after the close of hostilities, *The Lexington* (Va.) *Gazette* is the principal newspaper authority on Lee, but the papers of virtually all the cities visited by him contain accounts of his movements. As these publications are cited in the footnotes for all General Lee's journeyings, it has not been thought necessary to list them here. Generally speaking, newspaper material on Lee during the war is historically less valuable than might be thought. In the South it was fragmentary or laudatory, and in the North it was, in the main, uncritically hostile. Reports after the war were much more accurate and substantially supplement General Lee's correspondence.

INDEX

INDEX

INDEX

INDEX

Cheat River Bridge, I, 533-4
Chelsea, Banister homestead, IV, 339
Cherokee Indians, I, 204
Chesapeake and Ohio Canal Company, IV, 394
Chesapeake and Ohio Railroad, IV, 394-5
Chesney, Col. C. C. (British Army), I, 351
Chesnut, James, Jr., I, 535-6
Chesnut, Mrs. III, 218, 261
Chickahominy, I, 459; II, 15, 41, 46, 58-61, 64, 66-8, 72-3, 80-1, 96, 99, 104-6, 110-20; II, 117-26, 128-9, 133-8, 140-2, 145, 153, 155, 157-67, 169, 172, 174, 176, 192, 194, 219, 236-7, 243, 248, 254, 276, 518, *et passim;* III, 351, 362, 364, 369, 373, 382-3, 385-6, 393, 399-400, 402, 407; IV, 102, 153, 177, 198
Chickamauga, III, 206, 261; IV, 185
Chihuahua, I, 206-7, 209-10
Childe, Mr. and Mrs. Edward, brother-in-law and sister of R. E. Lee, IV, 309, 439
Childe, Edward Lee, nephew of R. E. Lee, IV, 380
Childe, Edward Vernon, I, 129 *n.*, 392-3
Childe, Mary, I, 392
Childe, Mildred Lee. *See* Lee, Catharine Mildred
Chilton, Emmie, I, 377
Chilton, Laura Mason (Mrs. Peyton Wise), I, 377; IV, 272-3
Chilton, Gen. R. H., C. S. A., I, 377, 530, 641-2; II, 169, 205, 207, 235-6, 249, 397, 443, 486, 525, 529, 566; III, 224, 228-9; IV, 191, 235 *n.*, 272, 306, 451
Chilton, Mrs. R. H., IV, 313
Chinn house, II, 334
Chippewa Indians, I, 144
Chisolm, Capt. A. R., C. S. A., III, 442-3
Christian, Col. Bolivar, C. S. A., IV, 218, 245-6
Christian, Lt. Col. C. B., C. S. A., III, 370
Church, Albert E., I, 55, 119, 319
Church, James C., I, 188
Churchill, Col. Sylvester, I, 210
Churubusco, I, 255-7, 266-9, 271-2, 287, 303; II, 342
Cicero, I, 36, 40
Cincinnati, Society of The, III, 234
Clark, Gov., II, 93
Clark's Mountain, I, 449; III, 267-9, 384
Clarke, Col. Newman S., I, 251, 282
Clarke house, III, 364
Clay, Henry, I, 340, 460
Clay house, III, 419, 422, 424
Clay's Farm, III, 416, 418-19
Clingman, Brig. Gen. T. L., C. S. A., III, 375, 379
Clinton, Fort, I, 48, 70
Clover Hill, IV, 60-1
Cobb, Gen. Howell, II, 489
Cobb, Gen. T. R. R., C. S. A., II, 211-12, 215, 226, 392, 397, 448, 458, 463, 471

Cockburn, Admiral, I, 29
Cocke, Charles L., IV, 434
Cocke, Mrs. Edmund Randolph, IV, 242
Cocke, Mrs. Elizabeth Randolph, IV, 209, 211
Cocke, Gen. P. St. George, C. S. A., I, 496, 505-6, 513, 540; IV, 212
Cockspur Island, Ga., I, 94-6, 100, 455; II, 420, 542; IV, 495
Codori house, Gettysburg, III, 95
Coggin's Point, II, 208-9, 275
Cohorn, I, 76
Coke, Lord (misspelled Cooke), I, 163
Cold Harbor, I, 460; II, 58, 111-12, 114, 140, 143, 146, 148, 150, 237; III, 373-403, 432, 436-9, 441, 446, 457; IV, 134, 170, 174, 198; order of battle, III, 385-6; evacuated by Grant, III, 401-3
Cole, Lt. Col. Robert G., C. S. A., I, 642; II, 493; IV, 55, 67, 71, 81, 453
Cole house, III, 257
Colfax, Schuyler, IV, 373
Collendar, I, 265
Colorado, Camp, I, 405
Colquitt, Gen. A. H., C. S. A., II, 215, 371; III, 467
Colquitt's Salient, IV, 14-17
Colston, Lieut. F. M., C. S. A., III, 129
Colston, Brig. Gen. R. E., C. S. A., II, 546, 559; III, 12; IV, 456
Columbus, Fort, II, 1
Comanche Indians, I, 363-7, 376, 405-6, 414
Confessions, by Rousseau, I, 72
Congress (Federal warship), II, 2
Congressional Committee to Examine Confederate States, IV, 249-56; Lee as witness, IV, 250-6
Congressional Globe, The, I, 436, 518; IV, 384
Connally, Jim, I, 219, 301
Conner, Commodore David, I, 223-4
Conness, Sen. John, IV, 361
Conrad, C. M., I, 326-7
Conscription, II, 25-9, 257; III, 254-5, 498-9, 517-18
Conscripts weaken morale, III, 507
Considérations sur l'Art de la Guerre, by Napoleon, I, 354
Contreras. *See* Padierna
Cooke, Maj. Giles B., C. S. A., I, 642; III, 423; IV, 158, 160, 212
Cooke, Col. John R., C. S. A., II, 91, 397, 458, 463; III, 181-3, 378, 445; IV, 16, 48
Cooke, Brig. Gen. Philip Saint George, U. S. A., I, 54, 84; II, 100
Cooper, Camp, I, 363-8, 374-7, 405
Cooper Institute, IV, 348-51
Cooper, James Fenimore, I, 81
Cooper, Peter, IV, 348
Cooper, Gen. Samuel, C. S. A., I, 536, 559-60, 579; II, 62, 188, 190, 242; III, 510; IV, 405, 451

580

INDEX

449, 461–2, 494–5; IV, 4–6, 8, 10–13, 20, 59–60, 107, 169, 180, 189, 195, 235, 240, 271, 450–1; his character, II, 45–6
Johnston, Mrs. Joseph E., I, 412
Johnston, J. W., I, 644
Johnston, P. C., I, 464
Johnston, Peter, I, 3, 51
Johnston, Preston, I, 260, 266
Johnston, Brig. Gen. Robert D., C. S. A., III, 297, 326, 332
Johnston, Robert E. Lee, IV, 404
Johnston, Samuel R., C. S. A., I, 643; II, 166; III, 86, 89, 94, 96–7
Johnston, Col. William Preston, C. S. A., IV, 299, 425, 429–31, 439, 491 and *n.*
Johnston, Mrs. William Preston, IV, 439
Johnston affair, IV, 345–58
Jomini, Baron A. H., I, 77, 354, 358, 456
Jones, A. Seddon, IV, 409
Jones, Mrs. A. Seddon, *see* Caskie, Norvell
Jones, Miss Anne Upshur, IV, 420, 433 *n.*
Jones, Gen. D. R., C. S. A., II, 174, 226–7, 246, 313–14, 316, 322–3, 330, 333, 372, 384–5, 395, 397, 400–401, 403
Jones, Fayette, I, 51
Jones, Col. Hilary P., C. S. A., III, 234
Jones, J. B., I, 607–8
Jones, J. R., II, 417
Jones, Brig. Gen. John M., C. S. A., III, 13, 103, 147, 305, 317
Jones, Rev. John William, D.D., IV, 419, 436, 441
Jones, Joseph, IV, 446
Jones, Paul, II, 433
Jones, Samuel, Gen., C. S. A., I, 487; III, 14, 18–19, 22–3, 29, 48–9, 52, 163, 168, 225–6, 254
Jones, Thomas L., IV, 384–5
Jones, Brig. Gen. William E., C. S. A., II, 479, 481–2, 492, 499; III, 62–3, 225–6, 280, 396; IV, 92
Journal, by Philip Fithian, I, 25
Joynes, Prof. E. S., IV, 265, 293, 431–2
Junkin, Dr. George, IV, 222, 243

Kanawha, I, 574, 577, 579–604; II, 12, 423
Kausle , *Atlas and Text*, I, 356
Kautz, Maj. Gen. A. V., U. S. A., III, 328, 333, 335, 399; IV, 38
Kayser, Henry, I, 147, 174, 182, 190, 196, 198
Kearny, Brig. Gen. Philip, U. S. A., I, 256; II, 342, 420
Kearny, Brig. Gen. Stephen W., I, 202
Keffer, John L., I, 51
Keiley, A. M., IV, 220, 343
Keith, Rev. Reuel, I, 106
Keitt, Col. Lawrence M., C. S. A., III, 377
Kelly, William, I, 41–2
Kelly's Ford, III, 190–3, 203
Kemble, Fanny, I, 198
Kemble, Gouverneur, I, 358

Kemper, Maj. Gen. J. L., C. S. A., II, 186–90, 322, 326, 333–4, 465, 471; III, 112, 122–7, 129–30, 348, 498
Kennedy, St. John P., I, 82, 104–5
Kennedy on Courts Martial, I, 357
Kennesaw Mountain, III, 461
Kennon, Mrs. Britannia (Mrs. Beverly Kennon), IV, 242, 382–3, 402
Kent, *Commentaries*, I, 79
Kernstown, II, 40
Kershaw, Maj. Gen. Joseph B., C. S. A., II, 90, 173, 212, 215–16, 387, 392, 463, 526, 545, 554; III, 99, 272, 282, 288–90, 375, 377, 379, 386, 388, 394, 413, 419, 421, 423, 425, 437, 447, 465, 479, 482, 494–5, 511, 518, 520, 523; IV, 23, 26, 30, 33, 42, 57–8, 63, 70, 72, 91
Keyes, Gen. Erasmus D., I, 84, 192, 294, 359, 431–3
Kiebert, I, 357
Kilpatrick, Brig. Gen. H. J., U. S. A., III, 187, 219
King, Col. J. H., C. S. A., III, 476
King, Gen. Rufus, U. S. A., II, 276–7, 280, 320, 323
Kinglake, A. W., I, 357
Kinsley, Lt. Z. J. D., I, 63, 70
Kiowa Indians, I, 406
Kirkland, Capt. Joseph, II, 252–3
Kirkland, Brig. Gen. W. W., C. S. A., III, 181–3, 221, 223, 277, 378
Kirkpatrick, Dr. J. L., IV, 431, 442
Kirkpatrick, T. J., IV, 218
Knickerbocker Life Insurance Company offers Lee supervisorship, IV, 394
Knights of the Golden Circle, I, 414
Knowlton, Miner, I, 56
Knox, Gen. Henry, I, 117
Kosciuszko, Gen. T., I, 49, 70
Ku Klux Klan, I, 414
Kumer, Lee's man, I, 375

Lacey, Capt. F. R., U. S. A., IV, 355
Lacroix and Bezout, *Application of Algebra to Geometry*, I, 58
Lacy, Rev. B. T., II, 496, 521–3, 560, 562
Lafayette, I, 9, 45–6, 52; II, 288; IV, 382
Lafayette, Fort, I, 186–91, 194; III, 211
Lafferty & Company, IV, 424
Laidley, Lt. T. T. S., I, 247
Laisne, I, 358
Lallemand, *Treatise on Artillery*, I, 77
Lane, Brig. Gen. James, C. S. A., II, 461, 467–8; III, 112, 123, 125, 127, 144, 185, 279–80, 319–20, 322–5, 353–5, 434; IV, 16, 48
Lane, Joseph, I, 413
Laramie, Fort, I, 348–9
Latané, Rev. J. A., IV, 365
Latrobe, John H. B., I, 70
Latrobe, Col. Osmun, C. S. A., IV, 153
Laurel Hill pass, I, 533–4

INDEX

Conference with Gordon, March 3, 1865, IV, 7–8

Court-martial service, I, 362–3, 368, 373–6, 384, 387, 393, 456

Courtship of Mary Custis, I, 99, 104; II, 461

Criticism of his acceptance of President's amnesty, IV, 205

Criticism of his operations, III, 3–7, 427–30, 432–3, 435, 438–40, 446

Daily habits, IV, 496–7, 499–501

Death, IV, 492; probable causes, IV, 524–5

Defeat, foreknowledge of, III, 36

Derwent, Lee's temporary residence, IV, 209–14

Devotion to R. E. Lee:
  Of civilian population, IV, 186, 335, 341, 396–9, 404–7, 447–67, *passim*
  Of his men, I, 173–4, 181, 346, 376, 378; II, 245, 497–8; III, 230, 239, 241–5, 247, 267, 320–1, 542; IV, 144–8, 185
  Of his students, IV, 275–98
  Of Negroes, IV, 404–5, 407, 450
  Of the South, IV, 335, 338, 404–7, 447–67, *passim*

Difficulties of Campaigns:
  Changed commanders, III, 427, 447; IV, 166
  Depleted cavalry, III, 440
  Dispersion of forces, IV, 166
  Heavy woodland favoring stolen marches, III, 440
  Inaccurate reports, III, 433, 442
  Inferior artillery, III, 427; IV, 166
  Insufficient numbers, III, 426; IV, 166
  Need to defend Richmond, III, 440–1; IV, 166
  Other difficulties, IV, 167
  Personal incapacity, III, 427
  Poor direction by generals, III, 437
  Reduction of forces by detachments, III, 440
  Scanty supplies, III, 427; IV, 166
  Transportation difficulties, IV, 166
  Unfit mounts, for cavalry, III, 427, 440

Discussion of the war, IV, 474–6

Disfranchisement, IV, 382

Dispatches:
  On evacuation of Richmond, IV, 49–50
  To Anderson at Bermuda Neck, III, 418
  To Jefferson Davis, after Spotsylvania, III, 337–8

Domestic happiness, I, 117, 301–2, 328, 360

Edits his father's *Memoirs*, IV, 415–19

Education:
  At Eastern View, I, 30–1, 36
  By his father's writings, I, 32–3, 65–7
  By home duties, I, 33–4, 36
  At Alexandria Academy, I, 36–7
  With James Hallowell, I, 46–7

At West Point, I, 48–85

In Mexican Campaign, I, 294–300

By experience, I, 455–9

Educational policy and system, IV, 232, 258, 275–98, 420–32

Elected president of Washington College, IV, 215, 221–2

Engineering Experiences:
  Florida, 304–5
  Fort Carroll, I, 303, 305, 308, 314, 316–18
  Fort inspections, I, 184–5
  Fort Monroe, I, 96, 100, 102, 119–21, 124–8
  Mexican Campaigns, I, 205, 207, 210, 212, 219, 222, 226, 228–9, 234, 238, 244, 250, 258–9, 273–8, 285–6
  Mississippi River, I, 138–40, 142–7, 150–5, 170, 173–7, 179–83
  New York Harbor, I, 185–91, 194, 199–200

Escape from death at Spotsylvania, III, 320; at Ellington, Fox homestead, III, 352

Estate difficulties, IV, 385–90

Estimate of:
  Alexandria Gazette's, I, 445
  Army officers' after Mexican campaign, I, 294–5
  As father, by his son Robert, I, 313–4
  As man, IV, 493–505
  As soldier and general, IV, 165–87
  Board of visitors', West Point, I, 346–7
  Brother officers', I, 378
  C. Anderson's, I, 415 *n.*
  Capt. Raphael Semmes's, I, 258
  Erasmus D. Keyes's, I, 359
  Fellow-cadets', I, 68;
  Gen. Schofield's, I, 346
  Gen. Scott's, I, 350 *n.*
  Henry J. Hunt's, I, 193
  James M. Porter's, I, 385
  Jefferson Davis's, III, 157–8
  Joseph E. Johnston's, I, 74
  Mayor J. F. Darby's, I, 174–5, 182–3
  M. C. Meigs's, I, 148
  On appointment to command in Virginia, I, 468–71
  On organizing Virginia army, I, 523–4
  Paul Hamilton Hayne's, I, 612

Estimate of situation after Spotsylvania, III, 337–8

Examination before Congressional Committee, Feb. 17, 1866, IV, 250–6; before Federal Court in Davis trial, 337

Exchange of Notes, Apr. 9, 1865, IV, 513–15

Executor of Custis estate, I, 380–92; II, 474, 476; IV, 385–90

Failure of campaigns, causes:
  Absence of Stuart, III, 147
  Commanders' state of mind, III, 149

592

INDEX

596

INDEX

598

INDEX

INDEX

INDEX

INDEX

INDEX

INDEX

INDEX

INDEX